P9-DYZ-003

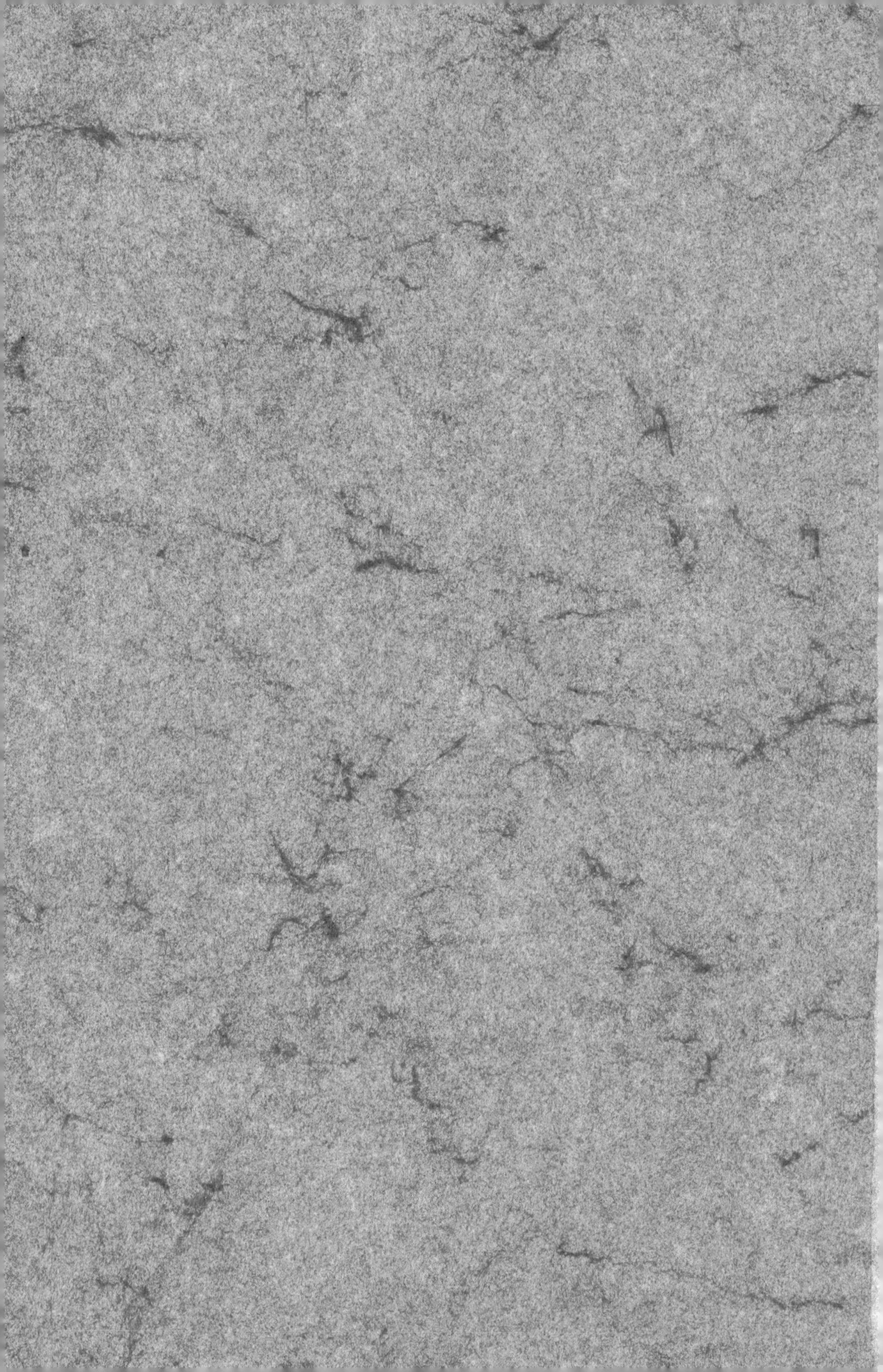

Kodomo no tame ni

Kodomo no tame ni

For the sake of the children

The Japanese American Experience in Hawaii

Dennis M. Ogawa

with the assistance of Glen Grant

foreword by Lawrence H. Fuchs

amplified by contemporaneous readings

THE UNIVERSITY PRESS OF HAWAII

Honolulu

Manufactured in the United States of America

Library of Congress Cataloging in Publication Data

Ogawa, Dennis M.
Kodomo no tame ni—for the sake of the children.

"Amplified by contemporaneous readings."
Bibliography: p.
1. Japanese Americans—Hawaii—Addresses, essays, lectures. 2. Hawaii—Social conditions—Addresses, essays, lectures. I. Title. II. Title: For the sake of the children.

DU624.7.J3037 996.9'004'956 77-18368
ISBN 0-8248-0528-3

For Quin and Owen

Contents

Foreword

PROFESSOR Dennis Ogawa has given us a dramatic story of how Japanese Americans in Hawaii have maintained continuity with their ancestral roots while contributing to a more peaceful, harmonious America. It is a story we need to hear and learn from as we read daily of how ethnic tribalisms in other parts of the world are tearing nations apart. The outcome is also quite different from that predicted for this country by Michel-Guillaume Jean de Crèvecoeur in his *Letters From an American Farmer* on the eve of the American revolution. Observing ethnic diversity around him—the English, Scots, Irish, French, Dutch, Germans and Swedes—Crèvecoeur predicted that out of this "promiscuous breed" would come "the American" who leaves behind "all his ancient prejudices and manners," acting only upon new principles. That the descendants of immigrants have acted on new principles is true, but ethnic cultures have not disappeared under the impact of liberal, individualistic principles as Crèvecoeur thought they would.

To the contrary. In the post World War II decades, the very time when liberalism made its greatest strides, we have seen a resurgence of ethnic consciousness. Instead of destroying ethnic identities, the emerging liberal civic culture of the twentieth century has made it possible for language and religious schools and other expressions of ethnic culture to flourish. The strength of liberalism is that it permits individuals to express their individuality through group identities if they choose; the weakness of liberalism is that it fails to offer the kind of deep, emotional enrichment which ties to organic ethnic history provide. Ethnic consciousness prospers on both accounts. Yet, liberalism has not suffered seriously thus far. Agreement on liberal constitutional principles has become the basis not just of American consensus but of a civic American identity. Because American identity is no longer defined by color, religion, language, or any other tribalistic symbol, the Amish, Hutterites, Hasidic Jews, Seventh Day Adventists, Jehovah's Witnesses, Hungarians, Cubans, or others are free to be as ethnic as they wish without being any less American as long as they abide by the noncoercive ideals and rules of the civic culture.

We owe much to Japanese Americans for our emancipation from a racist, linguistic, or religious definition of Americanism. Partly because of them, immigration policy is no longer racist; to a large extent because of them we no longer believe with Theodore Roosevelt or Woodrow Wilson that Americans *must* speak only English in public discourse; and almost entirely because of them we realize that the children of immigrant Americans can assert primary loyalty to the United States even when it is fighting a war against a nation to which their parents were deeply loyal.

While the Japanese Americans in Hawaii have contributed disproportionately to the civic meaning of American identity, they have also given something to its cultural definition. In this book we learn just how Japanese Americans have participated—and continue to participate—in a dynamic process of cultural diffusion within an ideal framework of protection for individual rights and reward for individual achievement. Rather than melting, ethnic groups have been molting as animals do when they shed feathers or skin in the process of renewal. But even the molting metaphor is misleading as we attempt to describe ethnic group acculturation in the United States. No single word or phrase can possibly capture the dynamic, complex process of cultural diffusion in which Japanese have changed over time but have also changed the rest of us. Ogawa gives us flavor and insight into that process in his description of *Urabon,* the annual Buddhist festival corresponding with the July full moon, held in the small rural community of Haleiwa. He takes us into the transmogrified *Urabon* from the perspectives of *issei, nisei, sansei, yonsei, haole*s and others. *Urabon* is no longer a Buddhist Japanese festival only, but a many-sided religious, secular, American, Hawaiian island, Buddhist, and Japanese occasion for expressing ethnic distinctiveness while sharing and modifying it at the same time.

As Ogawa takes us on a tour of the festival from many perspectives, he makes us realize that while few Japanese or non-Japanese understand the religious significance of the *Urabon*—the joining of the dead in a belief of *karma,* wisdom, and compassion—it has acquired new meanings synthesizing the experiences of the Japanese in Hawaii.

The continuity with the past is explicit for the *issei:* "To sing the old chants, to dance the ancient steps, seems to link the soul with . . . ancestry as if the genetic code contained choreography and musical scores." But even for the *issei,* Buddhism could not remain as it had been in Japan. Just as Buddhism there became uniquely Japanized through the influence of Shintoism (and Confucianism and Taoism), Buddhism in Hawaii became Americanized by the influence of Christianity, the civic culture and other aspects of the American milieu.

While Professor Ogawa is particularly vivid in his descriptions and selections as to how the Japanese adapted to and were changed by the American environment, he makes it clear that such vital Japanese values as *enryo* (self restraint), *haji* (shame), *on* (obligation to family and community), *kosai* (the kin and friendship networks to which one is obligated), and *giri* (reciprocity to obligation) have not disappeared. They have been renewed and changed and given new modes of expression, and not for Japanese only. All non-Japanese who live and work in Hawaii are touched by such values, especially those who marry with *sansei* or *yonsei*.

One Japanese value, *seiko* (success), fits the American environment extremely well. Without some basis for achievement motivation, the American principle of economic reward for individual achievement becomes a punishing illusion. *Seiko,* of course, was linked to family pride and obligation in Japan and even in Hawaii. One studied and worked hard to succeed for the family, not for oneself. But the results in terms of economic mobility were the same. Impelled by *seiko,* many *issei* and *nisei* found mobility ladders even in the repressive, restricted plantation system and especially beyond it in the towns of Honolulu and Hilo. By the time of the *sansei* and *yonsei,* pure *seiko* had been combined with the American drive for individual success.

One of the most fascinating things about the Japanese experience in Hawaii is that economic success has not destroyed *on* and *giri* among family members. Contrasted to Jewish Americans, for example, whose high mobility has been accompanied by great difficulty in maintaining extended kin networks, the third- and fourth-generation Japanese in Hawaii show considerable reliance on families through various forms of *giri*. The Japanese patriarchal *ie* (household) was weakened, of course, but the Japanese *kosai,* the large network of close family, relatives, and friends to whom one felt obligated and who, in turn, reciprocated, was maintained and adapted to island circumstances. Hawaii's island insularity kept the *kosai* active since economic mobility did not mean physical movement from one end of a big continent, or even from one city to another.

Of course, as Ogawa shows, new problems have replaced old ones and new roles and functions must be negotiated between the sexes and the generations under the impact of the American emphasis on independence and equality. In these matters, Ogawa shows no sympathy for the patriarchal hierarchy of old, although he reveals great sensitivity and concern—perhaps stemming from his Japanese roots —over the neglect and hurting of the aged so common in the United States. In addition, he displays an empathy for Japanese American women who suffer new conflicts because of the new expectations and demands which the American environment encourages. The family-mindedness of Professor Ogawa—as he looks at the strains and stresses of the *nisei* and *sansei* families—helps him to lift ethnic history into a larger humanistic context.

That humanism is reflected in the importance which Ogawa gives to such *haole* leaders as Miles Cary, Benjamin Wist, Frank Midkiff, John Burns, David Thompson, and Andrew Lind, and especially to the important places which he has assigned to the Reverends Yemyo Imamura and Takie Okumura in the unfolding of the Japanese story in Hawaii. Imamura, the bishop of the Buddhist Honpa Hongwanji until 1932, often criticized for redirecting Buddhist institutions to accommodate to Christianity, is no Uncle Tom to Ogawa, but a loving, compassionate man trying to help *issei* and *nisei* live comfortably in a new and disorienting place. Okumura, who was a vigorous Christianizer and Americanizer is not portrayed here as "selling out." Rather it was Okumura's vision of American pluralism which eventually materialized in Hawaii. Like Ogawa, he foresaw a way of life for Americans of Japanese ancestry which would synthesize elements of the old and new without leading to political and economic servility.

An expression of synthesizing with which Ogawa is in sympathy is the emergence of pidgin English, that remarkably emotive mixture of many languages which came from the multiethnic experience of

Hawaii's plantations. Ogawa correctly calls on the writings of *haole* John Reinecke, the scholar whose work on the two disparate fields of language and labor in Hawaii remains unrivaled, to tell about pidgin.

If there is anything missing in this fascinating saga of the Japanese-American experience in Hawaii it is a touch of pessimism. The optimism in this book prevails even in Glen Grant's concluding essay on race relations in the Hawaiian school. Grant shows convincingly that it is possible for school children of different ethnic backgrounds to negotiate points of commonality even when they openly express hostility to each other in school. Perhaps in another book Ogawa will face head-on the serious threats to his vision of pluralism in Hawaii. Now that they are relatively successful and powerful, Japanese Americans have become the targets of antagonisms expressed by the relatively poor and powerless Filipinos, Samoans and part Hawaiians. But Ogawa does not permit darker themes of resentment against Japanese success to mar his positive view of the Japanese experience in Hawaii or his hopes for ethnic harmony in the islands.

The author is an idealist who correctly finds confirmation of his humanism in his experience of Japanese Americans in Hawaii. At a time when retribalization the world over often results in torture and murder, Ogawa shows us how men and women can have some of the best of their tribalism and humanism, too. Perhaps they can, at least in the United States (with the possible exception of those natives who were conquered by the Anglo-Europeans), since First Amendment freedoms do permit one to be as ethnic as one likes while at the same time they impose limits to the destructive expression of ethnic values and interests. That is the hope implicit in this remarkable story.

By insisting that ethnic differences can enrich rather than destroy humanity, Ogawa hitches his scholarly talents and poetic insights to the party of hope. As impressed as he is by his inheritance from the past ("Okage sama de"—"I am what I am because of you") and by his obligation to the future ("kodomo no tame ni"—"for the sake of the children"), his sense of hope is contagious. For his scholarship, insight, and optimism we should all say *mahalo nui loa*.

LAWRENCE H. FUCHS

Preface

BY 1974 the descendants of Japanese immigrants to Hawaii had come to occupy influential and powerful positions in Island society. As a result of the state election in that year, Japanese American men and women not only occupied Hawaii's top political offices of Governor and Lieutenant Governor but also sat in significant numbers in the State House and Senate. In the economic life of Hawaii, Japanese had become major business figures helping to guide Hawaii's financial destiny. In public education, in civil service jobs, and in the statewide administration, Japanese could be found exercising a significant degree of power.

Forty years earlier suspicious voices in Hawaii had predicted the eventual takeover of the Islands by the offspring of Japanese immigrants, who were described as clannish, conniving, and disloyal, the forerunners of the oncoming "Yellow Menace." The doomsayers argued that one day, when too many Nipponese had been made eligible to vote, the Japanese race would inundate Hawaii's elected offices. They would then control the economy, buy up the land, and totally disregard American mores and traditions.

By 1974 the predictions had evidently fulfilled themselves but without the dire consequences that had been forecast. There were no anguished cries over a Japanese "takeover." When the people of Hawaii elevated Japanese Americans to their highest state offices, the bugaboo of the "Yellow Menace" was not resurrected. Obviously, in the decades between the Thirties and the Seventies significant changes had occurred in the status of Japanese in Hawaii. During World War II, Japanese Americans had proved their loyalty to America, dispelling doubts over their national affiliation and their degree of adaptation to American ways. During the Fifties, out of a deep-felt desire to improve the quality of their lives, second-generation Japanese Americans, the Nisei, had been in the forefront of those working for social progress in Hawaii. The children of that generation, the Sansei, had been raised in a community where schools, shopping centers, recreation areas, and social occasions were nearly wholly multicultural in complexion. Indeed, by 1974, Hawaii was well along in that process of racial maturation the objective of which is the unqualified accommodation of all ethnic groups into the flow of Hawaiian life.

As Japanese Americans evolved into full participants in Island society, a significant change in their social identity also took place. These descendants of the early Japanese immigrants no longer identify with Japan, nor do they feel the need to prove their Americanism. Rather they have become reasonably content to call themselves "locals"— a term used in Hawaii which has many meanings in many contexts. For some, a "local" is someone born and raised in Hawaii regardless of race or social background. For others, the term has a racial connotation and is used to distinguish nonwhite or "local people" from white people, or *haoles*. Despite the various specific usages of the term, a fundamental spirit is conveyed by the label "local." Those who say they are "local" are saying that they distinguish themselves from people who they believe are not sensitive to the racial and cultural forces operating in Hawaii. It means that they share a special language, a special mode of behavior, a special value system, and a special racial experience which separates them and other "locals" from the "outsiders." As "locals" they believe that they respect the diversity of people around them while also appreciating their commonness of lifestyles and attitudes. It has been the ability of Japanese Americans to involve themselves in this multicultural focus of "localness" which, in addition to World War II and social mobility, helped to ameliorate the tensions and suspicions of the previous decades and allowed Japanese to emerge not as a "menace" but as partners in the designing of Hawaii's future.

What I have sought to do in this book is interpret the history and the cultural growth of Japanese Americans in Hawaii, from the first contact made by shipwrecked sailors, through the years of major immigration, the plantation years, the war years, the years of growth in the dynamic Fifties and Sixties to the present and the emergence of a "local" identity. In the text of each chapter I have attempted the interpretation of broad Island social developments. The documents and articles placed at the end of each chapter provide the reader with contemporaneous accounts that illuminate the context in which the described events occurred.

I wanted also to make this book more than just an objective history of an ethnic group or a standard cultural investigation of Japanese American lifestyle. Since I have proposed that the Japanese American experience and identity evolved out of the complex multicultural environment of Hawaii, by extension this study is also concerned with the humanistic implications of pluralistic Island living. Various social questions are discussed in the chapters that follow: What are the relationships between Japanese Americans and the other racial groups comprising Hawaii's population? In what directions are the forces of ethnicity, economic mobility, and culture moving? How have technology, media, tourism, and the impact of modern urban society affected the many facets of Island life? What are the alternative futures open to the people of Hawaii as they attempt to strengthen their way of living? And more specifically, how can Japanese American culture contribute to the perpetuation of cultural pluralism in Hawaii?

With these questions, some answers are both explicitly and implicitly suggested. But underlying the answers and more important than them is the attitude suggested in this text, an attitude of "ethnic optimism" that I feel is indispensable to Hawaii's future. This optimism can be understood in terms of a number of value judgments: The "local" culture of Hawaii, the culture in which so many diverse people share values and behaviors, is valuable and needs to be preserved for the future. Why? Because at the basis of such a culture is a commitment to the human values of loving, caring, mutual obligation and respect, all of which enhance the quality of the human experience. The genius of Hawaiian race relations, the remarkable process of interracial harmony among a multitude of people on a minuscule island chain, grows out of the sharing of "local" culture. And most crucially, the ethnic peoples of Hawaii have the power to significantly improve the quality of their lives. Racism, economic oppression, and all the other evils of the American system or any other system are obstacles but not insurmountable barriers. Ethnic peoples in American environments are still capable of achieving equitable levels of power, freedom, and pride.

These value judgments might seem to many as simple platitudes. In the field of ethnic studies it is frequently fashionable to label such "ethnic optimism" heretical. Too often the study of an ethnic group is aimed at pointing out the frustrating conditions of their physical and psychological lives and creating attitudes of racial jealousy and confrontation. Some view Japanese Americans as ethnic "casualties" of an American racist system and their experience as one of unbearable suffering, or when it is pointed out that the ethnic group has been successfully upwardly mobile then the Japanese are a people who "sold out" or who were "whitewashed." In Hawaii, the pessimists reason, the future is dismal for both Japanese Americans and other "local" peoples. They say that forces of racial intrusion, cultural genocide, and capitalistic exploitation will be made manifest in mainland-style racial violence, crime, poverty, pollution, and alienation with the result that "local" culture will be destroyed. The ethnic individual is left with no real choice save to be bitter about the past, suspicious of the present, and fatalistic about the future.

The alternative attitude of "ethnic optimism" presented in this book is not an attempt to obscure or sugarcoat Hawaii's problems. It is, I believe, a humanistic approach to dealing with the complexity of the future as learned from the Japanese American experience. The impinging problems of today are no more dire, no more seemingly overwhelming than those met by generations in the past. The Issei lived in a world of overt racial oppression, imposed poverty, and social rejection. The Nisei not only inherited a world of limited opportunity but had to confront the catastrophe of a war which seemed to spell doom for their way of life. But rather than succumbing to fatalism or racial bitterness, both generations were sustained by the belief that for the sake of the children, *kodomo no tame ni,* the quality of life in Hawaii could be improved. If one worked hard, saved, sacrificed, and gathered strength from one's cultural roots, then material, social, and spiritual well-being would be possible for the coming generation.

Such a positive commitment to posterity is the basis upon which all ethnic groups in Hawaii have been able to improve the conditions of their lives. For the sake of the children, the racial and social systems of Hawaii have continually been made more flexible and durable. If Islanders earnestly wish to achieve more racial openness, to improve the quality of their lives, and to perpetuate the values and traditions of their "local" culture, then Hawaii's future will continue to rely upon this spirit of *kodomo no tame ni.*

Acknowledgments

THIS book would not be complete without acknowledging the individuals who helped make it a reality. First I am indebted to the scores of men and women pioneers in Hawaiian social research who developed the area of Japanese American studies. Scholars such as Yukiko Kimura, Bernhard Hormann, Andrew Lind, Katsumi Onishi, Jitsuichi Masuoka, Ernest Wakukawa, Romanzo Adams, Kiyoshi Ikeda, Louise Hunter, George Yamamoto, Take and Allan Beekman, and Harry H. L. Kitano have shared the conviction through their diverse works that the study of a relatively small ethnic group can provide creative inroads to understanding the American experience. The intellectual debt owed to them by any scholar in the field is beyond measure. In addition I must acknowledge the warm camaraderie of my colleagues, high school and community college teachers, research assistants, students, clergymen, community leaders, and businessmen with whom I have shared a myriad of insights and dialogues useful to illustrate an evolving Japanese American "local" lifestyle.

I wish also to thank Seymour Lutzky, Chairman of the American Studies Department at the University of Hawaii, whose continued support and sound advice have carried me through not only this publication but the demands ensuing from my work in the area of Japanese American studies. Special gratitude is also owed to Marcella Barcelona, Eileen Ebesu, and Sharon Uyeda, who conscientiously helped in the preparation of this manuscript, to Janyce Blair for her editorial assistance, and to Keiji Kawakami for his perceptive comments.

Funding for this book was made possible by the Rockefeller Foundation through the American Studies Department at the University of Hawaii and the Juliette M. Atherton Trust through the Japanese American Research Center.

Lastly, I am thankful to Amy, my wife, for her warm understanding and positive encouragement. Through her I have learned a special beauty of the "local" spirit.

CHAPTER ONE

Like Waves They Came

TO the small group of starved, sunburnt fishermen, the challenging cliffs, white beaches, and tropical greenery of Makapuu Point on the Hawaiian island of Oahu must have looked like heaven. For months their disabled boat had been drifting aimlessly in the treacherous current known as Kuroshio, the Black Current, which sweeps eastward from Japan across the Pacific Ocean. Their supply of food and water had been depleted; the sun had mercilessly shrunk and cracked wooden boards and human skin; the gods had seemingly deserted them. But now the vision of an island sanctuary aroused expectations of fruits, fresh water, shelter, and the more humane securities provided by the solid earth. The incoming ocean current captured the small craft in the sweep of its relentless waves, peaked to a wall of water, then finally exploded into a torrent of foam, rushing men and vessel to shore.

To the natives who lived near Makapuu Point, the shipwrecked fishermen must have appeared as a bewildering sight. The strangers' smaller stature, the slant of their eyes, their customs and language were wholly alien to the natives who for centuries had been isolated from the influences of the American and Asian continents. But now, in the thirteenth century A.D., the Polynesians stood face to face with a few disarrayed representatives of the Japanese race, wondering whether the *akua*s (the gods) would scorn or embrace the interlopers.

The legends of an ancient people are, more often than not, contestable factual histories. Wrapped in the myths and symbols of the natives' cultural vision, legends are interpretative forms of storytelling indifferent to modern concerns of objectivity. What happened to these Japanese fishermen stranded in the Pacific is an irrelevant question to the natives' stories and chants. Did the Japanese return to Japan? Did they continue their journey to the Americas? Did they remain in Hawaii, fusing their blood and culture with that of the natives? Legend simply does not say.

But ancient legend does indicate that these early Japanese fishermen were not the only shipwrecked visitors to Hawaii in the ageless era before Captain James Cook's arrival in the Islands in 1778. Between the thirteenth and nineteenth centuries, the Kuroshio's treacherous waters swept numerous Japanese ships and their frightened passengers out across the Pacific, depositing them rudely on the coral reefs of the Hawaiian archipelago. Inadvertently, the Kuroshio became a rough-hewn bridge between the civilizations of feudal Japan and the stone-age world of the Hawaiian native. Across this bridge came not only castaways but the artifacts of Japanese culture, several of which became incorporated into the indigenous lifestyle of the tolerant, friendly native. For example, the Hawaiian game of *konane* perhaps evolved from the Japanese game of *go*. The plumed standard of state which Hawaiian royalty retained, the *kahili,* was possibly derivative of the Japanese *keyari,* the feathered or haired pike carried in feudal Japan as a symbol of rank.[1] Early Japanese castaways probably even brought the first sugar cane to Hawaii.[2]

In the year 1804, the visits of Japanese to Hawaii ceased to be merely legend and became permanently recorded history. In that year a shipwrecked sailor named Tsudayu and three other men were picked up at sea by a Russian ship and then put ashore in Hawaii. Tsudayu later returned to Japan and wrote of his experiences in a journal entitled *Hawaii Kenbun Roku, An Account of Things Seen and Heard in Hawaii.* Though a colorful account of adventure and exotic lands, Tsudayu's published journal had little impact in Japan. No adventurers or explorers set sail for the curious isles in the Pacific to whet their appetites for exotica. No merchants or traders outfitted their ships with merchandise to be exchanged with the Polynesian natives for a healthy profit, for since the year 1636, the people of Japan had viewed travel to foreign lands with suspicion and justified fear. In that year, the imperial government ruled by the Tokugawa clan, had expressly forbidden all travel to or from Japan. To disobey this edict had meant death for the Japanese citizen. Even castaways, who through no fault of their own found themselves in the remote regions of the Pacific Ocean, knew that they risked execution by returning to Japan.

Under the reign of the Tokugawas (circa 1600 to 1868), Japan maintained this policy of isolationism for almost 230 years. Fearful of the damaging and exploitative influences of outside powers, cultures, and ideas, mistrustful that Japanese emigration would mean "contamination" by alien ways, the Tokugawa government attempted to forestall as long as possible the inevitable emergence of Japan into the nineteenth-century world. Nevertheless, more and more castaways returned to Japan to speak of the world outside. Manjiro, one of the most famous of these shipwrecked sailors, had landed in Hawaii in 1841 and later was educated in America; he was known also by his Anglicized name, John Mung. Returning to his homeland, Manjiro urged, at the risk of his life, the loosening of Japan's isolationism so that she could benefit from the knowledge and progress of other nations. His voice joined a chorus of other Japanese politicians, intellectuals, and business interests who began to realize that Japan could not remain indefinitely aloof from the rest of the world.

By 1868 these internal pressures within the island nation had culminated to a point where the opening of Japan's doors to the outside world seemed inevitable. In 1853 Commodore Matthew G. Perry, seeking to expand markets for American trade, had forced his steam frigates into Tokyo Bay, making Japanese policy-makers acutely aware of the need to strengthen the nation against Western encroachment. Also, political power shifted from the isolationist Tokugawas to the Meiji clan with the restoration of the Meiji Emperor in 1868. The new Meiji government was clearly more inclined to speed up the Westernization of Japan's economic and military system, and consequently the attitudes in Japan became less hostile to foreign emigration. And, as a consequence, one of the first foreign lands to which Japanese would travel would be the islands of which so many castaways had spoken—Hawaii, for concurrent with the developments in Japan, changes were occurring in Hawaii which would create a need for Japanese immigration. In the Islands, an environment once characterized by a peaceful and self-sustaining native economy and later by whaling and the selling of sandalwood was being transformed under Western influences and control into a blustering sugar-cane-plantation economy. During the American Civil

War, the price of sugar leaped nearly eightfold, making sugar production in Hawaii economically profitable—fortunes could be made which dwarfed the profits of sandalwood or whaling enterprises. After the war, as well, the Hawaiian sugar market continued to grow, firmly establishing power and prestige for several Island plantation families such as the Baldwins, Castles, Cookes, Rices, and Wilcoxes. Due to their sugar interests, these families became firmly rooted in the Islands' political, economic, and social life. Indeed, "King Sugar" revolutionized the old patterns of life in the Islands and initiated changes which would be the basis of a modern Hawaii.

Sugar production had an important impact on the racial makeup of the Islands. The primary need of the sugar planters was cheap foreign labor. The planters reasoned that what was necessary to the happy perpetuity of the plantation was a contented labor force that would work for a pittance, would not have "rising expectations," and would not question the power of *haole* (white) authority. In its ideal form, the plantation system would be predicated on the unchallenged but benevolent rule of the white man and the complacent obedience of the nonwhite man. To implement this system, the planters convinced the Hawaiian royalty to approve the Masters and Servants Act in 1850, establishing beyond question the power of the managerial class and the subservience of the workers. Labor immigrants would be required to sign a three-year contract which in effect made them indentured servants.

Yet, though they had developed a perfect institution of managerial control, the planters had a continual problem in finding adequate numbers of laborers. Initially, Polynesians were considered by *haole* planters as being unsuited for plantation employment—they were not "ambitious" enough for the planters. More accurately, the cultural and physical decimation of the Hawaiian population after the introduction of Western mores in the early nineteenth century had left a once robust, energetic people largely listless, in a cultural stupor. In addition, the long, continuous hours of monotonous work for a meager wage, coupled with the subsequent disruption of normal family and social patterns, were consequences of plantation labor which were wholly incompatible with the stable Hawaiian way of life. Consequently, the plantation owners turned to China as a source of cheap labor. But the Chinese workers soon proved themselves "unreliable" by leaving the plantation and starting small businesses in the towns. Perhaps, the sugar planters then hoped, a source of subservient, compliant labor could be found in Japan.

To secure a legal arrangement for the importation of Japanese laborers to work on the Hawaiian plantations, entreaties were made by the Hawaiian Foreign Ministry to the Japanese government. With forces of change ripe in Japan and with the diplomatic maneuvering of Eugene Van Reed, the Hawaiian representative in Tokyo, it was agreed that an experimental group of immigrants might at first be best. Approximately 150 Japanese artisans, criminals, ex-*samurai,* intellectuals, and an occasional farmer were subsequently recruited off the streets of Yokohama to work on the plantations in Hawaii. The year was 1868, or "Meiji One." These "first-year men" to Hawaii, the *Gannen-mono,* were the great experiment to determine the feasibility of further Japanese labor immigration.

Unfortunately for the sugar planters, the *Gannen-mono* did not prove to be a fully successful venture. Unaccustomed to field work, resentful of the poor treatment and the need to take orders from non-Japanese, the laborers drifted into Honolulu and refused to continue their plantation employment. Word soon reached Japan that her citizens were being maltreated, and eventually the *Gannen-mono* were recalled home. About 100 of them, though, chose to remain in Hawaii, where many intermarried with Hawaiian women.

The primary result of the 1868 episode of the *Gannen-mono* was to forestall the major waves of Japanese immigration for another seventeen years. The imperial government had become critical of the words and gestures of a government and its sugar interests which promised to handle Japanese citizens in a fair and equal manner and then subjected them to questionable working conditions and harsh treatment. As a consequence, not until nearly two decades later, in the 1880s, did the sugar planters finally succeed in loosening the reluctant and isolationist attitude of the Japanese government, allowing once again the movement of laborers from Japan to Hawaii.

In addition to the sugar planters, the concern for Japanese immigration to Hawaii was also being echoed by the Hawaiian monarchy, though for wholly different reasons. While the *haole* planters sought cheap labor from Japan, the monarchy, most notably King David Kalakaua, looked to the Japanese as a possible rejuvenating source of racial blood for the dying native population. From the hundreds of thousands of Hawaiians who lived at the time of Captain Cook's arrival in 1778, the native population had been reduced to fewer than 50,000 natives in 1880. Measles, smallpox, venereal diseases, and cultural shock—the "gifts" of Western civilization—were decimating the last vestiges of the ancient race. Many Hawaiian nationalists, especially King Kalakaua, considered the Japanese to be affinitive to the Polynesian race in blood and genetic background. Through intermarriage, the Japanese laborer could thus greatly help to bolster an otherwise waning people.

Conscious of the demands of the sugar planters and concerned with the survival of his race, King Kalakaua met with emperor Meiji in 1881 to encourage closer ties between the two Pacific kingdoms. The king even proposed to the emperor a union of the royal houses through a marriage of Kaiulani, the king's niece, and young Prince Komatsu of Japan. Although the proposed royal matrimony was declined by the emperor, positive relations between the two nations and the monarchs were enhanced.

The final culmination of Kalakaua's and the sugar planters' eagerness for Japanese immigration came on February 8, 1885. On that day, more than 940 Japanese labor immigrants, the first substantial group of Japanese to arrive in Hawaii, stepped from the gangplank of the steamer *City of Tokio* onto the dock of Honolulu harbor. The *Gannen-mono,* enshrouded in doubt and ill-feeling, had been an experiment—a trial balloon for both the Japanese and the sugar planters. But the immigrants of 1885 and the years following, most of them young, single males and indigent farmers from Hiroshima and Yamaguchi, came to Hawaii to become an integral part of the Hawaiian labor force—providing the bulk of the manual labor needed to plant, harvest, and cultivate sugar.

Between 1885 and 1907, thousands of Japanese came to Hawaii, bolstering, supporting, and giving wealth to the Island economy. So great was the inundation of Japanese laborers that by 1897 Japanese constituted the largest single ethnic group in the Islands. The growing use of Japanese workers was rapid, but controlled and structured due to careful agreements between the governments of Japan and Hawaii. In 1886, representatives of the two nations, after a series of major diplomatic maneuvers, negotiated a set of rather well-defined immigration guidelines and work provisions. An important priority for the Japanese government during these talks, as noted by Alex Ladenson in his essay "The Background of the Hawaiian-Japanese Labor Convention of 1886,"[3] was an insistence on the overall protection of Japanese citizens. Maintaining an attitude of distrust and reluctance, the government of Japan would not allow her emigrants to be exploited or abused in foreign countries. The imperial government demanded adequate working conditions for Japanese laborers, ranging from the employment of nonwhite overseers to the provision of daily hot baths. Later, when the harsh realities of life on the Hawaiian sugar plantation became known, efforts were made in Tokyo to further strengthen the treaty regulations and provide greater control over working conditions. But despite such attempts to rectify plantation injustice, the government of Japan, the Japanese consul in Hawaii, and various labor arbitrators in actuality were ineffectual in improving the life of the Japanese plantation worker.

In the 1886 negotiations, the Japanese government also demanded a provision that Japanese and Chinese laborers be kept separate—a stipulation wholeheartedly supported by the sugar planters. In the importation of foreign labor, the risk always existed that if nonwhite workers united, the managerial elite would be overwhelmed. But by keeping races apart and in competition with each other, by encouraging cultural diversity, the fear of a united labor force crippling the economy by strike or riot was dissipated. Consequently, the separation of Japanese and Chinese laborers was an action highly desired not only by the Japanese government, traditionally at conflict with China, but by the sugar planters as well. While keeping the Japanese content, such separation helped to maintain peacefully the plantation policy of "divide and rule."

Besides the practice of ethnic divisiveness, another device used to regulate the plantation worker was the enforced labor contract. As negotiated and formally outlined in the Masters and Servants Act, Japanese laborers working on the plantations had to sign three-year, nonviolative contracts which in effect made them indentured servants. This three-year contract system, perpetuating the racial caste-like rule of the planters, existed in Hawaii until the annexation of the Islands to the United States in 1898. The elimination of the contract system was stipulated in the annexation act because many members of the United States Congress viewed this form of labor contract as involuntary servitude and therefore a violation of the Fourteenth Amendment of the Constitution.

For the majority of Japanese immigrants, though, the three-year contract defined their Island experience—an existence before 1898 characterized by harsh physical work, oriented toward only those with an unusual amount of human fortitude. The feelings, frustrations, and expectations of the Japanese laborer in this environment are perhaps best understood if one analyzes the motivations behind his leaving Japan. Treaties, conventions, and negotiations between governments explain the legal, formal means by which immigration is carried out. But why would a young man, proud of his race, loving his homeland and devoted to his family, pull up stakes and take the risk of encountering unknown conditions and hardships on a Pacific isle? What, after all, would compel a Japanese to leave Japan?

In 1909, with the perspective of contemporary insight, Yosaburo Yoshida investigated what he felt were the reasons behind Japanese immigration to Hawaii and America. In his article, "Sources and Causes of Japanese Emigration,"[4] he suggested three major factors which created the conditions for a patriotic and proud people to leave their homes. Rather than religious, political, or social upheaval as a cause of emigration, Yoshida postulated: 1) an increasing homeland population made living conditions in some rural areas undesirable, 2) a rising cost of living beyond the range of wages as a result of fluctuating economic conditions caused money to be scarce, and 3) the inducement to migrate as propagandized through the "Horatio Alger" stories of a "get-rich-quick" life in Hawaii and America made emigration alluring.

As a result, in almost all cases the Japanese immigrant saw the journey to Hawaii as merely a chance to make money and then return to Japan. Unlike many immigrant groups who came to America to find a new home, the Japanese immigrant did not see working and living in Hawaii as a reason to sever his relations with the land of his ancestors. To the contrary, after completing his contract and earning his "wealth," he intended to return to Japan with new status and prestige. Emigration was not the beginning of a permanent new life abroad but meant a temporary job which would enhance his life in the homeland. Not until the illusions of a paradise in the Pacific gave way to reality did the immigrant find himself economically tied to a place which he had hoped only to visit.

Historians, sociologists, novelists, and artists have made some attempts to recreate different aspects of plantation life as encountered by the Japanese worker. The decision to come to Hawaii, the disorienting travel across the Pacific, the cultural shock of Island life, and the grueling labor have been described with varying degrees of success by several authors. One fictional account of the immigration experience is Margaret N. Harada's novel, *The Sun Shines on the Immigrant.*[5] The protagonist in Harada's story—Yoshio Mori—is a young man, son of a poor peasant family, who goes to work in a Kyoto hotel. There he hears of Hawaii and the fortune to be made, and he takes the risks that sometimes only youth can appreciate or understand. The author reveals through Yoshio's eyes the grim realities of plantation labor, the linguistic and cultural difficulties, and the unalterable truth that for three years Yoshio would be a servant to the plantation system.

The story of Yoshio Mori is largely romanticized fiction. But from 1885 to 1907, when Japanese labor immigration to the United States

and Hawaii was sharply curtailed, almost 180,000 immigrants similar to Yoshio Mori traveled to Hawaii. Like progressively mounting waves, Japanese swept across the Islands. In 1888, there were 6,420 Japanese in Hawaii; in 1890, 12,360; in 1896, 24,407; in 1900, 61,111.[6] Each immigrant came to find his wealth by laboring on the plantation. Each intended to return to Japan a successful man. And each found hardship, ceaseless toil, and, eventually, an unexpected racial prejudice denigrating to his ethnic pride.

Indeed, with each new wave of Japanese immigrants, the fears and racial distrusts of the Island *haole* elite were exacerbated. Japanese had been imported for labor, to bolster a dying race. But many *haole*s began to reevaluate the wisdom of unchecked Japanese immigration. By 1900, the *haole*s constituted about 5 percent of the total population of Hawaii, though they had virtual control of the political and economic life of the Islands. Numerically, the Japanese population was by 1900 the largest in Hawaii, nearly 40 percent. With such a large alien population, doubt and uncertainty in the *haole* community began to solidify and took the form of anti-Japanese sentiment. Could the *haole*s trust Japanese? What did the white man really know about Japanese? The immigrants provided good labor, but could they always be counted on to be subservient? What was the nature of their allegiance to Japan, a foreign nation with growing interests in the Pacific? Could a person such as Yoshio Mori be legitimately considered a vital member of a civilized Island community?

One of the earliest expressions of the distrust for the Japanese came in 1898, during the revolutionary period in Hawaiian history when the *haole* political leaders were establishing a new government with close ties to the United States. In that year, Thomas C. Hobson's article entitled "Japan's 'Peaceful Invasion' " appeared in the *Hawaiian Almanac and Annual.*[7] Several aspects of the article revealed an anti-Japanese sentiment, laced with impressionistic stereotypes. The immigration of Japanese, Hobson feared, was merely a long-range Japanese scheme to dominate the Islands. With the large numbers of Japanese on the plantations and in the cities, the *haole* would lose the ability to successfully control the political and economic future of Hawaii.

Hobson believed that the laborers, because of their refusal to return to the homeland, were part of a clear-cut policy of political intrigue designed and controlled by the imperial government in Tokyo. For Hobson, the only solution to the Japanese threat would be the establishment of closer ties between Hawaii and the United States.

Only America, acting as a counterbalancing power, could save Hawaii from the abhorred "Yellow Peril."

Attacked as infiltrators and agents of Japan, the Japanese immigrants were not without their response to the notion of a Japanese imperial conquest. To rebut the popular image of Japan's supposed "takeover" of Hawaii, Keijirō Nakamura wrote in 1897 an article entitled "Hawaiian Annexation from a Japanese Point of View."[8] Nakamura pointed out that Japan had never planned to include Hawaii in its sphere of interest. If anything, the annexation of Hawaii was seen as a threat to Japan's peaceful relations with the Islands. According to Nakamura, previous treaties with the Hawaiian monarchy, guaranteeing rights of passage and equal employment, would be jeopardized by the American government's discriminatory practices against Asians. He concluded with foreboding that "Japan would never nourish any ambition to fight with this great Republic, for she knows too well its powers and resources, but at the same time, she would not allow any party to snatch away her treaty rights." The stage had been set for forty years of American-Japanese entanglements, with the Japanese immigrant and his children caught in the resulting tensions.

By 1900, the Japanese community in Hawaii, due to its size, its relationship to Japan, and its noncommunications and misunderstandings with the *haole* community, had begun to experience some forms of anti-Japanese sentiment. Overall, the resentment which occurred was not manifested in the shape of dangerous racial outbursts or blatant expressions in public. The discrimination and prejudice encountered by Japanese in Hawaii were of a quality and quantity different from those they faced in areas of the mainland, such as California. The Hawaiian tradition of *aloha,* inbred into the lifestyle of Polynesians and even into the *haole* governance of the Islands, fostered subtlety and obscuration in the handling of racial matters. Discrimination on the social level was not openly practiced without a backlash of resentment and moral condemnation from several sectors of Hawaii's people.

On the mainland, such constraints on racism were rare. And, though Japanese laborers in Hawaii were relatively secure in their separate plantation camps, insulated from the social realities of the *haole* community and somewhat protected from overt racial oppressions, the racism directed against Japanese on the mainland had its residual effects on the Islands. Certainly the vociferous and dangerously persuasive rhetoric of the Yellow Peril on the mainland, particularly on the West Coast, injected its venom into several Island

haoles who had economic, educational, and social ties to the United States. The demagoguery against the Japanese and other Asian immigrants was being expressed not only by the rabble-rouser but by individuals in positions of power—labor leaders and progressives of both parties, mayors and state senators, governors and national policy-makers. Such a prevalent fear of Japan and Japanese immigrants could not have helped but influence the attitudes of the Island elite.

As inchoate mainland prejudices were transformed into action and legislation, national attitudes also affected the circumstances and conditions of the laborer's life. In 1907, the Gentlemen's Agreement, a voluntary pact between the United States and Japanese governments, virtually ended the immigration of male workers from Japan and, in addition, prohibited Japanese laborers from leaving Hawaii to work on the mainland. Whether he liked Hawaii or not, the plantation laborer was given little alternative except to work in the cane fields or to return penniless to Japan. The opportunities offered by the mainland United States had been closed.

The lack of knowledge concerning Japanese culture and people, the hostile influence of outside attitudes and legislation, the political and economic needs of annexation, and the unstable numerical position of *haole* dominance were all factors which helped cultivate the growth of anti-Japanese sentiment in Hawaii. The expression of that sentiment was somewhat tempered by the Hawaiian traditions of racial amiability and open acceptance. Nonetheless, the subtleties of Island prejudice and dehumanization continued to define the laborer's life in the first decades of the twentieth century. Like the victims of Kuroshio, these laborers had been helplessly swept into the involuntary forces of a plantation system impervious to human needs and emotions. Once, Hawaii had been viewed by the immigrant as a cornucopia of wealth where a man's dreams could be earned with perseverance and hard work. But the cornucopia had been found wanting, while men's dreams became idle scorn. In the rhythm of slashing cane and hauling loads, in the squalor of crudely improvised shacks and camps, the wounds of the system's drive would be soothed by the immigrant's song:

Hawaii, Hawaii
Like a dream so I came
But my tears are flowing now
In the canefields.[9]

NOTES

1. For a discussion of the cultural influences resulting from Japanese contacts with Hawaii, see John F. G. Stokes, "Japanese Cultural Influences in Hawaii," in *Proceedings of the Fifth Pacific Science Congress, Victoria and Vancouver, B.C., Canada, 1933,* Toronto: University of Toronto Press (1934), pp. 2791–2803.

2. United Japanese Society of Hawaii, *A History of Japanese in Hawaii,* ed. by Publication Committee, Dr. James H. Okahata, Chm., Honolulu: United Japanese Society of Hawaii, 1971, pp. 6–7.

3. Alex Ladenson, "The Background of the Hawaiian-Japanese Labor Convention of 1886," *Pacific Historical Review,* v. 9, no. 4 (December 1940), pp. 389–400.

4. Yosaburo Yoshida, "Sources and Causes of Japanese Emigration," *The Annals of the American Academy of Political and Social Science,* v. 34, no. 2 (September 1909), pp. 157–167.

5. Margaret N. Harada, *The Sun Shines on the Immigrant,* New York: Vantage Press, 1960, pp. 26–35.

6. United Japanese Society of Hawaii, p. 113.

7. Thomas C. Hobson, "Japan's 'Peaceful Invasion,' " *Hawaiian Almanac and Annual for 1898,* Honolulu: Thomas G. Thrum, 1897, pp. 131–134.

8. Keijirō Nakamura, "Hawaiian Annexation from a Japanese Point of View," *Arena,* v. 18, no. 97 (December 1897), pp. 834–839.

9. The only known song of Japanese immigrants in Hawaii referred to in this chapter is known as the "Hole Hole Bushi." For more information, see Gail Miyasaki, " 'Hole Hole Bushi': The Only Song of the Japanese in Hawaii," *The Hawaii Herald* (February 2, 1973), pp. 4–5.

The Background of the Hawaiian-Japanese Labor Convention of 1886

ALEX LADENSON

ON February 8, 1885, the *City of Tokio* arrived at Honolulu with 943 Japanese immigrants on board. These consisted of 676 men, 159 women, and 108 children. Extra precautions were taken by the Hawaiian authorities in the transportation of these people and not a casualty occurred during the passage.[1] With the immigrants came Jiro Nakamura, first Japanese consul to Hawaii.[2] Included in the first party of immigrants, also, was one G. O. Nacayama who was employed by the Hawaiian Board of Immigration as interpreter and general intermediary. On June 17, 1885, a second contingent of immigrants arrived consisting of 939 men, 35 women, and 14 children.

Advising his government of the shipments, Mr. Irwin[3] declared that the Japanese immigrants were not "laborers" in their native land but small farmers. They held land which in some cases had been a possession of their families for hundreds of years and which originally had been granted to their forbears as a reward for military service. Irwin also sent rather specific directions for the treatment of the Nipponese emphasizing the desirability of not placing them under white or native overseers. Moreover, he cautioned that they be supplied with hot water each day for bathing purposes.[4]

The new arrivals were promptly hired out to the planters. They were described by the American minister at Honolulu as "a hardy and tractable class of laborers."[5] The Hawaiian government guaranteed them a minimum wage of nine dollars per month in addition to food and lodging. The laborers had the option of supplying their own food in which case, individually, they would be allowed six dollars additional. The government of Hawaii engaged to provide them with rice at five cents per pound. Twenty-six working days of ten hours each constituted a month for purposes of payment. Five hundred of the immigrants agreed to work thirty minutes extra each day in return for the privilege of being permitted a quarter of an acre of land for the purpose of raising vegetables.[6]

A few months after the arrival of the Japanese emigrants, Katsunoske Inouye was sent from Tokyo as special commissioner to Hawaii. He carried a dispatch from Count Inouye, the Japanese foreign minister, addressed to Walter Gibson, minister of foreign affairs. In this note Count Inouye expressed his satisfaction with the manner in which the first shipment of laborers was conducted but desired to bring certain matters to the attention of the Hawaiian government. First, in view of the prospective emigration of thousands of Japanese to Hawaii, Count Inouye felt that one interpreter was not sufficient to dispose of the difficulties which might arise for want of a common medium of expression. He suggested that the authorities employ several Japanese who could speak the English language to assist Mr. Nacayama.

The foreign minister of Japan next dwelt on the question of Chinese immigration. He reminded Mr. Gibson of the promises made by the Hawaiian government that it would limit the entrance of Chinese into the islands to a number not exceeding 600 for any three months. Inouye complained that this figure had been exceeded. He, therefore, requested a renewal of the assurances made, limiting Chinese immigration, and suggested ultimately the termination of this traffic. His reasons for desiring the proscription of the subjects of China were frankly set forth explaining that the imperial government viewed with disfavor the association of Japanese and Chinese abroad.

Lastly, Count Inouye informed the Hawaiian foreign minister that a Japanese corporation was being chartered for the purpose of carrying on business between Hawaii and Japan. One of the objects of its establishment was to provide the Japanese in Hawaii with certain necessities of life. Inouye asked the Hawaiian government to consider the feasibility of granting to this company a rebate of duties paid on rice. In addition he observed that the company contemplated the operation of a line of steamers between Yokohama and Honolulu, to be connected also with San Francisco by a line under the Hawaiian flag. In view of the fact that Japan was prepared to guarantee a regular service between Yokohama and Honolulu, the minister inquired whether the government of Hawaii was ready to insure a like regularity of service between Honolulu and San Francisco. Since the Japanese government proposed to bestow a subsidy upon this company, Inouye desired also to know whether Hawaii could extend similar aid. On all the above points Katsunoske Inouye, the Japanese envoy, was instructed to confer with the Hawaiian authorities.[7]

On July 18, 1885, a conference was held at the Hawaiian foreign office between Walter Gibson and Katsunoske Inouye. Count Inouye's note served as the basis of negotiations. With respect to the request for additional interpreters Minister Gibson proposed the creation of a permanent Bureau of Inspection and Interpretation charged with the duty of facilitating intercourse between the Japanese laborers and the planters. For the present the board was to consist of Mr. Nacayama and at least four other Nipponese members. Inouye then suggested the appointment of several Japanese physicians as government employees. He explained that many of his countrymen objected to being treated by Caucasians. Gibson promptly granted this request stating that the Hawaiian Board of Health would be pleased to obtain the services of Japanese doctors. Next the conferees turned to the question of Chinese immigration. Mr. Gibson denied that his government had removed or relaxed restrictions on the immigration of Chinese into the islands. He reiterated the assurances previously made by Major Iaukea relating to this matter. Then followed a discussion of Count Inouye's final point with respect to a Japanese mercantile company and his request for a rebate of duties to be paid by it on importations of foodstuffs. Gibson announced that the government was willing to permit the importation from Japan free of duty of all provisions to be used by the laborers.[8] As a subsidy for a line of steam communication between Yokohama, Honolulu, and San Francisco, the foreign minister promised to recommend to the Hawaiian cabinet the annual payment of $25,000. This declaration, however, was subject to approval by the legislature. In conclusion Mr. Gibson raised the question of unpaid wage deposits. Under the original contracts, the Japanese laborers received only part of their wages in cash; the remainder, amounting to twenty-five per cent, was to be paid them at the expiration of the term of service. The unpaid portions of their wages it had been agreed were to be deposited by the planters in a government savings bank at five per cent interest. Gibson, now, suggested that these deposits be made in Mr. Claus Spreckels' bank instead, with payment to be guaranteed by the Hawaiian government. A précis of the conversations in the nature of a protocol was drafted and signed by the conferees.[9]

Three days later another conference took place between Gibson and Inouye. Certain other matters were examined and embodied in a stipulation to which they also affixed their signatures. By this instrument the Hawaiian government promised to regard the Japanese laborers as its wards. The planters, it was agreed, while employing Japanese were to be considered agents of the government. It was understood, moreover, that only duly authorized government officials were permitted to make arrests or seizures arising out of a breach of contract. In all cases of arrest the Nipponese were to be entitled to the services of an official interpreter connected with the immigration board. Finally, the government of Hawaii engaged itself to notify the planters that under no circumstances was a Japanese laborer to be beaten, and that a violation of this order would be ample grounds for the removal of the employee.[10]

But no sooner had these negotiations been concluded than Katsunoske Inouye received a message from Tokyo complaining of ill treatment of Japanese in the islands. The dispatch also disclosed the fact that the government of Japan had suspended immigration to Hawaii until a favorable report should be forthcoming from its envoy. Foreign Minister Gibson promptly wrote to Count Inouye. He asserted that the charges of ill treatment arose out of misunderstanding. They were not deliberate. Gibson assured Inouye there would be no recurrence of such complaints in view of the precautions taken by his government.[11] Added to these assurances, R. W. Irwin, Hawaiian representative in Tokyo, pledged his government to a scrupulous observance of the protocol concluded during the previous month at Honolulu. As a result of these many professions, Count Inouye agreed on August 17, to the resumption of emigration.[12]

The asseverations made by Gibson were not idle words. Early in August two additional interpreters were appointed under Mr. Nacayama. On August 10, a circular was issued by the Board of Immigration and distributed among the planters. In it attention was directed to the engagements made by the Hawaiian authorities in their negotiations with Japan. The planters were informed that the Japanese laborers were under the guardianship of the Hawaiian government. Therefore the onus of settling disputes between employers and employees fell upon it. The planters were further informed that a special commission of Japanese inspectors had been created under the direction of the immigration bureau. All complaints by employers, as well as by laborers, were to be referred to this commission for investigation and adjudication. Finally, the planters were admonished in no uncertain terms that force was not to be used under any circumstances except in self-defense. Disregard of this order by any employer would be considered sufficient cause for the withdrawal of the assignment of any person mistreated.[13]

While officials in Hawaii were bringing to fulfillment the provisions of the protocol, R. W. Irwin was pressing the Tokyo government for a formal labor convention. In Japan there was considerable opposition to the conclusion of such an agreement. In a speech made at Nagoya on August 24, the Chief Secretary of the Agricultural and Commercial Department exhorted the Japanese farmers not to go to Hawaii "and become slaves." This speech was printed several days later in the *Nichi Nichi Shimbun,* an important Tokyo newspaper.[14] Notwithstanding adverse opinion, a labor convention between the governments of Hawaii and Japan was signed on January 28, 1886.

Article 1 extended the terms of the convention to Japanese already in the islands as well as those who might emigrate in the future. In article 2 Japan agreed to permit her subjects to emigrate freely to Hawaii. Nippon, however, retained the right to limit, suspend, or prohibit this traffic. Under article 3 Yokohama and Honolulu were to be the ports of exit and entry respectively, and the transit was to be conducted under the supervision of the Ken Rei or governor of Kanagawa and a special Hawaiian agent. Article 4 stipulated that all emigration should be by contract; the term of service was not to exceed three years. The Hawaiian government undertook all the obligations of employer towards the immigrants and proffered to the latter the full protection of its laws. Article 5 provided for free steerage passage, including food, between the above-mentioned ports. By articles 6 and 7 Hawaii agreed to furnish Japanese inspectors, interpreters, and physicians. By article 8 Nipponese diplomatic and consular agents in Hawaii were granted freedom of access to all of their countrymen. Article 9 reserved to Hawaii the right to deport undesirable Japanese. Article 10 provided that the convention was to be in force for five years, and thereafter until one of the contracting parties, by a six months' previous notice, signified its intention to abrogate it. The signatories to this agreement were R. W. Irwin for Hawaii and Count Inouye for Japan.[15]

Before concluding the convention, Count Inouye wrote to Irwin demanding assurances that the proposed formal agreement should not supersede the engagements made by Hawaii in the protocol of July, 1885, and in the subsequent correspondence exchanged between the two governments. In addition, the Japanese foreign minister asked for the concurrence of the Hawaiian representative to the following supplementary terms: first, no emigrant was to be assigned, or reassigned to labor without the emigrant's written consent; second, whenever any laborer had just grounds for complaint which could not be satisfactorily adjusted, the Hawaiian government was to withdraw the laborer from his present employment and provide for him until a new job was found; third, suitable burial grounds for the laborers were to be provided; fourth, the government of Hawaii was to furnish hospital accommodations, and so far as possible to allow Japanese women to act as nurses; fifth, in suits instituted by Japanese emigrants, the latter were to have the assistance of the Attorney-General or such counsel as he might assign; sixth, vital statistics were to be kept by the Hawaiian government which were to be open to Japanese consular officers; seventh, the emigrants were to be encouraged to eat fresh meat and vegetables. Count Inouye also expressed the wish that the Hawaiian authorities should suppress immorality, inebriety, and gambling and to see "that the guilty parties would not be permitted by their continued presence in Hawaii to contaminate the better element among the emigrants."[16] Irwin accepted these conditions unreservedly. Upon request of Inouye, Minister Gibson shortly thereafter also joined in this acceptance.[17]

Thus a large-scale enterprise was launched. The convention with modifications remained in force until 1894. Under its terms twenty-six shipments of Japanese emigrants were made involving more than 28,000 persons.

The Hawaiian-Japanese Labor Convention of 1886 operated to the immediate mutual advantage of both countries. For Hawaii the convention made possible an adequate supply of labor at a time when the planters were in great need of it. The expansion of the sugar industry was facilitated to no small degree by Japanese labor. For Japan the convention meant economic opportunity for a considerable portion of its population. It marked, also, the beginning of a policy of Japanese emigration which has had, to this day, far-reaching effects in other quarters of the globe.

NOTES

[1.] *Report of the President of the Bureau of Immigration to the Legislative Assembly of 1886* (Honolulu, 1886), 227.

[2.] Rollin M. Daggett to F. T. Frelinghuysen, February 14, 1885, No. 215, [U.S. Department of State, Dispatches, Hawaii, XXII (hereinafter cited as H.D.)]. The following year this office was elevated to the rank of Diplomatic Agent and Consul-General. [G. W.] Merrill to [Thomas F.] Bayard, February 26, 1886, H.D., XXII.

[3. R. W. Irwin, Hawaiian representative in Japan (Ed. note).]

[4.] Immigration Report 1886, *op. cit.*, 227–28.

[5.] Daggett to Frelinghuysen, February 14, 1885, No. 215, H.D., XXII.

[6.] Immigration Report 1886, *op. cit.*, 228.

[7.] Inouye to Gibson, June 2, 1885, [U.S. Legation Archives, Hawaii, Notes from Hawaiian Government, IX (hereinafter cited as N.H.G.)].

[8.] Rollin M. Daggett, American minister to Hawaii, was asked to explain to his government the reasons for this agreement inasmuch as such an arrangement might be construed as being inconsistent with the reciprocity treaty.

[9.] Protocol of July, 1885, [*Report of the Minister of Foreign Affairs,* 1886 (Honolulu, 1886), cxl–cxliii].

[10.] Foreign Report 1886, *op. cit.,* cxliii–cxliv.

[11.] Gibson to Inouye, July 22, 1885, *ibid.,* cxlv–cxlix.

[12.] Irwin to Gibson, August 31, 1885, *ibid.,* cxlix–clii.

[13.] Immigration Report, 1886, *op. cit.,* 234–36.

[14.] Irwin to Gibson, August 31, 1885, Foreign Report 1886, *op. cit.,* cxlix–clii.

[15.] A copy of this convention is contained in enclosure 1 to accompany dispatch No. 54, H.D., XXII. It is also found in *Treaties and Conventions* [*Concluded Between the Hawaiian Kingdom and Other Powers Since 1825* (Honolulu, 1887)].

[16.] Inouye to Irwin, January 20, 1886, Foreign Report 1886, *op. cit.,* clxiii–clxvi.

[17.] Gibson to Inouye, March 5, 1886, *ibid.,* clxx.

Sources and Causes of Japanese Emigration

YOSABURO YOSHIDA

WHAT are the causes of Japanese emigration? I recognize and shall discuss three: increase of population, economic pressure, and inducement, or attraction.

Increase of Population

Increase of population is closely connected with economic pressure upon the laboring classes. But I shall describe here chiefly the former, and will discuss the latter afterwards.

No statistics of Japanese population are reliable until 1872. The increasing rate since that year has been as follows:[1]

Year	Per Cent	Year	Per Cent
1872	.57	1882	.86
1873	.98	1883	1.17
1874	1.11	1884	1.11
1875	1.00	1885	.84
1876	—	1886	.84
1877	—	1887	1.46
1878	—	1888	1.38
1879	.45	1889	1.17
1880	1.20	1890	.95
1881	.94	1891	.66

In *The Annals of the American Academy of Political and Social Science,* v. 34, no. 2 (September 1909), pp. 157–167. Reprinted by permission of the American Academy of Political and Social Science.

1892	.91	1900	1.25
1893	.73	1901	1.39
1894	1.03	1902	1.29
1895	1.09	1903	1.54
1896	1.04	1904	1.14
1897	1.22	1905	1.13
1898	1.24	1906	1.14
1899	1.14	1907	1.15

The above figures show that population is increasing year after year, and if the increase continues at the present rate the population will be doubled after sixty years.

Population increases, but the area of the land is limited, consequently the density of population per square ri[2] has been increasing at the following rates: 1872, 1,335; 1882, 1,385; 1892, 1,657; 1903, 1,885.

According to the general statistics, Japan in density of population ranks below only Belgium, Holland and England. These three nations get their food materials by importation from other countries; Japan is feeding herself.

I have described the rapid growth of population in Japan as a whole, but, if we ask ourselves whether those districts where population is most dense are the districts which contribute the largest number of emigrants, our answer is negative. The districts of Hiroshima, Yamaguchi, Wakayama and Fukuoka are not very dense in population, and their birth rates are also less than the average rate for the whole of Japan.[3] Yet these districts always contribute the dominant number to Japanese emigration. The districts of Kinai, where the successive emperors fixed their capital for more than twenty-five centuries, and where consequently the population is the most dense in the country, are not sections which drive emigrants abroad. Because of these facts, some writers urge that there is no direct connection between increasing population and Japanese emigration.[4]

But I consider the density of population a cause of emigration if we take the country as a whole. It is not the cause if we take district by district. The reason is very evident. Although some districts are very densely populated, if their economic capacity is sufficient to maintain their population, then it is not necessary to migrate. Furthermore, the peculiar character and environment of the people differ by districts. For example, the region of Kinai, with charming scenery, although crowded with a toiling population, renders the nature of the people very strong in home affection. Moreover, the family system is very ancient, and the people are amiable and submissive. On the contrary, the people of the regions from Hiroshima extending towards the southwestern districts, are venturesome and enterprising. The districts in Kinai have been the home of poets, artists and men of letters, while the southwestern part has supported pirates and warriors. That the increasing population is a profound cause for emigration can be seen more clearly if we consider it in connection with the economic pressure upon Japan's lower classes.

Economic Pressure

In this world-stage of the twentieth century, where many nations are competing with each other to become the dominant power, the rapid growth of population is a rather happy and desirable thing for our island empire, situated on the Eastern Sea. But this great movement, necessary from the viewpoint of further expansion of the empire, has a bad effect upon the classes who are toiling at the bottom of the present community. "The more poor the more babies," the Japanese proverb frankly runs. It is from these lower class people that the largest number of children come, and consequently the increase of population brings more laborers. The competition among the working classes in a country where the area of land is limited, where no national labor organization exists, where no labor legislation operates, results in vast millions of struggling creatures spending their daily lives under the economic pressure of landlords and capitalists in a hopeless and stricken condition.

The area of the cultivated land was only 5,193,762 cho in 1904,[5] that is, 17 per cent of the whole area. The average holding of land owned by one farmer is only 9 tan 8 se.[6] The annual yield from such a small piece of land, less than three acres, even under the most perfect system of utilization, is absolutely insufficient to support a family according to modern standards of comfort. Under such an economic condition the peasant class, which constitutes the bulk of the Japanese emigration to the United States, are spending their days. The fact that the districts which contribute the largest number of emigrants contain always the greatest percentage of the peasant class is shown below.

Geographical Sources of Emigrants

Basing our figures upon the number of passports issued by each district during the five years from 1899 to 1903, the number of emigrants to foreign countries, excluding Korea and China, is as follows:[7]

TABLE I.

District	No. of passports issued	District	No. of passports issued
Hiroshima	21,871	Fukushima	1,613
Kumamoto	12,149	Yehime	948
Yamaguchi	11,219	Aichi	767
Fukuoka	7,698	Fukui	683
Niigata	6,698	Shiga	646
Wakayama	3,750	Saga	624
Nagasaki	3,548	Twenty-seven other districts	5,041
Hyogo	3,532	Total	84,576
Okayama	2,176		
Miyagi	1,613		

Although the above statistics include emigrants to all foreign countries excepting China and Korea, more than 80 per cent of the total number came to the United States. The area of farm land cultivated by the Japanese in the State of California in 1908, classified by their native districts, was as follows:

TABLE II.[8]

Cultivated by immigrants from the district of	Area of farm land in California—acres
Hiroshima	33,443
Wakayama	30,905
Fukuoka	14,833
Kumamoto	14,827
Yamaguchi	10,598
Aichi	10,268
Okayama	6,334
Other districts	33,594½
Total	154,802½

The table indicates that the immigrants from the district of Hiroshima[9] cultivate the largest area of farm land. Next comes the district of Wakayama. Each district controls about one-fifth of all the farm land cultivated by the Japanese in California. In 1905 nearly 50,000 of the 74,000 total Japanese population in Hawaii were from the three districts of Hiroshima, Kumamoto and Yamaguchi.[10]

I have already mentioned the geographical section of Japan from which most of her emigrants come. Then, what is the peculiar character of those people? What are the economic conditions in those districts? Generally speaking, the people of the Sanyodo, where the districts of Hiroshima, Yamaguchi and Okayama are situated, were warriors in the feudal ages; and, the districts being along the coast, the people were accustomed to go to sea, and were venturesome and eager to satisfy new wants. The fundamental cause of emigration is the economic condition of the districts. The percentage of small farmers in those districts is as follows:

TABLE III.[11]

Districts	Percentage of agricultural families which cultivate less than 8 tan
Hiroshima	70
Wakayama	Unknown
Fukuoka	56
Kumamoto	Unknown
Yamaguchi	61
Aichi	Unknown
Okayama	66
Hyogo	73
Yehime	68

The number of small farmers is more than 50 per cent in all the above districts. Hyogo is the district which is populated with the largest percentage of small farmers of all districts in Japan. The district of Hiroshima, the center of emigration, comes next with its 70 per cent of peasant families. If we investigate the average area of cultivated land per capita of the agricultural population in the respective districts, the effect upon emigration can be seen with more clearness.

TABLE IV.[12]

Districts	Tan
Hiroshima	.11
Wakayama	Unknown
Fukuoka	.19
Kumamoto	Unknown
Yamaguchi	.17
Aichi	Unknown
Okayama	.15
Hyogo	.14
Nagasaki	.15
Yehime	.18

The average amount of farm land per capita in Hiroshima is not only the smallest among the above-mentioned immigrant districts, but also among all districts in Japan. Yamaguchi, Ohayama and Hyogo are also below the average.

A remarkable fact is noticeable here, that the district of Hiroshima, where the average holding of farm land was smallest among all Japanese districts in 1888, contributed the largest number of Japanese who cultivate farm land in America in 1908.

More than this, the wealth per capita in those districts is below the average amount of wealth per capita in Japan. According to Messrs. Igarashi and Takahashi,[13] the average wealth per capita of Japan is 505.755 yen, while that of Hiroshima is 381.895, of Yamaguchi is 489.005, of Wakayama is 351.675, and so on.

Inducement and Attraction

No advertisement has ever appeared in the Japanese newspapers inducing emigrants to go to the United States. But the most effective advertisement is the stories of success of Japanese in America, which occasionally appear in the papers and magazines. Whenever certain Japanese return to Japan they talk with the newspaper reporter, telling how they struggled in a penniless condition, how they saved money, what industry they started, or how many acres of land they own in America. Such articles in a local newspaper, accompanied by illustrations, usually make a strong impression upon the young peasant or rough country lad. Thus, the account of success of Mr. Kinya Ushizima, the "potato king" in California, appeared many times before the public and, it seems, induced many emigrants to leave home, especially from the district of Fukuoka, from which Mr. Ushizima himself emigrated many years ago. The success of Mr. Domoto, as the greatest flower raiser west of the Rockies, attracted many young farmers from his native district of Wakayama.

There have been many pamphlets published, some printed in more than thirty editions, under such titles as "How to Succeed in America," "Guide Book to Different Occupations in America," "Guide Book to America," "The New Hawaii," etc. All these books are written by those who returned from America or are still resident in this country. Generally speaking, they have exaggerated the abundance of opportunities in the United States and have stimulated emigration in over-attractive descriptions. Correspondence with Japanese laborers who are already in this country has also some influence.[14] But the sphere of this kind of inducement is very narrow, limited to the correspondent's relatives or friends at home. The inducements and attractions above mentioned are the result of the simple fact that labor earns more in America than in Japan.

The conclusion which can be drawn from the facts already mentioned in this paper is this, that a large proportion of the Japanese emigration comes from the peasant class in the districts of the south; and growing population, economic pressure and inducement or attraction combine to cause their emigration. No doubt there are countless minor causes operating on individuals, such as ill-luck in business, a bad crop of rice, sudden death of the devoted wife, frequent visits of the bill collectors, or simply desire to see great America. But the fundamental and principal causes are those already mentioned.

NOTES

1. "The Financial and Economic Annual of Japan," 1905, p. 3; 1907, p. 2.
2. Square ri equals 5.9552 square miles.
3. "Movement de la population de L'empire du Japon," 1905, Proportion, P. l.
4. Okawahira, "The Nippon Imin-ron," Tokyo, 1905, pp. 36–37.
5. M. Togo, "The Nippon Shokumin-ron," Tokyo, 1906, p. 180. A cho equals 2.4507 acres.
6. Tan equals 0.2451 acre, Se equals 119 square yards.
7. M. Togo, "The Nippon Shokumin-ron," pp. 269–271; also Okawahira, "The Nippon Imin-ron," pp. 38–40.
8. "The Japanese-American Year Book," 1909, the first appendix, pp. 3–4.
9. "Most emigrants in the district of Hiroshima come from the counties of Aki, Saeki, Takada, and cities of Hiroshima and Toyoda. When they start as emigrants, their land and houses are in the hands of landlords; their position is that of small tenant. But when they come back after four or five years' labor abroad, they usually buy a house and two or three tans of farm land, and become independent farmers, or merchants. . . . About six-tenths of all emigrants succeed in this way," etc.—"The Osaka Mainichi Shimbun," November 9, 1904, quoted by Okawahira.
10. T. Okawahira, "The Nippon Imin-ron," p. 89.
11. These statistics are based upon an investigation made by the Department of Agriculture and Commerce of Japan in 1888; it is presumed that there is not much change in the present condition.
12. M. Togo, "The Nippon Shokumin-ron," pp. 141–143.
13. E. Igarashi and H. Takahashi, "The National Wealth of Japan," Table I.
14. "The Seventh Biennial Report of the Bureau of Labor Statistics of the State of California," 1896, p. 103.

From The Sun Shines on the Immigrant

MARGARET N. HARADA

IT was in May, 1900, when the *Yamashiro Maru,* a small boat, carried many hundreds of young men and a few women to Hawaii. The rooms were dark and dirty. Yoshio was one of the many who sailed on the boat. The day was unusually hot and stuffy; perhaps it was due to the numbers of people who were crowded into such a small boat. Yoshio watched the harbor of Yokohama until it vanished beyond the sea.

He was doing a very unusual thing to leave his home and his parents, for he was the eldest son, who was to carry his family name to posterity and to look after his parents until they died. He was the heir of the house, and according to Japanese custom, he was being unfaithful to his parents in running away from home. "What was my heritage?" Yoshio questioned himself. "Nothing but poverty and shamefulness. I would gladly look after my father and mother, if my father only proved to be a good father. I am not unfaithful," he said to himself. "I have done the right thing. I have debts to pay which are not my own but my father's. I have made a wise decision."

Thinking these thoughts, he went into the cabin which he shared with the other immigrants. He had been given a blanket and a

Published by Vantage Press, New York, 1960, pp. 26–35. Reprinted by permission of Margaret N. Harada.

pillow. The room was ghostly during the night with only a glimmer of light from the kerosene lamp. The immigrants were talking to each other; and Yoshio listened.

"I am from a good family," said a woman. "I was once a rich man's daughter, but due to an unfortunate fate, my father lost all his fortune and had to sell his land, and the whole family moved into a little house, each year meeting more and more hardships. I heard that Hawaii is a good place to work, so I am here, sailing to look for better fortune."

He heard one of the young men say to his neighbor, "My father is a drunkard. He drinks whether he has the money or not. He beats my mother when he comes home from drinking, and he also beats my sisters, brothers and me. I became disgusted with my father, so I am running away to Hawaii to work on the plantation, which I think is far better. But I will write to my mother that I am in Hawaii working when I reach there."

Yoshio realized that the groups in the boat were practically in the same unfortunate circumstances as he was and were sailing to Hawaii to look for better fortune. How significant the words became: "A very bad lot. Decent people would never leave their beloved Japan." Yes, they were all laborers, and relatively uncultured and uncouth. They were ready to grab and hold any good opportunity. They looked strong, vigorous and ambitious. They, too, had *koris* as the only baggage. Each had a look of being willing to work, and somehow or other, able to attain the life and luxury of the rich, some day in the far future.

Yoshio walked along the deck and saw nothing but the blue skies and the large waves of the blue ocean. He wondered how many days he was to gaze upon only the blues which surrounded him. He soon got tired of looking at the ocean and went back to his cabin. It was suppertime. He ate the simple supper of rice, pickled turnips, fish soup and red-dyed plums. The same kind of food was served every day.

That night the ocean was rough. He could hear the waves washing the deck. The boat rocked to and fro, and although he was a good sailor, he felt nauseated. He saw several women vomiting, and helped them by bringing them his large pottery bowl as a container. In such times of emergency the people in the boat helped each other, but otherwise they were selfish and unkind.

The group yearned for the day of arrival. They felt the air become warmer and warmer as they neared Hawaii. The immigrants were happy to know that the boat was nearing the harbor of Honolulu. The long, thirteen-day journey which they had little enjoyed was coming to an end, and their hearts beat to see what was coming next.

Yoshio looked at the blue sky and thought the color different from the skies of Japan. The blue was deep, clear and crystalline. He saw the Diamond Head which stood loftily overlooking the Pacific Ocean. The mountains were blue-green. The coconut palms swayed lazily with large fruits under the leaves. The atmosphere of Hawaii seemed balmy and calm.

The boat soon anchored in the harbor of Honolulu. The laborers went on deck. After they had waited for twenty minutes, a dozen wagons approached, driven by sturdy Hawaiian men.

Yoshio looked at the Hawaiian men curiously, for they were brown-skinned, and their stout stomachs protruded. They were smiling and looked kind and good-tempered.

One of the Hawaiian men shouted, "Come on, come on, all in. All right."

The group were herded into the wagons as though they were hogs or cattle. Yoshio did not mind what was going on around him, for he was interested in the people. On a corner he saw a group of Hawaiian women, brown and fat, sitting or walking among myriad flowers and paper leis. They wore long *holoku*s, holding the left side of the dresses in their hands to avoid dragging the cloth on the ground and stepping on it. The women were stringing the flowers and papers to make more leis, which they sold to passers-by or people whose friends were sailing.

The wagons drove into the town. The large wheels made a clatter on the street. Yoshio saw many Chinese women in their trousers of black, shiny cloth. They had small legs, small as a child's, and walked slowly, taking careful steps. He saw tall, handsome, smart-looking Caucasian men in white suits and Panama hats. Puerto Rican women with wavy hair were walking leisurely along the streets, and Portuguese women were shopping, dressed in black and with black veils covering their faces.

The town was clean. The buildings were tall and the roads, many of them macadam, were good. The wagons drove toward the country districts, and the road turned rough and dusty. The wagons bumped heavily over the rocks, and the immigrants jostled each other. All through the ride Yoshio saw algaroba trees and large fields of sugar cane, and the rocky mountains covered with cactus and lantanas with tiny purple, orange, yellow and red blossoms. His eyes were attracted to the greens around him, and he stayed awake, while some of his companions dozed.

The wagons drove up to the plantation homes. The drivers shouted, "All right! Get down, come down."

The shouts were loud enough to wake everyone. Yoshio and the others were led to a house—a single long bungalow, a tenement house. He was given a small room to sleep and eat in. The kitchen was located outside for all the laborers to use. He did not let this bother him, for the conditions in his home in Japan had been just as bad.

Nearby was a plantation store owned by a Japanese family. He went in the store and asked for two cotton blankets, one to spread on the floor and one to cover himself with, and a pillow. He had only a small amount of money to buy these comforts.

His next-door neighbor was Nishi, who was about thirty years old. He had come from Japan about two years earlier. Yoshio went to Nishi and presented his best compliments. "I am a worthless lad, but please help me, for I am a newcomer."

Nishi greeted him warmly and wished him good luck.

The first night Yoshio was called by Nishi to share the simple supper. It was the same kind of food which had been served to him in Japan and on the boat, on a low, square, four-legged table.

Nishi squatted on the floor, and said proudly, "It is a plain supper, but share it with me."

Yoshio said gratefully, "Thank you for all the trouble."

Nishi explained to Yoshio that there was a large kitchen with long benches and long tables where the laborers had their food prepared every evening, but since he wanted to save his money he cooked his own meal.

"The laundry man comes to collect our laundry every week, but I do my own washing," said Nishi.

"What about breakfast and the lunch?" asked Yoshio.

"The cooks in the kitchen prepare them for us," answered Nishi.

"Oh! Then I shall have mine prepared. I am not much of a cook myself, so I shall eat my meals in the kitchen," said Yoshio. "I shall have my laundry washed, too. And what about getting our hair cut?"

"We do it for each other. For instance, I cut yours, and you cut mine," explained Nishi.

"I am not much of a barber, but I shall do my best when I am cutting yours," laughed Yoshio.

Nishi went on to explain that the work was not going to be easy, for one could not rest even for a moment, because foremen watched to see that the work was carried on without playing.

The night was getting darker, so Yoshio thanked Nishi and bade him good night and walked to his own room. He lighted the kerosene lamp, spread the cotton blanket on the floor and slept soundly until the following morning. At dawn the laborers were awakened and hurried to the kitchen. After breakfast, they received their square tin cans of prepared lunches, and started for the fields carrying picks and shovels on their shoulders.

The sky was cloudless and clear. The sun rose from the east, first with a soft tint of orange, then gradually turning the sky to fervid red. Yoshio looked at the beautiful colors, which suggested vigor and life. He had never seen a sunrise so meaningful and full of cheer. The shades of red touched him deeply, and the blood in his veins began to run rapidly, for from this day forward he would face a new life, working in a different land. With a fire burning in his body as red as the colors of the sunrise, he waited for instructions.

A dark, hairy Hawaiian approached with heavy steps. He gave each a working suit, a large hat to protect the skin from the strong sun, and a pair of Japanese shoes made with rubber soles.

Yoshio and the others changed immediately from their Japanese kimonos into their working suits. They were led to a railroad track where they climbed into a large truck, which was waiting for them. On his way to his destination, Yoshio saw many Japanese women cutting the leaves of the sugar cane with huge knives. Five strong-looking German and Hawaiian foremen cried, *"Go hey, go hey,"* meaning "Go ahead and keep on working," holding long horse-whips in their hands. He noticed that the women wore dresses made of thick material. The long sleeves fell to their wrists. Their legs were covered with thick stockings. On their feet they wore Japanese shoes. They wore towels tied around their necks, and straw hats with a piece of white cloth covering the backs of their heads and tied in front of their hats to shade their faces.

To Yoshio they seemed to be dressed heavily. They were perspiring, but they couldn't worry about the heat, for the sting of the whip was worse than the strong beat of the sun.

The truck finally drew up to a large, barren field. It was uneven, with large rocks protruding from the ground. There were some men already working on it. Yoshio was instructed to dig the ground and loosen the soil with his pick. Two foremen, who looked unsympathetic, stood one in front and one behind the workers, holding long whips and shouting, *"Go hey, go hey!"*

Digging without stopping to rest was a strain for Yoshio, as it would be for even the most muscular and healthy man. Yoshio noticed that some men were whipped brutally because they were working too slowly. He learned that *"Go hey"* was the pet expression of the foremen, and an alarming word for the laborers.

The lunch hour came, and the foremen called in loud voices, *"Kaukau, kaukau."* Yoshio wondered what they were saying. But he guessed that lunch hour was at hand, because his stomach was calling for food.

He ate his simple lunch with his chopsticks. He gazed at the large, rocky land and thought that digging this piece of ground for three years with the cry of *"Go hey"* in his ears would be sickening. Suddenly he braced up and said to himself, "Endure, no matter what hardships you encounter."

After an hour's rest, Yoshio again heard the foremen calling, *"Go hey, go hey!"*

He took up his pick again and began to dig the rocky ground.

He wrote to his mother that he was working hard and was expecting to receive his first pay soon. His mother, worrying constantly about her son, was happy to hear that he was well and safe. She wrote to him saying that everyone at home was well, except that his father persisted in his bad habits.

On payday, he was called into a little cottage, where he received nine dollars, a month's earnings. He was unutterably happy and excited. He had never held so much money in his hands in his whole life. He was inspired to work much harder.

He dug and dug. He glanced to one side and saw a foreman pulling a laborer's ear so hard it looked as though he might pull it off. He looked in front of him and saw another foreman kicking a laborer's back with his heavy boots, all because the work was done too slowly. The laborers did not complain, but took the blame upon themselves and started to work faster. The Japanese are wonderful people, for they can endure any hardship, thought Yoshio, admiring the patience of the two laborers.

The large field became even and soft. The laborers added some fertilizer to make the soil richer. Yoshio was given the job of planting the sugar cane, which was much easier than digging.

Soon the sugar cane started to grow, with green leaves on the top, side and bottom. Yoshio was set to work cutting the leaves to halfway up the cane, to stop the leaves from taking the vitality of the stalk. He wore a long-sleeved shirt, a hat, and a towel tied tightly around his neck. He was dressed almost exactly as the women he saw on his first day, except that he wore his trousers. A foreman had showed him with gestures that he had to be dressed as he was because the stickers on the leaves would stick deeply into his skin and annoy him a great deal. He did not understand what all the gestures were about. He wanted to laugh, but held it back for fear that the foreman might get angry with him. He ran into the field and started to cut the leaves. The edges of the leaves were as sharp as the knife. He cut himself on his fingers and hands, and was pricked by the invisible stickers of the leaves. He tried to pull them out, but he couldn't for they were too small for the naked eye to see. When he felt the surface where they had entered they hurt him terribly.

"I must pluck them out with a pair of tweezers when I get home," said Yoshio to himself wearily. "Had I known what the foreman meant I could have escaped this predicament. Oh, what bad luck!"

The foremen called *"Pau hana, pau hana,"* meaning that work was finished for the day.

Yoshio rode in the truck with other tired, weary-looking laborers. The truck carried him as far as his village. He walked in the dusty, red dirt and saw some laborers going into a wayside restaurant to have their supper. The restaurant was small, and from the kitchen floated the oily odor of coffee and toast. He thought of his supper, which would be the same dish—rice, pickled onions, pickled turnips, dyed plums and tea. He said to himself, "Some day I will walk in there and get a taste of coffee and toast. I am dying from eating the same dish every day. But today I'd better go home and remove these stickers."

He reached home, boiled his own hot water in a caldron, poured it into a tub and washed himself. His cuts burned. He dressed himself in a kimono and started to pluck the stickers out with his pair of tweezers, when a dark Puerto Rican woman appeared and began to make motions of circles and squares with her hands. He did not understand what she wanted, shook his head and said, "No, no," with perplexity. After a few seconds, she returned with a knife and threw it on the floor. He was frightened and thought she had come to kill him. He ran to Nishi and told him that a barbarous woman had come at him with a knife. Nishi went out to see what the woman wanted. She said, "Fire burn," and made motions that she wanted some wood. Nishi, who had lived in the neighborhood longer than

Yoshio, knew some of the woman's language and understood what she wanted. He told Yoshio that she had come to ask whether she could have some wood. Yoshio gave her as much as she wanted. He thought, laughing to himself, "Oh, I see! She brought a knife to show me she wanted some chopped wood."

After the evening meal Nishi and Yoshio talked about the day's events. Yoshio was still suffering from the pricks. Nishi said sadly, "Today a young lad ran away from the plantation, because he could no longer endure the treatment he received from the foremen. A cowboy hired by the plantation whirled his rope around and around and caught the young lad by the neck and dragged him to the court."

"What is going to happen to him?" asked Yoshio sympathetically.

Nishi continued, "If he is dead it is sad, but if he is alive it will be sadder still, for he will be thrashed and will not be paid at all for months for what he will do out in the fields; and his work will be doubled."

Nishi then said, "It is wise to serve out the three-year contract. Two years ago about twelve of my friends ran away from the plantation and went to California. They had a very hard time getting there. They reached Mexico one night and swam the shallow river to reach the border. In the river were alligators and crocodiles which dragged some of the men deep into the river and gobbled them up. When they reached the shore, only eight were left. They bought a few acres of land in the southernmost part of California and started to plant. When summer came the poisonous snakes and insects destroyed the crops and endangered the men. They sold the land and crossed the mountain. They were starving when they crossed the mountain, and then suddenly out of the clear blue sky appeared a lean horse. The eight men cut into the flesh of the bony horse and ate the raw meat. Surely, they thought, this was heaven-sent. Finally they arrived at Pomona, and today they are working as gardeners for some white men."

"You're not telling me a tall tale, are you?" asked Yoshio. "It was as exciting as a story."

"No, these friends of mine wrote to me. Poor men, they went through a lot. But I feel very sorry for the four ambitious men who became prey of the alligators and crocodiles," said Nishi. "Don't you ever run away from here until you are free."

The story was a good lesson for Yoshio, for he often thought that the work was too much for him to do. When the fire in his body died down a little and the flames got less hot, he would think that the labor was unbearable. But this story kindled the flames.

His whole body ached that night from the few leftover stickers that pricked him now and then when he moved to get a more comfortable position in which to sleep.

Japan's "Peaceful Invasion"

THOMAS C. HOBSON

THE matter of the "Peaceful invasion" of Hawaii by the Japanese is one entitled to all the consideration, and more, than is given it by the people of the United States. Residents of Hawaii paid little attention to the influx of Orientals until it was almost too late to check it, except by legislative enactment, a step not deemed advisable at this time.

Representatives of Japan in Hawaii, during the past five years, have vigorously denied the rumor that their government had any intention of taking the islands, coupling with their assurances of a contrary nature, the statement that Hawaii could not be governed advantageously by Japan owing to its geographical position. However that may be, the fact remains, that during the past twelve years, up to October, 1897, according to the records of the Board of Immigration, 37,451 Japanese contract laborers have landed in Hawaii; and during that same period less than one-third have returned at the close of their contracts.

Japan may not have intentions on Hawaii, by either war-like or diplomatic methods, but that it may gain control through strategy is possible, even probable. The Okuma policy is to land as many of Japan's subjects in Hawaii as is possible—the plan has been made public, innocently perhaps, by officials of the Japanese government,

In *Hawaiian Almanac and Annual for 1898* (Honolulu: Thomas G. Thrum, 1897), pp. 131–134. Reprinted by permission of Star-Bulletin Printers, Inc.

and then by force of superior numbers demand the right of franchise for its citizens. This obtained the rest would be easy, and so long as Hawaii, in its isolated position, retains its autonomy without the support of a stronger power, the interests of the Anglo-Saxon are in jeopardy.

It must be admitted that the Japanese are progressive to the extent that they are copyists. It has been stated by Americans who have visited Japan since the Japan–Chinese war, that there is not an article manufactured in the United States which cannot be produced in Japan and sold in America, even with the high tariff, at thirty per cent less than it can be made for in Chicago. This may be attributed to the low cost of living in Japan, and up to this time the use of silver as a monetary standard. With the change to gold, the cost of production may be increased; but even then Japan would still be a strong competitor of the American producer.

Mention has been made of the number of contract laborers who have arrived here since the signing of the Hawaiian–Japanese treaty in 1871, but those figures do not represent the entire number of citizens of that country who have assisted in forming the masses making the "Peaceful invasion." During the past two years Hawaii has had to contend with a class known as free laborers, men and women, brought here through the instrumentality of immigration companies. After 3000, approximately, of this class had sought domiciles here the Hawaiian government discovered that their advent in the country savored somewhat of fraud, and through the efforts of the Executive 1100, who came during the early part of 1897, were refused a landing. It was not until this action was taken by the Hawaiian government that Japan openly asserted its position in the premises, claiming for its subjects, privileges unthought of by the framers of the treaty. The question is one which attracts the attention of the diplomats of the world. Figuratively speaking, Japan has exposed its hand in the question of supremacy in Hawaii; its attitude is such as to strike terror in the breasts of every lover of republican principles and American institutions, for Hawaii is essentially American and the citizens are ready to foster republican principles.

. . .

During the past two years these people have made inroads upon the Anglo-Saxons engaged in mercantile pursuits, and in the trades, until there is scarcely a line but what has its Japanese representative. Single and alone the government of Hawaii cannot combat this condition of affairs successfully; it requires a stronger arm to maintain the rights of the people who have made Hawaii what it is to-day. The period of immigration to Hawaii from Japanese ports covers only about twelve years, and yet one hundred per cent more Japanese in Hawaii own their dwellings than do Americans. Of course the value of the property owned by the Americans is many times greater than that of the Japanese; the figures are given more to show the advance made by the Orientals, and as they have become property holders only within two years past the percentage is not a tithe of what it will be, should the islands be allowed to continue under the present conditions. The people of the United States, in view of the vast commercial interests, can ill afford to stand by and see this continue. For the safety of American capital and civilization, Hawaii must have closer political relations with the United States.

Hawaiian Annexation from a Japanese Point of View

KEIJIRŌ NAKAMURA

WHAT is the influence of the Japanese inhabitants in Hawaii? Truly, the Japanese inhabitants in the Sandwich Islands are steadily increasing in number; but they are merely laboring people, the people who work under the management of American capitalists. But, though they are under the system of a republic, they have no political power, because they cannot satisfy the property qualification for franchise. Of course, some Japanese capitalists might immigrate into the islands to start a certain new industry, and thus become citizens of Hawaii. But, even so, the number of Japanese voters would likely be very small, since the greater portion of the property in Hawaii is owned by the white race. What, then, is to be feared about the Japanese inhabitants in Hawaii? There is not the least possibility of danger which might arise from them.

It is, indeed, very ridiculous to see so many American papers speaking as if Japan were fostering some political intrigue in Hawaii. Suppose Japan should take possession of the islands by force; what interest would she derive from them? Since the economic and social fabrics are under the control of Americans, annexation of the islands by Japan would by no means promote any material interest she is seeking. Japan, though anxious to colonize her people, would not waste her power in gaining an inch of territory which would not yield her any material interest, or which she would not be able to

In *Arena,* v. 18, no. 97 (December 1897), pp. 834–39.

control. Therefore, the rumor that Japan has a certain unworthy intention about Hawaii is altogether unfounded.

It is very surprising, indeed, to see the United States acting so seriously upon mere rumor. So far as the United States is concerned, the proposed annexation would hardly yield her any additional gain. For even under the government of the native queen, the United States had always exercised a great influence politically, socially, and commercially, so that these islands were practically, though not in name, owned by this country.

In such a case, however, the mere name is a very important thing, and the transferring it from one country to the other may involve most serious international complications. On this very account, though England practically governs Egypt, she cannot claim a sovereign right over her. The absorption of one sovereignty by another is not such an easy matter as the union of one private corporation with another; for it may involve the question of balance of power, and when such a revolutional change is carried out by force it means a menace to neighboring countries.

In the case of Hawaii, the United States has not used any means of violence, but, as we have already seen, a certain group of adventurers claiming citizenship of this country have taken the right of sovereignty through violence from the queen, and now the mother country has nearly been persuaded to count the islands among her own territories. If such an attitude of the United States toward her neighboring islands in the Pacific Ocean should become established, it means to the Japanese people something new and also very alarming. They naturally construe this attitude of the United States as an opening policy of colonial expansion; and even though neither the President nor the Secretary of State may intend to establish this policy, it may nevertheless become developed out of the present example set forth by them. This policy means, of course, to get as many inches of land as possible whenever any opportunity offers itself. Therefore, it practically amounts to the same thing as a public announcement by the United States to follow the example of Peter the Great of Russia, who is said to have laid out a secret plan of political aggrandizement. Thus, Japan is about to be flanked by aggressive nations on both sides. Why should she not feel uncomfortable about the new tide of things? This is the reason, I think, why the Japanese minister said that the independence of Hawaii is necessary for the good understanding between the powers that have interests in the Pacific Ocean.

Of course, the United States does not, I imagine, intend to make any violent change in her foreign policy as above-mentioned and to create a new departure in her history, hitherto free from political intrigue and aggressive movement. Let us grant this, and let the Japanese minister withdraw his protest relating indirectly to this particular point. Even then Japan has another reason to complain against the proposed annexation. It is this, that the annexation treaty totally ignores the treaty rights that Japan has enjoyed in Hawaii. When Japan was first asked to send her workingmen to Hawaii, she demanded from the latter a careful consideration in the way of protecting the personal rights of laborers. The result was Hawaii's promise to observe the principle of the most favored nation in behalf of Japan. So the Hawaiian government is bound, by virtue of that treaty, to treat the Japanese people as well as the European. But now, in the relation between Japan and the United States, this favor is not guaranteed by the treaty, and in the matter of naturalization this country discriminates against the Mongolian race, including the Japanese inhabitants. Therefore, after the absorption of Hawaii by the United States, Japan would theoretically lose her privilege to be treated like any other nation, and practically her people would lose their right to become citizens of Hawaii. On this account, Japan cannot overlook the coming event of annexation, for she is bound to protect her treaty rights, the rights that have been acquired in favor of her people.

. . .

Of course Japan would never nourish any ambition to fight with this great republic, for she knows too well its power and resources; but at the same time she would not allow any party to snatch away her treaty rights. For it is a question of right or wrong, and not a question involving intricate political affairs in which a shrewd diplomatic skill and national power are to be tested. Supposing Japan loses all that she claims, it is not Japan that we should dishonor; and supposing that she gains, it is not Japan that we should praise. The whole moral responsibility in the pending question lies with the people who are asked to respect a certain human right, and whose moral pride has been for one hundred years towering over every selfish nation on the face of the earth.

Chapter Two

Their Great Thirst

IN the illumination of the multihued Japanese lanterns and torches, the festive crowd of Japanese men, women, and children eagerly awaited the commencement of the colorful evening *urabon* celebrations. To honor one of the first *bon* festivals in Hawaii on July 14, 1902, the grounds of the Honolulu Honpa Hongwanji Mission Temple had been impressively decorated; a stage with sliding curtains and dressing rooms had been erected at one end of the lawn. From the podium, speakers had spent the long afternoon extolling Buddhism, lauding the community services of the Hongwanji Mission, and leading the densely packed audience in chants, prayers, and the Japanese national anthem. Moving through the crowd, serving cool drinks and slices of watermelon, fantastically attired young men wore what one local reporter noted were "odd-shaped paper hats on their heads, bandoliers across their breasts and some [wore] false queues to impersonate Chinamen." The Japanese audience evidently relished the nationalistic jabs at the Chinese through the outlandish impersonations of the young men.

The highlight of the *bon* festival was surely the colorful dances and songs and the laughter planned for the nighttime entertainment. In addition to the traditional *bon* dances, a variety of amusements was to fill the evening activities, including prizes, foods, young dancers with swords and parasols, and wandering *tejinashi*—sleight-of-hand artists—to keep the young children amazed:

> On the stage the entertainment was of a very amusing character and young and old were kept in a humorous mood throughout the evening, the handclapping and laughing often drowning out all other sounds. There were phonographs which alternated in rendering Japanese and English music. Then came two little dancing girls, who went through the fantastic gyrations of a mixed sword and parasol dance. Sleight-of-hand movements were deftly given and long strings of pretty little flags, caps, clothing, oranges and many other things were made to appear from and disappear in apparently empty cans with puzzling rapidity, much to the delight of the younger element, which was given an opportunity to eat the fruit and wear the clothing.[1]

The joy of traditional celebration is often the elixir for loneliness. To sing the old chants, to dance the ancient steps seems to link the soul with the belongingness of ancestry as if the genetic code contained choreography and musical scores. For the Japanese immigrants celebrating on the grounds of the Honpa Hongwanji Mission Temple in 1902, the traditions, customs, and beliefs expressed through the *bon* festival must have also been an elixir to soothe with the security of ethnic ethos the uncompromising conditions of a new life. The *urabon* season was one of the most important and enjoyable occasions of the Buddhist holidays—the sacred season when the spirits of the dead returned briefly to the land of the living. Through the elaborate speeches and Buddhist chants, the singing of the Japanese national anthems and the paying of homage to the emperor, the delightful dances and the humorous acts of sleight-of-hand artists, the sojourner recalled the spirit of the homeland and renewed his bond to his ethnic community.

It was not unusual that the Japanese immigrant should have found his cultural continuity with Japan through the religious institutions and celebrations of Buddhism. Since the introduction of the religion from mainland Asia in A.D. 552, Buddhism and Japanese culture had been closely linked if not nearly synonymous. The Buddhism which spread throughout Japan became uniquely "Japanized" with influences of Confucianism, Taoism, and Shintoism. As the *dharma,* the teachings of the Buddha—the Four Noble Truths which explained human existence and the Noble Eightfold Path to spiritual enlightenment, or Nirvana—became popularized, various Japanese sects *(shū)* of Buddhist belief filtered into the lifestyle of the people. The *Jōdo-shū* (Pure Land Sect), *Jōdo-shin-shū* (True Pure Land Sect), *Nichiren-shū,* and *Zen-shū* were four dominant sects of Buddhism which presented Buddha's teachings with varying emphasis but in a distinctly Japanese manner.

The amalgamation of Buddhism, Confucianism, Taoism, and Shintoism into the various Buddhist sects resulted in a religious world view which permeated the social, cultural, and political institutions of Japan. By the Meiji Era (1868–1912), religion was omnipresent in the life of the nation. As one Japanese scholar has noted:

> A saying ascribed to Prince Shotoku, the founder of Japanese civilization, compares the three religions and moral systems found in Japan to the root, the stem and branches, and the flowers and fruits of a tree. Shinto is the root embedded in the soil of the people's character and national traditions; Confucianism is seen in the stem and branches of legal institutions, ethical codes, and educational systems; Buddhism made the flowers of religious sentiment bloom and gave the fruits of spiritual life. These three systems were molded and combined by the circumstances of the times and by the genius of the people into a composite whole of the nation's spiritual and moral life.[2]

The closeness of man to nature, the importance of the family system and of filial piety and ancestor worship, the interwovenness of religion and everyday life, the sense of *on* (obligation to community), and the link between religious beliefs and the Japanese imperial nation were values extolled through Buddhist institutions, saturating Japanese culture and reaching even the poorest peasant.

Religion was the essential underpinning which tied the Japanese individual to his family, community, and nation. Whether silently praying at the *butsudan* (the family altar), making flower or rice offerings, burning incense, chanting the sutra, or hanging the colorful *chōchin* (lanterns) at Buddhist festivals, the Japanese was expressing himself as a participant of an exclusive cultural community. Characterized by single, male laborers subjected to the isolation of plantation life, which was devoid of the homeland's religious institutions, the early Issei population was culturally and spiritually disjointed. Although nearly all the immigrants were Buddhist, before 1895 Hawaii had no established temples or priests to serve as a community focal point. The dead were buried without proper ceremony; religious festivals and observances were neglected; the *dharma*s of the Buddha were forgotten; alcoholism, wife-swapping, prostitution, gambling, and violence were not uncommon. When Sōryū Kagahi, the first Buddhist priest in Hawaii, worked among the plantation laborers of the Hilo district in the late 1880s, he found men who were under "heavy burdens both in the physical and spiritual [and who were distressed] and wandering, as sheep not having a shepherd."[3]

Instilling a consciousness of community and perpetuating a

cultural pride were the objectives of those Japanese religious leaders who came to Hawaii to serve as "shepherds" for the floundering Japanese plantation workers. The earliest "shepherds" among the Issei were not Buddhists but Christian evangelists. Hawaii in the 1880s was still very much a Christian nation, firmly rooted in the heritage of the American missionaries who had replaced the *akua*s and *kapu*s (taboos) of the native Hawaiian with the Gospel of Christ and the Ten Commandments. Since most Christians viewed any religion except their own as "pagan," the evangelists considered it imperative that Japanese immigrants should abandon their primitive beliefs so as to fit into a society dominated by the austere missionary. As a Buddhist, they felt, the Japanese was without the benefit of an enlightened, meaningful, spiritual vision of life. He was without the key to heaven, the prospect of life everlasting. As a United States Commissioner of Immigration had observed in a 1900 report on the nature of Japan and Japanese Immigrants:

> Japan is yet a pagan nation and the present tendency, as they break away from their ancient religion, is to drift into opportunism politically, and into agnosticism religiously, with the moral effects which follow such views among the ignorant and uneducated. The result is that the nation, as a whole, presents the aspect of being morally mad. There is apparently no sense of responsibility to society or to Deity.[4]

To correct this moral madness, to instill Christian beliefs in Buddhist immigrants, Dr. Charles M. Hyde, a Massachusetts pastor, was appointed superintendent of the Japanese Mission of the Hawaiian Board and was "willing and . . . indefatigable in carrying on . . . work for the Japanese."[5] By 1887 he was delivering sermons to clusters of Honolulu's Japanese population in Queen Emma Hall, the Young Men's Christian Association headquarters (YMCA), holding out the promise of Christ to those who would hear. Another *haole* preacher, Francis M. Damon, helped organize and became vice-president of a Japanese YMCA. Both Hyde and Damon were determined to see the word of the Gospel spread among the Japanese.

But perhaps the most successful Christian evangelists working with the Issei were of Japanese ancestry. Outstanding among these early preachers who risked ridicule and insult to bring the "foreign god" to their countrymen and arouse a sense of community spirit was Kanichi Miyama, an evangelist of the Methodist-Episcopal Church, who arrived in Honolulu in 1887. Touring the Neighbor Islands, speaking to large crowds of Issei plantation workers, Miyama was able to incite an interest among Japanese unmatched by any of the efforts of Dr. Hyde or Mr. Damon. His most dramatic impact on the Japanese community was his conversion of Japanese Consul General Taro Andō, which resulted in a "remarkable movement toward Christianity among the Japanese of the Hawaiian Islands."[6]

The Consul General Andō, during his term of office in Hawaii, had heard the Gospel of Christ as preached by Kanichi Miyama and had been deeply moved. Andō began reading the Bible, attended Japanese sabbath services, and convinced his wife and staff to embrace the Christian doctrines. He personally gave up liquor and tobacco, organizing a Japanese Blue Ribbon League—the first temperance society among Issei, dedicated to driving out the evils of demon *sake*. As Miyama's most influential convert, Andō zealously helped proselytize Christianity among the Japanese immigrants.

The efforts of Miyama to Christianize the plantation laborer were naturally given extensive publicity by the American religious press. In an article entitled "The Japanese Church in Honolulu,"[7] published in the February, 1889, issue of *The Friend,* a Church of Christ magazine, Miyama was described as "a man of great sweetness, spiritual fervor, magnetic power, and cultivated intelligence." The article lauded the efforts of both Miyama and Andō, revealing the earnestness with which American Christians viewed the conversion of Buddhists.

In part, the article also revealed the well-grounded fears of many Christians that Buddhism had to be challenged not so much for the souls of the immigrants but as a means to forestall the repaganization of Hawaii. Certainly the increasing numbers of non-Christian Japanese would mean doom for a God-fearing Hawaii. In this land of "darkness and sin," with the churches "saturated with inherited superstitions" and with a horde of "Asiatic heathens," the need for implanting Christianity in this "heathen field" was "ripe and urgent."

Despite the popular appeal of Miyama and the optimistic hopes of Christianizing the "heathen field," Christianity made only little headway with the Japanese plantation worker. Though various traveling evangelists would make successful tours of Oahu and the Neighbor Islands, laborers who had been baptized would later simply revert to the religion of their homeland. Japanese Christian ministries were established by Reverend Shirō Sokabe on the Big Island; Jenichirō Oyabe in Paia, Maui; and Jirō Okabe, who founded a church in Hilo for those workers eager "to leave this miserable earth any time to be with the Lord forever."[8] But the response was far from overwhelming. The early Japanese Christian Church could not overcome the cultural and religious barriers posed by the unstable, amoral nature of the plantation community and the entrenched Buddhist beliefs and customs of the Issei.

In the face of such discouraging conditions, the first Christian evangelists must have seemed out of place among other Japanese. They condemned alcohol to men who found spirit libation their only relaxation. They cursed adultery and fornication to men who had no wives. They spoke of Christ to men who knew only Buddha. They preached of a heavenly Kingdom Come to men whose muscles were being exhausted by the Hawaiian soil. But failure for these evangelists would be subdued by conviction; resolution would be sustained by self-righteousness. Such fortitude was especially the sustenance of Reverend Takie Okumura, the most remarkable of the early Japanese religious and community leaders. The taciturn gaze of his zealousness was stern as if here were a blend of a New England preacher and a *samurai*. His language was often abusive, riddled with the intolerance and indignation of fire and brimstone. But his purposes, buttressed by gaze and language, were always pellucid—to win souls to Christ; to strike down immorality and evil; to coalesce a disjointed, disgraceful immigrant population into a responsible, productive ethnic community.

Born in Japan in 1865, young Takie Okumura had been converted to Christianity at the age of twenty-three and attended the theological seminary at Doshisha University. During his studies he had heard a Japanese Christian evangelist speak of the Hawaiian mission and the need for young Christians to dedicate themselves to the needs of their immigrant countrymen. Filled with enthusiasm and anticipation, the newly ordained Reverend Okumura arrived in Honolulu in July, 1894, as a missionary for the Hawaiian Evangelical Association. Brash and insistent, Okumura quickly immersed himself in the not-always-pleasant task of bringing the Gospel to the Buddhist. Though labeled by many of his countrymen as an "adulterous minister," a "man without a country," "traitor," "conspirator" and "anarchist,"[9] Reverend Okumura still believed that with effort and faith the Japanese immigrant—the laborer, the prostitute, the alcoholic, and the dutiful—could be led into a clean and honest Christian life. Equally important, the Japanese immigrant could be encouraged to think of himself as a member of a healthy community, not as a vagabond.

"It was no easy task to preach Christianity in the midst of such a topsy-turvy community," he was later to write.

> I could easily have shut myself within the church walls and preached the gospel. But that would be ignoring the needy people and would be defeating my whole work. I went out, therefore, on the streets, determined to preach the gospel, at the risk of any danger. Just as I expected, when I tried to preach salvation, men ridiculed and even threw stones at me. When I explained the evils of excessive drinking, men laughed at me, thrusting empty bottles before my face. While fighting vigorously for about a year and a half, I felt most keenly the need of removing the causes of all lawlessness and immorality among the Japanese—the spirit of drifters and the frightful scarcity of women. I thought that the best way of combating these causes would be to encourage permanent settlement and the building up of homes in Hawaii. If not, no social or evangelistic work could be a success.[10]

In November of 1902, Reverend Okumura began an independent evangelical crusade in the eastern part of Honolulu, including the sparsely populated districts of Makiki, Manoa, Kaimuki, and Waikiki. Walking through areas filled mostly with fields and rice paddies, he went door to door, seeking Japanese converts for a Christian congregation which initially consisted solely of himself. In one year, he had been able to bring only ten men and women into the fold. When the Makiki Church was founded under his leadership in April, 1904, its charter members numbered twenty-four, predominantly Japanese.

In spite of its small membership, Reverend Okumura's Makiki Church directly served the diverse economic and social needs of the Japanese immigrant. English instruction classes, child day-care centers for working mothers, and a boarding home for orphans were a few of the services instituted to facilitate the immigrant's adaptation to Hawaii. During labor disputes, plagues, and natural catastrophes, the Makiki Church provided food, clothing, and shelter to impoverished Japanese. Always the Okumura ministry aimed at the evils of the immigrant population, attempting to build a stable, moral community.

Reverend Okumura's indefatigable zeal in confronting the social abuses of plantation life was particularly apparent in his war on the Japanese prostitute and pimp, recalled in his memoirs, *Seventy Years of Divine Blessings*. In a section entitled "Drive Against the Gangsters," the Reverend remarked on his early attempts to outlaw Japanese crime.[11] In his colorful recreation of minister versus prostitute, pimp, and gangster, he depicts not only the crude conditions of life in Honolulu but the efforts of a religious leader to arouse a sense of community among sojourners. While Okumura might have been dumbfounded momentarily by the prostitute who invoked her Japanese patriotism by extolling the wages of sin, he could not have been swayed by the immigrant's concern for money without regard for pride. The Japanese immigrant, Okumura believed, should protect the honor of his ethnic community as well as perpetuate Christian principles. As representatives of the Japanese race abroad, the immigrants must consciously join together to avoid the stigma of social castigation or incrimination.

Though Reverend Okumura was promoting the consciousness of a Japanese community through his unique ministry, he had been no more successful at Christianizing the Japanese immigrant than had been Reverend Miyama. For as stubbornly as the evangelists believed that Japanese must be brought into a Christian way of life, the old patterns and attitudes still stubbornly existed. Spiritually and culturally, the immigrant was not seeking a community through a strange theology, but through the ethnic intuitiveness of traditional belief. When speaking of the arrival of Buddhism in Hawaii, Reverend Okumura had recognized with little understatement that a "formidable foe loomed up."[12]

The "formidable foe" had not "loomed up" in Hawaii until Sōryū Kagahi of the *Jōdo-shin-shū* arrived in Honolulu in March, 1889, to inspect the spiritual conditions of the immigrants. Finding the plantation worker in a spiritual malaise, Kagahi became intent on establishing a Buddhist mission in the Islands. He helped to organize the first Hawaiian Buddhist temple—the Hilo Honpa Hongwanji on the Big Island—and then returned to Japan where his arguments for a Buddhist mission in Hawaii were to be ignored. Since the Japanese laborers were thought to be merely transients, many authorities felt no need for a Hawaiian mission.

Without the necessary financial and moral support from Japan, Buddhism could not establish solid footing in the Islands during the 1890s. Without benefit of Buddhist temples or priests and yet without yielding to the "foreign gods," Issei continued to bury their dead without ceremony, continued to neglect the traditional customs, continued to be a highly unstable, shifting population. At this time, opportunists from Japan who collected donations to build Shinto shrines or establish Buddhist temples only to embezzle the funds, exploited the religion-starved workers. Also, during this inactive period, the Christian community mounted their attacks on the "pagan" religion of the plantation worker. The future of Buddhism in Hawaii seemed bleak.

To withstand the onslaught of frauds, a growing amorality, and Christian evangelists, several Japanese merchants and businessmen in Honolulu sought the formal establishment of Buddhist institutions in the Islands. Petitioning the Honpa Hongwanji headquarters in Japan, they requested that Buddhist missionaries be sent to Hawaii. The plight of the Issei Buddhists was clearly revealed in the language of their petition dated June 5, 1897.[13] The urgency of this petition revolved around the need for community stability—a stability achieved through religious institutions and the revival of cultural commonalities among the immigrants. The unsettling experience of adapting to a new land as well as the need to maintain the integrity of the Japanese in Hawaii demanded institutional and spiritual harmony generating community cohesiveness. The thirst for Buddha's teachings, for the cultural security of the homeland, had to be quenched.

Buddhists in Japan, made aware that the Japanese immigrant had become more than a transient in Hawaii, responded to the petition enthusiastically. In a short time, the "thirst" for Buddha's teachings was wholly satisfied. After Kagahi established the Honpa Hongwanji in Hilo, the *Jōdo* sect was introduced in 1894 by Jotei Matsuo, the Higashi Hongwanji in 1899 by Shizuka Sazanami, the *Nichiren-shū* in 1902 by Gyōun Takaki, the *Shingon-shū* in 1902 by Hogen Yujiri, and the *Sōtō-shū* in 1903 by Senyei Kawahara.[14]

The rise of Buddhism in a predominantly Christian environment was due, in part, to the deeper expression among Japanese immigrants of their need for a sense of community. Since the Gentlemen's Agreement of 1907 had prohibited immigrants from leaving the plantation for work on the mainland, laborers were less free to move—economically, they were tied to Hawaii. With this loss of mobility came their growing need to normalize the community and to perpetuate cultural ties with the homeland. Buddhism, appealing to the cultural affinities of the immigrant population, restored certain simple, daily customs and reinstituted traditional celebrations lost in the years of disruptive plantation labor.

Another contributor to Buddhism's popularity was the sympathetic role played by the plantations. While non-Japanese sympathy with Buddhism was sparse in the general Christian community, the religion was strongly supported by a number of plantation owners. Although the more Christian-spirited such as Henry Baldwin of Maui or "Father" George Renton, manager of Ewa plantation, balked at the idea, other sugar planters provided several Buddhist missions with monetary and moral backing. To effectively bring Buddha to the doorsteps of the laborers, the plantation even donated free parcels of land near the immigrant camps for the construction of temples. At Waipahu, Kahuku, Aiea, and Waianae on the island of Oahu, at Kealia and Lihue on Kauai, and Naalehu, Olaa, and Papaaloa on Hawaii, Honpa Hongwanji temples were constructed on plantation property. The *Jōdo-shū* built temples on similarly donated land on Hawaii and Kauai, as did the *Sōtō-shū* of Waipahu. With the defrayed costs of land ownership, the Buddhist temples enjoyed an initial period of social acceptance facilitated by the plantation owners who, as the U.S. Commissioner of Labor observed, "rather encourage the building of temples."[15]

The motivation behind the plantations' support of the "pagan god" was a curious mixture of paternalism with socioeconomic self-interest and indifference. The plantation owners were interested in appeasing the workers so as to create a happy, satisfied labor force whose members maintained ethnic ties with their homeland. Paternalistically, the owners were prepared to take care of the laborers' basic material and spiritual needs. By encouraging Buddhism, they would be promoting a more stable and dependable plantation community. And, in accordance with their scheme of "divide and rule," a strong ethnic identity instilled by religion would help drive even further the wedge between workers of different racial groups. Indifferent to notions of "spreading the Gospel" or turning the "little yellow men" into Americans, the planters were more concerned with the equilibrium between profit, labor, and race.

The financial support given Buddhism was also intended to fortify labor-management relations against recalcitrant workers. Buddhism preached nonviolence, peace, and tolerance—emotional appeals conducive to ameliorate labor unrest. In 1904, such a philosophic assumption seemed to reap profitable rewards for the planters. At the Waipahu plantation in that year, Japanese laborers refused to work in protest of the vicious activities of a particular *luna* (overseer); not until the Honpa Hongwanji Temple of Honolulu was asked to intervene was the strike finally settled. Buddhism indeed seemed to replace hostility with docility in an otherwise firebrand racial group. The plantations continued to give their financial sanction to the religion, and by 1910 Buddhism was spreading throughout rural Hawaii—at Wailuku and Paia, Maui; Kohala and Papaikou, Hawaii; and Kilauea, Eleele, and Waimea, Kauai, temples were erected on land offered by the plantations. Exasperated, the Christian community could only angrily denounce the planters for encouraging Buddhism, "an open enemy of our Master and His Kingdom of Righteousness."[16]

But the plantation support was recognizably ephemeral, dependent on the whims or strategies of the owners. To survive in Hawaii, Buddhist institutions also required effective internal leadership which would ameliorate the more grating or "un-American" aspects of the religion. In an American community fearful of alien domination, the Buddhist leadership had to temper outside hostilities and doubts by adapting Buddhism to the Island environment. In this regard, one of the most effective Buddhist leaders was Reverend Yemyō Imamura. Arriving in Hawaii in 1899 at the age of thirty-three to serve as a priest of Hawaii's largest Buddhist sect, the *Jōdo-shin-shū,* Reverend Imamura's youthful zeal, loving compassion, and dedication were to win him the respect of both Japanese and non-Japanese as one of Hawaii's most outstanding clergymen. Appointed bishop of the Honpa Hongwanji, a position he held until his death in 1932, Reverend Imamura redirected Buddhist institutions to accommodate the uncertainties of Christians, yet instill spiritual stability in the immigrant community.

The adaptation of Buddhism under Reverend Imamura began earnestly in 1900 after the construction of the Fort Street Honpa Hongwanji Temple. Hoping to involve young immigrants in the activities of the temple, Reverend Imamura established the Young Men's Buddhist Association (YMBA), patterned on the YMCA model. The function of the YMBA was to teach English to immigrants, to assist in their adjustment to Hawaiian society, and to give religious training and solace. Opening a night school and publishing a magazine called *Dōbō* (Brotherhood), the YMBA began activities which were to range from lectures on Buddha to social amusements to athletic events.

Revealing the style of leadership which would sustain the early Buddhist institution, Yemyō Imamura wrote in 1918 *A History of the Hongwanji Mission in Hawaii*[17] to explain the temple's activities to the American public. His intentions in the small pamphlet were explicit—Buddhism must be made palatable for the Island population. If the immigrant was living on an American island, then his religion also had to reflect the attitudes and cultural tastes of his ambivalent social environment. If his ancient beliefs and practices were blasphemed as pagan and un-American, then efforts had to be made to show the similarities of Buddhism and Christianity.

"I take here the liberty of announcing in no ambiguous terms," he emphasized to the American public,

> that our mission as a whole advocates Americanizing the people of this territory in every possible way. I, more than anybody else, am aware of my incompetency in carrying on this work. Born a Japanese, brought up as a Japanese, I am a Japanese through and through. Whatever honest intention and pure motive I may have, this sense of incompetency has always kept me from pushing to the front as an active participant in this work of Americanization. . . .

The problem confronting the Honpa Hongwanji was more complex, however, than simply arguing that Buddhists were committed to Americanization. The leaders had to convince non-Japanese that the immigrants, by being Japanese, by preserving many aspects of their traditional values and beliefs, and by establishing a stable community, would in effect become better Americans. As the young plantation population congealed into a cohesive immigrant society, the identity of the ethnic community would enhance, not destroy, the adaptation of the Issei.

But with the congealing of the ethnic community occurred a concomitant revival of cultural practices and beliefs actually quite alien to the American lifestyle. As formal institutions perpetuating Japanese culture were established, the immigrant's cultural affinity with his homeland became greater, reinforcing Japanese customs and beliefs in a generation which had largely neglected many of the old ways. These beliefs and practices, comprising the lifestyle of the Japanese Buddhist, reflected a multitude of observances and daily habits. In part, they included the traditional celebrations during the year—New Year, when *mochi* (rice cake) was pounded and a feast of foods was prepared; *setsubun,* when the evils of the past year were cast out and a year of good fortune and hope began; *Hanamatsuri,* the Flower Festival, when the birth of Buddha was celebrated with flowers and ceremonies; the *urabon* season, the holy festival of ancestor worship; and *Bodhi* Day, the celebration of the enlightenment of Buddha.

The impact of Buddhism went beyond the observance of yearly holidays. From sunrise to sunset, from the sustenance given by daily practices to remembrances of the past, custom, habit, and belief could not be separated from the world view of Hawaii's Japanese Buddhists. Tradition and cultural practices touched every part of their lives—from the rituals at birth to the rituals at death. Especially in rural areas of Hawaii where the Japanese plantation village maintained a community pattern similar to those found in Japan, the funeral was an extremely important religious ceremony conducted with traditional ritual and solemnity. The custom of *kōden,* the presenting of money envelopes to the bereaved in lieu of flowers; the *otsūya,* the wake service; the complex ritual of the *shōjin,* or the calm, discreet way of life to be followed by the bereaved, including the abstinence from meat for a specified length of time; the annual services held on the *hinichi,* the date of death, were but a few funeral customs increasingly intertwined with the lifestyle of the Japanese immigrant.[18]

In addition to celebrations and customs, the stabilization of the Issei community also meant a perpetuation of the more fundamental cultural values and beliefs of the immigrant. Many of these values were the formal tenets of Buddhism and the extensive *Bushidō* ethic —self-sacrifice, hard work, getting an education, and the attitude of *shikata-ga-nai* ("it cannot be helped") so as to achieve success. The immigrant also revived the indigenous folk beliefs of the peasant class to which he had belonged. Complex interpretations of phenomena, intermingled with religious overtones, became a network of perceptions dealing with the supernatural; ghosts, fireballs, communications with the dead, gods and devil-gods, fortune-telling, magic, spiritual healing, and possession by demons played as much a role in the early Issei community as did plantation work, *luna*s, sugar cane, Reverend Okumura, or Reverend Imamura. The quirks of being human, the mysterious insights which pale "normal" behavior, frequently superseded the purely rational. The supernatural as a force in Issei lives, as a dimension of their ethnic and religious identities, continually stimulated a sense of cultural continuity.

From a land rich with folklore and supernaturalism, the Issei carried with them to the Islands a multitude of beliefs which became integral to daily living: "Don't cut your fingernails at night or you won't attend your parents' funeral." "It's *bachi* (bad luck causing harm) to poke *mochi* with chopsticks." "Don't sweep your floors on New Year's Day or you'll sweep out your good fortune." "Before entering a home after a funeral, throw salt to ward off any evil spirits." "To protect a house on a windy day, hang a sickle from a bamboo pole facing the direction of the wind—in the fiercest wind the house will be undamaged."

But even more than holding a multitude of simple beliefs, the Japanese community witnessed phenomena of a more astonishing nature—spirits and communications with the dead were part of many Issei experiences. As is true in most cultures, the ability to talk to the dead, to employ supernatural powers, was institutionalized in the immigrant community. Specific men or women, called *odaisan* or *kōbō-daishi,* were recognized as being clairvoyant or capable of healing illnesses by invoking the power of the spirits. These *odaisan* were highly respected in the immigrant community and served as spiritual comforters to the suffering and bereaved. You have a strange skin disease which doctors diagnose as untreatable—the *odaisan* blesses, heals. Your daughter is bothered by visions of a male ghost—the *odaisan* wards off the evil, gives protection. Your mother has died, but her spirit is restlessly reappearing—the *odaisan* slips into a trance, speaks to the dead. You want to know about the future—the *odaisan* has visions, divines omens. Especially in the small rural Japanese communities, the *odaisan* became supernatural "brokers." Imploring the spirits of the dead, satisfying the needs and fears of the living, their role was indispensable.

In several cases, the *odaisan* would also be required to exorcize the spirit of demons who had possessed the soul of a living human being. In Japan, forms of possession were usually described as being caused by one of several animal spirits—the fox, cat, badger, or snake. One such animal spirit which the immigrant transported to Hawaii was the *inu-gami,* or dog spirit. Barking like a dog, running about on all fours, attempting to commit violence, the person bewitched by the *inu-gami* would terrify the village, evoking ancient fears of witchcraft. The use or abuse of the *inu-gami* spirit was related in the following description of Issei religious experiences in Hawaii:

> *Inu-gami* is a form of witchcraft. Although the dog's supernatural power may be used for a good cause, namely to protect mankind against evil influences, the *inu-gami* is feared by the people as a formidable enemy, which brings illness, misfortune, and even death. . . . If a man has *inu-gami,* and if he hates somebody, the "dogs" will possess the hated individuals, bringing illness or some other forms of misfortune. When the person who employs *inu-gami* desires something such as food or clothing, enjoyed by another man, he will cause the "dogs" suddenly to possess the man. For this reason the employers of *inu-gami* have no intercourse with other people, and they are shunned in marriage. In Hawaii, however, the discriminations against them are not clearly made except in the matter of marriage.[19]

Two startling accounts of possession by the *inu-gami* and subsequent exorcism by a healer are told by Diane Matsunaga in her article "*Inu-gami:* The Spirit of the Dog."[20] The events described in this factual story are seen through the eyes of the author's father, Senator Spark Matsunaga. As a young boy growing up on Kauai, Matsunaga had numerous experiences of witnessing the healing powers of his Issei father, an *ikibotoke,* or living saint. Imploring the spirits to drive the evilness out of frantic victims, his father challenged the dog spirit with a mixture of Buddhist prayer and fundamental Japanese folk beliefs. In both cases—one in which a man was seeking cure of possession and the other of a young lady who tried to kill her son, the *ikibotoke* played a vital role in the village community—he was the balancing force between the supernatural and reality. Poignantly, Matsunaga concluded that his father's powers reveal "something more to life . . . . There is an entity called spirit, whether it be good or evil—a spirit with which some of us can communicate."

Whether these spirits actually existed and whether the supernatural in these instances was "real" are secondary concerns to the simple fact that the early Japanese immigrant in Hawaii had found in such religious beliefs, practices, and institutions a stability of community and ethnic identity. Christians, Buddhists, *odaisan*s, or *ikibotoke*s within the immigrant population might have represented a diversity of religious expression, but each served as catalyst for the development of human cultural bonds between an otherwise chaotic people. Through the early efforts of Reverends Miyama, Okumura, or Imamura and the sometimes fervent religious appeals, the immigrant began to recognize himself as a participant in a young, oftentimes rambunctious Island community.

As the lifestyle of the Japanese plantation worker began to coalesce into these regular cultural patterns revolving around religious institutions, the need for more permanent social relationships became apparent. If life in Hawaii was to be more than temporary, the single man would need a family—the plantation worker's great thirst for common social bonds would be satisfied only through the humanness of familial relations. Only through the interplay of family, cultural institutions, leaders, and religious custom could the Issei population truly feel comfortable in an alien land, for without a wife, children, the Bible, sutra, *mochi, kōden, kami, odaisan,* or the *bon* festival, the Issei would forever be the sojourner.

NOTES

1. "In Honor of Buddha," *Pacific Commercial Advertiser,* July 14, 1902, p. 2.

2. Masaharu Anesaki, *History of Japanese Religion,* London: Kegan, Paul, Trench, Trubner, 1930, p. 8.

3. Louise Hunter, *Buddhism in Hawaii: Its Impact on a Yankee Community,* Honolulu: University of Hawaii Press, 1971, p. 42.

4. William M. Rice, *Immigration of Japanese,* United States House of Representatives, House Document 686, 56th Congress, 1st session, Washington: 1900, p. 17.

5. Hunter, p. 48.

6. Reverend W. D. Westervelt, *The Japanese Consul,* Honolulu: Paradise of the Pacific Print, 1904, p. 2.

7. "The Japanese Church in Honolulu," *The Friend,* Honolulu, Hawaii, v. 47, no. 2 (February 1889).

8. Hunter, p. 52.

9. Takie Okumura, *Seventy Years of Divine Blessings,* Kyoto: Naigai Publishing Co., 1940, p. 7.

10. Okumura, pp. 2–3.

11. "Drive Against the Gangsters," in Okumura, pp. 21–29.

12. Takie Okumura, *Thirty Years of Christian Mission Work Among Japanese in Hawaii,* Honolulu: Takie Okumura, 1917, p. 2.

13. "A Petition to the Honpa Hongwanji Headquarters in Japan," in Hunter, pp. 60–61.

14. Hunter, pp. 59–60, 70, 101.

15. Hunter, p. 71.

16. Hunter, p. 73.

17. Yemyō Imamura, *History of the Hongwanji Mission in Hawaii,* Honolulu: The Hongwanji Mission, 1918, pp. 1–11.

18. For discussion of funeral practices of the Japanese immigrant, see Sueko H. Kimura, "Japanese Funeral Practices in Pahoa," *Social Process in Hawaii,* v. 22 (1958), pp. 21–25.

19. Masako Agena and Eiko Yoshinaga, " 'Daishi-Do'—A Form of Religious Movement," *Social Process in Hawaii,* v. 7 (November 1941), p. 18.

20. Spark Matsunaga, "*Inu-gami:* The Spirit of the Dog." Interview conducted December, 1972.

The Japanese Church in Honolulu

THE evangelization of the Japanese in this city has been the most immediately and largely fruitful of any Christian work lately conducted in these islands. The Methodist Church are to be congratulated upon the rich harvest of souls which their Mission here is gathering in. Account is to be taken, however, of the diligent labors of Dr. Hyde and his co-workers who for several years prepared the soil and sowed much seed and who still continue in the work. At the right time, the right man was sent to lift up the work and push it to a great success. Rev. Mr. Miyama, of whom we have spoken before, is a man of great sweetness, spiritual fervor, magnetic power, and cultivated intelligence. He wins both the high-placed and the lowly among his people. The Lord has greatly blessed his devoted labors.

Since his arrival here last spring, Mr. Miyama has baptized 84 new converts, including the Japanese Consul and his entire household. The majority were baptized during the last three months. Nearly 30 of the above live on the other islands. Seven women are among those baptized. There are now about thirty probationers under instruction. The Revival spirit continues to pervade the church. Many of those already received, have obtained a second blessing. Two have strayed and back-slidden, but have been reclaimed. None of those gathered in during the nine months have been lost from the church fold; all

In *The Friend,* v. 47, no. 2 (February 1889), p. 1. Reprinted by permission of the Hawaii Conference of the United Church of Christ.

are following the Lord. During the late week of prayer, a new spirit of work for Christ arose among them, a deep sense of duty to bring others to the Lord. A new organization of Classes has been made, to promote their going out after their heathen brethren.

Opposition from the others has much abated. Drunkenness has nearly ceased among the Japanese in Honolulu. The Consul Mr. Taro Ando has been very zealous in this work of temperance among his people. He and Mrs. Ando feel very decided to devote themselves to temperance work for the Japanese, as well as other Christian work. He has written an able and excellent letter to urge upon the Government in Japan the promotion of Temperance and the prohibition of intoxicating liquors.

Mr. Miyama has at the present time one trained helper in Honolulu, one on Hawaii and one on Kauai. This small force has to meet the demand for evangelizing the seven thousand Japanese who are now here, including about 800 women. The progress and success of the good work illustrates the readiness of the Japanese people to receive the Gospel of Christ. It also illustrates the great advantage offered in the presentation of Christian truth, by the presence of Christian institutions. The Japanese here are greatly instructed and influenced by the superior worth of character embodied in strong Christian churches, as well as by the noble working of Christian civilization, in society and in government administration. With all the darkness and the sin prevailing here, Hawaii is still a land of powerful Christian light. Probably in no other country, are the conditions equally favorable for the conversion to Christ of heathen people residing therein. Among those favorable conditions is undoubtedly the fact that Chinese and Japanese find most friendly treatment here, and are made very much at home. We wish that our Home Boards would perceive how very hopeful and fruitful a field this is for work among the Chinese also, with whom Mr. F. W. Damon is laboring with most inadequate means, yet important results. His working force and funds ought to be multiplied forthwith. But—"Hawaii has been already evangelized, and must take care of itself"; although our Hawaiian churches are saturated with inherited superstitions, and an Asiatic heathen population has been added nearly equal to the Hawaiian. Never was there a heathen field more ripe and urgent in its call upon the American churches than the Chinese and Japanese work is now in Hawaii. . . .

Drive against the Gangsters

TAKIE OKUMURA

IMMEDIATELY after my arrival, I was entertained by a clerk of Yokohama Specie Bank, Kichitaro Furukawa, by name. Although he was regarded generally as "very eccentric" or "shieky king," he treated me unusually well. Two or three times a week he invited me to a grill or hotel, teaching me table manners and etiquette, and helped me in mastering them so thoroughly that I was able to attend any gathering or function of American people without any feeling of embarrassment.

On the evening of my first day, Furukawa took me on a stroll around the city. On the corner of Pauahi and Nuuanu streets, he pointed to a group of women dressed in white holokus (Hawaiian clothes), and said that they were Japanese harlots. He said that there were then 200 harlots and about 300 pimps living on these women's earnings. Being on foreign soil for the first time in my life and filled with zeal, I felt really indignant, and at that very moment resolved to clean up the evil, and wipe out my country's disgrace.

The pimps and procurers had organized among themselves, three groups, called Hinode, Gikyo and Isshin, and were running a publication called *Hinode Shinbun* with Goro Sato as chief editor. Brazenly they went about squeezing out the lifeblood of the harlots,

In *Seventy Years of Divine Blessings* (Kyoto: Naigai Publishing Co., 1940), pp. 21–29.

operating gambling dens and saloons, and unscrupulously molesting innocent, law-abiding residents.

One day I visited the home of one harlot, and urged her to return to clean, decent life and work. She said: "Doesn't a big, healthy man on the sugar plantation get only $14 a month? I'm far better off, for in this work I can save up and send back $200 a month to my home in Japan. Am I not a real patriot who enriches our country?" Taken by surprise, I was dumbfounded and speechless.

. . .

From the early part of 1896, the *Advertiser* commenced a big clean-up drive against the red-light district of Honolulu. Toru Hayashi, who had just come from San Francisco, California, was asked by Theodore Richards and several other prominent Americans to secure signatures of influential Japanese to their petition, requesting the removal of harlots and pimps from the neighborhood of Pauahi and Nuuanu streets. The Hinode club people grabbed Hayashi, beat him up and took away the petition. Then, in groups of seven or eight, they visited the homes of men who signed the petition and threatened their lives. Led by gang leaders like Karikawa and Fukushima, some fifteen hoodlums also came to my home.

I heard from Mr. Theodore Richards the plan which he and his friends were drawing up to recover the stolen petition. I did not want to see so many Japanese thrown into prison, so I called to my home Rinnojo Uyemura, supreme head of Hinode club, whom I had known rather intimately because of my connection as guardian of this boy. I advised him and finally induced him to return the petition. Immediately, I handed it over to the director of the drive, but he was not very pleased with the conciliatory action that I had taken.

The incident closed peacefully, but in no time *The Hinode Shinbun* commenced to attack me, clamoring "Why Can't We Drive Out Okumura?" For one whole week, it came out with stinging editorials, urging that "Okumura must be got rid of, for he would sooner or later do the same thing." It howled loudly, and needlessly agitated the people. But nothing serious resulted.

In December, 1899, black plague broke out in Honolulu, and the section west of Nuuanu, commonly known as China town, was placed under quarantine. All traffic and communication were cut off, and houses of the suspects were burned. On January 20, while a little section was being burned, a big storm that arose unexpectedly caused a huge fire and wiped out the whole of China town. About

3,500 Japanese were made homeless. For these unfortunate people, special lodging camps were hurriedly erected at Lewers & Cooke's lumber yard in Kakaako, Kawaiahao church ground and armory, while I, opening my Boys' Home on Kukui Street, cooked 1,600 pounds of rice and fed them. Emergency aid was freely given to them. Meanwhile, detention camps had been built in Kalihi and on Vineyard Street, and the people in quarantine were removed there. Rigid quarantine regulations were still in force, and outside people were not allowed to take even one step into the camps. Fortunately, I was provided with a special pass from the Board of Health, and after a thorough check up of the needy ones, distributed thousands of shirts, trousers and holokus (Hawaiian woman clothes), which were made by women folks.

During this time, I had an excellent chance of looking up the names of higher-ups among the pimps and procurers and the number of harlots in their service. Three months later, when the people were discharged from detention camps, some thirty higher-ups of the under-world were placed under the custody of the police pending trials for deportation to Japan. Some were released on $1,000 bail.

. . .

There was one Mosaburo Shiomi among the arrested men. He had some education and, being rather well versed in the English language, was acting as an adviser of Gikyo Club. The day after he was arrested, he put up the $1,000 bond and was bailed out. That night he came to me and said, "I've taken the wrong road, and I have no grudge against anyone even if I am deported to Japan. But I can not bear to see my own brother, Tomokichi, treated in the same way as myself. I alone am to be blamed. I brought him here to Hawaii, made him a member of our wicked organization, and even made his wife become a harlot. His wife died later from a disease. I can not think of dragging him along with me. Won't you help him, and make a new man out of him?" His brother, Tomokichi, had not yet been caught in the police net. I comforted him, "I admire your spirit in coming to me, though I may seem to be your enemy. I'll see what I can do for him." Shiomi went home very happy. From that night, I took Tomokichi Shiomi to live in my own home.

Later when I came to know him better, I told him frankly, "I have no grudge against those men. I had to do something in order to preserve my country's honor, and safeguard the trust and confidence of American people in my fellow countrymen. My conscience and motives are perfectly clear. I have nothing to hide in secret," and thus I laid everything on the table. After that Tomokichi went almost every night and admonished the wicked men. At the same time, he came and repeatedly warned me of the dangers I was facing. Time and again, he acted like a body-guard against the threats or plans of the gangsters to kill me.

Later, Tomokichi confessed his sins, and was baptized. He started a bookkeeping school, as one of my church activities, and helped many a young man who entered the business. As weeks and months passed, I came to know him very intimately, and he turned out to be one of my closest and most trusted men. Although unfortunately illness forced him to return to his homeland, he fully recovered, and made a success in business. Today he has a most happy home. . . .

. . .

The trial of the thirty gangsters came up. Lorrin Andrews, a Christian attorney, took charge of the case, and it was decided to start with the prosecution of a certain Higuchi whose offense was most clearly established as a test case. But many persons who had been victimized refused to stand on the witness stand, and the chances of a sure victory became slim, so much so that we suddenly had the case nolle prossed, and thrown out of the court. The gangsters did not expect such a move, and were instead terribly frightened. Suspecting that we would gather more evidences to convict them, they scrambled for cover. Some escaped to other islands, while others became vegetable growers and turned a completely new page in their lives. So, without the aid of laws, we had the gangsters chased out of the city, and had order and decency restored in our community. It was for this case that I was nicknamed "litigant minister."

The harlots who had been in hiding gradually began to show up, and with the help of someone who advanced big capital and had many cottages erected in Iwilei district, re-opened their vicious business. In no time there were hundreds of harlots.

"IWILEI" became a great disgrace to Japanese. I felt a most piercing shame, because the man who was operating the business was one of my acquaintances. Unable to remain indifferent any longer when I thought of Christian principles and of the honor of Japanese, we launched forth another big clean-up drive.

Near the red-light district, a certain Rev. Ashville of the Christian Church and Japanese evangelist by the name of Otohiko Ota opened a mission center, and preached fearlessly night after night against the evil of prostitution. For our part, we attacked it vigorously, with our own paper, *The Honolulu Shinbun,* while Theodore Richards and other social workers commenced their drive which finally moved the police authorities to close up the houses of ill fame and clean out the whole district. Against this social evil, I worked for years, facing many a danger. When I recall those exciting experiences, I cannot help but refresh my gratitude to God and unseen friends who stood by me and encouraged me through the thick and thin of all the battles.

A Petition to the Honpa Hongwanji Headquarters in Japan

A GROUP OF HONOLULU BUDDHISTS

WE, the undersigned Buddhists, have acquired some property and established positions in Honolulu, the capital of Hawaii, since we immigrated after traveling thousands of miles from Japan.

Although we have no worry in our living, we feel as if we were treading on thin ice when we come close to the burial of dead fellow workers, which happens almost every day.

In spite of this situation, the religion here is dominated by Christianity. Towns bristle with Christian churches and sermons, and the prayers of the missionaries shake through the cities with the church bells. To strong Buddhists like ourselves, these pressures mean nothing. However, we sometimes get reports of frivolous Japanese who surrender themselves to accept the heresy—as a hungry man does not have much choice but to eat what he is offered.

While strong Buddhists eagerly wished and waited for missionary work here in Hawaii, few priests, introducing themselves as special envoys from headquarters, came to Hawaii. They deceived honest believers by indescribable actions such as fraud and trickery, and then disappeared from the Islands. We, twenty thousand immigrants in the Hawaiian Islands, experienced this disappointment and grief again and again because of ignorance on our part about the relation-

In Louise Hunter, *Buddhism in Hawaii: Its Impact on a Yankee Community* (Honolulu: University of Hawaii Press, 1971), pp. 60–61. Reprinted by permission of The University Press of Hawaii.

ship between headquarters and priests. We have no intention whatsoever to complain about the situation but eagerly wish to have real priests to be sent here.

In the middle of January, a certain "priest" came to Honolulu and claimed to be a special commissioner sent by order of headquarters in Japan for the purpose of observation and missionary work among the immigrants. He tried to pretend that he was headquarters' appointee. Having learned from our past experience, we could hardly believe him. Nevertheless, he made an assertion firmly and he showed us a written appointment. We finally acknowledged him as special messenger from headquarters for whom we had waited for a long time. You have no idea how glad and thankful we were. . . . We all thanked the benevolence of the headquarters for saving us from [a] chaotic situation, and this even encouraged many Buddhists.

After overcoming many difficulties, we managed to establish a Teaching Hall on Fort Street through campaigns and donations. We even hung our sign which said "Shinshū Honpa Hongwanji Branch." Knowing the weak position of the Shinshū religion here, we made every effort to support the priest, who was alone and unfamiliar with the conditions of this land. We raised Buddha's flag and did everything to serve Buddhists in Honolulu and the Hawaiian Islands to show our gratitude to the headquarters.

Quite unexpectedly, when Master Miyamoto came from headquarters, we discovered that the priest was an impostor. We were not only thrown into consternation but "lost our faces" to many people —the Christians and other religious people who are cruel to Buddhists. . . . We were so shamed that we could not walk [the] streets in daytime. In addition, the Teaching Hall, where we tried so hard to keep the faith, had to be closed. We fear now that the missionary work of the Shinshū cannot be carried out because of this disgrace.

We realize our mistake but we are very disappointed for having been trapped again by intrigue like this.

Since we cannot cry endlessly over spilled milk, we asked Master Miyamoto to ignore the past and make use of the Teaching Hall . . . for missionaries, observers, or bishops from headquarters. We hoped that the place would be used, in the future, as branch sermon hall of the headquarters. In reply, Master Miyamoto said that nothing can be approved without headquarters' directions. Although mistakes were made on the part of our believers, they are resulted from enthusiasm of Buddhists who eagerly wished to have missionary work done in this land. It is, therefore, necessary for the representatives of the Buddhists here to report everything that has happened to the headquarters and to ask for leadership.

We hereby report the whole matter to you and ask for assistance. We request that special consideration be given the matter and a suitable priest be sent to reside in the Teaching Hall so we can be healed from this thirst for the Buddha's teaching.

From History of the Hongwanji Mission in Hawaii

YEMYŌ IMAMURA

LOOKING back on the twenty years, during which I have had the privilege of identifying myself with the activities of the Honpa Hongwanji Mission in Hawaii, I can not help expressing my sense of sincere gratitude and obligation, first to the home authorities of our mission, and then to the government of this Territory and the public in general. If there is anything worth mentioning in the result of our activity it is entirely due to the mercy which our Lord never fails to extend to his followers, to the fair and just treatment received from all the officials of this Territory, and to the sympathy and manifold help of the community at large in our missionary and educational efforts. I know, better than anybody else, that our work here in this Territory does not amount to much. That does not mean to say I and my colleagues have not done our best. On the contrary I think I can say, without exaggeration, that we have gone through the bitter experiences of every description which foreign missionaries must endure. They were the first experiences for me as well as for my colleagues and it is always the first experience that costs. So I hope we may be forgiven for the little we have done towards the cause of our religion and the spiritual well-being of our fellow-men.

The name of the Rev. H. Satomi, my predecessor in the capacity of Bishop of our mission here, must first be mentioned in the nar-

Published by the Hongwanji Mission, Honolulu, 1918, pp. 1–11. Reprinted by permission of the Honpa Hongwanji Mission of Hawaii.

rative of our activity in this territory, for it was he who brought with him the first message of the Honpa Hongwanji Mission in Japan to this Paradise of the Pacific, and by the sheer virtue of his amiable personality won the hearts of the Japanese. The old Mission Building on Fort Street above Vineyard Street, bears unmistakable testimony to the immense gratitude the local Japanese felt for his paternal solicitude for their well-being. He was recalled to Kyoto after three years' toil.

I was painfully conscious of the tremendous responsibility I should have to carry on my shoulders, when I had the honor of being appointed his successor. My first step was to organize the Young Men's Buddhist Association, and with their co-operation I opened the night school to teach English to the Japanese. We live in an English speaking community, and it is needless to say that the first duty and privilege of every good resident should be to equip himself with the command of the spoken language. I cannot say that our work along this line during these twenty years has been entirely satisfactory. As an alien institution we have been handicapped in more than one way. But it is not without some pleasure I remember that our English school has had more than two thousand enrollments during its existence and its numerous graduates are now occupying quite important positions both in stores and in the plantations. Special thanks are due to those American ladies and gentlemen who were willing to render their services in this connection. . . .

The next task I had to cope with was to impart stability to our plantation laborers. I do not intend to cite in detail the various causes which contributed to stir up in their minds constant worry and agitation. They are old, old stories of immigrant communities which you will find almost everywhere in the United States. Suffice it to say that the Japanese were not settled. They did not care in the least to settle. "Like waves they would come and like waves they would go." This was more than lamentable, both for the sake of the plantations and of our countrymen. In order to bring about a state of more or less permanent settlement, however, there must be something established in the plantation on which the forlorn minds of the working men can fall back, in woe and in happiness. That this spiritual support through storm and sunshine could be found nowhere but in the church, the abode of eternal light and love, was my honest conviction. It is my special honor to announce that our mission has now more than thirty churches in the leading plantations, administered by as many ministers, each trying his best to maintain this abode of light and love for the good of his fellow-men. Since my early days a great change has occurred. The early period of agitation and exodus is gone forever. Those who left their wives and children in Japan have them now beside them. Most of the bachelors have got married. They are settled, and are prepared for permanent residence. It is preposterous to say that this state of desirable stability has been secured solely by the efforts of my colleagues.

More than anything else, that "Gentlemen's Agreement" which put an end to the flow of our population to the mainland, has had its effect. Japanese newspapers in this territory have also had their ample share in the desired result. Neither must the beneficent influence of the Christian ministers be omitted. The fact that our country-men began to see the importance of "stick-to-it-iveness" in achieving any sum of success has done much. But I shall not be accused of pretentiousness if I say that our mission has done its humble share of duty in realizing this much-hoped for state of stable and steady pursuit of work and happiness in the plantations. Managers of the Plantations were not slow in their appreciation of our honest efforts, and soon after the strike agitation in Waipahu Plantation in 1904 was amicably settled owing to the intercession of our mission, our activities in the plantations enjoyed the hearty co-operation of the plantation officials in various ways. Our sincere thanks are due to them all.

. . .

I take here the liberty of announcing in no ambiguous terms that our mission as a whole advocates Americanizing the people of this territory in every possible way. I, more than anybody else, am aware of my incompetency in carrying on this work. Born as a Japanese, brought up as a Japanese, I am a Japanese through and through. Whatever honest intention and pure motive I may have, this sense of incompetency has always kept me from pushing to the front as an active participant in this work of Americanization. But it was our mission that extended its ready hand when the local Y.M.C.A. asked us to co-operate in the proposed citizenship educational campaign. It was our mission that published, when the war broke out, a reprint of the five great state papers of American history with a Japanese version, in order to inform our public of the true idea and principle of the great Democracy. In the Food Conservation Campaign, in the Red Cross movement, our mission was second to none in doing its very best. In saying all this I am perfectly aware that our mission has done nothing more than the level best of a level man. Strange to say, however, our mission, during its existence of twenty years in this territory, has often been accused of strong autocratic or anti-American tendency. Let our accusers have their day. I have no mind to say anything against them. Our record is our best defence.

Inu-gami: The Spirit of the Dog

DIANE MATSUNAGA

Inu-gami no sawarimono, or illness caused by the use of the dog spirit, used to be very prevalent on the island of Kauai in the late 1930s and immediately preceding World War II. There were individuals in Japan, particularly from the Hiroshima prefecture, who had the power to use the spirit of the dog to bring about illnesses on others, a power inherited from generation to generation within a family. Whenever a person who had the power of the dog spirit wanted someone or something which a person possessed very badly, then he would set a curse and the person would fall ill. The victims of the *inu-gami* would become weak, would be unable to eat or sleep, and would finally just waste away.

As an *ikibotoke,* or living saint, my father was recognized on Kauai as sort of a spiritual healer. He healed people of all kinds of illnesses. And one of the illnesses that my father was capable of curing, and one which doctors could do nothing about, was the illness of the *inu-gami.* One of my father's most frightening experiences, and one which I witnessed, was the case of a Mr. I____ who was possessed of this evil spirit. He came to my father and asked if anything could be done to cure him. My father took him to the temple, had him kneel before him and then started praying. My father must have

The following personalized description of supernatural events is based upon a series of interviews with the author's father, Senator Spark Matsunaga. It is printed here by permission of Diane Matsunaga.

prayed for almost an hour or more, hypnotically chanting: *"Namu-Myōhō-renge-kyō, Namu-Myōhō-renge-kyō, Namu-Myōhō-renge-kyō."* As my father chanted, he swayed the *gohei,* or the pom-pom-looking instrument which he used in praying, over the head of the victim, touching him from shoulder to shoulder.

Suddenly, Mr. I____ got up on all fours and started barking like a dog, running out of the temple onto the highway. Others who had been present at the ceremony ran after him until he fainted from exhaustion. They carried him back to the temple where my father said a few words waving the *gohei* over Mr. I____. And Mr. I____ opened his eyes, cured of his illness.

A second case which happened about 1937 involved a classmate of mine. Soon after high school graduation, she married and eventually gave birth to a baby boy. One morning, shortly after giving birth, she suddenly grabbed a butcher knife and, with an insane stare in her eyes, was about to slay the boy. When her husband tried to stop her and took the baby away, she started chasing the husband with the butcher knife. The police were called, who finally subdued her. Since this incident happened in Hanapepe, Kauai, the police wanted to take her to the sanitarium at Kaneohe on the island of Oahu, the *pupule* house. But the parents of the young victim begged the police to permit them to take her to Mr. Matsunaga, the healer, to see whether he could cure her. So with handcuffs on they brought her over to my father's temple. As soon as she saw my father, though, she cowered away, as if dreadfully afraid. My father commanded her, the victim, to approach him. And she obeyed as if she were a little puppy, turning her head away from him, but then gradually obeying the command to approach him. My father ordered her to kneel before him over the Japanese *goza* or straw mat, covered by a *zabuton,* a little Japanese cushion. Then my father turned to the altar to pray, and he prayed and prayed and prayed, *"Namu-Myōhō-renge-kyō,"* waving the *gohei.* Here again the prayer must have lasted about an hour.

Then my father stopped and asked the girl, "Who are you?" *"Omae wa dare ka?"* "Who are you?" as if he was talking to an unknown person. Now in most cases of those who are inflicted with the spirit of the dead, the victim speaks almost as if a ghost from the past; the voice is the voice of the dead. Relatives who have been sitting nearby, witnessing the scene, have later testified that the victim would speak not with their own voice, but the voice of the spirit of the dead person who happened to be in the victim. This young lady responded to my father in a voice not her own, "You know who I am. I don't need to tell you who I am. You know who I am." Of course, my father knew who used the dog spirit, but would never relate it to others. He however confided to my mother who warned us against close association with certain families who lived on the island of Kauai.

After the young girl spoke to my father, she sprang up on all fours and started barking like a dog and whining. She ran out of the temple onto the yard and towards the highway, trying to elude my father. Her husband, her brother and my brother-in-law chased after her and she must have gone about a hundred yards on all fours until she dropped from exhaustion and fainted. Upon the instructions of my father, she was carried back into the temple where he waved the *gohei* and said a few words. She suddenly opened her eyes, looked up and said, "Where am I? How did I get here?" She was cured.

The police officer who had accompanied her to the temple was amazed. After questioning her, the girl appeared absolutely sane, so he turned her over to the husband and her parents. For years afterwards this cured victim of the dog spirit visited my father's temple, giving thanks, almost on a daily basis.

The stories which I have related seem impossible, almost incredible to believe. I perhaps would not have believed them myself if they had been told to me by others. But I have actually witnessed with my own eyes these happenings. As an educated man, I have tried to rationally and scientifically understand these strange occurrences, to look for reasonable explanations. But without logical answers, I am inclined to believe, at this time, that there is something more to life, something more than what the sciences have been able to explain. There is an entity called spirit, whether it be good or evil—a spirit with which some of us can communicate. And I am convinced that my father was one of those blessed with the supernatural powers to perceive things one step beyond the rest of us.

CHAPTER THREE

Eijū Dochyaku

TWO photographs, yellowed by time, are prominently mounted in the pages of the family album. A lovely young girl in kimono, her hair pulled back and bundled on the top of her head, gazes emptily into the camera. A mask of duty covers fear. A young man dressed in a plain black suit, probably rented from the photographer, sternly confronts the lens. The dark tan, the resolute strength of character, the broad shoulders speak for his years in the plantation fields. He had been an adventurer, independent and ambitious. But he had become lonely—he needed a wife and family. Asking his relatives in Japan to arrange a marriage with any eligible young female in the village, he had exchanged photographs with his prospective bride. At the docks of Honolulu harbor, they had carried the photos so as to be able to recognize each other at their first, anxious meeting.

For countless Japanese of Hawaii, two small photographs like these are nostalgic symbols of the "picture bride" marriages. In most cases, the Issei couple had never met each other before their arranged union; they risked their futures on a celluloid promise. The woman had not only accepted an unknown husband, but had traveled alone to a new land where life would prove, at best, to be uncertain. The man had foregone the freedom of his bachelorhood so as to support a wife and children in a dubious island environment. But both would sacrifice their personal wants, suppress their fears, and dedicate themselves to their family. As a result, a stable, moral Japanese community would flourish in Hawaii.

The immigrant institutions, the Buddhist and Christian churches and their respective leaders, had not been unsuccessful in instilling a spirit of community in the plantation worker. Cultural beliefs, values, and customs had been reinforced; the identification with an ethnic commonality had been promoted. But without the responsibility of a family, the plantation worker tended to be a member of an unsettled population. The impetus to leave the Hawaiian plantation, to migrate for more amicable and profitable conditions, became evident when the contract labor system was abolished after the United States' annexation of the Islands. The contract system had kept the immigrant legally obligated to remain on the plantation. But freed of such restrictions and tempted by employment agents of various West Coast fishing and agricultural industries, the Japanese laborers began a significant exodus from Hawaii. In one month alone in 1905, more than 1,000 laborers left for the mainland United States. Until the Gentlemen's Agreement of 1908 prevented Japanese workers from leaving Hawaii for places such as California, anywhere from 40,000 to 57,000 Japanese chose to leave the Islands.[1]

While the Gentlemen's Agreement prohibited Japanese immigrants from migrating to the mainland, other factors ebbed the flow of laborers back to their homeland. The forces of rising expectations that a little more money could be made with maybe just a year's more effort deluded the immigrant into believing that wealth and success as a plantation worker could be achieved. By the time he realized that plantation life was not the panacea to social status in Japan, the immigrant found himself in a personally frustrating predicament. He had very little money with which to return to Japan, and travel to the mainland was prohibited. If he did return home empty-handed, how could he ever face friends and families who surely assumed that he would be successful in golden Hawaii? The years of work and the isolation from cultural roots wore down the spirit of many immigrants. Picking up and reestablishing themselves took an energy which apathy, compliance, frustration, and routine had effectively eroded. In any case, Hawaii had become engrained in the lifestyles of many Japanese. The sense of community promoted by religious and cultural institutions, the island environment and climate, had provided a setting more than suitable to the psychological needs of many laborers. What remained in order to create a more permanent community life was the establishment of the family.

The establishment of such an institution necessitated a large number of eligible females of child-bearing age. For the Japanese immigrants, finding such females for marriage was extremely difficult—a significant shortage of eligible women existed in Hawaii. The overall demographic profile of the Islands well into the twentieth century indicated that the local population was characterized by an excess of men—the immigrant populations were especially male oriented. For every 100 females, there were 447 males.[2] But even if the general population had contained more eligible females, the dutiful Japanese immigrant would still have been extremely hampered in his desires for a wife. True to his family wishes, obligated to his ancestral heritage, the Issei man could marry only a Japanese woman. Interethnic marriage, though not unheard of, was inimical to the Japanese pride of race and ethnic integrity. The family honor, even if removed by an ocean, demanded a proper Japanese wife to raise well-trained Japanese children who would be reared in a well-maintained Japanese home. To obtain his Japanese wife, the unmarried immigrant had to write home to have a marriage arranged.

The period of summoning families—of arranged "picture brides" and the sending for close relatives, wives, and children—has been termed *yobiyose jidai*. The voluminous traffic in women and children after 1907 remodeled the character and nature of the Issei community. During the peak years between 1911 and 1919, 9,500 picture brides buttressed the Islands' female population, stabilizing the Issei sex ratio.[3] And, as can be expected, the early period of stabilization of the family coincided with a high birth rate. The peasant extended-family tradition of the Issei resulted in an initially high birth rate of the second generation, the Nisei. In the years 1920 and 1921, the Japanese birth rate climbed to a level exceeded only by Part-Hawaiians. In the period from 1920 to 1937, the second generation was to catapult from 39,127 to 113,289.[4]

Through the period of *yobiyose jidai,* the Issei population and the growing Nisei generation they fostered matured into a fully cohesive ethnic community. The interplay of family, churches, cultural institutions, and effective leadership acted on the immigrant, mollifying his urge for mobility, tempering his taste for adventure. Although many of the Japanese newspapers had warned single men with talent and ambition to venture into Mexico or South America, to leave the Islands where "no chance of success or opportunity" was to be found, the message for the family man was clear: "Men with large family, whether they like it or not, must settle in Hawaii permanently. Permanent settlement for such people is very good."[5]

By word of mouth, through the media, through the process of individual decision-making arose the prevalent attitude of *eijū dochyaku*—live permanently, remain on the soil. Perhaps the basis for such an attitude was pessimistic: it's too late to return to Japan; life is simple here; you have no choice. But the ramifications of *eijū dochyaku* were to have redounding effects on the evolution of the Japanese family in Hawaii.

Understandably, in the course of permanent settlement, the family which the Issei was to create in Hawaii would be fashioned by the roots in the rural villages of Meiji Japan. In that world of subsistence struggles, the young child was acculturated into a mazeway of attitudes, values, and behaviors which had developed after centuries of human interaction with the natural environment. Through this cultural inheritance, the child learned to contend with the varying contingencies of an agrarian economic base; behaviors and values suitable to the harmonious perpetuation of a communal society were developed; personal and individual needs and ambitions were synthesized with the demands of community and of religious and social order. Most importantly, the young child learned meaningfulness and social worth through the devotion and care of the family.

The Japanese rural family, which formed the primary social referent of the young child, was called *ie,* meaning "house." The *ie* was an extended-family pattern comprised of not only the family of procreation but a large array of members associated by kinship or affiliation. As a large social network of kin relations, the *ie* also was a critical economic unit, providing a stable agricultural work force in rural communities. Due to this economic function, the family was viewed as a corporate group, property and land being shared communally rather than individually.

Survival in a constantly demanding environment meant that the child's individual will and effort had to be funneled into a group consciousness. Familial communalism demanded the suppression of individualism to the needs of the extended family. The suppression of individual desires and motivations was insured by a social system which clearly defined the child's place within the family—a world view predicated on a vertical, hierarchical order of the universe. Every family member had a specific, delineated role of behavior differentiated by status and power.

Extending from the family, the hierarchy of social order formed a comprehensive "natural law" of Japanese society. From the symbolization of language to the everyday routines of behavior and value beliefs, the Japanese world view was marked by the emphasis on social order. The child understood that the "natural" hierarchy presupposed that some should govern and others should be governed —that authority and influence be rigidly inbred in the roles and statuses of the vertical arrangement of the world. In the following diagram of the Japanese hierarchy,[6] each pairing is listed in relative order of importance, status, position, and authority. The role on the left is dominant over the one on the right:

kun-shin	emperor and subject
fu-shi	father and child
fu-fu	husband and wife
cho-ya	elder and junior
shi-tei	teacher and pupil

Permeating this sense of hierarchy and order was a feeling of obligation and adoration to one's place in the scheme of things. The child was taught not to begrudge restrictions of status and position, but to emote a strong sense of *on*—obligation to family, community, teachers, and emperor. The *ie* was idealized by ancestor worship into a quasi-religious deity, a symbol of social order and meaning.

This deification of the family ancestral lineage elevated the prominence of the *ie* and subjugated the child's self-will and independence of action. Out of social and economic necessity, integral to survival in an unstable agrarian community, independence and individualism were replaced with dependence, obligation, and the sense of duty innate to the status system.

But an *ie* system harmonious to the world of Meiji Japan would not be completely compatible with the skills and values necessary for the family to survive in Hawaii. The most startling "social shock" the immigrant would encounter in Hawaii was the realization that the spirit of *ie* was challenged by an environment of rapidly expanding capitalism, industrialization, and urbanization. The bond of implicit love and understanding underlying his rural world view was threatened by the bludgeoning effects of an increasingly modern society. Self-reliance, the ability to exert self-will, and independent initiative were the skills useful in the Island plantation economy, not order, cooperation, reciprocity, or love. The extended family, a sociocultural burden in an economy based on growth, profit, and saving, was replaced with the smaller nuclear family. The industrialization and urbanization of rural patterns modified the internal relationships and structures of the family institution.

Caught in the tensions of a rural institution confronting the disorientation of modern society, the Japanese family was reshaped as it adapted to the Hawaiian environment. The immigrant and his family had naturally sought to recreate the implicit bonds linking the communities of the homeland—to wholly transplant the *ie*. But the need for modification became immediately apparent. The disorganization of plantation life, the general inability to purchase land and develop independent farming communities, the urbanism of Honolulu—all demanded new behaviors and family relationships. Internally, the fragmented character of the Issei family also impeded the full duplication of the *ie* system. The Issei couples were, after all, separated from their homeland kinship systems. No elderly grandparents and few uncles and aunts, brothers and sisters, lived under the same roof. The immigrant had come as a loner; consequently, the family he created in Hawaii did not represent the diverse *ie* pattern of Japan. A sociologist observed of the immigrant population in Hawaii:

> The Japanese family system is undergoing changes. Immigration has resulted in the creation of conditions that tend to weaken moral bases of the family. The removal of the immigrants from their families and home communities meant that they left behind all the prestige which went with their family names. They left behind, too, the living symbols of land, house, family cemetery, and the village shrines which constantly reminded them of the love and affection of their illustrious forefathers. The economic system of Hawaii, with its money wages, has tended to undermine family solidarity. The presence of other peoples whose family systems have different moral bases has helped to weaken family sentiment among the Japanese.[7]

Thus the Issei family was a curious potpourri of Meiji Japan values and institutions modified by the social contingencies of the Hawaiian experience. But while the Island home was not an exact replica of the *ie,* several Japanese cultural world views were reexpressed which had a significant impact on family, peer group, and community patterns within the Japanese population. Though tempered by urbanization and industrialization, these old-world values permeated the early human relationships of the Issei and Nisei.

Within the familial institution, one of the more pervasive Japanese values was that of filial piety, a Chinese Confucian concept transplanted into the Japanese conceptualization of *ie* and ancestor worship. Essentially, filial piety can be defined as the oath of empathy which links a person to the hierarchical order of the world. "Be loyal to the land and be filial to the parents"[8] was a tenet of the Japanese ethical code. And the loyalty was engrained as an unquestioned emotional attachment to parents and siblings. Elders were to be respected, the authority of the *ie* was beyond reproach, the individual was committed and obligated to the family:

> The filial duty of a son is a continuous obligation as long as the family is in existence. It is handed down from one generation to another. "Fathers may not be fathers but sons must always be sons," and they must learn to be more pious than their fathers were to their forefathers.[9]

In the Issei home, the deference shown parental authority and the obligation shown the parents through duty and compliance were highly respected aspects of filial piety. Remembering her early home environment, one Nisei, for example, stressed the effect of filial piety on her relationship with her parents:

> One of the basic ideals of Japanese life is filial piety. This ideal has been stressed in the home education of the second and third generations through gestures and definitions by parents. The Japanese revere age. Japanese custom demands that courtesy be shown to elders on all occasions. This is expected especially of youth. The thought of sending the aged to the poor house is inconceivable to them. The first as well as the second generation cannot understand how *haole*s can send their parents to charity institutions. Parents and elders are addressed as superiors. Even to this day, I say *Tada ima itte kaeri masu* (May I leave now) when leaving and *Tada ima itte kaeri mashita* (I have returned) when I return.[10]

The deference shown to authority was especially important when the young Nisei was dealing with the Issei father. In the rural family of Japan, the father was a patriarch with unchallenged authority and explicit rights. The patriarch controlled the assets of the *ie,* was the final authority in all decisions, and assumed total responsibility for family members. As a major relational power and head of the hierarchical familial order, the patriarch in the Island Issei home thus attempted to perpetuate his role.

The position of the female within the Japanese family, on the other hand, reflected submission and deference more than equality. The major characteristic of the Issei wife–husband relationship was the female's subordination to the male. Although the wife was the ruler of the household, in charge of running day-to-day familial operations, she did so under the direction and influence of the husband. The sphere of her role was completely overshadowed and dominated by the patriarch.

With time, however, the demands of a new Island environment modified the traditional familial roles of the male and female. The lack of family property and the disruptive plantation existence undermined the patriarch's position of power in the Island Japanese home. The sociologist Jitsuichi Masuoka in the 1930s conducted a number of sociological studies of the Japanese family in Hawaii, concentrating on the evolution of the patriarch from Japan to Hawaii. His article, "The Japanese Patriarch in Hawaii,"[11] traced the historical and cultural background of the patriarch, suggesting that in the Islands the father had succumbed to external forces demanding an internal restructuring of roles and values.

"The core . . . of the Japanese family," according to Masuoka, "is the body of sentiments which are clustered around the patriarch–heir relationship." The patriarch was the guardian of ancestry, land, economics, and family unity; his prominence was sanctioned by legal rights and unquestioned obedience. The eldest son was the inheritor of patriarchal status and therefore enjoyed a special respect and responsibility. The emphasis on male authority in terms of family inheritance was such that this relationship took precedence over even the husband–wife relationship—the bonds between mates were secondary to the bond between father and son.

Turning his analytical attention to the patriarch in Hawaii, Masuoka described an authoritarian figure being undermined by social and environmental circumstances. Masuoka pinpointed four causes of the waning of patriarchal authority. First, the ambitious young immigrant was culturally ambivalent toward the traditional values of his family system and more easily impressed by the cultural systems he encountered in the Islands. Second, the basis of patriarchal authority, the inherited ancestral land, simply did not exist in a community where the immigrant rarely could afford or find available fee-simple property. Third, the economic system of Hawaii demanded that the patriarch be a wage-earner outside the home, eroding his authority and prominence within the familial system. Finally, the social environment indifferent to the patriarchal system sapped the role of the traditional father of both its external and internal rationales and sanctions. Masuoka concluded that:

> With the waning influences of ancestor worship, family property, the family name, and the family line, on the one hand, and with the

> growing influences of the ideologies, the family etiquette, and the mores of the American people, on the other, the traditional patriarch-heir relationship weakens. The established relationship between husband and wife is also affected by the rising social status of women in response to the local situation. The experience of the Japanese people with the American culture is too short to indicate the later trend but the evidence seems to show that the emphasis is shifting from the patriarch-heir to a husband-wife relationship.

Indeed, with the change of the patriarch, the declination of male authority, the female found herself in a newer, potentially more productive role. The nuclearization and assimilation of the basic Issei family unit provided the female with greater equality and prominence within the household. Economically, it became important for the female to work outside of the home, exposing her to broader experiences and instilling economic independence. Even in the early Issei family the female was becoming more assertive as a family member. A Nisei recalled that though her Issei mother seemed submissive, her outside income altered her status in the family:

> Mother has a seemingly subordinate role, but her dominant personality makes her the most influential member of the group. Important matters of business, which are usually discussed between father and son, are further supplemented by the opinions of my mother.[12]

While filial piety and the nature of sex roles within the family were undergoing modification due to the influences of an impinging Island economy and social system, the integrity and "honor" of the institution remained unimpaired for the Issei—the Japanese notion of "family honor" was deeply imbedded in the relationships of the Island home. For if the family was an important social and economic unity demanding obedience of its individual members, then the status of the family in the community had to be protected. The family must not be shamed. The individual must do nothing which reflects negatively on the image which the family projects to neighbors and friends.

The impetus to protect and enhance the family image through individual effort and suppression of self-will was a value enculturated at the earliest age. A Nisei remembered:

> At night when I was in bed, my father used to kneel by me, his eldest son, and say, "When you grow big you must become a great man and distinguish our family name." This instruction was given me repeatedly and it went deeply into my heart.[13]

Childhood was a period in which the individual was given models of propriety to emulate and taught to achieve higher levels of status, bringing honor to the family. Independence and individualism were secondary to the family image.

Essentially, subordination to the family organism involved the functions of several behavioral mechanisms embracing psychological norms of self-restraint. Most prominent of these mechanisms was the use of *haji,* shame, to regulate individual behaviors. "What will others think of you?" "What will the neighbors say?" Such behavioral injunctions reinforced family honor and image.

The shame orientation of the Japanese individual, as opposed to one of guilt or self-appraisal of personal actions through conscience, was a highly valued and effective tool of social conformity in the rural Japanese community. In the Japanese world of relationships, the judgment of your peers and family, what others thought of you, was an important determinant reinforcing bonds of love. If you failed to perpetuate the open relations of love and trust, then you irrevocably threatened your position in the society—you were shamed.

The suppression of individual will to the family organism was also maintained through the cultural norm of *enryo. Enryo* involved a complex of deference behaviors helping to establish the perimeters of the individual's freedom. According to Harry H. L. Kitano in his definitive study, *Japanese Americans: The Evolution of a Subculture:*

> *Enryo* helps to explain much of Japanese-American behavior. As with other norms, it had both a positive and negative effect on Japanese acculturation. For example, take observations of Japanese in situations as diverse as their hesitancy to speak out at meetings; their refusal of any invitation, especially the first time; their refusal of a second helping; their acceptance of a less desired object when given a free choice; their lack of verbal participation especially in an integrated group, their refusal to ask questions; and their hesitancy in asking for a raise in salary—these may be based on *enryo*. The inscrutable face, the noncommittal answer, the behavioral reserve can often be traced to this norm so that the stereotype of the shy, reserved Japanese in ambiguous social situations is often an accurate one.[14]

Highly sensitive to the feelings of others, reactive to the opinions of peers and relatives, deferent to status and age, the Japanese individual became hesitant to express himself verbally—once the words had been said, they could not be retracted. The shame, the confrontation, the highly emotional charge had already been released. The individual learned the value and advantages of "keeping the mouth shut" when necessary, demurely acquiescing in unpleasant situations and *kuchigotae suru na* (don't answer back) in the face of authority.

Shared patterns of family respect, obligation, parental authority, the sensitive regard for honor, image and status, and the intense personal identification with the family unit were aspects of the family which became fundamental to the early Issei home. The expression of these diverse Japanese familial patterns as they were adapted to a Hawaiian environment is vividly depicted in a short story, "I'll Crack Your Head *Kotsun,*" by Milton Murayama, a Nisei.[15] The setting for Murayama's story is a plantation camp in rural Hawaii. Told through the youthful eyes of Kiyoshi, the story touches upon the commonalities pervading the Japanese family and personality. Filial piety, the maintenance of family honor, and the intuitive feelings of loyalty to family emerge from the delightful tale of a simple Island way of life.

The key plot of the story revolves around Kiyoshi's friendship with a youngster whose family is not considered reputable. Kiyoshi is admonished that by being friends with the boy, "you will bring shame to your father and me . . . . People will say, 'Ah look at the Oyama's number two boy. He's a *hoitobo* [beggar]! He's a *chorimbo* [bum]!' " Through the intimidations of family image, the stern control of the patriarchical commandments that if he doesn't comply, "I'll crack your head," Kiyoshi is finally coerced into abandoning his friendship with the youngster from the mysterious and ostracized family.

Another important theme emerging from Murayama's story is the role which peer groups played in shaping the individual's behavior. Outside of the family, the immediate social referent of the Japanese individual was his peer group. The friends one made as a schoolmate, co-worker, or acquaintance had a major part in shaping and reinforcing ambitions, needs, and interests. The intimacy of peer-group friendships permeated the individual's world view.

As with family relationships, Issei peer-group relations were characterized by a pattern of rural interdependencies. Within the family the individual learned a network of highly sanctioned obligations. Obligation to family, status, and position, to one's parents, teachers, or elders, fell under the value of *on*—an all-pervasive commitment to family and community. Between friends and acquaintances, the individual also acquired certain reciprocal obligations known as *giri*. Especially in rural communities, the reciprocal nature of exchanging goods, services, or affiliation was fundamental. One learned how to share property and feelings because selfishness was socially dysfunctional. In the rural community, nothing could be altered or changed without a loss of energy, without a chain reaction of multiplying effects. Gifts, energy, or emotions were given openly, but such exchanges left a vacuum demanding reciprocal replacement. After all, giving implies losing, and in a subsistence community an unreciprocated loss could be disastrous.

Therefore each individual understood that if he received something from another human being, he was obligated, for his own survival, to return that energy. For if he failed to do so, he was not only abnegating future help from his neighbors, but he was establishing a dangerous precedent—when he gave assistance or support, it might not be reciprocated, leaving him in personal difficulty. Reciprocal obligation also had a humanistic dimension—the dependency between human beings reinforced the bonds of affiliation. By being obligated one was not only economically involved with his neighbors but emotionally linked in mutual help and concern. Friendship became more highly valued than personal sacrifice or selfishness.

In the Issei community, *giri* was a highly formalized practice. The values of gifts, energies, or emotions were exactly calculated and had to be promptly reciprocated within a set time. The precision of *giri* could sometimes be measured to the dollar:

> As a marriage gift I received a $25 Mix-Master from a family which has six daughters. It had the $25 price tag on it, but I suppose this was an oversight. In any case, every time anything very important happens in that family, I am supposed to give in return something of as much or greater value. Soon the first of those girls will be graduating from college, and I will have to remember them at that time. Then they will be getting married, and I am supposed to remember that. If the daughters have babies, I must remember that. If the father dies, I have to remember that, or if any of them are sick I am supposed to go to the hospital with some bottles of fruit juice. That is how complicated the exchange of gifts can become.[16]

Between intimate friends and acquaintances, immediate family and relatives, the character of reciprocal obligation was more generalized and less exact—it would be humanly impossible to maintain an exact account book of exchanges on the intimate, day-to-day level. But beyond the generalized reciprocal obligations, the immigrant was keenly aware of a circle of friends, acquaintances, and relatives which comprised the *kosai,* or network of persons to whom the individual was obligated. This large circle of affiliated relatives, friends, and acquaintances required relationships based on a formally equivalent reciprocity.

The human relationships established through the obligations of the *kosai* were also the basis of a broader interrelatedness of ethnic community. The importance of cooperation with individuals and families sharing a common cultural background served to arouse a sense of community cooperation among the immigrants as well as stimulate the economic interdependencies of Issei relationships. As an immigrant institution in a new land, the Japanese family naturally tended to view itself as an extended member of an ethnic community. Cultural commonalities, socioeconomic stability through group cooperation, and the Japanese pride of race combined to accentuate the "clannishness" of the Japanese community. This "clannishness" could be seen in the establishment of exclusively Japanese organizations. *Kenjin-kai* groups composed of Issei who originated from the same Japanese *ken,* or prefecture, *sonjin-kai* groups composed of immigrants from the same village, social welfare associations such as the Japanese Benevolent Society, or broadly based community organizations such as the Honolulu Japanese Merchants' Association were chartered as a response to ethnic community cohesiveness and the social services provided through cooperation. As long as these organizations could serve a function, either economically, culturally, or psychologically, they would continue to be the focus of ethnic community identification.

Probably the most revealing study of such activity in the community was anthropologist John F. Embree's article, "New Local and Kin Groups among the Japanese Farmers of Kona, Hawaii."[17] Examining the lifestyles of pre-World War II Japanese in Kona, Embree hypothesized that the immigrants in a new environment, without extended-family kinship patterns, formed community groupings which served as "kin substitutes." The emotional, economic, and communal cooperativeness inherent in extended-family systems were replaced in function by newly established, geographically propinquant patterns of community organization.

Comparing the Japanese *buraku,* the village of interrelated family households, to the Japanese farmer cooperative groups (the *kumi*) in Kona, Embree believed that the *kumi* had replaced to a certain degree the relational groupings of old Japan. The emotional bonds through cooperation and celebration, pervasive in the extended Japanese family, were perpetuated for the dislocated immigrants through "kin substitutes" such as the *kumi.* Civic, agricultural, cultural, or mutual-help functions of the *buraku* were assumed in Kona by the kin-substitute *kumi.*

Another kin substitute which had importance for the Issei was the *tokoro-no-mono,* the "same place people." Without relatives in Hawaii, according to Embree, the immigrant naturally gravitated toward the closest thing to a family member—the man who shared a common background and prefecture in Japan. Embree recognized this form of community cooperation as one of the more relevant kin substitutes to emerge for the Japanese immigrant. In summary, what Embree emphasized was the importance of community organization as the functional replacement for the extended family:

> When a change takes place in the society or when members of a society form a new group in a different locality, there is an attempt to keep or recreate the old kin and local groups. It is comparatively easy to rearrange the local group, though frequently many of its old functions are lost. To recreate the old kin organization resort may be taken to *kin substitutes* such as neighbors or, more important, same-place-of-origin people, for instance the *tokoro-mon [tokoro-no-mono]* of the Japanese coffee farmers in Hawaii.

The ties which bound the Issei to his community were based not only on an emotional feeling of cooperativeness, but also on an economic self-interest. The ethnic community functioned not only for racial and cultural continuity but for very pragmatic economic reasons. To offset the uncertainties and pressures of the Island economy, Issei used the ethnic community as a source of financial stability. One example of such ethnically based economic dependencies was the *tanomoshi,* a mutual financing group. Usually from ten to twenty friends entered into membership in the *tanomoshi* as a means to raise money either to help one of the members or to make an investment of long-term reward. This self-help economic system was predicated on the mutual respect and obligations growing out of the socioeconomic interdependency of members of the community. The *tanomoshi* was such a popular means of investment and economic assistance that some studies indicated that several million dollars a year were invested in the *tanomoshi* up until the 1930s.[18]

The *tanomoshi* worked on the basis of a monthly investment of members into a communal pot which was then given to the highest bidder:

> Members agreed to put up a specified amount of money, say $5.00 or $10.00 per month. The promoter, or the person in charge of keeping accounts, took the first "pot." Beginning with the second month, the pot went to the highest bidder, the bid being divided among the remaining members in lieu of interest. Once a person took the pot, he was no longer eligible for dividends, therefore the longer he refrained, the larger was his return.[19]

A brief study of the *tanomoshi* as it operated in the immigrant community was conducted in 1937 by Ruth N. Masuda for a University of Hawaii sociology journal. In her article, "The Japanese 'Tanomoshi',"[20] Masuda explored the origins, functions, and style of expression of this uniquely Japanese mutual-self-help institution. The operation of the *tanomoshi,* as noted by Masuda, was based on the implicit trust of the rural community, serving also as a social gathering for the members. Functionally, the institution served as both a reaffirmation of community obligation and as an economic means of self-help within the ethnic group.

From such cultural and economic cohesiveness symbolized in the *tanomoshi,* the Japanese immigrant and his family gained the security of a resilient community identity. Although the institutions imported to Hawaii had been altered from the simpler *ie* patterns of rural Japan, fundamental relational values of filial piety, honor, obligation, and community interdependency had found significant reexpression for the Issei. With the birth of the second generation, the Nisei, the permanency implicit in the slogan *eijū dochyaku* was rapidly becoming actualized. Increasingly the immigrant began to speak of Hawaii as home. And as he did so, he also spoke of changes, improvements, and great expectations.

NOTES

1. United Japanese Society of Hawaii, *A History of Japanese in Hawaii,* ed. by Publication Committee, Dr. James H. Okahata, Chm., Honolulu: United Japanese Society of Hawaii, 1971, p. 162.

2. Andrew W. Lind, *Hawaii's People,* Honolulu: University of Hawaii Press, 1967, p. 33.

3. Seiko Ogai, "From Picture Brides to Pictured Brides," *Nisei in Hawaii and the Pacific,* v. 6, no. 2 (June 1952), p. 6.

4. Colleen L. Johnson, "The Japanese-American Family and Community in Honolulu: Generational Continuities in Ethnic Affiliation," Ph.D. dissertation (Anthropology), Syracuse University, 1972, p. 58.

5. *Hawaii Shimpo,* March 3, 1923, in *Translations from the Japanese Press in Hawaii,* Honolulu: Hawaii Sugar Planter's Association, 1923, unpaginated.

6. M. Hilo and Emma K. Himeno, "Some Characteristics of American and Japanese Culture," *Social Process in Hawaii,* v. 21 (1957), p. 37.

7. Jitsuichi Masuoka, "Changing Moral Bases of the Japanese Family in Hawaii," *Sociology and Social Research,* v. 21, no. 2 (Nov./Dec. 1936), p. 164.

8. Masuoka, p. 161.

9. Masuoka, p. 162.

10. Misako Yamamoto, "Cultural Conflicts and Accommodations of the First and Second Generation Japanese," *Social Process in Hawaii,* v. 4 (May 1938), p. 44.

11. Jitsuichi Masuoka, "The Japanese Patriarch in Hawaii," *Social Forces,* v. 17, no. 2 (December 1938), pp. 240–48.

12. Emi Yoshizawa, "A Japanese Family in Rural Hawaii," *Social Process in Hawaii,* v. 3 (May 1937), p. 56.

13. Masuoka, "Changing Moral Bases of the Japanese Family in Hawaii," p. 160.

14. Harry H. L. Kitano, *Japanese Americans: The Evolution of a Subculture,* Englewood Cliffs, New Jersey: Prentice-Hall, Inc., 1969, p. 104.

15. Milton Murayama, "I'll Crack Your Head *Kotsun,*" in *All I Asking For Is My Body,* San Francisco: Supa Press, 1975, pp. 1–11.

16. Forrest E. LaViolette, *Americans of Japanese Ancestry, A Study of Assimilation in the American Community,* Toronto: The Canadian Institute of International Affairs, 1945, p. 61.

17. John F. Embree, "New Local and Kin Groups among the Japanese Farmers of Kona, Hawaii," *American Anthropologist,* v. 41, no. 3 (July-Sept. 1939), pp. 400–407.

18. United Japanese Society of Hawaii, p. 215.

19. United Japanese Society of Hawaii, pp. 214–15.

20. Ruth N. Masuda, "The Japanese 'Tanomoshi,' " *Social Process in Hawaii,* v. 3 (1937), pp. 16–19.

The Japanese Patriarch in Hawaii

JITSUICHI MASUOKA

THE family in Japan is a continuing organization embracing not merely a man and his wife and children but also all others connected by blood or adoption. Not only the living but also the dead are included, and one might even say that those not yet born are members. The family is thus based on a vertical relationship—on successive super-imposed generations—from parents to children with primary emphasis upon the patriarch-son relationship.[1] As the continuance of the family is recognized through the male line only, it can be represented comprehensively for generations by a genealogical tree.

In general the status which every individual has and the role which he assumes in the family are determined more or less by customs and traditions of the group. The degree to which the future is "mapped out" for him differs according to the degree to which the cultural pattern is integrated and the degree to which any particular form of relationship is emphasized. In the traditional Japanese family organization the role of each member, particularly that of the patriarch, is definite and non-problematic. Thus the traditional Japanese family can be studied by considering the relations of patriarch and all other family members, related either by blood or adoption.

The Patriarch, His Status and Role

Sociologically speaking, the patriarch does not exist apart from the group which recognizes his authority and accepts the role he

In *Social Forces,* v. 17, no. 2 (December 1938), pp. 240–48. Reprinted by permission of University of North Carolina Press.

assumes. The patriarch has his status mainly because he performs his duties and obligations as dictated by custom and law, and in accordance with the expectations of others. His duties and obligations as defined in the Japanese Civil Code include

> . . . The right of consent to the marriage and divorce, the adoption, of each member of the family, right of determining his or her place of residence, and the right of expelling such person from the family, or of forbidding his or her return to it. He has also the right of succession to property in default of other heirs. But the headship of a family carries with it also duties and responsibilities, the duty of supporting indigent members of the family, the duty under certain circumstances of guardianship, and responsibility for the debts of all. . . .[2]

In reality the patriarch has daily his pressing problems; he must look after the welfare of every member; he must safeguard the family property and other family heritages; and he must uphold law and order within the family, and make peace, harmony, and collective well-being the keynote of family life. He accomplishes this by emphasizing the importance of laboring collectively, by upholding respect as the norm of conduct, and by creating a reverential attitude toward the cult of his ancestor. In a final analysis the "we-feeling" originates *in* and continues *through* the family in a form of gratitude toward the family ancestors.

Since so much of his social status and his role depends upon the continuance of his family property and the family, his paramount desire is to keep them intact. His sentiment toward his ancestral land, for example, is very deep seated. How deep seated is his sentiment toward his ancestral land and the ancestors can best be seen in the experience of a returned emigrant. In general, an immigrant is not notoriously faithful to ancestral worship because he is usually too busy in accumulating money, but when he returns to the original cultural situation he regains the sentiment toward his ancestral lands. Mr. O______ after living in Hawaii for nearly thirty years and having acquired the western conceptions of land and money, made a short visit to his old village with the expectation of selling his ancestral land. But he said:

> I could not sell the land which my ancestors handed down to me. When I witnessed the way the farmers worked from early morning until late in the evening tilling the land which they have inherited from their ancestors, I realized that my forefathers too must have worked as hard as they in order that I might have the privilege of owning a few acres of paddy fields and the forest land. I could not help but

weep and bow before my ancestors in deep gratitude and regret that I had thought of disposing of the land. Now I do not think of selling it, for I know that it is worth a million although it could not be exchanged for so much money.[3]

Law and custom have given the patriarch absolute control over the family property, but strictly speaking it does not belong to him.[4] He cannot dispose of it as he pleases, for the family property belongs to his ancestors and prospectively to his descendants. He is merely the manager of the property and if he must dispose of it he must do so only after the approval of the family council.

The patriarch is accorded the right to demand absolute obedience from every member in the family, and in the perfectly functioning family his authority is accepted unconditionally by all. An excerpt below illustrates the role of a patriarch in Japan when the traditional family is already undergoing some slight modification. He demands absolute obedience from every member in the family even at the risk of creating a psychological barrier between himself and the rest of the family. It should be noted that in spite of the apparent conflict, this family has been successful in maintaining its unity.

> My general recollection of my father is that he was a cold, stern, taciturn, rather cruel person. I remember clearly that during my boyhood, I never felt warm affection toward him. Our relation was, I thought then, more of the relationship between a master and servant. What he said was absolute and final in the family. I cannot recall any incident in which I ever disobeyed him. I simply dreaded him. . . .
>
> We always obeyed his every command. In the morning, before he went out to work, he always told us what to do after school. We were mindful of his orders, but sometimes we would forget and then we felt like a criminal appearing before a judge when we saw our father in the evening.[5]

. . .

The patriarch's primary concern is the family and he stands always for the welfare of the family from the standpoint of its institutional relations.

The Patriarch and His Wife

Where the continuance of the family is of supreme importance, marriage is of vital concern because it ensures the perpetuation of the family. Since it always means establishing a relationship between two families as well as introducing a new member with more or less different family customs, the head of the family is very particular in the choice of his or her son's wife.[6] A good marriage usually means a union with a family of the same standing in the community. Therefore, love before marriage is strongly disapproved, for it usually jeopardizes the social status of the family. "Love makes no distinction between high and low" *(Koi ni Joge no, Hedate nashi)* says the Japanese proverb.

The wife becomes a new member of the family. She is the bride of a house as well as of an individual. Her expected role is to bring forth an heir and the norm of behavior toward her husband and other members of the family is that of respect but not necessarily of love and affection. In the eyes of the patriarch and the family a good wife is a woman who, by bringing forth sons, helps to safeguard and perpetuate the family name, and by being obedient, properly humble and diligent, helps to maintain peace and order in the family.[7] As manager of domestic affairs she must be competent and thrifty so as to raise the economic status of the family.

Her failure to perform any one of these duties is regarded as sufficient ground for divorce by the family and the community. Being an affectionate and lovable wife to her husband is a secondary matter. They are desirable if she possesses the other qualities of a good wife. She is, thus, frequently divorced on the ground that she does not fit into "our family tradition" *(Kafu ni Awanu)* or on the ground of sterility. To these reasons for divorce social opinion makes no protest. Just as it is a moral obligation for a patriarch to marry in order to perpetuate his family line, so is it also his moral obligation to divorce his wife should she prove incapable of performing her duties, and thereby threaten the very existence of the family. Divorce, therefore, is in the mores.

. . .

If a patriarch always stands for the welfare of the family from the standpoint of its institutional relations, a mother is the chief creator and molder of human nature. Among the members family affection and a spirit of common devotion are created and nourished chiefly by her. Her role is that of mediator between the patriarch and the children, making it easier for the latter to adjust themselves to the former. The case below is a student's conception of his mother's role in the family:

As I look back upon her life from the beginning to the end, I can not help but love and admire her, and sympathize with her. Her life

> has been one of continuous self-sacrifice, labor, subjection, and cares and anxieties for others.
>
> There was no equality between my father and mother. During the meal times my mother always sat at the lowest end of the table. Of course this fact does not indicate that her status was the lowest in the family. She never sat beside her husband. . . . She always seemed to be contented with the least thing in the family. Whenever we had fish or meat she gave the best and the largest piece to my father and smaller pieces to us, while she took the smallest and the worst for herself.[8]

. . .

The Patriarch and His Natural Heir

Among the children the first in the order of importance is the heir because he is the future patriarch. In the past he received special education concerning the family law and regulations and other duties and obligations. The task of educating the nobility and the *daimyos* (war lords) fell to the family tutors.

Like the patriarch, the heir receives respect and special treatment from other members of the family and from the whole community. He is seated above all others and served first in the family save his father and grandfather. In addressing him others members use more honorific speech. This practice, as shown in the case below, still persists in a majority of the homes in Hawaii:

> We are taught to respect parents, elder brothers and sisters, relatives and strangers. Any violation of the above laws are seriously dealt with. We are not allowed to answer "no," nor refute any of my parents' commands. What they command is immediately obeyed. Younger children, too, are made to obey their elders. They have to call their elder brothers and sisters by certain titles, *niisan* (older brother) and *nesan* (older sister) and not by their own names. Thus, I being the eldest in my family, all my brothers call me *niisan,* instead of calling me by my Japanese name, Haruo, or by my American name, Alfred. Being called Haruo or Alfred by any one of my brothers in the presence of my parents would, without doubt, result in a very fiery lecture or reprimands from them.
>
> However, in spite of the large size of my family, I, being the eldest, can demand more things and have more privileges than the rest of my brothers. I do not know why this should be the case in all Oriental families, but it seems to be an accepted axiom that the first born child, or *chonan*—to be exact, the first born male child—should be ranked above the rest of the children of the family. In this connection I

> would like to mention some typical remarks that I received frequently from other people. I was still yet in high school when some one remarked: "Oh! you're lucky. Surely, your parents will send you to college." I guess, it is in the mores of the Orientals that one's parents should give their best to the eldest son, so that he would maintain the good name of the family. . . .[9]

However, if the heir fails to live up to the expectation of the family or appears to be incapable of managing the family property, or disgraces the family name by committing a crime or marrying against the wishes of the patriarch and the family, he is likely to be disowned and have his name taken off the family register *(Kando Seido)* or to be compelled to give up the right of succession to the headship. This is in one sense a face-saving device, not for the individual but for the family. If, for example, some member of the family insists on marrying a woman of lower social standing or has disgraced his family name in the eyes of the community, he is sometimes disinherited and thus becomes an individual having no connection whatsoever with his original family. Such an individual may create a new house of his own. It frequently happens that a disinherited heir returns to his house after proving himself worthy of reinstatement.

The Patriarch and His Adopted Heir

"The longer husband and wife are associated the more enduring their affection," goes a Japanese saying, showing that the personal sentiment often runs counter to the institutional practices and it may even endanger the very existence of the latter. Personal bonds may grow so strong that divorce becomes difficult. However, where the continuance of the family is of primary importance, the major institution has provided, so to speak, an auxiliary institution for its protection. Through the adoption of an heir a man is able to keep his wife and still have an heir.[10]

The practice of ancestor worship and the desire to perpetuate the family name and keep property in the family are incentives for sanctioning the institution of adoption. Death without an heir is considered to be the greatest filial impiety. So it is the duty of the head of the family to adopt an heir in the absence of a natural son.[11]

The most common form is the adoption of the son-in-law *(muko yoshi)*. This apparently originated out of a situation wherein the woman had no legal right to succeed to the headship of the family. The ancient law used to consider a man without an heir even though he had a daughter, because only men had the right to practice ancestor worship and to succeed to the family headship. Those who had daughters only, therefore, had to adopt a son, but since it was necessary, if possible, for the blood of the ancestor to be continued in the family, the head of the family adopted a son fitted to be his daughter's husband.

The adopted son legally acquires the same position as the natural-born legitimate son. He relinquishes his original house and enters into the house of the adopter, taking the latter's family name and becoming the legal presumptive heir to the headship. In reality his status in the adopted family is somewhat like that of a wife. His also is an insecure position, for the adoption may be dissolved for any cause by mutual agreement. But if the parties could not come to a mutual agreement a compulsory dissolution may be brought about by one of the parties on the basis of many grounds specified in the Law. One of them is: "If the adopted person commits a grave fault of a nature to disgrace the family name or to ruin the house property of the adoptive house, the adoptive parent may bring an action for the dissolution of the adoptive tie." [12] The reason for this is that the name of the ancestral house of the adopter is sacred and, therefore, it is not only the adopter's legal right, but also his moral and religious duty to dissolve the tie. The adoptive house is not the house of the adopter and the adoptee alone but it is the house which the adopter inherited from his ancestors. From the point of view of the adoptee, he does not truly become the important person until the death of the adopter. Even after his death he is still under the influence of his wife and her kinfolk and cannot exercise as much power and authority as the natural successor to the headship. The unpopularity of this practice is voiced in the proverbial saying: "If there is a mere handful of rice in the house one should never be adopted."

In passing we might point out the relationship of the patriarch to a retired father *(inkyo)*. The patriarch always considers the latter's will first and his opinion is given great weight in matters of grave importance. He is seated above all others and given the respect due him.

Other members of the family are given consideration according to their age and sex. While the oldest male receives first preference and respect, the second son also is treated with respect, for he is an important substitute for the heir. In case of the death of the heir or of his disinheritance the second son succeeds to the headship.

The core, therefore, of the Japanese family is the body of sentiments which are clustered around the patriarch–heir relationship.

The Japanese Family Relationships in Hawaii

Some understanding of the experience of a typical Japanese immigrant to Hawaii is helpful in acquiring deeper insight into the forces operating to modify the traditional family relationships in Hawaii.

The experience of an immigrant tends to be something like that of an urban man. His personality is affected by a series of crisis-situations. Leaving his family group, his native village, and his folk culture, and adjusting himself to a changed milieu, he is face to face with infinitely variable and perplexing problems which provide him with shocking and baffling experiences. Unlike his old village community which rested on a subsistence economy, the new community flourishes through a money economy. In his effort to find a new foothold in the new community he breaks away from his old culture and merges into the new culture life of the dominant group. His daily experience demands that he be assimilated and that he incorporate into his life some practices that are in harmony with the dominant culture. Moreover, he is credulous and susceptible to the new culture, for he was young when he left his village not in despair, but in hope —hope of acquiring money in order to raise his family status in his old village. In this sense he is an optimist, adventurer, and pragmatist eager to take advantages of the new community. Therefore, if in the new community a kindly relationship exists between his group and others and more particularly the dominant group, and if the infusion of the new culture does not radically undermine his group mores, he develops favorable attitudes toward the new culture.

The fact that his group always occupies a subordinate economic and social status and the fact that his community is located near the dominant group, explain in part why the cultural diffusion proceeds rapidly in spite of the existing language and other cultural barriers. Because of proximity in space, he and his descendant observe, feel, and develop an attitude of appreciation toward the culture of the dominant people. The longer he remains and the more successful he becomes, the more does he approach the cultural and personality types of the dominant group.

His community in Hawaii is economically, politically, and culturally never completely self-sufficing. Once he is brought to participate in the development of the local economy, he is, by this very fact, unable to confine his activity strictly within his own immediate community. Furthermore, in his quest for a high social status locally or elsewhere, he encounters competition and conflict with the members of other groups. In attempting to adjust himself to life outside of his *ghetto* he faces the need of learning other languages, customs, etiquette, and the law and moral obligations of the larger community, and consciously or unconsciously he incorporates in his life practices of other groups.

Finally, as the duration of his residence is lengthened and his family established, his children become Americanized through their wider participation in the larger community. Their education and their life in political activities make them understand the culture of the dominant group. They introduce American culture to the home and become more or less Americanized through their children.

In Hawaii the patriarchal control prevails to a large extent, but the patriarch's status and role are rapidly being modified in response to the demands of local situations. His traditional rights and privileges are fast becoming relative rather than absolute. In the following pages are presented in a broad way, some of the significant factors which explain the shifting status and role of the patriarch in Hawaii.

In the first place, the Japanese immigrant to Hawaii was an ambitious young man when he left his home. He was not strongly impregnated with the traditional attitudes toward the patriarchal family system. Moreover, being young and impressionable he was able to adopt, more or less readily, the culture of the West.

Secondly, in the absence of family property—the ancestral land and the house—his authority, which was vested in the cult of ancestor worship, lost its intrinsic value and began to be questioned by the members. The exercise of absolute control over his family became difficult for a patriarch in the highly mobile society of Hawaii.

Thirdly, the Japanese family as a unit in Hawaii became a consuming rather than a productive and consuming entity, as in rural Japan. In Japan the control of the family expenditures and incomes as well as the economic activities of each member was under the direct authority of the patriarch. But in Hawaii the patriarch earns his money outside of his home and the control of the family expenditures and incomes is now largely in the hands of his wife, if not of his son's wife. In general, as soon as he ceases to be the chief supporter of the family, his status is lowered and his role modified.

Fourthly, in the absence of a concerted social opinion in support of the patriarchal family within and without the Japanese community, plus the fact that the larger community sentiment and the law are not in sympathy with the typical traditional family, the value of continuing patriarch-heir solidarity even at the expense of the "happiness" of the young married couple is now questioned by both the first and the second generation in Hawaii. Sentiment in support of the traditional patriarch-heir centered family is rapidly being changed. Nevertheless, some families continue this form of relationship largely, if not wholly, for economic reasons. "It is much cheaper to live that way."

All of this is involved in the acculturation of both the first and second generation which inevitably affects the traditional status and role of the patriarch. Gradually as this process gains momentum the whole system of relationships comes to be modified. The status and role of patriarch take a different meaning both in the eyes of the members of the family and of the community. The excerpts below are presented to show the modifications and consequent effects on the family and the community.

> My father is no longer a "commander" or a "dictator." He himself has changed immensely in accordance with the changed environment according to the times. As I recall my childhood days, I believe I can say, he was the "boss" of the family. He was the one who decided what the members were supposed to do. I quite well remember the days when he tried to keep us away from luxuries. . . . But it was my mother who, accustomed to luxuries, defended us, saying that we are living in a different age. Now, we do not take father's words as seriously as we once did.
>
> My mother has influenced him a great deal. For example, in the past my father used to invite his friends regardless of whether mother liked them or not. But now whenever he makes a list of guests he submits it for mother's approval, and he is quite apt to leave out those whom my mother dislikes.
>
> Formerly father was rather a "dictator" on family problems such as marriage, etc. He used to say that he and his wife were to choose my brothers' wives. But today, odd but true, he has discarded such an idea and says: "It is up to my brothers. . . ." My father stresses the importance of the family status of a prospective bride or groom, but my mother does not agree with him. I believe, father's attitude is tempered by the fact that he "climbed" from a low economic status to a higher one, whereas my mother was never troubled with any economic problem. Whenever financial questions are raised in the family there is apt to be a conflict between my parents.

> It is interesting to note that he still keeps the seat at the dinner table which he had when we used to regard him as a "boss." Everything is served to him first. We try to prepare menus which we think will meet with his approval. We never think of taking our bath until he has had his. . . .[13]
>
> Mr. M______'s wife, a typical Japanese wife, is petite in stature and as polite as she is small. She keeps her humble plantation house immaculately clean, and slaves from sunrise to sunset in catering to her husband and her fine daughters. (It is very unfortunate that she did not bear a son.) In her home, even to this day, strict Japanese customs prevail; after all, that is what "his lordship" wants. For example, no matter what she may be doing, when she sees her husband coming down the bend of the road she will drop everything immediately, in order to greet him properly. As soon as the greeting is over she hands him his towels, soap, and slippers so that he may carry them to the bath house. Irrespective of whether or not he shows his appreciation for her effort she never fails to perform her wifely duties politely and respectfully. This couple observes all Japanese holidays in typical native style even though the other Japanese families no longer celebrate them in that manner. The community points out this family saying that they are *baka teinei* (foolishly and ridiculously polite). They make themselves conspicuous amongst the others who are rapidly adapting themselves to more of the western manners through the humble medium of plantation life.[14]

Thus with the waning influences of ancestor worship, family property, the family name, and the family line, on the one hand, and with the growing influences of the ideologies, the family etiquette, and the mores of the American people, on the other, the traditional patriarch–heir relationship weakens. The established relationship between husband and wife is also affected by the rising social status of women in response to the local situation. The experience of the Japanese people with the American culture is too short to indicate the later trend but the evidence seems to show that the emphasis is shifting from the patriarch–heir to a husband–wife relationship.

NOTES

1. Inazo Nitobo, *The Japanese Nation,* p. 159; S. Toda, *Kazoku to Konin* (The Family and the Marriage); and also by the same author, *Kazoku no Kenkyu* (Research on the Family); also, J. Masuoka, "Changing Moral Bases of the Japanese Family in Hawaii," *Sociology and Social Research,* 21 (1936), 158–69.
2. "Introduction," to *The Civil Code of Japan,* by J. H. Gubbins (trans.), pp. XXVI–VII; also, W. J. Sebald (trans.), *The Civil Code of Japan,* pp. 169–70.

3. Manuscript Document.

4. The Civil Code of 1898 recognizes individual property within the family circle. "Property acquired by members of a house in their own name constitutes their own separate property." See, Article 748 in *The Civil Code of Japan,* by W. J. Sebald, p. 169.

5. Manuscript Document.

6. Since the promulgation of *The Civil Code of Japan* a woman could be the head of a house, under certain conditions.

7. A. K. Faust, *The New Japanese Womanhood,* chapters 4 and 7.

[8]. Manuscript Document.

[9]. Manuscript Document.

[10]. In the past the institution of concubinage was resorted to by a few men of the privileged classes to secure an heir. At present it is widely separated from family and is a means of satisfying not only a man's sexual desire but also his wish for power and prestige.

[11]. N. Hozumi, *Ancestor Worship and the Japanese Law,* chapter 8.

[12]. N. Hozumi, *op. cit.,* pp. 166–67.

[13]. Manuscript Document.

[14]. Manuscript Document.

I'll Crack Your Head *Kotsun*

MILTON MURAYAMA

THERE was something funny about Makot. He always played with guys younger than he and the big guys his own age always made fun of him. His family was the only Japanese family in Filipino Camp and his father didn't seem to do anything but ride around in his brand-new Ford Model T. But Makot always had money to spend and the young kids liked him.

During the summer in Pepelau, Hawaii, the whole town spends the whole day at the beach. We go there early in the morning, then walk home for lunch, often in our trunks, then go back for more spearing fish, surfing, or just plain swimming, depending on the tide, and stay there till sunset. At night there were the movies for those who had the money and the Buddhist Bon dances and dance practices. The only change in dress was that at night we wore Japanese zori and in the day bare feet. Nobody owned shoes in Pepelau.

In August Makot became our gang leader. We were all at the beach and it was on a Wednesday when there was a matinee, and Makot said, "Come on, I'll take you all to the movies," and Mit, Skats, and I became his gang in no time. Mit or Mitsunobu Kato and Skats or Nobuyuki Asakatsu and I were not exactly a gang. There were only three of us and we were all going to be in the fourth grade,

In *All I Asking For Is My Body* (San Francisco: Supa Press, 1975), pp. 1–11. Slightly different version appeared in the *Arizona Quarterly,* 1959. Reprinted by permission of Milton Murayama and *Arizona Quarterly*.

so nobody was leader. But we were a kind of a poor gang. None of us were in the Boy Scouts or had bicycles, we played football with tennis balls, and during basketball season we hung around Baldwin Park till some gang showed up with a rubber ball or a real basketball.

After that day we followed Makot at the beach, and in spearing fish Skats and I followed him across the breakers. We didn't want to go at first, since no fourth-grader went across the breakers, but he teased us and called us yellow, so Skats and I followed. Mit didn't care if he was called yellow. Then at lunchtime, instead of all of us going home for lunch, Makot invited us all to his home in Filipino Camp. Nobody was home and he cooked us rice and canned corned beef and onions. The following day there was the new kind of Campbell soup in cans, which we got at home only when we were sick. So I began to look forward to lunchtime, when we'd go to Makot's home to eat. At home Father was a fisherman and so we ate fish and rice three times a day, and as my older brother Tosh who was a seventh-grader always said, "What! Fish and rice again! No wonder the Japanese get beriberi!" I was sick of fish and rice too.

Mother didn't seem too happy about my eating at Makot's. About the fourth day when I came home at sunset, she said in Japanese, "You must be famished, Kiyo-chan, shall I fix you something?"

"No, I had lunch at Makoto-san's home."

"Oh, again?"

Mother was sitting on a cushion on the floor, her legs hid under her, and she was bending over and sewing a kimono by hand. It was what she always did. I sat down cross-legged. "Uh huh. Makoto-san invited me. I ate a bellyful. Makoto-san is a very good cook. He fixed some corned beef and onions and it was delicious."

"Oh, are you playing with Makoto-san now? He's too old for you, isn't he? He's Toshio's age. What about Mitsunobu-san and Nobuyuki-san?"

"Oh, they still with me. We all play with Makoto-san. He invited all of us."

"Makoto-san's mother or father wasn't home?"

"No, they're usually not home."

"You know, Kiyo-chan, you shouldn't eat at Makoto-san's home too often."

"Why? But he invites us."

"But his parents didn't invite you. Do you understand, Kiyo-chan?"

"But why? Nobuyuki-san and Mitsunobu-san go."

"Kiyo-chan is a good boy so he'll obey what his mother says, won't he?"

"But why, Mother! I eat at Nobuyuki's and Mitsunobu's homes when their parents aren't home. And I always thank their parents when I see them. I haven't thanked Makoto's parents yet, but I will when I see them."

"But don't you see, Kiyoshi, you will bring shame to your father and me if you go there to eat. People will say, 'Ah, look at the Oyama's number two boy. He's a *hoitobo!* He's a *chorimbo!* That's because his parents are *hoitobo* and *chorimbo!*' "

Hoitobo means beggar in Japanese and *chorimbo* is something like a bum, but they're ten times worse than beggar and bum because you always make your face real ugly when you say them and they sound horrible!

"But Makoto invites us, Mother! Once Mitsunobu didn't want to go and Makoto dragged him. We can always have Makoto-san over to our home and repay him the way we do Mitsunobu-san and Nobuyuki-san."

"But can't you see, Kiyo-chan, people will laugh at you. 'Look at that Kiyoshi Oyama,' they'll say, 'he always eats at the Sasakis'. It's because his parents are poor and he doesn't have enough to eat at home.' You understand, don't you, Kiyo-chan? You're a good filial boy so you'll obey what your parents say, won't you? Your father and I would cry if we had two unfilial sons like Toshio . . ."

"But what about Nobuyuki and Mitsunobu? Won't people talk about them and their parents like that too?"

"But Kiyoshi, you're not a monkey. You don't have to copy others. Whatever Nobuyuki and Mitsunobu do is up to them. Besides, we're poor and poor families have to be more careful."

"But Mitsunobu's home is poor too! They have lots of children and he's always charging things at the stores and his home looks poor like ours!"

"Nemmind! You'll catch a sickness if you go there too often," she made a real ugly face.

"What kind of sickness? Won't Mitsunobu-san and Nobuyuki-san catch it too?"

She dropped her sewing on her lap and looked straight at me. "Kiyoshi, you will obey your parents, won't you?"

I stood up and hitched up my pants. I didn't say yes or no. I just grunted like Father and walked out.

But the next time I went to eat at Makot's I felt guilty and the corned beef and onions didn't taste so good. And when I came home that night the first thing Mother asked was, "Oh, did you have lunch, Kiyo-chan?" Then, "At Makoto-san's home?" and her face looked as if she was going to cry.

But I figured that that was the end of that so I was surprised when Father turned to me at the supper table and said, "Kiyoshi . . ." Whenever he called me by my full name instead of Kiyo or Kiyo-chan, that meant he meant business. He never punched my head once, but I'd seen him slap and punch Tosh's head all over the place till Tosh was black and blue in the head.

"Yes, Father." I was scared.

"Kiyoshi, you're not to eat anymore at Makoto-san's home. You understand?"

"But why, Father? Nobuyuki-san and Mitsunobu-san eat with me too!"

"Nemmind!" he said in English. Then he said in Japanese, "You're not a monkey. You're Kiyoshi Oyama."

"But why?" I said again. I wasn't being smart-alecky like Tosh. I really wanted to know why.

Father grew angry. You could tell by the way his eyes bulged and the way he twisted his mouth. He flew off the handle real easily, like Tosh. He said, "If you keep on asking 'Why? Why?' I'll crack your head *kotsun!*"

Kotsun doesn't mean anything in Japanese. It's just the sound of something hard hitting your head.

"Yeah, slap his head, slap his head!" Tosh said in pidgin Japanese and laughed.

"Shut up! Don't say uncalled-for things!" Father said to Tosh and Tosh shut up and grinned.

Whenever Father talked about this younger generation talking too much and talking out of turn and having no respect for anything, he didn't mean me, he meant Tosh.

"Kiyoshi, you understand, you're not to eat anymore at Makoto's home," Father said evenly, now his anger gone.

I was going to ask "Why?" again but I was afraid. "Yes." I said.

Then Tosh said across the table in pidgin English, which the old folks couldn't understand, "You know why, Kyo?" I never liked the guy, he couldn't even pronounce my name right. "Because his father no work and his mother do all the work, thass why! Ha-ha-ha-ha!"

Father told him to shut up and not to joke at the table and he shut up and grinned.

Then Tosh said again in pidgin English, his mouth full of food; he always talked with his mouth full, "Go tell that *kodomo taisho* to go play with guys his own age, not small shrimps like you. You know why he doan play with us? Because he scared, thass why. He too *wahine*. We bust um up!"

"Wahine" was the Hawaiian word for woman. When we called anybody *wahine* it meant she was a girl or he was a sissy. When Father said *wahine* it meant the old lady or Mother.

Then I made another mistake. I bragged to Tosh about going across the breakers. "You *pupule* ass! You wanna die or what? You want shark to eat you up? Next time you go outside the breakers I goin' slap your head!" he said.

"Not dangerous. Makot been take me go."

"Shaddup! You tell that *kodomo taisho* if I catch um taking you outside the breakers again, I going bust um up! Tell um that! Tell um I said go play with guys his own age!"

"He never been force me. I asked um to take me."

"Shaddup! The next time you go out there, I goin' slap your head!"

Tosh was three years older than me and when he slapped my head, I couldn't slap him back because he would slap me right back, and I couldn't cry like my kid sister because I was too big to cry. All I could do was to walk away mad and think of all the things I was going to do to get even when I grew up. When I slapped my sister's head she would grumble or sometimes cry but she would always talk back, "No slap my head, you! Thass where my brains stay, you know!" Me, I couldn't even talk back. Most big brothers were too cocky anyway and mine was more cocky than most.

Then at supper Tosh brought it up again. He spoke in pidgin Japanese (we spoke four languages: good English in school, pidgin English among ourselves, good or pidgin Japanese to our parents and the other old folks), "Mama, you better tell Kyo not to go outside the breakers. By-'n'-by he drown. By-'n'-by the shark eat um up."

"Oh, Kiyo-chan, did you go outside the breakers?" she said in Japanese.

"Yeah," Tosh answered for me, "Makoto Sasaki been take him go."

"Not dangerous," I said in pidgin Japanese; "Makoto-san was with me all the time."

"Why shouldn't Makoto-san play with people his own age, *ne?*" Mother said.

"He's a *kodomo taisho,* thass why!"

Kodomo taisho meant General of the kids.

"Well, you're not to go outside the breakers anymore. Do you understand, Kiyo-chan?" Mother said.

I turned to Father, who was eating silently. "Is that right, Father?"

"So," he grunted.

"Boy, your father and mother real strict," Makot said. I couldn't go outside the breakers, I couldn't go eat at his place. But Makot always saved some corned beef and onions and Campbell soup for me. He told me to go home and eat fast and just a little bit and come over to his place and eat with them and I kept on doing that without Mother catching on. And Makot was always buying us pie, ice cream, and chow fun, and he was always giving me the biggest share of the pie, ice cream, or chow fun. He also took us to the movies now and then and when he had money for only one treat or when he wanted to take only me and spend the rest of the money on candies, he would have me meet him in town at night, as he didn't want me to come to his place at night. "No tell Mit and Skats," he told me and I didn't tell them or the folks or Tosh anything about it, and when they asked where I was going on the movie nights, I told them I was going over to Mit's or Skats'.

Then near the end of summer the whole town got tired of going to the beach and we all took up slingshots and it got to be slingshot season. Everybody made slingshots and carried pocketsful of little rocks and shot linnets and myna birds and doves. We would even go to the old wharf and shoot the black crabs which crawled on the rocks. Makot made each of us a dandy slingshot out of a guava branch, and he'd made each of us a big barbed spear out of a bedspring coil during spearing-fish season. Nobody our age had slingshots or spears like ours, and of the three he made, mine was always the best. I knew he liked me the best.

Then one day Makot said, "Slingshot waste time. We go buy a rifle. We go buy twenty-two."

"How?" we all said.

Makot said that he could get five dollars from his old folks and all we needed was five dollars more and we could go sell coconuts and mangoes to raise that.

"Sure!" we all said. A rifle was something we saw only in the movies and Sears Roebuck catalogues. Nobody in Pepelau owned a rifle.

So the next morning we got a barley bag, two picks, and a scooter wagon. We were going to try coconuts first because they were easier to sell. There were two bakeries in town and they needed them for coconut pies. The only trouble was that free coconut trees were hard to find. There were trees at the courthouse, the Catholic Church, and in Reverend Hastings' yard, but the only free trees were those deep in the cane fields and they were too tall and dangerous. Makot said, "We go ask Reverend Hastings." Reverend Hastings was a minister of some kind and he lived alone in a big old house in a big weedy yard next to the kindergarten. He had about a dozen trees in his yard and he always let you pick some coconuts if you asked him, but he always said, "Sure, boys, provided you don't sell them." "Aw, what he doan know won't hurt um," Makot said. Makot said he was going to be the brains of the gang and Mit and Skats were going to climb the trees and I was going to ask Reverend Hastings. So we hid the wagon and picks and bags and I went up to the door of the big house and knocked.

Pretty soon there were footsteps and he opened the door. "Yes?" He smiled. He was a short, skinny man who looked very weak and who sort of wobbled when he walked, but he had a nice face and a small voice.

"Reverend Hastings, can we pick some coconuts?" I said.

Makot, Mit and Skats were behind me and he looked at them and said, "Why, sure, boys, provided you don't sell them."

"Thank you, Reverend Hastings," I said, and the others mumbled, "Thank you."

"You're welcome," he said and went back into the house.

Mit and Skats climbed two trees and knocked them down as fast as they could and I stuck my pick in the ground and started peeling them as fast as I could. We were scared. What if he came out again? Maybe it was better if we all climbed and knocked down lots and took them somewhere else to peel them, we said. But Makot sat down on the wagon and laughed, "Naw, he not gonna come out no more. No be chicken!" As soon as he said that the door slammed and we all looked. Mit and Skats stayed on the trees but didn't knock down any more. Reverend Hastings jumped down the steps and came walking across the yard in big angry strides! It was plain we were going to sell the coconuts because we had more than half a bagful and all the husks were piled up like a mountain! He came up, his face red, and he shouted, "I thought you said you weren't going to sell these! Get down from those trees!"

I looked at my feet and Makot put his face in the crook of his arm and began crying, "Wah-wah . . ." though I knew he wasn't crying.

Reverend Hastings grabbed a half-peeled coconut from my hand and grabbing it by a loose husk, threw it with all his might over the fence and nearly fell down and shouted, "Get out! At once!" Then he turned right around and walked back and slammed the door after him.

"Ha-ha-ha!" Makot said as soon as he disappeared, "we got enough anyway."

We picked up the rest of the coconuts and took them to the kindergarten to peel them. We had three dozen and carted them to the two bakeries on Main Street. But they said that they had enough coconuts and that ours were too green and six cents apiece was too much. We pulled the wagon all over town and tried the fish markets and grocery stores for five cents. Finally we went back to the first bakery and sold them for four cents. It took us the whole day and we made only $1.44. By that time Mit, Skats and I wanted to forget about the rifle, but Makot said, "Twenty-two or bust."

The next day we went to the tall trees in the cane fields. We had to crawl through tall cane to get to them and once we climbed the trees and knocked down the coconuts we had to hunt for them in the tall cane again. After the first tree we wanted to quit but Makot wouldn't hear of it and when we didn't move he put on his *habut*. *Habut* is short for *habuteru,* which means to pout the way girls and children do. Makot would blow up his cheeks like a balloon fish and not talk to us. "I not goin' buy you no more chow fun, no more ice cream, no more pie," he'd sort of cry, and then we would do everything to please him and make him come out of his *habut*. When we finally agreed to do what he wanted he would protest and slap with his wrist like a girl, giggle with his hand over his mouth, talk in the kind of Japanese which only girls use, and in general make fun of the girls. And when he came out of his *habut* he usually bought us chow fun, ice cream, or pie.

So we crawled through more cane fields and climbed more coconut trees. I volunteered to climb too because Mit and Skats grumbled that I got all the easy jobs. By three o'clock we had only half a bag, but we brought them to town and again went all over Main Street trying to sell them. The next day we went to pick mangoes, first at the kindergarten, then at Mango Gulch, but they were harder to sell so we spent more time carting them around town.

"You guys think you so hot, eh," Tosh said one day. "Go sell mangoes and coconuts. He only catching you head. You know why he pick on you guys for a gang? Because you guys the last. That *kodomo taisho* been leader of every shrimp gang and they all quit him one after another. You, Mit, and Skats stick with him because you too stupid!''

I shrugged and walked away. I didn't care. I liked Makot. Besides, all the guys his age were jealous because Makot had so much money to spend.

Then several days later Father called me. He was alone at the outside sink, cleaning some fish. He brought home the best fish for us to eat but it was always fish. He was still in his fisherman's clothes.

''Kiyoshi,'' he said and he was not angry, ''you're not to play with Makoto Sasaki anymore. Do you understand?''

''But why, Father?''

''Because he is bad.'' He went on cleaning fish.

''But he's not bad. He treats us good! You mean about stealing mangoes from kindergarten? It's not really stealing. Everybody does it.''

''But you never sold the mangoes you stole before?''

''No.''

''There's a difference between a prank and a crime. Everybody in town is talking about you people. Not about stealing, but about your selling mangoes and coconuts you stole. It's all Makoto's fault. He's older and he should know better but he doesn't. That's why he plays with younger boys. He makes fools out of them. The whole town is talking about what fools he's making out of you and Nobuyuki and Mitsunobu.''

''But he's not really making fools out of us, Father. We all agreed to make some money so that we could buy a rifle and own it together. As for the work, he doesn't really force us. He's always buying us things and making things for us and teaching us tricks he learns in Boy Scout, so it's one way we can repay him.''

''But he's bad. You're not to play with him. Do you understand?''

''But he's not bad! He treats us real good and me better than Mitsunobu-san or Nobuyuki-san!''

''Kiyoshi, I'm telling you for the last time. Do not play with him.''

''But why?''

''Because his home is bad. His father is bad. His mother is bad.''

''Why are his father and mother bad?''

''Nemmind!'' He was mad now.

''But what about Mitsunobu-san and Nobuyuki-san? I play with them too!''

''Shut up!'' He turned to face me. His mouth was twisted.

"You're not a monkey! Stop aping others! You are not to play with him! Do you understand! Or do I have to crack your head *kotsun!*"

"Yes," I said and walked away.

Then I went inside the house and asked Mother, "Why are they bad? Because he doesn't work?"

"You're too young to understand, Kiyo-chan. When you grow up you'll know that your parents were right."

"But whom am I going to play with then?"

"Can't you play with Toshi-chan?"

"Yeah, come play with me, Kyo. Any time you want me to bust up that *kodomo taisho* I'll bustum up for you," Tosh said.

That night I said I was going to see Mit and went over to Makot's home. On the way over I kept thinking about what Father and Mother said. There was something funny about Makot's folks. His father was a tall, skinny man and he didn't talk to us kids the way all the other old Japanese men did. He owned a Model T when only the *haole*s or whites had cars. His mother was funnier yet. She wore lipstick in broad daylight, which no other Japanese mother did.

I went into Filipino Camp and I was scared. It was a spooky place, not like Japanese Camp. The Filipinos were all men and there were no women or children and the same-looking houses were all bare, no curtains in the windows or potted plants on the porches. The only way you could tell them apart was by their numbers. But I knew where Makot's house was in the daytime, so I found it easily. It was the only one with curtains and ferns and flowers. There were five men standing in the dark to one side of the house. They wore shoes and bright aloha shirts and sharply pressed pants, and smelled of expensive pomade. They were talking in low voices and a couple of them were jiggling so hard you could hear the jingle of loose change.

I called from the front porch, "Makot! Makot!" I was scared he was going to give me hell for coming at night.

Pretty soon his mother came out. I had never spoken to her though I'd seen her around and knew who she was. She was a fat woman with a fat face, which made her eyes look very small.

"Oh, is Makoto-san home?" I asked in Japanese.

"Makotooooo!" she turned and yelled into the house. She was all dressed up in kimono. Mother made a lot of kimonos for other people but she never had one like hers. She had a lot of white powder on her face and two round red spots on her cheeks.

"Oh, Sasaki-san," I said, "I've had lunch at your home quite a few times. I wanted to thank you for it but I didn't have a chance to speak to you before. It was most delicious. Thank you very much."

She stared at me with her mouth open wide and suddenly burst out laughing, covering her mouth and shaking all over, her shoulders, her arms, her cheeks.

Makot came out. "Wha-at?" he pouted in Japanese. Then he saw me and his face lit up, "Hiya, Kiyo, old pal, old pal, what's cookin'?" he said in English.

His mother was still laughing and shaking and pointing at me.

"What happened?" Makot said angrily to his mother.

"That boy! That boy!" She still pointed at me. "Such a nice little boy! Do you know what he said? He said, 'Sasaki-san . . . ' " And she started to shake and cough again.

"Aw, shut up, Mother!" Makot said. "Please go inside!" and he practically shoved her to the door.

She turned around again, "But you're such a courteous boy, aren't you? 'It was most delicious. Thank you very much.' A-ha-hahaha. A-hahahaha . . ."

"Shut up, Mother!" Makot shoved her into the doorway. I would never treat my mother like that but then my mother would never act like that. When somebody said, "Thank you for the feast," she always said, "But what was served you was really rubbish."

Makot turned to me, "Well, what you say, old Kiyo, old pal? Wanna go to the movies tonight?"

I shook my head and looked at my feet. "I no can play with you no more."

"Why?"

"My folks said not to."

"But why? We never been do anything bad, eh?"

"No."

"Then why? Because I doan treat you right? I treat you okay?"

"Yeah. I told them you treat me real good."

"Why then?"

"I doan know."

"Aw, hell, you can still play with me. They doan hafta know. What they doan know won't hurt them."

"Naw, I better not. This time it's my father and he means business."

"Aw, doan be chicken, Kiyo. Maybe you doan like to play with me."

"I like to play with you."

"Come, let's go see a movie."

"Naw."

"How about some chow fun. Yum-yum."

"Naw."

"Maybe you doan like me then?"

"I like you."

"You sure?"

"I sure."

"Why then?"

"I doan know. They said something about your father and mother."

"Oh," he said and his face fell and I thought he was going to cry.

"Well, so long, then, Kiyo," he said and went into the house.

"So long," I said and turned and ran out of the spooky camp.

New Local and Kin Groups among the Japanese Farmers of Kona, Hawaii

JOHN F. EMBREE

WHEN a new social group—such as a group of immigrants in a new land—is organized, new social relationships must be formed. The structure of these new relationships is, as a rule, based on the pattern of the old network of relationships as they existed in the original social situation—for an immigrant group, as they existed in the "old country."

Of all the relationships involved in any social organization kin relationships, real or fictitious, are among the most important. This is especially true of preliterate and folk communities.

According to Davis and Warner, "Kinship is a concept that touches two levels of phenomena. On the one hand it refers to a relatively fixed biological structure, on the other to a relatively variable social pattern based on this biological structure."[1] The biological basis of kinship is the same in all human society: a primary sex relationship between a man and a woman, a parent-child relationship between these two and their offspring and a sibling relationship between the offspring. From these elementary groupings kin relationships may be traced indefinitely upward, outward, and downward from ego. The extent to which the kin relationships are recognized in a society determines the *range* of that society's kinship system. This recognition of kinship relationships is a social phenomenon and as such varies from society to society.

. . .

Reprinted by permission of the American Anthropological Association from the *American Anthropologist,* v. 41, no. 3 (July-September 1939), pp. 400–407.

In Japan, especially rural Japan, the extended family is one of the more important social groups. In Hawaii, on the other hand, there are almost no extended kin groups among the older, first generation Japanese. This paper attempts to show how the functions of the old kin group are still carried on by other special groups which we may term *kin substitutes*.[2] In Kona, a coffee growing district on the island of Hawaii, the Japanese community, including storekeepers and coffee farmers, is about twenty-five hundred, distributed over an area of some fifty square miles. While the oldest Japanese inhabitants came over forty years ago, most of the "old folks" have been in Kona only fifteen or twenty years. With few exceptions the families now growing coffee were first employed on sugar and pineapple plantations in other parts of the Territory.

Almost forty percent of the older people in the district were born in the one prefecture of Kumamoto, and as the writer spent a full year in a small village in Kuma County, Kumamoto Prefecture, during 1935–36[3] he is in a position to compare the social forms of Kona with those of Kumamoto.

In rural Kumamoto, as in most of rural Japan, the most important local groups are the household or small family and the small, geographically contiguous local community called *buraku*. Most villages *(mura)* contain several such *buraku* which were perhaps once separate villages. To give a brief outline of the social life in rural Kumamoto it will be necessary to outline both the functions of the household and the extended family on the one hand and of the *buraku* on the other, as the two are in many ways interdependent.

A household contains, as a rule, a master *(koshu),* his wife, first son *(chonan),* first son's wife, the unmarried children of the master and any children of the first son. In addition there may be an old father who has retired from active life besides a manservant and a maidservant. The group of households are united by a common territory, but their paddy rice fields and upland vegetable fields may be widely scattered all over the village or even in the next village. Population in a *buraku* is reckoned by households rather than by persons.

The *buraku,* made up of fifteen or twenty such households, functions chiefly as a cooperative entity. The cooperation takes several forms, the chief of which are:

1. *Civic cooperation.* When roads are cleaned or repaired or a bridge built a member of each household, either man or woman, turns out to do the work. *Buraku* heads oversee the work and decide

the day on which it is to be done. When the work is finished a small drinking party is held, financed by a contribution of ten *sen* or so from each house.

2. *Helping cooperation.* One man from each household in the *buraku* helps a man to build a new house or repair a roof. This involves an obligation on the part of the householder to feed the helpers and in turn to help any of them when they build a house. Similar cooperation comes into play at funerals. After any such helping cooperation a drinking party is given at the expense of the person aided.

3. *Exchange labor.* At rice transplanting it is desirable, almost necessary, for many people to work together. For this purpose a specific group of five or six houses joins together to transplant the seedlings of each member in turn. At the end of transplanting the exchange group holds a party together. The members of such groups remain constant from year to year and the party at the end rotates from house to house each year.

4. *Rotating responsibility for certain buraku affairs by small groups.* Thus, at the celebration of *buraku* festivals a given three or four families will gather in a small wooden structure *(doh)* where a deity, usually Buddhistic, is enshrined and serve tea and beans to visitors. One group will serve one year, a different group of three or four houses the next year and so on.

The various cooperative and exchange systems act as integrating forces in the *buraku* by bringing people together in common labor followed by drinking parties which engender a feeling of friendliness and well being. Furthermore, these systems can be used as a form of social sanction. A farmer who does not meet his obligations may be effectively disciplined by withholding cooperation from him at rice transplanting, housebuilding and burial.

The role of kinship is most important in the elementary family contained in the household unit with its three to four generations living together. Here the master's word is law. Most daily farm labor is done by this relatively permanent kin group, even the servants being hired on a yearly basis and treated as members of the family. It is not unusual for a man to adopt a man servant and, on the other hand, a servant is often a nephew or niece of the head or his wife.

The eldest son is born, marries and dies in the same house. Other children remain in the family of orientation till of age when through marriage, adoption or the establishment of a branch family they set up separate families of their own.

Almost every family has relatives in the village and in nearby villages. This extended kin group functions at all life's crises and on special occasions such as New Year's. At a naming ceremony only a few nearby relatives are invited, also a few neighbors.

At marriage all arrangements are made by the families involved with the aid of go-betweens, the immediate principals having little to say in the matter. From the point of view of social value to the family the marriage is the most important of life's crises. Through marriage come heirs and on heirs depend the future welfare of the family; and through heirs one's memorial tablets *(ihai)* are properly cared for. It is not surprising, then, to find the go-between who acts as intermediary for this event becoming thereafter something of a relative—being invited to naming ceremonies and often coming as a mourner to a funeral in the family. At the wedding, with its great importance to the family, relatives from far and near are called and there is a great banquet. The *buraku's* interest in the event is recognized by the *chanomi,* a *buraku* party given the day after the wedding.

There is a regular form of action at funerals and help given in case of disaster. While relatives in and out of the village gather inside the house and, as mourners, do nothing toward helping except for those close relatives who assist in putting the body in the coffin just before the funeral service, two people from each house of the local *buraku* come to help in preparing funeral things such as the coffin and grave lanterns, cooking funeral food and digging the grave. During the funeral service and banquet the *buraku* helpers eat and drink food provided by the family outside or in a back room, while relatives partake of a more elaborate feast together with the priest who reads the funeral service. Relatives gather together at several regular intervals, seven in all, after the funeral for memorial services. At death the family loses a member and comes together to mourn the event. The *buraku* also loses a member, but being larger than the family is not so seriously affected, so while they turn out to aid the unfortunate family at the funeral itself, they have no concern with the memorial services.

Beside the three crises of life there are certain other occasions for the gathering of the extended family—at New Year's, at *Bon* and for a family council.

New Year's time is an important one for the family in Japan. The holidays usually last several days and during this period relatives call on one another, take gifts, and give banquets. Usually a family makes a round of calls on the husband's relatives in one year and on the wife's kin the next, the whole family going together. There is no special activity by the *buraku* as such at New Year's time.

Bon season in July is the festival of the dead, at which time, it is believed, the spirits of the dead return to their former earthly abodes. Any house in the *buraku* that has lost a member during the past year holds a *First Bon* party. Members of the *buraku* call with gifts of lanterns or incense, and relatives do the same. The banquet itself is primarily for the relatives but *buraku* people are also welcome.

Besides these recurrent occasions, whenever a man contemplates any important step in life such as the marriage of one of his children or the purchase or sale of land, he calls a council of the extended family to discuss the matter.

The extended family, then, comes together and functions as such on five important occasions: (1) marriage, (2) death and memorial services, (3) New Year's Festival, (4) *Bon,* [and] (5) family council. Other lesser occasions in which some members of the kin group beyond the household cooperate and gather together are: (1) exchange labor [and the] (2) naming ceremony.

In only two of these seven various meetings is the *buraku* as such directly involved—both matters concerning the dead—at funerals where its cooperation is needed to provide the necessary articles for a funeral and food for use and consumption of the mourners, and at *Bon*. Exchange labor, also, is frequently within the *buraku* as it is not practical to exchange at too great a distance; and a few *buraku* neighbors may come in to a naming ceremony.

We may now contrast the social situation in Kumamoto with that to be found in Kona, Hawaii.

. . .

In Kona the Japanese population is predominant, forming over 70 percent of the total. Of the heads of eight hundred odd Japanese families, very few have any blood relatives in the Territory of Hawaii and still fewer have any in Kona itself. This is a natural corollary of the fact that the Japanese in Hawaii form an emigrant group, the emigrants being made up of the following types: (1) Men of families who were poor in Japan and hoped to make a fortune by coming to Hawaii; (2) Men recently discharged from the army after the Russo-Japanese War with a bonus in hand who came to Hawaii to seek a living; (3) Young men, often in their teens, who left Japan to seek adventure and become independent of their families.

Most of these individuals set out across the seas to solve some personal problem, and in so doing left all their relatives back home. After a few years, not making the expected fortune with which to return to Japan, many men sent back to their native prefectures in Japan for wives. Thus arose the well known custom of the picture bride. To this day, however, there are many old bachelors among the Japanese in Hawaii, a situation in sharp contrast to rural Japan, where all but the lame and the halt are married.

The Japanese in Kona have organized themselves into cooperative groups *(kumi)* of fifteen to twenty-five or more households each with a name and a head. In some parts of Kona these groups are united into *mura* just as *buraku* are united into *mura* in Japan. The *kumi* are purely geographical just as the *buraku* are geographical in Japan and, similarly, their primary function is mutual aid in such events as funerals and housebuilding.

Unlike the *buraku* in Japan where houses are in close clusters, houses in Kona are far apart and frequently people scarcely know some of the members of their own *kumi*. Houses are isolated, hidden away in the coffee lands. The local group in Hawaii, though based on that of rural Japan, is less closely integrated socially.

The roads and bridges are taken care of by the government, so that the *kumi* does not function in civic cooperation. There is less cooperation in general than in rural Japan, partly because in the American capitalistic environment there is less occasion for it; other reasons are that members of a *kumi* are not at all related, they are comparative strangers to one another and, since everyone came to Hawaii to make money, each man prefers to work his own field for whatever cash he can get out of it.

A notable thing about the *kumi* is that it participates in and comes together on the occasion of weddings and New Year's parties which are primarily occasions for the gathering of the extended family in Japan. It has thus come to replace to a certain extent the relative group of old Japan. At a wedding the *kumi* frequently comes on the first night together with relatives and close friends; at a funeral the help is rendered by the *kumi,* the same as *buraku* in Japan, but it is feasted with the same food as the relatives which is not done in Kumamoto. If there are very few relatives, *kumi* members might help in dressing the corpse, a task restricted to close relatives in Japan.

At New Year's time, instead of the round of extended family banquets, each *kumi* has a banquet, held in rotation at the house of a different *kumi* member each year; whereas such parties are among relatives in rural Japan, the host rotating from year to year.

There are, however, other *kin substitutes* of greater importance than *kumi* members. Of the first generation, as already pointed out, very few have relatives in Kona. The nearest thing to a relative is a man from the same region in Japan. There is a special term for such "same place" people: *tokoro-mon.*[4] Real *tokoro-mon* come from the same county in Japan or better still from the same or neighboring villages. It is these *tokoro* people who are first notified in case of a funeral by couriers from the *kumi* of the deceased. It is *tokoro-mon* who are first invited to a wedding. They are closer than *kumi* people, just as relatives are closer than *buraku* people. The closer to one's home village a man lived, the closer friend he is. A man from the same village is practically a brother. It is the *tokoro* people, in preference to *kumi* members, who are asked to help in preparing the corpse. If a man needs advice or money he goes to a *tokoro-mon* in Kona, as he would to a relative in Japan. While in Japan frequently a young widow is married by the younger brother of the deceased, in Kona it is a *tokoro-mon,* if there is one available, who performs that duty.

Another function of the *tokoro-mon* comes into play during exchange of labor at the time of fertilizing the coffee lands, an arduous task comparable to rice transplanting in Japan. Just as a man prefers to exchange labor in Japan with a relative, so in Kona he prefers a *tokoro-mon*. In both places, however, a certain amount of exchange labor goes on between close neighbors regardless of kin relationships.

The *buraku* and *kumi* are the neighborhood groups of rural Japan and Kona respectively; the extended family and the *tokoro-mon* of a man are scattered here and there for many miles around. The *buraku* and *kumi* are close geographically and thus have a definite social cohesion. The extended family and *tokoro* groups, while scattered, are still closer than *buraku* people because of blood, and what comes to almost the same thing, common origin.

In addition to *tokoro* people another group of relative substitutes consists of people in Kona who worked with one another at some plantation before coming to Kona. Still another group, but not so close, are people who came over on the same boat. Probably one reason these groups of people are less close is that they have been associated together such a short time.

These kin substitutes, especially the important *tokoro-mon,* apply in particular to the first generation and will probably die out in fifteen or twenty years with the demise of that first generation whose average age in Kona today is sixty years. Real kin groups are being established among the second and third generations, but along rather different, more western patterns than the original Japanese kin groups. The second generation has already acquired a group of relatives through siblings and marriage. They have a tendency to do away with some of the more elaborate rituals of funerals and other kinship gatherings.

The data from Kona tend to confirm the thesis set forth at the beginning of this paper. To summarize briefly: Two important aspects of social organization are kin and geographical group relationships. When a change takes place in the society or when members of a society form a new group in a different locality, there is an attempt to keep or recreate the old kin and local groups. It is comparatively easy to rearrange the local group, though frequently many of its old functions are lost. To recreate the old kin organization resort may be taken to *kin substitutes* such as neighbors or, more important, same-place-of-origin people, for instance the *tokoro-mon* of the Japanese coffee farmers in Hawaii.

NOTES

1. Kingsley Davis and W. Lloyd Warner, *Structural Analysis of Kinship* (American Anthropologist, Vol. 39, No. 2), p. 292.

[2]. While some studies have been made of the reorganization of kin groupings in immigrant communities, most of these have been made in cities, e.g., *The Ghetto,* by Louis Wirth, and *The Polish Peasant in Europe and America,* by Thomas and Znaniecki.

[3]. On a grant from the Social Science Research Committee of the University of Chicago. The Kona Research was made under the auspices of the University of Hawaii.

[4]. Or *tokoro-no-mon.*

The Japanese "Tanomoshi"

RUTH N. MASUDA

Introduction

THE word *tanomoshi-ko* is used in western Japan and is derived from the word *tanomu* meaning dependable. In Tokyo and Edo it is called *mujin* which means limitless, in this case meaning that there is no limit to the amount of money one may desire to raise. The use of this word *mujin* in Tokyo is especially significant of the money economy that has developed in this part of the country whereas, in western Japan, the word itself reflects the nature of the agricultural people.

The *tanomoshi* dates back to days before there was any knowledge of the western world. In the early days the word *ko* meant a lecture or religious sermon to which the people would listen. These meetings gradually developed into clubs and associations, cooperative in nature. Each participant paid small sums of money and when enough was saved they went on pilgrimages to chosen shrines and temples. They generally had a manager who took charge of the money and collected it every month. Sometimes when the funds were insufficient they drew lots and a privileged few would be allowed to go. (This idea still prevails in the form of bidding today in the *tanomoshi.*) It is believed that this plan spread and developed gradually until sometime in the Tokugawa Era (1700 to about the middle of the 19th century) when the poorer people conceived of the economic benefits that may be derived from such cooperative action.

In *Social Process in Hawaii,* v. 3 (1937), pp. 16–9. Reprinted by permission of *Social Process in Hawaii,* by Edmund H. Volkart, chairman, Department of Sociology, University of Hawaii.

The *tanomoshi* is carried on in a slightly different manner in some rural sections of southern Japan. Because many of the members are farmers without regular cash incomes, payment is made semi-annually or annually. Usually payments are made at the time of harvest when the produce is sold. Hence, if a *tanomoshi* with ten or fifteen members is started it runs for that number of years and frequently, a *tanomoshi* started by one generation easily carries on to the next, burdening the family endlessly. However, in the cities where life is based on a money economy, monthly payments are prevalent. The amounts invested, however, are very small for wages are low. Another difference is that when a member wishes to borrow that month's sum, he bids on the principal and not on the interest he is willing to pay, as in the Hawaiian practice. For example, if it is a *tanomoshi* of $100, he writes on his bid $95 and the rest is divided as interest among the different members.

Types of Tanomoshi

All *tanomoshi* operate in much the same way. They may vary somewhat as to the number of members and the size of the investments. They may also vary as to purpose. An interesting *tanomoshi* was once started by several women who wanted wrist watches. They solicited friends and made up a group of ten members, each agreeing to pay $5.00 a month. In this way each received her watch eventually. Sometimes a jeweler who wishes to increase his trade initiates a similar enterprise. Suit *tanomoshi* are also practiced among men.

> Mr. A, a tailor, finds that his business is not as prosperous as it should be. As a result he goes on a house to house canvass for customers. He succeeds in interesting seven persons to make suits from him. But a suit costs thirty-five dollars and they cannot afford to pay him the amount at once. He starts the *tanomoshi* with his seven customers as the members. At the first meeting each member brings $5.00. That makes a total of $35.00 and Mr. A is ready to make a suit for one of the members. Then each one writes the amount of his interest which is usually very small. The one bidding highest gets the first suit. At the second meeting Mr. A gets another $35.00 and another suit goes out. Thus at the end of seven meetings all of them have their suits and Mr. A is prosperous again. The watch *tanomoshi* operates in much the same manner.

Tanomoshi of this character are usually conducted on a friendly basis and the monthly meetings become social gatherings for the members.

It was formerly the accepted rule that only friends enter the *ko,* but with the economic expansion of the Hawaiian frontier, exceptions were made. When occasion demands, strangers may now participate. They must however, have good recommendations, their characters are investigated and the necessary witnesses must be procured before they are accepted by the group. The organizer of the *ko* is obliged to select members who are acceptable to the group. Otherwise, he will be unable to get the necessary number to form the *ko.*

The highest of morals are expected in a *tanomoshi.* A person is bound by his honor to the group. Actually some people do slip out, leaving their witnesses to pay for their shares. There is nothing that can compel a dishonest person from refusing to pay after he gets his share. Unless he has overdrawn on the rate of interest, legal action cannot be taken against him. There have, however, been many instances when a person, after drawing out his amount, quietly returned to Japan, leaving the unpaid burden to his witnesses. In such cases all friendship bonds are broken and the individual becomes an "outcast" from the group thereafter. Wherever he goes, if his history is known, he is branded as a "cheat" and not worthy of normal associations. It is surprising how few are these cases when compared with the number of *tanomoshi* in existence. If a person is of "good character" and he really cannot pay his share, he does not take the easiest course by running away, but will work the harder to meet the situation. Sometimes the witnesses will agree to pay for him temporarily and the amount is later returned to them.

Functions

The *tanomoshi* is essentially a plan whereby an individual who is hard pressed and in need of ready money may borrow a sizable sum from his friends for whatever purpose he wishes. This person perhaps needs a hundred dollars within a certain time. He may then ask nine friends (besides himself) to subscribe a sum of ten dollars per person each month to his *tanomoshi.* When the *ko* is formed, the members decide on a date that is most convenient for them all to meet.

In Hawaii the meeting is usually on a Sunday as most men are free. (In plantation communities meetings are held a few days after pay day.) They gather at the home of the promoter who is called *oya,* meaning head. The *oya* is obligated to make this a social gathering and has in readiness delicacies and tea for his friends. But business must be attended to first. Each member deposits with the cashier his monthly share of ten dollars, making a total of one hundred dollars. The first month's receipts always go to the promoter, who is the beneficiary and gets the total amount of one hundred dollars without paying any interest whatever. He is thus aided by the subscribers and for this reason a *tanomoshi* is often said to be an "aid for a friend in need." Of course he pays in his share of ten dollars just as the other members, the only "aid" being that he does not need to pay interest to the other members who are required thereafter to pay interest besides their ten dollars when they want to use the total amount.

Each month thereafter for nine months all the members contribute their regular ten dollar shares and depending upon their immediate needs, bid for the use of the capital. At all subsequent meetings the members who wish to draw the principal submit bids of the interest they are willing to pay for the use of the money. At times there is considerable competition for the use of the money and the atmosphere much resembles that of an auction except that the bidders do not voice their amount and the auctioneer has the satisfaction of first knowing to whom the share is going. The member who put in the highest bid secures the principal for the month but he must also pay to each shareholder the amount of interest he bids. If the highest bid in the second month is two dollars, the bidder has to pay this amount to each member who has not yet received his share. Thus, he would have to pay out a total of sixteen dollars to the eight members whose shares had not yet been drawn, leaving him with only eighty-four dollars. After a person draws his share, he does not benefit henceforth, from any interest, although he continues to make his monthly payments until the *tanomoshi* has run its course.

A *ko* may thus be a "savings account" for those who can delay drawing their share, while [for] others a considerable element of speculation may enter. When times are bad and many people need money, each member seeks to outbid the others for the immediate use of the principal. Well-to-do members of a *tanomoshi* who can afford to have their money in the *tanomoshi* until the end, receive in addition to the capital, extra payments made by the impoverished members who took their shares earlier. A shrewd and wealthy person sometimes enters two or three *tanomoshi* at the same time, using the interest derived from one to pay his shares in smaller *ko,* thus making money for himself.

Another important phase of the *ko* is the security. Each member before receiving his share must have at least two persons to stand as witnesses for him. These persons must be members of the *ko*. In case anyone cannot finish his payments after drawing his share these witnesses are obliged to meet his payments hereafter. In case they are unable to pay, their share is withheld from them.

The majority of the *tanomoshi* in Hawaii arise from the desire to help a friend and the members, as we have seen, are selected usually from the friendship group. It was unheard of to have people of other races in a *ko*. However, with the mingling of peoples in Hawaii these restrictions have been broken and now the *tanomoshi* is open to other races. This is especially so in the rural communities. *Tanomoshi* are frequently found whose members no longer form a close friendship circle, but are mere acquaintances or business associates of a foreign race. Of course these "foreigners" must be of good character and dependable. They usually are store clerks, plantation overseers, school teachers, and men of the upper classes. When a *tanomoshi* assumes this status, it becomes a purely economic organization and relations although flavored with friendship are more impersonal. The personal and friendly elements disappear.

Although the *tanomoshi* is widely used throughout the territory, it is losing its status among the more educated classes. It savors too much of moral claims in an area of purely economic relations. To start a *tanomoshi* is regarded as evidence of economic distress and is avoided by people of means, although they will join a *tanomoshi* which someone else has initiated.

The Hawaiian born generation are generally indifferent to the *tanomoshi*. They would rather do business with a bank, which is recognized by the state. The *tanomoshi* with its funds secured by honor seems crude and costly as a credit device.

Chapter Four

To Weep into Silence?

AS immigrants they had come to squeeze dollars out of the land. They were ambitious men who otherwise might have been the nondescript farmers, preachers, merchandisers of their native nations. But in their island home the drives of expectations could be realized when enough cunning, determination, and sinew had been tilled into the fertile soil; when a man with fortitude, by God, squared his shoulders, saved his money, and kept his wits, he could achieve almost anything.

Scots-Irish–Germanic was their stock—a blood which had pushed back the frontiers of the western hemisphere to even the farthest outreaches of this tiny Polynesian archipelago. They had brought to the Islands their two-storied, wooden-framed houses and shops, their Bible, diseases, steam engines, and constitutions. They had brought their carriages, trains, and electric lights, their English tongue, and grid patterns overlaid with macadam and gravel roads, and trolleys clamoring along the commercial district of Honolulu. They had pushed back the pagan with their insensate civilization based on sound American dollars, pushing back the native from his land and government, from his song, his dance.

These immigrants were called *haole*s, foreigners, by the people whom they had dispossessed. Fatefully, the native would be the foreigner in Hawaii. The ancient lands were parcelled into productive estates of sugar and pineapple industries, owned by the powerful class of planters and sugar agents. The crude frontier town of Honolulu had become a bustling international port where native stevedores and servants labored for menial wages and lei-makers lined the shaded sidewalks of the city selling their culture to the visitors who found it quaint. In the recesses of the sacred valleys where taro patches had fed a race, the *haole*s built their stately, rococo homes with palmed lanai and tropical motif, the leisurely domicile of a *nouveau riche*.

As *nouveau riche,* the *haole* men concerned themselves with the stockmarket graphs of Honolulu's Merchant Street businesses, recent political developments in the Territorial legislature, the alarming statistics of Asiatic immigration, and the most recent activities of the Outrigger Club. The women dedicated themselves to charitable work, cultural luncheons in the afternoon, the promotion of Christian principles, and the latest fashions from the mainland. Their children were sent to a special school called Punahou where the younger generation learned the requisite skills to wield power, and to play polo as did their fathers in Waikiki's Kapiolani Park.

Such was the worldly contentment of the self-satisfied *haole* immigrant. But other immigrants had also come to Hawaii to squeeze the dollars from the land. They, too, had ventured as ambitious men, eager to fulfill expectations, to use their brawn and cunning so as to expand their wealth. As laboring wage-earners providing the economic basis of the sugar industry, they too sought to establish homes, raise families, and insulate themselves in a self-contented community.

But for these Japanese immigrants, such expectations had to be continually deferred. Though the largest single racial group in the Islands, they stood outside the powerful system of wealth perpetuated by the *haole*. They owned no land. They had no political leverage. They had no personal capital. The men did not use their wits as much as their backbone in the fields. The women did not have the leisure of clubs and charity work but slashed the cane along with their husbands. Their children did not go to Punahou, or play polo in Kapiolani Park; instead, when they were old enough, they joined their parents in the fields. As immigrants from Japan, their greatest expectations seemed as futile as the endless cycle of plantation work, as barren as the rural shacks or backstreet shanties in which they eked out a living. The frustration of their world was certainly not the promise which Hawaii had once seemed to hold.

Two immigrants in two worlds. In one world, a world of *haole* power and authority, the forces of the status quo reigned supreme.

Steeped in a cultural elitism, comforted by a leisurely social life and partially blinded by a preferential status, the *haole* immigrant saw little reason to forsake his *noblesse oblige,* to relinquish any power and influence to the uneducated laboring classes. And to preserve his power, to maintain the social status quo, the *haole* had developed an elaborate plan of governance and racial control. First, the laborers had to be racially divided so that they could be more easily ruled. By keeping the races segregated, by encouraging ethnic distinctions of religion, custom, language, and taste, by utilizing a racially disproportionate pay scale to arouse racial jealousies, and by allowing the natural human tendencies of envy to disrupt interracial cooperation, the development of a unified labor force would be stifled. Second, the laborers' confidence had to be won by providing them with the necessities of life. Paternalistically, the worker would be taught to view the *haole* world as the source of cultural enlightenment and economic well-being, as a son would view a father. The result of both tactics—"divide and rule" and "paternalism"—would be the perpetuation of King Sugar and the wealth, power, and status of the *haole* world.

In the other world, a non-*haole* world of nonautonomy, the forces of "rising expectations" had taken root. As year after year passed, the Japanese immigrant realized that the Hawaiian plantation did not offer wealth and promise but backbreaking work for a subsistence living standard. It offered harsh discipline, often inhumane treatment, and an insulting racial discrepancy in the value of one's labor. It offered a "vicious cycle" of economic dependence and impotency, precluding return to the homeland. In such a world, discontent, cultural isolation, and unrectified grievances led to an ambience of muted hostility. Dutifully obligated to the plantation, intent on diligently doing their work to earn their meager wages, some laborers adjusted to plantation life with quiet, bitter acquiescence. Others tried to use any excuse, take advantage of any unguarded moment to escape the drudgery of their futile employment. For some, any gross insult or injury would be responded to with violence and anger. Gradually, though, even the most submissive workers became receptive to the ascending voices decrying the inequities, the low wages, and the miserable working conditions. By 1900 some plantations were beginning to witness small wildcat strikes, rowdy groups of workers threatening the lives of *luna*s and formal protestations of grievances by labor representatives. Listening to the harangues of "agitators," coping daily with an economically and psychologically unsatisfying world, the laborer found his existence becoming increasingly frustrating and volatile. These frustrations, enshrouded in a bitterness for the wealthy and profitable system, gave vent to the growing expectations that the *haole* was perhaps not invincible, the chances for improving the quality of life perhaps not impossible. With the necessary sacrifices, with the strength of numbers and sustained spirit—*Yamato damashi,* the pride of Nippon—the laborer could begin to feel that the system was alterable.

Not unexpectedly, the desire to maintain the status quo in the one world would grow in positive correlation with "rising expectations," unrest, and bitterness in the other. Also not surprisingly, a point would come in Hawaiian history at which these forces would converge, resulting in a period of conflict and crisis.

To locate the point at which the forces of preservation under *haole* leadership and the forces of frustration sustained by the Japanese plantation workers would engage in social combat, one must look to the year 1909. In that year, Japanese plantation laborers on the island of Oahu, aroused by the injustices and inequities of the established system, refused to work. The plantation owners, appalled at the ingratitude and audacity of the Japanese and terrified at what their actions could do to their established economic system, refused to meet the strikers' demands. As the events of the Oahu Sugar Strike of 1909 unfolded, it became increasingly obvious that a crisis of considerable proportion was to engulf the *haole* and Japanese communities of Hawaii.

This crisis and its ensuing chaos would require from both communities a critical demand for effective leadership. For the *haole* community in 1909, leadership was well-developed and well-exercised. In an intricately interlocked oligarchy, the *haole*s formed a tight network of extended relationships. Common uncles, aunts, nephews, nieces, and cousins helped to maintain a common outlook and use of power. The Territorial government, the legislature, the Hawaiian Sugar Planters' Association, the massive sugar agents—Castle and Cooke, Alexander & Baldwin, C. Brewer, and Theo. H. Davies—and the major daily newspapers were controlled by the *haole* elite, who were ready to meet the challenges posed by recalcitrant strikers.

But in the Japanese community, leadership in 1909 was still in a confused infancy. As contract laborers, Japanese in the early years of immigration had naturally looked to the Japanese government to provide guidance on the plantation. If a laborer needed economic advice or wished to send money home to Japan, he went to a specie bank established in Hawaii under the auspices of the Japanese government. If a grievance arose between laborers and a *luna,* the Japanese filed a protest with the Japanese consulate. In fact, among the Japanese throughout the Islands the Japanese consul, by virtue of his vested imperial authority, had an important social prestige and influence. For example, in 1887 Japanese Consul Taro Ando was instrumental in the formation of the Japanese Benevolent Association which gave medical and social assistance to Japanese laborers. Also, Consul Miki Saito in 1903 organized the Central Japanese Association whose primary interest, reportedly, was to serve and protect the Japanese in Hawaii.

Yet, it became apparent to many Issei that the growth of a spirit of *eijū dochyaku,* of a permanent Island home for a stable Japanese family, necessitated a community leadership dedicated to the needs and the relief of the frustrations of the immigrant. When one of the specie banks, the Keihin Bank, was found to be exploiting the immigrant, the Central Japanese Association did little or nothing. Indeed, many leaders of the association, it was later learned, had also served as representatives of the Keihin Bank.[1] And, in 1904, the association had supported management over the Japanese laborers during the labor dispute at the Waipahu plantation, attempting to persuade the workers to accept the planters' demands. Many Issei began to wonder what kind of leadership the Japanese government and its representatives were willing to give the immigrants.

The need for leadership became especially acute in 1909. The laborers, feeling the frustrations of a racially disproportionate pay scale, responded eagerly to individuals who spoke of striking for higher wages. As a result, a united and aggressive Japanese leadership emerged in Hawaii, seeking to oppose the forces of "rising expectations" against the formidable opposition of the planters. According to Take and Allan Beekman in their description of the 1909 strike in an article entitled "Hawaii's Great Sugar Strike,"[2] a number of historical figures and personalities with various styles and modes of leadership developed during this time of imminent crisis. In particular, Frederick Kinzaburo Makino, Yasutaro Soga, Motoyuki Negoro, and Yokichi Tasaka emerged as leaders and spokesmen of the Japanese laborers' Higher Wage Association, the first Hawaiian plantation trade-union movement. They utilized a keen intellectual and political skill against the tactics and maneuvers of the planter oligarchy.

For Makino, Soga, Negoro, and Tasaka, the power of leadership in the Japanese community was fundamentally a tool to protect and defend the Japanese laborer. Proud of their race and ethnic heritage, determined to rectify the subjugating position of the plantation way of life, these leaders used the open demonstration of grievances to challenge the entrenched labor system of Hawaii. Other Japanese leaders, however, viewed unfavorably this "politics of confrontation." These leaders dreaded the outcome of the activities of men like Makino and Negoro. They feared the power of the *haole* elite and shunned the thought that Japanese should challenge such an awesome force. The reasons behind a decision to oppose confrontation also included a respect for established authority, a disdain for the lowly Japanese laborer, personal greed or ambition to gain the favor of the powerful, faith in the plantation's paternal system, and a sincere belief that confrontation would mean only hatred and further oppression for the Japanese in the Islands.

One of the less scrupulous of these leaders, Sometaro Sheba, felt that only by conciliation or accommodation to the planters' system could Japanese benefit in Hawaii. As editor of the *Hawaii Shimpo,* a Japanese-language newspaper, Sheba was vehemently opposed to the strike—a vehemence subsidized by the planters' treasury. While receiving monthly payments from the sugar interests, he attempted in all his efforts to demoralize the strikers and their supporters, discredit their leadership, and urge a policy of conciliation.

This schism of leadership typified in the conflict between Sheba and the leaders of the Higher Wage Association characterized the Japanese community between the years 1900 and 1925. Many Japanese intellectuals, businessmen, and laborers favored forthright confrontations with the *haole*s when the Japanese found themselves in unjust and discriminatory situations. They maintained that where rights were concerned, the Japanese must openly attack those who disgraced the law, regardless of their social power and prestige. Such action, after all, was supportive of the American tradition of constitutional guarantees. If life in Hawaii were to be liveable for the Issei, then the inequities of the *haole* oligarchy had to be directly and courageously challenged. But to the proponents of conciliation, it seemed the Japanese would live happily and prosperously in Hawaii if they simply bent with the wind. Rather than challenging the *haole*s outright, the Japanese community had first to show its loyalty and devotion to the Island way of life. The arousal of *haole* revenge had to be avoided at all costs. In the end, the paternalistic system of

Hawaii augmented with various cultural values of Japan would succeed in incorporating Japanese both comfortably and rewardingly into the mainstream of Island society.

The question as to the usefulness of confrontation or conciliation seemed to be answered by the end of 1909. Through the combined energies of the *haole* planters, the strike had been broken; its militant leaders had been tried and found guilty on a variety of charges. Two million dollars had been spent to support the foundations of the Hawaiian plantation system, and all indications seemed to prove that the forces of status quo had outlasted and subdued the forces of frustration. The policy of confrontation, some believed, had done nothing constructive except to prove the hopelessness of the Japanese position in Hawaii.

Yet, in retrospect, the results of confrontation were perhaps subtly more successful than the defenders of conciliation would admit. The objectives of the strike, which had called for improved working conditions and salary adjustments, were eventually met by 1910. By exposing the issue, by exerting what power they could muster, the Japanese immigrants had put the planters into a vulnerable position. The laborers could no longer be depended on to be submissive or humbly patient. Social change and progress could no longer be exclusively planned and scheduled by the oligarchy. New forces and leaders within the Island community were beginning to challenge those who had ruled in the nineteenth century.

Recognizing the impact which the politics of confrontation had on both the Japanese and *haole* communities of Hawaii, perhaps a more comprehensive perspective of the ethnic experience in the Islands can be appreciated. While to view the nonwhite minority as the proverbial sacrificial lamb of Anglo-Saxon racism could be fashionable, such an attitude overlooks and underrates the various forms of responses developed by the ethnic community. Whether through outright conflict or subtle accommodation, the Japanese immigrants in the first quarter of the twentieth century were laying the foundations for a drastic alteration of Hawaii's social institutions. History and social systems are fluid. No one person or group of persons, in spite of their skin color, can permanently and indefinitely be in complete control of a society, even a small Island community. Countervailing powers and the frustrations of the have-nots necessitate a perpetual interchange and restructuring of priorities and social relationships.

Although the Japanese laborer of 1909 was defeated in his efforts, he set in motion that which the oligarchy had dreaded—the labor union movement which would redefine the plantation and paternalism. And as would be expected, the 1909 strike was merely the first step. Using the powers of confrontation to achieve more equitable working conditions, Japanese plantation laborers on Oahu struck again in 1920. Initially referring to themselves as the Japanese Federation of Labor, then later as the Hawaii Laborers' Association, the leaders of the striking workers argued that, since World War I, the cost of living had risen well above any increase in plantation salaries. The impoverished laborers, they pointed out, earned approximately seventy-seven cents for a ten-hour day.

A sense of interethnic unity was developed in the strike of 1920 under the leadership of the Japanese Federation of Labor. The Japanese leaders realized that if the strike were to be effective, it had to gain the support of other ethnic workers. The Filipino Labor Union under Pablo Manlapit was induced to join the Japanese strikers so as to strengthen the impact of the strike on plantation profits. Previous strikes had been stymied because of a failure to overcome ethnic barriers created by the planters' "divide and rule" policy. But in 1920 the attempts to supersede interethnic hostilities were partially successful. Two thousand Filipino and 4,000 Japanese plantation laborers and their families, amounting to 13,000 individuals, refused to work.[3]

But in spite of the number of strikers, the overall politics of the 1920 confrontation were costly. Pushed from their plantation homes, ravaged by influenza, the individual laborers bore the brunt of the physical and financial burden of the six-month strike. At least $200,000 was spent by the Japanese community to sustain the strike and help feed and house strikers. In turn, the planters spent nearly $12,000,000 in that period to maintain their resistance to social and economic change.[4] As in 1909, the strike was broken, but what followed were important repercussions and improvements on the sugar plantations.

Yet during this same period, when the Japanese leaders of confrontation came to the forefront of community leadership a stately Japanese Christian minister began to turn what had been an improbable idea into a small but risky undertaking—an undertaking which was to give an air of respectability to the leadership of conciliation. While maintaining his ministry at the Makiki Christian Church, Reverend Takie Okumura with the aid of his son Umetaro launched in 1921 an educational campaign among the plantation laborers which would help to generate an entirely new image of the Japanese in Hawaii.

The intention of the educational campaign for which Okumura would gain the reputation of "traitor" among many of his countrymen, was the Americanization of the Japanese. Rather than holding on totally to the ways of the old world, Okumura believed that Japanese should look to an incorporation of the American lifestyle which existed in Hawaii. Although Reverend Okumura might have appeared as a fanatical Americanizer to his opponents, his style of leadership was really a more sophisticated recognition that the Japanese population of Hawaii should embody a mixture of both Japanese and American elements. In his sermons he made analogies between the *samurai* sword and the Bible; he found traditional Japanese values of filial piety embedded in Christianity; he compared the age-old Japanese warrior with the Christian soldier; he stressed the similarities between Confucianism and Christianity. The epitome, perhaps, of Okumura's conceptualization of Americanization was in the construction of the Makiki Christian Church. Designed by the Reverend, the church resembled a Japanese castle with a 100-foot tower dominating the Makiki skyline. In style and purpose, the intention was to combine Christianity with Japanese culture.

The concept of cultural amalgamation for the Japanese immigrants and their children was forthrightly stated by Okumura in his writings:

> The Americanization, however, that I speak of is not a servile Americanization. I do not say that we should be Americanized in everything good and bad. On the contrary, I have been urging every youth to pick the good things of America and assimilate them, and thus become desirable elements in our community. Just so long as Japanese blood flows in their veins, they should grasp the real spirit of Bushido, Americanize it, and carry it along with them.[5]

In its most honest form, the policy of which Okumura was a leading proponent was one of conciliation. While Sometaro Sheba and others had urged accommodation to the *haole*s because they sought personal power and wealth or viewed the challenges of aggressive leadership with reservations, Okumura's intentions were more idealistic. His integrity and devotion to seeing Japanese peacefully and totally accepted into the Hawaiian social structure far outweighed any material or political influence which planters could exercise over him. Okumura sincerely believed that friction or hostility between the *haole* and Japanese arising from the politics of confrontation had to be avoided at all costs. Japanese should think of themselves first as Americans, in peaceful harmony with other Americans, even if that meant temporary hardship or self-humiliation. If friendship between the two races could be instilled, then eventually the Japanese people could become an integral part of the Island population.

With these thoughts, Okumura and his son began an educational campaign in 1921. Bothered by the hatred and violence generated by the plantation strikes, hoping to ameliorate conflict through Americanizing and instilling patient compliance among Japanese laborers, Okumura traveled from plantation to plantation, from island to island, year after year, hoping to ameliorate the friction between Japanese and *haole*s. In his account, entitled "Hawaii's American Japanese Problem: A Campaign to Remove Causes of Friction Between the American People and Japanese,"[6] can be found the methodology and activities which characterized the campaign. From this report can be discerned some significant features of the policy of conciliation and its effectiveness on Japanese leadership in Hawaii. That the Americanization of laborers began to receive the welcomed support of the plantation management can be seen. For the sugar planters, Okumura began to serve as an important balance to the "agitators" who had for years tried to create labor unrest. Americanization, especially the type promoted by Okumura, seemed to instill a docility and acceptance of the status quo. Good citizenship implied apathetic agreement and would forestall the radicalizing effect of "anarchist" leaders. As an important outcome of Okumura's campaign, not only the Reverend but the *haole* community were beginning to use the rhetoric of Americanization.

Emerging from Okumura's report are also insights into the creation and perpetuation of the new American image as it pertained to the Japanese immigrant. By imploring Japanese to "forget the idea 'Japanese'," to bring their children up as "good and loyal American citizens," Okumura was an early initiator of the 100-percent American image that the Japanese American community, specifically the second-generation Japanese, the Nisei, were to inherit. Conciliation necessitated a harmonious and humble style of adaptation—the immigrant must project the image that he has done all he could to fit quietly, at times even submissively, into the social system. Although some leaders challenged that such an attitude of 100 percentism was demeaning and self-destructive to the Japanese, no one could at that time foretell the important influence which the policy of conciliation would have on the social image of the Nisei generation.

But even as Okumura was making his small inroads on the plantations, at Iolani Palace in Honolulu the Territorial Legislature was putting into motion other developments which would once again put the test of leadership to the Japanese community. For in 1920, the Territory of Hawaii had decided to wage war against the Japanese language schools, striking at a sensitive nerve of ethnic pride and autonomy.

One of the first language schools had been founded in 1896, ironically, by Reverend Okumura, who later would be one of its most outspoken critics. The school had initially been intended by the Reverend to instruct young Nisei in Japanese, to enhance family stability as well as to teach Christian principles and institutions. Soon the idea of teaching the Japanese language to Nisei became extremely popular, especially since the schools facilitated communication and cultural transmission within the Issei family and provided a child-care center for working parents. With the proliferation of Buddhist institutions, the Japanese language schools came under the control of a more "Japanesey" leadership. Besides instruction in the language, reverence for the emperor and a strong attachment to things Japanese dominated the curriculum of the Buddhist-operated language schools. Many young Nisei would therefore attend not only public school, learning American culture and language, but would study the ways of Japan at the language schools.

Such was the popularity of the language schools that one of the major activities of, for example, the Honolulu Honpa Hongwanji temple was the education of Nisei children. In 1918 the temple was operating thirty-one education homes, serving about 4,700 children, and two advanced educational homes serving 500 students of high school level. The original schools from which the education homes evolved were merely language schools perpetuating a Japanese education for Nisei children. But by 1914 the church leadership realized the need for more sophisticated instruction, designed to complement an American education as well as facilitate the familial relations in the Japanese home:

> Lessons in the mother tongue, to enable the children to speak and write in Japanese, will be given in the morning, or in the afternoon, but they will be for only an hour or so, lest they overtax the children's

> minds. Historical descriptions will be given at times, when the curiosity of the children is excited by some incident, but care will be taken that they do not amount to more than stories and descriptions given by parents in enlightened families. Moral lessons will have their place—an hour every week—though they will not be based on national traditions but on a broader basis; the aim being to render some help in fitting the children for American life. In a word, the school will be an Educational Home, and the teachers will act as mediators between the public schools and the homes.[7]

But as optimistic as the Honpa Hongwanji might have been about the effects of the educational homes and language schools, some people were more frightened than reassured.

In 1920, the Federal Commission on Education, reporting on the status of public instruction in Hawaii, noted the extensive number of Japanese language schools in the Islands—163 schools educating nearly 20,000 students. The Commission concluded that attending the language schools was detrimental to the health of Nisei children; their progress in American schools was retarded and their loyalty to the United States was confused and neglected. Quoting teachers and parents as to the negative effects of the schools, the report recommended that the language institutions be abolished and their functions assumed by the public school system.

To many people in Hawaii, such a recommendation coincided with their belief that the maintenance of language schools was an un-American act by minorities who wished to preserve their ties with an alien homeland. Influenced by the surge of patriotism and the attitude of "America First" which swept the nation and Hawaii during World War I, many *haole*s became hostile to the notion that small children should be taught reverence for the emperor of Japan or the intricacies of Japanese culture. Since the Nisei were born as American citizens, the assumption was that they had to be fully immersed in American institutions. "One language under one flag" was the slogan which filled editorial columns and social conversations.

But for the Japanese immigrants, the continued operation of the language schools was essential. Uneasy parents saw their offspring becoming cultural hybrids in Hawaii without knowledge of Japanese culture or language; they felt their children needed a proper Japanese education. After all, the possibility still existed, no matter how remote, that the family would one day leave Hawaii and return to Japan. Other Japanese spoke in support of the language schools because of a belief that such institutions were valuable for the Americanization process. In 1927 an article by Yōichi Hanaoka, entitled "The Japanese Language School: Is It a Help or a Hindrance to the Americanization of Hawaii's Young People?"[8] suggested that the schools actually aided the Japanese children to become better Americans. Through learning the Japanese language intergenerational dialogue was enhanced, promoting discipline and greater mutual understanding between parent and child and a stronger, more moral family. Such a stable, moral family, according to Hanaoka, contributed to the building of good American citizens. Moreover, the moral and religious instruction imparted by the language schools was compatible with the American demand for "high moral and deep religious character in youthful manhood."

Although the language schools taught foreign culture or a worship of the emperor, Hanaoka stated that no "hyphenated loyalty" was created on the part of the young people. The language schools did not make Nisei obedient subjects of the Mikado. If anything, they produced a group of bicultural individuals who were essential for peace and industry in the Pacific: "Hawaii's young people of Japanese parentage are peculiarly destined to solve the problems of peace in the Pacific area . . . . The key to the true friendship of Japan and America is in the hands of the young American citizens, who understand both the ideals of the West and culture of the East."

Regardless of the arguments as to the benefit of language schools, steps were taken in 1920 by concerned legislators to implement the Federal Commission's recommendations. A special session of the legislature was called with the only order of business being the abolition of the schools. But due to the opposition from the Japanese community, a compromise bill, the Irwin Bill, was worked out. The Irwin Bill essentially required that language-school teachers receive a permit from the Department of Public Instruction and pledge to teach nothing which would contradict American ideals or institutions. Although seriously limited in operations, the language schools felt secure that the compromise would protect their peaceful operation.

But in 1922, the Territorial Legislature, seeing the advantages of gradual control and then elimination of the language schools rather than outright abolition, took steps to gain further control through enrollment qualifications and textbook regulations. Children of a certain age could not attend language schools, and the subject matter of the textbooks came under government scrutiny. Then in April,

1923, determined to make the existence of language schools impossible for the Japanese community, the legislature enacted the Clark Bill which imposed a $1 tax per language-school student per year. The bill was designed to curb the operation of the language schools and in response many of the schools temporarily closed their doors rather than pay the discriminatory tax.

As in the labor disputes of 1909 and 1920, the language school controversy found the Japanese community divided between those who felt Japanese should confront the injustices of the legislature and those who felt Japanese should conciliate, bend with the times, and patiently wait for the system to right itself. Reverend Okumura followed an accommodating pattern by supporting the Clark Bill and what it represented. He was joined by Yasutaro Soga, editor of the *Nippu Jiji,* who felt that in regard to the education of Nisei, "government authorities are within their rights to supervise the curriculum as taught in the schools."[9]

Others felt that a policy of conciliation had overly compromised the integrity of the Japanese ethnic community. Although Reverend Imamura had helped quell labor disturbances in 1904 and had supported accommodation to the Americanization programs, he now was forced to place the prestige of the Hongwanji Mission behind social action. Under Imamura the Hongwanji temple now stood ready to defend its language schools against the power of the *haole.*

Another individual, perhaps the most outspoken to champion the cause of confrontation by challenging the state laws in the courts, was Frederick Kinzaburo Makino, editor of the *Hawaii Hochi.* Makino, the son of an English businessman and a Japanese woman whose maiden name he adopted, was only twenty-two years old when he arrived in Hawaii in 1899. Working as a clerk at the Kona Sugar Refinery and Honokaa plantation, Makino in 1901 was able to open a drug store in downtown Honolulu. But his taste for confrontation, for the intellectual challenges of social power and change, soon led him into the forefront of controversy. His role in the 1909 Oahu Sugar Strike cast him as one of the strongest and most outspoken leaders in the early Issei community.

Whether because of his part-Caucasian background, his educational training and aggressive personality, or the brashness of his youth, Fred Makino expressed little hesitancy in attacking the injustices of the *haole* oligarchy. He seemed to gain personal strength and fortitude from confrontation—a strength he would pass on to thousands of Japanese immigrants. Establishing the *Hawaii Hochi* in 1912, he created a newspaper which became a source of frank and sometimes overly blunt opinions. As his biographers were to state, "*Hochi* was Makino, and Makino was synonymous with *Hochi*."[10] Undoubtedly, the Japanese language press was an extremely important source of leadership in the Issei community. The first Japanese newspaper in Hawaii was established in 1892 and was called the *Nippon Shuho,* or *Japanese Weekly*. By 1912, the two major Japanese newspapers in Honolulu were the *Nippu Jiji* and the *Hawaii Shimpo*. The *Hochi* was soon to be also recognized as an aggressive newspaper by taking the lead on many community issues.

After the 1909 strike and the establishment of the *Hochi,* Makino launched his first attack on the *haole* establishment. The issue was assembly-line marriages for picture brides, but the motive was to arouse both Japanese and non-Japanese public opinion around the fact that immigrants from Japan had to be treated with human dignity. And if injustices should arise, the immigrant and his leaders would demand and even insist on proper retribution and social adjustment.

Makino's involvement in the issue of assembly-line marriages developed as a result of the large number of picture brides who began arriving in Hawaii after 1907. Although they had been properly wed in Japan according to village custom, the picture brides were not recognized by immigration officials as being legally married. Consequently, a Christian minister would be brought to the immigration station to perform a single wedding ceremony for all the picture brides and their husbands. Not only did this practice degrade marriage, but it violated the rights of freedom of religion, since almost all of the Japanese were Buddhists. "The Japanese residents," wrote Makino, "similar to Americans, should be allowed to enjoy the freedom of worship."[11] Eventually under his protestations, the ceremonies were discontinued.

Other issues which Makino spearheaded that often caused confrontations between the Japanese and American communities were the rights of citizenship for Issei veterans of World War I, the unification of Japanese residents in the islands through the formation of the Japanese Association of Hawaii, and the protection of legal entry for Japanese language-school teachers into Hawaii. But in 1923 with the challenge to the existence of the language schools, Makino was to enter his most difficult and yet most satisfying struggle against certain sectors of the *haole* community as well as the Japanese promoters of conciliation.

The strategy of Makino and his legal advisers was to contest the legality of the language-school control bills in the courts. The first school to test the propriety of the language-school bills was Palama Japanese Language School, which filed a petition for injunction in the Territorial Circuit Court. Under the leadership of Makino and the *Hochi,* by the end of 1923 eighty-seven other schools had joined Palama School to test the constitutionality of the laws.

In using the *Hochi* to sway public opinion, Makino criticized those who by "weeping into silence," *"naki neiri"* had let the legislature slowly take more and more steps which now doomed the language schools. Selections from an editorial in April of 1923, "Unity Essential,"[12] demonstrate Makino's dynamic and aggressive editorial style. In the editorial the Japanese community was asked to unite totally behind the movement to save the language schools or "we would become a laughing stock of the community."

Makino was willing to see the language school become responsive to outside criticisms, but unlike Soga or Okumura, who were willing to accommodate the school authorities, Makino would not tolerate outside control. "We would compromise if the matter is tackled with the spirit of cooperation," he argued. "But we see no reason of weeping into silence, when we are forced to accept the measure which we cannot approve."

In an unexpected maneuver, the defenders of the language schools in 1925 took the litigation out of the Territorial courts and filed in the United States District Court. After legal battles and appeals, the United States Supreme Court rendered a decision on February 21, 1927, which struck down the Territorial Legislature's language-school control laws as unconstitutional. The decision was based fundamentally on the fact that the "Japanese parent has the right to direct his own child without unreasonable restriction" and that the Territorial laws sought to control the schools "for no adequate reason."[13] The politics of confrontation, the Japanese community, and Fred Makino had won.

On March 29, following the Supreme Court decision, Makino spoke before a gathering of Japanese at the Hawaii Chuo Gakuen school in Honolulu. The topic of his speech was "Did We Hurt the Feelings of the English Speaking Community?" Makino pronounced:

> The Americans feel it only proper that we took the action we did. The Americans are only too well cognizant of the fact that it is the

> right of the people living in a free democracy to advocate their rights guaranteed under the Constitution and to seek legal clarification of doubtful points in the enforcement of laws. The Americans are not giving the Test Case a second thought. They believe in sportsmanship and they shake hands and become good friends after a violent fist fight. It behooves us, who live in this country, to understand the characteristics of the Americans. Individuals and organizations alike must never forget to stand up for their rights and freedom.[14]

The politics of confrontation had taken on an air of respectability and success. Though leaders like Okumura might not wholeheartedly agree with Makino's words, the fact remained that confrontation, not conciliation, had helped to preserve the Japanese language schools.

For more than twenty years the leadership in the Japanese community had struggled over the direction in which the immigrant and his children would go. Makino had viewed adaptation to America as a process in which Japanese had to stand up unequivocably for their rights and struggle for an equal position in Hawaii's society. Okumura thought of adaptation as a process of Americanization, of first proving the humility of the Japanese in accepting the status quo of Hawaiian life.

To be accurate, both forms of leadership made significant impacts on the evolution of the Japanese community. Confrontation aroused the stability and unity of the ethnic community, instilling pride and defiance when that community was faced with the rigidity of the Hawaiian oligarchy. On the other hand, the leaders of conciliation worked effectively to prove that Japanese immigrants, especially their Nisei children, were anxious to become complete American citizens. Their rhetoric, both within and without the ethnic community, served to offset the harsh racial encounters between Japanese and *haole*s by helping to create the notion that in spite of agitation and resistance, the Japanese immigrants and their children were becoming loyal Americans. In attitude and behavior, showing patient accommodation when necessary, a great number of Japanese in Hawaii began to project what would later be a vitally useful image: "We Are Good Americans!"

Yet whether in a style of conciliation or confrontation, the leadership of the Japanese community had one impact which is indisputable. After 1909, 1920, and 1927—after the forces of resistance, change, and accommodation had reached florescence in the Japanese community—Hawaii would never be the same. The *haole*s' stranglehold on Island life had been loosened. New forces and leaders had to be considered. The rulers of Hawaii found themselves in a twentieth-century society comprised not of ignorant, submissive laborers but a dynamic multiethnic community which increasingly became more difficult to manage. Around the *haole* now swirled the threatening Kona winds of change, the currents of ambitions and expectations over which he would increasingly have little control.

By 1927, the divergent strains comprising the world of the Japanese immigrant had at last solidified into a permanent way of life. The spirit of community had been internally strengthened through religious and cultural institutions; the family and home had been established; values, beliefs, and customs had been largely transposed. The controversies of the last two decades had aroused an ethnic cohesiveness so that one could justifiably speak of a Japanese community in Hawaii. Even more important, the optimism of success and hope for a future had been reinstilled through the adaptations and struggles. Perhaps life was not tied forever to the old-style plantation cycle of crushing expectations. Perhaps Hawaii still offered more for the immigrant and his children.

NOTES

1. Ernest Wakukawa, *A History of the Japanese People in Hawaii,* Honolulu: The Toyo Shoin, 1938. The episode of the Keihin Bank controversy is related on pp. 153–56.

2. Take and Allan Beekman, "Hawaii's Great Japanese Strike," *Pacific Citizen,* v. 51 (December 23, 1960), pp. B1–B8; B23–B24; A14.

3. United Japanese Society of Hawaii, *A History of Japanese in Hawaii,* ed. by Publication Committee, Dr. James H. Okahata, Chm., Honolulu: United Japanese Society of Hawaii, 1971, p. 186.

4. United Japanese Society of Hawaii, p. 186.

5. Takie Okumura, *Seventy Years of Divine Blessings,* Kyoto: Naigai Publishing Co., 1940, p. 11.

6. Takie and Umetaro Okumura, "1921 Campaign," *Hawaii's American-Japanese Problems. A Campaign to Remove Causes of Friction Between the American People and Japanese, Report of the Campaign, January, 1921, to January, 1927,* Honolulu, 1927, pp. 9–12.

7. Yemyō Imamura, *History of the Hongwanji Mission in Hawaii,* Honolulu: Publishing Bureau of Hongwanji Mission, 1918, pp. 22–3.

8. Yōichi Hanaoka, "The Japanese Language School: Is It a Help or a Hindrance to the Americanization of Hawaii's Young People?" *The Friend,* v. 97 (1927), pp. 79–80.

9. United Japanese Society of Hawaii, p. 225.

10. Compilation Committee for the Publication of Kinzaburo Makino's Biography, eds., *Life of Kinzaburo Makino,* Honolulu: Hawaii Hochi, 1965, p. 43.

11. Compilation Committee for the Publication of Kinzaburo Makino's Biography, p. 20.

12. "Unity Essential," *Hawaii Hochi,* April 21, 1923.

13. United Japanese Society of Hawaii, p. 223.

14. Compilation Committee for the Publication of Kinzaburo Makino's Biography, pp. 65–6.

Hawaii's Great Japanese Strike

TAKE AND ALLAN BEEKMAN

ON the evening of January 15, 1909, in the Honolulu Theater, Aala Lane, Honolulu, Island of Oahu, Territory of Hawaii, some members and supporters of the recently formed Higher Wage Association sat down to enjoy a drama with the fanciful title: *A Play To Be Given in Formosa Fifty Years Hence.* Among these spectators were Yokichi Tasaka, Fred Kinsaburo Makino, Yasutaro Soga, and Motoyuki Negoro. Each of these men had particular reason to be interested in the performance, and in the reaction of the audience to it, for the play dramatized a movement of which they were the guiding spirits.

Negoro's interest, perhaps, was keener than the others, for he was the author. Thirty-five years of age, gaunt, ascetic, scholarly, he had whipped the play together at the request of the producer, Tsukasa Saito, who had seen in such a vehicle an opportunity to capitalize on the great interest that had been generated for higher wages and improved working conditions for the 30,000 Japanese who toiled on Hawaii's sugar plantations.

A handy man with a writing brush, Negoro was to record his impressions of this evening in a book entitled, *Meiji Yonjuichi-ninen Hawaii Hojin Katsuyakushi—Dai Hiko Kaikoshi* (History of Ha-

In *Pacific Citizen,* v. 51 (December 23, 1960), Section B: B1–B8; B23–B24; A–14.

waii's Japanese, 1908–1909, or Memoir of the Great Strike), a work which he prefaces with such remarks as,

> I compiled this history of the higher wage movement of Hawaii's Japanese laborers, 1908–1909, because the movement was an unprecedented, magnificent undertaking among the personal movements of the Japanese abroad, and also to bequeath it to our posterity, and to memorialize the great works of the men abroad of true Yamato spirit, who participated in the movement. . . . Excepting for the records of the recent Japanese-Sino War, Japanese-Russian War . . . and, in ancient times, the foreign invasions of the Empress Jingu and Hideyoshi, there are few records of the activities of the Japanese outside of Japan. . . . When we look for a victory of the Japanese abroad, fighting empty-handed against the foreigners, we must list this higher wage movement of Hawaii's Japanese.

The drama opened with the spectacle of Japanese and European laborers toiling together on a Hawaiian sugar plantation and illustrated that the Japanese, though accorded poorer living conditions, were no less efficient than the Europeans.

There followed a bit about a poor Japanese laborer whose friends tried to enable him to bring a bride from Japan by forming a lending fund *(tanomoshi)*. By the time the bride arrived, malnutrition had taken its toll of the groom, who lay stricken with beriberi. Unable to work, he could not pay his bills at the plantation store, and the store cut off his supply of food and other necessities. He could not pay the monthly installments on the lending fund, and to his bedside came pitiless collectors and usurers.

The play showed some public-spirited men, who had observed the pitiful state of the laborer, calling a great meeting to discuss relief measures. They unanimously agreed that such pitiful situations could be corrected only by pressing for higher wages, and so a movement for higher wages began.

As one means of promoting the movement, the fictitious higher wage advocates sent a committee to Honolulu to enlist the support of the Japanese language papers. Of the four papers, only the *Nippu Jiji* showed wholehearted sympathy and promised full support. The representatives of the other papers listened with sneers and rejected the request with abusive language.

A man named Chiba, who represented one paper, said, "I'm not against it, in fact, I'm greatly for it. But the time has not yet come when the demands can be made. And as for the ways and means of such things, country bumpkins like you do not know well—leave it up to me." He tried to bewilder the delegates with "vague and boastful words." But it was easily seen that Chiba was scheming, "and his duplicity caused the audience to grind its teeth in vexation."

When a mass meeting was held at the request of the plantation delegates, Chiba attended and quickly opposed the higher wage movement. After a hot argument, Chiba was on the point of striking Machida, the most zealous in promoting the movement, but was restrained by the crowd. No violence resulted. But the incident greatly impressed the audience, "who unconsciously ground its teeth in vexation."

Despite the opposition of Chiba, the higher wage movement grew, and the time came when Chiba must have felt inclined to grind his teeth in vexation: the circulation of his paper, and that of the other papers which opposed the movement, felt the effect of loss of popularity.

In his despondency, Chiba went to a tea house, and, after eating and drinking heavily, fell into a coma in which he had a weird dream: the ghosts of the many laborers who had died in bitter poverty because Chiba, by becoming the tool of the Planters, had prevented the great benefit to Hawaii's 70,000 Japanese—for all of Hawaii's Japanese were assumed to be potential beneficiaries—swarmed around him. Chiba "suffered as if forced to drink molten lead, or as if roasted in Hell's pot."

In contrast to Chiba's suffering, the scene changed. From yonder, music was heard—heralding the victory of the Higher Wage Association. A group approached with banners emblazoned, "Higher Wage Success," and "22.50." This was the parade of the Japanese laborers celebrating the final achievement of the (monthly) wage of $22.50. The drama thus ends.

The drama may have thus ended for some of the audience at the Honolulu Theater, but for Tasaka, Makino, Soga, and Negoro it was only approaching the crisis, and the play itself was to contribute to the climax and denouement.

Soga, who was to cover the events and the causes from which they sprang in his book, *Gojunenkan no Hawaii Kaiko* (Memoirs of Fifty Years in Hawaii), published in 1953, though an intellectual, knew the problems of the laborers from first hand observation. Born March 19, 1873, in Tokyo, Soga studied at the Tokyo Pharmacy School and the English Law Institute, but graduated from neither. He came to Hawaii, at the age of 23, in March, 1896, and for the next three years acted as clerk and manager of stores operated by

C. Shiozawa at Waianae and Waipahu, on Oahu, and also at Kaunakakai, on the Island of Molokai. He was often called upon to serve as interpreter between management and labor, and thus gained insight into the relations between the groups.

. . .

Negoro had come to America at 17 and worked his way through high school in California. He had matriculated at the University of California, Berkeley, in 1896, received a Bachelor of Letters Degree in 1901, and Bachelor of Laws in 1903. After a sojourn in Hawaii, he returned to Berkeley in 1907, and, in 1908, received a Juris Doctor Degree. With this impressive educational background—extraordinary for a Japanese in Hawaii at that time—Dr. Negoro returned to Hawaii, where the fuse of the powder keg of Japanese dissatisfaction was to be ignited by the writing brush of Gunkichi Shimada.

Shimada was a writer for Hanzo Tsurushima's *Nichi Nichi* newspaper, which had recently opened on the second floor of the stone building, on the northwest corner of King and Maunakea Streets. Shimada had been sent by his employer to all the islands of Hawaii to gather material for a book which was published by the *Nichi Nichi* under the title *Hawaii Seikosha Jitsuden* (True Stories of Successful [Japanese] People of Hawaii).

Knowing the situation of Hawaii's Japanese from first-hand information, Shimada wrote an article for the August 25, 1908, issue of the *Nichi Nichi* which was substituted for the editorial and which made the point that "prices had recently increased more than 20 per cent, but that the wage of the Japanese laborer, if he worked 26 days a month, did not exceed $18.00, and this made it difficult for him to gain a livelihood. . . . " His not unreasonable argument was that it was proper that the laborers' wages should be increased more than 20 per cent.

Soga had followed his employer, Shiozawa, into the newspaper business, and Soga was now editor of the puny, struggling *Nippu Jiji*. His reporter, Yokichi Tasaka, on the Island of Maui—where the *Nippu* had from 25 to 30 subscribers—read Shimada's article and decided that Shimada had uncovered the burning issue of the day.

Thirty-three years of age, a small, cherubic appearing man, Tasaka had come to Hawaii about 13 years previously as an official of the Morioka Immigration Company. He had a high school education, a knack for writing, imagination, and enterprise. He was the first, for example, to organize groups (kankodan) to tour Japan, a movement which, after this initial impetus, grew, flourished, and became traditional.

A *Nichi Nichi* reporter had been chaffing Tasaka because of the *Nippu*'s meager circulation. Tasaka put down Shimada's article with the remark that after returning to Honolulu he would write on the timely issue of the depressed wages of the Japanese and thus increase the circulation of the *Nippu*. This decision was, in a few months, to make the name of Tasaka a household word throughout Hawaii.

Tasaka carried out his promise, and Negoro, who had found work as clerk in the A.L.C. Atkinson Law Office, read the argument. Negoro, like any other Japanese, was barred from American citizenship; and being an alien, despite his impressive legal background, he was barred from the practice of law. Emotional, disputatious, flamboyant, smarting from the discrimination that put him below men of inferior ability, a crusader by nature, Negoro was impressed by Tasaka's argument, and took up the writing brush to elaborate on it.

Negoro wrote a long treatise, entitled "How About The Higher Wages," which begins, "We regret that wages in Hawaii are disproportionately low in comparison with the large profits," and argues that the Japanese government should intercede for the Japanese laborers, "for the Japanese government is well aware that its subjects are not born to be slaves of the capitalists of Hawaii. . . . The Japanese laborers who are placed in the position of slaves by reason of the prohibition of immigration to America do not have the courage to ask for higher wages. . . . [The] Japanese government, taking great courage itself, should request the American government to dissolve the prohibition of emigration of Hawaiian Japanese to the Mainland. The time is ripe. Though the Hawaiian immigrants do not say it in so many words, it is their hope of years and their silent prayer that they recover the lost liberty of choosing and changing their place of abode, and becoming full-fledged men, and to be in a position to earn a just reward for their labor."

Negoro took the treatise to Sometaro Sheba, editor of the *Hawaii Shimpo*—the man later to be lampooned as "Chiba" in Negoro's play. With what, to an ardent Japanese patriot like Negoro, must have seemed inexplicable obtuseness, Sheba rejected the treatise.

Negoro had only surface appearance by which to judge Sheba, though these appearances, it is true, gave some clue to the behavior of Sheba towards the movement for higher wages. Born of a *samurai* family in Ehime Prefecture, Japan, Sheba had studied for three years in the English Department of Aoyama Gakuin, Tokyo. In Kobe he had acted as interpreter and language teacher to the missionaries, and taught English in private schools. He came to Hawaii, at the age of 21, in 1891, and for 11 years worked in the stores of C. H. Bishop at Lihue and Hanamaulu, on the Island of Kauai.

Excepting for a slight accent, Sheba spoke, and wrote, English as well as an educated American, and was a crack translator. Some of his teachers at the Methodist School, Aoyama Gakuin, had been Americans, and he was early accustomed to turning to the Americans for his standards. He described himself as an "earnest Christian," and there being few Christians among the Japanese in Hawaii in those days it may have seemed natural for him to associate with Americans who shared his faith.

There was, perhaps, an even deeper reason why the Americans exercised a fascination for him: the Americans were the rulers. Sheba was drawn to men of wealth and power as steel is drawn to a magnet. He was like a forest vine which finds its glory and fulfillment in embellishing the mighty tree trunk around which it entwines itself. From the solid foundations of those mightier than he, Sheba drew strength and security.

Supercilious, handsome, physically powerful though small in stature, regular features set off with a large moustache, ears close to his skull, and thick black hair above a high forehead, Sheba was later to boast, "No other Japanese has arrived at the point I have. I have many Caucasian friends among the government and Territorial officials and among the capitalists of Hawaii."

When Sheba was criticized for making friends principally among the Americans to the detriment of his countrymen, he denied the charge, saying that he had as many friends among the Japanese. But in 1908, for a Japanese to have even as many American friends as Japanese was highly unusual.

Beneath the surface, where Negoro's keen eyes could not probe, there were stronger reasons for the repugnance which Sheba manifested for Negoro's treatise—reasons that Sheba, naturally, did not consider prudent to reveal, and that was to become generally known only much later.

On Kauai, where he had published the *Kauai Shuho,* Sheba had received financial assistance from the manager of Lihue Sugar Plantation. Just the preceding year, when he had come to Honolulu, Sheba had borrowed $5,000 from the Bank of Hawaii, over the endorsement of Bishop, an executive of the Hawaiian Sugar Planters Association, to found the *Shimpo.* Sheba was now the president of three papers—even called the Hearst of Hawaii. He was not, however, his own man. In addition to the aforementioned favors from the sugar interests, Sheba was receiving $100 a month from the Planters.

Consequently, Sheba must have felt compelled to rebuff Negoro's treatise, but Negoro, who was not easily discouraged, straightway took the treatise to Soga.

"First," said Soga, "I had him leave the treatise with me. I read it and found the argument splendid and just. I willingly consented to publish it. Thereafter, it began to run serially in the *Nippu Jiji,* with the full support of the whole paper. . . . The *Nippu Jiji* asserted that the Japanese laborers, when compared with laborers of other countries, were competent laborers, and not one whit less efficient, and that persons of equal labor capacity should be given equal wages and equal treatment. . . . "

Interest in the movement grew, and about November 1, 1908, in response to circulars which had been sent out, about 14 persons met at the Asahi Theater to discuss means of translating the growing sentiment for higher wages into action. It was apparent that the movement evinced a vulnerable spot: Sheba's *Shimpo* was opposing the course of Soga's *Nippu.*

Editor Sheba did not deny that higher wages for the Japanese would be a good thing, but he counseled that it should be achieved by representations to the Planters, rather than by making it a newspaper issue. Prudence! Prudence above all!—this was the watchword of Sheba.

Those attending the meeting consequently concluded that the division among the newspapers imperilled the higher wage movement and that a meeting should be held to persuade the opposing Hawaii *Shimpo* and the doubtful *Nichi Nichi* into presenting a united front.

Tsurushima, of the *Nichi Nichi,* who had published Shimada's article which had precipitated the movement, had drawn back in alarm. Tsurushima, as did every intelligent man, well knew the power and ruthlessness of the Planters. Under the monarchy, the Planters had been content to pull the strings to which the aboriginal monarch danced. But when Queen Liliuokalani began to have notions that she might rule as well as reign, the Planters dropped their mask of allegiance and showed that they could and would back their decrees with guns and bayonets.

. . .

Tsurushima, therefore, knew quite well the danger of opposing the Planters. A group who could, and would, oust a monarch, when that monarch dared oppose them, might crush a Japanese editor, who took up cudgels against them, with the ease and lack of compunction with which they would crush a mosquito.

Also, Tsurushima was frequently wined and dined by Sheba. He had heard Sheba speak of the supporters of the higher wage movement as "rabble" *(yajiuma)*. Tsurushima felt he had far more to fear from the displeasure of Sheba than from that of Soga, whose paper seemed weak and uninfluential. Fear suppressing idealism, Tsurushima paused to consider if the issue were not growing into something bigger and more dangerous than he had anticipated.

At the time of the proposed meeting, Tsurushima was on the Island of Maui, but he was represented at the meeting by his reporter, Yoshigoro Kimura. The meeting was held at the home of Yukichi Ishii, a druggist, on Vineyard Street. Negoro and Makino were present.

Sheba, who seemed bent on frustrating the object of the meeting, immediately objected to the presence of Negoro and Makino on the ground that they were not newspapermen. He seemed to feel a particular antipathy toward Makino, used vulgar language towards him, and even aimed a blow at him—but missed and struck his own knee.

The charge that Makino was not a newspaperman was certainly valid, though it scarcely seemed reason to exclude him from the gathering. The movement was the kind of activity that commended itself to a person of Makino's talents and temperament, and he had been active in it. He was, indeed, the "Machida" of Negoro's play.

Born in Yokohama in 1877, of an English silk merchant named Higgenbotham and a Japanese mother, Makino had adopted his mother's name. After attending primary school like any other Japanese, he had attended English-Japanese School. Equally fluent in English and Japanese, he had come to Hawaii at 22 to join a brother who resided there.

Now 30, a big, burly man compared to his confreres, and with many contacts among the Americans, Makino ran a drug store. He had a keen interest in law, and over the drug store he had a "law office," for his bilingualism made demands on his time as an intermediary between the Japanese and the American courts—though he was not, in the modern sense, a lawyer.

The prosaic tasks of running a drug store and "law office" must have weighed heavily on one of Makino's adventurous spirit. Where Sheba, by his own admission, was incapable of carrying out dangerous tasks, Makino thrived on such assignments. Vigorous, dynamic, articulate, iron-jawed and imposing in carriage, Makino found in the higher wage movement a vehicle to challenge and evoke his potentialities.

The behavior of Sheba, however, frustrated all efforts to achieve harmony and unity, and the meeting dispersed. Thereafter, the *Shimpo* was to devote itself wholeheartedly to attempting to frustrate the higher wage movement, and in its wake, oscillating occasionally in the stormy seas but always returning to course through the exhortations of Sheba, followed Tsurushima.

Despite the opposition of Sheba and Tsurushima, the movement gathered momentum. On a motion made by Negoro on December 1, 1908, at a meeting at the Japanese YMCA, attended by 42 persons, with Makino as chairman, the Higher Wage Association was formed.

Ishii was made president; Makino, vice-president; Negoro, secretary; and Matsutaro Yamashiro, treasurer. Makino declared that they must proceed in the spirit of old Japan—"Yamato damashii . . . the spirit that drives everybody away, no matter who the contestants may be." Tasaka, as a representative of the *Nippu,* the organ through which the "spirit of old Japan" was to be given voice, said, "We must do our best, and in order to accomplish that purpose we must stick together."

Ishii was soon to withdraw, and Makino moved up to fill the office of president while the other offices remained unchanged. And the Yamashiro Hotel, on Beretania Street, across from Aala Park, became the unofficial headquarters of the organization.

. . .

Soga, though he had no official connection with the organization, Makino, Tasaka, and Negoro, the Big Four of the movement, held almost daily meetings at the hotel. From this hub, lines of communication radiated to the farthest perimeter of the islands and reached all plantations. On the plantations autonomous higher wage associations sprang up, and these associations turned to the Big Four for guidance.

Makino and Negoro, kept busy with speaking engagements, hired an automobile and roared about the countryside in it to plantation after plantation, where they harangued the laborers who gathered in worshipful thousands to hear them. The *Nippu*'s circulation soared, and that of the *Shimpo* and the *Nichi Nichi* fell off correspondingly.

The Planters became alarmed. Even Governor Walter F. Frear began to take cognizance of the situation in correspondence with his superior, the Secretary of the Interior.

The American press directed streams of ridicule and abuse at the Big Four. And Sheba, fallen into such opprobrium with his countrymen that they would not accept delivery of his paper, his employees deserting him, found a new way to serve his American masters. His bilingualism and lack of scruples made him an ideal spy in the Japanese camp.

Since Sheba could no longer catch the ears of the Japanese, English became his medium. He ceaselessly denounced the Association. His biased translations of the contents of the *Nippu* began to be published in the American press. Through this activity, the name of Sheba acquired an unprecedented celebrity, and he became known far and wide as the lackey of the Planters and the enemy of the Japanese.

The Association made representations to the Planters, and though some among the Planters thought the requests reasonable and favored granting them in whole or in part, the majority was opposed. The majority ruled. With a facade of unanimity that was never to crack, the Planters peremptorily denied the requests.

The Association decided that equal wages and equal quarters and treatment could only be obtained through a strike. They formed a strike fund and ordered provisions for the anticipated siege. They also sought about for a suitable attorney to represent them in any litigation that might arise in connection with the strike.

The task of finding an attorney was not easy. Most of the ablest attorneys had prohibitive price tags for services to a cause that would bring them into community disfavor. Moreover, most were in some way connected with the Planters.

Finally the Association had the good fortune to engage Joseph Lightfoot, who undertook all defense in connection with the proposed strike excepting that involving violence on the part of the proposed strikers. It was hoped, of course, that there would be no violence.

The Japanese laborers, Soga says, "were repeatedly made aware that they should observe all laws and completely refrain from violent and riotous acts. We feared that if we had any unlawful point the planters would immediately exploit it. . . . We went about exhorting them that once violence was practiced the laborers would be routed."

The laborers were even instructed that during the duration of the strike they must not drink alcohol, lest such beverages lead them into intemperate or unlawful acts. They were also instructed that the leaders of the Association would assist in prosecuting them for any unlawful act.

The strategy of the Association was to have the laborers on Oahu bear the brunt of the conflict by striking, those on the other islands continuing to work but to donate money to the strikers. House servants on the plantations were also supposed to strike, with servants off the premises continuing to work and contribute to the support of the strikers through donations. It was felt that here was an issue that should appeal to the patriotism of all Japanese, and all Japanese were supposed to contribute directly or indirectly. The Japanese struck at Aiea and were ordered from the plantation, the Planters rightfully believing the power of eviction to be a potent weapon, and with it they proceeded to belabor the Japanese unmercifully.

At Waipahu Plantation, near Honolulu, Masso Haneda, a man of about 23, mobilized the strikers before evacuation, "and cleaned the camp inside and out, not leaving a speck of rubbish. At the time of departing, he especially invited the plantation manager, and, as the representative of all, he expressed his thanks for the kindness shown during the stay at the plantation. With the band leading, they made a grand parade, and quietly left the plantation."

This was a brave gesture on the part of a people turned out on the roads with their families, without money, shelter, or prospect of employment. Even Soga, from whom the above quotation is taken, concedes that this gesture may have seemed theatrical. Nevertheless, it seems to characterize the perfect courtesy of the Japanese towards their opponents, and the strikers' scrupulous observance of law and order.

As plantation after plantation struck, the thousands of strikers moved to places assigned them, most of them travelling by foot, and those from far-away Kahuku spending a night on the road. The largest contingent of strikers straggled into Honolulu where they were quartered in several places around town. The largest concentration of strikers was in the Aala district, where huge tents had been erected and volunteer women had tucked up their sleeves and fallen to to feed and care for the evicted.

"But most of the strikers," says Soga, "had families, and there were many small children. And among them were some pitiable persons with sick persons in their care. Their plight seemed wretched in the extreme."

Baffled by the strikers' decorum, the Planters concentrated on recruiting the strikebreakers. They paid the strikebreakers $1.50 a day plus transportation—not only far more than the 69 cents a day they had paid the Japanese, but far more than what the Japanese were asking.

The daily Pacific Commercial Advertiser, whose owner held sugar stock and had been a key figure in the overthrow of the monarchy, gave the legal definition of riot, in the presumably wistful hope that some part of the act could be used against the Japanese.

It was obvious, however, that hiring strikebreakers, some of whom earned their pay by sleeping in the cane fields, though a sound psychological weapon, was not a permanent solution. Something stronger must be used to bring the Japanese to heel. And gradually, the direction pointed by the tenacious Sheba, the Planters seemed to form a notion for appropriate strategy against the strikers.

It was impossible to find any fault with the strikers' dealing with the non-Japanese. But there were a handful of Japanese "sycophants," of whom Sheba was the chief, who did not sympathize with the movement. Against Sheba and his fellow "sycophants" the strikers felt such hatred that it showed. The Planters who, without a qualm, had, for decades, treated the thousands of Japanese laborers worse than animals now began to manifest the most touching solicitude for the "sycophants."

The April 19, 1909, issue of the *Nippu* warns against violence, so does that of April 24th and May 10th. The May 10th issue also draws attention to a sign before the Aiea strike headquarters, which reads, "Do no act of violence. This is a model strike. Be united, obey the words of your committee, and never act with carelessness or violence."

Makino and Negoro, speaking at Aiea, had exhorted the strikers against violence. They had warned that anyone engaging in violence would be excluded by the Japanese.

Nevertheless, Sheba was sure that the Association wanted violence. He asked for police protection and received it, as well as a ten thousand dollar life insurance policy paid for by the Planters. The Planters took another great stride towards protecting the "sycophants" when they succeeded in having the Planters' law firm—perhaps the most able firm of lawyers in Hawaii—Kinney, Ballou, Prosser, and Anderson, made deputies of the Hawaiian government to assist in prosecuting cases arising out of the strike.

Provocative incidents were hard to come by, but the Planters could be depended upon to make the most of such windfalls as came their way. On May 26th an incident occurred that must have seemed to the beleaguered Planters as almost too good to be true.

The *Advertiser* headlined the incident: How A Loyal Laborer Was Mobbed By Thugs. "The injured man . . . Tsuchiya Giichi, was badly handled by four thugs, who broke his arm, made ugly bruises on his back and just over his kidney, damaged his face and lamed his legs. . . ."

As a result of this incident, 21 Japanese were arrested and detained without warrants.

As soon as Makino learned of the attack he wrote a letter to William P. Jarrett, Sheriff of the City and County of Honolulu, deploring the incident, expressing sorrow for it, insisting the Association would never countenance such things, and offering whatever assistance it was in his power to give to bring the culprits to book.

The sheriff's office, of course, like every government agency, was quite under the Planters' thumb. The letter was made public amidst journalistic cries of derision. For the Planters had now come up with strategy to fit the situation: an act of violence by any of the striking Japanese could be attributed to inflammatory articles in the *Nippu* and the counsel of the Association officers; consequently, those responsible could be held accountable. Therefore, Makino was a coward seeking to escape just punishment for his acts. Among other uncomplimentary things, he was to be likened to a "rat, showing his teeth, but seeking a hole in which to hide." And his colleagues were described in terms no less derogatory.

The Planters finally seemed to have forged a lethal weapon, and they probably chafed at not being able to put it to the test immediately. But prudence evidently counselled that they seek more evidence to link the assault with the editorial content of the *Nippu* and the speeches of the Association leaders.

Since the strike had now become Hawaii's foremost issue, with the American press devoting reams of space to attacks on the "thugs and agitators" considered responsible, the U.S. Attorney General may have felt he might be considered derelict in his duty if he did not invoke his powers to help chastise the offenders. Accordingly, he had one Uchiyama, a minor Association functionary, arrested for violating the postal regulations by returning some copies of the *Shimpo* through the mails after marking them "Planters' Dog Sheba." For by the name "Planters' Dog" had Sheba become popularly known among his countrymen.

The U.S. Attorney General also discovered that the Japanese newspapers sometimes contain what, by the American standards of that day, could be construed as obscene material. He easily made the front pages and earned editorial encomiums by making some arrests on this score—his victims, by curious chance, always from the side opposing the Planters.

K. Yokogawa, editor of the *Maui Shimbun* and president of the Maui Strikers Aid Association, was arrested three times on such a charge. The arrest of Yokogawa, though in a way that neither he nor the U.S. Attorney could envision, was to dramatically affect the course of the strike.

At the time, however, the arrest of Yokogawa, though strategically sound as a means of shutting off the flow of information to the strike sympathizers, must have seemed a minor skirmishing action to the Planters. They were looking for important things and soon found them at Waipahu.

The strikebreakers not being equal to the task of caring for the cane, the cane was drying. Fearing that some incendiary might throw a torch into the parched cane, the Planters had armed men patrolling these areas, and, it was said, any striker seen entering a field was to be shot. The police were also supposed to serve as escorts to any Japanese who might choose to return to work.

Since it was inconceivable to the strikers that any self-respecting Japanese could choose to work on the Planters' terms, the sight of a Japanese proceeding to the fields between two armed men raised the suspicion that the man was going to work under duress. And on June 9th something occurred to evoke such a suspicion.

Two policemen, one, Wills, a regular; and one, Scoville, the head pumping engineer of Waipahu, who had been deputized, were seen escorting a Japanese down the main street of the plantation town of Waipahu. Ignorant of what was happening outside, Makino was addressing a group in the Togo Theater. Perhaps because of his presence, there were many Japanese in the area, along the route the two policemen were proceeding.

According to Negoro, a striker, Jotaro Mikawa, approached the escorted man and asked if he were returning to work voluntarily. Scoville and Wills give a different account. Scoville claimed that Mikawa tried to beat the escorted man and was, consequently, placed under arrest.

A crowd gathered. The police drew their guns. Scoville, a truculent man, fired into the air.

Holding on to their prisoner, the police then backed into a room which was the headquarters of the local Association. "Once inside," according to the *Advertiser,* "they closed the door, barred it, and shouted that they would shoot the first man who attempted to force an entrance."

The *Advertiser* headlined the story: Officers With Drawn Revolvers Hold Angry Mob At Bay In Waipahu.

In addition to Mikawa, charged with riot, although under arrest all the time the alleged "riot" was being carried on, about 30 Japanese were arrested, without warrants, and lodged in Oahu Jail.

The Planters' ace attorney, William Ansel Kinney, now felt he was in a position to find some connection between the *Nippu* and the Association officers and the assault on Tsuchiya and the "riot" at Waipahu.

. . .

Sheba had translated the *Nippu*'s editorials calling for the "extermination" *(bokumetsu)* of "sycophants" *(okintama men),* and the translations had been widely circulated. Sheba had solemnly asserted that plans for his assassination reposed in Soga's safe at the *Nippu*. Getting such evidence legally might not be easy, but in the service of the all powerful Planters it might not be necessary to be overly punctilious about legality.

The afternoon of June 10th seemed especially propitious for Kinney's project because Governor Frear, who might have had qualms about the matter, was absent from Oahu, visiting another island. William Henry, High Sheriff of the Territory of Hawaii, and Chester Doyle, for years a police official and Japanese interpreter for the courts, were, accordingly, given the assignment of arresting—without warrants!—the leaders of the Association and the staff of the Nippu.

. . .

They, and their fellow officers, called first at Makino's drug store, where the employees denied that Makino was present. One employee went to the phone and spoke into it in Japanese, and Doyle, in derby and high collar, the image of the old, small-time, police official, listened closely. From the conversation, Doyle learned the whereabouts of Makino, went there, found him with Negoro, and arrested both.

The police then went to the *Nippu* and arrested Soga and some of his staff, including Katsuichi Kawamoto, Shinichi Ihara, Yasayuki Imai, Hidekichi Takemura, and Tsurumatsu Okumura.

The unfortunate Tsurumatsu Okumura had an older brother, a Christian minister, the Rev. Takei Okumura, who must soon have been informed of these happenings. The Rev. Okumura, however, is not an important figure in the happenings of this day, though later an important role in the drama was to be assigned him.

After the raid on the *Nippu,* word of the arrests had circulated through town. When the police reached the Yamashiro Hotel, a sullen crowd had gathered.

The police began a search of the premises, found Yamashiro in a closet and dragged him out. They paraded him before the unappreciative crowd outside, Yamashiro's pudgy frame and round face taut with anger and defiance, while Doyle, in gentle self-congratulation at this exhibition of his prowess, grinned genially beneath his walrus mustache.

The day's work, however, was far from done. That night, at Oahu Jail, Henry and Doyle approached Makino with a scheme they had for getting the evidence they believed reposed in his safe. Makino refused to cooperate.

Far from being deterred, they and their husky confederates went to the Makino drug store and "law office," broke in, dragged out the safe and carted it off on a wagon. Later they opened the safe with a cold chisel.

It was now about midnight, and the party split up for the labors which awaited them. The group headed by Henry and Doyle went to the Miyake Ice Cream Parlor, on Fort Street, and went straight to the room of Negoro, in the north corner of the second floor. Negoro, of course, with his colleagues, was still in jail, and the door of his room was locked.

Doyle broke down the door. He and Henry entered and searched the room. They gathered up one or two books and a manuscript and shoved these into a pillow case, which they appropriated.

As they were leaving, Mrs. Miyake confronted them and charged them with the crime of breaking in and searching her home. They shouted her down. "Later she broke down and wept as if she had lost her mind."

The police officials, their blood up, and in full cry, swooped down on the Yamashiro Hotel, where they seized a diary, record book, and letters. They struck at the Waipahu Association headquarters in order to seize copies of the *Oahu Jiho,* a mimeographed sheet put out by Editor Akira Mitsunaga, of the Waipahu Association, and any other printed matter that might come to hand.

Soga was taken from the cell, where he had been held incommunicado and in partial ignorance of the other prisoners who had been arrested in connection with charges to be made against the Association, and marched to the jail yard. There Kinney and Prosser confronted him and told him the prosecution required him to open the safe of the *Nippu* and give up the books and papers of the *Nippu.* The prosecution had been informed that only Soga knew the combination. Soga objected. He was then told by Henry that if he did not open the safe it would be blown open.

Soga was then conducted to the second floor of the *Nippu,* where stood the safe. Drawing attention to the duress under which he acted, Soga opened the safe.

The police gathered up what they wanted and took Soga back to jail. Thus, healthily tired from their orgy of housebreaking and burglary, the police concluded the activities of the night.

When he learned of the plight of his clients, Attorney Lightfoot petitioned for a writ of habeas corpus. And though June 11th was a Sunday, argument was heard in the court of Judge Whitney.

. . .

At 10 o'clock, when the prisoners were brought to court in the patrol wagon, a delegation of several hundred strikers were waiting to cheer them. Each time the prisoners reappeared, at noon, at 2 o'clock, the crowd grew, the demonstrations of approval were greater. *"Banzai,"* some one would cry, and 1,500 voices, in a great roar, would repeat the cheer.

In order to avoid the sympathizers, at 5 o'clock, when court adjourned for the day, the prisoners were taken out the little used southern entrance. The move had been anticipated. The strikers were there.

"Banzai," the strikers shouted, *"Banzai! Banzai!"*

"It sounded," said Negoro, "as if heaven and earth would shatter."

The authorities hastened the prisoners into the patrol wagon and put the horses to the gallop. As they departed in this unseemly haste, the *banzai*s seemed to carry a note of derision for the faint-hearted police officers. And when Kinney appeared the strikers jeered at him.

Sheriff Henry, intimidated by this fanatic devotion, and thinking one such experience more than sufficient, caused placards to be printed in Japanese and displayed in various places about Honolulu, advising the strikers that they must not gather in large groups. Hereafter, they were informed, only 40 representatives of the strikers might attend the hearings.

There followed then a game by which the authorities tried to shut down the *Nippu* and break the strike by arresting the leaders on charge after charge. Makino, Negoro, Tasaka, Soga, Kawamura, Mitsunaga, Shigeta, and Hamada were released and immediately rearrested on a charge of conspiring to murder Sheba. Arrested for rioting at Waipahu and holding prisoner a uniformed police officer were Fushino, Mitsunaga, Takayama, Kawakami, Miyauchi, Morita, Kawamura, Toromatsu, Miyoi, Higashi, and Nagata.

When released on bond, the leaders were rearrested on new charges, again and again, in proportion, evidently, to what the authorities considered their importance. Soga, being considered the brains of the strike, and whom, consequently, it was most necessary to immobilize, was complimented with the most charges: ten altogether.

. . .

Finally, before a jury of aborigines, aborigine-Caucasian, and Caucasians, the Big Four were brought to trial. The charge was Conspiracy—that is, conspiring to impoverish the flourishing plantations by intimidating the Japanese from working on them.

Sheba was put on the stand and testified that the defendants had put his life in danger, and that he was confident that it was the aim of the defendants to do bodily harm to him. Terada, manager of the *Shimpo,* testified that the play presented at the Honolulu Theater on January 15th had been written by Negoro—Henry and Doyle had found an outline of it in Negoro's handwriting when they had raided Negoro's room—that he, Terada, had heard Negoro drilling the actors, that the play had greatly excited the audience, which had cried, "Sheba, Sheba! Kill him! Fix him!"

Next came Prof. Walter Dening, a 30-year resident of Japan brought to Hawaii by the government for a fee of $2,000, plus expenses, to testify as an expert translator.

Dening had proven his devotion to the Planters' cause, almost as soon as landing, by going to Waipahu and exhorting the strikers there to return to work. Later he was to bitterly denounce the Association leaders in the newspaper. An old man, steeped in the traditions of feudal Japan, obviously disturbed by the way the Japanese peasants of Hawaii were absorbing notions that they were as good as their betters, he proceeded to do his best to restore order.

To show that the defendants had incited violence, the prosecution had introduced as exhibits numerous translations from the *Nippu* of editorials, and of letters to the defendants. Some of these letters had been printed, after inflammatory lines had been deleted by blue-penciling. The printed letters, along with the deleted portions, were admitted as evidence. Furthermore, the unpublished letters to the defendants were admitted as evidence.

Sheba had testified that "Zokyu Kisei Kai" (Higher Wage Association) suggested violence. Dening disagreed. Nevertheless, he seemed conscious of his inferiority to Sheba as a linguist and manifested a reluctance to be drawn into a controversy over the meaning of words that might result in having that inferiority drawn to the attention of the court. Dening seemed content to testify along the same lines as Sheba.

Dening testified that Sheba had correctly translated the word *okintama* as "sycophant," but that the Japanese term was obscene and that he had never heard it until he came to Hawaii. He could not—Horrors, no!—translate its literal meaning. He translated *hikokumin* as "traitor," *taiji* as "get rid of," *bokumetsu* as "destroy," *tettsui wo kudasan* as to "swing an iron hammer," and all these meanings he implied suggested violent designs on Sheba and the other "sycophants."

Negoro, who had been lolling in his chair, tilted back against the wall, took the stand for the defense. He testified that the Higher Wage Association had always cautioned against violence. But occasionally he let his tongue run away with him.

"It is a credit to Mr. Sheba," said Negoro, "that he has consistently opposed the higher wage movement in the face of overwhelming opposition, for he is the only Japanese who is not in favor of the movement. He is a brave man, a man of courage."

As Negoro spoke, Sheba was entering a situation that would put his courage to the test.

The cracks in the strike situation had become too great to be ignored, even by the most sanguine. The Planters had succeeded in getting an injunction against the Association, and some of the strikers, including the Big Four, had been charged with contempt for allegedly violating it. Funds were almost exhausted. Strikers were drifting back to the plantations—not actually to work but they seemed to be eager to be in the vicinity when work became available. The delegates of the Association had been summoned from the outside islands for a conference.

Among the delegates was a dapper, smiling young man from the Island of Maui, named Tomekichi Mori. Mori had once been employed in Makino's store. And when he was a schoolboy there, five years before, he sometimes saw Sheba in the establishment. Sheba, of course, who did not condescend to give his time to a mere schoolboy, took little notice of Mori, but Mori never forgot Sheba. On Maui, Mori had earned a reputation as a law-abiding person and was employed as interpreter in the Circuit Court at Wailuku.

Mori was the devoted friend of the unfortunate K. Yokogawa, editor of the *Maui Shimbun,* who languished in jail on three charges of sending obscene material through the mails. Twice Mori had succeeded in raising bond to get his friend out of jail, the third time he had failed. All available money seemed to be taken up in keeping the strikers and their leaders out of jail. No one seemed ready to come forward with money for Yokogawa, who was from another island.

Mori had come to Honolulu partly as a delegate to the Association conference, and partly to try to raise money for his friend. The matter of the bond seemed uppermost in his mind just then, and he had come round to believing that Sheba, who had close relations with the U.S. Attorney, was blocking Yokogawa's chance of freedom.

This morning, Mori had bought a pocket knife. Finding the sharp blade not sharp enough to suit him, he had taken it to the knife grinding and sharpening shop of George Washington Lincoln, where Mr. Lincoln, for ten cents, gave the blade a razorlike edge.

Mori was standing outside the U.S. District Court, the knife in his pocket, beneath his coattails, when he saw Sheba emerge from the building. Instantly his attention became fixed on Sheba.

Earlier, Sheba had gone to the courtroom where the Conspiracy Case was being heard. He had been excluded, on a motion of Lightfoot's, on the ground that he might be called as a rebuttal witness.

Since he had expected to spend the day in court, Sheba was without his bodyguard and unarmed. But after being excluded from the courtroom, Sheba went to the nearby office of the U.S. Attorney General.

Finishing his business in the U.S. Attorney General's office, Sheba left the building and set out in the direction of his own office. Mori followed.

Sheba proceeded down King Street toward the business district. They had passed Nuuanu when Sheba heard his name called and turned to see Mori.

Mori approached Sheba and said in Japanese, "You are no good."

"What's the matter?"

"You're not doing good for the country."

Sheba was accustomed to insults. He turned away with a sneer, and the two walked along together, Mori on the side towards the road.

They turned into Smith Street and walked a few paces toward the mountains. Mori said, "Why do you oppose bond for Yokogawa?"

Over the space of more than half-a-century we can visualize the scene in the moment before crisis. Nearby, J. S. McCandless, foreman of the Tom Sharp Sign Store, was up on a ladder painting a "Bull Durham" sign on the side of a house. Approaching was Erling E. Mahlum, manager of C. B. Hofgaard and Company's store in Waimea Island of Kauai, and acquaintance of Sheba's.

We can imagine Sheba, his fortune at the flood, the reputation of his enemies torn to tatters by the American press, the cause to which they had given themselves crumbling, the men they had led broken in purse and spirit, their staunchest allies harassed and jailed by the authorities, they, themselves, in court at this moment, fighting desperately, against great odds, for their freedom.

And Sheba, in contrast, is lauded by the American press, he is the confidant, the adviser of the rich and powerful. Never had Sheba's future been seen in such rosy colors. And now this Mori—this country bumpkin whose friends are not powerful Americans, but broken, impotent Japanese—this Mori questions why Sheba does a thing!

Sheba gives a patronizing laugh. "You are too young to understand such things."

We see Mori take a step backward, as he might have recoiled from a venomous serpent. "You are a traitor to your people."

They face each other in the bright sunshine of the Hawaiian morning—Sheba, worldly, cultivated, mature, sneering at his gauche companion. We see Mori, white with rage, taut as a drawn bowstring, his hands under his coattails as he fumbles to open his knife.

Then Mori's fist goes up, and the sunlight glints on the open blade of his knife. "Traitor, I'll punish you!" And he lunges for Sheba's throat.

In the courtroom Negoro is still on the stand. His spirits, and those of his co-defendants, are beginning to rise as they feel they have begun to score against the prosecution. Kinney is called to the phone. He returns, white-faced, and whispers to the judge. The judge's mouth falls open, and he turns to stare, aghast, at the defendants.

The judge announces that court is adjourned for the day. The defendants are told that an assassin has seriously wounded Sheba.

As the defendants went outside the newsboys were already hawking extras about the attempted assassination. "And I felt," said Soga, "that the passersby who glanced at us had a strange glint in their eyes."

What a field day was this for the American press! With what gusto did they serve up this piece of fare for their readers! The papers went into the attempted assassination in great detail.

"Higher Wage Fanatic Attacks and Stabs Editor of *Shimpo,*" screamed the *Advertiser.*

When Mori had lunged at Sheba's throat, the blade, though coming perilously close to the jugular vein and carotoid artery, missed them, opening a gash a half inch deep. Mori had swung again, the blade going through the scalp to the skull and opening a wound an inch-and-a-half in length, the blade-point breaking. Sheba had then grappled with the assailant and Mori had inflicted two cuts on Sheba's left arm.

Sheba had pinned Mori to the ground, the young man's arms spread out so that he could not wield the knife. And as they had wrestled there, Sheba feeling his life's blood, with which both he and Mori were drenched, draining away, the editor had lifted his head beseechingly, and his gaze had fallen on Erling E. Mahlum, an American of the class for whom Sheba had sold himself.

Mahlum stood watching the two combatants.

Sheba cried, "Come and help me! Come and help me!"

Mahlum did not move.

Sheba mustered his ebbing strength. "Come and help me! Come and help me!"

"How can I help you?" said Mahlum.

J. S. McCandless, the sign painter, heard Sheba's cry, and responded in different fashion. He slid down the ladder on which he had been perched, seized Mori's knife hand and commanded him to drop the weapon. Mori obeyed.

Sheba saw the brother of U.S. Attorney Breckons in the street, and begged him, "Take me to a doctor—any doctor. I'm losing too much blood."

Instead Mr. Breckons took the two to the police station. And it was this bungling that had posed the greatest threat to Sheba's life, for he had lost a great deal of blood, though his wounds were superficial, by the time he was finally taken to the hospital. He was hospitalized about ten days, but made a complete recovery.

If anything had been needed to deliver the *coup de grace* to the higher wage movement, it had been supplied by Mori, who, in trying to punish treason, had betrayed his countrymen into the hands of their enemies. The Conspiracy defendants were thoroughly disheartened. For though the jury would be officially instructed to disregard the attack, unofficially they would not be permitted to do so.

That night, August 5th, the delegates to the convention passed a resolution urging the strikers to return to work: the Planters had gained their objective.

Though the delegates recognized defeat, they did not permit the defeat to degenerate into a rout. At the Higher Wage Headquarters, an employment office was set up. Delegates agreed to seek work for those wishing to transfer to other islands, and to have the prospective employer furnish travelling expenses. The Association, itself, was to attempt to help with such travelling expenses through another anticipated donation.

The Conspiracy trial was to drag on for 21 days. Soga was called to the stand by the defense. And though Soga qualified as an expert translator, he chose to speak through an interpreter—perhaps he thought that hearing the question in two languages gave him valuable time to formulate his answers. Small, soft-voiced, grave, imperturbable, deliberate, he testified that he had no official connection with the Association.

"Is it not true," said Kinney, "that you have published everything without thought and with criminal recklessness?"

"I just wrote the facts. I don't think it was criminal recklessness."

Soga denied, and the authors feel his denial is valid, that the words from the *Nippu* singled out by the prosecution as urging violence were not meant to be used in a literal sense. Lightfoot was to point out that such figurative meanings are not peculiar to the Japanese language.

Said Lightfoot, "We saw the statements made by prize fighters the other day. Cordell [one of the fighters] said, 'I'm going to take the scalp of Dick Sullivan [his opponent] to San Francisco on my belt. . . .'

"Mr. Kinney said the other day, 'I'm going to nail Mr. Negoro to the cross.' "

But the jury of eleven men—one had been driven from the court in disgrace for twice appearing too drunk to serve—had sitting with them the specter of the assault on Sheba, which Kinney's innuendoes did not permit them to forget. They listened to the arguments of Kinney, who pleaded the cause of Americans like themselves.

"Gentlemen," Kinney addressed the jury, "a plan that contemplates getting 70,000 men in line means something greater than the strike. They [the defendants] were going to do more than raise wages. They were going to dominate the commercial life of the country. And they wanted every man in line. Whatever the plan was, it required a solid Japanese front before they moved—they were an army. . . .

"They figured there was a Japanese spirit, but they didn't know there was an American spirit."

In an address lasting five hours, Lightfoot ridiculed the translations the prosecution had introduced, said the Higher Wage Associations of the plantations were not responsible to the Honolulu Association and that, consequently, the defendants could not be found guilty of crimes with which they had no connection. He said that Sheba was a "sycophant," a "sneak" who richly deserved all the contempt and aversion the Japanese felt for him. Lightfoot defended the right of the Japanese to organize.

"Why shouldn't we combine together, as the Planters combine?"

His wit, his eloquence, his logic fell on deaf ears. The assault on Sheba interposed itself between Lightfoot and the men in the jury box. And the jurors could not bridge the gulf of nationality, language, culture, and citizenship that separated them from the defendants. The jurors did listen when Kinney spoke in rebuttal.

"This situation," said Kinney, "is not going to be cured by turning over $2,500,000 a year to the Japanese, but by sending out of the country every year 5,000 of them."

After deliberating for six hours, the jury brought in a verdict of guilty in the third degree. The defendants were sentenced to 10 months in jail and $300 fine each. Lightfoot appealed to the Territorial Supreme Court, and the Supreme Court ruled against him. The defendants were committed to jail on March 10, 1910.

. . .

While the Big Four languished in jail, there came to their assistance . . . Rev. Takei Okumura. Calligrapher, author, founder of a home for orphans and the first Japanese language school on Oahu, renowned for his good works among the Japanese among whom he had tremendous prestige, he also, by virtue of his Christian ministry, had the ear of a number of influential Americans. Untrained in law, he knew human nature and the seat of real power in Hawaii. He worked to get a pardon for the Big Four.

A number of Americans sympathized with the efforts of Rev. Okumura and gave their assistance. But there seemed to be one American whose approval was vital to the project: Joseph Platt Cooke, President of Sugar Factors Co., Ltd., and director of the Hawaiian Sugar Planters Association. Rev. Okumura went to Cooke and persuaded him that the Big Four should be granted a special pardon. And lo and behold, through the softening of Mr. Cooke's heart the Big Four were transformed from loathsome pariahs to innocent lambs.

The acting governor, confronted with a petition bearing the signature of Joseph Platt Cooke, readily signed the pardon. The Big Four were released from jail on Independence Day, July 4th.

Mori had been found guilty of the assault on Sheba and sentenced to five years and $1,000 fine. He was released after two years on condition he return to Japan.

The defendants in the contempt case were found not guilty. The riot charges brought against those at Waipahu twice resulted in a hung jury and then, in accordance with Hawaiian law, the charges were dismissed. A charge against Soga as a disorderly person was withdrawn, ostensibly so Prof. Dening, who had been subpoenaed by the defense as a witness, could return to Japan immediately after the Conspiracy trial. Soga paid a fine of $100 on the charge of sending obscene material through the mail. And so it went. The strike was over now and the attention of the government, and the public, was on other things.

The Japanese, themselves, had had time to take stock of what they had gained or lost by the cold, hunger, sickness, privation, idleness and humiliation they had suffered. What had they gained by their rebellion against the oppression of the Planters? They had gained respect.

The time when the Nikkei would gain full equality was still far off. But a bridgehead had been won. The Japanese had insisted that they were equal to other nationalities, and the Planters had spent two million dollars to prove them wrong. But now came time for sober reflection. If the Japanese felt so strongly about the matter of equality, if the situation were not corrected might not these proud people make trouble again?

The Planters began replacing the "pig sty" quarters with better dwellings. Within three months of the end of the strike, the Planters proclaimed that, thereafter, pay would be proportionate to individual ability, without regard to nationality.

Thus were the principal objectives of the strike achieved.

1921 Campaign

TAKIE AND UMETARO OKUMURA

IN our 1921 campaign, we emphasized, in simplest and clearest ways, two ideas which we believe will serve to dispel the mistaken ideas of the Japanese:

(a) Forget the idea "Japanese" and always think and act from the point of view of the American people, as long as you live under the protection of America, and enjoy many privileges and blessings.

(b) Inasmuch as your children were born in Hawaii, and expect to live here permanently and work shoulder to shoulder with the American people, you should educate and build them up into good and loyal American citizens. If you dislike your children to live and work in Hawaii, if you prefer them to be educated into Japanese, you should send them back immediately to Japan and have them educated in that country, for when they grow up, they will become not assets but liabilities.

In our speeches to the Hawaiian-born Japanese on the plantations we have emphasized their opportunities for service and their duties to the plantations and Hawaii.

From January 7th to 11th, Takie Okumura went alone to Kauai,

In *Hawaii's American-Japanese Problems. A Campaign to Remove Causes of Friction Between the American People and Japanese. Report of the Campaign, January, 1921, to January, 1927* (Honolulu: published privately, 1927), pp. 9–12. Reprinted by permission of the family of Takie and Umetaro Okumura.

made a careful survey of the field, and prepared for the launching of the campaign. On January 27th we went back to Kauai, and finally started the campaign, beginning at Lihue. We met Manager Moler and secured from him a list of about 15 representative Japanese laborers in different camps. We called on every one of these men, exchanged our views, and enlisted their support. But we discovered that this method of campaign would require so many days, and that we would not be able to cover the definite number of plantations in a limited period of time. After three days at Lihue, we changed our tactics, and requested each plantation manager to pick a certain number of good, reliable Japanese on his plantation and have these men meet us in a quiet, face-to-face conference. This plan proved to be the best one, and we kept it up right through the first campaign.

We were amazed by the great changes which are taking place among the Japanese, particularly in their ideas. About ten years ago the ideas which we have emphasized in the first campaign would have been attacked and ridiculed as ideas of "betrayer," or "traitor." But today it is entirely different. When we approached the Japanese with these ideas, we found them very receptive and keenly interested in our campaign. Many were hitherto unable to express themselves in the open for fear of being branded "traitor" to Japan and Japanese. They were eagerly waiting for some one to come out and lead them. Naturally when we told them the views of leaders in Japan, like Viscount Shibusawa and others, that Japanese in Hawaii can serve their country best by removing all causes of friction between the American people and Japanese, and by training whole-heartedly their children born in these islands into not half and half, but 100 percent American citizens, many Japanese pledged themselves to stand and work for the ideas we have urged them to follow.

Unlike the early immigrant days when laborers were seeking a fortune in get-rich-quick fashion, and hurriedly returning to their native country, many are today working on the plantations with a definite idea of settling in Hawaii permanently. The Japanese of Halaula camp just above Kealia, Kauai, are a good example. According to the statement of one headman, there are 53 Japanese families in that camp. With the exception of four families which returned to Japan, all the rest will make Hawaii their permanent home. He said, "We will see to it that our men live up to their resolution and build up themselves into desirable laborers." The gradual change of Japanese in their ideas is a most splendid thing not only for themselves and their children, but also for Hawaii.

With the exception of one plantation manager who declared: "Americanization work is no use, no good; a Jap should always be a Jap. Hawaiian-born Japs are no good. They're too weak. All they want is a soft-snap job. We don't want them," all the plantation managers assisted us, and gave us many valuable suggestions. We were impressed greatly by the frankness and readiness of plantation managers to do all that they can for the laborers. We believe in some cases too much has been done and no efforts were made to have the laborers realize that they must work in order to secure any reform or improvement. With the exception of a few plantations, living or working conditions on the whole are excellent. In reply to our questions men on the plantations have invariably declared: "We have no complaints to make. We are satisfied with the present conditions and are proud of our manager!" We believe that their utterances are sincere and they will surely come to show their appreciation in concrete manner.

To some of the plantation managers we made following requests:

(a) Efforts must be made to make the laborers feel "at home." In this connection we have very little to say since the plantations are speedily improving the living conditions. We urge, however, that plantations which have hitherto never attempted to do anything should immediately map out their programme of improvement, for improved living conditions is the best inducement to the laborers to work permanently. The feeling of "at home" cannot be roused among Japanese laborers by movies, volleyball, basketball, or games at the community house, because they do not have any interest, nor do they understand or care for them. A moderate house with particular care to the kitchen, like the plan of Manager Valentine of Olowalu will satisfy the laborers more than anything else. But it would not do for the plantations to give everything or too much and make the laborers too dependent. The laborers must be made to realize that they must work in order to secure what they desire.

(b) Support the Language Schools on Plantations. As long as the adult Japanese in large numbers exist, the Japanese language schools must be kept up on the plantation. If the Plantation Japanese Schools are removed or abolished, we would surely see Japanese laborers moving away to the plantations which maintain Japanese schools. It is well, therefore, that plantations help the parents secure a well-qualified teacher and have him conduct the school. On the plantation, the language school teacher is a big figure and the school is the central meeting place. Today more money is being contributed by parents to the school than to the Buddhist Temple or Shrine. Remove this institution and we would surely be forced to face the restlessness and constant shifting of Japanese laborers.

(c) Discourage Anti-Japanese Sentiment on Plantations. The constant nagging of Japanese must be discouraged on plantations, for anti-Japanese sentiment is the easiest thing that incites restlessness and discontent among simple-minded Japanese laborers. Once an impression is created in their mind that they cannot work in these Islands peacefully and contentedly, all idea of permanent settlement will disappear and many Japanese laborers will be forced to go away. In order to encourage their permanent settlement in Hawaii, anti-Japanese sentiment must be discouraged by plantations. . . .

The Japanese Language School: Is It a Help or a Hindrance to the Americanization of Hawaii's Young People?

YŌICHI HANAOKA

. . . The Japanese Language School of Hawaii, which has been in operation since 1896 to instruct Hawaii's young people of Japanese ancestry in their native tongue, is questioned, "Is it a help or a hindrance to their Americanization?"

. . .

The Japanese Language School of Hawaii provides the necessary and the only medium of communication between the parents and the child. The home is the unit organization of the nation. It is the home where the child first forms his language, and his personal conception of matters relating to government. The impression that he gets at home will influence him to a great extent in his life. Before the language school was established, there was a grievous misunderstanding in the home life of the Japanese laborer, between the child and the parents. What the child wished to say, the parents could not understand because of his queer mongrel dialect, and the parents found considerable difficulty in making the child understand their language. There was an unnecessary misunderstanding in the home before the language school saw the evil. It is easy to see what kind of a citizen a child with no language school training would make. No per-

In *The Friend,* v. 97 (1927), pp. 79–80. Reprinted by permission of the Hawaii Conference of the United Church of Christ.

son can be expected to make a good American citizen if he misunderstands his parents and disobeys them. If he cannot make a good citizen at home, he cannot make a good American citizen. The Japanese Language School is a great influence in Americanizing the child by affording the only medium of communication between the parents and the child at home and thereby eliminating all misunderstandings that tend to break up family relationship.

The language school serves as a home for pupils from the time they are dismissed from the public school till their parents arrive home from the field labor. Both father and mother quite generally engage in field labor. When the children return from the public school after the close of the session, they find nothing to do and truly, as exemplified in the saying that "an idle mind is the Devil's workshop," they fall into bad company. Without the proper parental care offered by the language school after the close of the public school session, it is evident that we would have the serious girl-and-boy problem to face. In this respect the language school is a great help in preventing the young people from going on the wrong path and becoming a problem to the community.

The moral and religious training that the language school imparts to the children is worthy of commendation and is an important step toward making them good American citizens. America today demands a high moral and deep religious character in its youthful manhood. The Japanese children outnumber the other nationalities in the islands, but the boys' and girls' industrial schools have few children of Japanese parentage.

The session of the Japanese language school does not interfere with the progress of the child at the public school. It is a fact that the English used by the Japanese children is better than that of the Hawaiian and Portuguese in the elementary schools, and it is also true of their scholastic standings.

There is no "hyphenated loyalty" on the part of the young people. The language school does not stamp the young people as obedient subjects of the Mikado. It teaches them to be loyal to that flag under which they are to serve and die. During the World War, when the fate of the conflict depended upon the valor and patriotism of many young men, hundreds of young Japanese joined the army to prove their patriotism to America. In schools, the Japanese children bought more liberally of War Savings Stamps than the others. The Japanese teachers took the lead in Liberty Bond and War Savings Stamps drives. It cannot be said that the language school which produces so good a citizen is un-American and a hindrance to the Americanization of Hawaii's young people.

. . .

The two great nations of the Pacific basin are Japan and America. The peace of the Pacific depends upon the cooperative spirit of the two nations. America, with the ideals of the West, and Japan, with the culture of the East, must demonstrate to the world that two great nations unlike politically, economically and socially, can live together in harmony and peace. To effect this great and noble task, it is imperative for Japan to understand the high ideals of the American people, and the American people to understand to a certain extent the customs and culture of the Japanese people.

Hawaii's young people of Japanese parentage are peculiarly destined to solve the problem of peace in the Pacific area, because they have the advantage of the American and the Japanese education. The key to the true friendship of Japan and America is in the hands of the young American citizens, who understand both the ideals of the West and the culture of the East, and to a great extent they will be looked upon to unlock the golden doors to the "federation of the world." The Japanese language trains the young people to accomplish this task in the future. Is it not an attempt to "reveal in all their fullness the profit and the joy of working together for the common good and the attainment of our high ideals, to create the desire to have a part in the inspiring task, to show the way by which each may do his part best?" Is it not Americanizing the young people of Hawaii by preparing them to develop the future policies of America?

. . .

The Japanese language school offers the best of the Japanese people to their own young people. It enables them to take their part in the great democracy and be as good citizens as the people of other races. It makes it possible for them to contribute as their share to the great melting pot of the races the best qualities of the Japanese people.

The Japanese language school is a vital part of the social and educational structure of the community, and its activities are as important as those of other organizations or institutions that function within the territory. It is an important part of the machinery by which Hawaii's young people are trained for good American citizenship.

Unity Essential

AN EDITORIAL

THEORETICALLY Clark Bill should not have passed both houses of the legislature. That it is unconstitutional and is a direct violation of the American-Japanese Treaty is shown clearly by the legal opinion of foremost lawyers.

But Clark Bill passed the lower and upper houses. There is a good reason. It is not only because of the intensive campaign but also because there were among the resident Japanese those who favored the Clark Bill.

Dr. Tasuku Harada, Rev. Okumura, Soga of *Nippu Jiji* and others openly declared that they are supporters of the Clark Bill. The attitude of the legislature naturally became: "so long as there are men who favor Clark Bill among the Japanese, it is perfectly lawful to pass the measure."

In such fashion the bill has passed the legislature and after the approval of the governor it will become a law.

The governor will surely approve Clark Bill, judging from the fact that he has sanctioned the school curtailment regulations.

The fate of Clark Bill will determine the life or death of the entire Japanese Schools. We would have to close up the schools, if an instruction prohibiting the attendance of pupils who have not completed the entire grades from next month comes out.

. . .

Men who believe in temporizing measures advocate a test case against the $1 a pupil per year tax. These people do not understand the main issue. The most important point in the Clark Bill is that it delegates to the Department of Education the power to abolish Japanese Language Schools. Therefore in our test case we must fight first against this clause and then against the tax provision. We must utilize the opportunity which comes to us immediately after the approval of the Clark Bill, and for the purpose of solving the school question fundamentally we must institute a test case against the entire Clark Bill, on the ground that it is unconstitutional and is a direct violation of the American-Japanese Treaty.

Four schools which have already instituted a test case and eight schools which have hitherto fought against the litigation should join hands, and strive for the solution of the problem unitedly.

If perchance the same case is contested separately, we would become a laughing stock of the community. Every Japanese should think of this point very seriously.

We can no longer consult Harada, Okumura or Soga for they have favored Clark Bill. We are in the same mess. We must unite and strive for the solution of the school problem. Unity is most essential. If unity comes, all the hard feelings which have hitherto existed, . . . will disappear.

Every Japanese must join hands and cooperate on the question of the rights of Japanese Schools.

The work of *Nippu Jiji* from now on will be to disunite the Japanese in Hawaii. It will carry on all sort of slanderous attacks and incite dissensions among the Japanese. If *Nippu Jiji* succeeds, it will be a greatest disgrace to the Japanese.

Absolute Unity! It is the only way of solving the school question fundamentally.

. . .

People in general recognize the need of Japanese Language Schools. For the parents to have their native language taught their children is a right guaranteed by the constitution.

We would compromise if the matter is tackled with the spirit of cooperation. But we see no reason of weeping into silence, when we are forced to accept the measure, which we can not approve. The provision of $1 a pupil per annum tax is too unreasonable.

In order to destroy the root of future trouble, we must map out a plan of solving the school question fundamentally. The writer has enough of the school question. He dislikes to be troubled by it any longer. He wants to see the question made a question of the Japanese in general, for he sees an absolute necessity of fundamental solution.

How solve fundamentally? This will require time. Then, in the interval, in order to make the solution easy, strive to destroy the root of the school question. The school authorities, for instance, should investigate the views of Americans and Japanese. If the revision of text books is necessary, give a radical revision. If the knowledge of English language is necessary for the teachers, see that the classes are formed, and the teachers encouraged to take lessons. If teachers must have adequate knowledge of American history, ideals and institutions, in order to teach the children of foreign parentage who are to become American citizens, Teachers' Association should hold lecture courses. There are many other ways of improving the school and teachers. Call in efficient teachers, cut down the hours of instruction, and give real training to the children. Then it will be of great benefit to both parents and children.

Chapter Five

The New Americans

THE call to order had been made at 10:30 A.M., with the Reverend Takie Okumura initiating the proceedings. The small audience of fourteen youthful Japanese American Nisei delegates were understandably excited and nervous, for many of these bright young men and women, barely out of their teens, were in Honolulu for the first time and city life promised a special glamour that their communities on Maui, Kauai, or the Big Island could not offer.

But even those conference delegates from Oahu were eager on that August morning in 1927, for the coming six days of meetings, speeches, and roundtable discussions had an unparalleled importance. The Governor of Hawaii, Wallace Farrington; the Mayor of Honolulu, Charles Arnold; President of the University of Hawaii, David L. Crawford; former Governor of the Islands, Walter Frear; President of Kamehameha Schools, Frank Midkiff; economic magnate Walter Dillingham—all were scheduled to address the group, to extoll the virtues of American life and institutions and the benefits of the Hawaiian plantation system. Most of the delegates would be so close to the core of Hawaiian power for the first time.

This group of Nisei delegates, under the leadership of Reverend Okumura and his son Umetaro, called themselves the New Americans. Born of Japanese immigrant parents, they had gathered at their first conference to discuss the problems and tensions between Americans and Japanese, develop ways by which Japanese Nisei could mingle more freely with other races, pinpoint Japanese customs which hindered their occupational and cultural Americanization, and explore alternative styles of employment in Hawaii for the socially frustrated second-generation Japanese American.

After Okumura had made his opening statement and the Reverend John P. Erdman had given a short Christian invocation, Yasutaro Soga of the *Nippu Jiji* began an open discussion on "American Citizens of Japanese Parentage and the Japanese Language."[1] The auditorium of the Young Women's Christian Association rebounded with platitudes, debate, comment, and criticism. Some delegates, reinforced by that year's Supreme Court decision supporting the Japanese language schools, expressed the opinion that the knowledge of Japanese by Nisei was not only essential for family communication but for peace in the Pacific. By knowing Japanese, Nisei could act as mediators, entrepreneurs between Japan and America. Others warned, though, that Japanese should be learned only after Nisei had mastered English. The foremost responsibility of the Nisei, they reiterated, should be a healthy Americanization.

In many ways, it was very fitting that the New Americans were meeting in the recently dedicated headquarters of the Young Women's Christian Association (YWCA) to discuss Americanization and its implications for immigrant children. Indeed, the YWCA and the YMCA had been the more important institutions providing for the adjustment of the immigrant families to the lifestyle of the Islands. Supported by the munificence of various sectors of the *haole* community and intent on seeing the blessings of the American way of life adopted by foreign immigrants, the associations became focal points for many campaigns to spread the English language and American culture throughout Hawaii.

For example, in 1919 the YWCA established the International Institute. The purpose of this organization was to reach out to immigrant families, assist in the rearing of children, and facilitate the adaptation of the foreign immigrant to Hawaii. The Institute established a girl's home in Nuuanu Valley and taught a series of classes on English and American etiquette. In addition the YWCA sponsored the portable "Little House on Wheels." Looking somewhat like a mobile home, fully furnished and decorated, the "Little House" would be transported to various rural and urban areas on Oahu. Young immigrant mothers would be given a tour of the house and shown American living styles, housekeeping methods, and the care of children. As a "messenger of divine discontent," the mobile home was a demonstration of the YWCA's attempt to lift "better up to best."[2]

The YWCA, YMCA, and the New Americans were all part of the Islands' Americanization movement which could ultimately trace its origins to the missionary heritage that permeated the attitudes of many *haole kamaaina* (long-time resident) families. While plantation owners had initially shunned Americanization in favor of their "divide and rule" policy, other more religious *haole*s believed that the word of God could only be taught in the English language and that the Christian rule of life was an American progressive lifestyle. The responsibility of the white man was to raise up and guide the foreign laborer—to show him the benefits of the Christian God and the American flag.

Besides the influences of their missionary forefathers, two other factors helped to stimulate the Americanization movement among certain *haole*s. First, after the startling strikes of 1909 and 1920, the plantation interests began to see the connection between labor docility and Americanization. Laborers learning English, Christianity, good citizenship, and American customs could also be induced to learn that a good American is one who works quietly and obediently. The second development promoting an Americanization movement was the patriotism and nativistic propaganda following World War I. The war had made Americans aware of their disturbingly close ties with the rest of the world—a decadent world by American standards. The threats of alienism, Bolshevism, or foreign imperialism could only be countered by an attitude of "America First." A nation of immigrants, or an island of diverse immigrant laborers, had to be melted down and cast into a single American mold.

Armed with the popular notion of Americanization, these "missionary" *haole*s intended to see the Japanese and their children become integral parts of the Island community. Their design, of course, was paternal—the immigrant needed the benevolence and foresight of the *haole* benefactor. Their notion of what constituted the perfect community in Hawaii was racially stratified—the immigrant would become integrated into a system controlled by an enlightened elite of white men. Whatever their style or intentions, though, the primary outgrowth of the Americanization movement in the Islands was the establishment of an extensive public education system to teach Americanism to immigrant children; the Nisei were to become good Americans by attending good American institutions.

Most Japanese immigrants in Hawaii would have instinctively recoiled at the thought of their children becoming totally good Americans. Even though a spirit of *eijū dochyaku* had prevailed in the immigrant community, the Issei had expected their children to perpetuate traditional institutions, values, and customs. Although the Hawaiian experience had recognizably altered many of these traditions, by blood, culture, and allegiance the Issei still considered themselves and their children unadulterated Japanese. Nothing, they reasoned, could alter the fact that the Japanese way of life was fundamental to the home, community, and nation.

But the Japanese immigrants by the 1920s had made too many significant adjustments to the Hawaiian community to expect their children to be wholly "Japanese." The family system, the *ie,* the role of the patriarch and of community obligations had already been modified through the upsetting effects of immigration. Patterns of life more suitable to Island living had begun to appear in the day-to-day cycle of living; influences of the multicultural environment were constantly changing the direction and form of the Issei community beyond immediate perception.

Probably the most far-reaching development in the Japanese community was the movement of a great number of Japanese laborers off the plantation and into either independent small farming enterprises or businesses in Honolulu. After the strike of 1920, many Issei became discouraged with plantation life. Although improvements could be attained on a small scale through labor protests, the psychological and economic costs were too great. The violence and disease of the 1920 strike had convinced many Issei that their future in Hawaii depended on finding independent employment away from the menial labor of plantation work. Of the 25,000 Japanese working on the plantation in 1919, only 13,000 remained by 1924.[3] By 1932, Japanese plantation workers comprised only 18.8 percent of the labor force, a significant reduction from 73.5 percent in 1902.[4]

The reduction of Japanese workers on the rural plantation meant a swelling of their numbers in urban centers. Though in 1900 only 10 percent of the Japanese population was living in Honolulu, this number had climbed to 22.4 percent in 1920.[5] By 1930, one-third of the population of Honolulu was Japanese. Operating nearly 49 percent of the retail stores and influencing the composition of most blue-collar urban jobs, the Japanese filled the urban ghettos in areas such as Kalihi, Palama, Moiliili, and Kakaako.[6]

The outcome of urbanization for the Japanese immigrant was a competitive spirit of social mobility. The immigrant family, without the plantation's paternal protection, became keenly aware of the value of a rising standard of living. This in turn resulted in a decline of the early high birth rates and the subsequent reduction of family size.

Another consequence of urbanization for the Japanese immigrant's lifestyle was the disruption of the segregated Japanese community. In Honolulu, though residential patterns of ethnic housing would be maintained, Japanese came into greater contact with other ethnic groups. The cultural isolation of rural living, the insularity of the plantation world, could not be maintained when living amongst Hawaiians, Filipinos, Portuguese, and Chinese. The effects of a wider interethnic pattern of relationships were especially influential upon the lifestyle of the second generation. As the Nisei matured in urban settings, having contact with a broad spectrum of people and cultures, they became less comfortable with the traditional familial and community behaviors encouraged by their parents. A conflict of generations was increasingly inevitable.

The nature of this generational conflict continually shaping the Japanese family during the twenties and thirties was revealed in a personalized study by Misako Yamamoto, "Cultural Conflicts and Accommodations of the First and Second Generation Japanese."[7] The Nisei generation depicted by Yamamoto was generally an adolescent population comprised of youngsters under the age of eighteen. Their Issei parents, comfortable in the rural *ie* patterns of Japanese culture and language, had expected their children to retain many of the traditional patterns of the homeland. The immigrant families tried to maintain Japanese values such as filial piety, obligation to community and authority *(on),* reciprocal obligation *(giri),* a fatalistic acceptance of unforeseen circumstances in life *(shikata-ga-nai),* and a fear of shame *(haji)*. Education was highly valued as were hard work, perseverance, and frugality—the *Bushidō* Code of the *samurai*. And most important, instilled in the Nisei was the drive for success, *seikō*—a success measured in the attainment of social and economic prestige.

In addition to these traditional Japanese values inculcated into the family, the Issei expected the Nisei to understand and speak the Japanese language and perform when necessary the essential customs and rituals of Japanese behavior. Those parents who could afford it sent their Nisei children back to Japan for their education; later, they would return to Hawaii to rejoin their families. These

Nisei, called Kibei, were firmly acculturated in the Japanese lifestyle which many Issei found especially gratifying.

But Nisei were also being exposed to an American education and the diverse lifestyles of Hawaii which at times openly conflicted with the world view of the Issei. From children of other ethnic origins, radio and movies, instruction in the classroom, as well as the influences of social organizations such as the YWCA and YMCA and the pressures of the *haole* and Japanese Americanizers, the Nisei learned to value and appreciate the non-Japanese habits which they had begun to acquire outside the home.

This situation of multicultural lifestyles is explored in Yamamoto's article. For many Nisei, the retention of things Japanese was a normal and everyday routine of life. Filial piety and respect for the aged, as Yamamoto pointed out, were Japanese values which in her family remained fundamental. Yet the cultural conflict between parent and child over matters such as the hair bobbing among young women, going out to movies, or the practices of dating and marriage were equally as characteristic of the atmosphere of the Nisei's home.

Beyond the family, the cultural conflict between the Issei and Nisei generations also internally redefined the traditional beliefs and institutions of the Japanese community. Illustrative of these internal community changes was the role Buddhism came to play in the life of the Nisei. While the Buddhist religion had been the mainstay of the Issei lifestyle, Buddhism for the Nisei was rapidly taking on the stigma of old-fashioned, un-American beliefs incompatible with the lifestyle of the "New Americans."

"The problem with English-speaking young people," a Buddhist priest had observed, "is that they don't understand Buddhism enough. . . . While the young people may acquire Buddhism as a general knowledge, they don't have a so-called religious faith or conviction of Buddhism."[8] From the very earliest years in the development of the second generation, Buddhist priests, community leaders, and parents were concerned that the young Nisei would not have the necessary spiritual foundations of Japanese religion implanted in their lifestyles and attitudes. Since the immigrants' children generally had only a limited use of the Japanese language, the problem of religion was viewed as largely communicative. If, they reasoned, the children could be taught proper Japanese, could be instilled with Japanese values and outlooks, then perhaps they could grasp the finer truths and details of Buddhism. Though the language schools to some degree successfully imparted the Buddhist mentality to many

Nisei, they did not always provide enough language tools for the young child to fully comprehend the meaning and implications of Buddha's dharma, the folkloric beliefs, or the significance of ritual. Prayers could be memorized; rituals routinely followed. But the spiritual and cultural bond which Buddhism had for the Issei could only rarely be transposed to the culturally eclectic second generation. One Nisei, while describing the daily evening ritual of her family, stated:

> The prayers are difficult, and we children do not understand anything we are saying. However, we have been saying them since we were very young, even before we started for school. Everyone in our family knows them so well that we can say them without even thinking.[9]

Aware of the Nisei's waning interest in Buddhism, many priests recognized that if the Buddhist temple were to survive the passing of the Issei population, the institution would have to become adaptable to the Nisei. Consequently, leaders such as Reverend Imamura initiated a series of fundamental changes in the temple's activities and orientations. Besides establishing the YMBA to serve as a socializing agency for young Nisei, Reverend Imamura organized the English Department of the Honpa Hongwanji under the leadership of Reverend Ernest Hunt. A Britisher who had been attracted to Buddhism and become an ordained minister, Reverend Hunt's progressive style of arousing the interest of Nisei in their ancestral religion brought him a special popularity among the young American-born Buddhists.

The "Americanization" of the Honpa Hongwanji was to have repercussions on other Buddhist institutions and practices. Buddhist "temples" became Buddhist "churches" in the Christian nomenclature. Sunday, the Christian Sabbath, became the day of devotion and worship, as well as the time for Buddhist "Sunday schools." Gathas (Buddhist "hymns" written especially for use in Sunday schools) became reworded to sound strangely similar to Christian songs; the practice of the wedding ceremony, usually a civil ceremony in Japan, was expanded to meet its religious counterpart in the American practice.

The outcome of making Buddhism palatable to the Nisei was to turn religion into a socializing institution providing free-time activities and extracurricular interests for young children and teenagers. The Buddhist Church became for the second-generation Japanese the source of social gatherings with "their own kind." Dances, athletic events, social clubs—the opportunity to socialize with friends and meet members of the opposite sex—all these became primary functions of the religious institution. "That the Hongwanji plays a vital and important role in the lives of the second-generation Buddhist," a young Nisei educator wrote in 1937, "is evident. In the home, at school, at work, in his social, educational and religious life, through marriage and through death, the Hongwanji helps to direct and shape his future."[10]

But religion as defined by the Issei experience simply played a minor role for the great majority of Nisei. Even if some young Japanese diligently pursued the spiritual truths and rituals of their parents, a greater number could not fully internalize traditional meanings and beliefs. The trend toward the diminishing religious significance of Buddhist ritual and belief could be seen in the observance of events such as the *bon* dance. For the majority of the Nisei, the *urabon* season was a time of dancing, festivities, special foods, and meeting with friends. The meanings which the Nisei attached to the yearly festival were far removed from the spiritual celebration of the return of the dead. Some enterprising young Nisei even added newer, nonreligious elements to the *bon* so that greater numbers of non-Japanese and tourists would make the festivities a commercially profitable venture. One observer was perceptive in his evaluation of the Nisei's attitudes toward these "religious" events:

> The *Bon* festival, in spite of its religious significance, has become so secularized that most of its meaning is lost among the second generation in Hawaii. There seems to be a somewhat decreasing attendance among the ranks of the dancers as well as the spectators, but the crowds are still very large. Many of the second generation youths look forward eagerly to the coming of the *Bon* season as a social event. Others simply ignore the *Bon-odori*.[11]

The secularization of the Nisei's cultural world view was interpreted by many clergy as a "spiritual problem."

"Some of the young people," a Nisei wrote as early as 1923, "show a tendency to become passive in religious life, rather than active." Avoidance of problems was often the most expedient route and the writer found that of 6,550 Nisei interviewed in Honolulu more than 4,000 "are not touched at all by any religious agency."[12]

An assessment of the "spiritual problem" of the Nisei also revealed that for many second-generation Japanese the conversion to Christianity was viewed as a way to become integrated into the

Island Christian community. If the religion of their parents was heathen, then to be accepted as American meant converting to any of the varieties of Christian beliefs. The process of conversion, often acquiesced to by Buddhist parents, in effect tended to secularize the Nisei generation. Religion became a tool for social acceptance, not totally a matter of belief.

As the Nisei matured in Island society, then, a myriad of forces in the home, church, school, and community were shaping their culture, their spirituality, and their mode of life. Living in a multicultural setting, saturated with an American education and a Japanese home environment, the second generation truly existed in a cultural labyrinth—a mazeway of behaviors, values, and lifestyles. Forces of cultural rearing intermingled and interacted with forces of socialization; environmental surroundings created, sustained, reinforced, and destroyed behaviors, values, and priorities.

For some Nisei adolescents within the cultural labyrinth, the pressures of the home and the language school created a deep respect for the traditional values and priorities of Japanese culture as modified by the Island situation. These Nisei kept to a minimum the demands of the American and Hawaiian communities so that their lifestyles would be compatible with the expectations of their Issei parents. Other Nisei, engrossed with New Americanism, perhaps envious of *haole* status and power, attempted to emulate a 100-percent American pattern. For these Nisei, acculturation more often meant a negative rejection of their parents and the "old ways" than a positive striving for an ideal cultural goal.

Finally, the vast majority of Nisei began to identify with a "local" way of life. Through peer-group influences and non-Japanese contacts in the community and school, these Nisei recognized that living in Hawaii had resulted in a special Island identity. The use of "pidgin" English in personal or casual ways, the styles of dress, food, and entertainment as defined in an island environment, modes of affiliative behaviors, of an open and friendly attitude with friends and strangers, were features of an interethnic culture to varying degrees participated in by many Nisei.

The development of a "local" consciousness shared interethnically among non-*haole*s was largely the outcome of shared plantation experiences and the use of "pidgin" English. Young Nisei viewed their "cultural baggage" not so much as exclusively Japanese or American, but as a commonly accepted attitude of Island lifestyle shared with other young people of diverse ethnic backgrounds. The ruralness of Island life, the class differentiations between white and nonwhite and the use of language as forces shaping the Nisei generation were analyzed in an article by linguist John Reinecke, entitled " 'Pidgin English' in Hawaii: A Local Study in the Sociology of Language."[13] The major theme of Reinecke's analysis was that pidgin was a shared language of intimacy among the non-*haole* Islanders having varied emotional meanings for the user. Unlike Standard English, a largely denotative language, pidgin was a mixture of many languages which sprang from the multiracial plantation experience. The usage of pidgin also clearly defined class and racial cleavages. Those who could not speak the Island dialect were recognized as outsiders to the ethnic peer group. Those who were "ethnic" but spoke Standard English risked the threat of being called "haolefied." And those who did speak pidgin found many obstacles in their path, both in school and employment. At any rate, pidgin, the local *lingua franca,* became a cultural bond between Nisei and the culture of the greater Island community.

In the midst of their cultural labyrinth, in the midst of their adaptation of a "local" identity while family, church, and community strained to accommodate their needs, the Nisei were also experiencing an exacerbated feeling of frustration. At every turn, the second generation seemed to encounter the limitations of a rigid Island society. The inherent conservatism of the plantation system, the resistance of the Island oligarchy to change, seemed to tie the Nisei to the plantation. As one youth growing up on the plantation lamented, his greatest fear was that he would end up in the same predicament as his parents. "I hate to think that we're going to live on plantations all our lives."[14]

In part, Nisei frustrations were the result of their public school education which taught them American ideals and ambitions. The belief in equality of opportunity and the cultural drives toward success resulted in an outlook that menial labor was not good enough. Professional jobs or civil service employment in education, medicine, business, law, and even government—these were the roles to which Nisei aspired.

Instrumental in designing a public school system which had such an important impact on the character of the Nisei generation were men like Miles Cary, principal of McKinley High School, and Benjamin Wist, principal of the Territorial Normal and Training School, a teacher-training institution. From his arrival at McKinley in 1921 to teach history, Cary advocated a style of progressive education which sought to liberate the talents and creativity of children so they could be integrated into the Island community. Under Cary, McKinley High promoted democracy and student government and stressed equality of opportunity. The high school, located in Honolulu near the Japanese community of Moiliili, helped instill high social aspirations in many Nisei. McKinley, or "Tokyo High," served students from the town areas and the outlying plantation communities who rode to school on the Oahu Railway. Such were the Americanizing influences of McKinley that in 1922, when male students responded to a survey on future expectations, 15 percent wanted to become professional men, 50 percent skilled workers, 5 percent farmers, and less than 1 percent wanted to become menial laborers.[15]

Benjamin Wist, recognizing the fact that Hawaii's educational institutions in 1920 had very few Asian teachers, began a program to train more Japanese and Chinese teachers for the public schools. With Wist's efforts, the number of Asian teachers rose each year. By the 1930s, Japanese students comprised nearly 30 percent of the total enrollment in Normal School.[16] As teaching was a respected profession and Japanese families held teachers in high esteem, the opening of the Normal School to Asians provided the impetus for many Nisei to enter the field of education.

The result of such educative endeavors, in addition to the aspiration for a better job position, was the creation of an ethos of Americanism which also added to the frustration of the Nisei. Expressing this ethos of "American Success," a highly persuasive image among the second generation, was an essay by Kensuke Kawachi which in 1928 won first prize in a Japanese community essay contest. The topic was, "What Can American Citizens of Japanese Descent Do to Serve Hawaii and Contribute to Her Success?" Kawachi's essay, "How 'New Americans' May Serve Hawaii,"[17] revealed the Nisei ethos of education, democracy, social ambition, and a future in which Japanese Americans would play significant roles. Kawachi recognized that the responsibility of the Nisei was to get an education, secure "honest livelihood," participate in the political life of the community, and be concerned with the social welfare of the Islands. Although Kawachi's essay reflected a degree of "proving ourselves" to the *haole* American when he stated that New Americans "should try to erase permanently the criticisms that are made against them," that was not his major intent. Americanization was not totally a result of a hostile environment placing pressure on the ethnic community but also involved the ethnic group using Americanism as a means of social mobility. Employment, political participation, and educational attainment were intertwined with the rhetoric of Americanism so that Nisei, in effect, had channeled their social ambitions into a useful image of loyal and well-rounded New Americans.

This ethos of Nisei Americanism actually intensified the frustrations in many aggressive second-generation Japanese because the illusion did not reflect the more tangible realities of the Hawaiian system. Encouraged by teachers and parents to succeed in society, taught that they had an equal opportunity, many Nisei continually felt anxiety when faced with the limitations of the Island economy. Jobs in the professions were either scarce or filled by *haole*s; virtually no Island middle class existed to offer a means of social mobility. While racial discrimination in hiring was another factor contributing to the Nisei's frustrations, a more important determinant was the fact that Hawaii in the 1920s and 1930s remained predominantly an agricultural or plantation economy. Simply, little or no opportunity existed for the large numbers of educated Nisei who sought to find employment better than that of their parents.

As a response to the Nisei's frustrations and partly as a means to placate the sugar interests that had invested so much in their Americanization movement, Nisei who were part of the New Americans Conference directed much of their efforts toward working out the second generation's employment problem. Rather than leaving Hawaii or trying to attain professional positions which simply did not exist, the New Americans and their spokesman, Reverend Okumura, urged the Nisei to reconsider plantation employment. Under the slogan of "Back-to-the-Land," the New Americans argued that Nisei should have close ties to the plantations, improve the situation of wages and working conditions, and raise their families close to the earth in the American tradition of the yeoman farmer.

To raise the consciousness of the Nisei to the benefits of plantation labor, the annual New Americans Conferences would have guest speakers from the Hawaiian Sugar Planters' Association who would discuss the nature of employment on the plantation and the attractiveness of agricultural endeavors. Also, through their official newspaper, the New Americans encouraged Nisei to reevaluate their notions about plantation work, farming, and American traditions. An excellent example of such editorial appeals was the article "Japanese

Problem in Hawaii: A Solution," appearing in the May, 1929, issue of *The New Americans*.[18] The message given the young, confused, and jobless Japanese American was clear: accept your position, see the incentives and rewards in agricultural employment, and get back to the land. Invest in Hawaii's future by supporting the Island's major industries.

The tone and direction of the editorial stressed a major theme of the Americanization efforts of Okumura, the New American organization, and the *haole* community: Issei and Nisei must look upon Hawaii, not Japan, as their primary locus of identity. Issei were implored not to send money home to Japan but to invest in Hawaii's future. Immigrants should educate their children to be proper American citizens, not Japanese subjects. Nisei were told that they must work to make Hawaii comfortable and profitable for the Japanese community, that they should secure roots in the Islands by buying land or homesteading. Loyalty to Hawaii, to Hawaii's plantation system and *haole* oligarchy, was an issue of the utmost importance to the Japanese community and the great number of Nisei who were doubtful and worried about their future. The results of the "Back-to-the-Land" movement, though, were not as impressive as the New Americans would have hoped. The young Nisei began no major exodus from the city to the plantation. The idea of agricultural pursuits for the majority of Nisei remained tied to the subservient and meaningless positions their parents had once held. Returning to the plantation would be in their minds like taking a step back into the past—a past of grueling labor and second-class citizenship.

The Nisei had been instilled with ambitions and visions. The home, the school, the image of "New Americans," the comfort of a localized identity had all accentuated the drive to succeed, to surmount the limitations of the plantation world. Certainly Hawaiian adaptation had resulted in conflicts at home, the secularization of their religion, and deep and unabated frustrations. So great had been the cultural changes, the growth of the "local" feeling, that very few Japanese or non-Japanese could question that these "New Americans" had become firmly rooted in the Hawaiian soil. But a few voices did raise fears that the Japanese were too firmly implanted in Hawaii. Their roots went far too deep.

NOTES

1. For the text of Soga's speech and a description of the First Convention of the New Americans see New Americans Conference, *Proceedings,* 1st Annual, Honolulu, 1927.

2. Young Women's Christian Association, *Silver Anniversary Review of the Young Women's Christian Association of Honolulu, 1900-1925, Honolulu Star-Bulletin,* 1926, p. 19.

3. Lawrence H. Fuchs, *Hawaii Pono: A Social History,* New York: Harcourt, Brace and World, 1961, p. 225.

4. Andrew W. Lind, *Hawaii, The Last of the Magic Isles,* London: Oxford University Press, 1969, p. 45.

5. Andrew W. Lind, *Hawaii's People,* Honolulu: University of Hawaii Press, 1955, p. 52.

6. Fuchs, p. 123.

7. Misako Yamamoto, "Cultural Conflicts and Accommodations of the First and Second Generation Japanese," *Social Process in Hawaii,* v. 4 (1938), pp. 40–8.

8. Bernhard L. Hormann, *The Revival of Buddhism in Hawaii,* War Research Laboratory Report No. 12, Honolulu: University of Hawaii Press, 1947, p. 3.

9. Masako Tanaka, "Religion in Our Family," *Social Process in Hawaii,* v. 12 (August 1948), p. 14.

10. Katsumi Onishi, "The Second Generation Japanese and the Hongwanji," *Social Process in Hawaii,* v. 3 (May 1937), p. 48.

11. Katsumi Onishi, " 'Bon' and 'Bon-Odori' in Hawaii," *Social Process in Hawaii,* v. 4 (May 1938), p. 57.

12. C. N. Kurokawa, "Work Among Young Japanese is Rich with Opportunities," *The Friend,* v. 93, no. 11 (November 1923), p. 261.

13. John E. Reinecke, " 'Pidgin English' in Hawaii: A Local Study in the Sociology of Language," *American Journal of Sociology,* v. 43, no. 5 (March 1938), pp. 778–9.

14. Machiyo Mitamura, "Life on a Hawaiian Plantation: An Interview," *Social Process in Hawaii,* v. 6 (July 1940), pp. 51-2.

15. Fuchs, p. 288.

16. Fuchs, p. 283.

17. Kensuke Kawachi, "How 'New Americans' May Serve Hawaii," *Nippu Jiji,* June, 1928, pp. 3–5.

18. "Japanese Problem in Hawaii: A Solution," *The New Americans,* v. 10, no. 2 (May 1929), p. 1.

Cultural Conflicts and Accommodations of the First and Second Generation Japanese

MISAKO YAMAMOTO

PERHAPS in no other place do the conflicts and accommodations of culture become more evident than in the Japanese home. There are the conflicts of age and youth, traditions and customs of parents against American mores and folkways, and the second generation with the established group in the community. These processes are going on in every Japanese family where there is a member of the second generation. It also holds true of all immigrant groups, but the Japanese immigrants have more difficulty than the European immigrants in adapting themselves to the American ways. The contrast between the two civilizations is greater and causes deeper conflicts.

At home, we have beds as well as *futon,* or Japanese mattresses for use on the floor. We sleep on the one we prefer, but no one in the family, except mother, uses the *futon*. She will not sleep on a bed. Whenever we insist that she sleep on the bed she concedes; but it is not uncommon on such occasions to see mother wake up in the middle of the night to lay out the *futon* and sleep on the floor. We use chairs, but we also use *zabuton,* or Japanese cushions. A dresser stands in one corner, while a *kyodai* (Japanese bureau) stands in another corner of the bedroom. Japanese picture frames are hung beside American picture frames. The Japanese home of the typical middle class group in Hawaii is a mixture of both civilizations. The

In *Social Process in Hawaii,* v. 4 (1938), pp. 40–8. Reprinted by permission of *Social Process in Hawaii,* by Edmund H. Volkart, chairman, Department of Sociology, University of Hawaii.

homes show a certain amount of adaptation and adoption of phases of American life, even in the exterior appearances.

In a Japanese home the father is the head and is usually the one who directs the interests of the family group. He is the judge in all matters pertaining to the welfare of the family and is the official representative of the family in civic affairs. The mother stays at home and sees that the father has every possible comfort. She is considered a servant to her husband in the sense that he is her lord and master—his will is hers. This holds true to a large degree in our family; but more and more, mother is considered on an equal level with father. That is the position we children have given her and in most instances she seems to have the last word, just like an American woman! Gradually she is assuming the role of the boss of the family and holder of the purse strings. This does not mean that she no longer respects father. It is the economic and the social factors in the Islands which makes such a situation possible.

My parents never display affection for each other. They consider it bad form. Therefore, words of endearment are lacking in their conversation. The Americans call each other by their first names, but father, instead of calling mother by her name, always says *oi* which is equivalent to *hey* in the American vernacular.[1] Mother calls him *oto-san,* which means father.

Due to the traditional conception that the woman is inferior to man, a husband does not seem to have intimate companionship with his wife in the immigrant Japanese homes. The close intimate feeling that exists in the American homes does not exist in the Japanese homes. The social life of the first generation is very limited. Once a year my parents go to the prefecture picnic. They eagerly look forward to the occasion, for at this gathering, the *ken* (prefectural) people get together and talk of old times and of their homes in Japan. Aside from this, their only diversion is going to the movies or gossiping with neighbors. They prefer the Japanese movies since they do not understand English sufficiently to enjoy the American movies. My mother's experience is, I think, a typical one. Until talkies were introduced, she had never seen an American movie. When the talkies were first shown, I persuaded her to see one. She did not understand it, and furthermore she disapproved of the kissing scenes. That was the only American movie she has seen.

In the average Japanese home there is a noticeable lack of companionship between parents and children in the spending of leisure time. It is a very rare occasion in our family today when we ever have breakfast together. Each member prepares his own breakfast and goes about independently for the rest of the day. We seldom see each other in the mornings. Our evenings are never spent together—one goes to the library, the other to the movies, and another to work. We no longer go on family trips or picnics as we did when we were youngsters. I long to go on such trips with my parents, but this does not seem possible despite the fact that we have a family car.

Boys are considered superior to girls in the Japanese family. My eldest brother is deemed the legal heir to the family fortune. His comfort comes before ours, inasmuch as he is the one to perpetuate our family name. It is the custom of the family that the father and the eldest son are to be served first. Then, the younger boys are served and are followed by the mother and the girls according to their age. Being the youngest, I have always resented being served last. However, there are times when I am considered first because my brothers do not consider themselves superior to the girls despite the fact that they have been taught to expect special privileges.

The influence of authority and tradition cannot be overlooked in parent-child contacts. One of the basic ideals of Japanese life is filial piety. This ideal has been stressed in the home education of the second and third generations through gestures and definitions by parents. The Japanese revere age. Japanese custom demands that courtesy be shown to elders on all occasions. This is expected especially of youth. The thought of sending the aged to the poor house is inconceivable to them. The first as well as the second generation cannot understand how *haole*s can send their parents to charity institutions. Parents and elders are addressed as superiors. Even to this day, I say *Tada ima itte kairi masu* (May I leave now) when leaving and *Tada ima itte kairi mashita* (I have returned) when I return.

Birth control is a taboo subject in the Japanese home. In fact, many regard it as immoral. The second generation with its educational advancement is more informed along such lines. This knowledge has been gained chiefly through contact with friends and through medical sources and books. We do not believe in having large families. Both my brother and sister have been married for many years. My brother has remained childless for more than ten years of married life, while my sister had a child only recently. The second generation is not as prolific as the first generation. This is due to the acceptance of American cultural patterns and a desire for a better standard of living.

To the Japanese people, the three most important events in their life are birth, marriage and death. These are celebrated accordingly. Most of the second generation were delivered with the aid of midwives and in many cases their fathers were the only attendants. Such was the case in my family. Medical and hospital care were unthought of in the early days. It was and is still a great event in the life of the Japanese parents when their first born is a son. Great ceremony is performed in honor of the first born, and on naming him, a great feast is prepared. Gifts are received from relatives and friends. The names are usually derivatives of their grandfathers' or grandmothers' names. No American names are given, and those American names which the second generation Japanese have today were adopted by them at a later age or given them by their teachers who had a difficult time pronouncing their unfamiliar Japanese names.

Since marriage is one of the important events in life, the parents expect to pick the bride for their son. Marriage is looked upon as a family affair and not a personal matter. Parents believe that the welfare of the family (in future years) will come about with the successful marriage of their eldest son. This is one of the reasons why the second generation Japanese girl does not care to marry the eldest son of a family. She is afraid that she will find herself married not to the son, but to the whole family. The *baishokunin,* or "go-between", makes all the arrangements for the marriage. According to Japanese philosophy, love is not essential before marriage, but is something which comes after marriage. Americans often view Japanese marriages as forced unions, but this is not true, for before the betrothal is announced, both parties have a perfect right to make their decisions known. The second generation is getting away from the traditional modes and, if the "go-between" takes any part at all, he enters as a formality to please the old folks.

Because of the importance of marriage in one's life, no expense is spared to make it an elaborate affair. Families often spend all their savings for the occasion and newly-weds frequently start their married life with a large debt incurred from an elaborate ceremony. The marriage ceremony is usually held at a shrine or a temple.

American social life has equalized the status of the male and female. No longer is a girl regarded as inferior to the male, and thus, when the emphasis is placed upon the boy, conflict arises. The second generation idealizes the American type of marriage where intimacy and companionship exist between the wife and husband. Romantic love is the basis of their marriage. The American custom of giving showers for the bride-elect has been adopted quite extensively, and the groom usually gives a bachelor's dinner.

The desire of the second generation members is to secure a fuller life than that of their parents. They think of life in terms of progress and they are, unlike their parents, individualistic because of their contacts with the wider community. The first generation thinks of life as being static and unchanging and develops personalities which reflect the group patterns.

With the second generation Japanese, American folkways and mores have gradually displaced many of the customs and traditions of their parents. The young people of Hawaiian birth who are educated in American schools and who enjoy wider social contacts than their parents find it difficult to conform to the traditional Japanese standards. The second generation is educated in the Japanese forms of courtesy in the language schools, but their sentiments favor the freer American ways. We call each other "dear", "honey", and "sweetheart" just as casually as *haole* boys do. We walk arm in arm with boys and let them "date" us. The young people no longer bow to each other but shake hands and greet each other with "hello there" and "hi there". Even among our parents the forms of Japanese courtesy are no longer strictly observed. Despite the fact that boys are served first at home and taught to expect privileges, this does not prevail in their social life outside the home. The second generation Japanese boy, like any *haole* lad, seats and serves the ladies first. Though New Year is still one of the most celebrated events in the Japanese home, my family no longer stays home to spend the night together. We no longer have the customary last supper of the year together as in the old Japanese family. Instead, New Year's eve is spent in hilarity as in an average *haole* home. The young folks usually spend their New Year's eve at a dance. Then they return home in the early hours of the morning and sleep until noon. This situation which exists in many of the urban homes tends to undermine family solidarity and morale. Conditions are slightly different in the rural areas where the institutional aspects of the family are largely unchanged. This matter is of deep concern to our parents, who say that such actions will obstruct our chances to marry into a respectable home. This breakdown of familial control over the second generation is taking place in many Japanese homes as an inevitable result of the influences of American education and the freer American traditions.

Conflict is inevitable in this changing cultural situation. Conflict is severest where parents hold on to the idea of some day returning to Japan with their children and thus attempting to rear their children in the strictly Japanese fashion. However, the conflict is less severe in most homes where the parents are realizing that their children must become Americans, and are honestly attempting to adjust themselves to the situation.

There was a time when I was looked upon as the disturbing element in the family. I was radical, always dazzling my parents with something new. They said that I imitated the American boys and girls, that I was trying to be "haolefied". At first my parents insisted on my accepting Japanese customs, but they have gradually yielded to my desires to be like the other girls of the neighborhood. I distinctly remember the day I bobbed my long hair. Since all the girls were wearing bobbed hair, I didn't want to look different with my long hair. After begging and pleading for six months, my parents finally consented. I had it trimmed so short that I looked like a boy. They called me *otemba* or tomboy, but it did not concern me because now I looked like the rest of my playmates. On another occasion, I shocked my parents by nonchalantly walking down the lane into my home in a pair of slacks (they called it pants). Imagine what a step I was taking! I had borrowed this pair from a friend of mine whose parents were lenient. My parents ordered me to take them off, but I defied them. After much pleading, I finally prevailed upon them to let me dress like the other girls and by the time I began wearing shorts, my parents were well acquainted with my desire to be like other girls. They no longer protested.

Perhaps one of the most serious conflicts arises through the language difficulty. I tried to speak English at home because my teacher told me that if I wanted to be "smart" in English, I had to use it at home. My parents put a stop to this. They told me that I could speak English outside of home, but not before them. They could not understand English, and therefore, they didn't want anyone of the family to speak English before them. So, we speak Japanese before them, but English among ourselves.

The second generation does not speak Japanese fluently. Therefore, in their contact with parents and older folks, misunderstanding often develops. The younger folks, who no doubt mean to be polite, but who have not sufficiently, if at all, mastered the exacting Japanese language to adequately express themselves, are often misunderstood and berated for being rude and disrespectful to the elders in their speech. There is a tendency for the first generation to think that their children are deliberately trying to forget the Japanese language in order to become more Americanized, and with it, they fear the loss of Japanese customs and traditions which they cherish so dearly. The younger folks, at the same time, shun contacts with the elders due to this Japanese language deficiency.

Another source of conflict in a Japanese home lies in the divergent religious beliefs of parents and children—the one being Buddhist and the other Christian. I do not disapprove my parents' worshipping of the Buddha. Their ritualistic procedure such as incense burning, placing food before the shrine, and the shrine worship does not bother me at all as long as they let me worship in the manner I desire. This liberty of religious choice has been given me, although my parents are staunch Buddhists. Although I am a Christian, I still observe some of their rituals. I place food before the shrine and fast on the 16th of each month (the date on which Buddha was born). I follow these rituals not because I want to, but because I have found that it makes for harmony in the family. I have also learned not to contradict my parents' belief that the Emperor is God. When speaking of the Emperor of Japan, they use an altogether different and more respectful mode of expression. The "Son of Heaven", although respected by the children of immigrants, does not hold a place of reverence in their hearts as he does in the hearts of the members of the first generation.

My parents who came here thirty years ago to make their fortunes are still living in Hawaii. They have gone back to Japan from time to time, but they have always returned to the land of their settlement. They have found that going back to Japan involved difficulties in readjustment. They have changed, but they do not wish to forget Japan. They say that they still owe their allegiance to the Emperor. Though they emphatically state this, I am sure that the problem of rearing and educating their children has been shifting their interest from Japan to Hawaii and the regard they have for Japan is now just a sentimental attachment.

The processes of conflict and accommodation are taking place continuously in the Japanese families in Hawaii. The lot of my family represents a rather common experience among the average immigrant families. The problems arising between the first and the second generation are primarily caused by the clash of cultures and the struggle between age and youth. However, in this constantly changing milieu, there are still surviving some fundamental Japanese ideals as filial piety and respect for the aged.

The first generation, because of strong sentimental attachments to Japanese behavior patterns and because of infrequent and limited contacts with American cultural patterns, have resisted the changes which threatened to destroy their traditions and customs. Their adaptation took place because it was absolutely necessary for their survival on Hawaiian soil. On the other hand, we of the second generation, immersed as we are almost wholly in the ways of the West, have accepted American cultural patterns more rapidly. The American patterns have become an integral part of our lives. But the fact cannot be denied that we are not fully accepted by the race whose ways we have adopted. At the same time we are misunderstood by our own kind. What is to become of the bicultural product of Hawaii?

NOTE

[1]. More often the term used is *Oka-san* which literally means mother.

"Pidgin English" in Hawaii: A Local Study in the Sociology of Language

JOHN E. REINECKE

WHEN the Hawaiian Islands were opened to our civilization in the last years of the eighteenth century, a kind of broken trade language grew up in the ports and later (1820–80) on the whaling vessels. From the scanty references it appears to have been chiefly English adapted to Hawaiian syntax and pronunciation and containing a large number of native words though it never took a definite form. Whether the English or the Hawaiian tongue was the language of command on the plantations which about 1850 began to dominate Island economy is uncertain.

A reciprocity treaty with the United States, effective in 1876, precipitated complete dependence upon a plantation economy. The native population was submerged under a polyglot flood of imported laborers. On the plantations, under English-speaking foremen, English inevitably became the language of command, and consequently the chief lingua franca among the several linguistic groups. Based as it was on the mixed speech of the ports, this plantation idiom contains elements found in other English jargons of the Pacific, together with many Hawaiian words. It was called "pidgin English."

This "pidgin English" was of the familiar type of language found wherever a large number of menial workers (usually belonging to

In *American Journal of Sociology,* v. 43, no. 5 (March 1938), pp. 778–89. Reprinted by permission of the University of Chicago Press.

several language groups) are controlled for many years by a small class of alien masters who do not trouble to learn their servants' languages, and are not concerned to have these speak their own correctly. Because the servant already speaks the new language brokenly, the master often simplifies his own idiom, so that a very broken-down dialect results, marked by extreme simplification of form and, originally, by poverty of vocabulary.[1] This simplified dialect is learned by new slaves or coolies from their established compatriots, and thus linguistic corruption is perpetuated.[2]

Under plantation conditions as typified in the Lesser Antilles a Creole dialect usually displaces the servile workers' languages, becomes relatively fixed in form, and settles into place as the vernacular of the masses and the substandard dialect of the master class as well. Such a dialect generally gives rise to a folk literature and—usually through first serving the needs of religious instruction—may even be elevated into a literary vehicle, as has happened to the debased Spanish of Curaçao.

Hawaii was not, however, a typical plantation area. Certainly there were elements of servitude and caste in its plantation life, and its coolies were isolated and heard little native English speech. Nevertheless, many of the conditions of free immigration were present: there was much spatial and social mobility; in the cities contact with native English speakers was possible; immigrants could maintain their national individuality and languages, so that in their eyes broken English has remained a makeshift without sentimental value; and finally, there was free public education.

The school system of Hawaii was turning to the use of English when the immigrants began to arrive, and that tongue was the only practicable medium of instruction and assimilation for their own children.[3] So, even while the "pidgin" took shape in the cane fields, the schools were preventing its establishment. Immigration into Hawaii was continuous and heavy until 1932. The task of educating thousands of children in a tongue which they had not heard or heard only in a garbled form before entering school, in localities where not a single person may speak English as his native language,[4] would be a difficult one for a school system more wealthy and efficient than that of Hawaii. Yet, because the children had to use English as a lingua franca more frequently and intimately than their parents, because the youth were more aware of the cultural and economic compulsion of their new language, and because the teachers insisted on an approximation to standard English, a much more unified and a more nearly acceptable English took form on the playground and in the classroom than in the fields and shops.

Among the younger people every grade of English is spoken, depending upon their home language, schooling, associations, and ambitions. At the one extreme the youth speaks as acceptably as the average educated American, at the other as brokenly as the average immigrant speaker of "pidgin." In most cases his speech among his fellows is sufficiently deviant from standard English to receive, if not to merit, the epithet "pidgin," which is applied along the greater part of the English speech continuum in Hawaii. Yet even in extreme cases the English of those who have attended the schools is not the "pidgin" of their elders; it is more fluent, richer in words, and much nearer the structure of standard English—and they do most of their thinking in it, which few immigrants do in their "pidgin." In short, the makeshift language—thanks to the schools and to the economic opportunities of the immigrants—is passing over into a local dialect, for the most part substandard and confined to those who come of non-English-speaking families, but in its upper reaches comparable to standard English.[5]

. . .

The extent of the mastery of colloquial American English by the Island-bred is not generally realized in Hawaii. The application of the term "pidgin" to most of the spoken English hides the differences between the truly makeshift English of the father and the "bad," substandard English of the son. Any considerable deviation from the critic's individual standard of "good English" is "pidgin." And "pidgin" carries connotations of menial, contract-bound labor, of wide social distance, and of social discrimination. Hence arises much of the symbolic value of speech standards in Hawaii, with their emotion-charged attitudes, although between the attitudes toward the "pidgin" proper and toward the dialect there is a real difference.

With the crude "pidgin" of the immigrants and elderly natives is associated little of that preoccupation with language forms which gathers about the dialect. In the mouths of the old people "pidgin" is recognized as a makeshift, for it is realized that they have not had an opportunity to go beyond it. They, being for the most part outside the society and culture of the white Americans, do not feel themselves greatly isolated on account of their poor English.

Occasionally, indeed, the immigrants were unaware that there existed any better medium of communication with the whites than "pidgin." A friend of the writer tells of an experience he had two decades ago with a gang of Chinese workmen who were at the point of fighting with their field boss. He, an English university man newly come to Hawaii, was trying angrily to explain in pure English that the cane should be cut close to the ground and the tops lopped off and thrown between the rows for fertilizer. My friend interpreted to the gang foreman: "*Luna* [foreman], big boss speak, all men down-below cutch; suppose too much *mauka* [uphill, high] cutch, too mucha sugar *poho* [wasted]—*keiki* [shoots] no use. Savvy? All men *opala* [trash] cutch, one side t'row—byenby mule men come, *lepo* [dirt] too mucha guru [good]. Savvy?" "Savvy," replied the Chinese; then, with a look of ineffable disgust: "Huy! wasamalla dis Haole—he no can talk *haole!*"—("What's wrong with this white man?—he can't talk white man's language!")[6] Most immigrants have moved in a wider circle than these old Chinese and have been aware of a more adequate type of "haole," but they have found no particular need to learn it or had no opportunity to do so. In a plantation economy, and even at many other occupations, the immigrants could get along remarkably well with very little English.

Some immigrants, the favorably situated or ambitious few, learned adequate if "accented" English. Of late years the Filipino immigrants have broken away from the "pidgin" tradition to a considerable extent. Many of them studied some English in the Philippines; they are more clearly aware than were their predecessors of the cultural and economic advantages of using English correctly; and, most important, they are thrown into contact with Island-born persons who speak passable English.

Yet, so strongly ingrained is the tradition of "pidgin" as the language of command on the plantations that the petty foremen, usually men of little education, still frequently resent the use of good English on the job by the young Filipinos or Island-bred workmen. Several high-school lads, to excuse their poor English, have told the writer: "No use for us learn good English; the *luna* [boss] will wild us if we talk good English to him; he say we're too fresh."

Toward the old-time "pidgin" in its various national guises speakers of what they consider acceptable English generally show a good-humored contempt. The person who can skilfully caricature the speech of the old Portuguese, Japanese, or whoever it may be, is sure of hearty applause from the young people of all ethnic groups. Since the older people of every nationality speak broken English, no one can take offense at the limitation as being a thrust at one's own people. And the listener, like the imitator, congratulates himself upon his own superiority; for only one who understands English well can appreciate the takeoff! Likewise advertisements featuring the foreign English of the shopkeeper are popular.[7]

Quite a different picture is presented by the dialect of the younger people. The emotion-charged attitudes associated practically everywhere with the use of different levels of speech take on additional significance in Hawaii, for there the type of English spoken is connected with race as well as with class differences. The only persons to whom standard English is native are (roughly speaking) the few Americans and British, locally known as Haoles, who occupy an envied position of economic advantage. Good English and the Haole are associated in the popular mind. "A Haole," defined a Japanese girl, "is a person who speaks a beautiful language." To be like a Haole has been, by and large, to share in his economic and social advantages, to feel one's self more closely approximate to that state of a "real American" which the schools and press glorify. Yet at the same time it implies being "haolefied," dissociating one's self from one's class and racial group. Therefore the use of "good English," always a class fetish emphasized by the pedagogic mind, becomes in Hawaii doubly a fetish, about which play ambivalent sets of attitudes.

Nonspeakers are mostly hostile toward or contemptuous of the dialect. Schoolteachers, editors, and others, whose concern it is to reconcile Americanization with the castelike traditions of the plantations, attack its use in terms which the following extract from a radio address illustrates:

> Those who cannot, or will not, speak the English language well are at a disadvantage in our business and social life, and even in cooperative efforts; nor can they contribute their full part, as true citizens, to the common good. . . . This dialect, cramped and crude and chaotic, limited in expressive possibilities and unintelligible to the stranger, is surely not one to build a civilization and a culture on, a culture worthy of the intelligent, capable and kindly people of the most beautiful islands of all the world.[8]

Aware that its limitations are great—that its use makes for retardation and poor school work to a distressing extent, that occasionally it causes misunderstanding between mainlanders and Islanders, and that because of its habitual use Island youth are generally inadequate in public expression and appear at a disadvantage, thus acquiring feelings of inferiority—they attribute to it also the limitations of "pidgin" proper, with which they usually confuse it. Few have analyzed the differences between "pidgin" (dialect) and standard English; to get rid of "pidgin," therefore, unadvised suggestions are made, such as that of a former university head to teach the youth of Hawaii one thousand basic English words.

. . .

Among the speakers of the substandard dialect there are contradictory attitudes. They have been made speech-conscious to a much greater extent than is usual among Americans. The use of good English, they have had preached to them, is an essential part of the good Americanism to which they aspire, and a key to economic success. They have perhaps been treated with some contempt because of their poor diction. Above all they have struggled with the difficulties of expressing themselves adequately at school. All except the youngest children are quite well aware of the various levels of diction and seek to adapt their speech to the occasion. Unfortunately for them, long habituation to nonstandard syntax, idioms, and pronunciation keeps all except a very few from attaining an acceptable and easy diction. They usually attain only an error-sprinkled stiffness of expression.[9]

. . .

There is general agreement that the use of "pidgin" is an educational and often a social hindrance. In using it many know that they are losing prestige with the Americans, and they condemn themselves for using it, sometimes in strong terms. The idea that the "pidgin" might have the dignity of a dialect is foreign to them. In whatever qualities it may have of vividness, terseness, local color, few take any conscious pleasure.[10] It is to them, as to the Haoles, simply the despised "pidgin." When the worm turns it is to say, "But some Haoles use just as bad English, too," not to excuse the dialect as such. The teachers should eliminate the "pidgin."

. . .

Persons who exercise themselves over the prevalent bad English demand why those who can see the better continue to practice the worse. They fail to realize the weight of the obvious circumstances of the use of the dialect. The "pidgin" is impressed upon the young

Islander in his tenderest years and in his most intimate associations (excepting those with his parents if they speak a foreign language at home), those with his siblings and play group. The mere effort of changing from the dialectal idioms and pronunciation of one's childhood is itself extremely difficult even when removed from the social pressure of one's fellows. One's teachers usually cannot recognize or do not know how to correct many of the dialectisms. So long as there is a large polyglot population of elderly people, the young people must know and use the only practicable lingua franca—broken English. The necessity of speaking in "pidgin" with persons of another tongue, and especially with one's own parents whose language one does not know sufficiently well to converse in it freely, confirms the youth in his substandard speech habits. So-called "pidgin" is the young folks' native tongue, usually alongside an equally substandard variety of some foreign language, so that, "If we try to speak good English our hands are always trying to explain what we want to say." A girl whose elder sister refused to listen to her "pidgin" writes: "I tried to talk good English. This time I felt as if I were not a Japanese, but a 'haole,' and felt out of place." Thus the easiest course is to excuse one's self by remarking that only a Haole can speak English properly anyway, so why try? Even those who have learned to speak standard English with some ease feel, like most dialect-speakers, the warmth and intimacy which come of using one's childhood dialect within one's own circle, and the stiffness which would result from an attempt to talk "Haole English" there. Many a college graduate can be heard habitually relapsing into his juvenile speech. For, because of the racial lines in Hawaii, a young man who rises into the middle class there cannot so easily find congenial company among people careful of their English as does his fellow on the mainland.

Among adolescents, of all groups the most jealous of social conformity and unhampered by the necessity of speaking "good English" to hold jobs and maintain social prestige, the pressure to use dialect is strongest. Among them, too, is perhaps most keenly felt, or at least most plainly expressed, the racial and class implications of speech differences. These statements exemplify their attitudes:

> People using pidgin English can also convince their listeners to listen on to what they have to say. If you should speak good English they pay less attention to what you are saying because they think you are saucy [N. A.]. In Honokaa pidgin English are the common language

> they speak, because when we used good English they called it the hybolic [supercilious], so the boy put aside the good English and used pidgin English [P. K. O.]. Sometimes when I used good English some people say I act as if I know everything or acting fresh. Sometimes when we are in a crowd of people some people tease us saying "black haole" [M. A.]. And of course we hate to be called "haoles" because of many reasons [M. H.].

Such crude expression of the feeling that the choice speaker is overstepping the limits of his group and aping the manners of the dominant ethnic group—whose besetting fault in local estimation is "acting high-hat"—is not found so frequently among adults, but even among them the pressure of ridicule works against anyone whose manners either of action or of speech can be considered "haolefied," unless, indeed, his superior social position clearly justifies them.

NOTES

[1.] Joseph Vendryes (*Language: A Linguistic Introduction to History* [New York: A. A. Knopf, 1925], p. 295) says of Creole-speakers: "Their apprenticeship to this language was never completed. It was limited to its superficial characteristics, to expressions representing the ordinary objects and essential acts of life; the inner essence of the language, with its fine complexities, was never assimilated. . . ." See also E. Schultze in *Sociologus,* IX, 377–418; Otto Jespersen, *Language,* chap. xii; D. C. Hesseling, *Het Negerhollands der Deense Antillen,* pp. 49–61; Leonard Bloomfield, *Language,* pp. 471–75; G. S. Lane in *Language,* XI, 5–8; monographs by Hugo Schuchardt, Ch. Baissac, R. Lenz, S. R. Dalgado, William Churchill, S. Sylvain, J. Faine.

[2.] J. Graham Cruickshank, *"Black Talk"* (Demarara, 1916), pp. 13–16.

[3.] In 1876 English was the medium of instruction of 31.3 percent of the school children; in 1886, of 77.6 percent; in 1895, of 99.5 percent; in 1902, of all.

[4.] The "Anglo-Saxon" civil population, and "Anglo-Saxon" children in the schools, have averaged about 6 percent of their respective totals and have been concentrated in Honolulu.

[5.] The Hawaiian Island vulgar dialect is described in *American Speech,* IX, 48–58, 122–31. The 1930 census returned 301,514 English-speaking persons and 66,824 who spoke no English (though actually many spoke crude "pidgin"). Perhaps 55,000 spoke standard or "good" English, 130,000–160,000 (most of the persons under thirty-five included) spoke a dialect called "pidgin," and the rest spoke makeshift English—true "pidgin."

For a (too schematic) discussion of levels of speech see R. de la Grasserie, *Des parlers des différentes classes sociales;* see also H. Dauzat, *Les Patois;* L. Bloomfield, *Language;* G. P. Krapp, *The Knowledge of English;* H. L. Mencken, *The American Language.*

[6.] This sort of incident seems to be typical of situations where mixed jargons are spoken. Some Indians of our Northwest used to think that Chinook jargon was the white man's language, and some whites still think it is the Indians' only tongue. Both Norwegians and Russians took the "Russenorsk" formerly spoken in Finmarken to be the others' language.

[7.] Few generalizations are wholly true. The real "Musa-shiya the Shirtmaker," who in the advertisements speaks a marvelous exaggeration of Japanese English, has several times been approached by Japanese not of the Americanized generation who have tried to induce him to discontinue his advertising in this medium. They say it lowers the dignity of the Japanese people. But no Chinese has protested to "me, P. Y. Chong," about his pidgin advertisements.

[8.] Professor L. E. Bassett, reported in the *Honolulu Advertiser,* April 17, 1935.

[9.] Their contact with good English is, however, sufficient to keep them from using inflated, "babu" English, though some are a bit bookish in their careful speech.

[10.] Except in a patronizing way, as indicated above in discussing the use of "pidgin" in newspaper columns.

How "New Americans" May Serve Hawaii

KENSUKE KAWACHI

AMERICAN citizens of Japanese parentage or the "New Americans" are passing through a fascinating human experience in racial adjustment. Born to an Oriental heritage, brought up in a cosmopolitan environment, and imbued with American ideals, they are testing whether or not they can be loyal citizens of America. What can they do to serve and contribute to Hawaii's progress? As its progress is due to the intelligence, prosperity, loyalty and attitude of mind of its citizens in general, each "New American," it is obvious, should first resolve to do that which is required of a loyal citizen of any nation. To receive whatever education is claimed necessary for his position in life; to secure honest livelihood; to participate in the political life of his community; to appreciate and contribute toward social welfare; and to have a philosophy of life: let the "New Americans" first consider the achievement of these ends.

It is evident that American citizens of Japanese parentage should receive adequate public education. Having for its purpose the ultimate absorption of the fundamental American ideals and principles, this is the basis on which American citizenry is built. Students who have the means and possess mental ability should continue their education through high school, college, university and even graduate school in order that they may prepare themselves adequately in the

An essay contest entry in *Nippu Jiji,* June, 1928. Reprinted by permission of The Hawaii Times Limited.

field of endeavor or profession they find of more interest. Those who are handicapped financially should continue their education at home for personal cultural appreciation and for the ability to form individual opinion. Clear thinking and intelligence are not the monopoly of those who can pursue their scholastic endeavors. Freedom of thought is a precious gift to each citizen and it is his duty to exercise it in the fullest sense possible.

In addition to the training in English, the "New Americans" should study the Japanese language, art, literature and culture in order that they may understand and appreciate that heritage. Their tasks lie not only in the assimilation of American ideals and thoughts but also in supplementing these with the best of Japanese learning and culture. The East has something to give to the West; and the West has something to give to the East. It is essential that one understands their differences. The Oriental is subjective—he thinks about nature; he thinks about the mystery of the world. But the Westerner is objective—he inquires into the laws of nature; he inquires into the laws of the universe. The people of the East are interested in the soul of nature; but the people of the West are more interested in the body of nature. The East is temperamentally religious; but the West is scientific. Obviously our "New Americans" should serve Hawaii by fusing the best expressions of the East and the West.

American citizens of Japanese parentage should find honest livelihood. This economical outlook is doubtless the outstanding problem of today and many pessimistic assertions are made in regard to it, but it is not without solution. By virtue of education, by the general social pressure and influence of environment, and because of the prejudiced attitude of the parents toward plantation labor, most of the boys are seeking preferred positions in the secondary industries or professional careers.

. . .

The "New Americans" should try to erase permanently the criticisms that are made against them. They are often spoken of lacking in creative thought and action; and so having no ambition beyond the required—they do efficiently what is expected of them but do not take the initiative. Perhaps this lack of creative instinct is a heritage but it is within control when subjected to proper discipline. If they can add to their remarkable ability to learn, the creative habit, greater things are yet to be heard from them.

American citizens of Japanese parentage can serve Hawaii by participating in the political affairs of the community in which they reside. This contribution consists in playing a part with interest in the game of community life involving consideration of such problems as: public health, good roads, adequate hospital accommodations, proper school supervision, law observance, public celebrations, and protection of individual right and properties. Especially should the "New Americans" exercise the suffrage right with intelligence. In this respect, they should acquaint themselves with the history of American politics and government so that they can appreciate and understand its significance. There is an ironical stigma attached to their voting in that if the majority of them happen to vote for the same candidate, they are accused of having voted in a racial bloc and on the other hand if they happen to scatter their votes, they are spoken of as lacking in cooperative spirit. But the fact still remains that their service to their community is expressed when they exercise with judgment this right of voting.

. . .

American citizens of Japanese parentage can serve Hawaii by solving their social problems. They should raise their standard of living but in their eagerness should guard carefully against disillusion resulting from an over-emphasis of this motive. Materialistic interpretation of social standards may lead to a tragic consequence. It is essential that they should have a standard of living commensurate with their salaries and wages. If the standard is low, they should first demand higher remuneration. To raise the social status is a legitimate aspiration of any group of people and the "New Americans" particularly, should exert their energy toward this end. Another duty which is involved in this social adjustment is for them to appreciate and understand the status of their parents. Due to difference in training, especially in language, the parents differ in many respects with the "New Americans"; but the latter should exercise patience and forbearance and continue beautifully in practice the romantic tradition, the filial piety, of their fathers.

Moral and ethical standards also need to be adjusted and perhaps in this field the "New Americans" can contribute greatly to Hawaii and the Pacific world at large. There is as yet no definite moral and ethical standard. But with advancement in education and the fruitful assistance of the various social and religious organizations, the "New Americans" are adjusting themselves to the diverse moral and ethical standards of the different groups of people, particularly that of the American and of the Japanese groups. The natural outcome of the adjustment will probably result in a happy combination of the best of the two elements. With appreciation and respect the "New Americans" should find the best characteristics of their Japanese heritage and combine them with the best of American ideals and institutions.

Lastly, American citizens of Japanese parentage can serve Hawaii by having individually a philosophy of life which is indicative of the attitude of mind of a constructive citizen. Notwithstanding the complexity of society and the play of forces which sometimes run counter to their efforts, they should find meaning and value in life. Simply stated, they should have as the basis of their activities a religious motive which will stand the test of experience. They should attach their lives to some worthwhile cause to which they are willing to give their last measure of service. The cause may be peace in the Pacific, brotherhood of men, "Kingdom of God," religious unity, social justice, equal rights and privileges, adjustment of the East and West, economical solidarity; but whatever it may be, it should be one that will stir their souls to action.

Japanese Problem in Hawaii: A Solution

AN EDITORIAL

ONE of the serious problems confronting Hawaii is the large number of Japanese. According to the statistics, the Japanese population of Hawaii is somewhere near 120,000, and the majority of this number is American citizen. In other words, there are more than 60,000 second-generation Japanese in the territory, and the question confronting them is, "Shall they remain in Hawaii, or shall they migrate to some other countries?"

Some say that they ought to be educated in the Japanese way and sent to Japan for their field of activities. But this, as a matter of fact, is impracticable, and is nothing but an empty argument. Three years ago I visited Japan, and investigated its conditions. I found the opportunities very scarce, and the thousands of higher school and college graduates jobless. Even the university graduates were engaged in menial work like street car conductors, motormen, auto-drivers, or policemen. Were the Hawaiian-born Japanese to go to Japan, only a negligible number may be able to land positions. The great majority will have to join the vast army of jobless men.

Others say that they ought to go to the mainland. To discover whether or not abundant opportunities await the Hawaiian-born Japanese, I visited America last fall. I met various groups of Japanese in every city or village from San Francisco to Los Angeles, also

In *The New Americans,* v. 10, no. 2 (May 1929), p. 1. Reprinted by permission of the family of Takie Okumura.

Ogden, Salt Lake City, Chicago, and New York City, and reached this conclusion: Compared to Hawaii, America has abundant opportunities for the Hawaiian-born Japanese. But such opportunities are not white-collar jobs. They are hard manual or agricultural labor.

Whether in Japan, or America, the openings for white-collar job or soft-soap work, are very scarce. But there are abundant opportunities for the Hawaiian-born Japanese anywhere on this earth, if they are determined to engage in agriculture.

Moreover, the migration to America is something that is possible for only a small number of Hawaiian-born Japanese. Even if those having proper birth certificates should go, there is no doubt that more than half of the Hawaiian-born Japanese will remain in Hawaii.

Such being the case, it would seem best for the Hawaiian-born Japanese, if they are going to be plain, individual laborers, to remain and work in Hawaii, where their American citizenship is recognized, and where their parents and relatives live.

Then, WHAT SHOULD THE HAWAIIAN-BORN JAPANESE DO?

Honolulu might expand to some extent, but there is no likelihood of there being any great increase in corporations and stores to accommodate all those who are seeking white-collar jobs. There are talks of creating new industries to accommodate job-seekers, but from present indications there is no likelihood of early materialization of these plans. In the field of bookkeeping, typing, engineering, auto-mechanics, dentistry, and other occupations, the field is already congested even now. Each year more than one half of the high school and commercial school graduates are unable to secure positions. There is no doubt that the employment problem would become really serious within the next few years. After spending many years at high school, and even at college, they can not be sleeping just because they can not find any employment. As long as they live, they must eat. Then what kind of work should they do in order to eat?

During these five years we have been urging the idea of "return-to-farm," or agriculture as life profession, for we believe that agriculture is the most practical road for the Hawaiian-born Japanese to tread. There may be one or two individuals out of ten who may excel in scholarship or in other channels, but the exception is rare. The majority is therefore destined for agricultural pursuit.

When we speak about agriculture, we do not simply mean the

sugar cane or pineapple industries. The cultivation of corn and potatoes, raising of hogs and chickens, bees and honey, and any products that are obtained from the soil are included. We are not insisting that young people must engage only in sugar or pineapple or coffee industries.

The best possible way for the Hawaiian-born Japanese is to obtain a homestead, and become an independent farmer. Several of my former boys have purchased homesteads of 30 to 60 acres, and are making a success. Whenever large tracts of land are opened for homesteading, young people should obtain even a small homestead of five or six acres. Cultivating the soil with their own hands, and eating their own farm products, they can be more free and independent. They can, then, run for offices in government, if they have interest in politics. Men who are commercially inclined can seek positions in banks or firms. In the event of their loss of position, they can return to their homestead and cultivate the soil. To build such a foundation for independent living is the wisest step for every citizen.

Japanese parents, particularly on the plantations or in rural districts, should inculcate into the mind of their children the necessary ideas of farming, arouse their interest and encourage them to make farming a life profession.

The territorial board of education is establishing in various schools Smith-Hughes classes in agriculture. The pupils are being given practical training in cane cultivation, pineapple cultivation, poultry raising, or dairying. The aim of the classes is to turn out youths with a practical knowledge of farming. The parents who desire their children to become successful farmers ought to enroll them in these schools. If necessary, they ought to be sent to high school and college for further study in agriculture.

At the same time, the parents must decide to live in Hawaii permanently, stop sending back their money to Japan, and save it for their children. When opportunity comes, they should help their children buy homestead, or land, and strengthen their foundation of development. Or else they should invest their saving in the various enterprises. From 1911 to 1921, Japanese in Hawaii sent back to Japan more than 20,000,000 yen. What would have been the result if this staggering amount of money had been invested in Hawaii's industries?

Outside of the plains of Waimea and Kau, and small acreages in various parts of the islands, the lands actually available for independent farming is limited. The great portion of the fertile lands is controlled by the sugar and pineapple plantations. Hence to these plantations we must turn.

But under the present system of labor, it is extremely difficult to attract young men born in Hawaii, whether they be Japanese, Chinese, or other nationality, to the sugar plantations. The system, we earnestly hope, would be re-adjusted to meet the newer conditions.

We wish to propose that promising young men who have graduated from agricultural schools and who desire to take up agriculture be shown preference, and that they be allowed to hold ten to twenty acres of cane fields and cultivate sugar canes for a long period, say fifteen or twenty years. In other words, a system of leasehold tenant, we hope, would be adopted. The system would surely create greater interest and zest, for it makes the men feel that they are in semi-independent farming.

We strongly believe that a large number of young men would begin to remain on the plantations if this system is put into operation, for on the plantations where the system is in vogue, notably Kekaha and Ookala, we hear hardly any dissatisfaction and see no shifting of the workers and their families. The workers on every plantation want it. It gives reasonably good wages, and a fair degree of security.

Were young men allowed to "lease" for a long term, and cultivate the canes, their aged parents and family would work, with newer incentive, with them. Both will strive to increase year after year the yield per acre. This will be in turn a great benefit to the plantations.

To the sugar plantation, the production of canes is most important. If canes do not grow, the plantation will be a failure. The system of so-called leasehold tenant will most surely increase the yield per acre, for the workers will not hesitate to put in a greater amount of labor. This fact is proven by Ookala. Men on that plantation stated that this year's crop was estimated around 8,500 tons. But the actual harvest netted, they said, 9,400 tons. These figures may not be accurate, because they were quoted by the men. But that there was a larger harvest must be a fact. We believe that the yield per acre on some of the Oahu plantations will increase, if this system is put into operation, and workers aroused to work with new spirit.

Hawaii can not depend everlastingly on the labor from without. The importation of labor will be bound to become more and more difficult. This system, however, will attract labor from within, and will save the plantations from going into unnecessarily big expenses of importing labor from the outside.

We also believe that the operation of this system will do away with the *lunas*, bribery, vicious competition, race discrimination, deliberate refusal to increase the yield per acre, or sabotage. All sorts of evil prevalent under the present system can be gotten rid of.

The conditions on all plantations are not the same. Each has its peculiar conditions. But wherever this system is workable, we wish to see it given a fair experiment.

If the plantation managements put this system into operation, and attract young men born in these islands, who are congregating in the cities, they would be solving the problem of occupation, and rendering a great service to Hawaii.

Chapter Six

A Question of Loyalty

"JAPANESE Troops Invade Manchuria."

On the radio, in the headlines of the newspapers, in the daily gossip at home and at the office, the latest report of Japanese expansion in Asia caused alarm. The news contained references to a Manchurian railway being attacked by Chinese armed forces, the Japanese counterdefensive, invasion of Japanese troops from Korea, and the occupation of Mukden by the Japanese Imperial Army.

Probably only a handful of people in Hawaii on that September day in 1931 knew where Mukden in Manchuria was located. Few understood the complexities of Japan's involvement in Manchuria and Korea, the political entanglements after years of Japanese maneuvering to secure her position economically and diplomatically in Asia. And probably even fewer were aware of the violent struggles within the Japanese government between the foreign ministry and the military for control over Japan's foreign policy.

Yet regardless of the superficiality of public opinion, one sobering image emerged from the morning news which ominously pointed toward war in the Pacific. Japan, a nation which epitomized in American minds the notion of the "Inscrutable Oriental," was on the move. And in the Islands, rumors and opinions founded and unfounded, expressed the fear that Japan would not stop until she controlled mainland Asia, the Philippines, Australia, the South Pacific, and the Pacific Islands—including Hawaii.

"The political-military web around Manchuria is so vast, so complicated, so woven of ancient as well as latter-day issues," editorialized the *Honolulu Star-Bulletin,* "that judgment on the rights and wrongs of the situation is difficult. But its significance is plain —an ordered and tremendously powerful move by Japan to extend her 'sphere of influence' in highly important and strategic territory."[1]

As the Japanese immigrant and his children had learned during the period of annexation, events in Asia, especially as they concerned Japan, had a direct impact on the peace and security of their own community in Hawaii. Fears of Japanese expansion and the jealousy of Japanese competition for resources in the underdeveloped nations of Asia had aroused suspicions of Japanese designs for conquest of the Pacific. Naturally, such suspicions turned on the Japanese immigrant. Were the immigrants and their children an advance fifth-column movement to undermine internal security before invasion? Were the Japanese trained spies, saboteurs, and rabblerousers who had clandestine connections with the emperor and his war ministers?

And, if not, if Japanese Issei and Nisei were indeed loyal citizens, honest Americans, why did they persist in maintaining Japanese language schools and Buddhist temples? Why did they stubbornly insist on identifying with their ethnic community, perpetrating a racial pride and defiance? Were they preparing themselves for an eventual Japanese regime in the Islands? Were they waiting for the day when the flag of the Rising Sun would fly above Honolulu?

The question of Japanese loyalty became a very real issue to many non-Japanese in Hawaii in the decade preceding World War II. As events in Asia accelerated the possibility of war, the Island community became more anxious to understand the position of the Issei immigrants and their Nisei offspring regarding allegiance to Japan. This concern over the political loyalties of Japanese stemmed in large measure from the technical issue of citizenship. Japanese immigrants in Hawaii before World War II remained Japanese citizens, subject to Japanese laws and military draft. But the immigrants maintained their legal status as Japanese citizens not only because they desired to preserve their close ties with the beloved homeland but because, by American law, they were barred as nonwhites from becoming naturalized citizens.

The naturalization laws which had established the criteria of eligibility for citizenship of the United States from 1790 to 1906 had consistently limited naturalization to those persons "free, white and twenty-one years of age." The Issei had faced this clause as the barrier to American citizenship. To question the propriety of the naturalization requirements as they applied to Japanese, Takao Ozawa in 1902 and again in 1914 filed petitions in the U.S. District Courts to challenge the existing naturalization laws which he felt did not exclude Mongoloids from U.S. citizenship. Both petitions were dismissed.

Ozawa was a Japanese immigrant who had lived in California before coming to Hawaii to work for Theo. H. Davies and Company. As a student at Berkeley High School and the University of California, Ozawa, unlike the more typical Japanese immigrant, was well educated in American mores. Maintaining by law and by any social standard that he was "white," Ozawa was persistent in his endeavors to become a naturalized citizen and finally took his case to the U.S. Supreme Court. His culture, he argued before the court, as well as his children's and wife's culture, had been cleansed of anything Japanese. The foods they ate, the utensils they used, the magazines and newspapers they read, and the language they spoke were 100-percent American. Mrs. Ozawa was a member of the YWCA's International Institute which aided immigrant families in their Americanization. Ozawa had even moved his family from a predominantly Japanese area of Honolulu, Kalihi, to one which at that time was a *haole* district, Kaimuki. As Ozawa judged his life, he was American *ipso facto,* a "white man," and therefore entitled to citizenship in the United States.

The Supreme Court did not agree. On October 23, 1922, in a decision which would destroy any Issei hope for American citizenship, the Court ruled that the intentions of the framers of the naturalization laws had been explicit. Although to be commended for his efforts to become an American, Ozawa was still a nonwhite. The law as specifically designed in 1790 classified applicants for naturalization on the basis of racial ancestry, not cultural heritage or practices. Being Japanese, being Mongoloid, it was impossible for the immigrant from Japan to become an American citizen.

The Issei's children, the Nisei, also had citizenship complications. Because the Japanese government considered Japanese *jus sanguinis* (by blood) to be Japanese citizens despite their residence or place of birth, Nisei were technically subject to Japanese law and military draft. But, due to American law which recognizes citizenship based on *jus soli* (place of birth), Nisei were also *bona fide* American citizens with the accompanying constitutional rights and privileges. This dual citizenship was a cause of community distrust for the second generation. How could Nisei, many non-Japanese questioned, serve two nations with equal loyalty and reverence?

To ameliorate the suspicions of the non-Japanese communities and to protect their children against the Japanese military draft, some Issei sought to expatriate Nisei from their Japanese citizenship. In December of 1924, the Japanese government revised the citizenship laws, stipulating that children born of Japanese immigrants in the United States could not have Japanese citizenship unless within fourteen days after birth their names were registered with the Japanese Consul. As a result, by 1933 nearly 5,500 male and female Nisei had voluntarily expatriated their Japanese citizenships, while more than 32,000 Nisei had lost their Japanese citizenship by failure to register at the time of birth.[2]

But the expatriation movement could not dispel the lingering doubt that if Issei and many Nisei still owed allegiance to Japan in the form of citizenship, then the Japanese of Hawaii were in some way connected with the plans of the Japanese imperial government. It became imperative then to discern just what those plans were and determine to what degree the Issei and Nisei were implicated.

The first persuasive presentation of evidence warning against Japanese imperialism and the dangers posed by large numbers of unassimilated Japanese in Hawaii was by Stanley D. Porteus. A prominent psychologist influenced by the dubious racial theories of his time, Porteus in 1925 studied the comparative intelligence of Hawaii's various ethnic groups. His findings, including recommendations and conclusions, were presented in his book, *Temperament and Race,* coauthored with Marjorie E. Babcock, which stressed that most indications showed Japanese to be intellectually and temperamentally a superior race. Living on a small island nation, isolated from outside influences, strengthened by a lack of domestic strife, and free from the struggles of "humanitarian traditions," Japanese had been able to channel their racial energies into political, economic, and intellectual advances. Consequently, because Japanese could effectively compete with the white race, America had to be alert to Japanese interests in the Pacific. Japan might protest that it had no designs of conquest, but Japanese policies were shaped and hidden behind a "mask of inscrutability."

Even in Hawaii the white race had to be alert to Japanese penetration. Although Porteus admitted the possibility that the policies and ideas of Hawaiian Japanese and Japanese in Japan could in the future be quite different, the Issei and Nisei represented a formidable economic and political force which had to be seriously considered. Certainly the Japanese had not exercised their full powers in the Islands, Porteus reasoned, because they were biding their time until "their full weight can be brought to bear." The white race, to maintain its control over the Hawaiian Islands, must shield itself from the onslaught of imperialistic Japan and the racial energies of her people. Porteus argued that to expose America or Australia "to the dangers of Japanese penetration, peaceful or otherwise, would be to pursue a policy of race suicide."[3]

Porteus' suspicions of the Japanese and their relationship with Japan was but one rivulet of the darker undercurrents of prejudice which characterized Hawaiian race relations. Although undercurrents of racial openness and acceptance had helped stimulate the Japanese to share a "local" identity with other Island ethnic groups, concomitantly forces of suspicion, prejudice, and racial stereotyping also helped to color daily interracial contacts. Influenced by these currents of both friendliness and hostility, the *haole,* Chinese, Portuguese, Hawaiian, and Japanese learned to share a common identity and an ample supply of racial invectives against their neighbors—"clannish Jap" or "sneaky *daikon,*" "lazy *kanaka,*" "tight Chink" or "*pake,*" "loud-mouth Portogee," "dumb *haole*" or "knife-wielding *manong*" were derogative slurs not unfamiliar to the Island resident.

In Honolulu these racial attitudes were intensified due to a high degree of competitive racial jealousies. Since the Japanese were a highly mobile and ethnically conscious group, being in an urban environment especially reinforced the racist attitudes against them. As sociologist Jitsuichi Masuoka concluded in 1936, "the urban area . . . is an area of free competition for status, and acute as well as subtle conflicts accompany the competitive struggle among the various races. As a result the Japanese have tended to become race conscious."[4] This subtle race consciousness among Issei and Nisei, exacerbated by a pride in their Japanese blood, was translated into restrictive racial barriers against interracial marriages. Between 1912 and 1934 the percentage of total outmarriages for the Japanese community was consistently less than 10 percent of total marriages, a figure remarkably less than all other racial groups in Hawaii.[5]

The consciousness of racial differences prevalent in Hawaii was also reflected in Japanese intragroup relations. Within the Japanese community existed a diversity of subgroupings, each with distinct status, prestige, and historical background. The immigrants from the main islands of Japan were known as the Naichi. The Naichi were the earliest and largest population of Japanese in Hawaii, establishing themselves as the dominant subgroup. Another subgrouping was the *eta,* or "untouchables," a special class of outcastes who historically had been the people who handled the blood of animals, and who included butchers and leather-tanners. The *eta* were considered a highly undesirable people due to their unsavory occupations and were ostracized from the mainstream of Naichi society. Issei went to great lengths to insure that their children did not marry anyone with *eta* blood.

Another subgrouping subjected to subtle discrimination by the Naichi was the Okinawans. Japanese immigration from Okinawa had been later than that from the main islands of Japan, being spearheaded in 1899 by Kyuzo Oyama, the "Father of Okinawan Overseas Emigration." The total proportion of Okinawans who immigrated to Hawaii by 1907 was approximately one-fifth of the total Japanese immigration.[6] Subjected to discrimination by Naichi because they were considered "barbarians" or "pig farmers," Okinawans encountered special problems adjusting to the race-conscious atmosphere of Hawaii.

The nature of the Okinawan–Naichi relationship was especially illustrative of the undercurrents of group hostility evident in the competitive society of pre–World-War-II Hawaii. In their study, "The Okinawan–Naichi Relationship," Henry Toyama and Kiyoshi Ikeda investigated the hostility, competition, and resentment found among Japanese subgroups.[7] They noted that Okinawans encountered more hostility from the Naichi in Hawaii than they would have in Japan because 1) the Okinawans in relation to the rest of the Japanese population were in greater number than in Japan, 2) Okinawans and Naichi had closer personal contacts in Hawaii than they did in Japan, and 3) the Naichi had an established culture of which they were proud, while the Okinawans "suffered from a sense of inferiority owing to their 'peculiar' cultural practices and institutions." Toyama and Ikeda felt the situation for the Okinawan was especially acute in Hawaii because they had the "double problem of adjusting to Naichi culture as well as to American culture, with all of the maladjustments and disorganization attendant upon this transition."

At the level of intra- and interethnic relations, then, the Island society of the 1920s and 1930s was replete with cross-currents of racial uneasiness. Even as the urban setting of Honolulu acted as a catalyst for greater interracial contacts and a "local" identity, ethnic groups continued to demonstrate the weaker human instincts of viewing others as "evil," "contaminated," or "inferior." *Haoles*, Hawaiians, Chinese, Koreans, Filipinos, and Japanese—all were actors and victims of racism.

But what had made the race relations problem for the Japanese community in the 1930s especially acute, as so dangerously revealed in the Porteus study, was the continued identification of Issei and Nisei with Japanese imperialism in the minds of Islanders. Japanese shouting *"Banzai"* in movie theaters during newsreels of Japanese victories in China, language-school students sending packages to Japanese soldiers fighting in Manchuria, or money being sent home to Japan to be used in the 1910 annexation of Korea were incidents which infuriated immigrants from China and Korea and aroused the distrust in all Islanders fearful of Japanese aggression.

Consequently, to disassociate Japanese from imperialism became a wise course of action for community leaders worried about the ramifications of Island racial tensions. As part of its editorial campaigns, the *Hawaii Hochi,* for example, responded to the 1938 Sino-Japanese conflict by reaffirming that:

> Japanese people and the Chinese people are not enemies. The conflict is between principles, systems, abstractions. The people on both sides are caught in the terrible machinery of war which once started is no respecter of individuals or individual rights. Here in Hawaii the issues of the war are even more remote from the lives of the people. Neither Japanese nor Chinese are responsible for what the governments of Japan and China are doing. Though their sympathies lie on one side or the other, they are not permitted to develop animosities or hatreds —although agitators and partisans of other races seek to meddle and disturb the harmony of racial relations here.[8]

The subduing of non-Japanese fears was also attempted by Shinji Maruyama, an Island resident and city editor of the *Nippu Jiji,* in an article he wrote for the *Honolulu Mercury* in 1929, "Will the Island-Born Citizens of Japanese Ancestry Control Hawaii?"[9] Arguing that the Japanese had neither the strength nor the desire to control Hawaii economically or politically, Maruyama intended to discredit the logic which was the foundation for anti-Japanese sentiment. Nisei voting strength, Maruyama indicated, was only 9.5 percent of the total electorate in 1928 and in no way showed the rate of growth that was so commonly held to be true by those who were uncertain of the Japanese community's loyalty.

But even if the Japanese vote were to "dangerously" increase, Maruyama argued that the Japanese did not vote in ethnic blocs. Just because a candidate was Japanese did not mean that he would be assured of receiving the entire Japanese vote. The Issei and Nisei were not homogeneous groups without internal rivalries, competitions, and struggles for power; the notion of Japanese immigrants and their children having common goals, interests, and ambitions controlled from Japan was ludicrous. For Maruyama, the Nisei, the only Japanese in Hawaii with the franchise privilege, were reliable democratic citizens, upholding American institutions and ideals. "A ballot in the hands of an American citizen of Japanese ancestry is not like a razor in the hands of a baby."

By 1935 the question of loyalty as it concerned the large population of Japanese in Hawaii had become a hotly debated issue throughout the Islands. In that year the first in a series of numerous Congressional hearings between 1935 and 1958 took place regarding Hawaiian statehood. Many Congressional leaders and local spokesmen opposed statehood for Hawaii because they feared the racial imbalance in the Territory; the Japanese clearly outnumbered the *haole*. If Hawaii became a state, they asked, would it elect a Japanese governor and legislature? And would the allegiance of this Japanese-controlled state be to the United States or to Japan?

Before 1935, the major opposition to statehood had actually not been based on a fear of Japanese domination, but on the feelings of a great many *kamaaina haole*s that Hawaii's sugar interests would have greater benefits with Hawaii remaining a territory rather than becoming a state. However in 1934 Congress seriously hampered the Islands' sugar market by recognizing Hawaii as a nondomestic producer of sugar rather than as an integral part of the United States. The Hawaiian Sugar Planters' Association realized that the effect of this new status would be to cut Hawaii's sugar quota by nearly 10 percent. Therefore when Congressional Delegate Samuel Wilder King introduced a Hawaiian statehood bill in the House of Representatives in May of 1935, he did so with the backing of Hawaii's sugar oligarchy.

The Congressional hearings on statehood which subsequently took place in Hawaii during the 1930s exposed the various attitudes and opinions which existed among residents concerning not only the Japanese but the structure of Island power. Some disgruntled Hawaiians and middle class *haole*s opposed statehood because racially and socially Hawaii represented an oligarchy, not a democracy. The *haole* elite had created a "sugar-coated fortress" which contradicted the republican ideals and virtues of American society. Before statehood could take place it was necessary to revamp and democratize Hawaiian institutions.

But perhaps the most persuasive argument which successfully retarded Hawaiian statehood was the issue of Japanese domination. During the 1937 statehood hearings, a distinguished spokesman came forward to present persuasive evidence that Japanese immigrants and their children were closely linked to Japan and had plotted to place the Islands under Japanese control. John F. G. Stokes, a resident of Hawaii since 1899 and former curator of Polynesian ethnology at the Bishop Museum, testified before the Congressional investigators that since the 1880s the Japanese had planned the conquest of Hawaii as a spearhead in the Pacific.[10] Recounting the steps of Japanese imperialism in the Islands from King Kalakaua's early trip to Japan to the period of uncontrolled labor immigration and the coming of the picture brides, Stokes inferred that such historical events proved that Japan had vital interests in Hawaii.

The most interesting portion of Stokes' testimony was his argument that the *haole*s of Hawaii had been "Japanized" by the Issei and Nisei. *Haole*s had learned to accept and encourage the perpetuation of Japanese culture, behaviors, and institutions because the Japanese had cunningly allowed the *haole*s to think the white man was superior; as a result the *haole*s had to treat the immigrant paternally. "Unperceived by ourselves," Stokes stated, "the white population of Hawaii has become Japanese minded, and this fact constitutes a strong argument against statehood. The technique has been that of the Japanese 'Gentle Divine Spirit,' to which white people yield very readily—especially those of wealth and importance. It appeals to the white man's conceit and feeds his superiority complex to aid 'his little brown brother.' "

Nisei, according to Stokes, were part of the plans to control Hawaii, even though some second-generation Japanese Americans were earnestly Americanizing themselves. The fact remained that these young people were influenced by a home and community which vigorously clung to Japan. Language schools, dual citizenship, Japanese newspapers—all had the effect of counterbalancing any positive influences the public schools or non-Japanese Americans could have on the Nisei.

Not all Islanders, however, responded to Stokes' reasoning with acclaim. For example, many influential *haole*s who supported statehood did so with a minimal fear of Japanese invasion or takeover. Either so propelled by economic interests that they were willing to defend Japanese immigrants and their children at the risk of the Islands' security or genuinely sincere in their belief that Japanese were no threat to Island life, these leaders testified that Issei and especially Nisei were loyal to American institutions and culture.

Representative of this style of leadership which minimized the notions of a Japanese menace was the testimony of Frank Midkiff before the 1937 statehood-for-Hawaii hearings. Midkiff was not a *kamaaina haole,* but had arrived in Hawaii from Illinois in 1913 to teach briefly at Punahou School, an exclusive private school in Honolulu. While teaching at Punahou, Midkiff married Ruth Richards, who came from an established *haole* family, and then stayed in the Islands to become a highly respected educator in both the *haole* and non-*haole* communities. From 1923 to 1934, Midkiff served as president of Kamehameha Schools, the private educational institution for children of Hawaiian ancestry. Later, he became trustee for the Bishop Estate, a private trust fund for the Hawaiian people.

A progressive educator steeped in the background of his Danish-American home in Illinois, which he later said taught him to "respect the rights of everyone else regardless of race and creed,"[11] Midkiff looked upon the non-*haole* peoples of Hawaii with a greater objectivity than did men such as John F. G. Stokes. He was willing to accept the fact that the Island community held a place for Japanese. Prior to World War I, he had joined the Hawaii National Guard and helped to establish the first company of American Citizens of Japanese Ancestry—company "D." Following the war Midkiff aided in the formation of a social-political group called "The Society of American Citizens of Japanese Ancestry." Throughout the twenties and thirties the name of Midkiff appeared on the YWCA and YMCA rosters, on the list of contributors to numerous civic organizations geared to aid in the Americanization of the immigrant population, and on nearly every scheduled program of the annual New Americans Conference. Midkiff was a *haole* who, committed to his libertarian beliefs, was influential in creating the image of the loyal dynamic community of Japanese who added to the wealth and quality of life in Hawaii.

Midkiff's Congressional testimony clearly reflected the attitudes of many Islanders who agreed that Japanese were loyal to America.[12] For Midkiff, the Nisei through their Americanization efforts and committed beliefs in the United States had proven that the population of Japanese presented no threats to Hawaiian or American security. As to Stokes' argument that the *haole* must beware of Japanese in Hawaii because of their Japanese heritage, Midkiff responded that "it may be quite as unfair to impugn the loyalty of our American citizens of Japanese ancestry because of their origins and Japan's history as to impugn Dr. Stokes' fairness because he hails from Australia where the country is historically anti-Japanese."

Further, Midkiff encouraged some expressions of Japanese culture in Hawaii because they added to the cultural diversity and beauty of the Islands. Obviously, Midkiff's notion of Americanism was not a bland, look-alike lifestyle but an incorporation of many cultures in a common bond of interest. "To say that Japanese culture is pure nationalism is too narrow, for we know well the fine arts, the crafts, the manners, and the honesty, filial piety, sense of duty, etc., of the Japanese. We see other things featured here in Hawaii and on the whole we find the result good."

As the question of Japanese loyalty to America was tossed about in the statehood hearings, as Stokes and Midkiff exchanged views as to whether or not Americanization had been successful or whether deep-seated allegiances to the government of Japan remained, it became apparent to many Issei and Nisei that the entire issue was out of their hands. Whatever the Japanese were to do, the reactions of the greater community would be predictable. If Japanese professed their loyalty, Islanders who had encouraged their Americanization would wholeheartedly agree, while others would ignore such statements as part of Japanese subterfuge. If Japanese played a subdued role in political life, many Islanders would applaud their civic responsibility and fairness, while others would damn them for biding their time until a Japanese invasion.

As the 1940s approached, the Island community, a community criss-crossed by the undercurrents of racism, paternalism, and liberalism, would determine the acceptance or rejection of the Japanese as loyal Americans. Both the Issei and Nisei, to varying degrees, had adapted themselves to Island living, had become acculturized to patterns of life which were foreign to Japan. But significant traces of Japanese culture and ways of life remained even for the New Americans. And as relations between Japan and America deteriorated, these aspects of Japanism in Hawaii heightened tensions, fears, distrusts, and expectations.

The question of loyalty would ultimately be answered, the alarmists had warned, if war were to develop. Only when Nisei and Issei were put to the test of wartime allegiance would Islanders learn the true motivations and identifications of the group. The anthropologist in the field, determining degrees of acculturation and Americanization, could not predict how Nisei would behave under war conditions. Sociologists working on the voting patterns and census of the Japanese population could tell nothing of political allegiance. Government bureaucrats doing secret studies of Japanese activities in Hawaii could not definitively state whether Japan had any direct malevolent influence over the Issei or Nisei. The New Americans Conference promoting Americanism and an image of loyalty could not guarantee that sabotage or espionage were nonexistent among Japanese in the Islands. Even the Japanese, involved in the events of daily living and the Hawaiian lifestyle, bewildered by the suspicions of an outside community, could not unequivocally state that within their ranks no traces of Japanese nationalism or pride of race existed.

Only war between Japan and the United States could expose how far the roots had grown into the Island soil. Only conflict could unmask which of the two masters the servant had been obeying. So the question of Japanese loyalty could not be answered until in the early hours of that Sunday morning when the pilots, having tied around their necks the *sennin bari,* the good-luck scarves of a thousand stitches, boarded the crafts upon whose fuselages was brightly painted the red globe of the Rising Sun. Gradually ascending above the aircraft carriers in scores, leveling off thousands of feet above the Pacific Ocean, they set their compass direction for a steady course, south to the Hawaiian Islands.

NOTES

1. *Honolulu Star-Bulletin,* September 21, 1931, 6:1.
2. United Japanese Society of Hawaii, *A History of Japanese in Hawaii,* ed. by Publication Committee, Dr. James Okahata, Chm., Honolulu: United Japanese Society of Hawaii, 1971, p. 246.
3. Stanley D. Porteus and Marjorie E. Babcock, *Temperament and Race,* Boston: Gorham Press, 1926, p. 336.
4. Jitsuichi Masuoka, "Race Preference in Hawaii," *American Journal of Sociology,* v. 41 (1936), p. 640–1.
5. Romanzo Adams, *Interracial Marriage in Hawaii: A Study of the Mutually Conditioned Processes of Acculturation and Amalgamation,* New York: The Macmillan Company, 1937, pp. 336–9.
6. Yukiko Kimura, *Socio-Historical Background of the Okinawans in Hawaii,* Romanzo Adams Research Laboratory Report No. 36, Honolulu: University of Hawaii Press, 1962, p. 8.

7. Henry Toyama and Kiyoshi Ikeda, "The Okinawan-Naichi Relationship," *Social Process in Hawaii,* v. 14 (1950), pp. 51–65.

8. Edwin Grant Burrows, *Chinese and Japanese in Hawaii During Sino-Japanese Conflict,* Honolulu: Hawaii Group American Council, Institute of Pacific Relations, 1939, p. 73.

9. Shinju Maruyama, "Will the Island-Born Citizens of Japanese Ancestry Control Hawaii?" *Honolulu Mercury,* v. 1, no. 2 (July 1929), pp. 26–32.

10. "Testimony of John F. G. Stokes," *Hearings Before the Joint Committee on Hawaii Statehood,* United States Congress, 75th Congress, 2nd session (October 6 to 22, 1937), pp. 247–63.

11. Helen Altonn, "The Lively Seventies," *Honolulu Star-Bulletin,* July 7, 1964, 27:1.

12. "Testimony of Frank Midkiff," *Hearings Before the Joint Committee on Hawaii Statehood,* United States Congress, 75th Congress, 2nd session (October 6 to 22, 1937), pp. 304–5.

The Okinawan–Naichi Relationship

HENRY TOYAMA AND KIYOSHI IKEDA

LITTLE if anything is known about Okinawan–Naichi relationship in Hawaii by those who are outside of the Japanese group. Although many have touched on this subject, the comments have been incidental. This article is an exploratory study into the in-group–out-group relationship existing between the Naichi and the Okinawan groups in Hawaii. It is based on student papers in the Hawaii Social Research Laboratory.

Much has been written of the Japanese from the main islands of Japan—Honshu, Kyushu, Shikoku, and Hokkaido. They are usually referred to collectively as *Naichi* (insiders) or *Yamato no hito* (men of Yamato). Little need be said here of them.

The "Okinawans" in Hawaii come from the islands of Okinawa *(Okinawa Gunto)* which is part of the Ryukyu Archipelago *(Nansei Shoto)* stretching in a southwesterly direction from the southern tip of the Japanese mainland to the island of Formosa, which forms the anchor to this chain. The distance between the southern tip of the Japanese mainland to the island of Formosa is approximately 700 miles. The islands of Okinawa are approximately 275 miles from the southern tip of the Japanese mainland. The Okinawa Gunto is composed of a major island, Okinawa, and several smaller islands surrounding it.

In *Social Process in Hawaii,*" v. 14 (1950), pp. 51–65. Reprinted by permission of *Social Process in Hawaii,* by Edmund H. Volkart, chairman, Department of Sociology, University of Hawaii.

The majority of the Okinawans in Hawaii came from the southern tip of the main island, principally from Naha, the seat of the provincial government, and the surrounding districts of Oroku, Tomigusuku, Kanagusuku, Itoman, Takamine, Gushichan, Kuchinda, Tamagusuku, Chinen, Haebaru, Nishihara, and Shuri. However, almost all the districts of Okinawa have representatives in Hawaii. (Historically, Okinawa long enjoyed an independent status. Culturally, the Okinawans are closer to the Chinese than are the Naichi.) Most of Okinawa's early commercial and cultural intercourse was carried on with China. At some date, still unsettled by historians, the Okinawans began to pay dual allegiance to China and to the feudal domain of the Satsuma clan on the island of Kyushu, the southernmost of the main islands of Japan. There are some indications that contrary to the policy of Japan proper of keeping Western nations out, Okinawa maintained limited commercial relations with Western countries. The relations between Okinawa and China and Japan, were thus: 1) primarily of trade with China; 2) primarily for protection from other would-be invaders and conquerors with Satsuma. These conditions held true until approximately seventy years ago, at which time Japan began to establish its program of National Unity and incorporated the Okinawa Islands into the Empire.

The relationship between the Okinawans and the Naichi in Hawaii is somewhat like that between the Irish and the English: one group feeling superior to the other, and the other having a defensive pride. The situation is also comparable to the Jewish–Gentile relationship in that there are very seldom manifest dangerous, overt feelings, the attitudes being mainly covert. When an Okinawan is first asked about the relationship, he will say that there is nothing of consequence in it. However, as the personal relationship becomes closer between the two persons a "story" is unraveled in which at one time or another, the person was or is still emotionally involved in this "problem." On the other hand, among children the mutual attitudes are more openly expressed in the form of "scraps." But feelings between the two groups usually remain at the covert level and are not made public, and one finds Okinawans and Naichis doing many things in common, until it begins to appear that intermarriage between individuals of the two groups is imminent. At that time, attitudes very often become expressed in overt actions of rejection and resentment on both sides.

The Okinawan–Naichi relationship in Hawaii has been clearly "defined" by the two groups involved. In Japan there seems to be little if any clear "definition of the situation." Nevertheless, student papers seem to bring out the feeling that the prejudice against Okinawans was brought over from Japan:

> *Okinawan student:* Discrimination of the Okinawan people is actually an old prejudice which the first generation Naichi brought with them from the Mainland of Japan.
>
> *Naichi student:* . . . Japan was first made up of the mainland only, but later included the island of Okinawa. Here was found an aboriginal type of people entirely different from the Japanese. They were made subjects of Japan and were given equal status to the Japanese.

. . .

Contrast these statements with:

. . .

> *Naichi student:* My mother told me when I asked her about whether she knew about Okinawans before coming to Hawaii, "In Japan I did not see any Okinawans and did not know about them as when I came to Hawaii. All that I learned about Okinawa was from books.
>
> "On the boat we met some (Okinawan women) who wore their obi just tied loosely and not like us. You know, the women are dark. Well, they put on oshiroi (face powder) and they really looked funny. When they were asked to come up to the deck for inspection and to give their names, they came in clothes fit only for housework. The man (inspector) told the women to get their brooms. We had a laugh over that."
>
> My mother seems to have picked up a few notions about Okinawans which have some credence among the Naichi. "You know, Okinawans seem to be more *yaban* (primitive) than the Japanese. Look at their facial features. They look like Malayans or Filipinos. Some of their dances with all the waving around seem very primitive and look like the Filipino kind. Even their dress seems bright. Some Okinawans are very fair and look like Haole. These people are said to come from the province of Itoman. Seven Spanish sailors were said to have been ship-wrecked there and in time their blood became a part of all the people there."

Other students who have gone to Japan and have come back have commented on the relative lack of prejudice towards Okinawans in Japan itself. Perhaps this lack of prejudice in Japan towards Okinawans can be traced to these factors: 1) The relatively few Okinawans in Japan proper (in the urban centers) compared to the greater number of Okinawans in Hawaii; 2) The Okinawan visitors from Hawaii and the Okinawans in the Japanese urban centers were primarily there to study or travel and usually enjoyed better social status. They had enough Japanese "traits" to pass as Naichi or to be accepted on an equal plane. By the same token, the prejudice and discrimination in intergroup relationships is intensified in Hawaii because: 1) The greater number of Okinawans in relation to the rest of the Japanese population (of the 180,000-odd Japanese in Hawaii, 10 or 15 percent probably are Okinawans or of Okinawan parentage; 2) The closer contacts in Hawaii, making for cultural prejudgments of each other's behavior especially evident in the "gossip across the backyard fence" among those of their own group about individuals of the other group; 3) The Naichi and the Okinawans who came to Hawaii are predominantly in the economically lower class in the old country, and therefore many of their ways are regarded "crude" and "uncouth." The Naichi have a culture of which they are proud, while the Okinawans, on the other hand, have until recently suffered from a sense of inferiority owing to their "peculiar" cultural practices and institutions. The Okinawans in Hawaii have had the double problem of adjusting to Naichi culture as well as to American culture, with all of the maladjustments and disorganization attendant upon this transition.

Thus, although there seems to be little if any antipathy toward Okinawans in Japan, Okinawans have frequently expressed resentment toward Japan and these feelings may have been transferred to Hawaii. Some Okinawan students recall their parents telling them stories about Naichi "carpetbaggers" who "made their pile" in Okinawa off the residents. Enforced use of the Japanese language and culture by the Okinawans seemed to have aroused resentment among the Okinawans against things Naichi and encouraged a pride in the Okinawan culture. This may have occurred in some areas and not in others for some students bring out the fact that their parents did not have any grudges against the Naichi in Okinawa.

In Hawaii the situation can be somewhat more clearly and precisely defined, as the accounts by both Naichi and Okinawan students reveal. The student reports reflect the reciprocal stereotypes in the two groups with regard to each other.

> *Okinawan student:* The Okinawan is categorized as "loud, rough, and his speech guttural." During my childhood, I remember hearing Naichi children teasing Okinawans with a rhyme, "Okinawa ken ken, buta kau kau," implying that the latter ate pig slop. The Okinawans retorted, "Naichi, Naichi, chi ga nai (The Naichi has no blood, a pun involving two meanings of the word Naichi.)" Among the young

Okinawans, such phrases as "The Naichi think they're better than us," and "They take us cheap," were common.

. . .

Okinawan student: One day, when I was in the eighth grade, I was very embarrassed by one of my bosom friends (Naichi). He had somehow heard that I was an Okinawan and when I said I was, he could hardly believe it. I still recall that incident very clearly.

"Hey Satoru, somebody say you Okinawan, 'as right?"

"Who said so?"

"We—ll, somebody, 'As right or what?"

"Yeah."

"Gee, gees Christ, you no stay lie, huh?"

"No."

"But you no look Okinawan, yet."

"No can help, huh."

"Ahh, 'as all right. You good guy anyway."

This indicated that the Naichi children knew the difference between themselves and us, whatever the difference may be. I do not know whether the parents led the Naichi children to believe such a "false ideas."

The boy had told his friend, "You no look Okinawan." What is the "Okinawan look?" Many Naichis say that they can spot an Okinawan by his "hairiness, curly or wavy hair, big round eyes, short stature and dark complexion in comparison with the Naichi. The Naichi are less hairy, fair, and have slant eyes." Here the "definition" or preconception is in terms of physical traits.

But these definitions for both groups are quite unreliable in that individuals in each group are from time to time mistaken about the other.

. . .

Naichi student: Right in my home, I have an older sister who is very fair, not hairy, slant-eyed, and her appearance as a whole leads anyone to think that she is a Naichi. On the other hand, my younger sister is dark, more hairy, has big round eyes and her general appearance is that of a typical Okinawan. My best friend at the University looks like an Okinawan, and it was some time before I found out that she was really Naichi.

. . .

It is commonly thought that the family name provides positive proof of Okinawan origin. As might be expected, however, under conditions such as these, some Okinawans change their names to conform with those of the Naichi. Moreover, some of the same names are found in both groups, thus frequently creating situations of embarrassment and "shame" to the participants.

. . .

Over and above the conception of Naichi and Okinawan in terms of physical traits, "perceptible" culture differences in language, manners and certain other traits help to perpetuate the sense of difference and the consequent discriminatory treatment.

Student papers bring out the fact that there is an Okinawan "accent" which Naichi people judge as "uncultured" and even "obnoxious" to the ears.

> *Naichi student:* The first generation Okinawan's usage of the standard Japanese is very strange to the Naichi. The Okinawan people always seem to put their accent on the wrong syllables. One of the most evident pronunciations I have noticed was the way the Okinawan people said "*okazu*" (the dishes that go with the staple food of rice). The Naichi say *okazu* with the accent on the last syllable, but the Okinawans say the word by prolonging the last syllable.

Listed below are a few examples of the difference in language between the Naichi and the Okinawan:[1]

Naichi	Okinawan	English
buta	uwa	pig
ko	kwa	child
inu	ing	dog
okane (zeni)	jing	money
atsui	achisanu	hot
samui (hiyai)	hisa	cold
nagai	nagasanu	long

The difficulty of communicating between the two groups leads to the judgment that the minority group which deviates from the norms of the dominant group are "coarse and uncultured in their language."

. . .

Some of the other cultural practices of the Okinawans which make for prejudicial and categorical behavior on the part of the Naichis are: 1) Tattooing, 2) Hog-raising, 3) Restaurant and related business practices.

"One of the most interesting customs of the old Okinawan people was their custom of tattooing a woman's hand as soon as matrimony was expected or entered into. Blue blocks of about one square inch in size were tattooed on the woman's hands and arms. If the woman belonged to a very high class, she had a lot of blue tattooing on her hands and arms, but if the woman belonged to a very low class, she had very little tattooing on her hands."

How do the Naichi look at the tattooing of the Okinawan women? Some students say, "The Okinawans are aboriginal or primitive in tattooing their hands like other primitives to the South":

> As far back as I can remember, I have heard that the Okinawans are an inferior group. Many queer things were made up about them, especially when we were children. Children are an imaginative group but perhaps their imaginations only carry out the thoughts and doings of older people. I recall very clearly how we used to blacken the backs of our fingers with the ends of burnt sticks that we "borrowed" from mother's old-fashioned stove. Little did we know then that their hands were tattooed as a symbol of marriage. We had the queer notion that those women were born with such marks to distinguish them from others. Much fuss was made by those whose turn it was to be Okinawan for one day, for that meant being ordered by the others.

How does an Okinawan feel about his mother having tattoo marks?

> Some Naichi people just stare at the Okinawan women when they meet them on the street or in the bus. Therefore, there are quite a few Okinawan children who hesitate to go along with their mothers. My mother has tattoo marks on her hands, too, of which I am not ashamed. Those tattoo marks are a means of beauty to her and her friends.
>
> The Naichi women had their teeth painted black before. That was a custom which once made them conspicuous.

Hog-raising was practiced in Okinawa and it provided a means of occupational adjustment here for a considerable number of Okinawan immigrants who established their pig barn near plantation camps. As a result, Naichi children have coined epithets. The most famous of the jibes about "pig heads," *buta*s, and what have you, is *"Okinawa ken ken, buta kau kau,"* which was mentioned in an earlier context.

The Naichi children learned this phrase and oftentimes sang it in sing-song fashion as the Okinawan man or his son collected the *buta kau kau* or "pigslop" from the houses. The Naichi child regarded pig-raising as lowly work fit for only Okinawans who were dirty and smelly as they passed by hauling the slop for the pigs. Perhaps the disparagement of Okinawans for pig-raising may be traced to the fact that in Japan, the Eta do the raising and especially the killing of animals.

Restaurant and related business in Hawaii seem to have a majority of Okinawans connected with them. In this relationship, competition between members of the two groups make for ambivalent feelings on on the part of the Naichi of respect and envy and resentment against the Okinawans for being "smart in business." The idea of "let them take an inch and they'll take a mile" prevails in many Naichi circles. The Okinawans feel this too as evidenced by this Okinawan student's comment:

> There is a general attitude among the Naichi that the Okinawan is somewhat like a Jew in being shrewd in business. They think of the Okinawans as a people who are willing to take any kind of a job. As an example, I have heard that the Naichi considered working in a restaurant or an "eating business" as a job that would place them in a servant's status, so that the Okinawan usually took the jobs and learned the trade or business from the inside. As a consequence, among the Japanese restaurant owners today, one will see the majority will be Okinawans.

. . .

One naturally wonders what the effect of these stereotypes may be upon both Okinawans and Naichi—the extent of emotional involvement among both groups and the consequent relations between the two groups.

When first asked as to his attitudes, a Naichi states that he has no prejudice against Okinawans and that everybody ought to be treated equal in Hawaii. The Okinawan, on the other hand, will state that the situation doesn't bother him or that it isn't too bad nowadays, but as one goes deeper into the private attitudes of an Okinawan, then personal experiences involving prejudicial treatment are brought out. One of the first things mentioned is the marked feelings of inferiority and "shame." These attitudes seem to be learned very early in an Okinawan's experience as shown by these excerpts:

> *Okinawan student:* As a child, I always felt the ways of the Naichi superior. Our whole pattern of manners and speech was from them. My parents conversed with each other in their native dialect but sent their children to Japanese school to learn the Naichi language. In language school, the teacher and important school officials were

Naichi and children of Naichi parentage excelled in speech. The Naichi homes I visited were more orderly and showed a higher standard of living than ours . . . I considered what the Naichi ate tastier than what we had.

I early became aware that Okinawans were considered on a lower scale (socially) than the Naichi and felt Okinawan ways inferior and crude. This feeling went so far as to include Okinawan music. When mother played native records on the phonograph, the rest of the family would be concerned over whether they could be heard by nearby Naichi families. My sister would close the lid of the phonograph and adjust the volume to be heard only in our home. This attitude toward native music was characteristic in other Okinawan homes also.

. . .

The following statement by an Okinawan student reveals a sense of resentment for their prejudicial attitudes and behavior.

The ones (forms of discrimination) which hurt the Okinawan the most are social and psychological in nature. As an instance of social discrimination, to be classified lower than an "Eta" adds insult to injury. Added to this is the fact of taking good-naturedly abuses and razzings which are unbecoming of a human being and morally uncalled for. No one wants to be referred to as "hairy, *buta,* big rope" and the like. But the worst treatment anyone can receive is the "silent technique."

On dates it is customary to call at the home of the girl to meet the parents. Upon introduction, your ancestral origin is bound to come up or to be noticed. The following calls are made in a most cold and unpleasant environment. The "not wanted" sign is hoisted. It seems that equality of privilege or what have you, is not to be assumed if you're unlucky enough to be born an Okinawan. It may be that the old folks and the younger generation have no common ground to meet on but at least they could emit a miserly smile. There are many things that sicken the heart. Prejudice without knowledge is displayed by the Naichi towards the Okinawan in varying degrees.

The relatively larger number of papers written by Okinawan students about this "problem" may be an indication of their being much more emotionally involved than the Naichi students. Excerpts taken from the few Naichi student papers tend to show the more or less "unconscious" acceptance of this prejudice as a part of a typical Naichi's attitudes in Hawaii:

Naichi student: We ourselves avoid relations with Okinawan boys and girls, especially going steady with one of them. If there is a rumor that a friend of ours is going out with an Okinawan boy or girl, we tend to disapprove of it for reasons unknown. We laugh at the way they talk, sing, and dance, saying that they are queer and funny. Actually their ways are no more queer and funny than many dialects, songs, and dances of other parts of Japan. We do not stop to think how funny our parents' culture might seem to other people.

. . .

New Definitions Emerging

The stereotyped definitions of Okinawan and Naichi—of inferiority and superiority—and the consequent social distances between the two groups are still very much in evidence as indicated by the student papers. But there are also indications of new attitudes and definitions emerging. In the transitional period, one finds a continuum of groups and individuals from those who "stick to their kind," to those who associate freely with members of the other groups. Some Okinawans identify themselves as Okinawans first, while others tend to identify themselves as Japanese first and Okinawans second.

Ambivalent attitudes within individuals of both groups quite naturally tend to develop under these conditions.

Okinawan student: But I believe there must be covert conflict within an individual whether to marry his kind or out-marry, because I feel this conflict within me. Really I see no wrong in marrying out and sometimes I see nice persons in the other group and meditate and say perhaps they are all right. But on the other hand, if and when my emotions get the better of me, I cannot help but feel uneasy, gloomy, lonely, and even tense at the thought of marrying a Naichi. In the final analysis, I figure that I cannot marry one outside my own ethnic group the way I feel. It always comes back to me that my parents used to tell me time and again, "If possible, marry an Okinawan, they understand us better. Both families will be happier and have stronger and friendlier ties. It would be better in the long run."

Naichi student: Deep within me is an immutable conviction that I will never take a step toward intermarriage with an Okinawan. The fear of being rejected is too strong a pressure on me. It is a shame and wrong that I was exposed to such an unreasonable prejudice, but it is even more painful to have to confess my weakness.

. . .

The following statement by a Naichi student of a discussion with his mother about his Okinawan fiancee, reveals the shifting and equivocal attitudes toward intermarriage:

Mother: It is hard for me to give up my prejudice towards an Okinawan. I know that I ought to treat everyone on an equal plank whether they be Okinawans, Etas, Negroes, or Filipinos. But you must understand that we old folks have had to face a lot of resentment and prejudice from other kens from Japan proper who considered themselves better than us and marriage with their families would lead only to complications and squabbles. Okinawans are a little farther removed from the Naichis.

Son: But do you actually feel any resentment against Mi-chan for being an Okinawan?

Mother: I would not say that. . . .

Son: Then put it this way. How do the neighbors think of a marriage between an Okinawan and a Naichi? Would they gossip and object to such an idea?

Mother: If you ask that, yes.

Son: Then would you not say that of yourself in that you would feel "shame" in front of them?

Mother: Yes.

A typical expression of the new definition is shown in this excerpt:

I am an Okinawan. I am as normal as any other human being, mentally and physically. My parents are aliens and speak Japanese and their native dialect, Okinawan. I speak English, Japanese, and very little Okinawan, although I can understand most everything in the latter. Ever since I can remember, my parents have told us never to marry a *Yamato-no-hito* or "Naichi." Later, someone gave me the following explanation. "Long ago, Okinawa (the Ryukyu Islands) was an independent nation, but Japan conquered her. All prefectural groups such as Fukushima, Hiroshima, Niigata, etc. on the Japanese mainland are classified as Naichi. These people call themselves Japanese; they do not consider us as real Japanese; they say we were conquered; therefore, we are low-class and inferior." I was frequently told, "Don't associate with Naichi; they will always take advantage of you, etc."

Does this mean that all my friends are Okinawans? Certainly not! I have had very few Okinawan pals; my best friends are Naichi. What does this imply? Why, simply that this problem of adjustment depends largely on the personality makeup. What do I care what nationality, prefecture, etc., my pals come from, as long as they have desirable personal qualities.

I have never had too much trouble with the Naichi–Okinawan relationship because I usually laugh things off. However, I know some young people (indoctrinated the same way as I) who have a difficult time adjusting to the situation. They are so conscious of their background it is pathetic. If they should realize how narrow-minded their attitudes are, they would lead happier lives.

. . .

What can one expect of this Okinawan–Naichi relationship in the future? It seems that the old definition of inferiority–superiority is passing away. In its stead, equalitarian contacts are being stressed. This new definition has been fostered by the public school, the churches, and by public sentiment. Old attitudes will tend to become increasingly suspect and will be more difficult to justify. On a crucial question such as intermarriage, one can expect to find some measure of opposition. Until such a time as interracial or nonracial movements become an accepted part of the Naichi and the Okinawan groups as well as other groups in Hawaii, social movements within the Okinawan groups like the Hui Makaala[2] still tend to arise to meet the needs of the group.

To summarize, in the closer contacts in Hawaii and in the competition for a higher social status and a better economic position here, the in-group–out-group relationship between the Naichi and the Okinawans has been intensified to a degree not found in Japan proper. Most of the feelings have been relatively covert. The first definition of this relationship that developed in Hawaii has gradually been changing to one involving the equalitarian point of view. However, in this transition from the old to the new, ambivalent feelings have arisen, which in time will tend to pass away with the older generation and their ethnocentric attitudes.

NOTES

1. Editor's note: The word lists above are just one student's conception of difference in language between the two groups and we would like to make it clear that we do not hold the translations as necessarily accurate.
2. A social organization of second-generation Okinawans in Honolulu focusing major attention in the cultural and educational improvement of their group.

Will the Island-Born Citizens of Japanese Ancestry Control Hawaii?

SHINJI MARUYAMA

THE persistent effort of the sugar interests during half a century to import alien labor for industrial purposes completely changed the homogeneous character of Hawaii's population which more or less remained intact until 1850. We have now as a result of this effort, on which the sugar planters spent several millions of dollars, and as the result of the natural influxes of peoples which have taken place since annexation, a population consisting of Hawaiians, Americans, Portuguese, Japanese, Chinese, Filipinos, British and half a dozen other races and nationalities. The governor's report for 1928 shows that the estimated population on June 30 of that year was 348,767, of which almost half were alien.

The major racial groups in the Hawaiian population are the Hawaiian, Portuguese, Chinese, Japanese, Filipino, and "other Caucasian" which includes the American. The largest of these groups is the Japanese. There are at present in the Territory 134,600 Japanese. Of this number 83,242 are island-born.

The Fourteenth Amendment to the Constitution of the United States declares that all persons born in the United States and subject to the jurisdiction thereof are citizens of the United States. As Hawaii is an integral part of the United States, this constitutional provision makes all Japanese and other children born in this Territory citizens and as such grants them all the political rights and privileges incidental to American citizenship. They may elect and be

In *Honolulu Mercury,* v. 1, no. 2 (July 1929), pp. 26–32.

elected to public offices, municipal or territorial, and in the event Hawaii is admitted to the Union, to state and national offices, including the presidency of the United States.

While all this is true, it neither creates the "problem" nor causes the "alarm" to which uninformed people allude. The problem and alarm come to many people, especially in the continental United States, from the fact that children of Japanese descent—potential voters of tomorrow—outnumber all racial groups, and from the possibilities of the domination of the territorial electorate by representatives of this racial group. Their increase in number and steady growth of their voting strength have led those who are interested in Hawaii's future political situation to ask some pertinent questions. One of them is: What is the attitude of the rising generation of citizens of Japanese descent toward American citizenship and the United States? But the more common question asked here and on the United States mainland is: Will the island-born citizens of Japanese descent control Hawaii? Reserving the first question for discussion in the latter part of this article, let us proceed to consider the question with which we are more immediately concerned, namely, whether or not citizens of Japanese nativity will control Hawaii politically.

The present territorial electorate, based on the general election figures of 1928, is 46,058. Classified by race, there are 4,839 Japanese voters, 3,950 Chinese, 7,057 Portuguese, 8,964 Americans, and 18,952 Hawaiians and part-Hawaiians. The remainder includes British, Germans and others.

Twenty-seven years ago, in 1902, when the first Japanese cast their vote, the total number of electors in the Islands was 12,612. There were in that year 3 Japanese voters, 143 Chinese, 594 Portuguese, 1,932 Americans, 8,680 Hawaiians and a handful of voters of other races.

A comparison of the figures of 1928 and 1902 shows that during this period of 26 years the Japanese votes increased by 4,836, Chinese by 3,707, American by 7,032, Portuguese by 6,463, and Hawaiian and part-Hawaiian by 10,272, while the total electorate was augmented by 33,446.

At the general election ten years ago, in 1918, the territorial electorate was 20,124. The Japanese votes numbered 287, Chinese 954, American 3,810, Portuguese 2,844, and Hawaiian and part-Hawaiian, 10,901. This shows that during the sixteen-year period, from 1902 to 1918, the Japanese votes increased by 284, Chinese by 811, American by 1,878, Portuguese by 2,250, and Hawaiian by

2,221; and that, for the ten-year period from 1918 to 1928, the Japanese votes gained by 4,552, Chinese by 2,996, American by 4,154, Portuguese by 4,213, and Hawaiian by 8,051.

. . .

The foregoing official figures establish beyond a reasonable doubt the fact that the voters of Japanese descent are not increasing as rapidly as is commonly believed; that their increase during the last 27 years, with the exception of the Chinese, has been less than that of Portuguese, Americans or Hawaiians who make up the bulk of the voting population; and that their present voting strength is only 9.5 percent of the total electorate.

. . .

In considering the political situation in Hawaii we must not overlook the fact that while the Japanese voters are increasing voters of other racial groups are also increasing; and that the Japanese race is not as prolific as is erroneously believed; and that many children are moving out of the Territory, it being estimated that there are already in Japan some 20,000 island-born Japanese with little or no intention of returning to the Islands.

Taking into consideration all these facts and judging the future by the past and present, the answer must necessarily be "no," to the question, "Will the island-born citizens of Japanese descent control Hawaii?"

My personal belief and opinion are that island-born voters of Japanese descent will not attain a sufficient numerical strength to dominate politics in Hawaii. Most of them have affiliated themselves with either the Republican or the Democratic party. There is no bloc among them. The characteristic group solidarity of the first generation does not exist to any appreciable extent among the young people. This is best demonstrated at election times. During the last general elections two of their kind ran for the House of Representatives of the Territorial Legislature from the same district on the island of Oahu. When their candidacy was announced, it was naturally expected the Japanese voters would rally to their support by reason of nationality. Nothing of the kind happened. They split up in two factions, joined the rest of the voters of other races, and voted for the men of their choice. The result was neither polled sufficient votes to be elected.

There was another instance during the same election in another section of the Territory. A promising young man was a candidate for the Territorial Legislature. He did exceedingly well but failed of election by a few votes. One group of his own race had refused to support him. Leading members of the younger generation have often been heard saying just because a certain candidate is of the Japanese race is no reason why all the Japanese should vote for him, which is a healthy statement and augurs well for the political future of these Islands.

A ballot in the hands of an American citizen of Japanese ancestry is not like a razor in the hands of a baby. Experience shows that he can use it judiciously without injuring his own cause or menacing the welfare of others. There has not been an instance where he has deliberately abused it. Trained in the public schools, brought up in an enlightened environment, loyal to the ideals of America, and patriotic to the Stars and Stripes, he is in every sense American and does not wish to be set apart as non-American and classified according to the land of his parents' nativity. I believe this attitude is right, for a man who thinks himself as belonging to a particular national group in America has not yet become a true American.

Hawaii is conducting a great social and political experiment, testing whether its racial components can act as a single American unit with undivided allegiance to one flag. The American citizens of Japanese descent, one of the prominent racial components of this cosmopolitan community, in obedience to the mandate of true Americanism, are striving to live up to the ideals of American citizenship, and it will be a great disappointment to them if they are denied full participation in the American scheme of government on account of their race or color.

. . .

Leaders of the territorial and national government and those who are immediately concerned with the administration of their political affairs can rely on their fellow citizens of Japanese origin to stand unflinchingly by them in their determination to vindicate the faith that is in them and to demonstrate the vigor of their institutions. Shall Hawaii and the United States avail themselves of the aid of citizens of Japanese descent and thus rivet them with indissoluble bonds to America? Or shall they, by chilling their hearts with suspicions and weakening their loyalty by unreasoning hostility, add the force of conviction to the slanderous accusation maliciously disseminated by the apostles of violence, that America is a country of one race and one class?

American citizens of Japanese descent stand ready and willing, not only to offer their lives for the cause of the United States as they did during the last war but also to sever anything that savors of political ties to their ancestral land as evidenced by their fight against dual citizenship which they absolutely refused to countenance. What greater evidence is required to prove their worth as American citizens?

In short, the attitude of the rising generation of American citizens of Japanese descent toward American citizenship and the United States is this:

We believe that the Japanese born here should be given a fair chance to show themselves that they are capable of exercising properly the rights of American citizenship when political opportunities are offered them. Our belief and opinion are when the day comes the fear that the Japanese will have political control over Hawaii will not be observable. We are aware of the fact that along with the rights and privileges of American citizenship granted us, there are responsibility and obligation to assume and execute; that we have no less nor greater rights; that it is our duty to vote for the best candidate regardless of color or race; that we have to participate in the government with the interest of the country in which we were born first at heart and at all times; that having been born of a different race is no fault of ours; that our parents are Japanese is no reflection; and that it is our duty to prove that we are true Americans.

Testimony of John F. G. Stokes

CONGRESSIONAL TESTIMONY

Mr. Stokes. My name is John F. G. Stokes; born in Australia; 62 years of age and a resident of Hawaii for nearly 40 years. I arrived here in February 1899 and became an American citizen in September 1904. I was connected with the Bishop Museum for 30 years, part of the time as curator of Polynesian ethnology and part of the time as curator in charge. For the last 8 years I have been a research student in Hawaiian history.

. . .

Most arguments here against statehood have been based on the Japanese question, concerning which I propose to speak.

Local residents of Japanese blood number 150,000 out of a population of less than 400,000, or about 40 percent, and more than twice as many as the next largest number of any racial unit. On account of the high birth rate, the proportion is increasing. About 110,000 are American-born, nearly a quarter of whom have already reached voting age. Not all have registered, but those who have done so predominate in three out of the six counties of the Territory. Were all now registered, they would constitute the largest local voting group.

The parents of those American citizens, being Japanese subjects,

In *Hearings Before the Joint Committee on Hawaii Statehood,* United States Congress, 75th Congress, 2nd session (October 6–22, 1937), pp. 247–263.

have always been under the control of their home government, which has been reaching for the Hawaiian Islands for 50 years, and was openly aggressive against the Hawaiian Republic, as will be demonstrated presently. Since annexation, the aggression has continued, but not openly.

While it has been difficult to convince Americans here and on the mainland that Japan's great object is world conquest, keener students of world politics are now coming to recognize it as a fact. Japan is always studying, planning, and preparing, with oriental patience, and will move, as she always does, when the time is opportune. The ambition is not recent, it goes back 350 years, but in the past 50 years has become very definite. Observe this interesting picture (*China Weekly Review,* October 26, 1935) for home-consumption propaganda. It represents a Japanese soldier and a Japanese sailor wrapping up the world in a Japanese flag, the Japanese inscription being: "The Japanese flag will envelop the world." The design was on a sheet of wrapping paper found in Japan.

To one who has studied Japanese and local backgrounds, it seems that statehood for Hawaii at the present time might become dangerous to the United States in the near future. At best it would be risky, so why place Hawaiian control in the hands of an unproven group, especially one descended from subjects of an aggressive and ambitious nation which at any moment may become an active enemy?

. . .

Unperceived by ourselves, the white population of Hawaii has become Japanese-minded, and this fact constitutes a strong argument against statehood. The technique has been that of the Japanese "Gentle Divine Spirit," to which white people yield very readily—especially those of wealth and importance. It appeals to the white man's conceit, and feeds his superiority complex to aid "his little brown brother." Its effects are very noticeable in Hawaii, which is spoken of as a melting pot, but it is a Japanese melting pot wherein American culture is being melted. Illustrative of this Japanese-mindedness, I want you to observe the complacency and lack of comment in this alleged American community, with which the following incidents were accepted:

Here (*Honolulu Advertiser,* August 1, 1937) is illustrated the launching of an American registered 63-foot vessel *Kyo Maru,* covered with Japanese flags. On one side is a small American flag—a recent concession because in earlier launchings observed, it was absent. In the same publication is this other picture illustrating a ceremony in which two Shinto-Buddhist bishops bless a field at Waialua, this island, just prepared for the American game of baseball.

Another picture here (*Honolulu Advertiser,* September 4, 1937), a rather pretty one, shows two American girls of Japanese ancestry preparing sennin-bari. These are charmed jackets or waistbands, intended to guard Japanese soldiers in China from Chinese bullets.

Here (*Nippu Jiji,* December 6, 1933) is shown the ceremony of blessing a Hawaiian government bridge by Shinto-Buddhist priests. Prominent in the congregation is a Territorial legislator who did not expatriate from Japan until over a year following his election.

Enormous sums, stated to be $50,000 a month, are now being sent by the local Japanese to help the Japanese soldiers in China—rather a curious contrast to last year's united welfare drive when the local Japanese contributed $11,000 and received back $132,000.

Upon invitation, the publisher of the *Honolulu Advertiser* gave a very patriotic and helpful talk on the statehood question at the McKinley High School—locally nicknamed the Mikado High School. The alien editor of a Japanese-language paper condemned the excellent American address as "stirring up racial ill feelings."

. . .

Thus, an alien Japanese tells the young Americans of Japanese ancestry at McKinley High School that the patriotic American address they have heard from an American, of very many generations back, is prejudiced, lacks common sense, and is only stirring up racial ill feeling, and then he takes a dig at the military defenders in whom the young Americans should take pride, or whom they should at least respect. In this American Territory, then asking for American statehood, no adverse comment was heard on the editorial from any, not even Americans of white and Japanese blood who were vaunting their patriotism.

A few of us were awakened to the advance made in the Japanization of our ideas by the incident, when congratulations were being extended widely in Hawaii to the Japanese Emperor, on the birth of an heir to the throne. All local papers in English and Japanese were full of it, and flags were everywhere. One might have thought that Hawaii already belonged to Japan.

. . .

It must not be supposed that a local favorable regard for Japan and Japanese would be displeasing to the Japanese Government. Let us visualize the map of the Pacific. On opposite sides of the ocean are America and Japan, two unbeaten Nations, with interests between. Hawaii in the possession of Japan, which also holds Micronesia, becomes a spearhead threatening the United States. On the other hand, an American Hawaii, with people of unquestioned loyalty, is a bulwark against Japanese aggression.

Japan reaching for Hawaii is an old story. It may have begun in 1881, initiated by our own king Kalakaua.

This king was a constitutional monarch, elected by the business interests, mostly American, although previously he had been noted for his antiforeign sentiments. However, he was believed to be controllable. He was not the choice of the natives, who wanted Queen Emma as their sovereign. Despite Kalakaua's supposed willingness to collaborate with the business interests, he was constantly scheming for absolutism, and against potential American annexation. Being brought to time after an outburst in 1880, he asked and received permission to make a world tour. He was accompanied by two sons of missionaries, but no Hawaiians.

As Kalakaua approached Japan, he began to speak of himself as an Asiatic—an opinion previously unheard. Obviously he was preparing his anti-American plans. He was received with the greatest honors by the Japanese Emperor, with whom he had a secret interview when the emperor's nephew was affianced to Kalakaua's niece Kaiulani, then 6 years old. However, the main part of this interview was the proposal by Kalakaua that a "Union and federation of the Asiatic nations and sovereigns" be promoted under the leadership of the Emperor of Japan. The latter took the matter under advisement and later replied by letter.

The proposal was not refused by the Emperor of Japan who, however, explained that he was then fully occupied in providing his people with a constitution. Nevertheless, he "ardently hoped" such union might be realized and would keep it constantly in mind. He also proposed a further exchange of views on what might be "not only the fortune of Japan and Hawaii but also of whole Asia." The date of the letter is January 22, 1882, and it may mark the initiation of the modern drive of Japan in controlling Asia.

Following Kalakaua's visit a labor convention with Hawaii was signed by Japan, but on the understanding that future Chinese immigration to Hawaii should be restricted—a significant point. Japanese contract laborers began to arrive here in great numbers.

The next link in this chain of circumstances was a visit to Honolulu in 1892 by Sir Edwin Arnold, the noted Buddhist and poet. He interviewed Queen Liliuokalani, and may then have proposed annexation of Hawaii by Japan, because such proposal he did publish on his return to England.

In 1893, when the queen was dethroned, and as quickly as the news reached the Japanese Government, its powerful cruiser *Naniwa* was dispatched to Hawaii under command of Captain Togo. It is pretty clear, as then locally stated, that the purpose of the visit was annexation. The Japanese laborers (many of them army reservists) became very restless, and were supposed to cooperate with the aid of small arms supplied by the cruiser. However, the previous raising of the American flag then prevented any such action by Japan.

Evidence is also clear enough that the dethroned queen was negotiating with Captain Togo for her restoration. At this time also, it may be observed, Japan was attempting to gain control of Ponape, the most important island of Micronesia.

On the *Naniwa* came the emperor's nephew, betrothed to Kaiulani who was then in England. She was then 19 years old. Next year, the queen wrote to Kaiulani telling her "that Kalakaua had arranged she should marry the Japanese Emperor's nephew." The queen added: "I am pleased with it," no doubt having in mind her restoration to the throne under Japanese protection because the United States had already withdrawn from Hawaii. Kaiulani replied that the thought had troubled her much but if absolutely necessary she would agree, although she would much rather not, with the emphasis on the "not."

That year the Chinese war no doubt held Japan's attention, and in 1895 the queen surrendered all claims to the throne.

However, with regard to Hawaii, Japan was active in other directions, particularly following the queen's dethronement. Japan claimed Hawaiian voting franchise for her subjects and, the labor convention having lapsed, sent her people to Hawaii in excessive numbers in total disregard of Hawaiian laws.

. . .

The end of Japanese immigration is a good point to pause and take stock. Briefly it has been shown that Japan desired Hawaii and attempted its possession. The chief instrument employed was her emigrants, some allowed to come here as contract laborers, and others sent as free immigrants with official connivance, until their numbers constituted nearly half the local population. We may now understand the significance of the Japanese Government's insistence that Chinese immigration be restricted.

Of the original Japanese arrivals, 40,000 still remain and 110,000 of their descendents are American citizens, capable even now of dominating the local electorate. In view of their parents' training, characteristics, and background, how far may they be trusted?

The parents, on arrival and since, have maintained themselves as a separate community with national contacts, ancestral customs, celebrations of national holidays, and living as though they were still in Japan. They are directly under the thumb of their consul, who represents the Emperor of Japan and with whom their marriages and children are registered. They have not yielded to Americanization, except in material comforts, nor have they mixed or intermarried locally, as has been done by every other racial group here, nor as done by Japanese immigrants to other countries. Their children, drawn away by daily school and other contacts, are in frequent conflict with attempts to maintain Japanese thought, but which attempts, however, will succeed for awhile yet on account of the ingrained filial loyalty.

. . .

By Senator Gillette:

Q. Dr. Stokes, I have been following you very closely. As I understand your argument, you are opposed to statehood at this time for the reason that there exists here in these islands, in this Territory, two cultures, two civilizations, that appear to you to be nonassimilable; that because of religious differences, because of the attitude of the Japanese people who are dominant in numbers, there is no tendency or desire or hope to be amalgamated or assimilated?—A. Not quite as strong as that. I believe that if the influence of the Japanese Government, and of the societies and institutions controlled by that Government be removed from the new Americans, as well as from those of their white teachers who mislead them, they will advance rapidly toward Americanism and the trouble will cease. They cannot do otherwise if their environment is truly American.

Q. You cite as one of the main reasons why there is apparently no desire, that the Japanese Government keeps in touch with the religion, the adverse religion of the two beliefs, that Shinto, or Buddhist-Shintoism, as you have cited it, is based on the divine origin of the imperial family. Do you know how large a percentage of the Japanese population of the islands is Christian in religion?—

A. It is a very small percentage. I would say not more than 15 percent.

Q. You have tied up Shintoism and Buddhism as one religion. You did not intend to do that?—A. True Shinto and true Buddhism are very different, but in Japanese practice, Shinto has largely absorbed Buddhism. The great exponent of Shinto to foreigners claims that one can be a Christian, a Buddhist or a Confucian, and still be a Shintoist, and, in Japanese practice, it is so.

Q. You have also taken the position that down through this history of the last 50 years it was the apparent desire of the Japanese to keep the colonists as a separate culture. Do you believe it is still the desire?—A. Absolutely.

Q. You think that condition still exists?—A. To a great extent.

Q. That being the case, as you stated it, to what extent do you think the continuation of the territorial form of government will prevent the situation from being corrected, or state it in this way, to what extent do you think statehood granted would accentuate these two cultures?—A. I think it would be very serious for the United States should statehood go through, on account of the population. Mr. Brown gave you figures that 15,000 American voters of Japanese blood registered, and that 10,000 refrained, although entitled to do so. His excuse for them was that the 10,000 did not understand, but with the Japanese control on these new Americans it may be suspected that they were "pulling their punch" as I believe the expression is.

Q. Do you think with statehood granted the hold of the Japanese Government on the people here would be increased?—A. I believe so. The other 10,000 could register, and while we are already dominated by the Japanese-American voters, we would then be swamped.

Q. I was interested in looking over your testimony of 2 years ago. You stated here in one place that prime consideration—the word "prime" is mine and not yours—is the fact that the local financial interests had . . . and that influenced you to oppose statehood.—A. It still influences me. The power of the financial interests was so great that as long as they opposed statehood, it had no chance of going through.

Q. Then the fear of these cultures concerns you now because the financial and industrial interests have switched?—A. It is both. There is a curious combination between the financial interests and the local Japanese by which the latter exercises an influence over the personnel of the former. Highly educated and intelligent Japanese are put as servants in the homes of our most influential people and, by the exercise of the "gentle divine spirit" previously described, reach positions of trust. They can thus exercise a powerful though unconscious influence on our important people when questions come up regarding Japanese matters. Due to this influence, perhaps, or to some unstable reasoning, the financial interests and the local Japanese both put forward the same argument that as the financial people brought the Japanese here, they should do something for their children.

Senator Gillette. That is very well answered.

By Senator O'Mahoney:

Will the Senator yield to me? You said just now, highly intelligent Japanese were put into the homes, what do you mean by "put" into the homes?—A. I am giving information. I can produce the witnesses.

Q. By whom do you think?—A. By the Government of Japan through its local people.

Q. You want this committee to infer that the Imperial Government of Japan, through some method, induced the financial group to employ highly intelligent Japanese who in turn attempt to influence the families with whom they are associated?—A. That is the situation, except that they appear as servants.

Testimony of Frank Midkiff

CONGRESSIONAL TESTIMONY

THE only way actually to determine the loyalty of American citizens of Japanese ancestry in case of a war between America and Japan would be to try it out under war conditions.

It is my belief that many of the American citizens of Japanese ancestry have given more thought to their citizenship than have young people of "haole" and other racial stocks, and that their American citizenship means more to them because they have been challenged and therefore realize their citizenship has to be above criticism. I find among many of these young people a zeal for America that is not unlike the zeal of a new convert from one religious faith to another, when friends and relatives have taken sides for and against the new convert in his change to religious allegiance.

Without doubt the American citizens of Japanese ancestry realize full well that Japan is their origin and realize that they are generally spoken of and thought of as Japanese. Also they are proud of Japan and they desire to have the country of their origin well thought of and of high international consequence. In this they are similar to southerners or to New Englanders in America, who are always proud of their origin and stand up for their section of the country as well as for their Nation—and often in a stronger manner than they stand for America as a whole.

In *Hearings Before the Joint Committee on Hawaii Statehood,* United States Congress, 75th Congress, 2nd session (October 6–22, 1937), pp. 304–305.

Many people criticize these American citizens of Japanese ancestry for retaining certain Japanese customs and for attending language schools. Usually these criticisms spring from lack of appreciation of conditions. For many Japanese customs are valuable and appropriate in Hawaii and add to and enrich the culture of America. And the language schools, now supervised by the Department of Public Instruction, serve to teach a second and a useful language—it being advantageous to anyone to have ability in two languages—and stress ethical precepts such as filial piety, politeness, sense of duty, etc., in which none of us seem to be overdeveloped. As these customs and language schools now exist they seem to the writer to be beneficial to Hawaii and useful for the time being. They do good and need not really be feared. In due time the language schools will yield to similar instruction under public auspices. It does not appear that the language schools are political in influence or intention at present.

Although I enjoyed the historical review by Dr. Stokes this morning, I feel that to select data from the history and press of any foreign nation is dangerous. If we review in this manner the history and the attitude of Germany, for example, we might prove that persons in our country of German ancestry are not safe or loyal citizens. The same might may be said for other European countries from which our citizens originate, as well as for Japan, whose descendents were challenged by Dr. Stokes on the basis of excerpts from foreign sources and local foreign-language press published for alien Japanese now residing here.

To characterize Shintoism as a religion that teaches "Kiss the hand you cannot cut off" and claim that Shintoism implies cutting off hands, is too narrow and would not stand for any religion that has molded a great section of the world's people for ages. To say that Japanese culture is pure nationalism is too narrow, for we know well the fine arts, the crafts, the manners, and the honesty, filial piety, sense of duty, etc., of the Japanese. We see other things featured here in Hawaii and on the whole we find the result good.

It may be quite as unfair to impugn the loyalty of our American citizens of Japanese ancestry because of their origin and Japan's history as to impugn Dr. Stokes' fairness because he hails from Australia where the country is historically anti-Japanese.

Our concern must not be with certain phases of the history of any foreign country from which our citizens have originated, but with the actual qualities and attitudes of these young citizens themselves. For this alone can we hold them responsible. And while a view of foreign history may be offered to fill us with alarm, we become definitely reassured when we come into close contact with these young citizens in their everyday life among us. It is a case of theory and suspicious speculation as contrasted with existing facts and personal findings.

Very few of the young citizens wish to return to Japan, and those who do go back are practically always anxious to get back to American Hawaii. They do not feel at home or at ease in Japan. A Japanese parent once said to me: "They say my son, born in Hawaii and educated here, is not a real American. I know he is not a Japanese. What is he, then? He declares that he is American."

It seems to the writer that we should think carefully before stating that these young people are not good American citizens. They are very sensitive on the subject. One thing we do know: They are good members of our community. They are industrious, law abiding, polite, self-dependent; they have excellent family life and they contribute their full share to the wealth and development of our Territory. From among the many thousands of Japanese men and women servants in the homes of Hawaii for decades, I have never heard a single report of theft. The question of loyalty is of course a practical one, but it would seem wise to give fellow American citizens of whatever origins the benefit of the doubt. If we raise the issue with one group, how can we avoid implications against other groups?

Some years ago there were persons who advocated a plan of impounding within a stockade or on an island all persons of Japanese ancestry, whether American-born or not, in case of war with Japan. The harmful results from even the contemplation of such a plan are evident. To secure cooperation and loyalty, citizens must be treated as cooperative and their rights respected, otherwise suspicion and overt offense will engender resentment and noncooperation. In case of war, disloyal individuals could be dealt with on the merits of each case. This policy was wisely followed in our war against Germany.

And while the defense arm of our Nation must be conservative, from a practical standpoint of developing reliable attitudes it would seem wise to regard these young people as loyal American citizens.

CHAPTER SEVEN

Shall the Japs Dominate Hawaii?

THE sputtering of the crippled engine intruded upon the serenity of the tropical morning as the Hawaiian inhabitants of Puuwai Village on the tiny island of Niihau strolled in clustered groups to Sunday church services. Instinctively, the scores of worshippers looked upward to discover the source of the noises so untimely and unnatural on their remote island home. Shielding their eyes from the glistening steel, they could see two lightweight fighter airplanes flying low overhead, one spewing streams of black exhaust. Then, as suddenly as they had appeared, the unidentifiable planes passed the village and disappeared from view.

Later that afternoon one of the aircraft sighted earlier returned, wobbled erratically in the air and then slammed into a rocky lava field not seventy feet from the home of Hawila Kaleohano. Kaleohano rushed to the wreckage just as the pilot, dazed from the impact of the crash landing, was reaching for a concealed pistol. Yanking the pilot from his seat harness and throwing him to the ground, Kaleohano quickly subdued the intruder and confiscated not only his firearm, but his military papers. Realizing that something was seriously wrong, the Hawaiian sent for two Japanese residents of Niihau, Ishimatsu Shintani, an Issei, and Yoshio Harada, a Japanese American Nisei, to act as interpreters, for the pilot, the airplane, the weapons, and papers were Japanese.

Niihau, an island of approximately forty-eight square miles, was privately owned by the old *kamaaina haole* family, the Robinsons of Kauai. In 1941 the population of Niihau, consisting of caretakers and cowboys of the Robinson's cattle ranch, numbered 180 Hawaiians and three Japanese. Without modern conveniences, limited in communication with the outside world, isolated from tourists and the curious, the small island became a museum for the Hawaiian lifestyle of the nineteenth century—a lingering reminder of what Hawaii was like before the *haole,* the tourist, the immigrant, the military, and the *malihini* (newcomer).

Insulated as they were from "civilization," the inhabitants of Niihau had nevertheless been aware that war had loomed ominously in the Pacific. Japan's behavior in Asia and America's anti-Japan economic policies had made the approaching confrontation between those two powers all the more real. Throughout 1940 and 1941 preparations for war had preoccupied official activities in Hawaii as well as public opinion. If war was to come to the Islands, which seemed more than probable, then the government and populace must be thoroughly prepared. Intelligence units searched out possible saboteurs and spies, naval operations intensified at Pearl Harbor, army personnel increased at Schofield Barracks and Wheeler Air Base, and military spokesmen more frequently reassured an anxious population that Hawaii was prepared to withstand any foreign onslaught. War preparedness had even reached remote Niihau where furrows had been plowed across open fields to prevent enemy planes from landing.

Aware as he was of Japan's menacing posture in Asia, Kaleohano could not have known as he wrestled with the Japanese pilot that about one hundred and fifty miles away, Honolulu was reeling in panic in the wake of the Japanese attack on Pearl Harbor. He could not have known that Hawaii had been placed under martial law, that the fears of a Japanese land invasion had created among citizens and military a series of nightmarish rumors—paratroopers had dropped on Mt. Tantalus and in Palolo Valley; the water supply had been poisoned; submarines were landing soldiers on the beaches of Oahu. He could not have known that from December 7, 1941, Hawaii was going to be transformed into four years of blackouts, scare *puka*s (bomb shelters), gas masks, barbed wire, curfews, air-raid sirens, military courts, and hundreds of thousands of servicemen and mainland defense workers. He was unaware that the frightened and yet defiant aviator who had crashed into his field was but one member of a force which had brought the United States into World War II.

In fact, the most Kaleohano could learn from the pilot was that Oahu had been attacked but that the Japanese forces had been overwhelmed and destroyed by superior American fighting power. Speaking through Shintani and Harada, he reassured the Hawaiian that Japan's invasion had been a failure and that he was lucky to have escaped with his life. Although convinced that there was nothing to fear from the disarmed, defeated pilot and receiving his word that if left untied he would cause no trouble, Kaleohano started a signal fire to indicate to Kauai that an emergency existed on Niihau—an emergency soon to turn into a sequence of extraordinary occurrences later to be called the "Battle of Niihau."

Yoshio Harada had begun that morning as routinely as any other resident of Niihau, taking care of the Robinson home as he and his wife had done for the previous year. Harada was born and raised on Kauai, having what the casual observer would term a "normal" Nisei upbringing. Although Japanese by racial extraction and capable of speaking the Japanese language, Harada had been influenced by the interethnic nature of his environment. Living on Niihau had immersed him in Hawaiian culture and lifestyle; Harada spoke not only English but Hawaiian. Besides his wife and the alien Shintani, his personal day-to-day interactions for over a year had been entirely with either the Hawaiians or the Robinson family. As an American of Japanese ancestry, Harada had become firmly rooted in the Island way of life.

Or so it would have appeared. But after spending a short time with the pilot privately, Harada agreed to help the Japanese aviator arm himself, terrorize the village, threaten the lives of his neighbors, and burn homes in an attempt to regain the papers which Kaleohano had seized, hidden, and refused to relinquish. Possibly the pilot had duped Harada into believing that he needed his military papers to save face, the gun to commit suicide. Possibly he had told Harada that Japanese had actually taken over Hawaii and unless Harada cooperated the new imperial government would execute both him and his wife. Or perhaps Harada felt a closer affinity to the Japanese pilot than he did to his Hawaiian neighbors. At any rate, without the help of Shintani, who had run off into the woods terrified by the impending violence, Harada aided and abetted the Japanese enemy.

Harada's assistance of the pilot's reign of terror—helping to set up two machine guns in Puuwai Village and threatening to kill everyone unless the military papers were produced—seemed to show the depth of the Nisei's treasonous sincerity. After nearly a week of futile coercion and intimidation of the Hawaiian population, Harada and the Japanese pilot, in an unguarded moment, were set upon by Benehakaka Kanahele and his wife. Kanahele, though shot three times, picked the pilot up as one would a sheep and dashed his brains out against a stone wall. Harada, who was grappling with Kanahele's wife, broke free and shot himself in the stomach. A few hours later he died.

"The Battle of Niihau" made heroes out of Kaleohano and Kanahele—the Hawaiians who, risking their lives, had stubbornly subdued the Japanese invader and the local traitor. Yet the Niihau incident also cast a pall across the reputations and loyalties of the Nisei. Didn't Harada's actions prove that under the right conditions Japanese of Hawaii, even the Nisei, would join forces with the treacherous Japanese army? Turning their guns upon their neighbors, burning homes, and imprisoning men, women, and children, many of the frightened irrationally believed, was not beyond the cunning of the Nisei. As one more sober Navy investigator later commented concerning the Niihau incident:

> These facts indicate a strong possibility that other Japanese residents of the Territory of Hawaii, and Americans of Japanese descent, who previously have shown no anti-American tendencies and are apparently loyal to the United States, may give valuable aid to Japanese invaders in cases where the tide of battle is in favor of Japan and where it appears to residents that control of the district may shift from the United States to Japan.[1]

Actually, five months before the destruction at Pearl Harbor the military officials in Hawaii had reaffirmed that both Issei and Nisei were considered loyal American citizens. Speaking before an audience of 500 Japanese at Kawananakoa Intermediate School in Honolulu, Lieutenant Colonel Eugene M. Foster spoke on "What Should the Japanese in Hawaii Do in a Crisis in the Pacific?" The occasion of the address was the thirtieth anniversary of the *Jitsugyo-no-Hawaii,* a local Japanese magazine, and Foster spoke as the official representative of the Commanding General of the Hawaiian Department, Lieutenant General Walter C. Short. In effect, the message that the military wished to convey was that if war with Japan came, nothing would be done to local Japanese in the Islands:

> The army feels that it can depend upon the people of the Japanese race in Hawaii for full support, basing its conclusions on the fact that most of you are loyal to our government and its principles, and those

of you who are not sure of your own loyalty will support our institutions because you recognize their value and because your own self-interests dictate that you would not want to change your present way of life.

Therefore, I am authorized by the Commanding General, Lt. Gen. Walter C. Short, to assure you that the army in an emergency does not intend to treat the people of the Japanese race in Hawaii any different from those of any other race.

You are considered part of the team for defense.[2]

As late as December the government was issuing statements supportive of Japanese, especially the Nisei. Admiral Charles Blakely, in a statement printed on the front page of the *Honolulu Star-Bulletin,* was to say:

> The second generation Japanese or Nisei citizen has a definite place in our social structure, and we, as Americans, will be derelict in our duty to America if we fail to acknowledge this position and fail to assist these people in their ambitions to be true Americans.[3]

The *Star-Bulletin* responded positively to Blakely's remarks in an editorial which lambasted any attempts to connect young Japanese Americans with Japanese imperialism.

> Admiral Blakely's words will be both a comfort and an encouragement to these young Americans, in Hawaii and on the Pacific Coast, and will give them added incentive to stand firm in their American ideals no matter what the grave developments in the Pacific may bring.[4]

Three days after the *Star-Bulletin* made these comments, "grave developments" struck Hawaii. Hysteria had turned an Island community once acceptive of its Japanese neighbors into a frightened populace feeding upon rumor and innuendo, capable of lashing out at the innocent. Even as the billows of smoke poured from battleship row and naval anti-aircraft shells fell upon the city, untrue rumors of the most dangerous kind swept through Honolulu. Some said that local Japanese had had advanced warning of the Pearl Harbor attack, supposedly proved by the absence of some Japanese maids from their employment. Others pointed to an advertisement by a local Japanese importing company which was described as a veiled coded message to the local Japanese residents informing them of the event to occur on December 7. Based on no foundation of facts, the rumors reached ludicrous proportions: Arrows pointing toward

Pearl Harbor had been cut into the canefields by Japanese plantation workers to help direct the Nipponese pilots. Japanese had created traffic snarls and road blocks on the Pearl Harbor road to prevent personnel and supplies from entering the area. A milk truck loaded with Nisei suddenly opened up machine gun fire on personnel at Hickam Field. Japanese residents had hidden large amounts of ammunition on their property to be used by commando troops who had landed at various points throughout the Islands. Japanese pilots who had been shot down were wearing rings from McKinley High School and the University of Hawaii.

The rumors, coupled with the feeling that the air attack was merely a preliminary step for a land invasion, catapulted the instincts for survival above those of libertarian respect for private rights or an open attitude of *aloha*. On December 8, General Order No. 5 was issued under martial law by the new military government. According to the order, "all alien Japanese of the age of fourteen years and upward" were to "preserve the peace towards the United States, . . . to refrain from actual hostility or giving information, aid or comfort to the enemies. . . ."[5] Japanese were forbidden to possess weapons, firearms, explosives, short-wave receiving sets, transmitting sets, cameras, or maps of any United States military or naval installation. Issei could not travel by air, change residence or occupation, or move from "place to place" without written permission from the provost marshal.

The attack on Pearl Harbor, the rumors, the "Battle of Niihau" had aroused the inner conflicts, confusions, and mistrusts of a great many in the non-Japanese population. By the same token, the Japanese community was thrown into turmoil. The war that they had dreaded, had tried to prepare for psychologically and socially, had finally come. In shock and disbelief, Issei and Nisei in all parts of the Islands waited to see how the military and the community would handle the problem of the large numbers of Japanese in Hawaii.

Within hours of the Pearl Harbor attack the military began arresting various Issei aliens, Kibei, and others whose loyalty might be suspected. Certain Buddhist priests, language-school teachers, and those who had close ties to the homeland had been selected for imprisonment by prewar intelligence agencies in the event of hostilities with Japan. The purpose of the arrests would be twofold. First, possible espionage activities would be curtailed. Second, the Issei, left without large numbers of their leaders, would lose morale and effective unity. Making a well-planned and executed sweep of the

Japanese community, military authorities detained, questioned, and then imprisoned at Sand Island, Oahu, hundreds of Issei and Kibei. Those interned had not committed crimes or participated in espionage, but were judged "on personalities and their utterances, criminal and credit records, and probable nationalistic sympathies."[6] Pulled from their homes or places of employment, in some cases unable to tell their loved ones what happened to them, these internees and their families immediately felt the personal burden of war.

During the course of the war, 1,450 Japanese residents of Hawaii (about 1 percent of the total Japanese population) were interned at Sand Island. One of those imprisoned on December 7 was Kazuo Miyamoto. Born in Hawaii, a practicing physician in Honolulu, Miyamoto had spent two years in Tokyo vacationing and doing research work. As a consequence of his travels to China with varied Japanese officials and the publication of a monograph describing China under Japanese occupation, he was put under FBI surveillance when he returned to Hawaii. With the outbreak of war, without consideration for his American citizenship and honorable discharge from the U.S. Army, his only "crime" being his activities in Japan, Miyamoto was sent to Sand Island.

In his semi-autobiographical novel covering his experiences, *Hawaii: End of the Rainbow,*[7] Miyamoto captured some of the confusion, terror, and suspense of the first twenty-four hours of World War II. Through the fictional character Seikichi Arata, an Issei alien, Miyamoto was able to relate the psychological impact of confronting the hatred of the outside community and adapting to the fact that one's life was balanced on the whim of the military authorities.

As to the Issei's loyalties, Miyamoto, speaking through Seikichi, presented the notion that the first-generation immigrant had developed a deep and sincere attachment to the Hawaiian Islands. Hawaii was where he had spent his youth, raised his family, and expected to see the fulfillment of both his own and his children's ambitions. "Seikichi had lived longer in Hawaii than in the land that gave him birth. He was at heart a Hawaiian and he was going to have his bones interred in this soil together with his posterity."

While prewar parlor debates and Congressional investigations had inconclusively asked how Hawaiianized or Americanized the Issei and Nisei had become, the contingencies of war demanded immediate answers. If the Japanese had indeed developed an Hawaiian identity with a loyalty transferable to the United States, as Miyamoto suggested, then the military authorities had to determine the stability and depth of that identity. After all, loyalty to Hawaii did not necessitate loyalty to America—most Islanders had never left "the rock" and had only a faint idea of American history, landmarks, or institutions. Wouldn't it seem more reasonable that in case of a Japanese invasion, to save their own necks, Issei and Nisei would rush to the beaches shouting *"Banzai,"* welcoming their "yellow brethren"?

To resolve the question of internal security in Hawaii, America's first outpost of defense in the Pacific, Army, Navy, and British intelligence agencies, as well as the FBI, undertook investigations of the Island Japanese community. One such study was compiled by Curtis B. Munson, a government agent who also did extensive work on the mainland Japanese population. The Munson report,[8] completed in the early months of 1942, confirmed the notion that Japanese in Hawaii were closely attached to the Islands. Although not exceedingly loyal to America, they would do nothing to endanger their Island home. "The consensus of opinion is that there will be no racial uprising of the Japanese in Honolulu. . . . It may be well to state here in a general way that everyone in Hawaii . . . places loyalty to Hawaii first, and the United States second. This is not meant to impugn their loyalty—but they love the Islands."

In Munson's judgment, about 98 percent of the Nisei were loyal American citizens, and the 2 percent who were possibly disloyal had already been pinpointed by the military. If any danger from the Nisei existed, it was the possibility of race riots, especially between Japanese, Filipinos, and the large numbers of mainland *haole* defense workers. Noting the type of Japanese called the "bright young thing," Munson recognized that some Nisei would resent racial slurs or intimidations and would reciprocate in a like manner. These interethnic confrontations could cause a more serious problem in Hawaii than any treasonous actions among Japanese, for "the big majority anyhow would be neutral or even actively loyal."

On the West Coast of the United States, however, Japanese aliens and their American-born children were not being considered in so favorable a light. Racist organizations in California, such as the Native Sons and Daughters of the Golden West and the American Legion who had been active in the passage of the 1924 immigration law barring Japanese travel to the United States, had joined forces with those agrarian interests such as the Western Grower's Protective Association who saw Japanese landholdings and agricultural output as a competitive threat. The intent of these groups, with the acquiescence of some government leaders and the enthusiastic support of others, was the complete removal of all Japanese from the West Coast. Convincingly, they played upon the hysteria of the war situation and blasted Japanese as agents of Emperor Hirohito. Leaving the Japs on the West Coast, racists argued, would be a most foolish and irresponsible action. It would mean the beginning of the end for America.

And after all, wouldn't removal, relocation, incarceration, imprisonment of the Japanese be for their own good, their own protection? How could the government assure the Japanese that they would be safe from enraged whites looking for a Jap to kill, a home to bomb? If a father loses a son in the Pacific, wouldn't his blind revenge be taken out on the helpless Japanese Issei or Nisei? And what of Filipinos in California who would hear of atrocities committed in their homeland? Wouldn't it be natural that they would attack the Japanese communities in retaliation?

Viewing Japanese as a military threat, as well as arguing that for humanitarian reasons it was for "their own good," various factions of anti-Japanese lobbyists and policy-makers successfully created an atmosphere of public, military, and governmental support for the mass evacuation of all Japanese from the West Coast into a number of relocation, or "concentration," camps scattered about the country. On February 19, 1942, President Franklin Roosevelt signed Executive Order No. 9066 which gave authority to the Secretary of War or any military commander designated by the Secretary to establish military areas and to exclude therefrom "any or all persons." This order was carried out on March 3 when Lieutenant General John DeWitt, senior military commander of the West Coast, directed that all Japanese—alien and citizen—be evacuated into relocation centers.

The number of Japanese eventually interned in camps with such innocently picturesque names as Tule Lake, Heart Mountain, Manzanar, or Gila River totaled more than 110,000 men, women, and children. Under the direction of the War Relocation Authority (WRA), people, food, and materials were hastily concentrated in areas which became in actuality, confined barbed-wired cities. Suspending *habeas corpus,* neglecting the rights of American citizens, relocation violated if not the letter, then the spirit of the U.S. Constitution to meet the needs of "military and humanitarian necessity."

Halfway across the Pacific Ocean, though, a larger number of Japanese, about 150,000, lived and worked freely among an Island community. While Japanese in California were abandoning homes and possessions for nearly three years of uncertain confinement, the Japanese of Hawaii were generally unaffected by the emotional outrages of the military and public authorities on the mainland. And yet if fifth-column activities were anywhere most dangerous, if the consequences of racial riots anywhere the most real, it was Hawaii. Japanese comprised 37 percent of the population and provided the essential labor to carry on the war effort—the operations of Pearl Harbor were most vulnerable to Japanese sabotage. The large numbers of Filipinos, Chinese, and *haole*s living in such close proximity to Japanese would seem to inflame racial animosities as a consequence of events in the Pacific war. Still, except for the suspicious activities of a few Japanese who were imprisoned at Sand Island and then either interned at Honouliuli or sent to mainland relocation centers and internment camps, the Issei and Nisei population of Hawaii were accepted as part of the "team for defense."

Not that the mainland hysteria behind mass relocation of the Japanese in some form did not reach the Islands. Despite the military's intelligence reports which publically reaffirmed the sincerity and loyalty of Hawaii's Japanese, a few more skeptical individuals tried to encourage the government to consider relocating the Japanese of Hawaii. In the July 25, 1942, issue of *The Nation* magazine, Albert Horlings, a former resident of the Islands, wrote a persuasive essay, "Hawaii's 150,000 Japanese,"[9] in which he urged the evacuation of Japanese from Hawaii. Horlings' primary and indisputable assumption was that if West Coast Japanese were a military threat warranting mass relocation and the suspension of constitutional rights, then Hawaii's Japanese were an even greater risk demanding more extensive action. How could the government state that 110,000 Japanese dispersed over the immense area of the West Coast were a greater danger to security than 150,000 of them concentrated in small islands near America's foremost naval installation? The logic, as Horlings suggested, was irrefutable—if the government relocates Japanese on the mainland then it must do so in Hawaii for the same reasons.

More importantly, the Japanese in Hawaii were perhaps in a greater position to dominate the Islands with a foreign way of life. As Horlings wrote, ". . . to a remarkable degree Hawaii's Japanese are untouched by American ways; all their pride of race, family and religion binds them to Japan. Thousands see or hear almost nothing American, while they consume Japanese food, Japanese clothing, Japanese music, Japanese pictures, Japanese newspapers and magazines by the shipload.'' Victory of the Rising Sun over the Islands would be the very thing which Japanese residents would most welcome. The conquering army would need trustworthy administrators and policy-makers in the Islands who understood local lifestyles and temperaments; the resident Japanese would gain limitless power. The ownership of land, the profits from importation and sugar production would naturally be turned over to the willing Issei and Nisei. How could anyone, Horlings reasoned, believe that given the chance to dominate and colonize Hawaii the Island Japanese would decline? Evacuation and relocation were the only safe means by which to prevent that catastrophe.

In rebuttal to Horlings' position, a Japanese American named Thomas H. Ige wrote a letter to *The Nation* entitled, ''Hawaii's Loyal Japanese.''[10] According to Ige, Horlings had totally misread the success of American adaption among Issei and Nisei and the deep loyalty which they felt toward America. If a zero hour strike were to come, the overwhelming majority of Hawaii's Japanese would faithfully stand by America. Given the chance, the Japanese would demonstrate beyond any doubt that the Americanization of their souls and national loyalties had been complete.

Ige's laudatory remarks were continuously being echoed in the Islands by both the military government and the public media throughout the war period and helped to stem the anti-Japanese sentiment which on the mainland resulted in relocation. The loyalty of Issei and Nisei, their potential contributions to the war effort meant that they must be treated justly. The public was told to avoid the groundless fears and rumors which arose during war conditions. ''Beware of rumors always,'' editorialized a local magazine, ''avoid them like a plague and, when possible, kill them as you would a reptile. Don't repeat for a fact anything you do not know is a fact.''[11]

But the rumors, the fears of Japanese domination, and the mindless mainland hate campaigns could not always be offset by the local military and newspapers. Japanese in Hawaii were being constantly reminded that they were ''on the spot'' and many forces existed which would hope for nothing more than the relocation of Japanese Islanders. The confining situation in which Japanese were placed was demonstrated in the 1942 district supervisor's election on Kauai, when four Japanese, Noboru Miyake, an incumbent, Wallace Otsuka, Yutaka Hamamoto and George Watase won as candidates for office in the coming general election. The first reaction to the primary results came from the *New York Daily News* in an editorial calling attention to Hawaii's elections and the consequence of Japanese in positions of political importance.

> The Territory of Hawaii held its primary election Sunday and the sour part of the news is that five out of seven Japanese candidates who ran for various nominations won out over assorted White, Chinese and Hawaiian opponents. . . . It seems inescapable that we have got to exercise some old style imperialism in Hawaii for the duration of the war to be on the safe side. We cannot afford the risk of having any applecarts upset in those islands by the present or former subjects of the Mikado and if the Japanese in Hawaii do not like that attitude they had better go back where they or their ancestors came.[12]

Mrs. Clarice B. Taylor, editor of *The Garden Island* newspaper on Kauai, responded in an editorial that the national reputation which the primaries had created for Kauai needed to be resolved by the resignation of at least the three new Japanese candidates, if not the incumbent Miyake:

> We say frankly: 'It is undemocratic and an invasion of the rights of free men to place pressure on our three candidates at a time when we are fighting this war to preserve freedom.' But the answer to this is that it is better to relinquish our rights for the time being rather than to lose them forever.
>
> It was an invasion of the rights of the Japanese citizens on the Pacific coast to be picked up and shipped to the interior. To the credit of the American citizens of Japanese ancestry, they accepted it with good grace, and cooperated.
>
> It is an invasion of the rights of any citizen of Japanese ancestry on this island to suggest that he withdraw from the political race on account of his ancestry; but there is a difference in the comparison of the two problems. The mainlander was told to evacuate. The Kauai citizen must take the decision himself and whatever is done, must be done voluntarily.
>
> The point which every voter on this island should realize is that the mainland people do not care a hoot about the political rights of the people of these islands. They are frantically concerned with Hawaii's ability to stand as a bastion of military strength in the Pacific.[13]

After taking the advice of various counselors, Watase, Miyake, Hamamoto, and Otsuka withdrew from the Kauai general elections. The spirit of the withdrawal had been sacrificial—political careers had given way to unreasonable paranoia in the hopes of reassuring the skeptics that Japanese had no intentions of racially subjugating the Islands.

But some people would never be convinced that Issei and Nisei belonged to Hawaii's community. John A. Balch, president of the Mutual Telephone Company and a long-time critic of Japanese influence in Hawaii, wrote in July, 1943, a pamphlet entitled, "Shall the Japanese Be Allowed to Dominate Hawaii?" In this small tract, Balch argued that the bulk of Japanese in Hawaii should be evacuated to the mainland. Balch's concern was not primarily the military dangers posed by Japanese living near Pearl Harbor and other military installations but rather:

> . . . if the Japanese are left in their present numbers as the largest racial group in Hawaii the position of all other racial groups and that of their descendants will be jeopardized, and as these people gain even greater political and economic control we shall be forced out of our jobs and our homes.[14]

The public reaction to Balch's remarks, though, clearly showed the depth of the commitment which the military, government, and business interests had toward leaving the Japanese community under scrutiny but not harmed or unnecessarily disturbed. On the day the Balch pamphlet appeared in the newspapers, the military firmly denied that Japanese were going to be relocated. The newspapers showed no indication of giving Balch excessive publicity and the *Star-Bulletin* in reviewing the Balch pamphlet pointed out its exaggerations of the actual situation—Japanese were loyal members of the Island community.

Expectedly, the Japanese in Hawaii still reacted nervously to the admonitions of individuals such as Balch. Uncertain as to the depth of the military's commitment to not relocating the Japanese and fearful that the fate of the mainland Japanese might befall them, Island Issei and Nisei cautiously avoided any actions or behaviors which would reinforce the anti-Japanese relocation attitudes and opinions. For example, when the military considered in 1943 that 1,500 Japanese on relief rolls might be relocated to mainland concentration camps, many Japanese asked to be removed from relief so as to avoid evacuation.

Gradually, by 1944, the voices calling for relocation of Island Japanese died out; the pattern of peaceful acceptance and encouragement of the Issei and Nisei by the Island community was securely planted in the official statements of the military and the day-to-day interactions of the various ethnic groups. A question naturally arises, though, as to how Japanese in Hawaii were fortunately able to avoid the inhumane treatment and indiscriminate violation of civil rights which characterized the experience of Japanese on the mainland. Were authorities in Hawaii wiser, or more ignorant, than their mainland counterparts? Or were the Japanese of Hawaii simply luckier than Japanese on the West Coast?

The reasons behind the nonrelocation of Island Japanese were as complexly intertwined in military-economic-political-racial rationales as were the reasons for the relocation of mainland Japanese. But essentially the differences between the mainland and Hawaiian experiences were a result of how the Japanese community in each respective area stood vis à vis the greater community. From what positions could the ethnic group bargain for its liberties? What did they offer, or appear to offer, either the military or civil authorities which would make relocation improbable or even detrimental? What loyalties or bonds of friendship had been established between Japanese and non-Japanese which could work in favor of the Japanese community?

Clearly, Japanese in the Islands fared better than mainland Japanese when it came to establishing firm loyalties and bargaining positions with the non-Japanese population. On the mainland, the 110,000 Issei and Nisei who comprised the bulk of the Japanese population were scattered across the West Coast in diverse communities and situations. From Seattle to San Francisco to Los Angeles, Japanese were distributed in sparse rural and urban ghettos; no cohesive ethnic community with common leaders and goals existed. Regional and urban divisions placed Japanese in an extremely poor position to lobby for fair treatment. The Japanese American Citizens League (JACL), conceived in the 1920s and guided in 1941 by the youthful aggressive leadership of Mike Masaoka, had attempted somewhat successfully to organize Japanese in their national organization. However, with only scant support from various religious groups, the American Civil Liberties Union (ACLU), and the National Association for the Advancement of Colored People (NAACP), the Japanese were in no political position to counteract the forces of local and state governments and the agitation of racist and agricultural interests.

Numerically the Japanese on the mainland also represented an inconsequential ethnic grouping. Their manpower, in comparison to what was available from Caucasians or other minority groups, was too insignificant to be in demand. Removal of Japanese would have absolutely no impact on the war effort or the stability of the economy of the various communities. Relocation posed no serious logistic problems when dealing with a comparatively small handful of individuals. If anything, getting rid of the Japanese would boost the economic worth of those agriculturalists who would seize their lands, of those merchandisers who would make fantastic bargains on homes, cars, and other material goods hastily sold.

Political, economic, and numerical realities, then, could not seriously counteract the persuasive arguments of those who urged relocation for "national security" and "their own good." Due to prejudice encountered from without and a sense of ethnic distance generated from within, the Japanese and non-Japanese communities on the mainland had little or no sense of mutual understanding or friendly interracial contact. And when hysteria took control, the larger community could easily and often with benefit to themselves intern Japanese with manageable repercussions.

But in Hawaii, the Issei and Nisei had become socioeconomically interwoven with the greater Island community. Consequently, the military and humanitarian reasons for relocation would seem irrational in terms of the price to be paid for such an action. For Japanese removal would mean a severe reduction of the working force and a sharp curtailment of the market's buying and selling power. Disrupting the very core of the Island economy would mean crippling Hawaii and consequently the Pacific war effort; it would be analogous to removing every other strand of wool from a rug and then expecting the material to maintain its shape and strength. Profits, growth, and stability, many leading businessmen realized, would be seriously jeopardized if mainland fanatics got their way in the Islands.

Logistically, too, removal of Japanese would be difficult if not nearly impossible. Shipping lines between Hawaii and the mainland were already tied up with materials, food, military personnel, and evacuating families. The costs and cumbersomeness of using ocean liners to transport 150,000 Japanese to relocation centers on the mainland were prohibitive. Some argued that the island of Molokai could be turned into a huge relocation camp, and certainly Japanese could be shipped that short distance. More sober minds pointed out that the first invasion target of Japan would then be Molokai where disgruntled Issei and Nisei would comprise a deadly liberation army. The idea was swiftly abandoned.

But more than logistics, more than economic stability, the decision not to relocate the Japanese of Hawaii rested upon the political activities and ties of friendship which the Japanese community had established with the military, the civil government, the *haole* business community, and the vast numbers of non-Japanese.

In many ways the ties of friendship between Japanese and non-Japanese were an outcome of the Issei's and Nisei's identification with the "local" Island lifestyle—it is difficult to hate neighbors and friends who share the same interests, the same endearing attachment to their Island home. As the president of the Honolulu Chamber of Commerce had announced,

> . . . we have brought these people too far along the road to full partnership with us to drop them now. A little more faith, a lot more help and encouragement will build a strong and united citizenry. Our best protection against the few who might become disloyal under pressure is the strength of the many united in our common cause.[15]

The influences of neighborly racial acceptance, then, survived the prewar years of racial distrust, the attack on Pearl Harbor, and the period of war—the ferocity of anti-Japanese sentiments had been subdued. Not that the Japanese did not exist in a state of extreme public scrutiny; not that the old undercurrents of fear did not exist in the Island community. But when the crux of the issue centered on mass evacuation and relocation of neighbors, employers, employees, co-workers, schoolmates, and friends, the undercurrents of open racial relations prevailed.

The decision to leave the population of Japanese in Hawaii intact was the outcome therefore of the nearly fifty years of Japanese efforts to turn Hawaii into a permanent home and of non-Japanese to accept the Issei and Nisei as welcomed members of the Island community. Viewed from this perspective, the bargaining position which the Japanese held with the military and civil government was extremely advantageous—not only did Hawaii need Japanese to maintain social stability, but in most cases the Island people accepted and approved of their Japanese neighbors. Factors of affiliation, social assimilation, ethnic interaction and some political influence, almost totally absent on the mainland, helped to account for the failure of men like John Balch to destroy the efforts and ambitions of countless immigrants, their children, and their leaders who had hoped to establish a peaceful residence in the Islands. But if the military were still unconvinced, if Island neighbors still retained any shreds of suspicion, then the Japanese would employ their most precious bargaining commodity. If any doubt remained as to their loyalty to Hawaii, many Nisei were willing to offer their muscles, their sweat, their blood so that for their own sakes and the sakes of their parents and their children, they could unquestionably call the Islands their home.

NOTES

1. Gwenfread E. Allen, *Hawaii's War Years, 1941–45,* Honolulu: University of Hawaii Press, 1950, p. 46.
2. Andrew W. Lind, *Hawaii's Japanese: An Experiment in Democracy,* Princeton: Princeton University Press, 1946, p. 68.
3. *Honolulu Star-Bulletin,* December 4, 1941, 1:2.
4. *Honolulu Star-Bulletin,* December 4, 1941, 8:1.
5. Lind, p. 69.
6. Allen, p. 134.
7. Kazuo Miyamoto, "Pearl Harbor and Confinement," *Hawaii: End of the Rainbow,* Tokyo: Charles E. Tuttle, 1964, pp. 297–313.
8. Curtis B. Munson, "Report on Hawaiian Islands," in *Pearl Harbor Attack,* Hearings before the Joint Committee on the Investigation of the Pearl Harbor Attack, United States Congress, 79th Congress, 1st session, Part 6, pp. 2692–6.
9. Albert Horlings, "Hawaii's 150,000 Japanese," *The Nation,* July 25, 1942, pp. 69–71.
10. Thomas H. Ige, "Hawaii's Loyal Japanese," *The Nation,* August 8, 1942, p. 120.
11. "As We See It in Hawaii," *Paradise of the Pacific,* v. 54, no. 2 (February 1942), p. 3.
12. Allen, p. 145.
13. Quoted in Kauai Morale Committee, *The Final Report of the Kauai Morale Committee,* Lihue, Kauai, September 30, 1945, p. 30.
14. John A. Balch, *Shall the Japanese Be Allowed to Dominate Hawaii?* Honolulu, 1942, p. 5.
15. Lind, p. 64.

Pearl Harbor and Confinement

KAZUO MIYAMOTO

SEIKICHI Arata, at 69, was spry and healthy. The night before, on Saturday, his oldest grandson, Edward, had returned from Schofield Barracks where he was taking basic training with the last draftees. He had just finished his basic training. Because Honolulu was lit up with lights anticipating a very prosperous, unprecedented Christmas sale on account of the affluence that suddenly had descended upon certain segments of the citizenry doing defense work, Edward had taken the family out in the car to see this nocturnal splendor.

Like all his friends, Arata felt that times were difficult. Every day was trying on his nerves whenever he glanced at a newspaper. There was not a day that did not carry news or commentary that was not deleterious to the amity of the two nations. But Hawaii was his home. Because of the law that barred Orientals from becoming naturalized, he had to remain an alien until his death. However, he had lived longer in Hawaii than in the land that gave him birth. He was at heart a Hawaiian and he was going to have his bones interred in this soil together with his posterity. To see Edward in a uniform of the United States Army made him happy and proud. His thoughts wandered back about 50 years to the scene in the old country when he was rejected by the army because of his stature. He no longer thought a uniform glamorous, but it was nevertheless heartwarming

In *Hawaii, End of the Rainbow* (Tokyo: Charles E. Tuttle Co., 1964), pp. 297–313. Reprinted by permission of Charles E. Tuttle Co., Inc.

to see Edward assume the responsibilities and duties that must necessarily accompany citizenship.

On the night of the farewell dinner when Edward was inducted three weeks previously he had said, "Edward, you will proudly wear the uniform of a soldier from tomorrow. You owe everything to this country. Times are difficult for us with Japanese blood and you will have to work doubly hard and prove that in spite of your racial extraction you are a good American citizen. Your ancestors in the old country were *samurai.* I know you will be a good soldier. Let us all be proud of you." And Edward, in spite of his mixed blood, for his mother was native Hawaiian, nodded and seemed to understand the meaning he wanted to convey.

This morning, December 7th, 1941, at 8 o'clock the radio stations were announcing the events that were taking place in the skies over Honolulu and at Pearl Harbor. "Oahu is under attack by an enemy air force. Keep off the streets for the military needs all traffic lanes. Do not go to the hills and mountains. You are all doing fine. Keep calm. We shall from time to time let you know about developments. Keep your radio tuned to this station." The announcer was calm. There was no trace of panic and to hear this matter of fact voice was very reassuring at a time when any smoldering anger could be fanned to hysterical intensity and mob action. Seikichi was dumbfounded. He sat down and closed his eyes. His head felt tight. The thinking faculty was at a standstill, and he could only mutter a prayer that this be a dream only!

Then the special announcement came over the radio, "All soldiers on leave over the weekend return at once to your outfit. This order applies to all men in uniform, soldiers, sailors, and marines. Return at once to your barracks." Edward Arata left at once for downtown where buses for the various military installations usually congregated—at the Army and Navy YMCA near the Palace Grounds. There was not even a farewell: he just picked up his overnight bag and rushed out.

Seikichi Arata stepped from the house. Lower Alewa Heights was a vantage point from which to see some of the action that was taking place. Toward the West the distant Waianae Range was clear in the bright morning light, and about eight columns of black smoke and doughnutlike white smoke rings that signified anti-aircraft fire were increasing in number. Incessant crackling and booming noises came from that direction. Little planes were zooming over Pearl Harbor and looked like dragon flies in the distance. Just then there was a terrific roar as two groups of fighter planes flew low down Nuuanu Valley from the Pali, evidently advancing on Honolulu from the windward side. They flew so low that the amber colored wings bearing the blood-red sun insignia showed on the under surface.

To Seikichi there was now no doubt at all that these attackers were from his own country. What a shock it was and what a shame he felt toward neighbors who were non-Japanese. Just then a terrific explosion took place at the intersection of Liliha and Kuakini Streets. He heard later that these were misfires of anti-aircraft shells. What little bombs these attacking planes carried could not be wasted on ordinary targets: they were destined for military installations and battleships lying at anchor in Pearl Harbor.

Several children were injured, some were killed from these explosions, and Seikichi felt that if these shells had injured him, an old man, he might have felt better. He might have felt in his suffering a sense of expiation, of atonement for the destruction and killing that were taking place among the soldiers and civilians of his adopted country by the planes of his Japan, for in spite of the half-century he had lived in America, he could not have severed the ties with the land of his birth because the America he loved would not legally accept him as a citizen. He was old and had lived his natural life. No matter what befell him, he had no regrets. History was replete with incidents of massacre of minority races under emergency. His children would live and survive as Americans, but under the circumstances in this emergency how would they fare? Pogroms had no precedent in America but lynching was not unthinkable when people became hysterical and the mob got out of hand. Could one develop into another? So far everything was quiet. The rushing of the army trucks to points of vantage, the activity of the police cooperating with the military police was exemplary, and the directives over the radio had a reassuring and soothing influence on the mental state of the population.

In spite of this poised state, wild rumors started. "Some enemy soldiers parachuted in the mountains. They are clad in green suits. They are poisoning the water supply. Boil your water before drinking." was the advice circulated among the neighborhoods by block wardens. Seikichi half believed this and ordered his women folk to follow the instructions. Sadao was quiet the entire morning. He was in a state of partial shock from the events that developed so swiftly after he was told by neighbors that the graduation service for Red Cross trainees was not going to take place.

"That is ridiculous. If the drinking water was poisoned, the poi-son will not be removed by boiling. But is there food enough for several days?" irritably asked Sadao of his wife.

"Yes, we have plenty. Weekend shopping was done yesterday."

"Then it is all right, but I'll go out walking for a while. This waiting and doing nothing is getting me jittery." He sauntered out of the house and walked the sidewalks of the almost deserted city. The streets were clear of civilian traffic and at intersections policemen and military police enforced order. Military vehicles, both trucks and touring cars, were racing back and forth. An ominous quiet pervaded the Sunday morning atmosphere. A few loitering men were inspecting something on the telephone post on Kukui Street and a half dozen were milling around.

"See that noodle restaurant over there?" pointed a man in a gray sweater to a half-burnt small store with its roof caved in. "There were seven boys eating breakfast. A shell landed on the restaurant. Three killed and four badly hurt. Amateur boxer, Chinen, was one of the killed. Now, see the piece of flesh on the telephone post. This post is about 50 feet away from the restaurant, but with the explosion the bodies were shattered to shreds and the piece of flesh flew over here. I live over there in the lane and when the bomb fell, it was like an earthquake."

Toward one o'clock Sadao was home. Everybody was waiting for him. Silently they sat at the table for a light lunch of sandwiches and iced tea.

"What else was there different?"

"Nothing except that people remained at home and the streets were deserted."

"Yes, the sensible thing to do is not crowd the streets. The army will see to it that we are protected. But we must be prepared to be strong and cool-headed. Except for your mother and me, all of you are American citizens. You have been told at school all these years where your allegiance should be, and I have not told you anything different at home. Your son, Edward, is serving his country in uniform. Your turn to be useful to the country will come in some way. Be good citizens. It may be hard because you have Japanese faces and names. I do not know and nobody knows how hard our lot in Hawaii will be. We only have to conduct ourselves bravely. During the last war the Germans at Lihue were not molested and they lived without any trouble," solemnly lectured Seikichi.

"Oh, but they are Caucasians! They could merge with the rest, but we are of a different race," interjected Sadao.

"That may be so. It will take a longer time and the road may be more rocky for us. Because of that I am praying that you retain your calm and courage."

"I wonder if the rumor we used to hear several years ago is true. You remember I told you when the writer, Upton Close, returned from China and on his way to the mainland he made a speech at the University Club? You remember I attended that lecture and reported to you that if ever war should start, all Japanese would be concentrated on Molokai? It seemed fantastic at that time, but I wonder!"

"Hardly possible. In the first place, if they had such a plan, they could not let us live there like animals without any housing, and no news of any such construction work has been reported on that island. You must remember too, that only two months ago the general assured us that there was going to be no concentration camp as long as we obeyed the laws and lived peacefully."

"In that case we can relax. Since there is nothing to do, I am going to water the lawn. Father, you can take a nap."

Mrs. Haru Arata was in the kitchen early. From that night on there was to be no light after sundown. A complete blackout and curfew order was out for the civilians. But no home was prepared for such an emergency measure and the only alternative was to go to bed early. It was nearing a time of the year when nights could be long even in Hawaii. The sun set at 6 P.M.

Just sandwiches or rice and tea with pickled vegetable for those that wished a light, simple dish. Nobody had much of an appetite. The day was bright and sunny but toward evening it cooled rapidly. There was no moon. In no time the entire city was dark. The streets were deserted except for official cars that silently coursed back and forth with shrouded headlights. Sporadic firing could be heard from many quarters of the city. Jittery civilian guards must be firing at any moving object. It was risky to be stirring outside.

At 7 o'clock, Seikichi Arata was in pajamas. It was early to go to bed but it was a nerve-racking day and he was very tired. Just to stretch and relax would do him good. Just then there was a knock at the front door. Sadao went to the door.

"Is Seikichi Arata at home?"

"Yes, he is."

"Please call him here." There were two men and they produced badges. They indicated that they were from the police department.

"I'll go call him," and Sadao went to the bedroom to fetch his father.

"We are from the police department and want to take you to headquarters for questioning," explained the Caucasian member.

"For what?" asked Sadao.

"Oh, just a few questions. He will be detained only a few hours," soothingly explained the police officer.

"Then I have to change clothes," said Seikichi and turned to go to the bedroom.

"I'll go with you," said the officer as he entered the room and remained there while Seikichi dressed.

Haru Arata, instinctively felt something was wrong and followed the two. She took out his heaviest serge suit, added a few handkerchiefs, a comb and his pair of glasses. "You may or may not need any money, but just in case, I am putting two ten dollar bills in your pocket. These officers say it will only be for a few hours. We hope you will be back in the morning. Take care and be careful. Now officer, please drive slowly."

"OK mama-san. He will be all right."

Seikichi stopped to the doorway. "Sadao, I'll leave everything to you. Take good care of all." Somehow he felt it was going to be longer than a few hours. The two men helped him from each side to descend the front steps. Just to be escorted in such a manner gave him the feeling that his liberty was being curtailed: that he was being spirited away. In some inexplicable way he felt in his bones that this was like being kidnapped.

When they reached the street, there was a touring car with a man at the wheel. "All right, let's go, Joe," commanded the *haole* man.

"Papa-san, hands please," and when Seikichi raised his hand to a horizontal level he felt the cold steel of handcuffs applied to his wrist.

Shocked to his bones, Seikichi felt a cold anger rising in his chest. "Why this degradation! Can't these two giants see that a puny five footer at 70 years of age would not even consider escape? Why, in decency's name handcuffs?" He was seated between the two men on the back seat. He reclined and closed his eyes. When he opened his eyes because the car came to a stop, he found that all traffic was being scrutinized at a roadblock at the junction of Liliha and King Streets. Several men in plain clothes and military police with fixed bayonets were peeping into and inspecting cars that approached. The driver of each car stepped out to show identification badges to the sergeant in charge. Everything was done in subdued flashlight.

The touring car proceeded toward the waterfront and finally

turned to the right and stopped in front of a building. It was not the Police Station. It was the Immigration Station. Seikichi was led into a room where six army enlisted men were processing arrivals. The handcuffs were removed and he was led to a desk by the detective who laid a blue card on the desk. It bore the name Arata, Seikichi, alien. This name was checked on the list of names that filled several pages.

When he entered there was a bald, timid, and whimpering man in pajamas and wrapped up in a blanket. Evidently he was not given much time before he was snatched away from his sick bed. "I am sick, I have a fever of 101. Very chilly. I must have my medicine. My blood pressure is high and I must have medicine." To this plea the sergeant said nothing. There was no consideration. His duty was to process these prisoners into this readymade prison. Sick or dying, nothing beyond handkerchiefs and glasses were allowed. Medicine was not a permissible item.

"Now go over there and face the wall. Put both hands above your head and keep your hands on the wall." Seikichi did as he was ordered, while one of the sergeants searched his pockets and took out the wallet and fountain pen. These were confiscated and placed in a large Manila envelope marked with his name.

"All right, old man. Go up the stairway. It is dark. Hold on to the side railing. It is perfectly safe," said the not unkind sergeant. Then he yelled facing the second story. "Another prisoner!" Seikichi was ordered from home with the assurance that it was going to be an interrogation lasting a few hours; the truth of the matter was that he was now a "prisoner."

Up the stairway, he was careful to cling to the metal railing. At the top a soldier took him by the arm and talked to a guard that stood outside a door. The guard opened the door and pushed him into a room that was stuffy and reeking with the odor of human bodies. There was a continuous mumbling sound and there were some bodies on the floor. When his eyes became accustomed to the darkness he was able to discern the outline of three tiers of iron beds. It occurred to him that since he was not the first, he would not be the last. He had better look for a place to sleep if he were to rest at all. Most of the beds were occupied but on the farther end, he found empty spaces on the uppermost tier. He clambered aloft warily to avoid stepping on the persons on the lower two levels. Without taking off his coat, he stretched out on the mattress.

It was a strange feeling. He closed his eyes. It did not matter much because even with his eyes wide open there was nothing visible in this pitch dark night. He reviewed the turn in events of the last thirty minutes.

It was a short half hour, but during that interval a revolutionary change in human status had come over him. Never had he dreamed before that he would ever run afoul of the established laws of the country. He considered prisoners a different breed of men. He was an honest and upright citizen of the community. But then, here he was with that appellation preceding his name. In the seventy years of his life this episode could be the culmination and an inglorious end: to be considered a shame by his children and grandchildren. The low voices of the people in the room were strained, but devoid of any anger or hysteria. The conversation centered on the events of the day rather than the arrest which brought them together.

Almost every quarter hour the door opened to let in new arrivals. "Mr. Kagami, how is Waialua way?" came a voice from near the door. Evidently the newcomer was recognized.

"Four of us were brought in from Waialua by the FBI. Whereas ordinarily it is a one hour travel, today we were five hours on the way. There was another attack by Japanese planes after dark. Police stopped the car and crawled under it. We four sat on the side of the ditch, but nothing happened," related the new arrival and Seikichi listened to the talk as he had nothing else to do. His mind ceased to function and he was in complete passivity. Somebody opened the windows. It was discovered the following morning that in a room built for eighty persons, one hundred and eighty had been crowded in. The stifling oppressiveness resulting from the stagnation of air was somewhat ameliorated by the open windows, but in the wee hours of the morning it became chilly.

At about two o'clock, a commotion took place as twelve barefooted fishermen wearing raincoats were thrown into the room. These men were out fishing that morning, had been machine-gunned by planes, and were glad to be alive.

With every arrival there was conversation and the continuous hushed talk prevented any sustained sleep. When day dawned at six o'clock, the outline of faces became more distinct. Remarks such as these were heard all over the room.

"You, too! What a night! When did you arrive? I was escorted by an MP in the late afternoon. The Caucasian MP's were very gentlemanly and there was no rough talk."

"I came after dark. Oriental detectives came after me. I was watering the lawn wearing tennis shoes. Because I was told that this questioning was to take only several hours I did not even change clothes. I have thin summer pants and tennis shoes. It certainly was cold this morning. I wonder how long the several hours is going to stretch out?"

"Soldiers came after me. They had fixed bayonets and appeared fearsome but they were gentle. We were having supper when they arrived but they allowed me to finish my meal. I was allowed to change into a suit and hearing what you went through, perhaps I was the best treated," smiled a groceryman from Pawaa.

With the break of dawn, people began stirring and most headed for the lavatory. It adjoined the large dormitory and was open at all times, but contained only two flush bowls and two wash basins. To economize on water a gadget usually found on steamers was attached to the faucets. One had to grab the two flaring out-turned thumbs to turn on the water. Thus to wash one's face, the left hand had to grasp these blades to let water out while washing with the right hand. While the new immigrants from ships were accustomed to such devices, why the architect installed such a miserly gadget in water-plentiful Honolulu was beyond anybody's comprehension. With one hundred eighty men to use this limited facility, the room was packed continuously.

At about 9 A.M., the door opened and an MP stuck his head in and announced, "You will be taken out of the room to have your breakfast. Form in a single line and make it snappy!" The inmates lined up and marched into the hallway and descended a long straight stairway that led into the inner court of the Immigration Station. There were three MP's with bayoneted rifles stationed along this hall and stairway to direct and keep the file of men against the wall. They used the sharp instrument at a menacingly short distance from the men urging them forward.

To Seikichi Arata, this was the most degrading and humiliating experience he had ever gone through, but this was only the first experience of such a nature he was destined to undergo. He heard one of the soldiers growl, "What the hell! Let's get a machine gun and mow these bastards down. Lot of time wasted and good food thrown away." Seikichi could not help feeling sorry about the whole situation. Perhaps this soldier lost a brother or friend in the blitz. Naturally he had seen the sunken ships in Pearl Harbor. It was natural for one to become angered at the wanton destruction. Perhaps his own grandson, Edward, was feeling the same indignation as this lately arrived soldier to the islands.

The line passed a table out in the open courtyard and each was to pick an army aluminum mess kit and be given two slices of bread with strawberry jam. Each was to help himself to coffee which was in a large, thirty gallon container. The coffee was so hot it nearly burned Seikichi's lips and tongue. Most just drank coffee. Ironically, Japanese carpenters were busily constructing barbed wire extensions above the ten foot wall surrounding the inner court. The twenty minutes allowed out in the open air was a treat after the stuffy, cramped room. Men walked back and forth stretching their stiffened joints, and shaking hands with friends who were also caught in yesterday's raid. A shrill whistle blew and they were lined in single file and returned to the same room.

At about noon, Shoichi Asami's name was called and he was led downstairs. Because his name began with an A, there was a faint hope in everyone's mind that "hearings" had begun in alphabetical order and soon all would be returned home. All knew almost everyone else and there was none in the crowd that would have acted inimically to the security of the United States.

Mr. Asami returned after a short while. "There was no hearing. I was questioned about certain matters concerning the Nippu Jiji Publishing Co. But while I waited there, I overheard talk that there was a Japanese naval officer taken captive in yesterday's attack. I wonder how it happened but the talk was pretty excited about this captive." This was the group's first news concerning the operator of the midget submarine with whom they were to travel and share hardship for many months.

At about three o'clock, the door was again opened and the single file procession proceeded down to the inner court where two slices of bread, corned beef, and a cup of coffee were served. As the room could no longer admit newcomers, the men were able to arrange themselves so that as many as possible could sleep on the bunks. On Seikichi Arata's three-tier bunk, three slept in the place of the regular two. Two on the edges slept with their heads in one direction and the middle person had his head at the opposite end. This arrangement was all right as far as stretching their bodies was concerned, but being kicked in the face during the night was not very pleasant. On some lower bunks four slept across two beds.

. . .

On Tuesday morning after breakfast, the sergeant came into the room and read the names of about half of the men. These were ordered out of the room; where to nobody knew, but it was better than being locked up. Seikichi Arata's name was not on the list. For the first time in two days the remaining ones, being relieved of congestion, felt that they could at least sleep in comfort. Brooms and mops were handed to them and a general clean-up was undertaken with vigor. People were glad to do something. The atmosphere seemed to get cleaner and fresher after the sudden exodus and the common urge was to stretch at full length and catch up on sleep. Just about the time when they woke from their nap in mid-afternoon, the sergeant reappeared and called off a list of names. Seikichi was among them.

These men were taken out to the lawn in front of the side entrance facing Pier 2 amidst a drizzling rain that soaked them to their skin. Few had coats and there was no shelter. The list was checked twice. They were then ordered to board covered trucks which took them to Pier 6, the Naval Wharf. During this trip they were guarded by soldiers with fixed bayonets, three to a truck. Two armored cars were sandwiched among the vehicles. On the wharf, the men were lined up and again checked as to number and then ordered to board a large scow. A steam tugboat towed it. Fifty men that comprised this group were ordered to crouch down on the floor of the flat boat, while half a dozen soldiers with shotguns stood menacingly fore and aft with the muzzles pointed at the men huddled together in the center.

Perhaps one of the young soldiers could not help but crack a joke, in spite of the situation being anything but jocular, when he said, "You are all being taken out into the Pacific Ocean and will get scuttled to feed the sharks." This was bad enough, but the Germans had machine guns trained on them when they were ferried across later. A coast guard cutter was moored nearby, and its crew lined the rail watching these poor captives led away.

The radio of the coast guard cutter was turned on and its loud speaker blared forth President Roosevelt's message to Congress announcing the declaration of war against the three Axis Nations. It recounted the treachery of the Japanese in attacking Pearl Harbor while peaceful negotiations were being conducted at Washington. Since these men were ignorant of the events taking place in the world, this was the first news of the spread of the war to a worldwide scope. Honolulu looked like a deserted city. At the waterfront, the usual traffic at that time of day was conspicuous by its absence. It looked like a Sunday afternoon.

The tugboat pulled the barge out into the harbor and took it straight across to Sand Island which is situated on the west side of the harbor entrance. When the first contingent left the room in the morning, somebody said that they were to be shipped to an "island," and many thought it would be Molokai. Since pineapple crates are hauled from Molokai and Lanai on these barges, the destination could have been that island. When it turned out to be Sand Island everyone let out a sigh of relief.

A detachment of soldiers awaited them at the crude landing and the captives were marched two abreast. A dozen soldiers armed with shotguns flanked both sides. It was just getting dark but everything was still visible. In front of Seikichi Arata walked Mr. Komeya, eighty-four years old, who had been routed out of his sick bed. He could hardly walk, let alone keep up with the rest. Seikichi called the guard's attention to his plight. The captain came over and told the old man to step out of the line, for a truck was going to take him to the destination.

Just then a cold shower drenched them to their skin. It was a short march and a welcome exercise for most of them, but the tragic spectacle of a beaten group of men guarded with lethal weapons forlornly marching to an unknown destination in the gathering dusk was objectively and poetically felt by Seikichi even as a participant. It is said that Japanese love tragedy—love to shed tears over drama and stories—and they seem to have the peculiar quality of "enjoying pain." For any motion picture or drama to be a financial success among the Japanese there must be included in its plot scenes and episodes that wring the tear glands. Seikichi was detachedly imagining the scene of "retreat from Moscow of Napoleon's men" that he had once seen in a picture book. Surely the only common factor was the dejected manner of the marchers, but somehow he felt poetically elated. The procession ended at the headquarters of the Sand Island garrison made up of low, Spanish-type architecture.

The prisoners were lined up in single file in the hallway, which was lit by a very dim green light, for the windows were all covered by black board.

"Take off all your clothes and shoes. Hold them in your hands." As they stood without a stitch on their shivering bodies, a captain appeared and addressed them through an interpreter.

"You are now prisoners of war. I have been ordered to see that you are kept here. Strict discipline will be maintained, but I do not intend to be inhuman. Whether I shall be able to pursue this course and succeed in my purpose will depend on your behavior. I have respected the Japanese people in the past. I have studied your people a little and I think I know you. But after Sunday I know that we have a worthy opponent in the Japanese army and navy." Captain Coughlin, spare and straight, was well over six feet and his bearing was very military.

The immediate reaction to this speech of introduction was favorable and the men accepted the ensuing humiliating search of their person and belongings without resentment. It was a manly talk, straight and succinct. They were ordered to stand before several noncommissioned officers, to place their belongings on the desk. Money and valuables were placed in an envelope and after a search, clothes and shoes were returned. When ten or twelve put their clothes on, they were led outside. It was pitch dark. No light could be used and so they held on to each other's hand and followed a soldier. After walking about a quarter mile, they met their friends who had preceded them in the morning. These people had put up tents all day. The new arrivals were handed two blankets and assigned tents for the night.

When Seikichi Arata went to his tent there was no cot. Because of the rain the ground was wet and, since Sand Island is only slightly above sea level, brackish water seeped through the ground. The sergeant found cots for them and led them to the dining room for some sandwiches. The attack of mosquitoes was persistent and annoying, but before Seikichi knew it he was fast asleep. He was exhausted mentally. It was an eventful day.

Report on Hawaiian Islands

CURTIS B. MUNSON

THE consensus of opinion is that there will be no racial uprising of the Japanese in Honolulu. The first generation, as on the Coast, are ideologically and culturally closest to Japan. Though many of them speak no English, or at best only pigeon-English, it is considered that the big bulk of them will be loyal. This is especially so, for in Hawaii the first generation is largely on the land and devoted to it. It may be well to state here in a general way that everyone in Hawaii, especially in the dark-skinned laboring classes, places loyalty to Hawaii first, and the United States second. This is not meant to impugn their loyalty—but they love the Islands. The second generation is estimated as approximately ninety-eight percent loyal. However, with the large Japanese population in the Hawaiian Islands, giving this the best interpretation possible, it would mean that fifteen hundred were disloyal. However, the F.B.I. state that there are about four hundred suspects, and the F.B.I.'s private estimate is that only fifty or sixty of these are sinister. There are also a few Germans and Italians in the Islands who should be picked up. We do not at the moment remember the exact number, whether it was seven or seventeen. The Army Intelligence showed this reporter a secret map with pins of different colors to denote first generation, second generation, and other nationalities who are suspect, and their distribution in the Islands. Each one of these men's address is known and they showed me that

In *Pearl Harbor Attack,* Hearings before the Joint Committee on the Investigation of the Pearl Harbor Attack, 79th Congress, 1st session, pt. 6, pp. 2692–2696.

it would be a comparatively easy job to pick them up almost in a few hours, should the necessity arise. There is not the same danger as in Continental United States that if they escaped the first grab that they will completely escape, as of course they have nowhere to go but the Pacific Ocean. There will be, undoubtedly, planted Japanese and agents who are there for the purpose of sabotage. Though sabotage may be expected, it is a self-evident fact that the main things to sabotage in the Islands are the Army and Navy installations, and these are under the protection and complete control of the two services. However, materials are sometimes lacking to build, say protecting guard fences. Outside of the services' installations there are only two things open to sabotage; the commercial waterfront (this does not include Pearl Harbor), and the power stations and power lines. However, these power lines are especially important, for if one transformer is damaged in the Islands there are no replacements, and it would be a considerable time before a replacement could be secured from the mainland. Hawaii is particularly fortunate as regards water supply, possessing a large artesian flow along with numerous reservoirs. Fortunately, in the Islands there would be no "White" sabotage which could be purchased by the Japanese, as there is on the Coast, outside of the imported white defense workers. There are very few whites who would be anything except loyal.

. . .

One important difference between the situation in Hawaii and the mainland is that if all the Japanese on the mainland were actively disloyal they could be corraled or destroyed within a very short time. In the Hawaiian islands, though there are sufficient American troops and Navy present to overwhelm the Japanese population, it would simply mean that the Islands would lose their vital labor supply by so doing, and in addition to that we would have to feed them, as well as import many thousands of laborers to take their place. Since a large part of the vital and essential work of the Islands is ably carried on by the Japanese population, it is essential that they should be kept loyal—at least to the extent of staying at their tasks. If Imperial Japan were wise, she would devote all her energies in the Hawaiian Islands to trying to induce a spirit of mind which would cause a universal Japanese sit-down strike. She evidently has not thought of this as there is no sign of this type of propaganda. Propaganda, by Japan, is practically non-existent on the Islands.

. . .

The general background and characteristics of the Japanese are the same in the Islands as they are on the mainland. However, certain differences in the situation have tended to ameliorate these in some particulars. We believe that the best over-all method of expressing this is by the following observation: This reporter believes there is this fundamental difference between the Japanese "Problem" on the Coast and the Japanese "Problem" in the Hawaiian Islands. On the Coast, the Japanese are discriminated against on a racial basis. In Hawaii it is really only on a social and economic basis. This is peculiarly American. In our materialistic civilization one fits in socially largely on an income basis, provided he is willing to wash his neck and give up eating with his knife. In Hawaii, the Japanese fit in thus among the bulk of the inhabitants because the bulk are dark-skinned of one kind or another. The whites generally are on a higher economic plane than they are on the mainland. The few Japanese who reach a position economically where they can mix with the whites are not numerous enough to make much impression even if they do resent not being asked to tea. The bulk of the whites in Hawaii would not mix socially anyway with stevedores or dock laborers, black or white. On the mainland there are plenty of "Okies" to call the Japanese a "Yellow-belly," when economically and by education the Japanese may not only be their equal but their superior.

The result of this is that the Hawaiian Japanese does not suffer from the same inferiority complex or feel the same mistrust of the whites that he does on the mainland. While it is seldom on the mainland that you find even a college-educated Japanese-American citizen who talks to you wholly openly until you have gained his confidence, this is far from the case in Hawaii. Many young Japanese there are fully as open and frank and at ease with a white as white boys are. In a word, Hawaii is more of a melting pot because there are more brown skins to melt—Japanese, Hawaiian, Chinese and Filipino. It is interesting to note that there has been absolutely no bad feeling between the Japanese and the Chinese in the islands due to the Japanese–Chinese war. Why should they be any worse toward us?

The extreme Japanese "lover" in Hawaii is probably motivated frequently by self-interest. This is because he knows that the economic status quo is built largely on the fine industry of the Japanese labor, and he wishes to keep control of this as long as possible and is very loath to suggest to the Army or Navy that there is any danger from the Japanese. Any extreme anti-Japanese thought in Hawaii is probably due either to an unthinking element of the Navy which wants its base to be secure and of good service regardless of other consequences, or it is extremely anti-"Big Five" thought.

. . .

There is some danger in Hawaii of race riots. This is largely due to four elements. The Filipinos are intensely anti-Japanese and if they were attacked on the Philippine Islands they have threatened they would kill every Japanese in the Hawaiian Islands. The Intelligence Services, however, have made particular note of this and in conjunction with the sugar plantations, by whom most of the Filipinos are employed and controlled, have lectured the Filipinos kindly but firmly on this point. They have pointed out that if there is to be interference with any of the inhabitants of the Islands it must be by the properly authorized officials of the American Government. The Filipinos seem to have appreciated this and considerably toned down their patriotism. There is a type of Japanese who may be termed the "bright young thing," a bit loud, and liable to be openly resentful of insult. He is the prototype of his brother on the mainland. He has broken away from the fine character and parental control of his Japanese background while becoming too Americanized without fully comprehending what Americanization means. Fortunately, he represents a small group in the second-generation Japanese and contributes most of the juvenile delinquency which is found in this race. He gets drunk and frequents pool halls. There is danger that drunk sailors may push him off the street and call him a "Yellow-belly," especially if they have just returned from some Naval battle with the Japanese. Where other Japanese would take this in silent anger, this bright young thing might hit back and start some racial trouble. However, it must be said that the Army and Navy have this fully in mind and are very efficiently policing their own families. The sailors are extremely well behaved and it is a matter of common comment and approval. The real danger of racial trouble comes from the defense workers who have been imported from the mainland. Most of these come from the Pacific Coast and contain the dregs of the waterfront element. If they had been able to secure a job on the mainland, they would not have gone to Hawaii. They include many of the "Okie" class and to them any brown-skin is "Nigger."

. . .

In summarizing, we cannot say how loyal the Japanese in the Hawaiian group would be if there were an American Naval disaster and the Japanese fleet appeared off the Hawaiian Islands. Doubtless great numbers of them would then forget their American loyalties and shout *"Banzai"* from the shore. Under those circumstances if this reporter were there he is not sure that he might not do it also to save his own skin, if not his face. Due to the fact that there are more than enough soldiers in the Islands to take care of any Japanese, even if not so inclined, the Japanese will doubtless remain quietly at their tasks. However, in fairness to them it is only right to say that we believe the big majority anyhow would be neutral or even actively loyal.

Hawaii's 150,000 Japanese

ALBERT HORLINGS

THE United States is making one of the most dramatic bets of history in Hawaii. It is gambling the internal stability of its greatest base in the Pacific—the anchor of the whole Pacific battle line—on the loyalty of 150,000 Japanese and Japanese Americans, 40,000 of whom are aliens, the majority of whom cannot read or speak English, and few of whom have ever seen America or have a clear understanding of what America stands for.

This is no mean wager. A Japanese fifth column in Hawaii could do great damage during an attempted invasion. It could halt civilian transportation, block highways, destroy the vulnerable reservoirs upon which Honolulu depends for water, wreck gas and electric service, destroy food, and terrorize civilians. By diverting manpower from the exterior defenses this fifth column could turn defeat for the invader into success. Sabotage would be easy for it; the Japanese population is 40 percent of the total, and its members hold hundreds of strategic positions in public utilities, in civilian defense, and in other services.

We might deserve praise for risking so much on the human heart if only we were not making the bet for the wrong reasons. I suspect we are making it not because the military authorities in Hawaii really trust the Japanese but because pressure has been brought on them,

In *The Nation,* July 25, 1942, pp. 69–71. Reprinted by permission of The Nation Co.

and they have been told that the economic life of the islands will collapse without the Japanese. Hawaiian business men are variously motivated, but some of them appear to favor a liberal policy toward the Japanese simply because they favor business as usual. And in the background hovers the case for Hawaiian statehood. The Japanese in Hawaii have long been held up to the mainland as first-class Americans by those pressing for the island's admission to the Union, and many islanders fear that to cast doubt on Japanese loyalty now would ruin the chances of admission. The real conviction of the white islanders is shown by the large-scale evacuation of women and children that has been going on ever since Pearl Harbor.

In this historic gamble we have certainly something to win. First, we can win the confidence of some good citizens of ours. Japanese communities in this country have in general realized that their members could never blend physically into the American stream, and so far they have shown no evidence of wanting to be anything but a Japanese colony abroad. But a few individuals in these communities in Hawaii and in the states, have become truly Americanized in spirit, and it would be a tragedy if they were discriminated against by measures aimed at Japanese who merely live here. No one who knows the able, spirited, and likable American of Japanese ancestry will underestimate the contribution these people can make to American life once they choose—and once we permit them—to turn irrevocably to the West.

We gain something also by admitting that Hawaii has handled its peculiar racial problem sensibly and well, and by refusing unnecessarily to disturb the islands' equilibrium. Sociologically and genetically we have everything to win. Hawaii is one of the great anthropological laboratories of the world, and it would be easy to arouse antipathies that would destroy its value. The racial *aloha* of the islands is a real and priceless thing.

But the greatest thing we stand to gain is the aid of hundreds of millions of people whose skins are not the color of ours. Whether we win or lose the peace will probably depend greatly upon our success in convincing Asiatics, Indians, Negroes, and others that our plea for world leadership is not a screen for world domination. We must convince them that we are fighting not for an Anglo-Saxon world or a Caucasian world, but for a world in which humanity is the test of franchise.

However, our kindness to enemy aliens and enemy sympathizers at a naval outpost will avail us little so long as we needlessly affront our friends. The propaganda value of extraordinary solicitude for Hawaii's Japanese—and it is certainly extraordinary measured by Japanese and German standards, as well as by our own past performance—will be completely nullified unless we mend our manners. A Chinese seaman who was on our side years before the State Department knew which was our side is prohibited from coming ashore at an American port. And if it is true that an exclusion law aimed at all Orientals arouses more resentment than good treatment of enemy-alien Orientals can ever undo, then we must wonder whether we have not put the Honolulu cart before the Washington horse.

In any case Hawaii's safety is not a local matter, and a decision relating to control of a possible fifth column must be determined by national interests. How does our present policy look from that point of view? I am afraid that it looks crazy. I never found anyone in Honolulu, not even the most enthusiastic member of the Japanese Chamber of Commerce, who would say that Hawaii's Japanese were overwhelmingly loyal to the United States. Why should they be, and why should they want us to win this war?

The political and economic fortunes of a few depend upon our winning. Some have been released from stark poverty by living under the American flag. Some have washed away the stain of ostracism that attached to their family in Japan. Some believe that America's accent upon the worth of the individual will lead to greater happiness for themselves and the world. A few would rather see a defeated Japan than a militaristic one. Some have deeply rooted prejudices and sentiments binding them to our side.

But the proportion of these is not large. The majority have nothing to gain by the defeat of Japan. Their prestige as expatriates depends in large part upon the prestige of the Japanese empire. Their economic fortunes are often tied more closely to Japan than to America: they work for Tokyo banks and business houses; they import goods from Japan; they invest in Japanese securities. Even if they live entirely off Hawaiian land or its surrounding waters, their customers are likely to be members of their own race. When they work for the white man, it is in a menial position, one that is more likely to arouse resentment than regard. To a remarkable degree Hawaii's Japanese are untouched by American ways; all their pride of race, family, and religion binds them to Japan. Thousands see or hear almost nothing American, while they consume Japanese food, Japanese clothing, Japanese music, Japanese pictures, Japanese newspapers and magazines by the shipload.

In common with all the other races there, the Japanese love their purple islands, but they can imagine Hawaii without American rule. Indeed, Japanese propaganda has frequently drawn the picture for them. Instead of doing menial labor at the low end of a double wage standard, they would occupy lofty positions in the economic life of the islands. Instead of being crowded in slums, they would live in the cool valleys back of the city, from which deed restrictions now generally exclude them. Instead of seeing their children admitted to the best schools only in token numbers, they would enjoy all the emoluments of the ruling class. In hundreds of ways even the "good" Japanese would gain, not lose, by Japanese rule of Hawaii.

Nor are they unaware of these facts. In impressive numbers they fail to burn their bridges to Japan. Despite the numerous campaigns for renunciation of Japanese allegiance, there are still 60,000 dual citizens in Hawaii—in other words, the majority of American-born Japanese in Hawaii are willing to let the Japanese government claim them as its own. Some 15,000 Hawaiian-born Japanese have cast their lot permanently with Japan. Thousands of others shuttle between Tokyo and Honolulu, "taking my father's ashes to his homeland," seeking better jobs, or simply taking advantage of the low steamship rates through which Japan keeps in touch with its foreign colonies.

Only a Pollyanna could conclude that there is no danger in this situation. If only because it hides the emperor's agents, this large unassimilated group constitutes a real menace. Nor are the professional saboteurs who escape the FBI the only ones who would act with zest if they found themselves in a position to swing the balance against the United States forces. There are also congenital white-man haters (*haole*-haters in the island vernacular) among both the alien and citizen Japanese. The most innocuous *papa-san* could easily become their dupe. I do not say he will; the point is that we cannot be sure he will not. With no better material the emperor's men certainly welded efficient fifth columns in the Philippines, in Malaya, and in the Dutch East Indies. (There is another side to the coin, and in a happier time I would rather be polishing it—it presents the Hawaiianization of Japanese who can never be Americanized, for instance, and the human qualities which we must admire in these fine people whether they happen to be on our side or not.)

People who have been interned do not buy theater tickets or serve cocktails, and some islanders have argued that this is not the time to disturb matters in civilian Honolulu. Hawaii's Congressional delegate, Sam King, has worked assiduously to convince both Congress and the military that nothing should be done beyond apprehending known spies and treacherous ringleaders. Everywhere one hears repeated the testimony of Captain John Anthony Burns of the Honolulu police force that he has found the accounts of sniping at American soldiers untrue, and the touching story of Yoshio Yamamoto, who saves all his pennies for war stamps. Everywhere people emphasize that the Japanese are indispensable in Hawaii. But many of these are interested persons who overlook the Buddhist temples, the Japanese-language schools, the dozens of Japanese societies and organizations, some with official Tokyo connections, the ubiquitous pictures of the emperor, the Japanese holidays, the crowds flocking to see the emperor's cruisers, the subscriptions to Japanese war loans, the strongly nationalistic propaganda uncovered in Japanese-language publications.

The argument of the Japanese indispensability, the one that has been dinned into the ears of Congress and the military authorities, is a fallacious one. It would be inconvenient to get along without the Japanese, but it would not be impossible. The Filipino has long been the backbone of the plantation labor supply, and there are thousands of Chinese, Hawaiians, Koreans, Puerto Ricans, and Caucasians to carry on essential functions. If the plantations should stop raising sugar and pineapples, which they would be forced to do during a long siege, there would be an over-supply of labor. Conversion to food crops has not taken place in Hawaii to the extent always thought necessary.

One articulate group in Hawaii advocates internment of the Japanese. The leaders of this group are life-long islanders, some of whom were raised with the Japanese and speak their language. Those I know are not given to jitters, and when they say that the absence of sabotage on December 7 proves nothing, I agree with them. If Japan has a well-organized fifth column in Hawaii it would certainly not have exposed it prematurely, before any effort was to be made at invasion, and when the saboteurs could have accomplished nothing but their own extinction.

I cannot agree, however, that large-scale internment of Hawaii's Japanese would be wise. Not only would internment be sure to cause great hardship, but it would be ineffective in one particular—in getting out of the invader's reach a large and competent reservoir of manpower which could be depended on to carry on civilian life in the islands. For whatever doubt there may be about the attitude of the

Japanese before or during an invasion attempt, there is no doubt that the vast majority of Hawaii's Japanese will work with alacrity with the emperor's forces if Japan ever takes the islands. I favor evacuation, which would remove this labor force, bring less hardship, and reduce Hawaii's consumption of food, much of which is convoyed from California. Since ships return from Hawaii with only sugar and pineapples, which we can forgo momentarily, plenty of bottoms are available for the purpose.

We should not underestimate the importance of what we are gambling. Hawaii consists of seven islands—only one of them fortified—as against the 2,500 islands of Micronesia; it is virtually our only neutralizing agent for the vast insular system of "stationary aircraft carriers" that projects Japanese power south to the Equator and east to within bombing distance of Honolulu. Hawaii is indispensable to us if we are to protect our flanks in the Antipodes and Alaska, safeguard the Panama Canal and our West Coast, and eventually carry out a frontal attack on Japan. Without it we should be impotent in the Pacific.

If it was expedient to remove a scattering of Japanese from our Western coastal regions, the American people should be told why it is not many times more necessary to remove this heavier concentration of Japanese from islands which are in greater danger and harder to defend. We are playing for the highest stakes: Congress should investigate immediately and tell us what the odds are.

Hawaii's Loyal Japanese

THOMAS H. IGE

IN his *Nation* article of July 25, Albert Horlings scores the United States for its liberal or lax treatment of persons of Japanese extraction now residing in Hawaii. He argues that the great majority of them cannot be trusted; that we are taking a bad risk. The charges made by Mr. Horlings against these 150,000 Japanese, 110,000 of whom are American citizens, are numerous and serious. I wholly agree with Mr. Horlings that "Hawaii's safety is not a local matter, and a decision relating to a control of a possible fifth column must be determined by national interest." It does not follow, however, that a prejudiced, ill-considered presentation of the case will be any help in clarifying the situation. Being of Japanese descent, born and reared in Hawaii, I too may be biased, but let us look at the other side of the coin.

The degree to which people of Japanese blood have been assimilated into Hawaiian-American society has been, I feel, grossly understated. I doubt whether there is one island sociologist or any one else familiar with the island's racial problems who will go halfway with Mr. Horlings. The statement in his opening paragraph to the effect that a majority of us cannot read or write English is plain nonsense. For the citizen group, the extent of American schooling is as high as for other racial groups in Hawaii and compares very fa-

In *The Nation,* August 8, 1942, p. 120. Reprinted by permission of The Nation Co.

vorably with that of the mainland states. Alien Japanese recently arrived in Hawaii do as well, on the whole, as others of like circumstances. "Thousands see or hear almost nothing American, while they consume Japanese food, Japanese clothing, Japanese music, Japanese pictures, Japanese newspapers and magazines by the shipload," says Mr. Horlings. He does not mention the overwhelming majority who prefer Bob Hope, Bette Davis, and Gary Cooper; who read the *Reader's Digest,* the *Women's Home Companion,* the *Saturday Evening Post, Life, The Nation, Harpers;* who dress as Americans and sing American songs. It seems silly to deny that our attitudes are fashioned after American patterns. Where Mr. Horlings gets the idea that we of Japanese blood "imagine Hawaii without American rule" and picture ourselves as top dogs in this new Hawaii, I do not know.

The question of dual citizenship cannot be dismissed so easily. As Mr. Horlings states, it is true that a great number of American citizens have failed to burn their bridges to Japan. Nonexpatriation, however, is by no means an indication of disloyalty to the United States. Many are still dependents of aliens who cannot become American citizens because of the Immigration Act of 1924 and, therefore, cannot act independently. Many have been simply negligent, for expatriation is a cumbersome and time-consuming affair. The leaders among the citizen group are all expatriated, for it is impossible to make much headway in Hawaii without taking this step. As we go into the third and fourth generations, this problem will automatically be solved.

The question of our loyalty, of course, forms the hub around which all other considerations revolve, and loyalty is too much an intangible thing to permit of estimates or generalities. Most of our non-Japanese island leaders have vouched for the loyalty of Hawaii's Japanese. This was borne out during and after Japan's attack on Pearl Harbor and has been officially confirmed, but Mr. Horlings prefers to judge our loyalty on purely racial lines.

What of the solution? Can we gamble on the loyalty of the 150,000 Japanese in Hawaii? I will not deny for one minute that some agents of Tokyo and their dupes are still running loose, but the overwhelming majority of us here proved that we will stand by America when the zero hour strikes. We have brothers and relatives in the armed forces of the United States and are just as anxious for an Allied victory as other Americans.

Double or triple the FBI force in Hawaii. This would be more practical and wise than a wholesale evacuation which would involve innumerable hardships as well as seriously undermine our democratic concepts and the value of United States citizenship. That the Japanese on the West Coast have been evacuated is no reason for the same treatment in Hawaii. In reading through the Tolan Committee hearings and reports, I am far from convinced such drastic steps were necessary, especially since they were instigated not by the military but by hysterical civilians and interested groups. I suggest further that we young men of fighting age be given the same opportunities in the armed forces as other American boys and, secondly, some assurance of equality in the post-war world.

CHAPTER EIGHT

A Generation on Trial

FOR most individuals who lived in America or Hawaii during the years 1941 to 1945, World War II in the Pacific and Europe directly affected their lives. From household routines, work-day activities, and personal consumption to styles of recreation, the patterns of daily living were permeated with the tensions and demands of war. Even words took on new meanings. Gas rationing, food shortages, "day of infamy," gas masks, blackouts, air-raid sirens, GI Joe, Nazi, Jap, Victory Bonds, "loose lips sink ships," D-Day, "Kilroy was here"—all of these terms entered the lexicon of the American language. One could not read a newspaper or magazine, listen to the radio, or view a movie without being instilled with the spirit of victory or with hate for the enemy. Personal decisions concerning the future were temporarily suspended because, after all, the war effort came first. Young women went to work in bomb factories; grandmothers volunteered at the YWCA; lei-makers wove camouflage nets; Boy Scouts were activated as guards at roadblocks; young men worked in labor gangs to clear *kiawe* forests, dig shelters and trenches, string barbed wire along beaches, and build military installations—all able-bodied personnel were recruited into the armed forces to put their muscle and blood behind the destruction of Japan, Germany, and Italy. Even small children were made to realize that events of extraordinary and dangerous proportions raged halfway across the world—newspaper drives, bond sales, the collection of tin pots and pans, the funny cartoon characters who fought Nazis at the Saturday afternoon matinees, mornings at the babysitter while mother loaded ammunition belts for machine guns, father's oversized army hat or gas mask which provided realism to the children's mock war games. From the Hawaiian farmer in Makawao, Maui, who raised victory gardens to the housewife in Bangor, Maine, who conscientiously saved metal toothpaste tubes, from the infant wrapped in the "bunny" gas mask to the senior citizen who rolled Red Cross bandages—all would remember World War II as a period of sacrifice, hardship, grief, and finally exaltation—a period when generations of Americans would be tempered and matured by war.

For one generation of Americans, the Nisei, the war would also be remembered as a time when Japanese Americans would have to prove their sincere loyalty to America. Nearly thirty years of anti-Japanese sentiment had preceded the outbreak of war, a sentiment which cast aspersions on the character, integrity, and adaptability of the Japanese immigrant and his children to the American way of life. While in Hawaii those anti-Japanese forces were balanced by more rational individuals who could accept the Issei and Nisei as neighbors, lingering doubts still plagued the Japanese population of the Islands. With the advent of war, those doubts intensified to the point where the Japanese had to make swift and decisive decisions concerning their loyalties, customs, and daily habits so that their Americanism would be unquestioned.

Having the face, culture, language, diet, and dress of the enemy during a war necessitated caution and cultural suppression. It also necessitated superpatriotism. World War II was a popular war in that most Americans felt that they had to do their part to destroy the tyranny which threatened the world—Hitler and Tojo were devils who sought destruction and world mastery. While the Nisei were naturally swept into the intense patriotism of the period, many Japanese realized that they were expected to perhaps go just a little further in their denunciation of fascism and their complete repudiation of any ties with Japan. The Nisei were a generation on trial and the verdict would determine their future in Hawaii. As the McKinley High School newspaper, the *Daily Pinion,* wrote to the Nisei student body,

> You might as well admit it now that you are on the spot. There is nothing to be gained by fooling oneself at a time like this. Harm is

> apt to come from being indifferent. The outside world wonders about you.[1]

The chairman of the Oahu Citizens Committee for Home Defense, Shunzo Sakamaki, announced in a tone far from indifferent:

> Japan's dastardly attack leaves us grim and resolute. There is no turning back now, no compromise with the enemy. Japan has chosen to fight us and we'll fight. This is a bitter battle to the end; and to all loyal Americans and other lovers of democracy and human freedom that end is the complete destruction of the totalitarian governments that are blighting our world today.[2]

The first "grim and resolute" concern of the local Japanese in Hawaii during World War II was the complete disassociation with anything Japanese. To the Issei, this attempt at cultural suppression was extremely difficult and psychologically trying. Although Issei had become adapted to living in Hawaii and could remain relatively neutral throughout the war, to eradicate things Japanese in their daily lifestyle was profoundly traumatic. Language schools and Buddhist temples were closed down, and many Japanese believed that situation to be permanent. While before the war women could wear kimonos on the streets of Honolulu, such styles would arouse, during the war, jeers and gibes from non-Japanese. Speaking Japanese in public could result in insults; having Japanese flags or other nationalistic artifacts would be viewed as treasonous. At night Japanese families buried in their backyards or under their homes *samurai* swords, flags, or any treasures from Japan which they feared might link them with the enemy. Cherished photographs of a vacation in Japan were destroyed; the Japanese flag in photographs of Japanese language-school graduations or weddings were carefully blackened. Even name changes occurred. On the island of Oahu in 1942, almost 250 Japanese names were officially changed to Chinese, Hawaiian, Portuguese, or even Scottish names. The Fujita's became the Ah Nees, Haraguchi changed to Kanekoa, Matsugora to Figueira, and Nakamura to McFarlane.[3]

To facilitate the problems which would be encountered by Issei and Nisei during the uncertainty and bewilderment of war conditions, in February, 1942, the Japanese community in cooperation with the Military Governor established a morale group known as the Emergency Service Committee. During the war, this morale group was expanded to Kauai, Maui, Lanai, and Hawaii and in 1944 was called the Territorial Emergency Service Committee. These groups encouraged the Americanization of the Issei, giving classes in English and American history and culture. Japanese were urged to buy war bonds, donate their services to the war effort and support war relief funds. The Emergency Service Committee also aided in the liquidation of the property and assets of Japanese institutions and societies, some of which went to the Hawaii Veteran's Memorial Fund of Oahu. The Japanese Social Club at Ewa was given to the United Service Organization (USO), while the YMCA took over the buildings of the Kaimuki, Kalihi, and Wahiawa language schools.

In May of 1942, Police Captain John Burns announced the beginnings of an Americanization Program for Japanese which intended to contact every Japanese in the Islands in order to stress the importance of behaving like an American both privately and publicly. "A definite break should be made from those things and institutions which are or represent Japan itself,"[4] the program proselytized in the Japanese community. Issei and Nisei must actively engage in promoting an image reflective of the United States.

In conjunction with these Americanization efforts among the Japanese, "Speak English" campaigns were initiated in various communities. The "Speak English" movement was geared to teaching aliens how to speak, write, and read the English language. Illustrative of the movement's endeavors was a radio address directed to the Japanese community entitled "Speak American"[5] by Shigeo Yoshida, principal of Ala Moana School in Honolulu and an influential member of the Emergency Service Committee. Yoshida's speech illuminated the anxieties of the Japanese community concerning the continued use of Japanese language and customs. Although Yoshida believed that teaching English to the Issei would actually be futile because many of them were too far advanced in age to begin learning a new language, he stressed to all bilingual Japanese that they should "avoid the use of the Japanese language except in situations where it is absolutely necessary as a means of communication with persons who do not understand the English language." Issei and Nisei must remember, Yoshida admonished, that Americanization was not to be taken lightly—being fully Americanized was a part of the war effort. "I know that anything we Americans of Japanese ancestry can do to demonstrate our Americanism will redound not only to our benefit but the benefit of all Hawaii."

Understandably, for the Issei whose primary life orientation had always been Japanese culture such Americanization efforts had perhaps the severest repercussions. The enforced community Americanization, the "hate the Jap" war propaganda, the fear of strangers, generated subtle psychological disturbances within the Issei population. As one Issei said, "We are afraid. We don't know what to do. Even our own children don't let us go out. If we go out, we will be the focus of hate and revenge. So we stay in the house."[6]

An especially disruptive occurrence for the Issei community was the closing of the Buddhist temples. Taking advantage of the war situation, Reverend Okumura and other Christian leaders supported the closing of all such temples and language schools, hoping that they would never be reopened. Also, military authorities interned all but a handful of Buddhist ministers, successfully crippling the morale of the Issei community. The Honpa Hongwanji, for example, was left with a staff of only five assistant ministers—two men, one of whom was hospitalized, and three women.[7] Although Buddhist services were conducted on a small scale by the pitifully few ministers who remained to inadequately serve the vast numbers needing spiritual comfort, the social stigma placed on anything Buddhist predicated the Issei's cultural dilemma.

Without their spiritual institutions the Issei floundered—their common denominator, the nucleus of their lifestyle, was thrown askew. In situations of stress, frustrated by cultural suppression, an ethnic minority group invariably seeks outlets to relieve internal anxieties and repressions. Collectively they often became mesmerized by distorted visions of reality, so that racial hostilities could be vented and social stability restored. Not Japan, but "An evil human-faced cow possessed of supernatural powers and . . . beyond human control" had attacked Pearl Harbor, many believed.[8] For how else could the emperor allow his loving subjects in Hawaii to be placed in such a grave and threatening situation? Following the war many Issei simply found it impossible to believe that Japan could have actually lost. Rumors spread among the immigrants that the Japanese Imperial Navy was steaming into Honolulu to take over the Islands, that the emperor and his devoted countrymen had been victorious in their Pacific war. Other wild notions found eager ears among the suppressed Issei:

> A Japanese fleet is in Pearl Harbor to take over Hawaii.
>
> A Japanese fleet is sighted off Diamond Head.
>
> People in my neighborhood told me that the new Japanese Consul General was Mr. Yoshida. They saw him entering the Consulate, escorted by MPs on motorcycles. The Consulate was lit with bright lights the night of his arrival.

I heard that people saw a few Japanese officers at a restaurant, guarded by MPs.

A person told me that someone saw a Japanese army officer receiving $116 for a one yen bill at the Bishop Bank.[9]

In addition to the proliferation of distorted rumors, a suppressed ethnic group also demonstrates "cultural revivals," an expression of repressed traditional patterns refashioned by modern situations. Steeped in supernatural prophecies and messianic dreams, frequently adapting ancient magical beliefs to current crises, cultural revivals restore the spiritual vitality of a people. The most prominent of these cultural revivals among the Issei during the war was the *Seichō-no-Ie,* or House of Growth, a religious sect introduced to Hawaii in the 1930s but inconspicuous until World War II. The *Seichō-no-Ie* was founded in Japan by Masaharu Taniguchi, a self-proclaimed psychic whose earlier life had been characterized more by sexual predilections for ten-year-old girls and by venereal disease than by religious ardor. Believing that his physical deterioration had been purely mental, Taniguchi turned to mystic spiritual healing which was a combination of Shinto, Buddhist, and Christian Scientist beliefs. He established a small but devout following in Japan and began to publish a monthly magazine, the *Seichō-no-Ie,* which was eventually to find circulation in the Hawaiian Islands.

The *Seichō-no-Ie* became a popular movement among Issei when concerned parents began to seek out *Seichō* priests to pray for the protection of their Nisei sons fighting in Europe or Asia. These priests would come to the home and conduct fervent services over photographs of the Nisei soldier, supposedly guaranteeing their safe return to Hawaii. By November, 1944, regular public services of the cult were being held in Honolulu, and practitioners were being given supernatural insights into impending Japan–U.S. relations:

A member of my temple told me that Mrs. M. of *Seichō-no-Ie* is supposed to have spiritual eyes which foresee approaching events. According to him she told her followers that about 300 Japanese planes were to attack Hawaii on July 27, 1945, and she gave them amulets to protect them from the bombs. Nothing happened on that day. So someone asked her the reason. She answered that it was due to bad weather. They waited and nothing happened on the day she designated. So, people asked her again, and they were told that instead of planes a Japanese fleet would come. But the Japanese fleet did not come. Now she tells the people to wait until March 27. She also told the people that President Truman was called to Tokyo by the Japanese Emperor. The Emperor did not want to deal with MacArthur, and she saw Truman's party downtown on its way to Tokyo.[10]

While cult movements such as the *Seichō-no-Ie* might have salved the deeper psychological disturbances of the Issei, other wartime forces of cultural upheaval were to permanently alter the internal structures of the Japanese community. Especially within the home, the war repatterned roles and relationships. Due to the contingencies of wartime and the need to exercise 100 percent Americanism, the roles of parents and children were reversed—because the Nisei could maneuver easily within American society they became the authorities in the family. Disciplinary rules from the children such as "don't talk in Japanese," "don't use the telephone because you don't speak English," "don't wear a kimono," and "don't bow like a Japanese" reversed authority roles in the home.[11]

Husband-and-wife relationships were also altered by the war. Because many Issei and Nisei women joined in the war effort by volunteering services at the Salvation Army, the YWCA, the Red Cross, or the USO, they were not able to perform the necessary womanly chores customary in a Japanese home. Especially for many young Nisei women, the war imposed new alternatives and lifestyles which their Issei parents in years previous would have stubbornly suppressed. Taken out of the home and put into school, factory, assembly line, or professional job, the Nisei woman began a pattern of independent employment which exposed her to many forces outside of the ethnic community. Accustomed to the role of wife and mother, she found an equally challenging role as co-provider for the family. The working woman, as a secretary, clerk, or teacher, became an accepted role which altered the husband–wife relationships in the Japanese American household. No longer in the patriarchal manner could the Japanese male as the sole economic provider be the autocrat; the wife's opinion as a breadwinner had to be considered.

Nisei women were even recruited into the armed services during World War II. In October, 1944, the Women's Army Corps (WAC) sought Island enlistments. Eventually fifty-nine women were recruited in the WACs, twenty-six of them Nisei. In January, 1945, they left Hawaii for training and eventually served on the mainland, in Africa, Europe, and Asia. That Nisei women should engage in these sorts of activities seriously questioned the passive role of the female in the cultural practices of the Japanese family.

With the changing nature of the Japanese family due to the lessening of Issei parental discipline, the emergence of the Nisei as household authorities, and the liberalization of the female role, the character of the Japanese community was rapidly being transformed. The war was effectively disrupting the rigid ethnic boundaries which had separated Japanese from non-Japanese. No longer totally restrained by the traditionalism of the Issei culture, many Nisei in defense work, in the military service, and in their daily relations with the broader non-Japanese community expanded their contacts with people of all races. The outcome of these interethnic contacts was an increasing rate of interracial marriage for the second generation. Before 1940, only 9 percent of all Japanese marriages were outside of the ethnic group. By 1945 the annual rate had increased to 22 percent, a dramatic rise in outmarriages.[12] The assimilation of the Japanese community into the Island society was being accelerated.

But for the Japanese to be totally accepted as "locals" in an indisputable spirit, they had to do more than hide Japanese artifacts, speak English, rub shoulders on the assembly line, or intermarry with other ethnic groups. In addition, Japanese had to exert a total patriotism in the destruction of the Axis enemy. Proof of one's Americanism would only be accomplished when the offspring of Japan helped crush their homeland and her allies. "OK Tojo—you asked for it," read an ad in the newspaper signed by Akagi, Fukushima, Hiyama, Isoshima, Kanda, Kataoka, Kawashima, Komenaka, Ozaki, Ogata, Nagao, Yamamoto, and Musashiya:

> You dished it out with a head start by treachery—now we're going to see how you can take it.
>
> We're ganging up on you, Tojo, in a way you and your Nazi friend don't understand.
>
> . . . Get it Tojo? It isn't the Jap way, the Nazi way, nor the Fascist way.
>
> It's the *Free American Way*.[13]

Even before the Pearl Harbor attack, Nisei had volunteered for or enlisted in the armed forces. On December 7, approximately 200 Nisei were serving in engineering units, later known as the 1399th Engineering Construction Battalion, involved in the construction of bridges, water systems, defense enforcements, airfields, and training camps for combat soldiers. Eventually 900 Nisei comprised the total strength of the battalion, doing important defense work for which they received the Meritorious Unit Plaque.

Another all-Nisei group which performed important construction and military defense duties was a unit known as the Varsity Victory

Volunteers (VVV). The VVV was made up of young Nisei who were formerly with the University of Hawaii Reserve Officer's Training Corps (ROTC) and the Hawaii Territorial Guard (HTG). On January 19, 1942, the HTG was given orders from Washington that all men of Japanese ancestry were released from duty since their "services were no longer needed." Since the Nisei members of the HTG were associated racially with the enemy and involved in the vital defense of Hawaii, some military authorities had viewed them with suspicion.

Anxious to volunteer their services in any capacity, to prove that the rebuke of their loyalty was unfounded, the HTG Nisei petitioned the military governor of Hawaii, Lieutenant General Delos C. Emmons, to accept them unconditionally in the war effort:

> We, the undersigned, were members of the Hawaii Territorial Guard until its recent inactivation. We joined the Guard voluntarily with the hope that this was one way to serve our country in her time of need. Needless to say, we were deeply disappointed when we were told that our services in the Guard were no longer needed.
>
> Hawaii is our home; the United States, our country. We know but one loyalty and that is to the Stars and Stripes. We wish to do our part as loyal Americans in every way possible and we hereby offer ourselves for whatever service you may see fit to use us.[14]

The military governor accepted the Nisei's request and on February 23, 1942, the Corps of Engineers Auxiliary—the Varsity Victory Volunteers, as they were commonly known—was activated as a part of the 34th Combat Engineers Regiment. For nearly eleven months the 150 Nisei who made up the VVV lived at Schofield Barracks and labored on Oahu quarrying rock, building military installations, roads, warehouses, and dumps.

Other military units comprised partly of Nisei recruits before December 7 were the 298th and 299th Infantry Regiments. About 1,500 Nisei served in these units, guarding shore lines and military installations. Incoming mainland recruits however looked with disfavor upon working with "Jap" soldiers, and the military was uneasy about integrating Japanese with other servicemen. Consequently, in June of 1942, all Nisei military personnel, except those in the Engineering units, were gathered to form the Hawaii Provisional Battalion (Separate). Later called the 100th Infantry Battalion, these Nisei were sent to the mainland for training at Camp McCoy, Wisconsin.

While Nisei in the VVV, the engineering units, and the 100th Battalion had been given the opportunity to serve their country, other Nisei who were civilians before the war were barred from enlisting or being inducted into the military. How could Japanese prove their patriotism, many Nisei remonstrated, when they were not even allowed to take up a rifle in defense of their country? Early in 1943, the situation was remedied when General Emmons announced that Nisei were eligible for enlistment as combat volunteers.

"Open to distrust because of their racial origin," the general said of the Nisei, "and discriminated against in certain fields of the defense effort, they nevertheless have borne their burdens without complaint and have added materially to the strength of the Hawaii area."[15] The induction call was originally for 1,500 Nisei volunteers but, after an extensive campaign by the Emergency Service Committee, 9,507 men volunteered for service.

Of course some eligible Nisei did not respond to the opportunity to fight for the United States. Either reluctant to leave good jobs, resentful of the treatment accorded Japanese, or hesitant to succumb to induction campaigners who were described by the *Hilo Tribune-Herald* as "well-meaning enthusiasts who go around virtually clubbing their neighbors into joining,"[16] these Nisei elected to stay in Hawaii. The factors involved in the decision to volunteer in the army were revealed in an article entitled "To Volunteer or Not?"[17] written anonymously in a local Honolulu magazine. The article presented the reasoning behind the decision of many Nisei men to volunteer or to remain at home. Many simply believed that they could not serve the same government which had subtly harassed them and their families. These Nisei felt that they had nothing to prove and much to gain by staying in the booming Island war economy. Others reasoned that if they did not prove their loyalty when given the chance, their inaction would indicate that indeed the Japanese American was faithful and sympathetic to Japan. The decision to volunteer was a compulsion to guard themselves and their families from any further charges that Japanese were not worthy of American acceptance.

On March 28, 1943, thousands of these Nisei inductees, ready to be sent to Camp Shelby, Mississippi, to become part of the 442nd Regimental Combat Team, gathered on the grounds of Iolani Palace. Leis, tearful farewells, and gifts filled the occasion as one of the largest gatherings of people in Honolulu witnessed the *aloha* ceremonies which took place that day. A superpatriotic aura surrounded the whole proceedings, for the press, the Island community, and the Japanese community viewed these Nisei soldiers as the vindicators of the loyalty and Americanism of the Japanese of Hawaii.

Those Nisei who did not enlist quietly went about their business, engaged in civilian defense work or private enterprise, while the activities of the 100th Battalion and 442nd Combat Units began to be played up in the press in a zealous effort to turn the suspicions of the early days of the war into an appreciation and acceptance of local Japanese. The transformation of the Japanese from menace to friend in the minds of Island residents was an extremely influential message used by the military authorities, Japanese community leaders, and leading *haole* families to suppress anti-Japanese feelings and enhance the racial openness of the Islands. In this context one can speak of the "Go for Broke" image which was created out of the exploits of Nisei military units in war and the patriotic enthusiasm of Japanese on the home front. "Go for Broke," the motto of the 442nd, typified the image which Nisei acquired through news releases of military actions in Europe and even the Pacific: "The 100th Battalion performs valiantly in Italy against overwhelming odds . . . Due to heavy losses, 100th called the Purple Heart Battalion . . . The 442nd Combat Team, absorbing the 100th as its 1st Battalion, fights bitterly in France and Germany . . . The 442nd rescues troops of the Texas 'Lost Battalion' . . . Valor of 442nd Nisei soldiers earns combat unit the plaudit of 'Army's Most Decorated Unit.'"

Laudatory statements also enhanced the "Go for Broke" image:

"The courage, steadfastness and willingness of your officers and men were equal to any ever displayed by United States troops," read a message to the 442nd from the Texas 36th Division.[18]

"I have followed closely your splendid record . . . I have seen you in action and know your ability,"[19] General Mark Clark said in a statement to the 100th Battalion.

And a message from the 168th Infantry read:

> "In appreciation of the heroic and meritorious achievement of our fellow Americans in the 100th Battalion and the 442nd Infantry Regiment, we do hereby assert that our help can be counted upon to convince the folks back home that you are fully deserving of all the privileges with which we are ourselves bestowed."[20]

Praise came even from the Pacific war zone, where Nisei and Kibei Japanese language interpreters from Hawaii, part of the "Top Secret" Military Intelligence Service (MIS) served. After V-J Day General Charles Willoughby, Chief of Staff of Intelligence, would announce that "the Nisei shortened the war in the Pacific by two years."[21]

"Going for Broke" on the battlefield became translated into the stories and editorials which filled Island newspapers. Hardly a day passed when the *Star-Bulletin* did not include current news concerning the Nisei fighting men. An example of the hyperbole of publicity given the 442nd and 100th Battalion was a pamphlet published by the *Honolulu Star-Bulletin* entitled "Summing Up the AJAs at Shelby."[22] Written by journalist John Terry, the article was an attempt to build public support for the Japanese of Hawaii by projecting the "Go for Broke," "Proving One's Americanism" image of Nisei. Besides revealing many personal and daily events of life at Camp Shelby, Terry also permeated the article with the notion that Nisei had superior fighting, thinking, and morale capabilities. Nisei, according to Terry, were furnishing proof of their Americanism by preparing themselves for a superhuman effort in battle. "I'll take these men into battle," the commander of the 442nd was reported as having said, "without hesitation."

As in the case of the Nisei's "New American" image before the war, the "Go for Broke" image had kernels of reality but dangerously enshrouded men and events in highly pressured and unpredictable circumstances. The Nisei soldiers were obviously not as superhuman as the stories would have the public believe, and Nisei who did not enlist were not necessarily as unpatriotic or cowardly as rumor would imply. Yet as the Island community responded to the "Go for Broke" image, high expectations were demanded of the Japanese community; little deviation from the standards set on the battlefield would be tolerated.

The community was shocked, therefore, in July, 1944, when the newspapers reported that Masao Akiyama, a 27-year-old Kibei, was charged with violating the Selective Service Act. Born in Hawaii in 1917 and raised in Japan between the ages of six and seventeen, Akiyama had been working at a Honolulu dairy during the war. Before the Pearl Harbor attack his family and friends had left Hawaii to return to Japan. But because Akiyama felt obligated to repay a $300 debt, he remained in the Islands, only to be isolated from his family when return to Japan became impossible.

At the time the government began enlisting Japanese Americans, Akiyama received an order to report for a physical as required by the induction process into the United States Army. Akiyama did not appear for the physical but sent a note which declared that he "cannot be 100 percent American" because his "mind is with Japan." At his court trial he refused to speak English, using a translator. In a statement before the court Akiyama declared that:

". . . since my refusal to be inducted, I have been looked upon by people as being disloyal. Personally, I feel that I am disloyal. I know my father's wish is for me to be with him and not with this country, and if I were in the United States Army, I can imagine how my father would feel."[23]

Akiyama was the first Nisei to refuse induction; he was joined by another Nisei evader of the Selective Service in September, 1944. Both of them were found guilty and sentenced to one year and one day in prison, after which they expressed the desire to be repatriated and sent back to Japan.

Akiyama was disowned by the Japanese community and all his ilk summarily attacked. Dr. Ernest Murai, Chairman of the Emergency Service Committee, announced in the *Advertiser* at the time of Akiyama's trial that,

. . . the action of Masao Akiyama, an American citizen of Japanese ancestry . . . is a serious blot on the excellent record of the people of Japanese ancestry in Hawaii both aliens and citizens in the war. . . . Divesting him of American citizenship is not enough. If he valued his American citizenship he would not have acted as he did. There must be other ways to deal with him and his kind.

His action is contemptible and an insult to the rest of us, particularly to the boys who are serving in our Armed Forces and to those who have already paid the supreme sacrifice. It is a dirty slap in the face to the mother and father, many of them aliens, of these American boys.

We doubt that there are many others like Akiyama waiting to be discovered. But if there are, whether kibei or not, let them come forth and show their hand without waiting until they are forced to do so. If they don't, it will be the job of all of us to smoke them out.[24]

The Nisei "Go for Broke" image, then, successfully was able to create a favorable attitude toward the Japanese in Hawaii which aroused community support and overshadowed any anti-Japanese feelings stemming from events such as the Akiyama case. From the image emerged the romantic, yet vitally functional myth that World War II activities of the Nisei represented the ultimate demonstration of the Japanese American community in proving their rightful place in the Islands. Blood had been shed so that the Japanese could unquestionably assume a significant role in the Island economy and social system. As one young Nisei soldier was quoted:

If the American Japanese in Hawaii are still "on the spot" even after their AJ [American Japanese] soldiers come marching home, then the people themselves are to be blamed. If, during the course of this war,

> they have not won and earned for themselves a more secure and trusted status in the community, then we, who have left everything so dear to us in Hawaii, are fighting a losing battle as far as the home-front Hawaii is concerned.[25]

The romantic myth which has become an integral feature of the Japanese experience in Hawaii was certainly founded in truth. No one could deny that the Nisei soldier fought valiantly—the 100th and 442nd won seven Presidential Distinguished Unit citations, and nearly 6,000 awards were given to individual members. No one could deny that the Nisei gave their fair share of blood for American victory—the 442nd in their European campaign lost 650 men, with 3,506 wounded and 67 missing. And no one could deny that the Japanese of Hawaii proved their American loyalty—besides the energetic war effort, no acts of sabotage or treason were committed by a Japanese throughout the entire war. Yet the "Go for Broke" romantic myth loomed above facts; it drew upon unpleasant memories of the past, incorporated ambitions and hopes for the future, and interwound an ethnic pride with a respect and love for the Islands.

This powerful imagery which surrounded the Nisei war experiences and gave meaning to the Japanese community in Hawaii can perhaps best be seen in excerpts from Daniel Inouye's autobiography, *Journey to Washington*.[26] Inouye, during the war a young lieutenant in the 442nd, was a Nisei who had been caught up in the patriotism and fervor of his generation. Serving in the European campaign, Inouye wrote about the circumstances surrounding the famous "lost Battalion" episode when the Nisei saved a portion of a Texas division from annihilation in the forests of France. In another experience he described the events which led to his own injuries.

The facts as related are undeniable. But the strength of the "Go for Broke" myth pulsates behind each line. The Nisei camaraderie, the vision of victory for the Japanese back home, the determination to prove an unparalleled Americanism emerge from Inouye's description of events. While one is reading an exciting war drama, one is also reliving the "glory and guts" of the war experience which were widely shared by Nisei and the Island community who experienced the tensions and drama of World War II. Indeed, the "Go for Broke" myth functioned to instill pride and confidence in a community which had been more than confronted with social insecurity. The generation who had been on trial, who had tried to prove themselves as loyal residents of Hawaii, had successfully convinced themselves and the majority of the Island population that Japanese would

"Go for Broke" to dispel any doubts of their patriotic sacrifices for their Island home.

So when the Nisei GIs clamored to the railings on the multitiered ocean liner in response to the cheers and celebration from dockside, they were returning to Hawaii as the war heroes of a country, an island, and an ethnic people. They could see the multitudes of friends and relatives, the streaming confetti, the welcome home banners, the hula-skirted dancers, and the Hawaiian musicians playing songs of the Islands. The training, the fighting, the recuperating were over. The war in Europe had ended and the war in the Pacific would soon be triumphantly won. Hawaii would return to the daily routines and normalcy of peace and postwar restoration. But significant and maturing changes had taken place during the soldiers' absence. Aloha Tower still stood stately; the skyline of Honolulu had only slightly changed. But internally the Islands had been undergoing a revolution in power, economics, and social relations—a revolution to alter the fate of the Japanese community in Hawaii.

NOTES

1. Quoted in *Honolulu Advertiser,* February 28, 1942, 9:1.

2. *Honolulu Star-Bulletin,* December 11, 1941, 7:1.

3. United Japanese Society of Hawaii, *A History of Japanese in Hawaii,* ed. by Publication Committee, Dr. James H. Okahata, Chm., Honolulu: United Japanese Society of Hawaii, 1971, pp. 263–4.

4. *Honolulu Star-Bulletin,* May 13, 1942, 4:7.

5. Shigeo Yoshida, "Speak American," *Hawaii Educational Review,* v. 31 (1942), p. 106.

6. Yukiko Kimura, "Some Effects of the War Situation Upon the Alien Japanese in Hawaii," *Social Process in Hawaii,* v.8 (1943), p. 18.

7. Gail Miyasaki, "The Role of Buddhist Church," *Hongwanji Newsletter,* May, 1974, p. 5.

8. Louise Hunter, *Buddhism in Hawaii: Its Impact on a Yankee Community,* Honolulu: University of Hawaii Press, 1971, p. 193.

9. Yukiko Kimura, "Rumor Among the Japanese," *Social Process in Hawaii,* v. 11 (May 1947), p. 84.

10. Kimura, "Rumor Among the Japanese," p. 85.

11. Yukiko Kimura, "Some Effects of the War Situation Upon the Alien Japanese in Hawaii," p. 23.

12. Akemi Kikumura and Harry H. L. Kitano, "Interracial Marriage: A Picture of the Japanese Americans," *Journal of Social Issues,* v. 29, no. 2 (1973), p. 73.

13. *Honolulu Star-Bulletin,* January 23, 1943, 6:1.

14. Yutaka Nakahata and Ralph Toyota, "Varsity Victory Volunteers," *Social Process in Hawaii,* v. 8 (1943), p. 30.

15. Gwenfread E. Allen, *Hawaii's War Years, 1941–45,* Honolulu: University of Hawaii Press, 1950, p. 267.

16. Allen, p. 268.

17. "To Volunteer or Not?" *Paradise of the Pacific,* May, 1945, pp. 11–2.
18. United Japanese Society of Hawaii, p. 270.
19. United Japanese Society of Hawaii, p. 270.
20. United Japanese Society of Hawaii, p. 271.
21. United Japanese Society of Hawaii, p. 274.
22. John Terry, "Summing up the AJAs at Shelby," in *With Hawaii's AJA Boys at Camp Shelby, Mississippi,* Honolulu: Honolulu Star-Bulletin, 1943, pp. 23–5.
23. *Honolulu Advertiser,* July 8, 1944, 1:1.
24. *Honolulu Advertiser,* July 9, 1944, 1:4.
25. "Hawaii's Debt on Army Day," *Paradise of the Pacific,* v. 56, no. 4 (April 1944), p. 20.
26. Daniel K. Inouye, "Go for Broke," *Journey to Washington,* Englewood Cliffs, New Jersey: Prentice-Hall, Inc., 1967, pp. 131–4; 146–54.

Speak American

SHIGEO YOSHIDA

THE "Speak American" campaign sponsored by the Emergency Service Committee has the endorsement and cooperation of military and civilian leaders. It is worthy of the support of all who need the admonition to "Speak American" or who are in a position to help such people learn and use the language of America.

The idea of speaking English is not new. The schools and other educational agencies have been working on it for years. It is particularly important in Hawaii where we have many large groups of foreign-language-speaking people and where we have developed a jargon which is commonly referred to as pidgin English. And now with ruthless enemies seeking to destroy our way of life, it is essential that the people of Hawaii unite to maintain her position as America's main line of offense against Japan. One way to achieve this unity is through the use of one language, the language of America, by all residents of Hawaii.

The advice to "Speak American" should be heeded by all to whom it applies. I should like to direct my remarks, however, particularly to the people of Japanese ancestry who, because of their racial affinity to our main enemy in the Pacific, are a source of misunderstanding and suspicion to a great number of people. I want to speak to them because I'm one of them and I know that anything

In *Hawaii Educational Review,* v. 31 (1942), p. 106. Reprinted by permission of Shigeo Yoshida.

we Americans of Japanese ancestry can do to demonstrate our Americanism will redound not only to our benefit, but the benefit of all Hawaii.

In time of war, many things associated with the enemy are a source of irritation and suspicion. Japanese, being the language of our enemy, is especially irritating to many people. Used in the presence of others who cannot understand it, it also leads to suspicion. We should, therefore, avoid the use of the Japanese language except in situations where it is absolutely necessary as a means of communication with persons who do not understand the English language. If this were Japan, which it is not and we know it will never be, the use of the English language would certainly not be tolerated as the use of the Japanese language has been here. That is one of the differences between the American and the Japanese ways of life. But we should not take advantage of the tolerance which is part of America by using the language of the enemy in situations where its use is not desirable or absolutely necessary.

I have been a school teacher for many years and I know that many of our boys and girls speak pidgin or mix Japanese with English when they are perfectly capable of speaking good English. This un-American and irritating habit is often practiced even by those who have had the benefit of higher education. Perhaps they do not realize how it sounds to others who are more particular about the use of our national language. Perhaps they do not realize what a millstone they are carrying around their necks. But in times like these, there is no excuse for anyone to use anything but the language of America, unless, of course, he has been unfortunate enough to have never learned our language or is speaking to one who is equally unfortunate.

I am naturally interested in the Americanization of all our people. I do not believe that the ability to use the English language is the only factor in one's Americanism, but I do believe that it is a very important factor. It is the main tool with which one acquires the true meaning and appreciation of what America is and stands for. It is the medium of communication for all Americans in their business and social relationships. One's usefulness in an American community depends a great deal on his command of the English language.

I wish to mention one other reason for urging the use of English. We think in the language we speak. I believe it is more important than ever that we in Hawaii not only speak but think in the language of America. Our slogan might be: "Speak, think and act American.'' I believe that it is up to us to see that this is done. It is something that we've got to do for ourselves, for our own as well as our country's good.

What of the aliens? I don't believe that much can be done for them by way of teaching them the English language. Many of them are too far advanced in age to begin learning the language now. However, the younger ones should make every attempt to learn it and I hope that the various educational agencies in the community will make it possible for them to do so. The alien parents must also encourage the use of English by their children at home and refrain from using the Japanese language in situations where its use might be irritating or discourteous to others.

I hope that this campaign to ''Speak American'' will continue as long as there is a need for it. I know that it will be an asset to our community and particularly to the people directly concerned. I hope that it will add its part toward winning the war and help to lay the foundations of Americanism among our young citizens of today.

To Volunteer or Not?

ANONYMOUS ARTICLE

. . . EXAMINATION Week had finally come, when out of the clear came the announcement that the Army was going to accept 1,500 volunteers of Japanese ancestry from Hawaii. This important message was given to the students at the University before it had leaked out to the local papers. The announcement came at a special assembly held for the purpose. And of all times, it had to be given on the day before examinations were to begin. The instant it was announced, exams became secondary.

After the assembly, and at the assembly, most of the boys were enthusiastic and raring to go. I thought to myself: It's a good thing that the boys want to go, but I wonder whether they have given it any serious thought. If they are planning to volunteer on the spur of the moment, or because their friends are volunteering, it isn't being done properly. It isn't intelligent; it's just plainly stupid. Such a type of volunteer will make a poor soldier. I'm sure the Army wants us to think it over before we sign up.

. . . And yet our country has deemed us fit to serve her! She has called upon us in her need. Shall we refuse help? I should say not! All these years, the Japanese youth in Hawaii have said, "We are loyal. Give us a chance to prove it. It isn't fair to doubt us without giving us a trial." But is loyalty something that is only shown or

In *Paradise of the Pacific,* May, 1945, pp. 11–12.

proven by a trial, or only on a battlefield? No, loyalty is something that goes deeper than merely superficial action; it is a complex set of attitudes and ideals. Yet, how are people to know us? They can't see through us; they judge by what we do.

That night as I futilely tried to study, two "me's" begged and pestered to be recognized. Finally, in desperate effort to gain peace of mind, I let them in. One was light, the other was dark. The dark "me" spoke first and was answered by the other.

"Ah, what do you care about the things people think of you? As long as you believe in yourself, forget about the others."

"But you do care about what people think of you. You know that public opinion is important. Do the right thing."

"Sure, do the right thing. Remember, your life, your ambition, everything is at stake. Besides, this is a call only for volunteers; you can always do your share later. Maybe the draft, maybe a defense job."

"No, that's not the right attitude. Look at all the other American boys. They're giving their lives; they've forgotten their old ambitions; they know that they are needed. Volunteer; that's the only noble thing a man can do. Don't let the other fellow carry your share of the burden. It isn't fair."

"Fair, huh! It isn't fair for you to give up what you have planned for years; it isn't fair for you to ignore your parents' cherished ambitions for you. Participating in the post-war reconstruction period will be just as important as taking part in this war. Trained leaders will be needed. Stay and bear whatever comes your way."

"Why should you think about the post-war period when the present isn't secure. Remember, other boys are dying—dying for you."

"Sure, let them die. They haven't suffered as you have; they haven't been discriminated against as you have been. Their parents aren't 'kicked around' and looked down upon as your parents are. Let them die; they should be willing to die; they have everything to be thankful for."

"What would have happened to you if you had been born in Japan? Why, you'd be a farmer, a low-down, ten-sens-a-day farmer. You wouldn't be attending a university as you are doing now. You'd be a soldier, or even dead and rotting in China, or in the Philippines, or in the South Seas. A soldier you'd be, and a soldier with no choice but to die for the Emperor—an ordinary human being! You wouldn't have had any choice as you are having now. If you die now you will die for a concrete idea, not for a near-sighted human. You'll be dying for democracy, dying for the equality of man. Be a man by taking your share of the responsibilities."

"Be a man! What's a man if he doesn't stand for what he believes? Be a man; think about yourself. After all, this is a democracy, and you have your choice. And in a democracy the individual is paramount. You know what that means. You have the right to think about yourself first, last, and always."

"Is that what you want to do? Do nothing but think about yourself? It's selfish, that's what it is. And you don't want people to think that of you, do you? There's only one way out of this. Your country needs you; forget about your own selfish self."

"There are other ways out. Think about yourself . . . yourself . . . you—. Forget about volunteering and the war. Think about yourself and the tests you'll have to face tomorrow. Start studying, and forget about it, or you'll be a wreck tomorrow."

"Sure, study, study hard! But don't forget . . . you can't run away from it!"

"That's right, think about yourself. Forget about the tests, forget about volunteering, forget everything. What do you care if you 'flunk' and are 'kicked-out' of school; you can always 'sponge' off the old man. He's good enough for many more 'squeezings.' Take it easy, pal, take it easy."

"Don't take it easy that way. Relax with a clear conscience. Remember you can't escape it; it will always haunt you. . . . Don't be a man with a guilty conscience, a man who won't be able to sleep, a man who won't be able to meet his friends. You'll be a man in the psychopathic ward. That's what you'll be."

"Sure, you go ahead and join up and be a goddam buck private. You know what they're going to use you for—ditch-digging and as a source of cheap labor. You with a college education; you deserve a better break. Don't sign on the dotted line; don't be an ass."

"Do be an ass, an intelligent ass. You want to go, don't let him hold you back. The Army'll make a true man out of you. You're going to go eventually; why not go now? You're going on combat duty, not ditch-digging. Besides, you'll have your choice of Army service. You know what you're good for; you'll make good.

"Remember, it is one of the prime duties and obligations of a citizen to bear arms in defense of his country. You don't want to be a member of a conquered nation; you don't want to be shut up in a ghetto; and you certainly don't want to have your sisters used to bring forth more 'supermen' or even forced to be prostitutes. Remember what's happening in Europe and China. Remember you're fighting to preserve decency and the right to a peaceful pursuit of life for all mankind. It is your duty to fight for home, country, and humanity."

"Don't listen to him, big-head. Don't listen to him, I tell you. He's waving that same old flag. Don't fall for it, you lug. . . . Okay, okay, go ahead. Don't come crying to me later saying that I didn't warn you. So long, you wonderful ass."

. . . And so did I volunteer.

Summing Up the AJAs at Shelby

JOHN TERRY

THIS article, purposely left unwritten until now, is an effort to evaluate the 442nd Combat Team, that extraordinary U.S. army unit now training in the humid, sweltering pine forest surrounding Camp Shelby in southern Mississippi.

The writer has returned to this city after spending a week with the 442nd in camp and field.

Behind the impressions here set forth are personal observations, and conversations with scores of enlisted men, with many junior officers and all the senior officers of the 442nd, with its doctors, dentists and chaplains, with the commanding general of the camp, with several merchants in the nearby community of Hattiesburg and with one of those motorized philosophers—a taxicab driver.

. . .

We brought back with us from Shelby these two dominant impressions:

1. The 442nd Combat Team will make good despite all trials, of which battle will not necessarily be the hardest, and,

2. The combat team is receiving excellent training.

In *With Hawaii's AJA Boys at Camp Shelby, Mississippi* (Honolulu: *Honolulu Star-Bulletin,* 1943), pp. 23–25. Reprinted by permission of the *Honolulu Star-Bulletin.*

As for the first point, a lieutenant colonel commanding one of the 442nd's infantry battalions put it this way: "These men will come through, for the reason they are determined not to fail. They feel their whole future, and their children's future, is tied up in this thing."

Powerful factors have welded that determination. On the clear statement of the war department that their services would be used in battle, these men volunteered. They are American citizens, obviously proud of that allegiance and quick to resent any slur, as fights have illustrated on a number of occasions.

. . .

Furthermore, over and beyond the normal loyalties of a Caucasian citizen whose place is secure and unquestioned, these men feel they have to furnish striking proof of their Americanism, and that the battlefield offers them that opportunity.

. . .

Time after time at Camp Shelby, AJAs of the 442nd told us of their impatience to get through with the grind of training and go into battle. They were not talking heroics. Some expressed fears that delays of one kind or another might keep them out of combat until it is too late.

"If we should only become part of an army of occupation," one mainland AJA told us, "this whole thing is shot. We've GOT to get into battle."

An AJA from Hawaii, somewhat older than his fellows and a recent graduate of Columbia University, said, "If we want to see our children and grandchildren lead the sort of lives we want them to have, we feel we must do something about it right now.

"Really, that feeling is pretty basic with the boys."

As the lieutenant colonel said, these men will succeed because they are grimly determined not to fail.

There is another factor to be considered. The 442nd probably has the highest IQ of any unit in the United States army.

High officials in the war department told us that before we left Washington for Camp Shelby, and it was repeated to us many times in camp by officers who pointed to the swift progress made by the 442nd in training to date.

Good soldiers are not made out of stupid material, and the material in the 442nd apparently is unequalled, intellectually, anywhere in the army.

. . .

Officers of the combat team who have made the army their life profession told us that the organization has advanced farther in its training than any other army unit they have ever seen over a comparable length of time.

. . .

The thoroughness of the training given the 442nd is impressive to a civilian. Standard though it is in the new American army, it is far different from the hasty methods of 1917. The 442nd will go into battle with the advantages of every kind of training short of the ultimate experience of combat itself.

To the parents of these boys that fact should be a source of comfort. There will be casualties when the combat team goes into action, but there will be no needless waste of life. These men are not being trained like robots for cannon fodder. After following them in the field, we know.

They are being taught every trick of concealment, of their persons and equipment. They are being trained to strike with swift and deadly effectiveness, to get maximum results for every life expended, to save their own skins for the reason that the army needs live soldiers, not dead ones.

. . .

It was interesting to note that there has been some friction, especially in the beginning, between the Hawaii and mainland AJAs in the combat team. It has subsided noticeably, however, and will be adjusted satisfactorily, according to many comments from the men. All the evidence points that way.

One cause of friction was the high proportion of noncommissioned ranks held by mainland AJAs at Camp Shelby at the time when the Hawaii group arrived. The islanders had expected to serve under corporals and sergeants who were also from Hawaii.

The army, however, had to have a cadre of NCOs around which to build their organization, and the mainlanders were already in camp and available. Meanwhile normal adjustments are taking place. Current training activities are designed in part to determine what men have qualities of leadership. Men who meet the test will be recognized and will win NCO stripes. Every man in the combat team has a chance.

The mainland AJAs in general speak much better English than the islanders, who, for the first time in their lives, are learning that pidgin is not a sign of sophistication. The islanders are now somewhat aware of their shortcomings in this regard, and respect the mainlanders for their ability to express themselves effectively.

A growing mutual respect is replacing the early consciousness of differences. Daily association, a recognition of common problems and a common purpose, together with a more equitable distribution of NCO stripes, are influences leading to a more unified spirit. Individual friendships are forming without regard to places of origin.

. . .

The 442nd already has one physical characteristic which makes it distinctive—a distinctiveness attended by difficulties. We refer, of course, to the Japanese ancestry of these young American citizens. Racially, their stock is that of our enemies. Out of that biological fact grow difficulties and misunderstanding for the boys of the 442nd.

They have to prove themselves every inch of the way, even though they were born on American soil, have gone through American schools and have identified their lives with America. A mistake made by any one individual in the outfit reflects back with an immediate and inescapable directness upon the combat team as a whole. No other unit in the army stands in such a position.

. . .

They face the corroding influences of ignorance and misunderstanding. Nothing could be more strikingly apparent to one who understands them and has watched them in combat training than that these young men, despite their racial derivation, are a people different from their ancestors. To think otherwise is to make a fundamental mistake.

That is the solid rock on which this experiment is based. That is the premise on which the war department offered these men the opportunity of serving their country in battle.

. . .

Another characteristic which is making for their integrated personality as an army unit is their determination to succeed because failure would be intolerable.

Their future place in America, and the future of their brothers, sisters and children, and of their parents who are loyal to the Allied cause, is bound up in their record in battle as members of the 442nd combat team.

They know it.

. . .

On top of that, they have been catapulted into the deep south, and into its social distinctions. Through it they appear to be moving with dignity, with modesty, with pride, with self-respect. In nearby communities they enter theaters and restaurants along with Caucasians, and are accepted there without question.

They can not accomplish the impossible, but they are winning respect among people whose minds are not closed.

Four out of five merchants with whom we talked in Hattiesburg spoke well of the men of the 442nd. The fifth merely said they were good customers.

The editor of the *Hattiesburg American* is an ardent champion of the combat team. He is a southerner, born and raised. He and one other man, the latter the owner of a nearby stock farm, have done more for the 442nd than any other civilian in the Shelby area.

Incidentally, many of the officers of the 442nd are southerners by birth, education and lifelong residence ranging from a lieutenant colonel down to lieutenants. Their respect for the men under their command is genuine, and great.

. . .

Added to the ultimate test of battle, the soldiers of the 442nd, with their adolescence not many years behind them, are shouldering problems of adaptation which no Caucasian unit is obliged to bear.

Fortunately, so far as we could see, the men give every evidence of a healthy mental outlook.

The men do not go about with the appearance of persons carrying the weight of the world on their shoulders. They are a high spirited, cheerful lot, who delight in beer, sports and a good time. Even though they bear responsibilities beyond their years and beyond the lot of many another soldier, they don't seem to take themselves too seriously.

They do not seek trouble, although they do not always escape it. They have their pride, and they will not lie down as a doormat for anyone to walk over. There have been a number of fights, sometimes between AJAs and Caucasians, sometimes among the AJAs themselves.

When they fight they give a very good account of themselves indeed, and they fight clean. From what the officers tell us, these encounters have been no more frequent than in any other outfit.

. . .

We left Camp Shelby with the feeling that the boys of the 442nd are a credit to their country, to Hawaii, to their parents, to their uniform and to the Americanizing processes of the public schools. They are good citizens, ready to prove it with their lives, and without making too much fuss about it, either.

Ten days ago we watched the 442nd combat team march in review at Camp Shelby. The band went by, cymbals clashing and brasses blaring. Behind streamed the Stars and Stripes, and the regimental colors. In battle uniform, the infantry battalions, artillery, engineers and medical units swung crisply down the field.

As they strode past the colonel, unit commanders called out eyes right and put a snarl into it. Colors dipped down with a snap.

As the last company of the "Go for Broke" 442nd stepped off the field, Col. C. W. Pence, a regular army officer and commander of the combat team, said, with a jut to his jaw and a glint in his eye:

"I'll take these men into battle without hesitation!"

Go for Broke

DANIEL K. INOUYE

ON November 6, I started back to rejoin my outfit. By the time I reached them, the bloody battle of the "Lost Battalion" was over. My platoon, which had numbered 20 men when I left them only three days before, now had eleven GIs capable of carrying a weapon; and that included me.

What had happened was that the 1st Battalion of the 141st Infantry, part of the almost-all Texan 36th Division, had driven down a ridge east of Biffontaine. Clearing the enemy as it moved swiftly forward, the outfit had swept into a narrow valley between Gerardmer and St. Die, and here the Germans, having been rolled back on their own strong support positions, turned to fight. Furthermore, enemy units filtered in behind the unfortunate battalion and completely cut it off from any contact with the American forces. Twice the Texans tried to hammer their way out of the trap, and twice they failed. Nearly 1,000 GIs were effectively surrounded and desperately short of supplies and ammunition. That was when Major General John E. Dahlquist, C.O. of the 36th Division, had ordered the 442nd to the relief of the Lost Battalion.

They had jumped off right after I left. The bombardment from the German defenders was unbelievable; endless rounds of artillery and mortar shells, and at every roadblock a withering hail of rifle and machine gun fire. The casualty rate approached 50 percent and there

In *Journey to Washington,* copyright 1967 (Englewood Cliffs, N.J.: Prentice-Hall, 1967), pp. 131–134; 146–154. Reprinted by permission of Prentice-Hall, Inc.

were some companies without an officer or platoon leader left standing. Days passed and the men were still 1,000 yards short of the trapped Texans, whose situation had grown critical. A few planes had managed to drop some food and ammunition, but they were in terrible need of water and medical supplies.

And then a kind of universal anger overtook the "Go for Broke" outfit. Without orders, without even a plan of attack, men got up off the ground and began moving ahead, firing as they went, rushing to the cover of a tree and lobbing a grenade into a machine gun nest, closing with the Germans in deadly individual battles of bayonets and rifle butts and fists. And at last a platoon of B Company broke through the enemy line and made contact with the Texans. There were tears of relief and gratitude, a few exhausted embraces, but no time for cheers. The enemy was on the run and General Dahlquist ordered the 442nd to drive on. By the time I got back, the worst was over, but not until November 17, with St. Die firmly in our hands, were we relieved. The outfit had been engaged in the most desperate kind of fighting for 25 out of 27 days.

I lost even more weight in that time and looked like a scarecrow, but I had no complaints. I was alive. When General Dahlquist called the regiment out for a retreat parade to commend us personally, he is reported to have said to the C.O., "Colonel, I asked that the entire regiment be present for this occasion. Where are the rest of your men?"

And Colonel Charles W. Pence, as bone-weary as any dogface in the outfit, replied, "Sir, you are looking at the entire regiment. Except for two men on guard duty at each company, this is all that is left of the 442nd Combat Team."

And there we were, cooks, medics, band and a handful of riflemen, a ragged lot at rigid attention, without a single company at even half its normal strength. One had only 17 men and was commanded by a staff sergeant. My outfit, E Company, with a normal complement of 197 men, had exactly 40 soldiers able to march to the parade ground.

General Dahlquist looked at us for a long time. Twice he started to speak and choked on the overpowering feelings that took hold of him. And in the end, all he could manage was an emotional, "Thank you, men. Thank you from the bottom of my heart." And the saddest retreat parade in the history of the 442nd was over.

. . .

Our biggest single advance came on the day word reached us that President Roosevelt had died. Men just got up out of their holes and began fighting their way up. "Where the hell are they going?" the brass hollered at regimental headquarters, and of course no one in the S-3 section knew. But down on the line, we knew. Every *nisei* who had been invested with first-class citizenship by virtue of the uniform he wore knew. We were moving up for FDR. He had given us our chance and we had a lot of *aloha* for that man.

Ahead of us now was Mount Nebbione, guarding the critical road center at Aulla and the La Spezia naval base. If we could take those two towns, the enemy's line of retreat to the Po Valley would be cut off. The 3rd Battalion poked at the outer edges of the German defenses on Nebbione and was thrown back. The 2nd Battalion tried circling them from the south and they flung everything they had back at us. We were dead beat now. For two weeks we had been fighting our way up and down 3,000-foot mountains and the men were walking zombies, marching, firing, hitting the ground, marching some more and hitting the ground again, only out of some instinctive memory of what they were supposed to do. The situation cried out for fresh troops, but there just were no such animals in northern Italy in mid-April of 1945.

And yet we could believe that we were close to the end. One day the regimental C.O. called the officers together and said that there was word of German peace feelers. "There's nothing we can tell the men," he said. "It might last another year and they have to be ready to fight on. But it might end next week and I'm telling you so that you won't take unnecessary chances, so that if it does end next week you won't have to blame yourself for some rash action that cost lives you might have saved."

We regrouped on the twentieth and made a new battle plan. Our battalion was moved to the center of what was to be a three-pronged attack. E Company's objective was Colle Musatello, a high and heavily defended ridge. In the early evening, Captain Akins called the platoon leaders together and gave us our orders. All three rifle platoons were to be deployed, two moving up in a frontal attack, with my platoon assigned to skirt the left flank and come in from the side. Whichever one reached the heights first was to secure them against counter-attack, for momentum was vital.

I went back to my area and briefed the men. I watched them move off in isolated clusters, seeking some last moments of solitude before committing their bodies again to the fates of war. Many pulled out talismans which they felt, or maybe only hoped had guarded them through all the bloody months past: a St. Christopher medal, a Buddhist charm, a rusted .30 calibre bullet. Some fingered their *sen ninbari,* a piece of white cloth with 1,000 stitches, each of which, in the Japanese tradition, protected the wearer against 1,000 misfortunes. I remember old ladies standing on the street corners of Honolulu with *sen ninbari*s destined for their sons in the army, asking total strangers to sew in a stitch.

Was it all nonsense, a throwback to some pagan time when men did not realize that they could invoke the protection of an almighty God? Who knows? I only know that God was not neglected on that night of April 20. We prayed, deeply, devoutly. And I don't believe you can fault a man who is asked to face sudden death if he seeks a small measure of comfort in some earthly amulet.

The fact is that I had carried two silver dollars, won during my gambling heyday in Camp Shelby, through every campaign. But perhaps I had special reason to regard them as a lucky charm. One was bent and the other cracked almost in two from absorbing the impact of a German bullet during the Battle of Bruyères. Since I carried them in a breast pocket and wore a purple welt on my chest for two weeks after the incident, I had some grounds for believing they had done me some good.

And the further fact is that on this night of April 20, I was suddenly and acutely troubled because they had mysteriously disappeared. I searched the area as best I could in the darkness, and I asked around, but it was no use. Undoubtedly I had bent forward with my pocket unflapped and the coins had slipped out, to be unknowingly ground into the muddy earth by someone's boot. And I suppose they are still there, in that narrow valley that once served as an assembly area for the 442nd Combat Team.

I walked back to my tent, shivering a little for the night had grown cold. I fumbled through my pack for my field jacket, and *that* was gone. And I remembered: in the heat of the afternoon, miles to the south, I had put it on the ground beside me during a break, and when the break was over I had marched off and left it. I can call to mind the sad, sinking sensation that settled in the pit of my stomach. My brain commanded me to be sensible; so I'd lost a field jacket and two beat-up silver dollars; so what? But from the message center in my heart, I kept hearing forebodings of disaster.

I went over to First Sergeant Dan Aoki's tent and borrowed his camouflaged parka. I knew he treasured it and I promised to take good care of it. "But keep an eye on me," I said. "I have a feeling that tomorrow is not going to be one of my best days and you may have to peel it off my back."

He didn't laugh. He said, "You bring it back yourself or I don't want it."

We jumped off at first light. Off to the right, we could hear the crackle of rifle fire and an occasional machine gun burst as the 1st and 2nd platoons closed on the perimeter of the German defenses. For us, though, it was like a training manual exercise. Everything worked. I walked along directing artillery with my walkie-talkie. What little opposition we met, we outflanked or pinned down until someone could get close enough to finish them off with a grenade. We wiped out a patrol and a mortar observation post without really slowing down. As a result, we reached the western edges of the rise where the main line of resistance was anchored long before the frontal assault force. And we didn't mean to sit there and wait for them. We were right under the German guns, 40 yards from their bunkers and rocky defense positions, so close I had to call off our artillery. We had a choice of either moving up or getting the hell out of there.

We moved, hunching slowly up that slope that was so painfully devoid of cover, and almost at once three machine guns opened up on us. I can still smell that piece of unyielding ground under my face, and hear the *w-hisss* of the bullets tearing the air above my helmet. I lay there for a second, thinking about how neatly they had pinned us here and wondering how long it would take them to get us all if we just lay there hugging the earth. Then I pulled a grenade from my belt and got up. Somebody punched me in the side, although there wasn't a soul near me, and I sort of fell backward. Then I counted off three seconds as I ran toward that angry splutter of flame at the mouth of the nearest machine gun. I threw the grenade and it cleared the log bunker and exploded in a shower of dust and dirt and metal, and when the gun crew staggered erect I cut them down with my tommy gun. I heard my men pounding up the hill behind me and I waved them toward the left where the other two nests were adjusting their field of fire to cover the whole slope.

"My God, Dan," someone yelled in my ear, "you're bleeding! Get down and I'll get an aid man!"

I looked down to where my right hand was clutching my stomach. Blood oozed wet between the fingers. I thought: *That was no punch, you dummy. You took a slug in the gut.*

I wanted to move on; we were pinned down now and the moment was crucial. Unless we stirred, unless we did something quickly, they'd pick us off one at a time. And I knew it was up to me. I lurched up the hill. I lobbed two grenades into the second emplacement before the riflemen guarding it ever saw me. But I had fallen to my knees. Somehow they wouldn't lock and I couldn't stand and I had to pull myself forward with one hand. Someone was hollering, "Come on, you guys, go for broke!" And hunched over, they charged up into the full fire of the third machine gun. And I was so fiercely proud of those guys I wanted to cry.

Then they had to drop and seek protection from the deadly stutter of that last gun. Some of them tried to crawl closer but hadn't a prayer. And all the time I was shuffling my painful way up on the flank of the emplacement, and at last I was close enough to pull the pin on my last grenade. And as I drew my arm back, all in a flash of light and dark I saw him, that faceless German, like a strip of motion picture film running through a projector that's gone berserk. One instant he was standing waist-high in the bunker, and the next he was aiming a rifle grenade at my face from a range of ten yards. And even as I cocked my arm to throw, he fired and his rifle grenade smashed into my right elbow and exploded and all but tore my arm off. I looked at it, stunned and unbelieving. It dangled there by a few bloody shreds of tissue, my grenade still clenched in a fist that suddenly didn't belong to me any more.

It was that grenade that burst into my consciousness, dispelling the unreality of that motion picture in my brain, and the shock of that astounding and spectral moment in time. The grenade mechanism was ticking off the seconds. In two, three or four, it would go off, finishing me and the good men who were rushing up to help me.

"Get back!" I screamed, and swung around to pry the grenade out of that dead fist with my left hand. Then I had it free and I turned to throw and the German was reloading his rifle. But this time I beat him. My grenade blew up in his face and I stumbled to my feet, closing on the bunker, firing my tommy gun left-handed, the useless right arm slapping red and wet against my side.

My men were running up on both sides of the emplacement. It was almost over. But some last German, in his terminal instant of life, squeezed off a final burst from the machine gun and a bullet caught me in the right leg and threw me to the ground and I rolled over and over down the hill.

For a while everything was quiet. Maybe I passed out. But soon I could hear the 1st and 2nd platoons firing as they moved up in front. I saw blood pulsing out of the nearly severed arm in regular little geysers and I made a feeble attempt at putting a tourniquet on it. But there wasn't enough upper arm left to work with, so I just fumbled in that mass of muscle and bone until I found the artery and I pinched it closed.

There was a crowd of men around me and someone was saying, "Let's carry him back," and they were grabbing at my legs but I kicked free.

"Get back up that hill!" I said in a voice that didn't sound remotely like mine. "Nobody called off the war! I want you to set up defensive positions and hold until the rest of the outfit gets here! Report back when you're all set. Get me a casualty report as soon as you can! Now get moving!"

And so they left me there, all alone with what used to be my arm, until the medic came. I asked him to cut the arm off, but he paled and said he couldn't. Instead, he gave me a shot of morphine so that soon I quit wanting to scream out in pain, and before I could stop him he'd slit the 1st sergeant's beautiful jacket clear up the side. Then he finally managed to get a tourniquet around the stump so I could let loose of that artery. "I'll get a couple of men and we'll carry you out of here," he said.

"I'm staying until the rest of the outfit gets here," I said. "I'm okay. You go look after some of the others."

It didn't take long. Captain Akins was among the first to find me. He said I'd be okay, I'd be fine, and I said sure I would, and realized for the first time that whatever else I was going to be, I was surely not going to be a doctor, not with one arm.

I sent for my platoon sergeant, Gordon Takasaki. "You're boss now, Gordie," I told him, "the new platoon leader. Now listen to me. This thing is going to be over soon—a week, a month, soon. Take care of yourself and take care of the men. Don't let anybody get knocked off so close to the end. Understand?"

Dan Aoki came by as they were loading me onto a litter. A lot of men were watching. "So long, Dan," they called.

"I'm sorry about your jacket, Sarge," I said.

"I'll take it out of your hide, Lieutenant." But I noticed that he was crying.

Then they carried me down off that hill. And all the way down I could hear men calling, "So long, Dan."

It was April 21. The German resistance in our sector ended on April 23. Nine days later, the war in Italy was over and a week after that, the enemy surrendered unconditionally.

CHAPTER NINE

Okage Sama De

THEY were youthful, ambitious veterans, readjusting to a Hawaii which had gone through nearly five years of wartime conditions. For these veterans the victorious war in Europe and the Pacific had been not only a deadly hardship but a period of growth and maturity. The confines of Island living before the war had largely been accepted by most youth—Hawaii with its social and racial order, its hampered economic and professional potentials, its frustrating atmosphere of subtle second-class citizenship was their entire world. And they had learned to adapt somewhat to a society which imposed limitations on lifestyles and personal goals. But experiences gained during the war had instilled a confidence as well as a certain degree of brash arrogance. Traveling, meeting a wide variety of new friends and acquaintances, seeing outright racial discrimination in the South, dating and associating with white women, relying on themselves and their buddies in the horrors of combat had a telling effect on the veterans' self-attitude. Certainly Hawaii was their home and surely it was the best place in the world to live. But certain fundamental social conditions had to be improved—opportunities, first-class social standing, and a large measure of simple decency had to be achieved.

The Nisei veterans, like the majority of the Nisei generation after the war, could have best been described as being "on the make." Indeed, everything in their upbringing suggested that given the right time and conditions, personal ambitions would be actualized into a dynamic burst of social and economic advancement. Their training in the home stressing education, success, and economic stability; their training in the public schools teaching democracy, equality of opportunity, and a distaste for the status quo of plantation labor; the expectations of the Americanization movements, the patriotism of the period of national mobilization for war, and the opening opportunities of wartime Hawaii were influences congealing within the Nisei generation, waiting for fulfillment.

And such was especially the case for the aggressive Nisei veteran. Instilled with an optimism for success and a cynicism for second-class mentality, the veteran returned to Hawaii committed to ill-defined goals of social success. The veterans took advantage of the Servicemen's Readjustment Act of 1944, the "GI Bill of Rights," which gave a stipend to veterans who continued their education. Enrolling at the University of Hawaii, Nisei began to pursue careers in medicine, dentistry, teaching, law, accounting, and business. And in their pursuit of personal success, the veteran shed the deference he had once held for the *haole* elite. "After seeing some scum of the white race on the mainland," one returning veteran noted, "the instinct of looking up to the *haole* disappeared."[1]

Aside from infusing personal confidence, the war experience had also been a justification of ethnic pride and status. The veterans had proven Japanese to be patriotic Americans—about that there could now be no question. Some Nisei had given their lives so that the suspicions and hatreds of the past could be replaced with respect and trust. When the Nisei veteran returned home he had expected the total and equal assimilation of Japanese into the political, economic, and social communities of the Island.

As a consequence, returning veterans were especially sensitive about any sentiments which might have reinstigated the old wartime fears of dubious Japanese loyalties. Therefore when GIs discovered that many Issei, psychologically and culturally suppressed, had refused to accept the fact that Japan had lost the war, they were enraged. How could the rumors that Japan had won the war or that the Japanese Navy was heading for Pearl Harbor be allowed to exist? Rather than viewing as pathetic the scene of disillusioned Issei waiting on Mt. Tantalus for the victorious entry of the Japanese Navy, veterans felt such behavior cast an ugly shadow over their war efforts.

Moreover, many Nisei veterans viewed with equal consternation the reestablishment of Japanese cultural institutions. After the war the reopening of Buddhist and Shinto temples had been widely acclaimed by the Issei as a restabilization of the immigrant generation. But in addition to the temples, many Issei also sought the reopening of the language schools. Closed for the duration of the war, the language schools in 1943 had been subjected to laws and litigation which many community leaders hoped would "nail the lid on the coffin of Japanistic culture agencies." But the laws were declared unconstitutional and in the spring of 1948, to the delight of the Issei community and some Nisei, the language schools began to reappear with almost overnight rapidity. Within a period of three months the island of Oahu saw the establishment of fifteen schools, employing forty-five teachers and teaching approximately 3,800 students. Viewing this development in the same embarrassing light as the rumors among the Issei, members of the 442nd Veterans Club, on April 13, 1948, held a meeting to discuss the question, "What are these old fogies trying to do, destroy all we fought for in the war?" The club failed to issue a public statement against the language schools, fearing it would cause too much controversy. But one veteran described the general reactions:

> The mere existence of Japanese language schools will reflect badly in the eyes of non-Oriental groups. All the efforts of the 442nd and 100th will be for naught. The *haole*s are saying "Look at those guys—they're going back to their old habits!" We're trying to make the best of a bad situation.[2]

Though critical of those elements within the Japanese community attempting to revive dubious cultural practices, the overall optimism and self-assuredness of the Nisei veteran became a symbol with the ethnic community—a symbol of Loyal, Good Americans, "Having Proven Themselves," ready for an overdue social mobility. Illustrative of the symbolization of social mobility and equality generated by the Nisei veteran was an article, "The Nisei and the Future,"[3] by Dr. Katsumi Kometani, appearing in the magazine, *Nisei in Hawaii and the Pacific*. Dr. Kometani, a dentist, was a prominent figure in the prewar community of Japanese in Hawaii primarily due to his active involvement in local baseball leagues. Baseball, football, basketball, or volleyball teams organized on a small scale among nonprofessionals had been a respected and standard feature of the Island lifestyle for many years. Dr. Kometani owned and managed the Asahi Baseball Club, which he took to Japan in 1940, the first international athletic competition between Japan and Hawaii. During the war he served in the 100th Battalion and fought at the beaches of Anzio and later Volturno River.

Kometani's article revealed two facets of the Nisei's postwar attitudes. First, the Nisei generation was viewed as a monolith of interest, opinion, and motivation. "The Nisei," devoid of individual variation or intracompetitiveness, seemed to have a common ethnic identity—they encountered prejudice together; they sacrificed their lives to secure their position in Hawaii; they made possible peace and understanding in the Pacific; they should be grateful; they should feel a responsibility; they have a big job ahead. The ethnic group, consolidated by a common heritage and purpose, must strive to overcome racial barriers in the Islands—the ethnic member has his foremost responsibility to "his people" and their advancement.

The second facet of the Nisei's postwar attitude of social mobility and equality was the dominant, recurring emphasis on the future. No longer bound to a past of limited opportunity, no longer impeded by racial discrimination, the Nisei must help shape the future. Drawing upon the strength of the *samurai* ethic and the Bushido Code of hard work, perseverance, education, and diligence, the Nisei could redefine their lives and the lives of all Hawaii's people—"Competition and struggle make for vigor and strength." The Nisei have the choice to assume power and direction in the Islands and they "should be willing to assume that burden."

But as powerful as the feelings for social mobility, equality and future success might have been, the Nisei's choice to "assume power and direction" was also dependent on the structures of community power embodied in the Island oligarchy. The second generation might have been "on the make," but social mobility also depended on the dissipation of power in the seat of government at Iolani Palace and in the brokerage firms of Merchant Street in downtown Honolulu. A racial group that had been "making it" for a hundred years had now to face the inevitability of "rising expectations" and the tenuousness of nondemocratic institutions in an era of budding affluence and literacy.

Writing in 1944, an observer of Hawaiian history and politics noted that "for nearly a century there had been no true freedom for the individual in languorous Hawaii."[4] The idea that Hawaii had been totally controlled by a small elite of *haole* enterprises in a feudal system seemingly out of the antebellum South or medieval Europe was neither a totally new or wholly inaccurate characterization of the Island society in the first half of the twentieth century.

Sensing the tight network by which military, sugar, and racial interests manipulated Island affairs, one journalist labelled Hawaii "the sugar-coated fortress," a description which even thirty years later found a few proponents.[5] Through a system of interlocking directorates and economic interests, business committed to a common goal of wealth with a common management of brothers, uncles, cousins, sons, or nephews, the Big Five conglomerates had a monopoly in most areas of the Island economy. In the food he consumed, the house he lived in, the property he owned, the clothes he wore, and the goods and services he enjoyed, the resident of Hawaii could not avoid being affected by the power and influence of Hawaii's oligarchy.

But by 1945 the control of the Big Five was on the wane due to the impact of war, martial law, and defense production. Within twenty-four hours of Pearl Harbor, the control of Hawaii had passed from the economic elite to the military authorities—the governor and legislature seemed to become merely rubber stamps of the military governor and military courts. Besides the transference of power, the war also brought to Hawaii fundamental racial changes. *Haole* defense workers poured into the Islands, competing for housing in every area. Wherever one looked, *haole* faces would appear in an Island community which had known only nonwhite faces, the aloofness of the aristocratic *haole,* or the sanguine smile of the tourist. But these new *haole*s were different. They were not the professional crust, but middle- and lower-middle-class skilled workers. They brought with them a spirit of labor aggressiveness and unionism which could be channelled into Island labor movements. Many of these *haole*s intermarried with local girls, mingled with local people on a day-to-day level, helping to dispel the deference of intellect and power many nonwhites had learned to give the *kamaaina haole.* Moreover, the new *haole*s had no paternal associations or racial fear of the *haole* elite that had controlled Hawaii for so long. The impact on race relations of the new *haole* influx into Hawaii could be seen in the census statistics. Between 1876 and 1930, when the development of the plantation system had brought the immigrant populations, the growth of the *haole* population, excluding Portuguese, did not keep pace with other ethnic groups; from 1884 to 1900 the percentage of *haole*s actually dropped from 8 percent to 5 percent of the general population. But with the wartime experience, the *haole* element of the population rose to over 16 percent in 1950, the largest ever.[6]

In addition to racial changes, the war had turned Honolulu and its environment into a modern city. The war economy had provided what seemed limitless jobs in the urban areas, making impossible the "return to the plantation" which prewar sugar interests had hoped to instill in the unemployed young. New small industries, independent small businesses, the economic ramifications of the blossoming tourist industry—all developments stemming from the wartime boom—were sources of new wealth which undermined the monopolistic control of Merchant Street powers.

The war, then, contributed to the weakening of the oligarchical, political, and economic bases and strengthened the opportunities for the ambitious middle class. An enterprising young man in postwar Hawaii had a greater number of alternatives to choose from than the local college graduate before the war. While in 1950 *haole*s were still disproportionately represented in preferred occupations, with 34 percent of employed *haole* males in the professional and managerial classes as compared with 16 percent for all other groups, the non-*haole* races were showing marked social advancements. By 1950 Chinese males had nearly matched the Caucasian figure of 29 percent in preferred occupations, and the median income of the Chinese was nearly $100 greater than for *haole*s. While the Hawaiian ethnic group and more recent immigrants, Filipinos and Puerto Ricans, remained in the skilled or unskilled labor classes, the number of Chinese and Japanese men and women surpassed the *haole* in many professional jobs. Accountants, chemists, dentists, designers and draftsmen, pharmacists, physicians and surgeons, actresses and entertainers, retail traders, and restaurant operators were jobs especially occupied by Asians.[7]

Managerial positions also opened up for nonwhites in the postwar years. On the plantation and as officials and directors in the major corporations, Orientals were finding a broader range of opportunities. In part these changes were a result of major policy alterations in the leadership and management of the Big Five. To maintain family control and structure, the conglomerate of Hawaiian power had for most of its existence shunned outside influences—ownership and management of corporations was an incestuous affair which would hopefully breed a common economic and social attitude. However, in 1939 the door was opened to mainland corporation management which saw more value in turning a profit than in maintaining obsolete notions of paternalism or a distrust of Orientals. In that year Atherton Richards was president of Dole Pineapple Company, a subsidiary of Castle and Cooke, whose chairman was Richards' uncle, Frank Atherton. One of the young mainland executives who was influential in both companies was Alexander Grow Budge, a graduate of Stanford, who had won favor with E. D. Tenney. Tenney, previous head of Castle and Cooke and an in-law of the Castle family, had put Budge in the line of succession to head Castle and Cooke. When Richards considered the possibility of subordination to Budge, an "outsider," he went to the stockholders to have Budge ousted. Despite a heated struggle, calling on family ties and sentiments of the *kamaaina,* Richards failed to have Budge removed and in turn was fired. Following that struggle each of the Big Five firms eventually obtained mainland talent, professional executives, as managers.[8] Nonwhites increasingly found that traditional local restraints no longer impaired advancement and that local skills were in demand.

The "fall" of the *haole* regime in Hawaii may also have occurred because the oligarchy had been overly paternalistic in the prewar era. Paternalism manipulated effectively might enhance and strengthen despotic rule, but eventually the sons mature and demand their rights. The father who has taught hard work, education, and democracy while expecting filial obedience must one day succumb to the ungrateful demands of the progeny who consider themselves able to assume the role of social equals. Accordingly, the *haole* oligarchy in the 1920s and '30s had supported the New American Conferences and the educators who believed that the nonwhite child must be taught the democratic principles and institutions which reinforce notions of social achievement and good citizenship. Nisei were promoted as integral members of the Island society who should show good American aggressiveness and ambition. Lawrence A. Baldwin, of the *kamaaina* Baldwin family of Maui, had summed up the spirit of social mobility paternalistically instilled in the Nisei during an address to the New Americans in 1939:

> Don't be impatient of recognition, for recognition sometimes comes late. The opportunity to which I refer is the opportunity to cultivate and increase your own powers. Be efficient! Do everything you undertake with the fixed intention to do it in the best way that it is possible for that particular thing to be done. Merely doing it may not be much, but no man ever yet was conscious of having done this work to the very best of his ability without a distinct addition to his own powers. Efficiency! It's a great word. It's the world's passport along the highway to success.[9]

To some degree, then, the *haole* elite in the prewar era had inadvertently encouraged the development of countervailing powers which would eventually erode the oligarchy of the Big Five. The changes in Hawaii brought on by the war, the new racial stratifications, and the various pockets of ethnic pride and ambition combined with the new belief of many Island people that Hawaii's society must be democratized; the result was powerful forces beyond the manipulation of the oligarchy. And perhaps the most powerful of all forces to confront the *haole* elite in the postwar decade would be the labor unions.

Unionism in Hawaii before World War I was characterized largely by exclusive *haole* organizations of bricklayers, painters, iron molders, and plasterers. Opposed to admission of Orientals to the Territory, denying membership to Chinese or Japanese, these unions had alienated a segment of the working force which could have been for them a tremendous source of power. As the Japanese and Chinese began to learn the various skilled trades and established businesses in Honolulu, they would not join unions which barred their participation. With an increasing number of nonunion workers, the trade unions waned so that in 1929 the U.S. Commissioner of Labor would report that "labor organizations are few in number, small in membership, and, with the exception of the barber's union, have no agreement with employers."[10]

The greatest potential for established unionism, then, lay with the great bulk of non-*haole* laborers who comprised the working force of the plantations. As was seen in the Japanese workers' sugar strike of 1909 and the Filipino–Japanese strike of 1920, the primary need for effective labor organization among this group was interracial strength and effective leadership. Without such unified strength, the sugar planters had the resources and established power to effectively suppress labor unrest. For example, in 1924, 3,000 striking Filipino workers on Kauai, with limited support and chaotic organization, were routed by the planters. Their leaders were imprisoned and military forces were used to intimidate, disperse, and, in a few cases, kill the workers.

Laborers had sought in each of these strikes higher wages to meet inflation, improved working conditions and management–employee relations. To some degree the 1909 and 1920 strikes had been successful, but workers in pre-World War II Hawaii primarily relied on the plantation paternalism to ameliorate harsh or inequitable conditions. To overcome paternalism and the divisions among the races and to successfully contest the power of the oligarchy, a united labor force, organized on a scale strong enough to challenge the Big Five, was necessary. With this in mind, Jack Hall and Harry Bridges, leaders of the International Longshoremen's and Warehousemen's Union (ILWU), recognized that the realities of the Hawaiian system demanded a labor union which was interracial, based on the waterfront, affiliated with the West Coast ILWU, and covering all the business and employees which the Big Five handled. With the slogan "An Injury to One Is an Injury to All," the ILWU and Jack Hall began to unionize longshoremen on Hawaii's docks. After an abortive attempt in 1938 to unionize the Inter-Island Steamship Company in Hilo, the ILWU began to use New Deal labor legislation and apply mainland pressure to have the union recognized in Hawaii. In August, 1941, Castle and Cooke terminals signed an agreement with the ILWU covering longshoremen in Honolulu Harbor. As one labor relations historian observed,

> For the first time in one hundred years of Hawaiian industrial history a large employer was faced with the problem of operating under a contract with a legally constituted and endorsed union organization representing the majority of his employees.[11]

Though war had momentarily put a moratorium on union activities in Hawaii, the ILWU spread quickly in the postwar period among sugar workers suffering from a recession and anxious to have a unified, effective labor voice. In 1946 the ILWU staged a successful strike of all sugar workers in Hawaii's sugar industry. For 79 days, Japanese and Filipino laborers, the core of the plantation employees, refused to work, asking for an eighteen-and-one-half-cent general wage increase, a forty-hour week, and an end to paternalism. Management, surprisingly, dealt with the union in a rather liberal fashion—a twenty-cent wage increase was approved after the 1946 strike, and the fringe benefits of paternalism had been abolished. The ILWU had been established as a caretaker of the worker. By 1947 the ILWU numbered 30,000 members and two years later demonstrated its power again by staging what would be Hawaii's first serious dock strike—a 178-day shutdown which crippled Island shipping, destroyed many small businesses, cut wages, raised prices, threatened a food shortage, and portended a new periodic feature of Island living to reach into the 1970s.

With its immense power, the ILWU also began to play an important role in postwar Island politics. Along with various American Federation of Labor unions, the ILWU established the labor's Political Action Committee (PAC). By endorsing candidates, by door-to-door campaigning, and with a little arm twisting PAC helped to elect a prolabor majority to the Territorial legislature of 1946. In the fall of that year the ILWU had made major inroads into the control of the Democratic Party—fourteen of fifteen Democrats elected to office had been endorsed by the union.

Swollen with membership, success, and power, the ILWU was soon to encounter an issue which would weaken its Island credibility. In 1947 Governor Ingram Stainback, a conservative Democrat originally from Tennessee, was approached by the commanding general of the Army in Hawaii and handed a list which contained the names of prominent Communists operating in the Islands. At the head of the list was Jack Hall, influential ILWU leader. Dismayed that the labor force should be infiltrated with such enemies of the Republic, Stainback launched a campaign to expose Communist activities in Hawaii. Throughout 1947 at public addresses, Stainback deplored the power which Communists had been allowed to wield through the ILWU.

Communism as a political scare tactic was not unique to Hawaii—the McCarthyism which was occurring in Washington during the same period reflected the same combination of hysteria as a result of international tensions with the Soviet Union, fanned by the libel and viciousness of demagogues as well as the honest concern among some for national security. The fear of Communism in Hawaii, however, was magnified by the accusations that the ILWU was Soviet-controlled. With a power so immense as to cripple the Island economy, with a political influence so manipulative as to control the Democratic Party, the ILWU was a prime target for political and patriotic attacks of sometimes dubious credibility.

The first effect of the Communist issue seemed to be the reinforcement of the worker's support for the ILWU. As one union member recalled, "most of the boys did not know Communism from rheumatism, but they did hate the bosses, and they believed Jack Hall would help them." One Filipino worker said, "Befo' no Communista, befo' bus-ass, by 'n by little Communista, get mo' pay; if get plenty Communista, by 'n by mo' pay."[12] But such testaments of the worker's faith did not reassure the populace more easily swayed by fear and intimidation. In May of 1947, public anxiety was aroused when Robert K. Mookini, president of pineapple Local 152, contended that the union had suspended him because he refused to follow Communist orders. Then Amos Ignacio and Ichiro Izuka left the ILWU, charging the union with Communist domination.

Ichiro Izuka had served from 1941 to 1942 as president of the ILWU, Local 1-35, Kauai. His defection was followed shortly with a pamphlet, *The Truth about Communism in Hawaii,*[13] in which Izuka named people, places, and events linked to the Communist infiltration of the ILWU. Claiming that he had joined the party before the war, had been active in promoting its cause, he fell into conflict with other Communists. The severity of the breach was such that Izuka would say in the preface of the pamphlet,

> . . . you good people need to know the truth about the Communist situation in Hawaii. You need to know where and how they operate. Hawaii must wake up. *Especially union members must wake up.*

The effect of Izuka's sensational confession was to substantiate the fears which the campaign against Communism had initiated. "The Communist Party in Hawaii is a secret, underground organization," Izuka concluded. "It works in the dark—fears the light of day. It takes advantage of the simple faith of our people. . . ."

Izuka's revelations were reinforced three years later when Jack Kawano resigned from the ILWU. A popular and effective union leader, president of the ILWU Local in Honolulu, Kawano testified for five months in 1951 before the House Un-American Activities Committee, uncovering the operation of the Communist Party in Hawaii and its connections with the ILWU.

The consequence of Kawano's testimony was a series of arrests which were to challenge the civil liberties of several Island residents. Under the Smith Act, any person or persons conspiring to teach the overthrow of the U.S. government by force or violence were subject to imprisonment. During Kawano's lengthy recitation of Communist activities, seven individuals stood out as leaders or agitators of party policy. On August 28, 1951, these figures—six men and one woman—were arrested by the FBI and charged with conspiracy under the Smith Act. Four of the seven arrested were Nisei—Charles Fujimoto, self-proclaimed Chairman of the party; Mrs. Eileen Kee Fujimoto; Jack Kimoto; and Koji Ariyoshi. Also arrested were Dwight James Freeman; John Reinecke, a former McKinley High School teacher; and Jack Hall. The "Hawaii Seven" as they were called by the press, did not go to trial until a year later, and eventually were found guilty as charged on June 19, 1953. They were each sentenced to five years in prison and a $5,000 fine, a conviction which they appealed. Finally the United States Circuit Court of Appeals in San Francisco ruled in January of 1958 that the abstract teaching of Communism did not constitute conspiracy to overthrow the government by force or violence as defined by the Smith Act. The convictions of the Hawaii Seven were reversed.

One of the more articulate of the Hawaii Seven had been Koji Ariyoshi of *The Honolulu Record,* a labor newspaper. Born and raised in Kona, Ariyoshi had seen the poverty and inequality associated with the laboring class. He became committed to changing Hawaii and striving for social justice throughout the United States. As editor of *The Honolulu Record* Ariyoshi led aggressive editorial campaigns supporting labor and the ILWU. After his arrest, *The Honolulu Record* began a series of weekly articles which were to constitute an autobiography of Koji Ariyoshi. In Chapter 58 of "My Thoughts: For Which I Stand Indicted,"[14] which appeared October 10, 1952, Ariyoshi directly denounced the Smith Act, Jack Kawano, and the anti-Communists for denying the Hawaii Seven their civil liberties to advocate social change. The problems which Hawaii was experiencing, Ariyoshi explained, stemmed from the system of government and men which oppressed minorities and the poor the world over. The people of Hawaii must come to identify with these oppressed people—the black, the relocated Japanese American on the mainland, the injustices of conditions which confront the poor Southerner or the ghettoized Northerner. Anti-Communism was seen as a reactionary movement against social justice—a perpetuation of a "*haole*-boss" system.

Through the rhetoric, a profound sincerity surfaces in Ariyoshi's writing which typified the style of men maturing in the postwar era. As the forces of unionism, the Red Scare, and economic change reverberated among the foundations of the old order, a young generation of Nisei reinforced a tenacious commitment to social equality and improvement—a "better Hawaii" was the message not only of the left-wing labor leaders or editors such as Ariyoshi but a growing number of Island people.

The notion of success idealized in this period of social change was for the Nisei naturally very materialistic—success was usually measured not by Ariyoshi's criteria of social revolution but social status and the ever-present economic yardstick. How much money do you have? How much real estate? How many shares, in which companies? Business, finance and income, prestige, position, and status were the gods of Nisei materialism.

But the crass materialism of the Nisei notion of success was tempered with the cooperative spirit of the family. Nisei materialism was inclusive of the needs of family security and unity. One didn't succeed just for oneself but for the family. The successful Nisei businessman could bring pride to his parents, his relatives, his family name through an affluence historically denied his ethnic group. The value of *kodomo no tame ni,* for the sake of the children, implied hard work and self-sacrifice so that the family, the children, would always be secure. As an Island businessman revealed in a 1951 survey, success incorporated a dimension of *kodomo no tame ni:*

> My main concern is to help my children and keep them comfortably provided. My work has all been for the family. I am perfectly happy now with the way things are, but of course, I should like to make some progress every year and advance in our business and continue to build it up, my sons to continue it, with me in the background. It's no sense just keeping and accumulating money, but it should be put to good use, invested in bigger business, expanding business.[15]

The achievement of this materialistic success meant that the Nisei had to establish a *rite de passage* into the Island economy, an access to wealth partially opened through the dissipation of the oligarchy and the rise of the ILWU. For some Nisei this *rite de passage* was achieved through a strategy of ethnic exclusiveness—success and economic gain was achieved by drawing upon the cultural tastes of the community, catering to the ethnic needs. So for example, the Nisei language-school teacher, press editor, the Japanese restaurant owner, Buddhist priest, or *okazu-ya* (Japanese delicatessen) operator socially achieved success as they "sold" Japanese culture within the ethnic community. And in an Island society which appreciated cultural diversity, this exclusive strategy provided the profitable appeal for many Nisei businesses to perpetuate a highly valued Japanese cultural trade. Saimin companies, sake breweries, *okazu-ya*s, tea houses, Japanese restaurants, Japanese movie houses, or Japanese department stores owned by enterprising Nisei thrived in postwar Hawaii.

Another *rite de passage* for the Nisei was through an accommodation strategy—Japanese cultural identity was rejected to facilitate social assimilation and wealth. Rejecting any un-American cultural tie, isolating themselves from the "unhygienic" influences of the family, these Nisei met the powers of the Island economy "on their own terms." Especially on the upper-echelon levels of national finance, as the Hawaii-based businessman began to deal with national and even multinational corporations, his approach had to be somewhat "haolefied" to accommodate an array of individuals who could not understand the peculiarities of local style. And even on a small, role-playing level, the accommodating strategy was utilized in many day-to-day situations. Working for a mainland firm in the Islands required the employee to behave a little more haolefied. Speech patterns lost their trace of pidgin; a suit and tie replaced the *aloha* shirt; the standards of an American middle-class pattern were quietly accepted.

The accommodating strategy, like the exclusive strategy, did have very high social and personal costs. In each strategy the individual took a risk of group or social condemnation, even ostracism. If the accommodation went too far, the exclusiveness became too rigid, the result was a torrent of abuse. "You're too *haole,*" "you're too Japanese" were admonitions serving as barbed reminders of the limits of personal strategies.

Still another means to social success in postwar Hawaii was through the strategy of ethnic cohesiveness. Essentially the strategy of cohesiveness involved drawing upon the economic, social, and cultural stability of the family organism to achieve success in the assimilated society. In other words, the family environment, community connections, and extensive obligations acted in concert to stimulate individual social mobility. The Nisei was interrelated with other Nisei in the common goal of success. When a Nisei declared *okage sama de* (I am what I am because of you), he was not just extending platitudinal gratitudes; he was expressing the dynamic core of Nisei's strategic cohesiveness—the interdependency of ethnic members in a common wealth of interest, goal, identity, and mobility.

The success of ethnic coherency to attain social success was illustrated in the case of Japanese small business enterprises. Basically family businesses handed down from generation to generation, these enterprises formed the vital center of the Japanese community's economic wealth. The roster of the Nisei-controlled Honolulu Japanese Chamber of Commerce became a listing of family names behind some of Hawaii's more influential local businesses. Times Supermarket, Thrifty Drugs, Star Supermarket, International Savings and Loan, Servco Pacific, S. Horita Construction Company were but a handful of the family-based businesses eventually to evolve out of the Nisei strategy of cohesiveness.

The philosophy of *okage sama de,* from individual employment to family businesses, helped to explain the assimilative role which Nisei and the returning veterans began to play in the dynamics of postwar Hawaii. Unionism had loosened the reins of the *haole* oligarchy; the Communist controversy had wrenched the fabric of Island living. And as Hawaii was pushed into becoming a modern, democratic society, the Nisei used the resources of their background, their aggressiveness, ambitions, and strategies to gain economic, social, and moral power beyond the ethnic community. Of all the people of Hawaii, they alone seemed ready to become a new generation of rulers.

NOTES

1. Andrew W. Lind, "Some Problems of Veteran Adjustment in Hawaii," *Social Process in Hawaii,* v. 12 (August 1948), p. 67.
2. Andrew W. Lind, *Japanese Language Schools, 1948,* Hawaii Social Research Laboratory Report No. 15, Honolulu: University of Hawaii Press, 1948, p. 8.
3. Katsumi Kometani, "The Nisei and the Future," *Nisei in Hawaii and the Pacific,* v. 6, no. 1 (1952), p. 10.
4. Alexander MacDonald, *Revolt in Paradise: The Social Revolution in Hawaii After Pearl Harbor,* New York: Stephen Page, Inc., 1944, p. 2.
5. Francine Du Plessix Gray, *Hawaii: The Sugar-Coated Fortress,* New York: Random House, 1971.
6. Andrew W. Lind, *Hawaii's People,* Honolulu: University of Hawaii Press, 1955, p. 31.
7. Andrew W. Lind, *Trends in Post-War Race Relations in Hawaii,* Romanzo Adams Social Research Laboratory Report No. 25, Honolulu: University of Hawaii Press, 1959, p. 2.
8. Frederick Simpich, Jr., *Anatomy of Hawaii,* Toronto: Coward, McConn and Geoghegan Inc., 1971, pp. 115–6.
9. Lawrence A. Baldwin, "Opportunities for Youth in Hawaii," New Americans Conference, *Proceedings,* 13th Annual, Honolulu, 1939, p. 40.
10. C. J. Henderson, "Labor—An Undercurrent of Hawaiian Social History," *Social Process in Hawaii,* v. 15 (1951), pp. 50–1.
11. Henderson, p. 53.
12. Lawrence H. Fuchs, *Hawaii Pono: A Social History,* New York: Harcourt, Brace and World, 1961, p. 361.
13. Ichiro Izuka, *The Truth About Communism in Hawaii,* published in 1947, pp. 4–9, 30–1.
14. Koji Ariyoshi, "My Thoughts: For Which I Stand Indicted," *The Honolulu Record,* October 10, 1952, p. 1.
15. Clarence E. Glick and Students, "Changing Ideas of Success and of Roads to Success as Seen by Immigrant and Local Chinese and Japanese Businessmen in Honolulu," *Social Process in Hawaii,* v. 15 (1951), pp. 57–8, 59.

The Nisei and the Future

KATSUMI KOMETANI

. . . The Nisei are an important factor in Hawaii, not only at the moment, but they have been instrumental in the past in a most vital way. As little as ten years ago feeling ran strong against the Oriental, and particularly against the Japanese. There were tensions and dark suspicions regarding loyalty. It was the American-Japanese soldier who died in Italy and France by the hundreds in tremendous acts of bravery and self-sacrifice that proved to America that the Nisei were more than a hundred percent loyal citizens. This restoration of faith and trust by those heroes of the last war have in a measure established peace and understanding between the Occidental and the Oriental.

Perhaps the war has been a blessing in disguise. Americans have learned to know their Oriental brothers. They have discovered there is little difference except pigment. The war compelled the American and the Japanese to live with each other and thereby established a feeling of sympathy and understanding so sadly missing previous to that time. Now the American people have a better comprehension of the Oriental and can approach the difficult Far Eastern question in a wiser and more tolerant fashion. This, indeed, was made possible only by the Nisei and the war.

In turn the war shaped the Japanese way of life at home. Like a

In *Nisei in Hawaii and the Pacific,* v. 6, no. 1 (1952), p. 10. Reprinted by permission of Katsumi Kometani.

symbol of medieval restraint, the kimono has been almost forsaken, and women have been freed of the stiff obi bindings and wrappings. Japanese women are taking their place in the world of business and are successful. In Hawaii, especially, women are blessed. Women attend the University here and on the mainland and hold down good jobs in the professions, in the newspaper world and in the world of commerce.

The Nisei has an open field of endeavor. There is no class restriction; a boy or girl from the laboring class can have equal opportunity with the boy or girl of the more well-to-do. The Nisei should be grateful for this truly American community. The professional field beckons. There is always more room for dentists and doctors. The University offers courses in the social field as well as the teaching field. If students can afford to go away, no door on the Mainland is closed. But the Nisei should go to work, not depend on government handouts such as compensation. Competition, and struggle make for vigor and strength.

The Nisei should also feel a deep responsibility toward community life. Many Nisei are leaders in the labor unions of Hawaii. They have a chance to improve the working conditions of the people and to raise the standard of living. But they also can improve relations between the employer and employee. In a measure they can stabilize the economy of Hawaii. The Nisei has a big job ahead and should be willing to assume that burden.

The Truth about Communism in Hawaii

ICHIRO IZUKA

I. Fertile Soil for Communism

First, a few words of personal history. I was born in Hanapepe, Kauai, T. H., on June 5, 1911, the sixth of a family of nine. Most of my brothers and sisters were born on a rice farm to which my parents had moved from a sugar plantation in order to improve their living standards. Later economic pressure forced my parents to return to the sugar plantation and submit to the original labor contract.

When my parents came from Fukuoka, Japan, to Hawaii in 1900 as contract laborers, most plantation workers, recruited largely from the poorer people of Japan, worked under conditions of virtual peonage. When they were recruited my parents were led to believe they would make enough money in three years to return to the old country for my grandparents. Instead they spent 35 years in Hawaii much of this time toiling on plantations and barely making enough to live on. My parents truly worked hard. When I was small, mother would get up in the morning at about four o'clock to prepare lunch for my brothers and sisters to take to work. From then until late at night she worked, as did my father and older brothers and sisters. In those early years, my mother took me with her when she slaved in the fields for $17.00 a month, then the standard wage for women. My own first taste of work on the plantation came when I was ten. I

Published privately in 1947, pp. 4–9; 30–1. Reprinted by permission of Ichiro Izuka.

worked during the summer vacation for $7.00 a month and later, after finishing grade school, I received $18.00 a month. The hours in the fields were long. We commenced before sunrise.

Seven of our family worked for the pitiful plantation wages, and in addition there was our continual debt bondage to the plantation store. Our family had a debit there for nearly fifteen years. We workers had no incentive to go for our money on payday, for most often the envelope was empty, all charges having been taken from the pay checks. Because of our poverty and the need of income from the older children, only my youngest brother and I had the opportunity to go as far as the eighth grade in school.

When I was sixteen years old I decided to get away from the plantation into some other kind of work. My father and two of my brothers were employed at the Kauai Railroad Company (later the name was changed to Kauai Terminal). I went to work as a boatman, or lighter-bargeman, working in rough dangerous waters in all kinds of weather. During that whole period I was building up a resentment against our hard working conditions that was later to make me ripe for Communistic propaganda. Two of us worked in a boat, going out from the shore piers to unload the ship which could not come in. We went back and forth until the job was done and they loaded her in the same way with Hawaiian sugar for the Mainland.

When I was first employed in this dangerous, difficult work, I received 25 cents an hour, because the company claimed I was only a kid and not entitled to the 30 cents paid to other workers, although my work was the same. The pressure from the bosses was terrible and we sometimes were compelled to work 48 hours straight. High waves, sometimes 15 feet high, heavy cargo and poor working facilities often threatened our lives. Many workmen were crippled and some were killed. For all this work and danger we received about $75.00 a month. I should say here that these off-ship working conditions stopped in 1939 when a new pier was constructed.

In 1937 the workers finally got together and decided to strike the ship *Maunalani*. Although the quarrelling of our bosses for favors from the company, and their roughness toward us was the precipitating cause of the strike, all that most of the workers wanted was more money in the pay envelope, and better working conditions.

When the port was closed, we got a hint of the pressure industry can bring. Policemen came with a machine gun and other firearms and acted as though we were a bunch of criminals. However, John Waterhouse, President of Alexander and Baldwin, Ltd., came and told us that wages would be raised and conditions improved. We would get about 8 cents an hour raise, which seemed big money to us after the years of hardship. That was the first spontaneous strike in the history of Hawaii, I believe, where the workers really won.

II. Enter the Communists

The settlement did not come immediately after Mr. Waterhouse's offer, for the local leaders of the strikers had called Honolulu headquarters for help in negotiating an agreement. Maxie Wiesbarth, who is not a Communist, sent Jack W. Hall (now ILWU Director for Hawaii) and George Goto to Kauai to aid us. (This was before Hall's 99-year suspension from the Sailors Union of the Pacific.) At that time Antone Marcalino, who represented the company, offered a contract containing the provisions agreed to by Mr. Waterhouse. During those days, I and many other workers knew nothing about the union movement. We accepted the statements of Mr. Marcalino and signed the contract. But later we discovered the union recognition clause was phony. It gave the union recognition only so long as the union had a majority. It left the door wide open for splitting tactics. A real contract gives recognition for the life of the contract, which is usually for a period of one year at least.

Hall and Goto were members of the Communist Party. They had brought with them plenty of Communist literature and distributed it secretly. I was an active young fellow, very anxious for the improvement of the working classes, so Hall and Goto saw to it that I had plenty of Communist literature to read. I devoured it, and for the first time thought I had discovered a party that really had something to offer the workers. I soon decided that the Republican and Democratic parties were only interested in helping keep the workers in submission. This was my first introduction to the Communist Party and I was thrilled. A whole new world opened—at last I could really work to improve my lot and that of the other workers of Hawaii. It was so exciting and intoxicating that after a year I decided to join the Communist Party. I joined in 1938, giving my application to Jack Kimoto. He had come to me and asked me to join, because he knew from my militant attitude that I was heart and soul for the workers. This is the way most Communist recruits are gained here in Hawaii—they take enthusiastic workers and fill them with propaganda against the existing conditions and against the present government, and soon they have a new Communist dedicated to turning the world over to the workers. . . .

According to the story Kimoto told me, he was born and raised on Ewa Plantation. His father participated in the 1919 strike. The family was evicted from their home. Sometime between 1919 and 1928 Kimoto became a "left-winger." Sometime during the late 1920's or early '30s he went to Los Angeles to further his education in left-wing philosophy and tactics. He told me he was sent back to Hawaii in 1938 or thereabouts by the Communist Party of California to do the work of the Party in Hawaii. When I first knew Kimoto in the early part of 1938 he was staying with the manager of the weekly Japanese paper, *Yoenjiho Sha*. Hall and Goto were trade union Party members, whereas Kimoto directly represented the Party in Hawaii. When I first met him he had no other occupation.

I believe Kimoto is sincere. I recall he gave me a membership book and I treasured it as a symbol of the Party that was working for the common man. And too, I was thrilled by the secrecy of the Party and the influence we wielded in union meetings. At that time the Communist International organization meant nothing to me.

At our secret meetings, sometimes held in my home, sometimes in my automobile in lonely spots, we were taught how to control union meetings, parliamentary procedure, and, of course, Party principles. We were taught too, that the Big Five was a fascist organization, and that both political parties were like a coin—heads or tails, it's still the same coin. These lessons were given to us by Hall and Kimoto, sometimes together, sometimes separately.

This intrigue was interesting and when I could go into a union meeting and get hundreds of people to do what we had decided upon at our Communist meeting the night before, I felt powerful and important. Here is how it worked: I was vice-president of the ILWU, Local 1-35, and at the same time a leader in the Kauai Communist group. All during 1938–1939, and 1940, when I held these dual positions, we steered the union membership into doing our wishes. One Communist would get up and make a motion. Then, after discussion which was led by other Communists in different parts of the hall, it would be voted upon. At any time the discussion did not go the way we wanted it to, another person would jump up with some objection based upon parliamentary procedure. This system is still being used in the ILWU unions by Communist leadership, and the union members still do not realize what is happening to them.

We also used our Communist influence to control election of certain candidates. For instance, in 1938 we had the "Progressive League of Kauai." This was a Communist front political group, in which most of the members did not realize the Communist connection. We were especially anxious to prevent the election of Lindsay Faye, of the Kekaha Sugar Co., who ran for Senator on a Republican ticket against a Democrat, J. B. Fernandez. We were successful. This was my first introduction to the power a few people can wield secretly in politics. We were to get much deeper into politics at a later date.

In this period of the Communist Party growth in Hawaii, we were very careful about taking in new members. During most of this period, I was the one who decided who should be admitted on Kauai. We would pick out some sincere labor enthusiast, feed him ideas, and finally give him some Communist propaganda. We had to be very careful because if the bosses had learned anything about our Communist group they would have used it against us. My bosses never learned of my Communist connection, and for this reason I was able to continue effective work. We watched the reactions of men selected for Communist Party membership, and sometimes we decided against admitting one because he lacked the proper militant spirit or because he could not accept the iron discipline of the Communist Party. There was no room for weakness. The Communist method is to recruit only the strongest and most fanatical elements who know how to obey orders. We knew that with only a few members we could control hundreds of non-Communists through the unions, so we took no chances on admitting a doubtful person to party membership. That might have exposed our entire plan.

. . .

VII. Conclusion and Summary

I quit the Communist Party because it is not honest with the workers. With Adolph Hitler, the Party believes that the lie is a very useful means for gaining its ends. The bigger the lie, the better it works. The Communists propagandize the workers with any story, true or false, which aids their cause. Just as the Kremlin tells the Russian people it was the Soviets alone who defeated the Japanese, so the Communists have now told their victims in the pineapple unions, not that they lost a strike, but that they won a lockout. What an insult to the intelligence of our Hawaiian workers!

The Party has never undertaken a broad American style of program of worker education. The Party does not want an intelligent, well-informed rank and file in the unions. The Party will do the thinking for the masses. All the Party wants are handpicked Charlie McCarthys who know how to carry out orders. Prospective victims are sent to San Francisco for training and indoctrination. Then they come back to the paid positions in the unions.

Moreover, the Communist Party is not interested in the workers in Hawaii as human beings or as individuals. Nor is it interested in this community as a place in which to grow up and live. It is merely interested in Hawaii as a favorable battle ground on which to wage the class struggle and win converts to Communism. Its loyalty is not to Hawaii or to America, but to the Soviet Union. For this reason it will sacrifice American men and women, even its own existence as a "local party," if Soviet policy and needs so dictate.

Communist Party leaders, always deceitful and contemptuous of truth, will denounce anyone opposing their program or methods as a "fascist" or "enemy of labor." Character assassination and vilification are their standard weapons and they are ever alert to use them to shift the spot light from themselves.

But the truth comes out despite their frantic efforts to cover up and fabricate. The American people including the rank and file of labor are beginning to see the light.

I served the Hawaiian labor movement proudly and faithfully and believe in the American labor movement and social progress. Our American trade unions must be preserved. They are a vital part of our democracy but the termites who would undermine and destroy them must be exposed if democracy is to survive.

The rank and file Hawaiian workers, now innocent pawns of the Communist Party, must free themselves of the Communist leadership whose first loyalty is not to the American labor movement but to the political doctrines and policies of the Soviet Union.

I am hoping that they will not wait too long.

The Communist Party in Hawaii is a secret, underground organization. It works in the dark—fears the light of day. It takes advantage of the simple faith of our people and of their lack of knowledge and experience. We do not need that kind of influence in our growing Hawaiian democracy. Indeed, it is a serious threat to our American ideals, for it makes a mockery of democratic action and subverts it to its undercover objectives.

For these reasons I am doing my bit in exposing the Communist Party of the United States of America as it operates in the Territory of Hawaii.

My Thoughts: For Which I Stand Indicted

KOJI ARIYOSHI

We See a Growing Challenge to Reaction

The un-American Activities Committee[1] is on the run. In Chicago it packed up and scuttled back to Washington after three and one-half days of hearings, when it had announced a two-week affair.

In Los Angeles the un-Americans met the same kind of defiance. Trade unionists, housewives and professional people are taking the offensive to rout and finish the committee. This is the growing challenge during the high tide of reaction. The ebb follows.

More and more people are getting tired of being hounded and heaped with indignities. Some take courage in the growing resistance of people who refuse not only to crawl before the committee, but who fight back. They are fed up with the low congressional practice of making heroes out of stoolpigeons. They have faith in the Constitution and invoke its guarantees to prevent the witchhunters from stepping into their province of legal rights.

We remember the headlines of about three years ago when ten Hollywood screen writers and directors refused to answer the un-American committee. They invoked the First Amendment which guarantees freedom of speech in declaring their right to remain silent. They were convicted. Today, people speak of the "Hollywood

In *The Honolulu Record,* October 10, 1952, p. 1. Reprinted by permission of Koji Ariyoshi.

Nine'' because one lost courage and self-respect and went crawling to the committee, because he wanted to be ''respectable'' and feel the jingle of Hollywood dollars in his pocket.

The Fight for Bill of Rights Is Old

Exercise of intelligent courage made the Hollywood Nine stick to their guns. And while they served their time, they made their contribution in the struggle to outlaw the un-Americans.

Close at home, here in Hawaii, the ''Defiant 39'' invoked the Fifth Amendment, which guarantees one the right not to answer incriminating questions. Thirty-nine individuals were cited for contempt of Congress by the un-American committee. And the thirty-nine were upheld by the court on their legal stand in refusing to turn stoolpigeons. But here too, the Hawaii thirty-nine is now thirty-eight, for one has gone crawling. Jack Kawano has become the stoolpigeon, turning against his former union in joining the big bosses in attacking it.

Today in places like Chicago and Los Angeles, housewives, professionals and workers find protection under the Fifth Amendment as they fight back against the un-Americans. They take courage from the fight of others who made their fight earlier. They undoubtedly appreciate the integrity and understanding of the Hollywood Nine, Hawaii 38 and others like them, and that of the early fighters for democratic processes who insisted that the Bill of Rights be spelled out long, long ago.

Men of property and special privilege in the founding days of our country tried to assure the people that the rights of free speech, press and religion were implied in the Constitution. But the common people refused to accept this assurance as a guarantee, and refused to ratify a constitution that did not put down these inalienable rights in black and white.

Thus, the Constitution says ''Congress shall make no law'' abridging these rights. The struggle to win these provisions—the Bill of Rights—was a major event.

The Climate in Which Un-Americans Thrive

But the Bill of Rights is not safe. For example, it is not safe as long as 16 million Negroes do not enjoy their full guarantees. They actually have not been fully established because racists and vested interest elements with power, in and out of government, have found it profitable to keep them from general enjoyment.

In the South particularly, it has been unsafe for Negroes to speak their minds and to assert their minimum rights.

In Hawaii, as a national Negro magazine said in a recent issue, numerous Negroes here try to pass as Hawaiians. Why? Because of discrimination.

When 16 million Negroes are subjected to frameups, persecution, lynching, discrimination in housing, education and on jobs, indignities and what have you, the climate in the country is suitable for the un-Americans.

Smith Act to Get around First Amendment

The strategists of the un-American committees have generally been congressmen from the South. In their states they do not need the un-American committees to harass and persecute the Negroes. And they carry their prejudices to the far corners of the country.

Ever since I was indicted under the Smith Act, along with six others, on August 28, 1951, I have frequently thought that the persecution of people by the use of the Smith and McCarran Acts and the harassments by the un-American committee, bad as they are, are comparatively mild when we consider what the Negroes go through in our country year in and year out. Their growing struggle for freedom and equality is a common struggle of all democratic-minded people.

Rep. Howard Smith of Virginia, who authored the Smith Act, admitted that his law was aimed to "get around the limitations imposed by the First Amendment" (Congressional Record, May 19, 1940). He is a southerner who does not believe in the Bill of Rights.

There is growing opposition to the Smith Act, just as there is mounting opposition to the un-American committee.

Jefferson Would Be Unsafe under Smith Act

The Smith Act attempts to put ideas behind bars. This is impossible, for ideas grow out of actual conditions.

Thus, people fight for peace when they see the horrors, devastation and waste in wars. They realize the desirability of organization, like in trade unions, when they become aware that dog-eat-dog competition is against their interests. When they experience poverty amidst plenty, chaos in the economic setup and depressions, they begin to think of social planning.

The Smith Act is actually a plot to overthrow the Constitution of the United States. Rep. Smith admits that.

Thomas Jefferson would not be safe today. When he led the fight for the Bill of Rights, he said:

"If there be any among us who wish to dissolve this Union or to change its Republican form, let them stand undisturbed as monuments of the safety with which error of opinion may be tolerated where reason is left free to combat it."

People cannot say the same today. The spirit of the times has changed. But this is not a permanent situation.

While under Attack Defense Brings Improvement

In about three weeks the Smith Act trial here will get underway. More than a year has passed since our indictment. And as I look back I see that the Smith Act case has brought a favorable change to Hawaii.

The jury which indicted us and the jury list from which it was chosen were predominantly *haole* and people classed as and tied up with the big employers. The non-*haole*s, particularly the people of Japanese ancestry, were underrepresented, and so were the workers in the major industries.

The government prosecutors who are pushing the Smith Act case fought for the unrepresentative jury list, and Federal Judge J. Frank McLaughlin stood four-square behind that jury list.

Who's fighting for democratic processes and constitutional rights?

Today even the Big Five lawyers claim the former grand jury was not valid, that it did not represent a cross-section of the community. They put forth this argument in a current tax suit.

The old jury list is gone and the present one is more representative. Here, the Smith Act defense has brought a constructive improvement in the Federal court system. Decent and fair-minded *haole*s prefer this change. The advocates of the Smith Act want a *haole*-boss jury system.

Thus, the people fight for decency, equality and self-respect.

I Have Learned from Struggle of Others

As I look back to Kona, to the waterfront of my longshore days, to Georgia where I saw Tobacco Road conditions, to Manzanar[2] where we of Japanese ancestry were held behind barbed wire and to my experiences overseas as a GI, I see that there have always been people who struggled for improvement. I have learned from them. The conditions I've experienced have shaped my thoughts, raising in my mind protests to bad conditions and advocacy of improvement.

NOTES

[1. The House Un-American Activities Committee was an anti-Communist investigating body of the government during the 1950s and 1960s (Ed. note).]

[2. Manzanar Relocation Center, located in central California, was a Japanese relocation camp during World War II (Ed. note).]

CHAPTER TEN

The Bloodless Revolution

NOT since the regal coronation of King Kalakaua, not since the tumultuous days of the revolution and the establishment of the Republic, had the Victorian chambers of Iolani Palace, the stately old capitol, seemed so hectic—so full of anticipation, optimism, and a spirit of change. The young lawmakers who crowded into the throne room for the opening ceremonies of the 28th Legislature of the Territory of Hawaii were intoxicated with their newly acquired power. The great majority of them had won their legislative seats in the November, 1954, general elections, promising a new political order for the Islands. They were Democrats, harbingers of a "New Deal" for a traditionally Republican Hawaii. They were youthful, replacing the tired old guard of the oligarchy. They were "of the common people," sensitive to social evils, labor unrest, and racial discontent. They were of modest means, progeny of the plantations, distrustful of the entrenched wealth of the few. And not by chance, a great many of the freshmen legislators were Nisei veterans of the great war who demanded racial justice and equality.

The daily newspapers called the February 16, 1955, opening ceremonies of the 28th Legislature "a riot of color and confusion." From early that morning workmen had been decorating the House chambers with banners and flags in anticipation of the Democratic ascendency to power—for the first time in Hawaiian history both Houses would be controlled by Democrats. Baskets of flowers filled the tables and spilled over to the floor; hundreds of relatives and friends packed the gallery and *lanai;* television cameras and bright lights darted among the crowd; six Hawaiian musical and choral troupes entertained the chamber audience while outside the Royal Hawaiian Band played.

Upstairs in the governor's office while these preliminary festivities took place, a subdued stillness permeated the air. Governor Samuel Wilder King, former delegate to Congress and a stalwart Republican, had served only one year of his gubernatorial term before the electorate of Hawaii had ushered in a new Democratic era. Appointed governor by President Eisenhower in 1953, King, the first Part-Hawaiian to hold that high office, had the ironic task of representing a government and a people who largely viewed his party affiliation, conservative policies, and close ties to the "inner circle" of oligarchic power as inimical to the future of the Islands. Now, as the exuberant Democrats went through the gaieties of political triumph, a sober governor and his wife prepared to witness the legislative swearing-in rituals while his staff muttered about the "high-handed tactics" of the Democrats.

At 9:30 A.M., led by David ("Daddy") Bray, one of the last authentic *kahunas* (priests), the procession of Democratic legislators filed into the House chambers to be sworn in. Chanting in Hawaiian as he walked, "Daddy" Bray, who wore the scarlet and yellow feather cape of the ancient ruling *aliis* (chiefs), compared the legislators to "Majestic Keala and the Heavens Above." Speaker of the House Charles Kauhane came after the *kahuna,* followed by the legislators grouped into the Kauai, Maui, Lanai, Molokai, Hawaii, and Oahu delegations. As each group entered, the song of the Island was played and leis representing their Island flower were given to each legislator. After the Queen's Prayer and the singing of *Hawaii Ponoi,* the state anthem, Representative Raymond Kobayashi from the first district, East Hawaii, called the House to order.

Within ten minutes Republican representatives began challenging the new Democratic House leadership over an issue of procedure. The ensuing sorties of fired arguments were suddenly subdued when Democratic Representative Daniel Inouye interjected his disappointment in the Republicans' attitude. When the Republicans had controlled the House, Inouye admonished, Democrats had not harassed the majority party or hampered proceedings. "We are here. We have the majority. I suggest you let us proceed." The chambers resounded with the hearty applause of the rambunctious Democrats.

Whether tactless, inexperienced, boisterous, or overambitious, the new Democratic majority was intent on implementing its party platform as demonstrated by the nearly 300 bills submitted to the House and 50 bills to the Senate. While a larger number of these measures were pork-barrel legislation and GOP bills to increase veteran benefits, the Democrats also proposed major tax revisions to put a greater burden on the wealthy; supported a land reform act which would allow tenants to buy leased land, the controversial Maryland Land Law; sought increased education funds, particularly to "give proper dignity to labor"; and supported decent wages, more industrial safety, and increased workmen's compensatory benefits. The platform of the Democratic Party also strongly endorsed statehood for Hawaii and the need for Home Rule. Envisioning themselves as the guardians of the public interest, the designers of Hawaii's modern society, these young Democrats in 1955 represented a deep undercurrent of social change in the Islands, a change characterized and perpetuated by frustrated personal ambitions, heightened social consciousness, as well as a binding responsibility to the ethnic community. Many of the measures which the 28th Legislature proposed did not leave committee; others were vetoed. But regardless, 1954 and 1955 were to be watershed years for the evolution and democratization of the Hawaiian social and political institutions. The old guard had fallen to the new, never to be restored.

In the afternoon of February 16, following the swearing-in ceremonies, entertainment programs, and first submitting of bills, Governor King addressed the assembled lawmakers. Warning that many of their proposed bills and acts would mean higher taxes and greater government spending, which he felt would "penalize private enterprise to the detriment of our whole economy and reverse the upward trend we have been experiencing," King symbolized the last efforts to stem the tide of social change. The *Honolulu Star-Bulletin* was more direct in its misgivings about the new Democratic regime:

> . . . The lawmakers of 1955 are very much on the spot.
>
> When the people of Hawaii elected a Democratic Legislature last November, they were looking for fresh, vigorous, industrious men and women with new ideas.
>
> They were impressed by a campaign waged on issues and a serious approach to the problems of the Territory.
>
> To interpret the results of the election as a mandate to swing the Territory's rudder to the left is to misread the public will.
>
> The people of Hawaii are interested primarily in good government at a reasonable cost. There are certain minimum services they expect and should get. They do not need and do not want radical proposals of visionaries.[1]

Many of the "visionaries" of which the *Star-Bulletin* spoke in 1955 had been ten years earlier the returning Nisei veterans, intent on making an impact on Island society. Since their return to civilian life, having taken advantage of the education provided by the GI Bill of Rights these Nisei had begun to look to political action as a means of implementing a new era of social democracy in Hawaii. Sensing that the time was ripe for a change, in the turmoil of the labor movement and the Red Scare, they turned to the Democratic Party, which had been somewhat subjugated by the political arm of the oligarchy, the Republicans. To breathe life into the Democratic Party, to use the party as a vehicle for many young, mostly non-*haole* candidates, seemed for these veterans the most natural course of action.

Expressions of ethnic frustrations or ambitions through the ballot box were certainly not new in the American democratic process or in the Islands. In Hawaii the government before World War II had been run by a coalition of Hawaiians and *haole*s in the Republican Party. Certain candidates representing an ethnic community were elected occasionally to state offices before the 1950s. But generally the ethnic populations of Hawaii, especially the Japanese and Chinese groups whose first-generation immigrants were ineligible for naturalization and the franchise, were not active political communities. The second generation was generally under age before the war and constituted a small voting bloc.

To illustrate the difficulty Orientals had in exercising political power, not until 1920 was a Chinese elected to office. In 1930 two Japanese were elected to the Territorial Legislature. The inability to get a Japanese elected was in part due to the small number of voters among the Nisei; although 86 percent of the eligible Japanese voted in 1930, they comprised less than 16 percent of the voting population.[2] The following table reveals the disproportionately minor role which Japanese and Orientals in general played in the government of Hawaii before 1950:

PERCENTAGE OF ORIENTALS IN HAWAII IN GOVERNMENT POSITIONS IN RELATION TO ADULT CITIZENSHIP, 1920–1955

	Elected Officials		Appointed Officials		Adult Citizens	
Year	Oriental	Japanese	Oriental	Japanese	Oriental	Japanese
1910	0	0	0	0	3.1	0.3
1920	1.1	0	0.8	0	12.7	5.5
1930	5.5	2.2	4.1	1.6	23.9	15.3
1940	24.2	14.3	6.3	2.9	35.9	26.6
1950	37.4	25.3	17.5	10.0	48.2	34.7

Source: George Yamamoto, "Political Participation among Orientals in Hawaii," *Sociology and Social Research,* v. 43, no. 5 (May/June 1959), p. 360.

Evident from these statistics, however, was the steady rise of the Japanese voting population as a consequence of the maturing Nisei. By 1950, many young Nisei politicians were realizing that the rise of the Democratic Party as a viable power in Hawaii was imminent, given organization and progressive control.

The roots of the "Revolution of 1954," the rise of the Democratic Party, and the Nisei politician go back to 1948 when a young Nisei veteran, Daniel Inouye, made a political alliance with a tough Honolulu policeman, John Burns. In that year Burns was running for delegate to the U.S. Congress against popular Republican candidate Joseph Farrington. Burns had made many friends in the Japanese community due to his wartime activities and had hoped that the votes of the young Nisei generation combined with those of the discontented Hawaiian voters could catapult the Democratic Party into office. Inouye, then completing his undergraduate degree at the University of Hawaii, agreed that the potential power of the Japanese ethnic vote would be significant. When Inouye convinced Dan Aoki, Nisei president of the 442nd Veterans Club, that the energies of the 442nd Club could be implemented to improve the social and political status of the Japanese in Hawaii, the foundations of the powerful Democratic Party were laid.

Into the core of power were invited young Nisei who saw the possibility of social and personal goals being actualized into a better Hawaii. Matsuo Takabuki and Mike Tokunaga, both Nisei veterans reared on the plantation and tempered in war, became important leaders of the party, as did William Richardson, a Part-Hawaiian who saw the possibilities of a Japanese–Hawaiian voting bloc which could loosen the oligarchy's grip on Hawaiian politics.

Although Burns lost the 1948 election, the machinery had been established both to wrest control of the Democratic Party from the ILWU and to wage successful campaigns against Republican incumbents. Cognizant of the damage which the Communist issue would do to a party under ILWU leadership, personally stunned over the revelations of Izuka and Kawano as to Communist activities in the Islands, the Burns–Inouye coalition moved to control the Democratic Territorial Central Committee in 1950. Using their total influence, they were able to elect 25 of the 30 members to the committee. The ILWU's control of the Democratic Party had been seriously weakened.

But to overcome the Republican Party would require a *tour de force*. The critical year that the youthful Democrats thought could be turned into a major victory was 1954. Dissatisfied with the Republican Party, looking forward to a new style of government and progressive legislation sensitive to the working and middle classes, the electorate was certainly prepared for the young Nisei politician and his promise of a better Hawaii. In addition, and not unimportantly, the Issei community, a major portion of the population, was granted the privilege of naturalization and voting in 1952. The ethnic community was now prepared to act upon long-suppressed political frustrations and demands for action.

The story of the campaign of 1954 is perhaps best told by one of its foremost participants. In his autobiography, *Journey to Washington,*[3] Daniel Inouye related the background and important events which culminated in the fall of the GOP and the rise of the Democratic Party. The "Go for Broke" spirit revealed by Inouye in his recounting of his World War II experiences clearly emerges in the context of Island political campaigning. The excitement of the political challenge and the dramatic victory are accurately recreated in Inouye's story.

The prime campaign theme which the Democrats rallied around was that the Republicans represented the past and the Democrats the future. The past was replete with discrimination, injustice, hardship, and a political and racial reign of despotism. The future promised multiracial equality and social progress for an improved Island home. The GOP might lambaste the Democrats as Communists, tools of the ILWU, but the facts remained that the party represented the great majority of Hawaii's non-*haole,* nonelite. Inouye recalled of his fellow Nisei politicians:

> We had played a small but vital part in the great war, and now that it was won we were not about to go back to the plantation. We wanted our place in the sun, the right to participate in decisions that affected us. Day after day, at rally after rally, we hammered home the point that there must be no more second-class citizens in the Hawaii of tomorrow.

Election night, after the returns had been counted, a jubilant Democratic Party surveyed the results. John Burns had lost again for the delegateship but this time by a narrow margin. Overall the Democrats had secured more than two-thirds of the House seats and had a 6 to 9 margin in the Senate. Throughout the Territory, personalities who in the next decade would become the new power establishment began their political careers. Daniel Inouye, Spark Matsunaga, Stanley I. Hara, George Ariyoshi, and Nelson Doi, to name but a few, were Nisei who rode the crest of the new Island political tidal wave.

The political career of John Burns; the entrenchment of the Democratic Party in Island politics nearly to the point of making Hawaii a one-party system; the issues of land, taxes, liberal legislation, labor, education, and tourism became the salient issues of community affairs for the next decade. Perhaps Hawaii after 1954 was not totally "revolutionized" by the new coalition of Japanese Hawaiian Democrats. Perhaps land and tax measures relieving the burden on the middle-class resident were not always effectively implemented. But the 1950s was a decade of growth and expansion for Hawaii and the Nisei. Education, for example, was made top priority by the Legislature, increasing the size and scope of the Hawaiian public school system and the University of Hawaii. As a result of such expansion, Nisei teachers hitherto qualified but not given the job opportunities now eagerly applied for newly created jobs in significant proportions. Indeed by the 1970s, conservative estimates showed that teachers of Japanese ancestry numbered approximately two-thirds of the total number of state-employed teachers. Given the developments of the 1950s, the educational preparation of the Nisei, and the family stress on better professional jobs, as well as cultural esteem for learning, the predominance of Japanese in the public school administration and faculty was understandable.

Tourism in the 1950s also propelled growth in Hawaii, offering new jobs and professions to the skilled and professional workers. Niseis entered, for example, into the *aloha* shirt business, servicing the vast numbers of tourists who "just had to look Hawaiian." Actually, the *aloha* shirt had its beginnings in 1926 and was a home product. The popular plantation shirt before that was made of sturdy *palaka,* a plaid fabric, and the gentry wore solid-color cotton sports shirts. To help add color, tapa designs and Island flowers—birds of paradise and anthuriums—were hand-blocked on the backs of these shirts, soon to be followed by more elaborate and colorful designs. In the 1930s these shirts began to be produced commercially, partly as a response to demands by tourists for the comfortable shirt and by locals who had adopted the *aloha* shirt as a "must" for any Hawaiian-style party. As tourism became a major industry in the 1950s, local businessmen, many of them Nisei, saw the potential profit in producing and marketing such shirts.[4]

The total effect of the political, educational, and economic growth of the Nisei was their eventual assimilation into the mainstream of the Islands. Before the 1950s, Japanese had viewed their community, and their community was viewed by others, as an ethnic unit, having ethnic problems demanding an ethnic solution. What concerned the Japanese individual most was the protection and promotion of his community, which many times was considered an anomaly to Island society. For the Japanese community, vital issues were those issues which primarily affected Japanese. Assimilation, though, slowly altered this perspective. Japanese were in leadership positions in the 1950s; economically they had joined the *haole* elite in Merchant Street decision-making, and they constituted policy-formulators in the education system. Their problems were soon Hawaii's problems; their leadership, leadership for all the people. No longer could the ethnic community be viewed as totally separate and distinct from other ethnic communities. As both Japanese and non-Japanese leaders had envisioned over the seventy years of the immigrant experience in the Islands, the Japanese community had become an integral and influential part of a dynamic, multiracial Hawaii.

Moreover a final development was occurring in the Islands which would remove forever the stigma of second-class citizenship and separatism from Japanese and the people of Hawaii. Since the 1930s when the sugar interests and influential leaders had decided that the Islands should become a state, attempts had been made to enact statehood legislation. But powerful forces in the U.S. Congress, especially race-conscious Southern representatives, had consistently blocked such actions. Throughout the 1940s and 1950s, hearings were conducted in Hawaii, calling on several spokesmen to testify concerning the advantages and disadvantages of Hawaiian statehood. And consistently the arguments were repeated that because the Islands were not contiguous with the United States, had such a large nonwhite population, had accepted an undemocratic rule of law under the sugar interests, and had Communist infiltration in the labor movement, Hawaii was simply not ready for statehood status. But worst of all, Hawaii harbored more than 180,000 Japanese who were not only nonwhite and unassimilable, but were questionable citizens. As a Democratic representative from Georgia stated in 1947:

> What does it [the Hawaii bill] do? It makes citizens with equal rights with you and me of 180,000 Japanese. . . . It gives these people the same rights you and I have; we the descendants of those

who created, fought and maintained this country. . . . When you give these people the same rights we have today, you will have two Senators speaking for those 180,000 Japanese.[5]

Statehood, for a great many Japanese, would mean their acceptance as loyal American citizens. If the United States recognized Hawaii as a state then the intimidations and suspicions of racism would finally be removed. Not surprisingly, Japanese were the most solidified of all ethnic groups in support of statehood. Indeed, Japanese constituted the only ethnic group in which a majority supported Hawaii's becoming a state. In a 1958 survey, 62 percent of the Japanese community favored statehood compared to 44 percent of the Chinese, 39 percent of the Filipinos, 33 percent of the *haole*s, and 30 percent of the Hawaiians and Part-Hawaiians.[6]

Indicative of the type of anti-Japanese sentiment which continued to surface during the postwar statehood hearings was the testimony of Mrs. Alice Kamokila Campbell given before the House Committee of Interior and Insular Affairs in 1948.[7] Mrs. Campbell, a respected personage in the political and social circles of Hawaii at that time, bluntly expressed her fears and uneasiness about statehood. Japanese, Mrs. Campbell stated, had literally taken over Hawaii economically, challenged non-Japanese politicians with their ethnic tactics, and were arrogant in their "Americanism." Japanese were bringing Communism into Hawaii as well as using their political and economic power to intimidate public officials to support Japanese interests. For Mrs. Campbell, the Nisei were just as bad as the Issei. "The Japanese are not my people," she declared in pronouncing her American heritage and, "I don't want to see an unhealthy condition here in these islands. It is an unhealthy condition. We are not safe when in an American country one-third of the population are Japanese."

Concurrent with these perspectives to the Japanese issue, however, was a more favorable view of Japanese in Hawaii. Indeed, by the middle of the 1950s the whole question of Hawaii's Japanese was becoming moot. A number of people in Hawaii certainly thought that the Japanese community was becoming too powerful, too competitive, too much in control. A survey in 1959 revealed that in one electoral district more than 50 percent of the Hawaiians and Portuguese residents felt that Japanese had too much power in Hawaii.[8] But generally the community had come to be recognized as a functioning, equal partner in Hawaiian society. The Japanese had successfully assimilated and the old bugaboos of "Japanese Menace" were simply no longer proper or relevant.

An interesting example of the new attitude toward the successful assimilation of Japanese was revealed in the 1957 testimony of Mike Masaoka before the statehood hearings.[9] Masaoka, leader of the Japanese American Citizens League (JACL) on the mainland, was an extremely active and influential lobbyist for statehood. As a Japanese American, Masaoka felt that the war record of the Nisei and the assimilation of the ethnic community in Hawaii had been justification for full status for Hawaii as a state. As long as statehood was denied, second-class citizenship for Japanese and other Island nonwhite races would be perpetuated. "In this record of devotion and sacrifice," Masaoka argued, "lies an answer to those who question the loyalty of the so-called Japanese population in Hawaii. They have purchased with their blood the right to be accepted as Americans individually and to have statehood extended to the Territory that gave them birth and imbued in them that spirit of liberty and freedom that inspired their wartime gallantry."

Masaoka went on in this presentation to give a brief overview of the type of pro-statehood arguments which became the basis for the eventually successful statehood bill. Hawaii's position in Asian affairs, the strength of her racial relations, the Island's war record, and the deep commitment of Island people to Americanism—all were factors which showed that Hawaii's period of "pupilage" was over. "Statehood is the remaining step in that progress for equality of status."

In interchanges with representatives on the statehood committee, Masaoka stressed over and over the notion that Hawaiian statehood for the Japanese was a central ethnic issue. Second-class citizenship could no longer be tolerated by a people who had given so much, asked so little, and had assimilated so completely as loyal Americans. The response given to Masaoka, however, was equally as insightful as to the status which Japanese in Hawaii had attained by the late 1950s.

"I think the record ought to show here," declared Republican Rep. John R. Pillion of New York, "that never during any of our hearings has there been any statement made derogatory to the loyalty of the Americans of Japanese ancestry. I think the record ought to show that. There is no issue here or question of loyalty of these people."

Hawaii, the Japanese, and the American public had advanced a long way along the road of rational, democratic social justice.

The banner headline which the Honolulu dailies used to proclaim statehood on March 12, 1959, was even larger than the type used to proclaim war on December 8, 1941. The wailing sirens, the crowds cheering, the bonfires, the optimism and jubilation, as well as the bitterness and foreboding, seemed the perfect climax to two exiting and meaningful decades in the development of Hawaiian institutions and the maturing of her diverse peoples.

War, the returning veterans, social achievement of ethnic groups, unionism, tourism, Communism, revolution at the polls, and now statehood. Hawaii had entered the 1940s supposedly a quiet outpost of idyllic paradise. Her people, her society and her prospects for the future seemed secure in the languorous acceptance of the status quo. Of course the nostalgia remained among some for those old days when the *haole kamaaina* could dine gracefully in sublime Waikiki, serenaded by the melodious *ukulele* and Hawaiian song; when the Hawaiian father could enjoy his remote country home, the unspoiled taro patch, his freshly dug *imu* (underground oven), and evenings filled with song and friendship; when the Japanese *mama-san* could casually sweep out her small family grocery store, restock the shelves with *tsukemono* (pickled vegetables) imported from Japan, and look forward to a quiet afternoon "talking story" with friends or relatives.

But the nostalgia, however well-intentioned, tended to forget the uncomfortable, the bitterness, or the uncomely. Underneath those idyllic images of the old Hawaii were the volcanic frustrations and discontents of human beings in conflict, restrained by the economies and systems in which they lived. The natives had learned to cope with indignation and despair that their people were aliens in their own Island home. The immigrant stoically adapted to harsh conditions so as to optimistically forfeit present happiness for future rewards. And the rulers of Hawaii anxiously protected their wealth and status and yet were bewildered by their own religious obligation to equality and fairness.

The eruption of these human desires and the emergence of a new Hawaiian society struggling to be equitable to each of its parts was the bloodless revolution propelled in Hawaii's postwar era. Conflict and hate, cooperation and respect flowed through the course of events as individual men and women and groups sought to design a Hawaii which would not only be rewarding to them, but to their children and the Island people. And in the midst of this revolution, this emergence of modern Hawaii, were the Nisei—leading, following, influencing, instigating, and defending. The Nisei as a result had established themselves in Hawaii as a respected force and as equal participants. They had used their ethnic community, their ethnic identity to instill self-respect and social mobilization. They had created a successful community image to overcome the hate and suspicion of the past. They had played leading roles in unionism, politics, education, the Communist scare, tourism, and statehood. Yet, increasingly evident in this assimilation was the realization that the Japanese community had also been undergoing fundamental changes, from sex role to family structure. The Nisei, the second generation, had fostered a cultural world which bore but faint resemblance to the world of their Issei parents.

NOTES

1. *Honolulu Star-Bulletin,* February 16, 1955, 8:1.
2. F. Everett Robinson, "Participation of Citizens of Chinese and Japanese Ancestry in the Political Life of Hawaii," *Social Process in Hawaii,* v. 4 (1938), p. 58.
3. Daniel K. Inouye, "A Reckoning in Ballots," *Journey to Washington,* Englewood Cliffs, New Jersey: Prentice-Hall, Inc., 1967, pp. 242–52.
4. Ruth Revere, "Aloha Shirts Are Big Business with Nisei Men," *Nisei in Hawaii and the Pacific,* v. 10, no. 3 (1956), pp. 1, 8.
5. Roger J. Bell, "Admission Delayed: The Influence of Sectional and Political Opposition in Congress on Statehood for Hawaii," *Hawaiian Journal of History,* v. 6 (1972), p. 51.
6. Lawrence H. Fuchs, *Hawaii Pono: A Social History,* New York: Harcourt, Brace and World, 1961, p. 412.
7. "Statement of Mrs. Alice Kamokila Campbell," *Statehood for Hawaii,* Hearings before the Subcommittee on Public Lands, United States Senate, 80th Congress, 2nd session, January–April 1948, pp. 410–6.
8. Fuchs, p. 413.
9. "Statement of Mike Masaoka," *Statehood for Hawaii,* Hearings Before the Subcommittee on Territories and Insular Affairs of the Committee on Interior and Insular Affairs, House of Representatives, 85th Congress, 1st session, April 8, 9, 16, 1957, pp. 139–57.

A Reckoning in Ballots

DANIEL K. INOUYE

WE believed there was a chance that 1954 could be our year. Ever since the war we had been whittling away at the absolute dominance of the huge Republican majority in the legislature. Now there was a certain promise in the air, a secret and contagious spirit that whispered, "Go for broke!" This year. Now!

Again we nominated John Burns for Delegate. I was named his campaign chairman and my first statement to our people was a request for anybody who thought we were just going through the motions again to roll up their voters list and sit this one out. We meant to win this time, I said, not only the Delegateship, but control of the Territorial House and Senate, as well.

That summer, at a meeting at Dan Aoki's house, Jack Burns dropped his bombshell. We were discussing likely candidates and overall strategy when Burns, who usually sits quietly absorbing every word and intonation—but has only to clear his throat to gain everyone's attention—suddenly spoke up: "Dan, I think it's time for you to run."

I tried to brush him off politely—the idea seemed that outlandish to me—but everyone went quiet, staring at me as though my shirt were on backward. "Listen," I said, "why me? There are other guys who have been around longer, better qualified . . ."

In *Journey to Washington,* copyright 1967 (Englewood Cliffs, N.J.: Prentice-Hall, 1967), pp. 242–252. Reprinted by permission of Prentice-Hall, Inc.

"Because you can win," Burns said.

"In the Fourth District?" I thought he was kidding or crazy. In Hawaii's whole experience with representative government, only two Democrats had ever been elected from the old Fourth District, where I lived.

But he wasn't crazy, and he certainly wasn't kidding. "Who was it that made the big speech about going through the motions?" he asked quietly. "Who is it that keeps saying times are changing and that the people want a chance to come out from under 54 years of Republican rule? That was you, Dan, and this is your chance to prove you believe it."

I looked around at the impassive faces. I wanted to tell them that I did believe it, that my only concern was me: who would vote for Dan Inouye? I wasn't even thirty years old, had never been a candidate for an elective office and felt numbingly unready. I wanted to run, sure—but now?

Dan Aoki spoke up. I respected Dan. Everyone did. He had been a 442nd first sergeant, was now president of the Veterans Club and knew as much about the needs and hopes of the ex-GIs as anyone around. "They'll go for you, Dan," he said. "You've got the right combination—a war hero, a fresh face. If we want the vets to come into the Democratic party, we've got to give them somebody they care about, one of their own. You."

"You're on," I said to them. "I'll do it. And I'll give it everything I've got."

There was no cheering or back-slapping. For one thing, we had nothing to cheer about—yet—and for another every one of us took the whole thing as a deadly serious challenge.

That night I discussed it all with Maggie. "Go ahead, Dan," she said. "If you think you're ready for this, I'll be happy to be on your side and working for your election."

Next morning I walked over to Benny's Photo Shop—where, to this day, I have all my official pictures taken—and said to my old friend stooping behind the camera, "Make this a good one, Benny. It could have some bearing on my future."

When the prints were ready, I took them around to the newspapers with a short statement I had scrawled while I waited. The next day, there I was, on the front page of the Honolulu *Advertiser*, announcing to the world that it was going to be different this time, that the tide was coming in strong for the Democratic party in Hawaii and that we meant to ride it to victory. In the next several weeks, I had plenty of professional head-shakers bemoaning my foolhardiness. They told Maggie, they told my father—they even told me!—that I was a nice guy, but absolutely crazy if I really thought I had a chance against the Republicans. "Do you *like* beating your head against a stone wall?" someone asked me.

But the stone wall was crumbling. If you had a feel for the political mood of the people, you could sense it that summer and autumn of 1954, like a fresh breeze off the Pacific. For one thing, we were getting some topnotch candidates. Unlike past years when a sort of Democratic suicide squad—loyal workers but something less than inspiring candidates—ventured forth to have their brains beaten in by Republican opponents, 1954 was the year of the eager young hopefuls, better-educated, thanks to the GI Bill, unscarred by past election defeats, and all abrim with vigorous, forward-looking ideas about the management of the Territorial government. In the Fourth District, until this campaign a permanent graveyard for Democratic hopes, four of our six candidates were veterans and included persons of Japanese, Portuguese, Caucasian and Hawaiian descent. Let me say a word about them:

Spark Matsunaga, war hero with the 100th Battalion, lawyer and now the senior member of the Hawaiian delegation to the U.S. House of Representatives.

Masato Doi, member of the 442nd, soon to become chairman of the city council for the city and county of Honolulu, then to be appointed a circuit judge by Jack Burns.

Russell Kono, a war vet who fought in the China-Burma-India theater with Merrill's Marauders, a successful lawyer and now a magistrate.

Anna Kahanamoku, sister-in-law of Hawaii's beloved swimming champion, Duke Kahanamoku, had been a physical education instructor at Washington Intermediate School when I went there, a beautiful, gracious woman of Hawaiian-Portuguese-Caucasian ancestry who has since been chairman of the board of education and served in the Hawaiian state senate.

Daniel K. Inouye, now a United States Senator.

William Crozier, a long-time Democrat and one of the only two ever elected from the old Fourth District, the only one among the six of us who would fail to win in that crucial election.

This gives some indication of the caliber of our team. There were other straws in the wind. In one speech, I suggested that the best way for the electorate to make a judgment between the two parties was for every Republican candidate to get up on the platform with his Democratic opponent and debate the issues face to face. I even took a deep breath and said we'd foot the bill for radio time, although our treasury still suffered from chronic anemia. This, of course, was six years before the Kennedy-Nixon debates revived interest in this time-honored style of campaigning—and the point was that the Republicans didn't even respond to the invitation. Even if some of our own people hadn't yet realized it, our opponents had grown acutely aware that the day of the halfhearted Democratic way of battle—hula dancers, luaus, pretty balloons—had ended. We understood the issues and were prepared to talk about them—education, economic development, the kind of future Hawaii ought to aim for—and, more than anything else, this shook the Republicans' confidence. And as we slashed away at them, our audiences growing in size and enthusiasm, many a beseiged G.O.P. candidate must have sadly wondered what ever happened to the good old Democratic patsies who used to roll over and play dead for them, election after election.

The six of us running from the Fourth District campaigned as a team. Each of us had a particular issue—mine was education—on which we spent many after-midnight hours of study, but our central theme was progress, for all the people. We had played a small but vital part in the great war and now that it was won we were not about to go back to the plantation. We wanted our place in the sun, the right to participate in decisions that affected us. Day after day, at rally after rally, we hammered home the point that there must be no more second-class citizens in the Hawaii of tomorrow.

Then came the meeting at Ainahaina. Once again we had challenged the Republicans to a radio debate. Once again their reply was dead silence. But somewhere, at some strategy meeting, they must have faced up to the grim fact that we Democrats had a chance to win, and their reaction was that well-worn, John Wayne-to-the-rescue ploy, the "Truth Squad." So it was that the first of our speakers had been talking for about five minutes when, with a great flourish and determined air, in charged the "Truth Squad," their chairman grabbing the microphone to announce that they could no longer stand idly by while "these so-called Democrats" went on deceiving the people. He went right to the heart of what the "Truth Squad" had come to say: the Democratic party had been captured by the I.L.W.U., we were the willing tools of I.L.W.U. leaders Harry Bridges and Jack Hall and hence, at the very least, soft on communism.

For a long and electric moment I just sat there, the words ringing in my ears, and the realization that this infamy was going out over the air numbing me: in the space of three minutes we had been lumped with Bridges and Hall, made out to be either fools or traitors, and I could see all our high hopes, all our back-breaking effort, going out the window. True or false, a political charge travels with the speed of light, while a denial moves at a snail's pace and most often doesn't catch up until the day after the polls close.

I remember getting to my feet and moving to the microphone. It wasn't my turn to speak and, truthfully, I had no idea in that instant what I meant to say or do. As a matter of fact, until I actually began talking, everything blurred in my eyes. But Maggie was in the audience, and she remembers vividly:

"I was afraid," she told me later. "The skin on your face was all tightened up and you looked as though you were going to kill somebody. You said something under your breath to the moderator, then you just took the microphone out of his hand and you looked straight ahead and began to speak."

Once I heard the sound of my voice, all the ripples of faces in front of me stiffened into focus and became people. It was like the first instant of combat: one second you're scared to death, and the next you set out to do what needs to be done. I knew how desperately important it was that I win these people back, here and now, not tomorrow or next week when the smear had hardened to fact in their minds.

I put the notes for my speech into my clenched teeth and tore them in two with my only hand. I said that in my view the danger to our democratic institutions was less from communism than from the social conditions on which communists fed and flourished—poverty, slums, inequality of opportunity. These were the evils, the very real evils, that my fellow candidates and I were pledged to fight. If our opponents wanted to wage a shadow war, a smear campaign, that was their sad privilege.

"But I cannot help wondering," I said, "whether the people of Hawaii will not think it strange that the only weapon in the Republican arsenal is to label as communists men so recently returned from defending liberty on the firing lines in Italy and France. Let me speak for those of us who didn't come back—I *know* I speak for my colleagues on this platform, and for good Democratic candidates everywhere in these Islands—when I say that we bitterly resent having our loyalty and patriotism questioned by cynical political hacks who lack the courage to debate the real issues in this campaign."

I had never before called attention to my disability for the simple reason that I didn't consider it a qualification for public office. But at that moment, blinded with fury, coldly aware that I was engaging in a bit of demagoguery, I held up my empty right sleeve and shook it: "I gave this arm to fight fascists. If my country wants the other one to fight communists, it can have it!"

There was a moment of stunned silence, then a crashing of applause. A man ran to the edge of the platform and cried up at me: "It's about time somebody stood up to them!"

Arms waved, and handkerchieves, and sometime during that tumult, the Republican "Truth Squad" skulked off the platform—and with them went any chance they had to win the election. That was the turning point, and when the votes were counted a few weeks later, five of the six Democratic candidates running from the Fourth District were elected, a victory beyond our wildest imaginations. We had won 22 of the 30 seats in the House, and 10 of 15 in the Senate, besides gaining control of most of the city and county councils. My name led the ticket.

We had one disappointment, but it was a big one. Jack Burns lost the Delegateship to Elizabeth Farrington, widow of Joe and daughter-in-law of the onetime Governor. A mark of how far we'd come was that of 140,000 votes cast, Mrs. Farrington's winning margin was less than 1,000—and she could thank the heavily *haole* districts for those.

Jack moved slowly among the winners that night, congratulating us all. And whenever anyone offered him words of sympathy, the tough ex-cop shrugged them off: "Fifty-six is another election," he said. "I'll be back."

And he was.

Even today, there are some good Democrats in Hawaii who would just as soon forget the session of the Territorial legislature that was called to order in February of 1955. It was wild, full of sound, fury and confusion and, if you were looking for a log of solid legislative achievement—well, I'd have to concede that you'd come to the wrong place.

Of the 22 members of the Democratic majority, only 8 had any legislative experience whatever. Most were young, burning to set right out redressing evil. We were convinced that our zeal would see us through, that because our hearts were pure and our aspirations lofty we would prevail. We believed in ourselves. Thanks to the GI Bill and the fact that most of us were vets, few legislative bodies anywhere in the country could boast the level of professional and educational competence that we brought to our task. But when it came to the ways and means, the give and take of practical politics, we were pretty much in the dark.

Our first problem was organizing the House, a job that had been regularly and routinely handled by the opposition for all the years anyone could remember. We went at it with gusto, emotion and crossed fingers. Meetings and caucuses were held all over the Territory, nearly all of them concerned with the best way to conduct this first Democratic-controlled legislature. Since we five winners from the Fourth District represented an important block of votes, I was designated to express our preferences for the leadership posts to be assigned in the House. In order of importance, they were speaker, vice-speaker, majority leader and then the various committee chairmanships.

When the final choices were to be made, a group of us sat down for a long session of debate, discussion and decision. The selection of our speaker reflected a kind of idealism rarely found around statehouse caucuses. Though most of the Democratic members were *nisei,* we promptly decided that the Speakership should go to Charles Ernest Kauhane, a Hawaiian. Why? For reasons that most political practitioners would think laughable: because as a member of the minority in the past he had carried the ball for us through many lean years, and because short as we were on experience, Kauhane had as much of it as we could lay claim to.

We agreed on Elmer Cravalho as assistant speaker—which must have been a sound choice because he is now speaker—and then came the chore of assigning committee chairmen. It was a monumental task because, traditionally, each member of the majority party was to be given a committee to chair. On and on the meeting went—finance committee, judiciary, Oahu County—and so intent was I in getting the right people in the right places that when we were done and Charles Kauhane said, "Well, we've done a good job except that there's no committee left for you, Dan," all I could manage was a small, "Oh."

"The only thing left," Kauhane said, "is majority leader. Do you want to be majority leader?"

I shrugged. "Why not?"

And that's how it happened, which will come as news to some people who are convinced that I connived for the post. The fact is that it was a job with limited powers, small staff and still seeking definition, having been created only a few years before by the Republicans.

And still I took it very seriously. My personal problem was clear-cut: I had only the vaguest possible notion of what responsibilities were entailed in my new post as majority leader. And so, seeking guidance and moral support I took what I considered to be the most direct possible action. I wrote a letter to Sam Rayburn, who in 1955 had already served as majority leader of the U.S. House of Representatives longer than any man in history, and I told him how in more or less haphazard fashion I had been named to this important post. I had been studying everything I could find about a majority leader's responsibilities—which wasn't much—and asked if he could give me some basic human guidelines that would at least get me through this first session. And bless Mr. Sam's big Texas heart, he took sympathetic notice of this obscure Hawaiian legislator of whom he had never heard and whose name he wouldn't learn to pronounce for six years, and he said essentially this:

Though the rules of legislative bodies differed, it was generally true that a majority leader had few constitutional powers; that he knew of no constitution, including that of the United States, which made any reference to a majority leader; that the post, like others within the internal framework of the governing party, was a convenience and a tool to help keep the legislative business moving.

There would be further strictures, not only on my powers, but on my freedom of choice. Wrote Rayburn, if, for example, my personal convictions led me in direction A, but the clear-cut sentiment of the majority was toward B, I was duty-bound as leader to press for B, and if in good conscience I could not, I was obliged to resign as a party functionary, for at that point I could no longer represent the will of the majority.

What, then, makes a good majority leader? The understanding, appreciation and practice of good human relations, said Mr. Sam, and the Golden Rule was as good a guide as he'd ever encountered.

I don't think I have ever had better advice, and the days were upon us when I needed it desperately.

Statement of Mrs. Alice Kamokila Campbell

CONGRESSIONAL TESTIMONY

Mrs. Campbell. Now I don't know, Senator, just what you wanted to see me for. I am here to answer any questions.

Senator Cordon. Mrs. Campbell, I want your views on the advisability of the enactment by Congress of the pending bill granting statehood to the Territory of Hawaii. I have understood that you are opposed to the passage of legislation at this time. I am interested in the reasons which bring you to that contention.

Mrs. Campbell. First I will give it to you from the standpoint of a Hawaiian, the land being the land of my people. I naturally am jealous of it being in the hands of any alien influence. It took us quite a while to get used to being Americans—from a Hawaiian to an American—but I am very proud today of being an American. I don't want ever to feel that I am ashamed of being an American. But I think that in the past 10 years I have lost a sense of balance here in Hawaii as to the future safety of my land. This un-American influence has come into our country, and even in the report of the Governor you will see where he says one-third of the population are Japanese. If we are a State they would have the power to vote and they would use every exertion to see that every vote was counted, if we became a State. As it is now, I feel the confidence and I feel the sincerity of Congress, and know they are not going to forsake us.

. . .

In *Statehood for Hawaii,* Hearings before the Senate Subcommittee on Public Lands, 80th Congress, 2nd session, January-April, 1948, pp. 410–6.

Now there are two things that I have been thinking of. What could make the average American in his own land afraid to speak? It is a very unnatural thing.

First, there is the purchasing power of the Chinese and Japanese combination in this country. The outsider coming in says "Oh, no; the Chinese hate the Japs and the Japs hate the Chinese." Don't you believe it, Senator Cordon. The Chinese and Japanese are so tied up together in this community that if we ever went to war they could have a stranglehold on us. We cannot afford to talk. We cannot afford to talk to Russia, is what I claim today, because of that situation. Those for statehood come forward; those who are not for statehood won't make their statements showing where they stand.

Who supplies our fish? The Japanese. Who do they sell to? The Chinese storeman. Who supplies our chickens and eggs? The Japanese. Who do they sell to? The Chinese—Chun Hoon, C. Q. Yee Hop. Who supplies our pork? This is a pork-eating country. The Japanese. Who do they sell to? C. Q. Yee Hop, who is a wholesale man, and that combination goes on and on and on. I say Russia could afford to say—and I should take a chance as one born here in Hawaii—to have Russia say, "All right, you Chinese and Japanese, you come and fight for us. We will give you the Territory of Hawaii." Should I take these chances of giving my land up and permitting Russia for one minute to do it? We don't know where Russia stands. Russia does not want this Territory. Russia is out to get Europe. Congress knows that. I know it. I am not hiding it. If it was any other nationality I would have to say the same thing; that we must be careful. I don't want to have a Japanese judge tell me how to act in my own country, no more than you Americans over on the other side would want an Indian to overrule you, or a Negro, which are among your American people.

Senator Cordon. We have judges of both.

Mrs. Campbell. I know, but it is not racial prejudice with me. There is still a very bitter feeling; there is still a very great racial feeling there on the mainland, because when I went on a trip the Negroes were all put in one car; the Negroes were set aside, and yet they are Americans.

The Japanese are not my people. The Chinese are not my people. The Caucasians, yes, and by adoption it makes me an American, and I am proud to be an American, and as an American I don't want to see an unhealthy condition here in these islands. It is an unhealthy condition. We are not safe when in an American country one-third of the population are Japanese. The Governor himself says that in his report, at which I was surprised—one-third, in an American country. I cannot see it. I am too much an American, Senator, to see anything but Americans here.

. . .

Senator Cordon. Mrs. Campbell, let me ask you for your judgment as to the extent to which the native-born American, and that is what he is, in the islands, of Japanese extraction, has foresworn the Government and the ways of his ancestors, and adopted those of his native country—America.

Mrs. Campbell. Yes.

Senator Cordon. What is your judgment as to whether he has done that, or hasn't?

Mrs. Campbell. I would say a lot of them, maybe a great majority, have taken on American ways. Why shouldn't they?

Senator Cordon. Well, they should.

Mrs. Campbell. They are American people.

Senator Cordon. But I seek to determine whether they have. I don't mean as a cloak.

Mrs. Campbell. No, no.

Senator Cordon. Mrs. Campbell, I mean as an existing fact, in respect to their lives and beliefs.

Mrs. Campbell. I say a great many—in fairness to the Japanese, I say they have taken on the form of Americanism, and as to those I am proud of them; but I say "but"—because this is a great "but"—why do they keep insisting and emphasizing to an American that they are of Japanese ancestry? Why don't they drop it? Isn't it enough to say that "I am an American," and have us all understand that they are American "period." But when they try to keep saying "of Japanese ancestry"; "of Japanese ancestry," why do they do it? Why do they want to bring up the Japanese ancestry?

Senator Cordon. Perhaps because my dad, who was born in England, 'til the date of his death loved roast beef.

Mrs. Campbell. Why, any more than I should keep saying "I am an American of Hawaiian ancestry." Who cares? Another American only wants to know "Are you an American?" I am an American "period." My Hawaiian ancestry does not mean a thing. It is: What am I today? An American. I may be wrong, Senator, but I don't like having them ram down my throat all the time "I am an American of Japanese ancestry," trying to make me feel that they went away with the Four Hundred and Forty-second or the One Hundredth Battalion—they went away to fight for a foreign country because they were Japanese? No. Why don't they say "We went away to fight for our country"? It is always, "Americans of Japanese ancestry." Why? Because they want the praise of the Japanese—fighting for your country and my country. I can't see it. I am too much of an American. I am an American "period." That is all I know. And that is why I may be a little bit bitter down here, when they try to ram down my throat "Japanese."

No one but those who were in Hawaii, and lived in Hawaii, as I do, will ever forget December 7. Who was it that brought on that attack of December 7? The people who were here, right here in this country, whom I thought were loyal to my country. I thought they were Americans. They gave out the information to their own people in Japan. Blood is thicker than water. That is my contention. I cannot help it. I am basing a lot of these things on that. I am interested in the safety of Hawaii; in the safety of the people. It includes the Japanese too, but it is Hawaii first, last, and always in my heart, and I will fight and fight for that. Who wants Hawaii to be a State? They cater to the Japanese. Why? Because the Japanese vote is what everyone wants.

. . .

Mrs. Campbell. . . . That is the sad part about Hawaii today. There are many things that are not right. I was born here. It was through my interest as a representative family, and a member of a representative family of Hawaii, to watch the trend of the people that were permitted to come into this country, and I have watched it without prejudice. I have Japanese servants. I have a servant who has been with me—a Japanese, an alien—for 42 years, and that woman is still with me. I don't hate her because she is an alien, because she is a Japanese. No, I don't even suspect her, but it is not of the generation we have to watch.

Senator Cordon. You mean the new?

Mrs. Campbell. The new generation. They say they are the third and fourth generations. They are the first and second, if the truth were known, because the first generation to me is one that the alien parents; that is the first generation. You never hear of the *issei*; you hear of the *nisei,* which makes a generation in between; the *nisei* is the second generation. That is all you hear about, the *nisei,* the *nisei,* but no, it is the *issei* that I am after. They are misrepresenting themselves here, calling themselves the second generation; they are the first; their parents are aliens.

I did not approve of the bill, and I was in the senate when they introduced the bill, that all parents of Japanese aliens should automatically become American citizens because their sons and daughters all took part in this war. Why should we give them that privilege of being an American? I cannot see it. I said "No." I fought it, but I was only one in the senate. During the session when I sat there, and this was during wartime, Senator, they wanted to do away with the oath of allegiance. I never heard of such a tragic thing in my life, to do away with the oath of allegiance in time of war, and while we were right in the midst of it, and who was the one who had to fight it in the senate there? I had to fight it alone. Everybody was in favor of doing away with it, and the only backing I got, which was a wonderful backing, was by the American Legion; they came to my support, and they felt the same way I did. Why should we leave out the oath of allegiance right here in Hawaii during wartime? But that is the influence that goes on, all underground, here.

There were dual citizens, and dual citizens. A dual citizen appeared when I was on the judiciary committee, and he said that it is on record, and you can see it in the newspapers, that there was a petition sent on to Washington signed by 10,000 Japanese, favoring the bill, and it never arrived in Washington. Why? I said, "Why? Because you did not send it." That is what I told that individual. Ten thousand names to a petition. Don't you suppose if it ever got to Congress that we would have heard of it—that they wanted to become American citizens? It never came out.

Now, there are so many little things, Senator, that it would take hours, and your time is very valuable, and I cannot go into details; I am just trying to give you the highlights of what I know, Senator, and I am talking sincerely, as one senator to another, representing the people.

Statement of Mike Masaoka

CONGRESSIONAL TESTIMONY

Mr. Dawson. I would like to say a word about Mr. Masaoka before you go ahead. He is one of the outstanding Japanese of this country. He is a native of my State. He was a director of the University of Utah debating team. He is one of the most outstanding men I know and I know he is in a position to speak for the Japanese in Hawaii.

Mr. O'Brien. That is very fine.

Mr. Saylor. I would like to say that the next witness is of Japanese ancestry. To me there is a tremendous difference. I welcome him as an American citizen who was born in Utah and has been doing a tremendous job.

Mr. Burns. For the sake of the record, as an honorary member of the 442d Veterans Club, I want to welcome Mr. Masaoka to the committee.

Mr. O'Brien. Certainly we cannot doubt your welcome.

May I say before we start, I think we can wind up the hearings with this. I think we have covered it all. You do not know of anyone that has to be heard from the islands?

Mr. Masaoka. Mr. Chairman, I wish to thank my Congressman from Utah, and my good friends, the Congressman from Pennsylvania, and the Delegate from Hawaii, for their kind remarks.

In *Statehood for Hawaii,* Hearings before the House Subcommittee on Territories and Insular Affairs of the Committee on Interior and Insular Affairs, 85th Congress, 1st session, April 8, 9, 16, 1957, pp. 139–151.

At this time I would like to submit my statement and make some comments on what I think is a very important question.

Statehood for the deserving Territory of Hawaii has been one of the major postwar legislative objectives of the National Japanese American Citizens' League, JACL, the only national organization representing Americans of Japanese ancestry in the United States.

The JACL, which is composed entirely of American citizens, most but not all of whom are of Japanese ancestry, has some 88 chapters and members in 32 States and the District of Columbia. Interestingly enough, JACL has one or more chapters in each of the States represented by members of the committee that is considering this vital legislation.

. . .

Hawaii Qualifies For Statehood

As Americans, most of whose members reside in the western part of this country, and particularly along the Pacific coast, JACL members believe, as did so many congressional committees in the past, that by every legitimate standard Hawaii qualifies for statehood.

We are convinced that it is in our national self-interest that this island paradise that lies at the crossroads of the Pacific be welcomed into the sisterhood of States; that, from the viewpoint of national security, international commitments, economic and commercial implications, and social well-being statehood for Hawaii will benefit the Nation.

. . .

JACL's Special Concern

Moreover, as Americans of Japanese ancestry, JACL members also believe that we are equipped especially to testify to the reactions that statehood will activate among the peoples and nations of Asia at a critical time in your history, when our interests in the Far East and the Pacific are greater and more crucial than ever.

Because of its large population of persons of Asian ancestry, the treatment which our Nation accords to Hawaii is under constant scrutiny in the so-called Afro-Asian area, where more than two-thirds of the world's population reside, by the free nations, the neutral countries, and the Communist pawns, as reflecting the opinions and the feelings of the United States toward Orientals generally.

It is no secret in Asia, and one constantly exploited by the Communists, that a racist disinclination to accept persons of Oriental origin on the same footing with those of European background has been one of the strongest forces working against statehood for Hawaii.

This unfortunate attitude hampers our international efforts to gain for the free world the minds and the hearts of the peoples whose support may be pivotal to the survival of the world as we know and like it.

It is not enough to say that we believe in the equality of nations when, at the same time, we continue to deny to one geographical and political segment of our country the same equality of representation and autonomy that we extend to most of our country.

It is inconsistent that we call upon other powers to recognize the free determination of peoples when we refuse to practice that same principle in regard to a long-time territory whose population has overwhelmingly determined in free elections that they desire statehood status.

Japan's Position as an Ally

At the moment, the people and the Government of new Japan look with great favor on American leadership, though the Communist enemy is attempting to convert them into neutrals and subsequently into satellites. In this troubled era, we need to keep Japan as a friend and an ally, for of all the nations in the Far East she has the skills, the production, and the manpower to provide a truly formidable bulwark against Communist encroachment from the West.

Because the United States recognized the part that a new and free Japan could play in the post-World War II era, after the end of hostilities in 1945, we provided her with a benevolent and provident occupation, unprecedented in world history.

In 1952, the United States signed a treaty of peace with Japan that was more in the nature of reconciliation than of victor and vanquished.

In 1952, too, the Congress enacted the Immigration and Nationality Act that, among other provisions, repealed the Japanese—and other Orientals—Exclusion Act of 1924, and extended to Japan and all Asia token immigration quotas based upon the same national origins formula that governs all basic immigration into the United States.

. . .

Affirmation of Faith

To hold off Hawaiian statehood any longer is to nullify the great gains we have made in all of Asia, and particularly in Japan, at a time when the Soviet Union and Red China are mounting their greatest psychological and economic offensive in these same areas where we have given so much of blood and treasure.

It will mean to these peoples who have long been suspicious of the so-called western powers that the United States is not yet ready to throw off traditional antiorientalism. It will mean another potent propaganda weapon we have given gratuitously to the enemy.

To grant statehood to Hawaii now will be a reaffirmation of our new policy of giving equal concern and equal opportunities to all people interested in freedom and democracy. But more, it will give to the United States and to the free world a new citizenry which, by its very background, is best qualified to explain our ideals and our objectives to the peoples of Asia and to interpret for us the hopes and aspirations of most of the world's population.

Statehood for Hawaii is more than a political issue of the moment; it is an international token of our real intentions in dealing with the problems of this tension-filled world. Only illogically and self-defeatingly can we preach democracy to others while denying proper and long-overdue recognition to a deserving territory in our own front yard because of its Asian population.

. . .

War Record of Persons of Japanese Ancestry in Hawaii

In World War II, American citizens of Japanese ancestry—Nisei—in Hawaii formed the all-Nisei 100th Infantry Battalion.

Later, the 100th was integrated into the 442d Regimental Combat Team, an all-Nisei outfit composed of volunteers from Hawaii and the mainland of the United States.

In connection with this volunteer combat team, the Army called for only 1,500 volunteers from Hawaii. In less than 3 days, more than 10,000 responded; in a week, more than 15,000 had volunteered. The Army decided to accept 2,500.

Between them the 442d and the 100th made history without parallel in American military annals. According to the record, they were awarded more medals and combat decorations for their size and length of service in the line than any other United States infantry unit in the last or any previous war.

Fighting in Italy and France, the 100th and 442d became famed as the "Purple Heart Regiment." They were in 7 major campaigns, suffering 9,486 casualties, or 314 percent of their original strength.

The unit received 18,143 individual decorations and medals and 7 Presidential distinguished unit citations.

Pacific Service Revealed

In the Pacific, in the war against the land of their ancestry, thousands of Nisei Americans served with equal distinction. For security reasons, little publicity has been given to the activities of these Japanese-Americans against the Japanese enemy.

Today, however, it is known that Gen. Charles A. Willoughby, chief of staff for intelligence under Gen. Douglas MacArthur, credited the Nisei in the Pacific, who served mainly as combat intelligence troops, with shortening by many months the war against Japan. To them, General Willoughby attributed the savings of untold thousands of casualties and billions of dollars.

In the occupation of Japan, additional thousands of Nisei were called upon to serve as the eyes and ears of the occupation, in the role of interpreters and translators and administrators.

While this occupation duty did not have the color or the drama of active combat service, the work of the Japanese-Americans contributed in great measure to the unprecedented success of the American occupation in Japan and to the promotion of democratic principles and general good will toward the United States.

. . .

Record in Korea

More recently, on the battlefields of Korea, the men of Hawaii were again fighting and dying with their fellow Americans from the continental United States. As in World War II, Americans of Japanese ancestry carried their share of the load, for the records reveal that based upon population more than three times as many Japanese-Americans were wounded and killed in Korea than the national average.

Devotion and Sacrifice

In this record of devotion and sacrifice lies the answer to those who question the loyalty of the so-called Japanese population in Hawaii. They have purchased with their blood the right to be accepted as Americans individually and to have statehood extended to the Territory that gave them birth and imbued in them that spirit of liberty and freedom that inspired their wartime gallantry.

Japanese Americans and Politics

Because the Japanese comprise a third of the population in Hawaii, some fears have been expressed that Japanese Americans will vote as a bloc, once Hawaii becomes a State, and thus control the political destiny of the islands.

A quick look at Nisei participation in Hawaiian politics will dispel this fear and myth of bloc voting.

In Hawaii, as on the mainland, Japanese Americans are active in both political parties. In Hawaii they enjoy positions of influence in both parties; they have been elected and appointed to local and Territorial offices.

In the last election, and prior thereto, it was not uncommon to find Japanese Americans vying with each other as representatives of the Republican and Democratic Parties for the same post, or to find a Japanese American representing a predominantly non-Japanese district, or to find a non-Japanese representing an overwhelmingly Japanese area.

Among the Hawaiian Japanese Americans, as with any other group in the United States, party politics and voting are based upon the same factors of daily living and economic interests which motivate any other people to vote for the candidates of one party in preference to another.

. . .

Attitude of Nisei in Hawaii on Statehood

The overwhelming sentiment among Japanese Americans, as among the entire population, is for statehood. Before the war, the margin of Hawaiians favoring statehood was more than 3 to 1. Among the Nisei, the proportions were even more lopsided. And it is greater today.

The desire for equal status is the understandable spirit which motivates those who urge statehood.

When the Congress enacted the Immigration and Nationality Act of 1952, in effect, it lifted the legislative mark of inferiority from the Japanese people, by admitting them to citizenship through naturalization and extending to Japan, their ancestral homeland, immigration quotas.

That act was hailed in Hawaii as an indication of the acceptance of the Japanese as individuals by their own government.

In the last 4 years, 2 Japanese American attorneys were nominated and confirmed for the Federal judiciary, Ben Tashiro as judge of a district court, and Masaji Marumoto as an associate justice of the Territorial supreme court.

This means that in the judgment of the executive who nominated them and of the Judiciary Committee and the Senate that confirmed their appointments, Japanese Americans are qualified as individuals for even the most important responsibilities of citizenship in a growing democracy.

Remaining Step

Statehood is the remaining step in that progress for equality of status. Statehood will mean, not only for those of Japanese origin, but also for every American in Hawaii, acceptance as equal partners in the United States to which they have contributed so much and asked so little.

In 1950 the citizens of Hawaii held a constitutional convention and drafted a State constitution that could well serve as a model document for many States and governments. This action on their part shows their clear willingness to assume the responsibilities of being an active and integral part of the Union.

At the moment, they feel like the stepchild who is almost a member of the family. Their citizens feel their second-class status keenly, for they appreciate the fact that though their taxation without representation may not be tyranny, in the revolutionary sense of 1776, it does represent, nevertheless, a lack of appreciation for their capabilities and desires on the part of their Government which at times seems far more removed than by distance alone and which sometimes seems to be more solicitous and responsive to the requests of foreign nations.

Race Should Not Be an Issue

In spite of all this testimony, however, as a matter of principle, the racial composition of the Territorial population should be of no consequence in this matter, the fact that certain Asian peoples constitute the bulk of the peoples of Hawaii should neither be an argument for or against statehood. The fundamental question involves not the races of people who reside in Hawaii, but the kind of thinking and living they indulge in as citizens of that Territory.

On this basis, there can be no question that Hawaii's mixed population qualifies as American, as United States-minded, as an integral part of this Nation and Government.

Though Hawaii may be noncontiguous geographically, ideologically and sentimentally they are part and parcel of the continental mainland.

The only reason that JACL felt compelled to comment on the so-called Japanese of Hawaii is to demonstrate the innate Americanism of this significant group and to illustrate that they, as well as every other racial strain in Hawaii, are ready and eager for statehood.

. . .

Mr. Masaoka. . . . To the citizens of Hawaii, statehood is a kind of recognition of the many long years they have put in as public pupils of the democratic, American way. They think that they—and I agree with them—are entitled to graduate now summa cum laude, because they have made contributions to America equal to or greater than that of any other State.

They have given in the way of taxes and they have given in terms of contributions in industry, they have given in terms of blood, and, when they have met every standard by which other States have been admitted into statehood, it becomes difficult for them to understand any reason why, after all these years, they should continue to be denied what they consider to be their right and their privilege as fellow Americans.

Mr. Pillion. I think the record ought to show here that never during any of our hearings has there been any statement made derogatory to the loyalty of the Americans of Japanese ancestry. I think the record ought to show that. There is no issue here or question of loyalty of these people.

CHAPTER ELEVEN

The Romantic Revolution

KAZUHARU Hamasaki arrived in Honolulu on a balmy summer day with the photographs of ninety-four Japanese women. He came from Hiroshima, innocently enough, to pair the anxious females with proper and decent husbands from among Hawaii's Japanese population. Armed with his photographic bevy of *femmes fatales,* confident that an honorable tradition would be enthusiastically perpetuated among lonely Japanese bachelors, the matchmaker from Hiroshima also carried with him an array of introductory letters, extolling ideal virtues and describing ideal mates:

> I'd like a he-man aged 40–45.
>
> I don't mind a man who drinks a little sake or a little beer. But I do not want a drunkard.
>
> I have no police record.

Their photographs revealed the diversity of Japanese feminine beauty—from the pedestrian to the demure to the stunning. Their ages ranged from a youthful eighteen to a mature forty, though most of the women had wisely neglected to reveal their ages. Among them were an Osaka restaurant owner, a college-educated hospital secretary, and a divorcee who had graduated from a Taiwan high school and served as a hotel cashier in Hiroshima.

But despite the appeal of these ladies, the likely opportunity of obtaining a good wife, few Island Japanese were to respond to the marriage proposals. The Hiroshima matchmaker would, in the end, return to Japan sadly disappointed and bewildered. His scheme of finding Japanese brides for Japanese men in Hawaii would be a farcical failure—a joke to be played up by the media. The failure, he would no doubt have to conclude, could only be blamed on his timing. After all, 1966 was a very poor year for the "picture-bride" business.

"It's very interesting," commented Dr. Yukiko Kimura on the ninety-four eager picture brides, vintage 1966. "But, my opinion is that the Nisei in this generation won't respond to this sort of proposal. They're Americanized now, and they want to choose their own mates."

"The idea of picture brides," added the editor of the *Hawaii Hochi,* "is out of date."[1]

Indeed, the picture-bride phenomenon, of overseas arranged marriages with the use of exchanged photographs, had not occurred in the Islands since the 1924 Oriental Exclusion Act outlawed such practices. Since that time, it had naturally been assumed that the aspiring young Japanese male looking for a female companion would independently find one among the local population. Exchanging photographs through a marriage broker so as to wed someone you had never met was a traditional custom unsavory and irrelevant to the Hawaiianized Nisei.

Actually, though, the picture bride project stemmed from a lighthearted comment by a Hawaiian-born Nisei, James Nishi. Nishi was a member of the Hiroshima Kenjin-kai, a community organization of Japanese immigrants and their descendants who originated from Hiroshima *ken,* or prefecture. In 1965, four Hiroshima beauty queens, under the sponsorship of the Hiroshima Kenjin-kai, had visited Honolulu, turning quite a few Nisei heads. Several of the Nisei were so impressed with the attractive girls that they made ardorous marriage proposals, but to no avail. The beauty queens explained in their graceful declinations of marriage that wives in Hawaii not only had to perform domestic chores but worked outside of the home. Being from Japan, their command of English was certainly too inadequate to find suitable employment in Hawaii.

Although the beauty queens returned to Japan unwed, Nishi told a Hiroshima official that some Nisei men, especially older bachelors, might be inclined to favor a marriage with a Japanese bride—they had certain attributes of feminine grace, beauty, and submissiveness which made for excellent wives. Accordingly, an advertisement was placed in several newspapers in Hiroshima requesting picture brides for Hawaiian Nisei. The letters and photographs came in from all parts of Japan, revealing the resiliency of traditional customs and attitudes.

But Island Japanese males, on the whole, simply preferred Island Japanese females whom they met in person, not the eager picture brides of Japan. Very few Nisei were anxious to obtain a Japanese wife through a method which smacked of loveless arranged marriage, an interesting but archaic behavior of the past.

"I don't think it's so good," commented an Island Japanese on the idea of picture brides from Japan. "Plenty girls in Hawaii. Better marry local girl."[2]

Though Mr. Nishi had hope that the business could be covered "quietly," the phenomenon of picture brides in 1966 was given lively media coverage. The *Honolulu Star-Bulletin* ran photographs of thirty girls with accompanying highlights of their introductory letters. Frustrated and angry, Nishi finally terminated the whole comical episode with a short but effective resignation. He had agreed to follow through on the project only if it were done discreetly. "After all," he explained to the local female population, "I live here, and I don't want our local women . . . to become angry with me."

> I'm through. I've already had it. I'm no longer interested in this plan.
>
> If a Nisei or anyone else wants to marry a Japanese woman, let him go to Japan to meet her. Let's not consider the Japanese woman like we do a piece of merchandise.[3]

To be sure, one outcome of the picture-bride revival was the realization that as the Nisei generation were contributing to the development of a modern Hawaii, as political and economic revolutions opened new social opportunities, they had also undergone profound changes in their cultural lifestyle. The family, the peer group, the traditional values and beliefs were continually being affected by the evolution of an urban Island society. No alterations within the Japanese community, though, were to be so dramatic or so consequential for the Nisei as their evolving sex roles. In the world of the Issei, the female had been relegated to a secondary status beneath the male. The patriarch, though enervated by the unsettling conditions of Hawaiian life, had attempted to maintain an authority over the *ie,* the extended family. But with social mobility, a rising standard of living, and education, the birth rate in the Japanese community had been curtailed. The emphasis within the family narrowed on the husband–wife relationship, facilitating the nuclearization of the extended *ie* and subsequently elevating the female to an increasingly egalitarian status. The war had introduced the female to the workaday world, creating employment in offices, schoolrooms, and factories. As a breadwinner, the female gained new respect within the family, altering her traditional secondary role. In a 1950 survey of single women at a Honolulu business college, nearly 90 percent of the respondents said they intended to work after they were married and 93 percent of the males agreed that they would expect their wives to work:

> Is chivalry dead? "Not at all," protests one young man. "Housework is much harder physically, and less interesting than office work. Besides, my wife will get paid for her job and I'll help her with the housekeeping. Is that bad?"
>
> "If both husband and wife are working," said one young man, "it gives them a better start toward getting the things they want in life."
>
> Said a young lady, a bride of six months, "As soon as I finish my business course I'm going right to work. When I took my marriage vows I promised to help my husband in every way I could. When we have my salary with which to pay the rent and buy the food, my husband can quit his job and start his own business."[4]

And the war had also introduced the Japanese female to the once-unspeakable phenomenon of interracial dating and marriage. With the enormous number of single *haole* males in the Islands looking for female companionship and the depletion of local males by their service in the armed forces, many local girls discovered that more men than they could handle vied for their attention. Though many *haole* soldiers stationed in Hawaii during the war probably found some Japanese females unapproachable and even snobbish, it was obviously not the case for the entire female population. As one *haole* soldier advised his mainland comrades in a letter to a local newspaper:

> To those who are griping about the aloofness and frigidity of the Honolulu girls: Many of you come over here with the idea that these girls are barbarians. You barge into a cafe and, thinking that you have a lot of oomph, you try your line on the waitress, expecting to snow her under, and you often get coarse and vulgar.
>
> . . . Try being nice to these girls and they will be nice to you. Politeness doesn't cost anything and it pays big dividends![5]

For some *haole* soldiers the dividends were evidently handsome indeed, for the war accelerated the Japanese female outmarriage rate. While total outmarriages of Japanese females between 1939 and 1940 had been only 8.1 percent, by 1944 the annual rate had increased to 21.1 percent.[6] The broadening social roles of the female, coupled with the declining size of the family and increased intermarriage, changed the familial expectations of the Nisei female. And it also gave birth to a "romantic revolution" within the Japanese community.

In the extended *ie,* love was displaced throughout the kinship and community—the emotional attachment to the husband or wife could qualitatively be no greater than between offspring or relatives so as to maintain social harmony and obligation. In the nuclear family, though, love between mates was interpreted as sexual romance. The blissful American dream of romantic love assumed that the man and woman would meet, fall in love, marry, and raise a family.

The romanticization of the Nisei female and male was a sharp turn from the attitudes of their Issei parents. To fall in love and choose your own mate was now a Nisei liberty which arranged marriages or picture-bride practices largely ignored. Indeed, the development of romance as a theme in Nisei attitudes corresponds with the greater expression of female self-determinism and structural changes in familial roles and relationships.

In the post-World War II magazine, *Nisei in Hawaii and the Pacific,* the themes of romance and love were frequently used in story formats and in editorial advice to the newlywed Nisei. An early example of a very "un-Japanese" expression of female sexual freedom was a soap-opera short story entitled "Love among the Pineapples."[7] In this heart-wrenching romance between two Dole pineapple cannery workers, Ellen and John, the principal lovers are attracted to each other, over the pineapple conveyor belts, by "love at first sight." Though the "fiery" and "glamorous Filipino," Virginia, tries to steal John's heart, he remains faithful to his demure Japanese girlfriend, Ellen. With such electric attraction one would expect more to develop between the lovers—but the summer ends and they must return to school. A pledge of love is made, but left unrequited. Unfortunately, by the time school begins, the romance has cooled, and pineapple love has faded. Romance, the Nisei female brazenly learns, need not always be consummated in marriage.

The romantic Nisei female was dramatized in another story as the dreamy, bubbly, ever-happy wife whose marriage is a fairy tale of love. "Romance Is a Lot of Little Things,"[8] written anonymously by "Kathryn," is a living testament of Japanese American romance and the struggle of the female to find a measure of self-respect as an individual. The wife, often escaping into idyllic scenes of beach shacks, moonlit nights, and swaying palm trees, realizes that marriage must be a perpetual affair of the heart as it had been during courtship. The woman's responsibility is to look pretty, pamper the husband, and smooth over marital difficulties with a kiss and a sigh. "Marriage," Kathryn stresses, "really can be a romantic affair, with only a slight mutual effort, that what we call *affaire-de-coeur* could still exist even after a couple has passed the oomphie-doomphie stage."

Silly in its extreme, illustrative of the male notion of the prettified wife, this romantic attitude of the maturing Nisei female was nonetheless the first stage in the emancipation of her traditionally perceived role. The assimilating nuclear family could have little place for marriages built on convenience or family arrangement—the emotional feelings of the female had to be taken into account. Kathryn went so far as to suggest that where love in marriages does not exist, the couple should have a "magistrate cut off their unfortunate nuptial tie." Indeed, young girls today, wrote a Nisei mother in the 1950s, are different from the early Issei woman. "It is she who is going to decide whom she will marry, whether mom likes her idea or not. Rare the girl who will concede without objection to any arrangement which does not suit her ideology."[9]

In traditional Japanese culture, the choice of a mate for a young girl was usually arranged by the family. In Hawaii, arranged marriages, through the efforts of a middleman or marriage go-between, were called *shimpai*. The *shimpai* marriage was an outgrowth of the Japanese tradition of *baishaku-kekkon*, the *nakodo* system or the *miai* marriage:

> In this type of marriage the family of a boy sends a *Nakodo* or go-between to propose marriage to the family of a girl they would like for a daughter-in-law. The *Nakodo* plays the essential role of Cupid and first makes the proposal (to the family). If the families concerned are happy about the deal, the *Nakodo* then arranges the *Miai* or boy-meets-girl scene, which is more a family-meets-family time. This *Miai* was formerly arranged at a picnic, the theater or at the *Nakodo*'s house. Today it is usually set in a restaurant or tea shop.
>
> If the *Miai* is successful, the next step is the *Yuino* or exchange of presents which includes money, clothes and certain kinds of fish. This

Yuino corresponds to the engagement party and marks the wedding plans as final.[10]

For the Issei, the arranged marriage, achieved either through picture exchange or in person, was an unquestioned cultural practice. Among the Nisei, especially the older rural generation and the Kibei, *shimpai* marriages were also occasionally practiced. But clearly the romantic impetus was gaining ground with the assimilating Nisei:

> One does not often see the "go-between" bustling about looking for a prospective husband or wife. And at weddings they form only an atmosphere—a touch of solemnity. They are only a necessary feature to appease the family's desire for a symbol of the old authority and sanctions. The role of the go-between, once an essential part in the formation of a new family, is waning. Romantic love and courtship is gaining ground. Marriage is fast becoming a relationship between the two individuals concerned.[11]

Although the go-between was recognized as a continued feature of Nisei marriage practice in pre-World War II rural areas such as Kona,[12] the modernizing Nisei generally looked askance at arranged marriages and the use of go-betweens. However, to appease their parents, many Nisei allowed the go-between to play a perfunctory role in their marriage arrangements. Many Nisei couples, after falling in love and becoming engaged, often went through the *baishakunin* (go-between) so that the wishes of the parents might be placated.[13]

Eventually, though, such filial gestures would cease to have any use for the female who felt her position in the family to be equal and independent. A short story—"Yasuko Rebels"[14]—by Clara Kubojiri, appearing in a 1954 issue of *Nisei in Hawaii and the Pacific,* deals with this theme of the Nisei woman breaking out of the restrictions of her female role. When Yasuko, a young girl in rural Hawaii, discovers that a go-between is going to arrange her marriage, she is furious. She had been dreaming of falling in love, being whisked away to faraway lands, her feminine beauty accentuated by beautiful clothes and makeup. Now her illusions are shattered by the limitations of her family environment, the submissiveness she must display as a good Japanese girl. "To have herself married away in this unromantic, old fashioned 'shimpai' method was not only disappointing, but insulting, she thought. She did not want to marry that stranger. He was not impressive in any way."

So Yasuko rebels; she refuses to comply with her family's wishes.

Of course, her parents berate her for her impropriety and foolishness. She will be disowned unless she obeys her parents. Fortunately for Yasuko, the boy to whom she is betrothed is not without his own attractive qualities. In the world of romantic myth, conflict is resolved with the realization that the boy might possibly become the object of Yasuko's love. The confrontation of the independent female and family control is cleverly diverted by accidental circumstance.

Yasuko's rebellion as a Japanese woman, limited and diverted as it was, illustrated the attitude of the young assimilated Nisei girl—self-determination in love and romance in marriage were inviolable values. And the liberalization of Japanese femininity extended from the selection of the mate to the wedding ceremony, the reception, and the marriage itself. The wedding celebration in the Japanese community had always been a family affair—a means to gather the kinship and peer group for revelry and reconfirmation of solidarity. The guest list was carefully arranged to fulfill reciprocal obligations and great care was given to include all the important relatives and friends. As a matchmaker in Kona noted in 1936, the wedding reception was an elaborate, gala event:

> These folks must have a big feast to feel that it is a wedding, otherwise, they think that something is missing. They like to eat and drink and make merry. They make it an elaborate affair in order to impress upon the couple that it is the most important event in their lives. This puts them under a moral obligation to make good and forgive each other's petty grievances.[15]

Increasingly, though, the Nisei couple sought to express an independence in the nature of wedding ceremonies and receptions. While maintaining in most cases the familial aspects of the gala reception, the young couple sought to include more diverse tastes in the ceremony. After the war, Christian weddings had a brief boom among Nisei. The bride wore a Westernized gown instead of a kimono. Rings, in a Christian style, were exchanged after the nuptial vows. The reception itself lost some of the flavor of Japanese-style. "Who would have thought of serving *kalua* and *poi* with *sushi* and *sashimi*?" queried one Nisei who in the brief span of seven years had witnessed, within her own family, weddings ranging from the traditional to the multicultural.[16]

Indeed, the transformation of the wedding reception under the direction of the Nisei couple was an outcome of the idealization of the nuclear family and the liberalization of female roles. The changes occurring at the reception were generated by a couple who were assuming control over the first stage of their married lives. That the couple should arrange the wedding, a job formerly filled by the go-between, demonstrated that the integrity of the nuclear family would to a degree be protected. And in addition, the female, who would most likely play the major role in designing the wedding, would have the respect and freedom to make her own decisions, though not without family interference and conflict:

> My father let us have our way about most of the things, but he was fussy about the reception. One night at dinner time without consulting me about the kind of reception we were going to have, he instructed my mother and my sisters to make sushi, roast turkey, salad, etc., for my reception. I promptly told him that our reception was all planned and that we were having sandwiches, punch and cookies because that was all we could afford and besides we couldn't serve anything elaborate for a 2:00 P.M. reception. He snapped at me and said, "You can't invite people and serve them just that. People will talk." I told him, "Some people might but it didn't matter because it was accepted according to American custom. Besides, we are going to finance the wedding, not you, and we can't afford an elaborate reception." That really made him furious; he said, "What's so good about American style!" By that time I was so upset that I grabbed my plate and walked away from the table in a fury.[17]

But in spite of the conflict, the assertive position of the Nisei female as an equal partner was enhanced through the courting and wedding stages. And as could be expected, the equality of the female would extend into the husband–wife relationship—the attitude that the wife and husband are fifty-fifty partners in the marriage enterprise would gain prevalence in the assimilated Japanese family.

Of course, the defunct patriarch in the Issei and Nisei family could not tolerate a total subversion of his dominance. And assimilated American society, though promoting notions of independence and freedom for the female, saw the woman as a sweet, domesticated housewife. Marriage for the Nisei woman, though spiced with notions of "fifty-fifty-ness," would generally leave her in a subservient role, catering to the husband, tending the house, and forgetting for the moment a good measure of her own self-worth.

Again, *Nisei in Hawaii and the Pacific* presented a Nisei husband–wife relationship characterized by male dominance. Recognizing that the female in Hawaii not only served as a wife but as an economic breadwinner, many articles in giving advice to the young wife stressed her ever-demanding domestic role. Go to work; pursue an equal economic role within the relationship. But remember your most important function is to please the male—to pamper, comfort, encourage, and protect. One article stressed:

> A wife should be a mother, big sister, and sometimes a baby to her husband. She should pamper him and yet be pampered by him in turn. Thus, slowly, she can learn his habits, likes and dislikes in their daily living.[18]

A wife is not considered to be an ornament, an image of uncompromising adoration. She is a functional unit who comprehends her role and performs accordingly:

> The day of ornamental brides, whose gossamer qualities alone made a man go cuckoo are *pau* [finished]. Today's hubby wants a working partner who can darn his socks by the fireside, who can cook at least one decent meal that he can enjoy when he comes back from work all tired out. He is looking out for a lifetime partner who does not pester him with eternal demands for spending money, who knows the meaning of thrift and can tell you offhand today's ceiling price on carrots and onions.[19]

Even sexually, the Nisei wife must remember that striving for "equality" in marriage can be a trying and disappointing exercise. The young wife was urged not to read books on sex and believe she was capable of sexual satisfaction. Take the tragic case of Mrs. Ruth G. who innocently read a sex manual, a "how-to-do-it" book for the married couple:

> The book contained many eloquent descriptions of sexual activity. Ruth began to compare her own tranquil sex life with the frantic, abandoned ecstasy on the pages before her. Suddenly she was discontent.
>
> "Doctor," she asked me, "is something wrong? I don't know anything about such ecstasy. Why do I fall so short of normal? Am I at fault or is it my husband?"
>
> A woman at peace with herself and her husband had been jolted into doubt and insecurity. Why? Because she tried to mold her expectations not to her own capacity but to someone else's experiences. I urged her to forget what she had read.[20]

Indeed the advice given Mrs. G. and other easily beguiled wives was explicit: Do not be tempted by fraudulent claims that every woman can experience orgasms—for many women such sexual ecstasy is impossible to attain:

> It was not easy to reassure Mrs. G. It is not easy to reassure all the wives who have been lured by books into expecting, and at times demanding, what is for them impossible.[21]

Paradoxically, though, even as the Nisei woman was being influenced by advice columns that admonished the sexually curious female or the selfish wife to serve her husband, she was ideally convinced that the best marriage was one of an "equal" partnership. Romance, freedom from the old ways of the homeland, had liberated her, supposedly, to a new social position:

> Nisei brides would like to be treated like all modern brides in America. They do not feel that they could play the role of subservient and docile wife who is completely under the domination of her husband that seems to have been the lot of old-fashioned Japanese brides. The Nisei bride of today expects marriage on a fifty-fifty basis, no more and no less.[22]

And for many Nisei women, these American ideals of freedom in the marital relationship reached a pitch of absoluteness:

> My parents' ideas on the freedom of women, the independence of children, are entirely different from mine. They make their daughters obey them, and find the husbands and wives for their children and force them to marry. I believe in the absolute freedom of women, to go with whom they please, and wherever they want.[23]

This paradoxical illusion of "freedom and equality" measured against domesticated reality instilled in many Nisei females a frustrated drive for self-expression and self-worth within the marriage. Her humanness, her exposure to education, travel, and media, motivated her to fulfill her own potentials, to be treated with respect and consideration. Her environment, her peers, her social milieu idealized her freedom and equality to pursue her potentialities, her self-worth. But the role restrictions—being a wife, a mother—and the frequent expectations of her semi-patriarchal mate, not always imbued with an overgenerous attitude of "freedom," inhibited her personal development. She was expected on the one hand to be "free" to work, to pursue a secretarial or teaching career. But she must always be a wife in the traditional sense, serving the husband, protecting the children, cooking the meals, responding to the desires of the family. Romance, equality, illusions, and delusions did not minimize the fact that she was a domestic.

Not surprisingly, therefore, only with rare exception did the female Nisei publicly excel beyond the home. Although providing the primary concentration of employed females in private households, clerical, and saleswork occupations, the Nisei did not generally win individual recognition for her efforts. Homemaker, secretary, or clerk, the Nisei female continued to remain domiciled, though forces of nuclearization and romanticization had liberated her traditional roles.

Exceptions occurred. Most outstandingly, Representative Patsy Mink, a Japanese female, rose to political prominence in the 1960s and '70s as one of Hawaii's two United States Representatives to Congress. Representative Mink in 1962 had been part of the triumphant coalition of Democrats who had captured the key political roles of the new fiftieth state. Daniel Inouye was elected as United States Senator, Spark Matsunaga and Mink as U.S. Representatives, and John Burns as governor of Hawaii. The fulfillment of political ambitions stemming from the 1954 revolution was complete, and symbolically the Japanese female had participated in the process. An outspoken liberal, Representative Mink was in her career to defy the limitations of traditional roles, to exercise an independence and social equality usually not realized by the Nisei female.

Another extraordinary Japanese female to rise in Island prominence was Bishop Tatsusho Hirai. Though an immigrant to Hawaii and not a Nisei, the ministry of Bishop Hirai was to exemplify the expanding possibilities of the female role in Hawaii and the contribution of women's intelligence and drive to the life of the community.

Bishop Hirai arrived in Hawaii from Japan in 1941 and subsequently became a "cult hero" among the immigrant Issei population. Follower of the Tōdaiji sect in Japan, Bishop Hirai established that sect's first overseas mission in Hawaii. The matrix upon which her ministry was based was the reliance on elaborate ritual, the ancient beliefs in supernatural spirits, and the "healing power." Living in luxury, yet open and loving with her followers, she became, in many eyes, the *Ikigami*—the Living Goddess.

In the *Tōdaiji of Hawaii* a pamphlet published in 1956,[24] Bishop Hirai recalled her early life which led to her priestesshood and confronted many of the issues which had been used to discredit her style of spiritual healing. Her early life was marked with suffering and shame as a result of an early divorce. In a nation where divorce was looked upon as inexcusable, she turned to a monastic life with the Tōdaiji sect. Rising early, showering in cold water, fasting for days and meditating in cold weather, Bishop Hirai pursued an ascetic existence which tended to isolate human emotions and insights. The attention turned inward, the psyche searched out God and visions, and an *Ikigami* was born. As a Living Goddess, one of Bishop Hirai's roles was spiritual healing, a power which she felt stemmed not from magical forces but from sound psychosomatic principles. Most physical disorders, she reasoned, emanated from emotional tensions. So "by inculcating religion into one's self, one can obtain a peace of mind, and by developing a pure and secure faith he is able to control his emotional disorder."

Although not a typical Nisei female, Bishop Hirai represented, as did Representative Mink, the nontraditional opportunities opening for the Japanese female in Hawaii. Her self-image, her expectations and ambitions were evolving into new patterns wholly alien to those of her immigrant mother. And the effects of these new evolving sex roles and familial relationships were to have their greatest repercussions on the Sansei, the offspring of the Nisei marriage.

NOTES

1. Quoted in "Picture Bride Idea Is Almost Passe," *Honolulu Star-Bulletin,* August 11, 1966, p. A–1A:1.
2. "Picture Bride Idea is Almost Passe," p. A–1A:1.
3. "Suggestor Bows Out of Japan Brides Picture," *Honolulu Star-Bulletin,* August 20, 1966, p. A–2:1.
4. "Should Wives Hold Jobs?" *Nisei in Hawaii and the Pacific,* v. 10, no. 2 (1956), pp. 9, 12.
5. *Honolulu Star-Bulletin,* January 18, 1943, 4:3.
6. Otomi Inamine, Phyllis Kon, Yan Quai Lau, and Marjorie Okamoto, "The Effect of War on Interracial Marriage in Hawaii," *Social Process in Hawaii,* v. 9–10 (1945), p. 105.
7. Seiko Ogai, "Love Among the Pineapples," *Nisei in Hawaii and the Pacific,* v. 1, no. 2 (Summer 1956), pp. 8, 10.
8. "Kathryn," "Romance Is A Lot of Little Things," *Nisei in Hawaii and the Pacific,* (Autumn 1947), pp. 6–7.
9. Kathryn Yumeko Koi, "When Daughter Gets a Beau," *Nisei in Hawaii and the Pacific,* v. 10, no. 2 (Summer 1956), p. 1.
10. Clara Kubojiri, "Shimpai Marriage—An Out-dated Custom?" *Nisei in Hawaii and the Pacific,* v. 9, no. 2 (June 1955), p. 4.
11. Amy Akinaka, "Types of Japanese Marriages in Hawaii," *Social Process in Hawaii,* v. 1 (May 1935), p. 33.

12. Shiku Ogura, "Familial Survivals in Rural Hawaii," *Social Process in Hawaii,* v. 2 (May 1936), pp. 43–5.

13. Tamiko Yamamoto, "Trends in Marriage Practices Among the Nisei in Hawaii," *What People in Hawaii are Saying and Doing: Report No. 21,* Hawaii Social Research Laboratory, University of Hawaii, 1952, p. 9.

14. Clara Kubojiri, "Yasuko Rebels," *Nisei in Hawaii and the Pacific,* June 1954, pp. 10–1, 16, 18, 20.

15. Ogura, p. 45.

16. Chiyo Gushiken, "Wedding Ceremonies: 1938–1945," *Social Process in Hawaii,* v. 12 (August 1948), p. 10.

17. Yamamoto, p. 10.

18. "So You Want to Get Married," *Nisei in Hawaii and the Pacific,* v. 7, no. 2 (June 1953), p. 19.

19. "Marriage," *Nisei in Hawaii and the Pacific,* v. 2, no. 2 (Summer 1948), p. 11.

20. Lena Levine, "For A Better Marriage," *Nisei in Hawaii and the Pacific,* v. 6, no. 2 (June 1952), p. 8.

21. Levine, p. 8.

22. "The Editor's Desk," *Nisei in Hawaii and the Pacific,* v. 6, no. 2 (June 1952), p. 12.

23. Jitsuichi Masuoka, "Changing Moral Bases of the Japanese Family in Hawaii," *Sociology and Social Research,* v. 21, no. 2 (November/December 1936), p. 168.

24. Bishop Tatsusho Hirai, "I Owe Most of What I Am Today to My Mother," *Tōdaiji of Hawaii,* Pub. in 1956, pp. 1–5, 24–8.

Romance Is a Lot of Little Things

"KATHRYN"

I glanced toward John, comfortably huddled up in his easy chair, reading the latest dope on local sports. The lapping of the waves came drifting in from the lanai; for ever so long, it seemed to me, I had lulled myself to sleep with the sound of the waves slapping ceaselessly on the white sand. Tonight was moonlight, such a beautiful moonlight as only blesses tourist-famed Waikiki beach. My heart seemed to dance within me as I recalled what happy days John and I spent together in this tiny little shack by the beach we called home.

My memory took me back ten years into the dim past; sent me scurrying to the side of Margie who had taken me into her confidence the very day I started working for A—— Company as a clerk-typist. There were many things she taught me, about work and the people around me. Above all else, she filled my little mental cubby-hole with a chuck-full of information on men and how to get along with them, or shall I say, "kid them along," to use Margie's own vernacular. Some of the things she told me I just laughed off; some, I took to heart.

For instance; the subject of how to get along with hubby after wedding bells have pealed and the excitement is all over. John, like most men who adore their little woman, remembered our wedding date to a dot. That is, for the first couple of years at least. Then,

In *Nisei in Hawaii and the Pacific,* Autumn, 1947, pp. 6–7.

what with business interests and club activities taking up so much of his time, he forgot once, then (oh shucks) twice and so on, until by the fifth year I had to give him little hints; remembering Margie's advice, I never flared up. Men might forget wedding dates; that does not mean, however, that they have stopped loving you. I would have myself all made up nicely in the morning, and as certain as the delicate lovebirds would sing each morning on the twig facing our bedroom window, John would pop up with the remark, "Kathleen, you're as charming as a ripe peach this morning. What's up?" And, of course, my "Guess what," would instantly remind him of a date which to a woman is more important than the date of the battle of Sevastopol. John has always liked the way I hinted things nicely to him this way, instead of bringing down hell and heaven on him for forgetting our wedding date. If most men are like John, girls, take my advice, which is really a legacy from my prexy, Margie.

Other maxims which Margie handed down to me as being essential to a happy married life: 1) Don't appear at breakfast looking like a fine specimen of a dilapidated scarecrow; 2) Don't send off hubby to work growling; nine chances out of ten he will continue growling all day long at his office, and wherever and whomever he calls on; 3) When out at parties or visiting friends, don't contradict everything your man says, or to make him appear before his friends as though he were a numbskull, a moron; there are so many nice things you could say or do while attending socials with him; 4) Some men might like the clinging-vine type of a woman, but that usually lasts only during the courting days. A man usually tires of a woman who is continually hanging on to his shirttails for this and for that which in his mind even a child can perform without any effort.

Before I met John, I was constantly visiting Margie's home. Through these visits I learned that marriage really can be a romantic affair, with only a slight mutual effort, that what we call *affaire-de-coeur* could still exist even after a couple has passed the oomphie-doomphie stage.

They say a man marries for the sake of the woman; the woman for the sake of love. As a corollary, when a woman marries she gives everything; to a man marriage does not seem as serious as a matter of life and death affair. It seems that woman has a bigger stake in matrimony. Naturally, little things that concern her marital bliss mean a lot to her. A man can really make her life so much happier if he will only pay little attentions to her, even after wrinkles have started to appear on her once peaches and roses face. Margie always told me it meant more than all the money her hubby made to have him compliment her on her nice hair-do, or the new gown she just received from her dressmaker, or every now and then eat with gusto as proof or approval of what a good cook she is. There are men, and sometimes too many, whose only claim to existence is to lambast everything about the missus. The shortest cut to heaven for such cat-and-dog existence is to have magistrate cut off their unfortunate nuptial tie faster than he can handle the two-bit shears at home.

Yasuko Rebels

CLARA KUBOJIRI

A gleaming, black sedan drew up to an isolated farm house. It was a rural home typically Japanese with *geta* neatly lined on the porch. A hostile-looking poi dog had dashed out; he kept barking fiercely at the visitors. In the field not far away the family heard the dog and knew that someone had come to visit them.

"Okasan! Dare ka uchi kimashita." The sunbrowned, little girl shouted excitedly to her mother that someone had come to the house.

"So, na. Dare ka kita to mieru," the mother replied.

The barefooted boy threw down his hoe and started to leave. "Hey! Get back to work!" his big brother yelled.

"Somebody been come to da house! I go for see!" The younger boy called back, running away as fast as he could.

"Me, too!" his little sister yelled, and ran off toward home.

"Hey! Come back here!" their big brother shouted. But they were both gone. He swore angrily.

The old man, who was the father, had taken a pouch from his pocket and was rolling a cigarette. *"Mo itte shimatta,"* he chuckled. *"Kodomo wa hayai na,"* he said, marvelling at the agility of youth. His wife agreed. Then she said it was about lunch time, so they picked up their tools and started home.

In *Nisei in Hawaii and the Pacific,* June, 1954, pp. 10–11, 16, 18, 20. Reprinted by permission of Clara Kubojiri.

All but Yasuko. She was their eldest daughter. Like the others she was brown from working in the sun. She was a lovely girl and looked feminine even in the masculine clothes that she was wearing.

"Oi! Yasuki, kaero!" the old man called to her. Let's go home!

"Olai," replied the girl, awakening from her daydream. She picked up her hoe and followed the rest of her family. She did not hurry. She just plodded slowly home. She was so young, yet so weary! 'Such a miserable life for a girl,' she thought.

Yasuko looked at her hands. They were dirty, and her fingernails were black. She was young, but her hands were calloused and rough. To work day in and day out, month after month, year in and year out . . . was there no brighter future for her, she wondered?

She sighed, and went back to her daydreaming. She imagined that she was somewhere in a faraway city, dressed like a fashion-page model, wearing flaming red nail polish on beautiful white hands, and looking radiantly lovely. She imagined she had met someone very handsome. He was in love with her, and they were going to get married.

"Hey, Yasuko! Okasan said come home quick!" Jane, her younger sister called. "The okyakusan like see you," she said, running up to her. "Okasan said wear your good dress."

Yasuko stopped. "Wear my good dress? What for? Who like see me?" she asked. She could think of no one in particular who would come to visit her. Curious and excited, she started to walk faster.

"I don't know who," her sister said. "But they sure get one nice car."

When Yasuko reached home, she saw two elderly men, an elderly lady, and a young man standing before the house. They were admiring the lovely flowers and commenting on the peace and quiet of the country. They were most properly dressed.

Yasuko's parents were apologizing humbly for their unsightly attire, and for the dilapidated condition of the house and yard—which were not all true. The yard was very well kept. Her mother kept sweeping her hand over her forehead although she had swept all stray hairs in place.

Yasuko hurried into the house through the back door. She did not want to be seen in her working clothes. Her old trousers were not only dirty, but had patches on the knees and seat.

She scrubbed her feet and hands with the laundry brush and soap. Then she went to her room and took out her best dress. It was a simple, homemade dress which she had sewed herself.

The guests had come into the living room. Through the crack in the door, Yasuko could see them, seated on cushions on the floor. They were all strangers whom she had never seen. She wondered who the young man with them could be.

He was sitting very properly on a cushion. He looked thirtyish. Maybe not that old, she reconsidered. He did not look up at all, but kept his eyes on the floor. Once in a while he took a deep breath, very slowly, and exhaled very carefully so that it was hardly noticed.

Smiling and bowing courteously, her mother excused herself from the group. She came to Yasuko's room. Her face changed to a nervous, impatient frown.

"Yasuko, hayaku shina sai! Okyakusan wa mina matte imasu!" She scolded in a whisper. The guests were waiting, go to the living room, she told Yasuko.

Being very bashful, Yasuko protested. But her mother became angry and told her to go into the living room at once. She obeyed. Yasuko could not understand why her mother should be so peeved. She was usually told to remain outside when they had guests. Now all of a sudden, she was told to go and join them.

Yasuko blushed as she sat down on the floor in the living room. Her mother came and sat next to her. To her surprise and embarrassment, the guests began to murmur praise of her. Yasuko again blushed, and sat there without looking up. She was much too embarrassed to know what to do.

Her mother, with most gracious humility, smiled and said, *"Ie, so dewa arimasen. Yasuko was tsumaranai ko desu."* Then, one of the guests asked her if she was twenty-three years old. She said she was. Ah! he said in Japanese. Twenty-three! What a beautiful age to be . . . like a flower in bloom. It is wonderful to be young and blooming as Yasuko is, he said, full of animation. But, he added sadly, like the flower, even a young girl's loveliness soon fades away. Ah yes, he sighed.

Yasuko's blush deepened. As she listened to the words, she understood the nature of their visit. "Shimpai!" That's what they called this kind of match marriage. That old man was the matchmaker. And that young man was no doubt the suitor!

Yasuko's embarrassment changed to indignation. To have herself married away in this unromantic, old fashioned "shimpai" method was not only disappointing, but insulting, she thought. She did not want to marry that stranger. He was not impressive in any way. Just dark-complexioned, probably from working in the fields.

The matchmaker continued in elegant Japanese. So, Yasuko

heard him say, because she is twenty-three and at the height of her youthful beauty she should take the opportunity to be married to this fine young man, son of Mr. and Mrs. Taketa.

Her parents entered into a very restrained discussion. Finally, they replied to the matchmaker saying that it was a great honor to receive his proposal, and that they were very happy. Then they turned to Yasuko and told her to speak for herself.

Yasuko was a very obedient girl by nature. And she realized that her parents wished her to marry the boy. But she refused to accept the proposal. Impulsively, without looking up, she replied, *"Ie, watashi wa mada yome suru ki ga arimasen."*

She heard everyone gasp in astonishment. She wondered if she had said the wrong thing. It was the truth. As an after thought, she bowed her head courteously and said, excusing herself, *"Gomen nasai."*

"Ale—ma!" her mother gasped.

"Yasuko, nani?" her father demanded.

Yasuko knew that her father was violently angry. *"Gomen nasai!"* she said again, and left the room as quickly as she could.

Jane, who had been behind the door, followed Yasuko to her room. "What that man said?" she asked, full of curiosity. "How come okasan and otosan look angry?"

"Nothing, nothing," Yasuko said, trying to chase Jane away.

But Jane kept pestering her. "What the old man said?" she asked.

"Nothing," Yasuko replied. "He just like I marry the boy."

"Ah!" Jane giggled. She flew out of the room to tell her brothers.

Yasuko sat down, and began to wonder what her mother and father would do to her after the guests were gone. She had never in her life disobeyed them so boldly. She had never dared. After a short while, Yasuko heard the guests depart. She prepared herself to meet her parents.

"Yasuko!" her father called. She did not go to him.

"Yasuko! *Honto ni hagaii ko!"* her mother cursed, as she came to Yasuko. *"Anna hazukashii koto hajimete!"* She had never been so humiliated in all her life.

"Yasuko!" her father called again. He sounded even more angry. "Yasuko," he said angrily. *"Anna yukoto kikanai nara uchi kara dete yuke!"*

Her father's threat to disown her frightened Yasuko. And yet, she felt irrepressibly rebellious. *"Dete iku!"* she cried, and stalked out of the house because she was ready to cry.

She went to her flower garden and absently began to pull the weeds which grew in her flower beds. She cried a great deal, and thought much. Her temper slowly burned away, and she felt sorry and afraid. She wished she could be back in the good graces of the family again.

But if she could not, she knew what she would do. She would pack her things and go. She would go anywhere. To the city, probably. She could work as a maid, couldn't she? Perhaps she would find someone she knew.

"Yasuko, come eat kau kau," Jane said. Yasuko was startled out of her thoughts.

"What?" she said.

"Okasan said you can come eat, if you like," Jane said. She looked at Yasuko, half in sympathy and half in curiosity. "You make okasan and otosan angry, no?" she said.

"Otosan very angry yet?" Yasuko asked.

Jane nodded. "Mmmmm. He said he no going let you eat in the house no more," Jane said.

Yasuko wiped the tears from her eyes. "I going away," she said miserably. "I going someplace far away." She blew her nose. "And I no care if otosan no let me eat here!"

Jane gasped. "Ah, Yasuko! No tell like that," she said. Then she said impatiently, "Come eat kau kau. All coming cold already."

"I'm not hungry!" Yasuko said. But she went to have her supper.

No one said anything. Her father was not around. And her mother had kept the food warm for her. Her brothers did not bother her at all, but acted as though nothing had happened.

And it continued that way for weeks. There remained an uncomfortable feeling in the house. Otosan never talked to Yasuko after that day. And she never approached him to apologize.

Yasuko kept telling herself that she would go away. But she delayed, and kept on delaying. Finally, she made up her mind to leave definitely the next week. She could no longer stay with the rest of the family. She felt that she was the cause of all the unhappiness.

Then one day a car again drove up to the house. Everyone was working in the garden except Yasuko. She had stayed at home to pack her clothes. She heard the dog barking and went out to see who had come. Then, she recognized him.

The young man in the car was the same one who had visited them before. Only this time he had come alone. Yasuko felt very embarrassed to see him because she was dressed in her unflattering home clothes. She scolded the dog. He stopped barking, and began to wag his tail.

The young man opened the door and came out of the car. He was wearing a nice *aloha*-shirt this time, and looking more casual. He smiled self-consciously at Yasuko. "Ah . . . hello," he said.

"Hello," Yasuko smiled, shyly.

"Ah . . . your mother folks at home?" he asked.

"No," Yasuko replied. "But I can go to call them."

"No, never mind," he said. There was an embarrassed silence. Then, he looked at the flowers in the yard and said, "You folks get nice flowers, no?" Yasuko said that they had only a few, although the azaleas were all in bloom. "I like flowers," the boy said.

"I love flowers, too," Yasuko said.

"Yeah?" the boy said. "You like flowers too? You like roses?" Yasuko told him that they were her favorite flowers. And it was true. She had been trying to grow some roses herself.

"Oh!" the boy said, as though he had just remembered something. He went back to the car. "Ah . . . here," he said. "This is for you." He handed her a gorgeous bunch of brilliant red roses.

No boy had ever courted Yasuko with flowers. It thrilled her with romance. "Ah, my!" she exclaimed. "My goodness! Oh, thanks, yeah!"

The boy beamed happily. "Ah . . . this too," he said, handing her a two-pound box of candies.

"For me?" Yasuko was almost afraid to ask if it really was for her. But when the boy nodded with a big smile, she accepted both the candy and the flowers. "Oh, thank you, thank you!" she said happily. "Ah . . . come inside," she invited.

Jane and her brother had heard the dog barking. When they came from the fields, they saw the black sedan.

"Hey! Same car!" her brother noted.

"They come for see Yasuko again," Jane said. "Go for call okasan," she told her brother.

"No, you go," her brother replied. He was more curious to meet the guests.

"No, you!" Jane argued. And when he refused to go, she ran toward the house. Her brother did the same.

When they got home, they saw Yasuko and the visitor in the living room. Yasuko was arranging the roses in a vase. She was blushing and smiling prettily. The visitor was admiring her. Jane sighted the box of candy on the table, and pointed it out to her brother.

"Hey, I like eat boy!" her brother whispered.

"Me, too," Jane said. "We go for ask," she suggested. Her brother hesitated only for a minute, and agreed with the idea. They both went and stood by the door and smiled shyly at the two young people. They weren't sure whether they would like the young man. But they certainly wanted some candy. Yasuko called them in.

Munching on the delicious candy, the children decided that the visitor was a nice fellow after all. They had a hunch that he would be coming around often. And they were glad. He brought good quality candy.

I Owe Most of What I Am Today to My Mother

BISHOP TATSUSHO HIRAI

MY native village in Japan, where I was raised, is called Shiromura in the province of Hōtaku, Kumamoto prefecture. West of the village lay the extensive Kumamoto Valley and to the far south one could see almost the dream-like island of Amakusa off the coast of Ariake. The Shirakawa that runs near the village meandered through the Kumamoto Valley and finally flowed into the Ariake Sea.

They say I looked almost like a boy when I was a little girl, having always been very active from the time of birth. However, about the time I started going to school, it seems that I had quieted down considerably and that I played alone with dolls in the house to avoid trouble with the mischievous children in the neighborhood.

When I consider my present status, that of devoting myself to the ways of Buddha with my mother, and sharing my daily life with her in this land of paradise, Hawaii, I feel as though I am the happiest person in the world. At the same time, I believe, I have also loved and revered her more than any of my sisters or brothers.

After finishing elementary school in my native village, I enrolled in a private girls' high school in Kumamoto City. Soon after graduation, I came to Hawaii and here an arrangement was made for me to marry a second generation Japanese; I shall call him T. In comparison to the rich religious atmosphere in which I was raised under

In *Tōdaiji of Hawaii,* published in 1956, pp. 1–5, 24–28. Reprinted by permission of Bishop Tatsusho Hirai.

my mother's guidance, my husband had shown no particular concern for "faith." With this difference in our basic beliefs, a day of permanent separation came in the 11th year of our marriage . . . a result of infidelity, on his part.

When I was a little girl, I gave much thought to becoming a nun eventually. I do not know whether this deep-seated desire was in my nature or something I had acquired later. However, when I informed my parents of this, for good reasons of their own, they disapproved. When I was twelve, on a cold wintry day, I showered myself with cold water from the well. This is only one of my many recollections that I have of my days when I wished to become a nun.

Having had this deep-seated wish, the opportune moment seemed to have arrived when I was deserted by my husband nineteen years ago. My long cherished wish to become a nun was to be fulfilled. However, when I actually received my divorce decree in the mails from my husband, I was deeply grieved. I cried like a child on my mother's lap. "Oh Mother! Would you die with me?"—these were the words my mother heard from me for days afterwards. At that moment I can imagine how my mother must have suffered because of my misery.

"Fine, I will die with you, but, before we take that step, would you promise to listen to my last advice?" Thus she began to pull me out of my darkness. "Yes, Mother, what is it?" "Let us go to the 'Honzan' together immediately," said my mother. "You will enter there, and when you have finished your training, and if you still think you want to die, then your mother will come with you," was her reply.

Her words gave me strength. I found myself in front of the gates of Todaiji in Nara with her soon after this. From this day, the road to serve Buddha opened before me. However, when I began my training, instead of devotion to my training, my strong desire to live had continued to occupy all my thoughts.

I do not remember exactly how many days passed. I gradually came to like my training and this discovery of my own progress was somewhat of a surprise to me. Since I was fond of cleaning the house from childhood, the task most people dislike, I had no difficulty in getting up at 4:30 in the morning every day to clean the rooms and bathroom in the temple. I considered this early rising a joy. Four years passed and during these years I toiled under the strict discipline. It was similar to the training used hundreds of years ago of the Kegon Sect. I was thankful to this strict training because it gave purpose to my life for, at one time, life had become meaningless for me.

I never missed the Taki-gyo (the taking of a cold shower under the waterfalls in order to cleanse one's soul) which lasted fifty minutes every day. In addition I often fasted for a period of two to three weeks, and sat on a cold floor, meditating, on the coldest days of winter.

I gradually came to like the training itself and one day I said to my mother, "I no longer feel that I want to die, Mother, I want you to go home now. . . . My brother and his wife probably missed you all this time."

Upon hearing these words, tears came running out of my mother's eyes.

The next day, my mother left the Temple early in the morning. I went to the train station to see her off and at departing, she said to me, "Be a fine priestess. Promise me not to become a second-rate priestess."

"Yes . . . ," I nodded in tears.

"Work as hard as you can so as not to ruin our family reputation and remember not to become an object for ridicule."

With these compassionate words from her, we parted from each other.

Since then, she had visited me at the Main Temple of Nara at least once a month traveling over a great distance from home with numerous gifts on her back. Indeed, only one's mother could go through so much for her child.

Thus to remind me of the bygone days when I was a burden on my mother, I have risen early so that at 4:30 every morning, I would sit facing towards Japan to repent the past and at the same time, I would pray hard for her happiness and health.

When I finished the training, I came to Hawaii for the second time as the first overseas missionary from Todaiji. I rented a house on Waiola. With "Fudo-In" written on a sign board at the front of my house, I began my missionary work.

For me, one who had left Hawaii earlier in tears with innumerable sad memories, this was the second start in my life in these Islands in an entirely different role: that of a priestess. In any event, with fervent desire for our particular denomination to be accepted and understood by the people, I have diligently toiled despite the shame that had earlier fallen upon me for having been deserted by my husband. As a result, several hundred people gather every day at my place of worship. At the same time, I have been subjected to undeserved and unexpected criticism from priests belonging to other Buddhist sects.

However, thanks to my vigorous activities which were actually made possible after having struggled and conquered the desire for death, these criticisms did not perturb me at all.

I have realized that if one has learned to become humble, he will only take such criticisms lightly. Besides, don't we all know a well-known Senryu (Ode) which reads: "Regardless of whether you have won or lost in a religious argument, you have done a shame to Buddha"?

. . .

Regarding our sufferings and pains, we know it is wrong to possess the idea that such are caused by the fault of others. Needless to say, it is still more absurd to resort to resenting or even denying the very existence of God and Buddha because of our sufferings and worries. "One's own sufferings are the fruit of his evil deeds, and the agony consequent to the sufferings is a stern reality he faces in life" is a quotation from one of the sutras. I believe there is no other way but to develop faith in order for us to live our life courageously in the midst of all the sufferings. We should neither ignore nor avoid this suffering, but we should realistically face and challenge it.

While religion has a deep effect upon one's salvation of his soul, it should also function as a direct reminder for promoting his peace of mind in his daily living. However, when we take a close look at the present system of "Buddhist Invocation," for example, I regret to say that for many it has come to mean only a perfunctory function. This tendency is prevalent in Hawaii as well as in Japan. No longer does the system as fine as the "Invocation" seem to foster the spiritual feeling in people. It is also not recognized by the general public for its value. Today, religion is apt to be taken as an insignificant factor in living or an object of meaningless argument. It is regrettable to observe this tendency of misunderstanding the real essence of faith on the part of many people.

Some people in Hawaii make unreasonable criticisms. Some conclude that the incantation in the invocation, which is advocated by our Hawaii Todaiji as "something which makes use of the old religious idiosyncracies such as retribution." This is a thoughtless argument on the part of those who do not thoroughly comprehend the value of real faith. As the philosopher Ryotetsu says, "There is nothing greater than understanding and there is nothing more dreadful than ignorance."

Then what would faith mean to a man? Needless to say the utmost purpose of faith is to attain spiritual enlightenment. That is, to become a Buddha himself is to be the goal. If he lives to seek this spiritual enlightenment throughout his life, no doubt he would find the greatest comfort by the religious faith he practices.

The worship and incantation upheld by the Hawaii Todaiji is, in short, a means whereby a man is led to practice this true religious faith. I shall use an example to explain this so that the reader will not misunderstand this particular point I have so strongly tried to emphasize.

Our present mode of living has created a series of tensions in all of us, which is the result of the complicated social system and human relationships, and the rapid development of industrialization. This is hard on our nervous systems and interferes with the proper metabolism of our bodies.

Many of us are not able to adjust ourselves to the strain of this complicated environment. We are not able to control our own anxieties, consequently, our nervous system breaks down. This leads to neurosis, which is a common topic of conversation. This is not all. Various disorders of digestion, liver and kidney which have rapidly increased in recent years are the symptoms also caused by the series of severe tensions experienced within.

When we look around, we find many examples of those symptoms in our friends and acquaintances who have emotionally collapsed because of their family troubles or because of the anxiety they have experienced as a result of the meaningless rumors and explosive incidents of the world. Their internal systems have already broken down or are not able to face them in the near future.

The fact that the medical treatment is needed for these people need not be mentioned. However, it is also a fact that it is almost impossible to cure these disorders only by medical treatment. The emotional treatment for such patients is vital, and this consists of course of faith in religion.

By inculcating religion into one's self, one can obtain a peace of mind, and by developing a pure and secure faith he is able to control his emotional disorder. My incantation and prayers became a psychological treatment by bringing these patients in contact with religious life. Actual instances of people who have been cured by my incantation and prayers are countless. The motivation of ninety percent of the people who have become the followers of the Todaiji of Hawaii was this desire for their illnesses cured. This will indicate clearly the value of religious life which I have already mentioned.

"While religion has a deep effect upon one's salvation of his soul, it should also function as a direct reminder for his promoting of his peace of mind in his daily living," was what I have said earlier, and the majority of followers who have come to me because of their illness, and who have been cured by developing faith, would verify the fact that religion has attained this purpose of promoting contentment in their daily living. One can see the significant part religion can play in his life.

With the above statement you would probably understand that the meaning of the incantation and worship practiced by the Todaiji in Hawaii would not in any way contradict scientific thinking. My attempt to cure the suffering of my followers by incantation and prayers is not something that provokes criticism as being superstitious or unscientific. It is based on rational thinking.

Although there are many people who immediately conclude that religion, which brings benefit to one's life, is inferior, superstitious and paganish, I do not think this to be true. In this life where we weep or laugh according to the turn of events, the thing of importance in our lives should be the attainment of spiritual happiness. Buddhism has no place in this life if it did ignore the bodily and spiritual salvation of these people who are lost in the midst of life's many confusions and complications.

In the case of "having been cured by faith," which I have talked about, this was neither accomplished by miracles nor mysterious psychic methods. They were cured by spiritual treatment which is based on scientific knowledge.

CHAPTER TWELVE

The Spoiled Generation?

NO generation of nonwhite people in Hawaii, without the sacrifices of hard work and perseverance, had enjoyed so much of the affluence and abundance of Island living as had the Sansei. No generation of nonwhite students in Hawaii, gaining the intrinsic social rewards of education, had adapted so successfully and comfortably to the culture of the public school. Inheriting the homes, the small businesses, the stability of their Nisei parents, the Sansei had reached adolescence and adulthood in a Hawaii where middle-class "good living," where material success and comfort, obscured the glaring racial inequalities of the previous decades. And yet while the Sansei had become a "spoiled" generation they had also become the most complex of the generations of Japanese who had inhabited Hawaii.

The Issei came to Hawaii with a specific goal in mind—to make money and return to Japan. The wealth and the trip home never materialized in those early years, and the Issei found himself a sometimes unwanted visitor in a harsh environment. Yet, drawing upon the strength of their culture, with a drive to establish secure homes, the Issei generation successfully created the foundations of the Japanese community in Hawaii. And stubbornly, but humanly, they clung to their cultural roots.

The Nisei, too, as they grew up in their Island home, had a specific goal in mind—to be accepted as equal, participating neighbors in shaping Hawaii's future. As youths they had to learn Americanism; as young adults they had to prove their Americanism; as mature adults they had to actualize their social, political, and economic ambitions and responsibilities. To their credit, the Nisei were successful in elevating the Japanese community to a respectable position in Hawaiian society. They employed their American and Japanese natures to meet the most profitable and adaptable ends.

But what goals did the Sansei have in the late 1960s and 1970s? What challenges as a generation did they meet? What was expected of them? Like many of the youth growing up in the America of the fifties, sixties, and seventies, the Sansei were exposed to a myriad of influences which made more and more untenable the cohesiveness of ethnicity and ethnic identity that marked both the Issei and Nisei generations. Problems, goals, and ambitions for the third-generation Japanese became increasingly the problems, goals, and ambitions of the contemporary American youth, regardless of ethnic background. Unlike their parents and grandparents, Sansei grew up in a world and a Hawaii where mass media, dissemination of popular culture, and influential, multiethnic attitudes exerted an enormous effect. Fads and faddism, the influence of television, movies, and music, a leisure world of recreation, sports, and a healthy allowance from Dad helped sustain the free hours outside of school. The older generation of Sansei might remember "The Lone Ranger"; "My Little Margie"; Bill Haley and the Comets; Davy Crockett caps; American Bandstand; "drop-drills" in school; "I like Ike" buttons; James Dean and Ricky Nelson; the fresh, youthful face of the new President, John Kennedy, on TV; "I Love Lucy"; and the gyrations of an obscure teenager from Tennessee, Elvis Presley. Younger Sansei more likely associated their upbringing with more hectic and more frustrating times—hippies; "The Great Society"; Paul Newman; surfing; Robert Kennedy; discotheques and the "Twist"; flower children; pot; race riots; "All the Way with LBJ"; "far out, outasite and groovy"; long hair; McDonald's hamburgers; miniskirts; and four mop-haired serenaders from England, the Beatles. But regardless of the different influences exerted on the Sansei generation, one basic trend was common throughout—the Sansei generation was profoundly influenced by the world of mass media outside of Hawaii. Dress, habits, taste, and goals increasingly were altered by the explosion of popular culture which infiltrated the Japanese home through television, radio, stereo, and magazines.

The meaning, then, that the Sansei would impart to being Japanese, their perception of their ethnic identity, would be significantly different from that of the Issei or Nisei. On the one hand, "being American" in dress, habits, or tastes was generally accepted as a normal day-to-day style associated with the youth culture—growing their hair long, listening to rock music, dressing in the latest styles of *Seventeen* magazine was considered to be "in" for a generation which was learning to accept nonconformity in their lemminglike rush for conformity. On the other hand, "being Japanese" for the great majority of Sansei in Hawaii posed little problem. Japanese language school was compliantly attended, though with little enthusiasm or results. *Ikebana* (flower arranging), *origami* (paper-folding), karate, or judo intermittently became hobbies or avocations of a number of young Japanese. *Giri,* reciprocal gift-giving; the practice of giving to the bereaved family at a funeral, *Kōden*; or giving money to a person going on a trip, *senbetsu,* were traditional customs instinctively perpetuated by the third generation. And eating at Japanese restaurants, going to *samurai* movies, watching the local Japanese television programs and worshipping Japanese rock and movie stars was as natural for Sansei in the 1970s as any of their cultural Americanisms.

By the middle of the 1970s, the Sansei remained a youthful generation, not yet fully matured in character or social goals. But becoming more obvious was the fact that the new generation of Japanese Americans of Hawaii had incorporated in their lifestyles a unique blend of cultures. Being American, Japanese, and living in Hawaii's atmosphere of multiculturalism created a youth group which psychologically and socially appeared to be very secure in Island society. Their environment was free from the excessive self-righteous Americanisms of the past, the racial inequalities and injustices of an oppressive society. The open practice of Japanese or local non-*haole* behavior and customs was a normal and accepted part of everyday life. Interracial dating and marriage continued to obscure ethnic boundaries; outmarriage rates for Japanese climbed to over 25 percent in 1970.[1] Indeed, for the Sansei the unique blend of American, Hawaiian, Filipino, Chinese, Portuguese, and Korean cultures increasingly characterized their Island identity.

An expression of this Island Sansei identity which generally transcended either the ethnic exclusiveness or cultural confusions or contradictions of previous generations was a poem, "The Soliloquy of Hamlet Yamato," written by a Sansei, Kenneth Ono.[2] Ono, a student at the University of Hawaii in the early 1970s, participated with other Island youths in the development of University courses which examined the culture and history of Hawaii's ethnic groups. Involved in questioning the Sansei's identity and social position in the Islands, Ono wrote a poem in "pidgin" English which expressed what he felt to be the psychological perspective of the Hawaiian Sansei.

To those familiar with Sansei attitudes and social opinions on the mainland, "The Soliloquy of Hamlet Yamato" was a startling contrast. Instead of the feelings of social inadequacy and militancy which frequently permeated the attitude of the mainland Japanese Americans conscious of their minority status, Hamlet Yamato was confused but not embittered. The identity dilemma of "trying to be white" did not enter into Hamlet Yamato's consciousness as much as the primary concerns of everyday living. Being American or Japanese, confronting elusive white devils, were not the concerns of Hamlet Yamato:

> Ma name Ameriken, ma face Japanee.
> So wat! As up to me
> To be free an make it in Hawaii.

The primary identification of the Sansei as they strived to "be free an make it in Hawaii" was of course still the family and peer group. Outside pressures and influences might have intensified interracial influences, instilling a durable "local" identity, but the family institution, the network of peer-group relations continued to have an influence over the character, ambitions, and lifestyles of the third generation. Part of the traditional patterns of the more rural lifestyle continued by the Sansei included the extensive influence of cliques on entertainment, recreation, and revelry. Social clubs in high school and college, sexually exclusive male and female "gangs," picnics, organized sporting events, "drinking buddies" and the "girls' night out" were but a few of the numerous extended group activities distinguishing the Sansei's peer influences. The individual Sansei was usually a member of a clique of males and females who spent much of their leisure time together, especially, but not exclusively, before marriage.

Structurally it would have appeared, though, that the Japanese *ie* rural system of family relations had been dramatically changed for the Sansei's family. The urbanization of the Japanese family had remained a salient trend during the postwar decades. The population of Honolulu Japanese in 1960 was 37 percent greater than their general Island proportion. In the smaller towns as well, Japanese predominated. Forty-seven percent of Hilo in 1960 was Japanese and the ethnic group comprised the majority of the populations of various small urban centers including Wahiawa, Waipahu, Wailuku, Honokaa, Lahaina, and Lihue.[3] And except for the postwar baby boom, a phenomenon characteristic of national trends, the Japanese birth rate continued to decline in the same period. Indeed, the birth rate for the socially mobile Nisei generation was one of the lowest of any ethnic group in Hawaii. The size of the average Nisei household in 1960 had dropped to 4.1 persons.[4] Moreover, by 1970, the average Japanese family contained only 3.7 members.[5]

But though the family had become structurally attuned to urban society, patterns of relationships stemming from a spirit of *ie* tenaciously survived. The continuation of *ie* patterns in the family of the urbanized Sansei could be seen especially in the development of the Japanese modified-extended-family pattern. Though the procreating family had become increasingly nuclear in profile, these nuclear families were linked, attitudinally and socially, with an extended kinship pattern. In other words, nuclear families of average household size became connected in the Japanese American community in a modified extended network of relational dependencies and obligations.

In her study of Japanese families in Honolulu, Dr. Colleen Johnson investigated the familial identifications of a sample of Nisei and Sansei and demonstrated the emergence of this structurally modified extended family. Dr. Johnson's results showed a progressively strong identification of succeeding generations not with the nuclear family but with the extended familial network. So while a third of the Nisei respondents felt their families were nuclear in design, less than one-fifth of the Sansei responded in a like manner. In addition, nearly 60 percent of the Sansei studied viewed their families as a network of extended relationships, compared to less than 50 percent of the Nisei who held such a view.[6]

What these results indicated was that progressively for the Island Japanese family, as urban and economic changes resulted in nuclearization, the pattern of extended families found reexpression in a modified form. While the birth rate and size of family stabilized in nearly typical urban patterns, the extended relationships and identifications with kinship had intensified for the Sansei.

In part the psychological mechanisms behind the growth of a modified-extended-family attitude could be understood as a generational reaction to urbanization. For the Issei generation, without extended family relations, dependent on other immigrants, the identification was primarily with the Japanese ethnic community—in the alien world one gained strength through one's countrymen. But urbanization weakened the bonds between the immigrant's progeny and the ethnic community. By the Sansei generation, the community would have little geographical integrity, few self-help services not provided for more effectively by state agencies, few means to express itself as a single ethnic group since ethnic assimilation and social mobility had undercut exclusive ethnic identity.

The waning community identifications had been replaced by an increasing family identification for the Sansei. While the ethnic group as a whole had less relevancy to Sansei lives, the ethnic family had a significant impact. Uncles, aunts, cousins, nephews, nieces, grandparents, and even in some cases great-grandparents for the first time in the Japanese American experience played an effective role in creating cultural and psychological stability in the home. Even though the modified extended families did not live under the same roof, they were involved in relationships of extensive interdependency due to geographic propinquity. In Dr. Johnson's study, three-fourths of the Sansei respondents, compared with half of the Nisei respondents, indicated that thirty or more of their relatives lived on Oahu.[7] Such kinship solidarity implied that for the Sansei, familial values, behavioral influences, and structural relationships were becoming more prominent as a source of identification.

The Sansei modified-extended-family pattern also suggested that cultural transmissions between generations would become increasingly cohesive. As an enculturator of ethnic values, the Sansei family would have to deal less with the difficult social and cultural issues with which previous generations grappled. Language difficulties, value confrontations, and the radical variations between the immigrant trauma and the second generation's feelings of social ostracism were concerns outside the purview of the Sansei.

Moreover, for the Sansei and their children, the emergence of grandparents as active cultural transmitters also enhanced the ethnic integrity of the evolving Japanese family. Grandparents, especially in the extended family situation, are "caretakers of culture," passing on the cultural continuity of their world view to their grandchildren. Significantly, Dr. Johnson's study revealed that 60 percent of the Sansei respondents indicated that grandparents played an active, welcome part in family affairs.[8]

While the Sansei generation might have been characterized by a reexpression of traditional family patterns and a restabilization of the grandparent role, the conflict of sex roles continued to affect the relationship of the Sansei male and female—the sexual Sansei still felt the repercussions of traditionalism in conflict with individualism. The discrepancy between independence and sexual role limitations especially affected the Sansei female. More acculturated to the American attitude of female equality than the Sansei male was acculturated to a pattern of female egalitarian treatment,[9] the Sansei young woman was in no more secure a social position than her mother. First, she felt the restrictions and roles of the family—as a girl, she was expected to find a good husband and get married. A young woman without a boyfriend was considered a source of family concern: What is wrong with her? Why can't she find someone? And, though figures indicated that Island Japanese females were marrying at a later age than females of most other ethnic groups,[10] statistics did not reveal the "long engagement." Many young girls had steady boyfriends for numerous years to whom it was assumed by family and friends that they would eventually be married. The "long engagement" became in many cases a period of prolonged domestication so that the girlfriend at 18 would become the experienced wife at 24.

The marital limitations on the Sansei female, induced by family expectations and control, were also enhanced by the social restrictions on her femininity. Whether because of internal restrictions in family expectations ("Since you're a girl you had better just become a secretary") or in sex discrimination in the labor market, the Sansei female could not expect as diversified and as rewarding an occupational career as the male. Correspondingly, economic disparity and discrimination in pay scales confronted the young Island female. In 1972 the female employee in Hawaii earned a median income from 32.2 percent to 47.6 percent less than a male doing equivalent work.[11]

While over 40 percent of the professional occupations were filled by women, the predominant female roles were those of accountant, registered nurse, dietitian, and public school teacher.[12] The Sansei female, especially if she graduated from college, was more often than not channeled into a career as a teacher or a nurse.

The pressure to get married and to find a job, plus the subtle social inequalities confronting her in Island society, obscured the Japanese female's notion of self-direction—the need for independence was exacerbated by a growing trend for Sansei females in the 1970s to move away from the home, to live in an apartment with girlfriends or become economically independent. An openness in dating practices, in exercising equality in their interpersonal relationships, a modernization of their sex attitudes, indicated attempts by women to develop greater self-expression.

The difficult, often conflicting identity problem of the Japanese female was reflected by Colette Nakao in her fictional description of a Japanese family. Nakao, herself a recent Sansei graduate of the University of Hawaii and an aspiring journalist, wrote her essay, "The Wedding,"[13] for a university class delving into the ramifications of being a female in Hawaii. The problems many Japanese females had in handling their internal psychological conflicts could be seen in the author's character, Pam. A male is expected to be aggressive, rebellious, and somewhat independent—his "talking back," "moving out on his own," or demand for freedom can be tolerated as part of youthful manliness. But the Japanese female in many cases finds such untoward behavior difficult. She has learned from an early age her duty to the family—to play a domestic, reserved role. "I usually acquiesce into silence," is the reaction of Pam to her family "empire."

The paradox for Pam is her entrapment in a familial system which is at once comforting and prohibitive. The family offers stability, confidence, and assurance. Her "empire" is clearly the modified extended family operating at its best—control, honor, image, and filial piety permeate her secure world. But this very security also leads to restriction. The illusions of freedom and equality are insulted by racial prejudice, unreasoned expectations, and biases. Pam, the individual, seems consumed in her familial and sexual roles while she attempts to resolve her love for family with desire for self-expression. The conflict can hardly be resolved with her grudging final remark that "I would never get married," a defiance of family control. Yet the inability to settle the conflict is itself but one futile component of the female's identity dilemma.

Out of frustration and desperation for independence, the Japanese female in several cases developed the role of domineering girlfriend, wife, or mother. Power in the domestic household shifted from the impotent patriarch to a developing matriarch. The father, due to unstabilizing and unsupportive American social conditions, became somewhat ineffectual within many families. He works all day at the office; he's tired; he hasn't the time; he doesn't care; and who at any rate would listen to him?

Into this vacuum moved the Japanese female. She needed to feel important, to have a sense of self-worth. If she was expected to obligingly serve the meals, cater to the family, pamper the husband, then it was only right that she assume the patriarch's cast-off role. In Dr. Johnson's study of Japanese families, evidence indicated that the patriarchy was indeed waning, being replaced by a strongly matrifocal or bifocal family structure. In her interviews of Nisei and Sansei, 63 percent of the Nisei responded that the focus of the family was either bifocal or matrifocal. Only 28 percent of the respondents indicated that their families were patrifocal. Among the Sansei, 88 percent of the respondents said that the family was bifocal or matrifocal, while only 11 percent said the patriarch still held familial power.[14]

In part this shift from patrifocal to matrifocal power in the Nisei and Sansei families could be seen as a result of the emasculation of the father, the natural expressive role of the mother, and the outside employment of the wife influencing her familial independence and respect. Whatever the cause, the emergence of the matriarch had multiple effects on the Japanese male. Dominated at home, a few Nisei men, unmindful of their own role in frustrating the female, sought solace in the variety of bars in Honolulu. Served by attractive Japanese, Korean, or Vietnamese bar hostesses who pampered and catered to them, the men found these bars to be one outlet for the male's own powerlessness. Another was simply to "close up" and avoid the situation with silence. One Nisei wife in Dr. Johnson's study saw her eminence of household power as a result of her husband's quiet consent:

> My husband is a good man. I can do anything on my own. That's because he's quiet—never says a thing. You *haole* women [to interviewer] don't understand the Japanese man—how different they are from *haole* men. They're aloof and quiet. They won't listen to their wives. They turn their backs, say they don't want to hear about it. So they leave most decisions up to their wives.[15]

Or if the male did exert himself in the family, it was no longer as a patriarch. Especially among Sansei fathers, the emerging role was not as disciplinarian, but as "chum." In such a situation, the mother again assumed the function of greater family authority and influence:

> My husband has always regretted the fact that he hardly knows his father. His father was so stern and remote and even cruel at times that

he never came through as a real person. He doesn't want that to happen with our children. So he's their friend, and I'm the one with the paddle.[16]

The male–female role relationship for the third generation Japanese, then, continued to undergo major structural changes in the 1960s and '70s. Assimilation into Island society, the adjustment to employment, income, standard of living, family size, education, and attitudes of freedom and independence altered the meaning of the marital bond. But even as internal relationships were altered, the general stability of the modified extended family survived. This stability could be seen in a variety of remarkable assimilative successes by the Nisei and Sansei. Most notably, within the comfort and cohesiveness of the family institution, the Nisei couple, in spite of role alterations, continued to produce a highly productive and capable individual.

The ability of the Japanese population to compete in the Hawaiian job market alone indicated the stability of the modified extended family and the subsequent success of assimilation. In 1970 the percentage of employable Island Japanese actually in the labor force represented 79.7 percent of the males and 57.2 percent of the females, a percentage higher than the U.S. average. In addition, only 1.4 percent of Island Japanese males and 2.1 percent of the females were considered unemployed, figures lower than for Japanese Americans nationally or for the total U.S. population.[17]

The occupational status of employed Island Japanese also showed this pattern of marked assimilation. In 1970, 14.0 percent of the males and 15.9 percent of the female Japanese population had become professionally employed. Although the percentage of Island Japanese professionals was below the percentage of professional Caucasians in Hawaii, and below the national Japanese American average (21.3 percent male, 15.9 percent female)[18] Japanese still played a prominent role in Island life. Japanese Nisei and Sansei comprised an estimated 61 percent of the dentists, 60 percent of the optometrists, 26 percent of the architects, 25 percent of the physicians, and 24 percent of the lawyers in 1970,[19] though they constituted approximately 30 percent of the population.

As a result of this occupational assimilation, the Japanese gained economic parity with the other established ethnic groups in the Islands. In 1966 the annual median income of the Japanese population was $8,877, second only to the Chinese.[20] More revealing figures in 1970 showed that the average Japanese family income at $13,542 was over $1,000 higher than the Japanese American national average and $3,000 higher than that of the total U.S. population.[21] This higher family income was accredited to the economic pooling of resources encouraged through the modified extended family.

Although the statistics representing poverty among Japanese Americans were obscured by the cultural biases against accepting welfare or allowing family members to show economic failure, again Nisei and Sansei represented a group highly assimilated into Hawaiian society. Only 3.9 percent of the Japanese families in Hawaii were considered below the poverty level in 1970, while only 1.8 percent of the families received welfare assistance. This figure was considerably below the national figure of 11 percent families in poverty and 5 percent on welfare.[22]

The stability of the Nisei and Sansei families could also be seen in the attainment of educational levels within the ethnic group. The median educational level of Island Japanese in 1970 was 12.3 years, above the national average of 12.1 years.[23] By 1966 only 0.5 percent of the 25-to-44-year-old group of the population had four or fewer years of schooling, while the percentage completing one year of college or more was 16.3 percent. The University of Hawaii revealed in 1971 that 38.7 percent of the student body at the Manoa campus was Japanese American, while 64.6 percent of Hilo campus was of that ethnic group.[24]

Further demonstration of the resiliency of the Japanese American family was the maintenance of the lowest divorce rates among Island people. Of the in-group divorce rates, only 14 out of 100 marriages ended in divorce for Japanese in the sixties.[25] In a 1954 survey of cases at the child and family service, only 23 percent of the cases involved Japanese, a considerable disproportion from their total percentage of the Island population in that year (36.9 percent).[26] This structural stability of the family also had an effect on individual physical, psychological, and social well-being. Physically, the Nisei and Sansei were extremely healthy people. For the Japanese the rate of infant mortality, for example, had been consistently low. In 1974 the number of deaths of children per 1,000 live births was 14.8 for the Japanese, 15.4 for others on Oahu, and 16.5 for the nation.[27]

By virtue of days missed from work due to physical disability the Japanese also seemed to be the nation's healthiest ethnic group. The average number of days lost from work by Japanese in 1960 was 25 percent less than the national average.[28] Other statistics revealed a markedly lower profile of chronic diseases for the Island Japanese: Japanese had a 37 percent lower incidence of heart conditions than other Oahu groups and 60 percent lower than the national average.[29] Though asthma-hay fever and dental problems were statistically high among Japanese, rates for heart conditions, peptic ulcer, arthritis and rheumatism, hernia, chronic bronchitis, and visual impairment were outstandingly low.[30]

The physical well-being of the Japanese population was complemented by their mental well-being. Statistics compiled in 1960 showed that Japanese had the lowest admission rate to public and private mental hospitals.[31] Although sometimes the hiding of the mentally ill person to protect the family image obscured the data, on the whole ethnic cohesiveness—kinship and peer solidarity—evidently provided the Japanese individual with a secure and psychologically stable environment.

If illegitimate births could be viewed as a socially disruptive phenomenon undermining family structures, then Japanese again demonstrated how stable the family had become—the Japanese had the lowest rate of illegitimate births among Hawaii ethnic groups.[32] The evidence of crime among Nisei and Sansei was also markedly low. In 1968 only 7.4 percent of all admissions to Honolulu jail were of Japanese ancestry.[33]

But such consistently roseate pictures of the Nisei and Sansei families would also neglect the bottom of the Japanese American statistical curve. Affected by poverty, loneliness, illness, frustration, and rootlessness, some Japanese during the postwar decades had still not felt the intuitive spirit of family love. For them, the changes within the Japanese community had disturbed their patterns of well-being and security. For some the family could not keep up with the rapidly accelerating demands made upon the modern Sansei individual. Though not necessarily typical and certainly not modal for the Island Japanese home, the extremes, the maladjusted, served as sobering reminders that no institution, no matter how durable, could be without its sometimes dormant but tumorous malignancies.

For the large part, the synthesis of the modified extended familial bonds and the success of social assimilation contributed to producing a Sansei personality with secure psychological, cultural, and social skills. But in some Japanese homes, as internal structures stretched in response to social changes, families failed to meet individual needs. For example, many Sansei complained that their families, while protecting the family image, had misplaced more important value priorities. The couple who remained married because they feared the shame of divorce often created a family atmosphere of bitterness and insensitivity. The child whose problems were covered up because they might have caused family shame merely became more confused and socially maladjusted. A sense of pride, so often useful to the individual, could unthinkingly inhibit constructive action, thereby magnifying problems.

Figures indicate, for example, that Japanese American families in poverty did not utilize welfare assistance to the same extent as the national population.[34] The stigma of receiving welfare, or disgracing the family image by admitting that they failed to achieve, helped explain this discrepancy. But such a hesitancy to receive assistance when needed could be irresponsible and self-inhibiting. One Island Japanese American noted, "When father died, we hardly had enough to eat. Mother refused welfare of any kind, because if one of us became successful later, it would be a blot on the family name."[35]

One of the more tragic consequences of an overweening family image was the inability of many Japanese families to deal honestly and reasonably with mental illness. *Kichigai* ("crazy") behavior was not viewed so much as an illness as it was an irreparable scar on the family honor. The mentally ill person had to be hidden, removed from the sight of others, so that the family was not disgraced and shamed.

Harry H. L. Kitano in his study of mental illness among Japanese of Hawaii, Los Angeles, Okinawa, and Tokyo found marked similarities in the nature of Japanese "crazy" behaviors. Not only was the mentally ill person a social leper to be concealed, but in each area hospitalization was postponed for the sake of the family image, until the family and individual could take no more. Japanese families, Kitano observed,

> . . . resist the move towards professional labeling and categorization until the behavior literally tears the family apart. By then, it may be "too late," so that once a Japanese is hospitalized, the chances of recovery may be slim. However, once he is hospitalized, he does acquire the characteristics of the mentally ill role, which for many becomes permanent.[36]

Also noteworthy was the personality profile of the mentally ill. In each area the mentally ill individual was an isolated, lonely person from a lonely, isolated family.

This unrealism in many Japanese family attitudes, their inability to subjugate pride so as to deal intelligently with familial problems, was the source of much conflict between the Nisei parent and Sansei youth. Youngsters who were frustrated by unrealistic or self-serving familial demands felt hemmed in by threats to their independence. They were not allowed the respect to handle their own futures, to make their own decisions, to have their own friends. The family simply could not understand or deal with their problems.

In a modern world of information overload, the family seemed for the young to be restricting; out of touch. The Sansei had more choices, more decisions, and more information than most individuals could have hoped to sort logically—and less fundamental life roots with which to deal with personal problems. The years of religious conversions and indifference in the Nisei community, for example, had taken their toll on the Sansei. In a 1955 survey, well over half of the young Sansei respondents professed no religious identification whatsoever.[37] The Sansei had no other institution except the family or school to help handle a personal "identity crisis"—a crisis in most cases brought on at home or in the classroom.

A great many young Sansei hoped to deal with their crisis by reaching a compromise between family constraints and individual freedom. And, in turn, many families responded with parental flexibility. This responsiveness of Nisei families to the needs of the Sansei, their flexibility to balance love with parental guidance and obligation, allowed the adolescent Sansei to feel that his desire for individualism was encouraged and insulated by family concern. The child could make his own decisions, make his own failures, and understand how he fit into the family unit.

Other Nisei families were not so much flexible as they were simply inert. The child did as he liked, without guidance, because the parents were usually helpless to grasp the situation. "There is nothing we can do about it" became a rationale to spoil the child with apathy and powerlessness. Still other families responded to the Sansei "identity crisis" with silence or a reexertion of overcompetition. Parental expectations for the recalcitrant youth became unusually rigid—the child was even under greater pressure to conform to the family expectations—and little room was left for failure. Sociologist Bernhard Hormann described the silent and overly competitive Japanese families:

> One kind of family I like to refer to as the silent family. When the members congregate at home after their day's activities, there is no conversation. The sons and daughters are unable to talk over anything with their parents, who themselves are at odds. Or in such families we note the one withdrawn silent member, the old maid daughter who

could not marry the Haole or Hawaiian or Filipino man she wanted to marry and who refused to marry the man her parents proposed for her. One student wrote about the aunt who lived a lonely embittered silent life in her parental home.

The poisonous air in some of these families is intensified by the code of hiding one's feelings and never raising one's voice. So the married daughters, in one case, visited their mother who was living with the oldest married son. They entered her bedroom and behind closed doors gossiped maliciously about the daughter-in-law, the mistress of the home who was caring for her. The relentless disowning of children who do marry out against their parents' wishes has brought years of unnecessary heartache to many Chinese and Japanese individuals in Hawaii. If the Japanese have problems of schizophrenia, if the Japanese sometimes are shocked to find in their families sullen juvenile delinquents, here in the loveless silent families may be what is in the background.

Or these problems may have their beginning in the overly competitive families who push their children up the educational ladder even when they are not fit to climb very high. "Why can't you study hard like the neighbor children?" they prod. A girl wrote: "To them education was 'the' main thing, for with this education one could get a good job and be able to live comfortably. . . . In our family there was always the endless concern about 'what people would think.' "[38]

To a youthful population feeling loneliness, a need for love and a measure of individuality or self-worth, the silent and overcompetitive families became personal anathemas. "My father's a bastard," "My parents push too hard," "There's no love in my family"—these were but a few of the epithets that several Sansei youth learned to hurl, often subliminally, at their parents.

At the opposite extreme of youth, sometimes suffering from an equally ominous loneliness of human relationships within the Sansei family during this time, were the Japanese elderly with their own unique and demanding problems. The island of Oahu alone held in 1971 slightly fewer than 30,000 persons 65 years and older. Of this number, approximately 38.8 percent were Japanese.[39] Predominantly Issei, this elderly Japanese population comprised the largest bulk of Oahu's aged community and consequently shared the problems encountered by all Hawaii's senior citizens.

Although comprising only 7.6 percent of the total population of Hawaii,[40] the Island elderly—those over sixty years of age—had an acute economic and attitudinal crisis in the 1970s. The elderly were not, after all, a highly employable group—65 percent of the Oahu aged did not work at all in 1969.[41] And the 1970 census revealed that, of the over 10,000 households with a family head sixty-five or older, 13 percent earned incomes below the poverty level. Most economically impoverished were the elderly living alone. Of this group, nearly half were earning incomes below the poverty figure in 1970.[42]

Living largely on social security, the families below the poverty level were economically in an extremely disadvantageous position. Their fixed incomes were seriously jeopardized by the rising costs of living and inflation. Due to their advanced ages, susceptibility to ill health and inadequate modern training, they were beyond meaningful employment in a fast-paced, youth-oriented Hawaiian system. In addition, they experienced the attitude of futility and helplessness attached to old age. A significant portion of the disadvantaged aged were neglected by their children, put into rest homes, encouraged to go to "sun cities" where they might live out their lives undisturbed and undisturbing.

The care and role of the elderly in society had not always been so harsh. Especially within the Japanese *ie,* the aged were cared for and made useful within the extended family—their age earned them wisdom and authority, not neglect. But with the assimilated Japanese family, this care of the aged parent underwent transition. Progressively the assimilation of the family, the attitude of economic independence and the futility of age altered the meaning of obligation to the elderly.

Because the Issei in age were a relatively homogeneous population, the first impact of care for the elderly affected the Nisei generation in the middle of the 1950s. An estimated 10,000 Nisei families in that period had one member sixty years or older who was being provided for by the children.[43] The question of obligation for the second generation was by then becoming a very real concern. While many Nisei gladly accepted the care of their elderly parents, some evidently did so out of the threat of shame. Modifications of parental obligation were also evidenced. Traditionally, the eldest son had been responsible for caring for the parents, since he had been the sole inheritor of family property. Changes in the patriarchal system had minimized the status of the first son, and this resulted in a diffusion of sibling responsibility to the parents. Not only the eldest son but all the children, many Nisei believed, must assume the obligation of parental care:

> If my brothers and sisters can afford to, I'm going to want them to at least pitch in. The old lady can live in my house, but they should all give some money—even if I'm the eldest son.[44]

Other Nisei also noted that the burden of parental obligation was going to be limited to their generation. Because their parents expected to live with the children in old age, the Nisei had no choice—they owed the Issei too much. But the Sansei, many decided, would not be saddled with similar burdens. The obligation to parents, *oya-no-on,* would not be expected of the Sansei offspring by a self-sufficient Nisei population.

And evidently the Sansei wholeheartedly agreed. A study of Nisei and Sansei attitudes toward care for the aged by Dr. Johnson revealed that fewer Sansei saw care for the aged as part of their obligations, and more saw it as a burden than Nisei respondents.[45] Another cross-cultural survey indicated that although Japanese Sansei were generally more favorable about caring for their aged parents than other non-Asiatic young people, they were more negative than the generation of Japanese Americans a decade earlier.[46]

The result of these changing attitudes was the displacement and isolation of many old people in need of love and a feeling of self-worth. Certainly the majority of Issei were cared for adequately by the modified extended family—most Japanese elderly found the comfort and security of an appreciative kinship. But the lonely aged Japanese male or female, made to feel a burden, rejected, and isolated, was also a social fact, a malignancy of neglect. Statistics revealed that Japanese suicides in the Islands rose with age and that the cause was usually the personal displacement the elderly felt within the familial system:

> Mr. M. was a 71-year-old Japanese man who lived with his son, daughter-in-law, and grandchildren. He was born in Japan, came to Hawaii as a young man, and was now retired. About ten years ago, his wife died. Since his return from a trip to Japan, within a few months Mr. M. was unable to sleep and stayed up due to his insomnia. Moreover, he was alone during the day since the rest of the family was either at work or school. One day, his son found him dead of chemical poisoning after returning from work. His suicide note said: "I am sorry for having worried you so and having been a burden. Please forgive me." Recalling his previous behavior, Mr. M.'s son remembered that his father usually washed clothes for the family on Monday (the day he took his life) but had washed on Sunday. It was the first time that he changed his habit.[47]

The suicidal Issei; the cold, over-competing Nisei family; rebellious Sansei; the quarrelsome, self-destructive couple—all were the bleaker dimensions, then, of the Japanese American family experience. While most families did not encounter the extremities of these problems, did not have to deal straightforwardly with mental illness, poverty, or suicide, within their seemingly ideal structures were traces of these potential family problems. To help ameliorate these family difficulties, the Reverend Ted Ogoshi of the Makiki Christian Church wrote several position papers delving into various aspects of Japanese family developments. In one study, "Problems of Japanese in Hawaii: Youth and the Aged,"[48] the Reverend suggested some prospective outlooks and recommendations which provided alternative directions for the handling of the socially displaced.

Reviewing the social complexities of the Japanese elderly's situation in modern Hawaii, Reverend Ogoshi pinpointed 1969 as an important year altering the nature of old age in Hawaii. After the children were legally absolved from care of the parents in a 1969 act of the Hawaiian legislature, the elderly turned their property over to their children, applied for welfare assistance, and in increasing numbers went to live in homes for the elderly. Though this practice was an economically sound scheme, the psychological repercussions for the Issei, Reverend Ogoshi suggested, were disastrous. The diverse needs of the elderly were not being met in displacement—feelings of familial security and comfort, a sense of purpose, were lost in nursing homes. Reverend Ogoshi pointed to increasing suicide statistics and concluded that they indicate a trend of alienation detrimental to the Japanese aged.

The solution? Partially the elderly's future lies in the attitude of the third and fourth generations. The Sansei, on the whole, Reverend Ogoshi felt, were anxious to develop a rapport, a relationship with the aged. And generations of Yonsei and Gosei who have grandparents that play an active role in their upbringing would in the future be favorably inclined to share in the moral and economic support of the elderly Nisei and Sansei. Reverend Ogoshi concluded by supporting three measures which he hoped would reverse the destructive trends brewing in the ethnic community: 1) an improvement in parent–child communication, 2) a reorientation of values away from family success and to values of personal relationships, and 3) the repopularization of *on,* obligation as a means to offset the disrupting effects of getting old in Hawaii.

Probably the most important theme emerging from Reverend Ogoshi's paper was the need for a reemphasis of relational values within the Japanese extended-family systems. Not only the elderly but the youth would need an increasingly heavy reliance on relational in lieu of economic values. The young Sansei, desiring family flexibility to deal with their modern identity concerns, would need to feel greater degrees of familial love and compassion and less insistence on achievement, status, and success.

The continued flexibility of the Japanese family to balance individual needs, self-worth, and initiative with the demands of family unity and cooperation would for the Sansei be the future measure of the family's resiliency. Though they might have been a materialistically spoiled generation, the Sansei had inherited a complex, yet pressing burden. In essence, the modified extended family needed to become modernized and democratized without sacrificing any bonds of love. Relational priorities had to take precedence at times over family honor or image. The social and psychological stability of the individual became more important than "what others will think," or "you must do this because it is expected of you." Sex roles within the family and between mates needed to be more equalized and harmonized. Attitudes toward the aged had to be reevaluated and adjusted to offset the elderly's possible displacement generated by neglect. And it became the responsibility of the Sansei generation to incorporate these several social needs into the lifestyle of the Island *ie* so that the ethnic group could meet the dynamic technological and environmental changes of urban society, changes reshaping the meaning of race, culture, and ethnicity in Hawaii.

NOTES

1. Akemi Kikumura and Harry H. L. Kitano, "Interracial Marriage: A Picture of the Japanese Americans," *Journal of Social Issues,* v. 29, no. 2, 1973, p. 73.
2. Kenneth Ono, "The Soliloquy of Hamlet Yamato."
3. Andrew W. Lind, *Hawaii's People,* Honolulu: University of Hawaii Press, 1967, p. 52–3.
4. Colleen L. Johnson, "The Japanese-American Family and Community in Honolulu: Generational Continuities in Ethnic Affiliation," Ph.D. dissertation [Anthropology], Syracuse University, 1972, p. 112.
5. U.S. Department of Health, Education and Welfare, *A Study of Selected Socio-Economic Characteristics of Ethnic Minorities Based on the 1970 Census, Vol. II: Asian Americans,* Washington, July 1974, p. 57.
6. Johnson, p. 115.
7. Johnson, p. 111.
8. Johnson, p. 186.
9. Abe Arkoff, "Male Dominant and Equalitarian Attitudes in Japanese, Japanese-American and Caucasian-American Students," *The Journal of Social Psychology,* v. 59 (1964), pp. 225–9.
10. Lind, p. 102.

11. Honolulu, City and County, Office of Human Resources, *Profile: Oahu's Women,* Honolulu: July 1973, p. 27.

12. Honolulu, City and County, *Profile: Oahu's Women,* p. 27.

13. Colette Nakao, "The Wedding."

14. Johnson, p. 192.

15. Johnson, p. 153.

16. Johnson, p. 148.

17. U.S. Department of Health, Education and Welfare, p. 83.

18. U.S. Department of Health, Education and Welfare, p. 83.

19. Frederick Samuels, *The Japanese and the Haoles in Honolulu,* New Haven: College and University Press, 1970, p. 26.

20. Johnson, p. 98.

21. U.S. Department of Health, Education and Welfare, p. 105.

22. U.S. Department of Health, Education and Welfare, p. 123.

23. U.S. Department of Health, Education and Welfare, p. 70.

24. Johnson, p. 100.

25. Johnson, p. 102.

26. Makoto Araki, Marjorie H. Carlson, Kazuichi Hamasaki, Blossom M. Higa, Betty Ann W. Rocha, and Hiromi Shiramizu, "A Study of the Socio-Cultural Factors in Casework Services for Individuals and Families Known to the Child and Family Service, Honolulu, 1954," M.A. thesis [Social Work], University of Hawaii, 1956, p. 113.

27. Department of Health, State of Hawaii, *Statistical Report 1974,* pp. 4–5.

28. Charles G. Bennet, George H. Tokuyama and Paul T. Bruyere, "Health of Japanese Americans in Hawaii," *Public Health Reports,* Public Health Service, U.S. Department of Health, Education and Welfare, v. 78, no. 9 (September 1963), p. 754.

29. Bennet, et al., p. 758.

30. Bennet, et al., p. 761.

31. Johnson, p. 101.

32. Johnson, p. 101.

33. Johnson, p. 101.

34. U.S. Department of Health, Education and Welfare, pp. 122–3.

35. Johnson, p. 321.

36. Harry H. L. Kitano, "Mental Illness in Four Cultures," *The Journal of Social Psychology,* v. 80 (April 1970), p. 133.

37. Bernhard L. Hormann, "The Problems of the Religion of Hawaii's Japanese," *Social Process in Hawaii,* v. 22 (1958), p. 6.

38. Bernhard L. Hormann, "The Contemporary Family in Hawaii" [partly revised paper given to Hawaii Social Work Conference, Honolulu, 1964], p. 5.

39. Honolulu, City and County, Office of Human Resources, *Profile of Oahu's Aging Population,* Honolulu: 1973, p. 4.

40. Honolulu, City and County, *Profile of Oahu's Aging Population,* p. 1.

41. Honolulu, City and County, *Profile of Oahu's Aging Population,* p. 23.

42. Honolulu, City and County, *Profile of Oahu's Aging Population,* pp. 10–1.

43. Clarence E. Glick, Alice T. Higa, Irene S. Nose, Judith M. Shibuya, "Changing Attitudes Toward the Care of Aged Japanese Parents in Hawaii," *Social Process in Hawaii,* v. 22 (1958), p. 9.

44. Glick, et al., p. 18.

45. Johnson, p. 185.

46. Ronald Kazuo Ogitani, "Attitudes Toward Aged Parents: Symptom of Social Dysfunction," Senior Honors thesis [Sociology], University of Hawaii, 1969, p. 34.

47. Doman Lum, "Japanese Suicides in Honolulu: 1958–1969," *Hawaii Medical Journal,* v. 31, no. 1 (January-February 1972), p. 22.

48. Ted Ogoshi, "Problems of Japanese in Hawaii: Youth and the Aged."

The Soliloquy of Hamlet Yamato

KENNETH ONO

Be o' no be, as da queschen.
I Japanee o' I Ameriken?
In Inglish dey wen name me,
But ma face look Japanee!
Eh, mo noble for me suffa
O' fight da haole oppressa?
An die in da fight
To get ma right?
I gotta die! so I dunno
Fo wat I sca'ed fo.
But wen I die wat goin' happen?
I goin' Hell o' I goin' He'ven?
O' else, no mo notin';
O', one *mo worse* somptin'?
So now I kno
Wat I sca'ed fo.
If no was fo dis fe'a
I woud'nt be he'a.
No mo worry,
No need feel sorry;
No mo dis, no mo dat;

No mo good guy, no mo rat;
No mo suffa, no mo oppressa;
No mo axkin', "wa-sa-matta?"
I coud end ma life
Wid one sha'ap knife.
But das da ting;
Ma conscience keep tinking—
Afta dyin'
Get somptin' o' notin'?
You see, no body, afta det
Wen come back an said wat get.
As wy I still he'a—
Because of dis fe'a!
Conscience make me yallow
An I feel real hallow.
So, I tink, an no use da knife.
Instead, I stink, an stay in dis life.
But wait! I not pau.
Get somptin', some how.
Yea, still get me—
Ma name Ameriken, ma face Japanee.
So wat! As up to me
To be free an make it in Hawaii.
So, făk you, you făka,
I goin' be shăka.

The Wedding

COLETTE NAKAO

MARRIAGE was the last thing on my brother's mind less than two years ago. But on July 21, 1973, following their sudden engagement eight months earlier, Mark, then twenty-six, married Caren, two years younger than him, in an elaborate, double-ring, fifteen-minute Buddhist ceremony at the Pali Honpa Hongwanji temple. On that day, I bequeathed my only sibling and confidante, Mark, to Caren, my new sister-in-law. On that same summer day, my parents gained a second daughter.

July 21st was a busy day of last minute details in getting more liquor, ice and pupus for the gift-opening party after the reception. Unbelievably, eight months of planning and preparation, headaches, confusions and expectations were coming to a gala climax. And the excitement was growing as we neared the nuptial ceremonies, which seemed to me both awesome and final. This was, after all, the first wedding in the family since Ted, my mother's youngest brother, was married ten years ago. Since then, we had all been anxious for another lavish celebration, and Mark's wedding was the perfect opportunity to bring the family Empire together again on a grand scale.

"Empire" really best describes the size of the family which my grandparents have built in the heart of Honolulu: forty members

Reprinted by permission of Colette Mariko Nakao.

consisting of my parents, brother, aunts, uncles and twenty cousins. It is an empire of relationships, a tight-knittedness of purpose and attitudes which pervades the clan, family and individual. In lifestyle and outlooks, interests and values, there is a commonness overriding individual differences.

Grandpa Hamada, or "jitchan" as we call him, is still the symbolic patriarch of the Empire. In the pre-World War II days he owned a prosperous restaurant business which was located in downtown Honolulu. Now eighty years old, he lives with my grandmother in the same two-story house he built more than forty years ago. The house had been built to accommodate the needs of a growing family—to raise the children in the best possible environment. Even today my grandparents' home is the weekend meeting place for the entire clan. The old house gives continuity to my family Empire—it is an emotional bond that spans the generations.

And in many ways, the people who have grown up in my grandparents' house are just as unchanged and continuous. My aunts' and uncles' values reflect generations-old Japanese ideals, such as the importance of family image and filial piety. They are respectable, middle-class Japanese in whom belief in reputation, material possessions, traditionalism, and racial descent are ingrained. In part, this continuity of values and lifestyles is due to the physical proximity of members of the Empire. Through the more than twenty years which I have been part of the clan, all except two of the families have continued to live in the same community within fifteen minutes reach of each other. My parents and I, as well as four other families, live not more than a block away from my grandparents. The families' geographical proximity has reinforced the tight, almost impenetrable emotional bond within the family, which is a perpetuation of old values and close-minded visions of the world outside the family womb.

Stability, then, is one naturally understood rule of life for my family. And in many ways it is a beautiful, rare quality that my family is lucky to have. Keeping the family together has, through the years, been made possible without much effort, since family unity is so highly stressed. So while as individuals our interests, livelihoods and tastes are changing, at home the old-fashioned family life remains stable and unchanged.

"Pam, come. Help me make sushi!" My mother's harried plea for help sent me running to the kitchen. There she was, bustling about in that tiny, steaming kitchen in which all four burners on the stove were blazing under huge metal pots. Although she had already cooked and decorated two trayfuls of sushi, that would hardly be enough for the one hundred and fifty people who would attend Mark's and Caren's gift opening party. To add to the confusion, my father was running in and out of the house setting up chairs and tables in the adjoining penthouse where the after-reception party would be held.

As I helped my mother prepare the platters of pupus, I couldn't help but wonder why Mark would bother to go through all of this insanity. Why hadn't he and Caren just eloped, or better yet, simply lived together? I snickered to myself at the shocked faces and blackened reputations that last alternative would have caused. But at any rate, my brother was certainly going to be the first and the last of the family grandchildren to plan such a tradition-bound, formal wedding, with the usual church ceremony, two-hundred-plus guest reception, and the gift opening party. My other three cousins, who all graduated from college two years ago, and I hold negative attitudes about such an elaborate, expensive wedding ceremony. Why the persistence of this trend to get married? It must partly be because of the prevailing attitudes that if my friends are getting married, I don't want to be the only unmarried soul in the crowd.

Another reason no doubt stems from the local oriental style of family life. Unless the child is determined enough to move out of the house to live alone and to become self-supporting, he is expected to live with his parents until he eventually gets married. When the time comes to finally move away from the family, making that move with a partner would be financially easier than doing it alone.

One cannot also underrate the pressures of the family to get married—especially on a single girl. My cousin Beth, for example, graduated from the University of Michigan two years ago. Since then, she has returned home to work for a year and entered graduate school last fall. Just after returning home from college, my aunt confronted Beth with the topic of marriage.

"Now that you are out of college," she asked, "Don't you have any plans to get married?" Beth replied that she had no intentions of getting married in the near future, for school and a career were at the top of her list of priorities. The "now that you've completed college the next step is to get married and have kids" syndrome is as prevalent in my family as in others. And it is a syndrome which builds as the son or daughter, year by year, remains single or unengaged.

Even the wedding guest list reflects this intensity of family pressures. After months of guest list decisions—six different lists, with constant revisions and arguments between Mark and Caren and my parents over who to invite and who not to invite—I realized that the wedding was for the family, not the couple. The final list included not only immediate aunts and uncles as well as grandaunts and granduncles and my mother's cousins, but my father's business associates as well. What began as a simple, carefully budgeted affair for about one hundred and fifty relatives, under the insistence of the families, was gradually transformed into a grand affair for family, friends, acquaintances and who knows who else.

The stability, the tradition, the pressures to conform, the influences over our behavior, are features of my family which have withstood change. They were obvious in the preparations for my brother's wedding. And in the contentment of the womb I had once thought all Japanese families must be the same. But they really aren't. My boyfriend Ken, comes from a very loosely-knit family which seems to feel no need to get together on occasions like Thanksgiving, Christmas or New Year's day to express familial sentiments.

"You gotta understand," he would say to me straight-forwardly, "not all families have to get together every weekend in order to feel close and to be aware of each other. If anything happens, like an emergency, my relatives would never hesitate to help one another. . . ."

So true, I agreed. Only in recent years have I accepted the fact that not all families are like mine. And perhaps not all families ought to be. For in the sheltered realm of the Empire, you can become cut off from the rest of the world.

Until "jitchan" became ill last year, family activities had always been huge and plentiful, inclusive of very few persons outside of the clan. During summer vacation, while my friends were going camping together, I was tagging along with the family for weekends in a rented, run-down beach home in Laie, or a self-styled tent camp on Mokuleia Beach. For my brother, my cousins and myself, there seemed to be no need for YMCA or public school summer fun programs, because the family itself was so active that we were content with our own aunts' and uncles' improvised summer programs. It wasn't until I had graduated from high school that I realized how I had grown up separately from my friends because I had spent so much time away from them during the summer months.

And when an outsider is included in my family activities, he or she is always given the "once over." Recently I invited a friend of mine to my cousin Wayne's sixth birthday party in Nuuanu. During the course of this typical family gathering of more than thirty relatives, amid the raucous children running about and adults talking above the noise, I became aware of my guest's uneasiness. He seemed to be getting along with my uncles, drinking beer and talking story, but it was no later than nine o'clock in the evening when he nudged me.

"Hey, let's go," he muttered. As we were leaving he grumbled, "Your relatives really looked me over, yeah?" A usual reaction from friends who meet the clan for the first time. A kind of David meets Goliath situation (if you can see the analogy).

The cliquishness of my clan naturally makes them highly critical of "nonfamily." Outsiders always have to meet up to the standards, either racial or social, which the family sets.

"Don't you go out with *haole,*" my grandmother would always warn me. "You marry *haole,* you'll be sorry," or "you go out with *haole,* everybody going talk . . . shame you know. Everybody going say, 'look at her, so cheap.' "

"You still going out with that Ito boy?" another female relative will persistently warn. "You marry poor, you'll be sorry."

The suspicions my family has for outsiders even extended to my sister-in-law Caren. Caren is the younger of the two children in her family, but unlike her sister, she is adopted. My relatives had always been leery of adopted children, particularly because of the fact that their parents' identities remain unknown. Their cultural and racial origins could very definitely be "different," my relatives claim—a difference which will begin to show in later adult life. In Caren's case, her unusually round eyes and dark skin prompted my relatives' tactless criticisms that she could not possibly be "pure Japanese," but instead, part Filipino perhaps—which, they warned, was not at all a good choice for my brother. These types of feelings, which remained below the surface, created an inhospitable atmosphere around Caren whenever she visited the family. Only after nearly two years of marriage would the family sincerely accept Caren as the truly warm, beautiful person she really is.

Instead of confronting my family's exclusiveness, though, instead of arguing that perhaps the family Empire is not always right, I usually acquiesce into silence. During the five years that I have known my boyfriend Ken, he has yet to come away from an evening with my family without saying, "Why is it that you're so quiet with your family? It's just not like you to hardly say one word . . ."

I cannot transcend this feeling of futility that gnaws at me every time I choose to say nothing instead of trying to explain why it is not so deplorable for my cousin to have "mokie" Hawaiian friends, or why kids of my generation, including myself, are not deliberately rebelling against our parents the moment we accept the first marijuana joint while sitting with a circle of friends. I cannot transcend the feeling that not all the pressures, the expectations, the loving bonds of my family are always best for me.

My brother came into the living room between trips to and from the penthouse to remind me that Bev, Caren's maid-of-honor, was to pick me up at lunchtime to go to the studio to get dressed. Before going out the door, Mark muttered to me the same piece of advice he had been repeating for the past seven months.

"Remember, when your time comes, elope."

As I returned a quick glance at him, I noticed the anxiety on his face. He was more nervous and worried than Caren. I swore inwardly that I would never get married.

Problems of Japanese in Hawaii: Youth and the Aged

TED OGOSHI

On

Hawaii Japanese are the cultural inheritors of the Meiji period in Japan (1868–1912). Its norms were "*on* (ascribed obligation); *giri* (contractual obligation); *chu* (loyalty to one's superior); *ninjo* (humane sensibility); and *enryo* (modesty in the presence of one's superior)."[1] These norms reflect varying senses of obligation. My emotional memories of *on* describe this obligation as a *duty to be grateful*. The effect is gratitude, encased in ribs of responsibility. A typical Japanese school story might be of a widowed mother, laboring unknown at night at a second job, to keep her children alive and give them an education. So it might be with us, that outward appearances might cover inner sacrifices. Be grateful! Filial obligation is probably universal. But this quality of duty made it feel peculiarly Japanese.

One way this obligation to parents is met is through achievement, or at least the appearance of success in the community. Wealth is the most obvious; being a teacher *(sensei)* was close to it, better than being a minister. My passing the English-standard examination was a matter of great but unspoken pride. Success and prestige have served the Japanese community well. With them have come respect in the classroom, better jobs, accessibility to housing, inclusion in the political process, and corresponding social standing. By contrast, the black, who personally may have equal ability, is held back from the above because of the low prestige of his race. Achievement has been important to survival and well-being for the Japanese.

Another way obligation is met is through filial piety. "Filial piety is thought of by the Japanese as the core of all morality."[2] "A child is indebted to his parents for having received care and support from them. In other words, the child has received an *on*."[3] The most important duty of a child is to obey his parents. Another duty is to care for them in their old age. As a child, I remember visiting my father's uncle in Pearl City, a senile man who was simply vegetating, but who was cared for by his family for years until he died. The norm of caring for one's aged parents comes from such personal images. All the children of a man share in the duty of caring for him, but the eldest son is responsible for ensuring that the obligation is carried out.

Aging

In a little known play, "Time Limit," an army major is accused of betraying his country while in a Korean prison camp. In trying to explain his refusal to defend himself, his wife says: "Can't you understand how he feels? . . . Nobody wants him. The Army doesn't want him. His own men turned against him. He has no place to stand."[4] In a culture in which Age has had "a place to stand," there are signs of uncertainty today with the pain that that brings, when older persons do not know their place or role. Closely tied with the matter of role is the importance of achievement among Japanese. One has to do with relationships, the other, with productivity. While American values stress role and achievement, the Japanese sense of obligation to family gives these different psychic loadings.

In 1960, 8,244 Japanese were age 65 or over; in 1970, 14,522. In 1955, Wayne Kanagawa made a study of elderly Japanese on welfare and counted a total of 133 persons.[5] In March, 1973, I made a survey of nursing hospitals in the city and of those that gave me information, the following figures [Table 1] can give us some feel of the situation.

The State no longer keeps records by ethnic backgrounds so figures comparable to Kanagawa's study were not available. The hospital sampling, which does not include Japanese on welfare but healthy, shows 96.22 percent of the Japanese to be welfare recipients. It also shows 81.03 percent of these to have children. Has there been a shift in attitudes of filial piety?

TABLE 1. Japanese in Nursing Hospitals Who Are on Welfare, March, 1973

Hospital or Home	Bed Capacity	Jap. Population	Jap. DSS	DSS w/ Children
Convalescent Center	159	49	43	26
Hale Malamalama	31	25	20	19
Island	42	37	36	35
Kida	74	56	53	?
Kuakini	49	49	47	20
Laniolu	54	2	2	2
Maluhia (city operated)	144	59	57	56
Maunalani	101	14	12	?
TOTALS	654	291	270	Inc
Comparison totals of those reporting both Department of Social Services (DSS) recipients and number of recipients with children.			195	158

Acculturation

Gerald Meredith, using the "Edwards Personal Preference Schedule (1959)," shows needs that emerge in Hawaii sansei.[6] Compared to a normative mainland sample, Japanese male university students expressed greater need for:

Deference. To get suggestions from others, to find out what others think, to follow instructions and do what is expected, to praise others, to tell others that they have done a good job, to accept the leadership of others, to read about great men, to conform to custom and avoid the unconventional, to let others make decisions.

Abasement. To feel guilty when one does something wrong, to accept blame when things do not go right, to feel that personal pain and misery suffered does more good than harm, to feel the need for punishment for wrong doing, to feel better when giving in and avoiding a fight than when having one's own way, to feel the need for confession of errors, to feel depressed by inability to handle situations, to feel timid in the presence of superiors, to feel inferior to others in most respects.

Nurturance. To help friends when they are in trouble, to assist others less fortunate, to treat others with kindness and sympathy, to forgive others, to do small favors for others, to be generous with others, to sympathize with others who are hurt or sick, to show a great deal of affection toward others, to have others confide in one about personal problems.

Affiliation. To be loyal to friends, to participate in friendly groups, to do things for friends, to form new friendships, to make as many friends as possible, to share things with friends, to do things with friends rather than alone, to form strong attachments, to write letters to friends.

Order. To have written work neat and organized, to make plans before starting on a difficult task, to have things organized, to keep things neat and orderly, to make advance plans when taking a trip, to organize details of work, to keep letters and files according to some system, to have meals organized and a definite time for eating, to have things arranged so that they run smoothly without change.

Sansei female university students expressed a greater need than the mainland norms for Deference, Nurturance and Order. Sansei male and female students showed reduced needs for:

Male	*Female*
Dominance	Abasement
Aggression	Aggression
Exhibition	Exhibition
Heterosexuality	Heterosexuality

But an even greater surprise is that the male has a reduced need for Dominance. Colleen Johnson says, "The Japanese male (sansei, college students) is notably high on male-dominance attitudes, while the Japanese female is similarly high in egalitarian attitudes as they relate to the future marital role."[7] We have a picture of a Japanese man being lord of his castle and servant in his outside world. We also have the picture of a Japanese woman, moving out of this hierarchical world, having had opportunity for education, competing directly with men, baptized in an equalitarian environment, being "the neck on which the head rests," both at work and in the family. The picture that Meredith draws, comparing Japanese and Caucasian is as follows:

	Japanese	*Caucasian*
Male:	reserved	outgoing
	humble	assertive
	conscientious	expedient
	regulated by external realities	venturesome
		imaginative

	Japanese	*Caucasian*
Female:	affected by feeling	emotionally stable
	obedient	independent
	suspicious	trusting
	apprehensive	self-assured

Amae

Amae is a basic need to be cherished and loved. When this is thwarted or disturbed by conflict or a wrong done, a Japanese male feels *kodawaru,* an inner disturbance. He turns inward, analyzes and blames himself. Meredith theorized that this inward retreat or withdrawal has created a "leadership crisis" among Japanese males. Harry Kitano has observed the same thing and called it "social backwardness." Because of his need for *amae,* he is less likely to risk being in a position of being scolded or laughed at, or to have to report on a superior when the superior is acting wrongly or in trouble, or to assert his views against other peoples. I believe that with so many wives working and with many social and personal needs being met outside the nuclear family, there is a growing vacuum for such *amae* which will need to be met in new, responsible ways.

Japanese women, on the other hand, feel *sumanai* (guilt or obligation), when there is a disturbance in the relation. But this does not cause her to withdraw. She seems able to deal with the guilt and is becoming the strong one in the Japanese constellation.

The Sansei acculturation problem seems to focus mainly around male identity. Many of the counseling problems that I face have to do with this: "He's not a man . . . Why can't he stand up to his parents? . . . He won't make decisions . . . He lies all the time . . . Men are little boys . . . He can't keep a job." Often when husband and wife are together in counseling, the man has difficulty expressing what it is that he feels, becomes tongue-tied, unable to express himself effectively. I hear whining men, men who are dependent. Turning inward need not be pathological, but most men do not know how to be honest with themselves, do not know what to look for or what to do with what they find. The *kodawaru* anxiety is a symptom and can be used effectively for growth.

Behind the anxiety are the needs, shaped as they are by the cultural value of filial piety. As such, they are a collective unconscious, deeper and more pervasive than we are aware. Their value is that they give us the wisdom of our race. Their danger is that they can become death-dealing. They function as a legalism, demanding conformity, robbing a person of his selfhood. The crisis-of-leadership idea lifts this fact to our consciousness in order that we may deal with the values and decide whether these are what we want.

Conclusion

The *duty to be grateful* is a quality I appreciate about my Japanese background. It appears that we are reexamining the actual relation of gratitude today. What are we really grateful for? What do we owe? Can we be responsible and cherished at the same time? C. S. Lewis has described gratitude as "inner health made audible." Gratitude is highly desirable, but what form shall it take?

1. A mutual listening between parent and child. A child's parents may be no wiser than other parents, but they have an interest and stake in him that no one else does. If for no other reason, he should take what they say with seriousness. But a parent must understand that his child is to be self-governing, not a mere cog in tomorrow's machinery.

2. Japanese valuing personal excellence as much as they have, family success. A return to this value would correct much of the distortion we have had about people, particularly the role of the elderly. We need to learn a new and genuine appreciation for age.

3. Dramatists who will portray the essence of *on* for a democratic (not hierarchical) and urbanized (not rural) age. We need a clear image of what is already in us that can be used for the benefit of all. It needs to be a vision, not of a narrow family obligation, but it needs to include responsibility for others and the world. Japanese, like Hebrew, is a very picturesque language and there is, buried in our past, the possibility of storytelling that can reshape our images.

NOTES

1. Kitano, Harry, *Japanese Americans,* Prentice-Hall, Inc., New Jersey, 1969, p. 102.

2. Masuoka, Jitsuichi, quote from, "The Japanese Patriarch in Hawaii," *Social Forces,* XVII (December 1938), p. 246.

3. Kanagawa, Wayne, *A Study of Old Age Assistance Recipients of Japanese Ancestry Under the Honolulu County Department of Public Welfare, Territory of Hawaii,* January 1955. Thesis submitted to the Graduate Division, University of Hawaii, for Master of Social Work, June 1955.

4. Armstrong, James, quoted in *The Journey That Men Make,* Abingdon, Nashville and New York, 1969, p. 143.

5. Kanagawa, p. 53.

6. Meredith, Gerald, "Observations on the Acculturation of Sansei Japanese Americans in Hawaii," *Psychologia,* Vol. VII, No. 1-2, June 1965, Kyoto, Japan, p. 41.

7. Johnson, quoting Abe Arkoff *et al,* "Attitudes of Japanese-American College Students toward Marriage Roles," *Journal of Social Psychology,* XLIX (1963), 11-15; Abe Arkoff, "Male-Dominant and Equalitarian Attitudes in Japanese, Japanese-American and Caucasian American Students," *Journal of Social Psychology,* LIX (1964), 225-229, p. 141.

Chapter Thirteen

The New Hawaii

"FOR the first time, we have a candidate for Governor who is of Japanese ancestry."

The speaker was Dan Aoki, representing gubernatorial candidate George Ariyoshi. The audience was Nisei war veterans of the 100th Battalion, Club 100. The date: September 3, 1974.

"Just as I did not ask to be born a Japanese, I am sure he did not ask that he be born a Japanese. In other words, all of us are what we are because of the nature of things and yet, how often have you heard, time and time again, that we are not ready for a Japanese governor, or that no Japanese can be elected a governor?

"Isn't this also saying that no Chinese can be governor, or no Hawaiian can be governor? If you follow this line of reasoning, then we are being tested again as to whether or not we are Americans? Must you and I think, act, and live like the mainland Americans to be identified as an American? Is this what they are saying?

"If we concede this, are we then relegating our youngsters, our children, to a secondary role because of color?

"Is this the Hawaii we know?

"Is this the Hawaii that we love?

"Is this what we want Hawaii to be?"

A "breakthrough" for the ethnic community, Aoki stressed, would be the result of an Ariyoshi victory. "Didn't the election of

Dan Inouye to the United States Senate and Spark Matsunaga to the United States Congress also represent a breakthrough?''

''In closing, I ask you to recall the dreams you had in the battlefield and to cap those dreams by joining in our cause to fulfill the essence of what you had fought for as members of the 100th and the 442nd.''

Twenty years previously, in the heated debate of the 1954 general elections, Aoki's statements and sentiments would have been common. The second-class citizenship of Japanese in Hawaii was an all-too-accepted fact of life which hopefully the ballot box would have reversed. The appeal to ethnic pride and community was a legitimate, unchallenged necessity to shape the ''Revolution'' which would improve the status and self-image of Hawaii's diverse people. Even in 1974, the Japanese American romantic myth of the postwar decade could generate empathy and support.

But social undercurrents had for nearly a decade been shifting the substructure of Hawaiian communities and social attitudes. While some Japanese in 1974 would not question the propriety of ethnic politics, others, particularly some Sansei, would react with indignation.

''It sounds like you [Ariyoshi] and your campaign people,'' charged an enraged Paul Murakami, University of Hawaii student and supporter of gubernatorial candidate Tom Gill, ''are trying to bring race into the campaign.''

For Murakami, as for an increasing number of younger Japanese, the appeals to the past, to the ethnic cohesiveness of a community ''on the make'' and trying to ''break through,'' were becoming irrelevant in the 1970s. More important for a great many members of this generation was not the ethnic individual or the ethnic community but the social issues, the direction of Hawaii. ''Is the color of my skin tied to my vote?'' queried Murakami.

The interethnic perspectives of the Sansei generation's identity—the notion of being a ''local'' and sharing a ''local culture'' of food, dress, speech, and sport—had mollified the ethnic exclusiveness of the Japanese youth. They had been raised in a world where color, ethnic cohesiveness, or minority consciousness did not necessitate a special obligation, a special contribution of money, or a special vote. To judge a candidate solely on the basis of ethnic background seemed somewhat ludicrous to a generation proud of their youthful openness and racial maturity. For during their adolescence, during the political and economic changes of the fifties, the rapid growth and political advancements of the sixties and seventies, the Sansei had been permeated with a "world view" affecting all of Hawaii's peoples. This "world view," as expressed by the middle-class Island resident and his children, could have been stated thusly:

> Hawaii is my home, a home I love. My roots are in these Islands. Generations of my people have worked the land and enjoyed the richness of the earth and sea. Happily, Hawaii is comprised of many different people and we have a common goal. We want to see Hawaii grow as an example of world peace and prosperity. We want to see our children participate in a free and rewarding society. The "Good Life," a home, children, a family, being able to work hard and play hard in our Island paradise comprises the meaning and goals of our lives. To this end, racial differences are accepted and appreciated, but are secondary.

In its simplest form, this world view was the Hawaiian Consensus of political and social thought which in the 1950s and 1960s would have found few detractors. Within this Consensus, politicians appealed for votes, businessmen constructed high-rises, teachers struck for higher wages, and laborers demanded better working conditions. Always the appeal was for a better Hawaii for all people. Optimism, not a pessimism of "oppression" or "rebellion," was the overriding spirit of the Hawaiian Consensus. From Hawaiians to Japanese Nisei and Sansei to *haole*s, this Consensus, this basic notion of the good life, became an outlook on both ethnicity and everyday living. We, the people of Hawaii, might be diverse, but we want the same things for our families, our children, and the future.

Fundamentally the Hawaiian Consensus had three themes. First, it relied on an appeal to interracial harmony and a sense of united purpose. Second, it valued economic growth and expansion which meant more affluence for the individual. Third, it looked not to a past of hardship and bitterness but to a future which promised to bring prosperity and peace to the Islands, a racially torn nation, and the world.

The interracial aura which surrounded the Hawaiian Consensus was based on the traditions of Hawaii's racial *aloha,* the democratic principles of a society "of the people" regardless of race, color, or creed. In the past, social or political expressions of ethnicity by a racial group in Hawaii always had to be tempered by the realization that no one group was a majority. Rather, since each ethnic group was a minority, interracial cooperation was necessary if improvements for the ethnic community were to be successful. One had to appeal to "all the people" if an action or proposal was to be accepted and effective.

Perhaps the best example of how interracial harmony became an integral feature of the Island world view was seen in the influence of labor unionism on Hawaiian race relations. In the 1909 and 1920 sugar strikes, Japanese and Filipinos had used the ethnic community as the primary focus of organization. Japanese and Filipino unions were established which occasionally worked together but usually were incompatible in means and goals. Ethnicity clearly acted in these early years to hinder social reform or progress.

Recognizing this limitation, the ILWU had sought as its primary goal the instilling of a spirit of interracial harmony and purpose. Their slogan, "An Injury to One is an Injury to All," in effect helped to generate the notion that the problems of the ethnic community were really the problems of all Hawaii's people. And instead of working as compartmentalized units of interests and goals, the working people of Hawaii had to unite in a common purpose.

The effects of the labor movement on the ascendency of interracial harmony were explored in an article by David Thompson entitled "The ILWU as a Force for Interracial Unity in Hawaii."[1] Thompson, information director of the ILWU, discussed the history of the early attempts by the ILWU to bring the races together under a single union, the difficulties of making the practices of the union more integrating, and the procedures established to create a leadership which would be multiracial. Primarily the ideological success of unionism would rest on the subordination of ethnic differences to economic and social realities—the economic betterment and even survival of each worker depended on his ability to get along with and support a worker of another race. The ILWU in the Territory, Thompson concluded,

> . . . has been a powerful element in the whole complex of factors operating to transform Hawaii's former colonial social system, with its basic population of more or less unassimilated and exclusive immigrant groups effectively dominated by a paternalistic *Haole* ruling group into a genuine island commonwealth of self-governing people consistent with the basic American doctrines of democracy and equality and the corresponding Hawaiian public doctrine of racial equality and interracial *aloha*.

Certainly, interracial equality and unity had been integral to the general acceptability of the Hawaiian Consensus. However, the more visceral social attitudes stemmed more from concerns for growth and economic betterment which affected the Islander's pocketbook and bank account. The sugar and pineapple industries had been the basis of the Hawaiian economy before 1946 and had kept the Island locked in an upper-class–lower-class stratification. The middle class in Hawaii before 1940 was in many ways nonexistent. Except for some professional jobs, civil service employment, and small businesses, the major available occupations were non-skilled and semi-skilled labor either for one of the sugar conglomerates or for one of their subsidiaries.

In the fifties and sixties, however, the development of tourism and the expansion of the Island economy with mainland and foreign investments helped account for the financial growth of Hawaii. In turn, this growth was correlated with a lowering of the unemployment rate, a rise in the quality of living, and the establishment of a durable middle class. More nonagrarian jobs were available in urban and tourist centers which meant an expansion of urbanization and technology.

Hawaii had always symbolized the "lure of the Pacific," an image engrained in the minds of mainlanders and foreigners who dreamt of an ocean voyage. In the pre-World War II era, though, tourism was largely limited to the wealthy who could afford an ocean cruise and the expenses of Waikiki. Still, the promotion of Hawaiian tourism in the national media began earnestly in the 1930s. Matson Shipping Lines, which had a monopoly of all cargo and passenger travel between the Islands and the mainland as well as owning the Royal Hawaiian Hotel, hired an ad man named Sydney Bowman to promote travel to Hawaii. During the Depression of the 1930s, tourism had been seriously hurt, so Matson Lines believed that an all-out image campaign was necessary to sell Hawaii to the mainland. Exchanging free passage and accommodations to famed writers for favorable magazine articles, sometimes written by his own staff, or staging elaborate publicity stunts such as Amelia Earhart's solo flight from Hawaii to the mainland, Bowman helped generate the public responsiveness necessary to Hawaii's infant tourist industry.[2]

The successor to Bowman and Matson Lines as promoters of Hawaii's tourism was the Hawaii Visitors Bureau (HVB). The HVB was a privately operated agency, financed with matching funds from the private sector and the state government. Responsible for promoting

Island tourism, facilitating tourist accommodations and complaints, training tour guides and setting up "points of interest," the HVB had become by the 1970s the major coordinator of tourism's growth. In 1972 the HVB budget was nearly $2,500,000, three-quarters of it from the State.

But it was changes in transportation rather than promotion that gave tourism its greatest boost. Before statehood, travel to Hawaii was either slow or relatively uncomfortable. An ocean cruiser, though luxurious, took nearly four and one-half days from San Francisco to Honolulu. In 1946 air transport was an exhausting twelve and one-half hours. Later, jet travel was introduced to the Island-mainland traffic leading to an easy four-and-one-half-hour flight. The use of jets made tourist centers in the Midwest and the East Coast closer—seven and one-half hours from New York to Honolulu. "We're so close now," one Honolulu businessman said after the introduction of jet travel, "that we can be a part of the West Coast."[3]

The boom in Island tourism after World War II could be seen in the increasing numbers of tourists and the annual income from the tourist industry. Between 1946 and 1957 the annual number of visitors to Hawaii increased from 15,000 to over 169,000. Tourists spent over $6 million in Hawaii in 1946; by 1957 they were adding nearly $77 million to Hawaii's economy. The remarkable boom in tourism through the fifties and sixties meant that by 1970 tourism had become about 33 percent of Hawaii's source of income.[4]

Hawaii's growth into contemporary urbanized society was accelerated by increased mainland and foreign investment in Island industries. Kaiser, Del Webb, and Boise-Cascade on the mainland became investors in Hawaii's urban and tourist growth. Financing hotel and high-rise construction, suburban middle-class housing projects, or public services such as hospitals or clinics, mainland investment became by the 1970s a major factor in the Island economy.

Also by the 1970s, Japanese foreign investment was becoming significant to Island economic growth. Estimates for the period 1970 to 1973 suggested that from $50 million to $250 million had been invested in Hawaii by Japanese, primarily in the tourist industry.[5] Indeed, in 1972, 225,000 Japanese tourists visited Hawaii and yearly increments of nearly 10 percent were expected for 1973 and 1974.[6] Japanese investment had been concentrated largely in financing the service agencies which catered to Japanese tourists—hotels, restaurants, tour guide agencies, bus lines, and airport facilities. It was not unusual in 1975 to see large advertisements, printed in Japanese, displayed next to English signs along Kalakaua Avenue in Waikiki—Japanese investment and tourists had made an impact on the Hawaiian economy and lifestyles.

Therefore, economic growth and security, in addition to interracial harmony, became another one of the mainstays of the Hawaiian Consensus. Since nearly everyone profited from the skyrocketing boom of the fifties and sixties, few could criticize the prosperity and "good times" which Islanders were generally enjoying. Looking at the high-rise expansion of Honolulu, the construction of highways, and the growth of small industry, most Islanders viewed with satisfaction the fact that Hawaii was becoming a modern, productive part of the United States.

An expression of this attitude was illustrated in a speech by businessman Chinn Ho, "Our Future in Hawaii,"[7] to the Hawaii Newspaper Publishers Association Convention on October 6, 1967. Ho, a major multimillionaire financier in Hawaiian land and industry, was the grandson of a Chinese rice planter, an immigrant to Hawaii in 1865. Founder of the Capital Investment Company in 1945, Ho had sensed the postwar economic boom which would revolutionize the Islands. With Ho believing that wealth was based on the land and the proliferation of small industry, the Capital Investment Company expanded its land ownership and the selling of fee-simple estates and encouraged non-*haole* local businesses and industry to compete with the large *haole* enterprises. By 1950, Capital Investment could claim assets worth $2,000,000. And by 1959 the company had sold more than 1,500 fee-simple homes and had helped subsidize various small enterprises from apartment houses to a macadamia nut company.[8]

Committed to the financial growth of Hawaii, the expansion of the tourist industry and the modern development of Honolulu, Ho spoke in "Our Future in Hawaii" as a leading representative of the economic prosperity of the Hawaiian Consensus. In an optimistic tone of "unprecedented prosperity," he upheld the virtues of growth before the skeptics of urban ugliness or pessimism for Hawaii's future. Tourism as the only major industry "capable of providing the increasing economic wealth which the people of this state require in increasingly greater amounts to attain their social aspirations" was "assured" in the future. Ho clearly recognized the blossoming affluence of new generations of Islanders shunning the plantation limitations and poverty and seeking the material security of the middle-class "good life." While some might "write off" Waikiki as an irreparable loss, Ho maintained that since growth and prosperity were integral to the local people's lifestyle and attitudes, what was needed was not economic regression but better planning for expansion. "I believe," Ho stated, "that the people of Oahu need not endure the gap between what they would like for Waikiki and what is possible."

The development of training programs and increased education for the enlarged labor market, the modernization of tourist facilities such as at Hilo Airport, and the progressive city planning necessary for the rising demands of tourist housing were developments linked to the future which Ho foresaw in the 1970s. And, in a tone with which few Islanders would have taken exception, he reiterated his conviction that "Hawaii for the years ahead will have unprecedented prosperity."

That Hawaii was growing into a comfortable and rewarding place in which to live for all races and ethnic groups was an attitude which prevailed throughout the 1960s. Progressively, though, this Hawaiian Consensus which grew out of the postwar decade also needed a more altruistic goal or vision. In addition to wealth and interracial harmony, the promise of Hawaii had to stimulate the imaginations and dedication of not only Islanders but all those looking for an ideal society. Thus, the Hawaiian Consensus included a utopia in its future. The future was more than bright—it promised to initiate an "era of good feeling" which would be an example for the world. Multiracial people, living in peace and prosperity, would work together to design a future society which would be a New Hawaii, a Hawaii which would be the prototype of international peace and cooperation.

Understandably, this theme was closely coupled with the political rise and establishment of the Democratic Party in the 1960s. The party's platform of progressive education, land and tax reforms, low-cost housing, and increased social benefits had to a great degree forged the New Hawaii of multiethnicity and economic power. The Burns–Inouye coalition of the early 1950s had become the basis for the establishment of a political power that controlled Hawaii well into the 1970s. After statehood, nearly all of the most prestigious positions of power were held by Democrats. Besides the control of the State Legislature, Democrat Daniel Inouye became U.S. Senator; Spark Matsunaga was elected to the United States House of Representatives, as was Nisei Democrat Patsy Takemoto Mink. And John Burns in 1962 was elected Governor of Hawaii, a position he had long coveted and one which he would hold until 1974.

A theme which Burns promulgated and one eloquently presented in his Inaugural Address of December 5, 1966,[9] was the belief that Hawaii must become in the future a progressive, "Open Society." Hawaii is "our beloved home," it can be a shining example of a modern multiethnic society, but "we must not be deluded by past tradition and restraint." Education, housing, jobs, and growth demand great strides in social reform and change, but "we do not promise change merely for the sake of change, but only to meet the legitimate needs of our people and our changing institutions."

The goal of the Island people must ultimately be to fulfill the spirit which they symbolize—"a new vision of the cooperation and enlightened unity that all mankind must surely find one day." To do this "you, the people, must have the will to move ahead, to work for a better life, and to break the bonds of traditions when they become restrictive and inhibit creative growth." To the generations of Islanders who remembered the plantation system, a life of poverty, and second-class citizenship, to their children and grandchildren who sought a better life in the Paradise of the Pacific, the message was clear: "Let us go forth to build the New Hawaii."

This imagery of the future, the appeal to make Hawaii a better place to live not only for the family and children but as a model for all nations, was an undebatable facet of the Hawaiian Consensus. For the Nisei and the Sansei as well as for many other of Hawaii's peoples, it was an enticing social attitude, an optimistic outlook on life which stressed success, self-improvement, interracial harmony, and a new spirit.

The temperament and outlook of the Hawaiian Consensus was certainly to last well into the 1970s. Yet, at the same time, voices of dissent had begun to speak out against growth for growth's sake, profit without respect to environment, and an "open society" which increasingly became "closed" for certain ethnic minorities. Tourism had gotten out of hand; mainland investment was depriving local people of economic self-determination; Oahu had been turned into a concrete jungle of hideous high-rises, condominiums, and hotels. The Neighbor Islands and rural Oahu were threatened with ecological destruction, air pollution, and urbanization. The cost of living rose faster than the per capita income of Island residents, making living in Hawaii increasingly hard to afford. In addition, many local people of medium income could no longer find moderately priced housing. As for racial *aloha,* the Islands were being run by either arrogant *haole*s or ethnically exclusive Japanese. Moreover, the *malihini* newcomer—*haole,* Filipino, or Samoan—was accused of marring the multiracial beauty of the Islands. Especially young *haole* hippies who littered the landscape and *haole* professionals who flooded the labor markets caused alarm in the New Hawaii. In the face of a *haole* racial majority which many sociologists had predicted by the 1980s, even Governor Burns, the proponent of the "open society," was alarmed. "If any group goes over that," Burns told a reporter after writing the number 51 on a notepad, "then Hawaii is in trouble—everyone is in trouble."[10]

The Hawaiian Consensus of growth, harmony, and a bright future was by the late sixties undergoing a critical reexamination. Though generally the Islander would never question his love and pride for his home or his appreciation of Hawaii's unique multiracial beauty, he would begin to feel discontent. The national inflation following the end of the Vietnamese War meant even higher costs of living. By 1974 unemployment rates which had been as low as 2.7 percent in the 1960s soared to over 8 percent. Crime multiplied, as did the number of people on state welfare. Perhaps, many thought, the New Hawaii of the Burns' administration had been merely a ruse. Perhaps unlimited development would lead only to the eventual destruction of Hawaii.

This discontent with the Burns' organization and the Hawaiian Consensus led to the heated gubernatorial elections of 1970. Thomas Gill, considered by many to be a brash upstart of the Democratic Party, challenged the Burns' incumbency on the grounds that the New Hawaii needed a recommitment of priorities. Rather than just growth and expansion, Hawaii needed mature planning and progressive leadership with no political or financial ties to businesses or outside investors. Speaking of developments in Hawaii during the 1960s, Gill recognized that:

> The long period of plantation colonialism was over.
>
> Our legislature, filled with bright and feisty young men, had turned out a mountain of new and innovative legislation. Finally in 1962 our party also gained the executive power, and the ability to make things happen.
>
> Growth burst out all over. Development was progress and progress was good.
>
> Some of our people became rich beyond their every expectation; most of us gained more income and more things than we ever had before. Most agreed—and still would today—that, having been both poor and rich, "rich is better."
>
> But things began to happen to us.

Some of our poor and struggling public servants became less poor and struggled less. Some of the crusaders for a change decided that change wasn't so important after all. The result was a slow and insidious loss of momentum. We became more interested in the form of social innovation, not the substance.

There was talk of planning and proper land use, but action on variances and zoning giveaways. There was refusal to recognize the growing crises of housing and pollution until this election was almost upon us.

Those who sold tourism spoke of the "golden people of Hawaii," but turned Waikiki into an overbuilt human bog.

Belatedly, as the smog begins to blind our view of the mountains, some verbalize the need for pollution control, but then fail to fill necessary positions in the control agencies and hardly move to enforce existing laws and regulations . . .

There is a flutter of concern as the election approaches, a great deal of expensive public relations, but no real answers.

In Hawaii the sixties came in with a shout and crept out with an ominous shudder.

It seems clear: The seventies are a watershed.[11]

Indeed the 1970 gubernatorial election was another watershed in Hawaiian politics and social thought. To be sure, John Burns won reelection—the New Hawaii of 1966 was given voter confidence as was the power base of the Democratic Party. But in the 1970 campaign the complexities of modern Hawaii, the dynamics of interracial ties and conflicts, the influence of media and image, the fears of a *haole* racial invasion, the power of the Hawaiian Consensus to overcome ethnic lines, the old strings of the 1954 coalition which could still be pulled, and the emergence of social issues which undercut ethnic community concerns were countervailing influences in the 1970 election which determined that political social relations in Hawaii were no longer the easily manipulated affairs of the past.

One especially relevant aspect of the 1970 election was that issues and leadership had changed the nature of politics in the Japanese community. While the Burns' coalition had once sought strength through Japanese support, in 1970 this support was no longer a "sure thing." While on the Neighbor Islands, Japanese influenced by the ILWU could still pull the votes for the Democratic standard-bearer, the Japanese community was becoming less and less the monolith of opinion which it supposedly had been in previous years. Fully incorporated into the Hawaiian Consensus and assimilated in the social and political institutions, Japanese, especially the Sansei, realized that issues of Hawaii's social priorities and leadership demanded wider concern than that of merely supporting an ethnic ticket or feeling ethnic obligations. A breakdown of Japanese voting patterns in the 1970 election showed that while a majority still supported the ethnic coalition of 1954, a growing number of Japanese voters were willing to vote against the "establishment." Until the final days of the campaign, the Japanese voters had actually been split 50-50 between Gill and Burns, though with the final efforts of media and outer Island constituencies Burns' lead was improved to 58 percent, with 34.8 percent of the Japanese vote going to Gill. In 1970 "ethnic bloc voting" for the Japanese was no more evident than for the *haole* population that voted 59.2 percent for Gill and 34.8 percent for Burns.[12] Clearly, the elections had revealed that even among Japanese, dissatisfaction with the conditions of Hawaii had led to new political allegiances and diversities. Even John Burns recognized his waning Japanese support before the election. "I may have worn my welcome," Burns was heard to remark early in the campaign.

More and more evident was the growing diversity of political and economic interests stemming from the Japanese community. While many Japanese continued to support the Burns–Inouye coalition of 1954 and were attracted to the candidacy of Burns' protégé, George Ariyoshi, in his successful gubernatorial campaign of 1974, other Japanese were becoming disenchanted with the "Old Guard." What should concern Japanese politicians, educators, or businessmen, these Japanese believed, were issues and social affairs which confronted all of Hawaii's people. Responsibility and power meant a commitment to a better Hawaii beyond ethnic affiliations, interests, or obligations.

But even as the more "successful" ethnic groups began to increasingly identify with broader interethnic issues, other less assimilated minorities in the 1970s began to awake to the potentiality of their own ethnic self-interest. As a result, the Hawaiian Consensus theme of interracial harmony was to undergo serious reevaluation by certain nonwhite minorities who viewed "harmony" as a mask to conceal racial stratification and injustices. For these groups, integration of Hawaii's peoples represented suppression of ethnic diversity, a sham for ethnic heritage and community. Ethnic groups struggling for power, for their own style of identity and status, complained that other ethnic groups, especially the *haole* and the Japanese, had absorbed more power and wealth from the Hawaiian system than was justifiable or equitable. Lambasting the interracial harmony of the Consensus as "plastic *aloha,*" ethnic dissidents were willing to confront the *haole* or Japanese Establishment as readily as the group of Nisei veterans had challenged the *haole* oligarchy of the past.

This confrontation of the "Establishment" turned into a "hot war" on June 18, 1971, in the hallowed chambers of Kawaiahao Church in Honolulu. A large group of Hawaiian and Part-Hawaiian leaders and concerned citizens gathered in one of Hawaii's oldest churches to protest the appointment the day before of Matsuo Takabuki as trustee of the Bishop Estate by the chief justice of Hawaii's Supreme Court, William Richardson. As trustee, Takabuki, who during the 1950s was a part of the Burns–Inouye core of Democratic power, who was a 442nd veteran and a prominent Honolulu lawyer, would be in an influential position to set policies and directions for the Hawaiian community.

The concern expressed by Hawaiians over Takabuki's appointment centered on the nature and purposes of the Bishop Estate. Created in 1884 by the will of Princess Bernice Pauahi Bishop, the Bishop Estate was to manage the vast landholdings which the princess had held as the lineal granddaughter of King Kamehameha the Great. The income received from the land was intended by Mrs. Bishop to be used for the education of the "children of Hawaii," generally interpreted to mean Hawaiian or Part-Hawaiian children. As a result, Kamehameha Schools were established to aid children of Hawaiian or Part-Hawaiian ancestry in their adjustment to modern American society, as well as to help them retain forms of the cultural roots of their ethnic heritage.

Actually, the Bishop Estate had largely been managed for sixty years, without protest, not by Hawaiians but by *haole*s. The first Part-Hawaiian Trustee, Edwin P. Murray, was not appointed until 1940, and only two other trustees had been of Hawaiian ancestry—Samuel Wilder King and Richard Lyman. Although the first Asian, Hung Wo Ching, was appointed with the quiet acquiescence of the Hawaiian community in 1968, the Takabuki appointment in 1971 was made in an atmosphere of growing Hawaiian ethnic consciousness and discontent. With a resurgence of activism and misgivings for the Burns–Inouye political coalition, the Hawaiians resented the appointment of a non-Hawaiian. With significant numbers of their people living in poverty, on welfare, or in prison, they were realizing that the Hawaiian Consensus at times had little room for the original inhabitants of the Island. Although seething with internal factions and movements which sought to implement forms of "Brown Power," the Hawaiian community that met at Kawaiahao Church had little taste for compromise.

"With all due respects to Mr. Takabuki," announced the Reverend Abraham Akaka, beloved pastor of Kawaiahao Church and respected leader of his people, "I am disappointed in the choice." The appointment of Takabuki marked "a dark day for our native Hawaiian people," Akaka sermonized, who had become "strangers in their own land."[13]

Most of the arguments against Takabuki's appointment involved not so much his Japanese ancestry *per se,* but his ties with Chinn Ho's Capital Investment Company and the fact that a Hawaiian as Trustee would best know the needs of the people. As a lawyer for Capital Investment, which had extensive land dealings, many felt Takabuki would have a conflict of interest. And as someone not of Hawaiian ancestry, Takabuki would be insensitive or unaware of the educational needs of Hawaiian children and uninformed of the best ways to handle the vast estates to the best interests of the Hawaiian people.

"Undoubtedly Mr. Takabuki is a capable man," a reader wrote to a local paper. "But surely there is a capable Hawaiian to be found in these Islands."[14]

Samuel Crowningburg-Amalu discussed precisely this issue in his June 28, 1971, column in the *Honolulu Advertiser,* entitled "In All Hawaii, Not One Hawaiian Worthy of Trust?"[15] Amalu, a controversial figure in the Hawaiian community, descendant of the *alii*s of ancient Hawaii and an articulate, though at times Latinate, writer, had always been a spokesman for interracial harmony and unifying Americanism in the best tradition of the Hawaiian Consensus. Excessively calling attention to one's ethnicity would have been contrary to Amalu's notion of the *aloha* tradition upon which the Island society daily operated. But even for Amalu, the Takabuki appointment grated on the latent Hawaiian ethnicity which bound him to his people and community.

Critical of the mainland-style protestations, marches, and placards of Hawaiian demonstrators, Amalu also felt that to some degree the agitation over Takabuki's appointment was racially based. "It would be extremely difficult to dissuade me," he wrote, "from the persuasion that the objections against the appointment of Matsuo Takabuki are based on anything else but racial grounds.

"And if this be true, I am chagrined that such bigotry should arise from among my own people."

Although race should not be made an issue, Amalu contended that the Bishop Estate was to serve the Hawaiian people and "who else should be entrusted with the administration of these lands but persons of Hawaiian blood? Can I be led to believe that in all of Hawaii, there is not one single person of Hawaiian extraction worthy of trust?"

Caught in the paradox of believing in the *aloha* of Hawaii while feeling the need for ethnic awareness and unity, Amalu poignantly concluded that everything of the Hawaiian people—their crowns, their land, and their identity—had been taken from them save the Kamehameha lands. "And would any of the alien races whom we have welcomed upon these shores, would any of them take even these away from us?"

The bells of Kawaiahao Church tolled the laments of the Hawaiian people later that year when the appointment of Takabuki was confirmed.

During the controversy over his appointment, Takabuki had remained silent, reluctant to become embroiled in what could have become a bitter racial confrontation. But eight months later, in February, 1972, Takabuki addressed the Hawaiian Civic Club's annual convention.[16] Besides reassuring the audience that he intended to do his utmost as trustee to advance the best interests of the Hawaiian people, he also confronted the racial issue which surrounded his appointment.

The 1970s, according to Takabuki, had seen an emergence of ethnicity as a means of social and political power. "Black Power" on the mainland had been followed by "Yellow Power" and "Brown Power" movements in Hawaii. To be proud of oneself, one's ethnic heritage, was an accepted and healthy development. "Is it not true," Takabuki asked, "that to deny pride in one's ethnic identity is really to deny who you really are?"

But, in striving to be ethnically identifiable, did the races of Hawaii jeopardize the racial harmony and cultural sharing which had been the process of Island race relations for over a hundred years? Did not ethnicity contradict the "golden man" of the Pacific, which had so long been the dream of social scientists and novelists? "Is there any danger," Takabuki queried, speaking of ethnic identity, "that it may lead some to reject all that is not of its color?" Or "What happens when such ethnicity, such way, such right, or such truth sharply conflicts with other groups aspiring for the same thing within the same society?"

"I guess this was our dilemma in this incident."

The conflict between the recognition of one's ethnicity on the one hand, and the tradition of *aloha* and cultural sharing and mixing on the other, was accurately identified by Takabuki as the dilemma of Hawaiian society in the 1970s. By 1975 Hawaii had witnessed developments of contradictory and tumultuous proportions. Ethnicity and ethnic awareness were reaching levels of expression which would not soon disappear. At the University of Hawaii and in the public schools, young Hawaiians, Filipinos, Chinese, and Japanese were taking a variety of courses which aimed at giving students a sense of their cultural and ethnic roots. While some courses fell back on mainland-style Third World political rhetoric, others appealed to the student's simple need to know who they were and what their ethnic identity and heritage were all about.

In the community, the Takabuki incident sparked other movements of equal political and economic importance. Filipinos and Hawaiians being evicted from their rural homes of many years began to resist the land developers who had previously been unhampered in their manipulation of the impoverished. Speaking of "our people," "our community," Hawaiians, attempting to preserve some of their rural lifestyle, opposed the proposed developments of Halawa and Kalama valleys. And by 1974 through an organization known as Aloha, Inc., they were demanding reparations for lands allegedly stolen from the Hawaiian monarchy in 1893. At Ota Camp on Oahu, Filipinos were refusing to abandon their homes for land development until concessions could be won which would guarantee them resettlement compatible with their former modes of life. And in September of 1974, following a series of racial outbreaks in the public high schools between immigrant Filipinos and local students, including the beating-death of a young Filipino immigrant, the Filipino community began organizing to study what could be done to protect its children and ameliorate racial hostilities.

Even Japanese who had been exercising an ethnic power and community concern since the 1950s were in some ways participants in the emergence of expressive ethnic pride and awareness. Not only were the Sansei becoming educationally exposed to their ethnic heritage in the schools, but the gubernatorial elections of 1974 elicited a special meaning for some Japanese. For the first time in Hawaii's history, a Japanese governor, George Ariyoshi, together with a Japanese lieutenant governor, Nelson Doi, had been elected as heads of the state government. While many insisted that race was not an issue of the elections, some Japanese, especially Issei and Nisei, must have felt gratified that the injustices of World War II and the second-class citizenship of plantation life had been so totally reversed.

But if ethnic awareness, in a reaction against the Hawaiian Consensus, was finding a new avenue of expression in the Hawaii of the seventies, so too was the realization that the problems that confronted Island society were greater than those of any one ethnic group. While many could applaud the new Japanese governor, many others would say "So what?" The problems of urban development, population growth, transportation, ecological control, welfare, or the cost of living had very little to do with the slant of the governor's eyes or his skin color. The future of Hawaii depended on leadership and direction, not just the fulfillment of narrow ethnic interests or ambitions.

The Sansei inherited a place in Hawaii which generations before them had struggled to achieve. Through cruel and cheap labor, through the nightmare of war and through the conflicts of the contest for power, the Issei and Nisei had helped define the Japanese community of Hawaii. They had given shape and purpose to the status of Japanese as accepted neighbors in Hawaii. In so doing, they had relied on a style of ethnic identification which was flexible enough to maintain group solidarity and unity and at the same time allow for the adaption of their culture to the multicultural society in which they lived.

The newer generations of Japanese who would call Hawaii their home in the 1970s also were developing a pride of ethnicity, a commonality of culture and heritage. But at the same time they found themselves in a modern New Hawaii which was multiethnic in nature and straining from the radical political, economic, and social changes which had occurred since World War II and statehood. These young Japanese had been reared in a Hawaii where the Hawaiian Consensus at times superseded ethnic allegiances. The answer to making Hawaii a better home for all people, to coping with the changes which at times seemed too much for the Island people did not lie in the ethnic community or in their ethnic identity. Diversity to the point of separatism hardly seemed a solution to problems which demanded broad ethnic and social support. But unrest, confusion, and the seemingly uncontrollable influences of politics and economics, of media and outside forces, prompted skepticism and even distaste for the New Hawaii—the Hawaiian Consensus which at times provided more dilemmas than solutions.

So as they looked to the future of Hawaii, the Sansei and Islanders of all ethnic backgrounds would have to realize that many of their values and priorities would have to be redefined and reordered. While the "golden man" of the Pacific, a bland cultural similarity, was not the total cure-all of social ills, neither was excessive ethnic awareness or pride. Neither was the Hawaiian Consensus of the "good life" wholly enough—uncontrolled growth, profit, and success without planning for the conservation of land, resources, and the quality of life would render Island living stripped of the beauty and peacefulness associated with Hawaii's multiracial diversity and environmental charm.

The sojourners and natives who had made Hawaii a modern Island society had done so seeking personal and ethnic success. Many had succeeded in their endeavors, passing on to their children the responsibility of leadership and power. Others had encountered cultural and racial barriers demanding ethnic cohesiveness and passed on to their children the continued need to adapt and strive for an equitable share of available social rewards. But in the New Hawaii of the seventies, this success and ethnicity could no longer be adequate to complete the cycle which the sojourner and native had begun a hundred years previously. To become equal neighbors in a complex Island society which offered equal opportunity of employment and leisure, to harmoniously design the Hawaii of 2000 A.D., a new Hawaiian Consensus would be needed—a Consensus which would put interracial sharing and endeavors above ethnic separatism, the quality of Island life above the quantity of growth, an appreciation of cultural variations above the pettiness of exclusive provincialism or racial xenophobia, and a love of Hawaii and her future above personal or group gain. For Japanese, Filipinos, Hawaiians, *haoles*, Chinese, Koreans, Portuguese, Puerto Ricans, Samoans, and others, for the generations of immigrants and their progeny, this New Consensus would demand both self-examination and interracial cooperation. The tasks ahead seemed clear—the challenge was both thrilling and promising.

NOTES

1. David E. Thompson, "The ILWU as a Force for Interracial Unity in Hawaii," *Social Process in Hawaii,* v. 15 (1951), pp. 32–43.

2. Frederick Simpich, Jr., *Anatomy of Hawaii,* Toronto: Coward, McConn and Geoghegan Inc., 1971, p. 91.

3. H. McKinley Conway, Jr., "Progress is Jet-Propelled in Hawaii," *Industrial Development,* December 1959, p. 20.

4. Simpich, p. 101.

5. "Japan Investment a Concern," *Hawaii Tribune-Herald,* February 8, 1973, p. 12.

6. "10% More Japanese Tourists to Visit," *Honolulu Star-Bulletin,* February 21, 1973, p. D-8:4.

7. Chinn Ho, "Our Future in Hawaii," presented to the Hawaii Newspaper Publishers Association Convention, October 6, 1967.

8. Lawrence H. Fuchs, *Hawaii Pono: A Social History,* New York: Harcourt, Brace and World, 1961, pp. 397–8.

9. Governor John A. Burns, *Inaugural Address,* December 5, 1966.

10. Tom Coffman, *Catch A Wave: A Case Study of Hawaii's New Politics,* Honolulu: University Press of Hawaii, 1972, p. 10.

11. Coffman, p. 114.

12. Coffman, p. 181.

13. Theon Wright, *The Disenchanted Isles: The Story of the Second Revolution in Hawaii,* New York: Dial Press, 1972, p. 259.

14. *Honolulu Star-Bulletin,* June 24, 1971, p. A-17:5.

15. Samuel Crowningburg-Amalu, "In All Hawaii, Not One Hawaiian Worthy Of Trust?" *Honolulu Star-Bulletin and Advertiser,* June 27, 1971, p. D6-1.

16. Matsuo Takabuki, "Speech to the Hawaiian Civic Club's Annual Convention," February, 1972.

The ILWU as a Force for Interracial Unity in Hawaii

DAVID E. THOMPSON

The Logic of Union Interracial Policy

The objective of trade union organization is to create a situation in which the organized workers can effectively deny labor to an employer who will not meet their terms for the sale of labor. Fundamentally, the power to bargain for improved wages and conditions depends upon the extent to which such a situation is created. The only basic and stable guarantee of such a situation is support of this trade union objective by all workers available to the employer.

In a modern industrial community, the number of useful workers available to an employer is not restricted to a handful of skilled craftsmen; instead it tends to include the entire force of workers. To the extent that a community does not have actual race-caste restrictive laws or mores, or to the extent that these laws or mores become less effective, the useful workers available to any employer tend to include the entire force of workers regardless of race, creed, or color. Increasingly industrial methods of production and declining race or caste restrictions on job-competition have forced enlightened trade unionists to recognize the necessity of achieving unity of workers across and without regard to racial lines.

Many trade union leaders and workers still refuse to see these facts. In 1934, however, West Coast longshoremen felt they could

In *Social Process in Hawaii,* v. 15 (1951), pp. 32–43. Reprinted by permission of David E. Thompson.

not afford the luxury of such illogic in their bitter struggle to establish an effective trade union against great odds. When they had finally established their own West Coast union, the ILWU, they wrote the principles which had guided them in their successful struggle, into the Constitution, the basic law of their new union. Among the "objects" of the union, they wrote, "First, to unite in one organization, regardless of religion, race, creed, color, political affiliation or nationality, all workers . . ." and in the Preamble, they listed as one of their objectives "to banish racial and religious prejudice everywhere in the world"—an obvious corollary, for the prejudices which divide the community operate both to impede universal organization into trade unions and to intrude themselves divisively into the life of the union even after it has achieved universal organization.

If trade union logic demanded a program of interracial unity on the Mainland, the same logic operated even more powerfully in Hawaii where the main industries drew upon a polyglot community for a working force basically unskilled. Hawaii's workers learned this lesson the hard way; the "pre-history" of successful unionism here is replete with tragic tales of labor organizations, wage movements, strikes, and hopes shattered on the twin rocks of racial exclusiveness and racial strikebreaking; but this pre-history also contains bright interludes of momentary interracial cooperation and resultant increases in bargaining power. Throughout, this chronicle of a few strikes won and many others "lost" shows that every upsurge in labor militancy was followed by "voluntary" improvements by the employers in wages and conditions. The lesson was clear, collective action is the road to advance, and collective action can only be successful on a basis of interracial unity.

Thus in the late thirties when unionists from the West Coast, themselves newly armed with the principles of interracial, industrial unionism, pointed out the logic of these lessons, they found Hawaii's workers ripe for understanding. A brief battle of theory took place during the 1937 strike of the exclusively Filipino Vibora Luviminda on Maui. Although the leaders of Vibora Luviminda refused to see it, the course of the strike clearly confirmed the logic of the new unionism. The racial form of the strike limited its effectiveness. Harvesting was prevented, but other plantation operations essential to crop production were not. That the strike was even partially successful was due to financial support from the Japanese and financial and other support from CIO unions here and on the Mainland, including the vital contribution of the International Labor

Defense in preventing the strike from being decapitated through the incarceration of its leaders. Shortly thereafter Vibora Luviminda, the last of the big racial unions, died, an anachronism. For the first time in twenty years the Japanese were drawn back into the labor movement. Having once found the successful organization, Hawaii's plantation workers began to join into their first stable and effective union movement.[1]

The principle that workers of all races have common interests as workers and can only advance these interests by interracial unity has never been seriously challenged—as a principle—in the years that have followed. Indeed the principle of interracial unity or "brotherhood" has been one of the most popular slogans of Hawaii's unionists; it has been kept constantly before their eyes, not as an idealistic shibboleth, but as a practical working theory so powerful that both the main theory and its logical corollaries are looked to as the criteria of correct action.

It is not strange that this should be so. For every attempt of Hawaii's workers to achieve combined action has from the earliest days been faced with the unified opposition of employers who clearly understood that racial division was their strongest weapon against combination. This idea was well expressed by a plantation manager appearing in 1895 before a commission of the Hawaiian Republic, who testified that:

> Strikes will continue as long as men combine and the only measure that can be taken, which may be effectual to any extent, are those which will reduce their opportunities for combination and their inclination for same.
>
> It seems to me that this can be done by employing as many nationalities as possible on each plantation. If immigrants of various nationalities would come in until there are sufficient of them in the country to offset any one nationality, we would then be better off.[2]

A careful observer notes:

> Throughout its subsequent history, it has been part of the conscious strategy of the plantation interests to "divide and rule." The arrival of each new racial group has been welcomed not only as an addition to the labor force but also as a check upon the potential aggression of its predecessors. Japanese and Portuguese served to curb the rising ambitions and rebelliousness of the Chinese during the eighties, and during the following decade the roles were reversed, new shipments of Chinese restraining somewhat the protests of the Japanese. Still later,

> Puerto Ricans, Koreans, Spanish, Russians, and a number of other groups were introduced in small numbers to supplement and discipline the existing plantation labor force.[3]

Thus both the variety in the Island population and many of the prejudices and divisive attitudes which exist between races here can be traced to employer policy. Many of the familiar racial slanders made their appearance in the local culture as justifications for the importation of new immigrant groups, and much of the mistrust and resentment between racial groups can be traced to the employer policy of playing off one group against another, with the fundamental objective of preventing or disrupting collective action. While it would be completely inaccurate to say that all of the existing barriers to racial unity stem entirely from economic motives, the important fact for trade unionists is that all such barriers do constitute obstacles to successful combination for economic interest. Concomitantly with every struggle for their economic interest, therefore, Hawaii's organized workers have been forced consciously to struggle against latent racial prejudices and against the intensification, manipulation, and exploitation of these prejudices by the opposition.

The Interracial Practices of the Union

Given then the fact that the principle of interracial unity is an established and generally accepted principle in modern Hawaiian unionism, the sociology student's interest centers around the questions, "To what extent is this principle applied in practice?" "What forms does practical application take?" "How has this aspect of union program affected social process in Hawaii?"

The leadership of the International Union has prided itself upon a rigid adherence to the Constitutional provisions on "no discrimination," even when momentarily such a course appeared to certain "practical" critics to be imprudent. In 1942, for example, ILWU Secretary-Treasurer Louis Goldblatt was the lone trade union representative to appear at administrative hearings in California and to protest wartime relocation of the Japanese. Again, in 1945, when a small clique of officers in a Local Union of the ILWU in Stockton, California attempted to ban returning Japanese evacuees from work on the Stockton Waterfront, the International officers promptly moved into the situation. The offending officers of the Local were tried and suspended from the Union. The Japanese workers were returned to the job. Of course, this record has served the International well in the Territory in helping to break down the Local workers' mistrust of the *haole* and *malihini* representatives of the organization, as well as in competition with other International Unions whose records of discriminatory practices on the Mainland have proved acutely embarrassing to them here.

Similarly, the International Union has consistently used its influence in the internal life of the Territorial Locals to prevent the development of discriminatory practices within the Union. Statements of International officers and representatives to Union conferences and committees are studded with warnings against the danger of racial division, appeals to the membership to form an "unbreakable weld of interracial unity," and prideful reference to the way in which workers of all races have been drawn together in Union brotherhood.

More significant, however, has been the use of International Union influence to prevent the formation of racial power blocs within the Union, to prevent the domination of the Union by any one racial group, to protect some of the smaller racial groups within the Union, and more positively, to encourage and assist in the development of strong and effective Local leadership within the Territory which is representative of all racial groups. During and after the rapid postwar growth of the Union here the International frequently demanded that there be a strict proportional division of leadership positions among representatives of various racial groups. Because of the democratic constitutional structure of the Union, and especially the provision of Local autonomy, the International has been able to achieve these objectives only by appeal to correct principle. The fact that it has been largely successful is one of the strongest indications of the general acceptance and practical power of this principle among Hawaii's unionists.

Looking now to the practical applications of the interracial principle by individual Locals, we find a universal policy of organizing all eligible workers, regardless of race, into one Union with constitutional guarantees of equal rights.

Equally important is the policy of extending recognition and respect to members of various groups. An obvious example is the use of various languages in conducting meetings, so that all members are equally informed of the issues and enabled to have their say in decisions. It is common for a Union meeting to have reports given in three languages, English, Japanese, and Ilocano, with members of the various language groups sitting patiently through explanations in other tongues, and to follow this with floor discussion in which each contribution is interpreted. The Union uses the medium of three languages for its important publications and for its regular radio programs.

Another almost universal form of recognition is the policy of encouraging the election of representatives of each racial group to office in the Union.

Local Unions have also had a policy of protecting the interests of workers regardless of racial groups, as reflected in demands made in negotiations and the processing of grievances under the agreement. Further than this, in accord with the slogan, "an injury to one is an injury to all," Locals have given special attention to problems more or less unique to individual racial groups such as the various stock swindles and fleecing rackets injuring Filipino members and the problems of the McCarrran Act registration facing alien members.

But here again a statement of official policy fails to answer the question of how consistently these policies have been applied in practice and the extent to which they have overcome racial barriers. To be able to understand the answers to these questions, one must also understand the height and intensity of these racial barriers and emotions which had to be overcome. When the new Unionism came to the so-called island "melting pot" in the late thirties and during its expansion after the war, racial barriers were real obstacles to organization and collective work. Many of them still persist, although with diminished power. The local population then was definitely stratified, with the various groups occupying an economic and social status generally consistent with the date of their importation. Acute racial jealousies and competitive fears reinforced prejudices based upon cultural judgments, ignorance, or lack of understanding.

These prejudices and jealousies came quickly to the surface as the Union was organized. The Japanese, generally the most aggressive group in the formation of the Union, tended to under-rate the importance of other groups, dismissing the Portuguese as being generally "no-good" and not worth organizing, while the Filipinos were recognized as necessary to successful organization, but too "ignorant" to be admitted to leadership. Portuguese workers shared the Japanese scorn of the Filipino, but regarded the rising Japanese leadership with alarm and indignation as a threat to their own generally superior status on the job and in the community. Filipinos shared the Japanese suspicion of the more favored Portuguese, but were resentful of the condescending attitude of both groups toward them, and positively outraged by the thought that they as the largest group of workers should not enjoy a proportionate leadership position.

Conflicts and controversies growing out of such attitudes for a long time were at the roots of the thorniest problems of Union policy and administration. One of the most important contributions of the International officers and representatives in building and maintaining the Union here was in acting as a neutral force, restraining violently prejudiced factions. No one who has experienced those early conflicts in the life of the Union has any illusions about the lack of "racial aloha" and understanding among Hawaii's workers a short five or six years ago.

In this situation, the most immediate impact of the new Unionism upon the existent racial relationships was to bring workers and their leaders together for collective discussion and an effort to solve mutual problems of great import. It should be remembered that at that time the Union movement was regarded as fraught with danger for the individual member and especially for the leader. In the mind of the new unionists, any serious mistakes or failure of the movement carried the danger of discharge, blacklisting, individual ruin. The compulsion was strong upon those who dared to take leadership to be guided by the logic of unionism, to reach across barriers, to try to understand and to try to be understood. Inevitably, former prejudices and exclusive habits were corroded.

An example is that of two young Japanese community leaders, newly chosen as delegates to a Union conference in 1945. Both were appalled when they discovered that they were to share a hotel room with a Filipino delegate. But they were equally appalled at the thought of the effect that a display of their feelings might have should it reach the ears of their large Filipino memberships at home, and so they hid their feelings. In recent years, the writer has observed these same two Japanese leaders genuinely enjoying board and lodging from fellow Filipino trade unionists on other plantations.

In the same way, in membership meetings, the average worker shows an understanding of the need for mutual respect. In times of crisis, such as strikes, or momentous membership meetings, the reaction is usually a deeper one, a genuine expression of the warm emotion of brotherhood. An effective orator in a foreign tongue is admired, enjoyed, and applauded by workers who cannot understand his speech. The contributions to the common cause by one racial group are doubly appreciated, and doubly lauded by the members of other groups for the very reason that they reenforce the shared emotion of united strength. Outpourings of friendliness and exhibitions of acceptance, as in the sharing of national foods in strike kitchens, are greeted by all as positive contributions to the unity which they realize is essential to victory. Here too, former habits of withdrawal and exclusiveness are diluted or momentarily washed out; and while they reemerge with a return to old routines, they have been weakened and are now subject to challenge and popular censure by those who recall the values and attitudes shared during the crisis they met together.

Union logic has not acted as a universal solvent of crystalized prejudice, however. Frequently the prejudice prevails. Many units have planned a social dance, thinking that it would help cement friendly interracial relations, and instead created a situation of great bitterness because all the girls refused to dance with Filipino men. The policy of conducting meetings in three languages has frequently backfired when English speaking members refuse to attend meetings which they feel are unnecessarily drawn out.

Many times on a plantation level the tendency of leaders from one racial group to form a social clique has resulted in their acting together as a clique within the Union. Members of other groups immediately become suspicious that members of the clique are not motivated in their policies by consideration of the common good. And such suspicions are frequently quite sound because even with good intentions, the clique members' understanding and responsiveness to rank and file needs are limited by the exclusiveness of their associations. If the clique becomes dominant in Union affairs, a contest for control along racial lines may develop and debates on policy become distorted by considerations other than the common good. Another reaction is for the other groups to withdraw from activity. This may take a passive form, or it may take an actively spiteful one, such as campaigning against a general Union policy which is supported on that plantation by members of the clique. But here again, the logic of Unionism asserts a continual pressure for change; for all of these things weaken the Union and thereby deprive all involved of the ability to advance their interests effectively.

The leadership, beset by failures, can look to other plantations where wiser leadership has established warm interracial social relations; where a broad, representative leadership engages in informal bull sessions, social drinking, and other play activities; and where the intimate knowledge, understanding, and trust born of these relationships result in leadership and membership unity, esprit de corps, and outstanding trade union success.

It has now long been recognized as a general rule in union circles that where people play together they can work together better; and the compulsion is strong upon all active unionists to develop the social relationships prerequisite to good union work. This Union rule and the practical pressures which flow from it have had their primary positive effects upon the more active Union members or leaders in their male social activities. Where effective women's union auxiliaries have been established, family groups have been brought into interracial social activities which represent a much more complete acceptance of individuals from other racial groups. At the same time, the effect of Union program and doctrine in breaking down prejudices and exclusive habits has done much in an indirect way to accelerate the development of interracial social life among the membership at large.

This rule has its opposite which has also been long recognized by sophisticated Unionists here, the rule that the *existence of racial recrimination is a sure sign of Union weakness.* It is a particular example of the axiom expressed in the common saying, "It's easier to fight another worker than it is to fight the boss." Where Unionists are frustrated by their own weakness relative to the employer, it is very common to find leaders from each racial group blaming other racial groups for the general failure. Here old prejudices reemerge and find new reinforcement, in the repetition of all the old familiar racial slanders and stereotyped characterizations, plus a few new ones which have grown out of the actions of particular groups on the plantation since the Union came. But here again, the group only begins to solve its problems when it has once discovered or been shown that the "scapegoat" reaction is not only diverting its attentions and energies from the real tasks at hand, but is making those tasks more difficult.

In a situation, for example, where frustrated Union leaders complain that Portuguese workers are inactive, or are actively anti-Union, the obvious trade union objective is to enlist some Portuguese in the work of winning back this group. But by using the Portuguese group as a scapegoat for their own failure and repeating generalized slanders against all Portuguese, the frustrated leadership is itself making this objective impossible.

As a group finds its way out of such an impasse, the more perceptive and effective members of the group recognize the divisive role that racial slander has played and tend to use their influence against a repetition of the same mistake. The lessons of such experience are spread from one group of workers to another through Union channels. Workers from different racial groups, plantations, and islands have engaged in literally thousands of discussions of such problems of technique and tactics both in formal Territorial or Island conferences, steward council and executive board meetings, and in informal bull sessions. As the Union movement has matured, leadership and membership have shown increasing awareness that racial slanders play a dual role of splitting the unity of the workers and of diverting attention from the vital issues or making it more difficult to arrive at correct solutions to basic problems.

Some of the uses of the race level and racial slanders in controversy are reflected in statements such as:

> We cannot afford to decide the issue of a strike in a membership meeting because the Filipinos are too ignorant and easily swayed by emotion. The Filipinos are irresponsible because they do not intend to live here forever; they don't care if the plantation goes broke.
>
> The *haole* Union leaders are clever and selfish like all *haole*s, only interested in getting rich. What do they care if the strike ruins everyone? They'll go back to the coast with their money. Yes, they married local girls, but that was only to get an 'in' with local people. They'll leave their wives behind.
>
> The Japanese dominate the Union and are only using the Filipinos as tools.
>
> The *haoles* dominate the union and are only using all Local people as tools. We should form a Union with strictly local leaders.[4]

And perhaps the commonest expression of all in surreptitious use is the direct selfish nationalist appeal: "We Portuguese (or Japanese, or Filipinos, or Hawaiians) should stick together." The significant thing is that such appeals must be used surreptitiously today, while only a few years ago they could be openly expressed without drawing general censure.

Many of these slanders and racist appeals have had obvious uses in the struggle for representation in Union leadership. The development of trade union logic around the question of proper leadership in the effect of that logic upon social process has been most interesting. With its first startling successes, the Union suddenly emerged as an institution with great prestige. There was a natural tendency for individuals and racial groups to vie for positions of leadership. Frequently, plantation Unions would be effectively dominated by Filipino, Japanese, or Portuguese leadership. At the same time, however, if that leadership was to achieve unity of all workers it found it necessary to give recognition to each group, and generally the other groups were quite vocal in their demands for representation. The more cogent arguments for representative leadership were that only leaders from a given group could fully understand and respond to the problems of that group, that only people who can speak the language of the given group can make issues clear to that group, and finally that only a recognized leader from a given group can enjoy the trust of that group.

The counter argument, used by groups enjoying actual control, was that leaders should be chosen on the basis of their "ability" and that any other criteria were both discriminatory and against the best interests of the membership. (Interestingly enough some of the prime proponents of the "ability" argument had, in earlier days, used the "representation" argument in a bitter fight against *haole* leadership.) Proponents of the "ability" argument usually pointed out that language problems could be solved by using interpreters who need not be actual leaders.

The International Union's approach to these problems has consistently been that representative leadership is a necessity and that the ability problem should be solved by developing capable leadership from within each racial group. Experience has today produced a general agreement among active Unionists here. At the same time, consistent trade union emphasis upon the importance of basing decisions and action on issues rather than upon "personalities," and the emphasis upon developing rank and file control of Union program based upon understanding of issues rather than loyalty to leaders has tended to blunt former sharp feelings about the racial composition of leadership. The type of racial tension described in the foregoing pages—the tendency of leadership cliques to form along racial lines, the use of the threat to withdraw support by one racial group or another in controversies over policy or the composition of leadership has now generally disappeared. Today a leader who voiced the threat so familiar until recently, that he would walk out of the Union and take his whole racial group with him, would be a laughing stock. Everyone knows that today such a leader would take no one out but himself. Leadership groups which persist in acting as racial cliques are quickly repudiated by all sections of the membership as dangerous and ineffective.[5]

While everything noted to this point would indicate that the ILWU has acted as a force for better race relations, it is frequently charged by critics that the ILWU has "created race hatred," meaning anti-*haole* sentiment. This is not true. Anti-*haole* sentiment existed and found sharp public expression long before the Union came.[6] Certainly racial feelings were a powerful element in the whole complex of resentments and dissatisfactions which motivated the mass movement into the ILWU in 1944–45. What happened then can only be understood in the light of its background.

The plantation system created a situation of caste distinction along racial lines, with *haole*s comprising the actual ruling caste. It was generally felt among non-*haole*s that "the white men's floor is the colored men's ceiling." The inevitable result was resentment on the part of the less favored races. The situation was not only resented, but felt to be unjust. This feeling was reinforced by the disparity between actual plantation practice and the American ideology of equality of opportunity as learned by the growing second generation.

The impact of the war helped both to crystallize these feelings and to open the way to their freer expression. At first made doubly resentful by increased suspicion and discriminatory treatment at the beginning of the war, the Japanese found themselves vindicated and released from suspicion by their record during the war and in a position to speak freely. The influx of white working men, intimate association with white service men, and the increase in interracial marriages, did much to break down former awe and reserve, and much too to reinforce feelings of injustice. Plantation workers especially smarted under wartime government orders which froze them to their jobs and froze their wages while living costs and outside wages soared. When finally the whole situation of frozen labor and superheated passions erupted into a sweeping Union movement, the racial overtones which have always been associated with questions of economic justice in Hawaii were strongly felt. One of the most popular slogans and demands was for an end to discrimination.

If the Union movement opened new avenues for the sharp and open expression of anti-*haole* sentiment, it also channelized that sentiment along the constructive channels of demands for the removal of the economic inequalities from which that sentiment largely stemmed.

Aside from the fact that a deliberate policy of inflaming anti-*haole* sentiment would flatly contradict official ILWU policy, the whole idea becomes ridiculous when one thinks of the dangers such a policy would have for a Union movement which depends upon solidarity with West Coast workers for much of its bargaining power. Or from another viewpoint, blind anti-*haole* sentiment could make it impossible for *haole* representatives of the International Union to work in Hawaii. On the contrary, the experience of intimate work and association with *haole* Union members and leaders has had the effect of removing much of the original suspicion, resentment, and hatred of the *haole* per se. It is only since the formation of the Union that *haole* plantation workers have been integrated into the laboring community. The exceptional *haole* laborer in the old days was generally regarded as a person who was merely serving an apprenticeship for a supervisory position. In the recent past a good number of *haole* laborers on plantations have been elected as Union officers or stewards by electors who were entirely non-*haole*.

Effects of Union Policies and Practices

Let us turn now, briefly, to the impact of these Union policies and practices upon social process in Hawaii. A complete listing of the social effects to which these practices have contributed, or an analysis of the relative weight which should be given to ILWU influence among the other factors which have produced these effects, has not been attempted here; but rather a mere indication of a few of the more obvious examples of these effects as they appear to the writer, a trade unionist, with the thought that these may provide productive subjects for more scholarly investigation.

By bringing workers of all races together for a common effort, by providing them with many shared experiences, by providing a consistent, logical, and practical pressure against exclusive habits and the expression of prejudice, by a similar pressure toward the establishment of issues rather than labels or "personalities" as the criterion of judgment, the ILWU has done much to remove racial tension and promote interracial aloha and unity among its members.

By raising the demand in collective bargaining, of "no discrimination," the ILWU has made a major contribution to the establishment of free economic mobility in the community as a whole. The "seniority" and "no discrimination" clauses written into ILWU agreements covering 28,000 workers in basic island industries are guarantees of free mobility within the labor force. Equally important has been the reaction of many local employers who have sought to remove the potent discrimination issue from the Union's arsenal both by avoiding race discrimination in job placement under the

Union agreement, and by promoting non-*haole*s to supervisory positions. An incidental effect of this latter increasingly common practice is to create a group of non-*haole*s who identify themselves with the position of management, thus weakening the strong race-class identification which formerly reinforced anti-*haole* prejudice.

The purely economic impact of the Union in doubling or tripling basic wage rates for all of its members, thus raising their standard of living and expectations has also done much to enhance the status of all groups and to give them the feeling that they belong to the larger community and have a right and duty to participate in its affairs. It should be noted, too, that this influence has not been confined to plantation workers, for Union wage scales have exerted a definite leverage on community wage rates and living standards as a whole.

The feeling of belonging to the community is reflected in the modern tendency of immigrant workers to regard the islands as "home" as contrasted to the prewar "sojourner" attitude of the average Filipino whose ambition was to accumulate sufficient wealth here to return, a "success" to his native barrio, or the common ambition of the older Japanese to return to Japan to die. There can be little doubt that improved living standards here, stemming directly from Unionization, have done much to influence the former sojourner to adopt Hawaii as his home.

The ILWU has also helped to create a sense of belonging to the community, especially among immigrant groups, by its efforts to acquaint all of its members with their basic legal rights, to encourage them to defend and exercise these rights and to provide them with effective implementation therefor. In this the Union has been motivated in large part by the most elementary considerations of survival as an organization,[7] but the incidental effects have been profound. A few examples will give some ideas of what this has meant. In the field of enforcing beneficial labor legislation alone, such as wage and hour laws and industrial accident compensation laws, literally millions of dollars have been recovered for Union members and their families. More important is the way in which the availability of Union lawyers has protected members of immigrant groups, and especially Filipinos, against the harsh and high-handed treatment at the hands of police and the courts which is all too frequently the lot of the politically weak, "unimportant," or uninformed individual in every society.

The Union found this whole matter to be so vital to the protection of its members that in 1948 it issued a pocket-sized card in English and Ilocano entitled, "Your Legal Rights," in which basic rights affecting arrest, subpoena, search, deportation, and the right to legal counsel were outlined. The informed *kamaaina* will appreciate the significance which a Union lawyer attached to the incident when a Filipino who had been arrested for alleged presence at a cockfight walked into the law office and announced that his "civil liberties had been violated!" Even more important than the availability of sympathetic and able counsel, has been the effect of Union appeal to constitutional law in making available to the non-Caucasian working men a trial by a jury of his peers. The challenge by the Union of the racial and occupational composition of the Maui Grand Jury in 1947, has resulted in the wholesale revision of jury lists everywhere in the Territory to include representatives of all groups. A number of non-Caucasian lawyers have expressed to the writer the conviction that this has made it possible for them for the first time to get a "decent jury trial" for their clients. These three examples of the effect of Unionization in the field of law enforcement and legal rights provide only the barest indication of the extent to which Unionization has brought the actual substance of theoretical legal "rights" to the average member of the island community but it is obvious that to the extent that members of the community are familiar with, protect, and exercise these rights, a feeling of belonging to the community is enhanced, and former bitter resentments of injustice or "racial justice" are deprived of foundation both in fact and in feeling.

And of course the Union's concern with the law has not been limited to existing law, but has also been expressed in a program of political action designed to elect lawmakers and obtain legislative action responsive to the interest of laboring people. Here again, the Union was motivated in great measure by elementary considerations of survival as an organization,[8] but the incidental effects of political campaigns upon the Union membership and the various racial groups within the community have been profound. By drawing its members, and especially its Filipino members, and the wives of Union members into effective political campaigns, the Union has hastened the practical integration of large segments of the community and helped develop their appreciation of the concept of an island commonwealth and the rights and responsibilities which that idea connotes. At the same time, the emphasis upon issues rather than upon individual candidates in election campaigns and during legislative sessions has acted as a deterrent to "racial voting" among Union members and their families.

The Union has provided a medium through which groups who formerly were voiceless in the community can now make themselves heard and can honestly and independently express their dissatisfactions, opinions, and wishes without fear of reprisal. Moreover, the power which formerly impotent or ignored groups have gained through their Union gives weight to their expression. At the same time, responsibilities shouldered and skills and experience gained by newly developed leaders from every racial group have equipped them with both the ability and self-confidence needed for effectively asserting community leadership. The basis is being established for a much broader and more representative community leadership than formerly existed.

The ILWU in the Territory has been a powerful element in the whole complex of factors operating to transform Hawaii's former colonial social system, with its basic population of more or less unassimilated and exclusive immigrant groups effectively dominated by a paternalistic *haole* ruling group into a genuine island commonwealth of self-governing people consistent with the basic American doctrines of democracy and equality and the corresponding Hawaiian public doctrine of racial equality and interracial aloha.[9]

NOTES

1. Edward L. H. Johannessen, *The Labor Movement in Hawaii,* M.S. thesis, Stanford 1950, gives a concise but comprehensive account of unionism's "prehistory" in Hawaii.

2. *Report of the Labor Commission on Strikes and Arbitration, Republic of Hawaii,* Honolulu, 1895, pp. 23–24, quoted in R. A. Liebes, *Labor Organization in Hawaii,* M.A. thesis, University of Hawaii, 1938.

3. Andrew W. Lind, *An Island Community,* Chicago, 1938, pp. 218–219.

4. The latter two ideas were combined in the "Izuka" pamphlet with the idea that a dominant *haole*-Japanese clique was manipulating the union for ulterior purposes. (See Ichiro Izuka, *The Truth About Communism In Hawaii,* Honolulu, 1947.) A careful reading will show that no Filipinos are listed as members of the alleged clique. The leadership of the 1947 dual union movement, which was planned in part on the basis of the anticipated effect of this pamphlet, made strong appeals to Filipino members and leaders to leave the parent Union and form a new Union "free from Japanese and *haole* domination."

5. It is true that here and there in a given plantation or camp or district, the anti-union attitude of influential individuals within one racial group or another still acts to deter members of that group from active union participation. These are influences which are exercised from *outside* the Union, however, and such situations are both uncommon and decreasing.

6. Anyone interested in confirming this need only refer to the translations from the Japanese newspaper *Nippu Jiji* published in the *Pacific Commercial Advertiser*

in 1908–09. And on the other hand he will find enough vitriolic anti-Oriental statements in the pages of the *Pacific Commercial Advertiser* for those years as well as 1920 to satisfy him that the non-Caucasians have had no monopoly on racial incitement and vilification.

7. From the beginning, the modern Union movement has had to fight, as a precondition of existence, first for the enforcement of the Wagner Act in the Territory, and the second against the use of the courts and Territorial law to deprive workers of the right to free association and collective action. (See issues of *The Voice of Labor* for Spring of 1937 for story of Wagner Act enforcement. See also *Intermediate Report of Trial Examiner,* NLRB cases XX-C-455 and XX-C-578 [Castle & Cooke Terminals, Ltd.] 1940.) A good account of anti-labor law and law enforcement in the Territory is contained in the *Memorandum on History of Labor and the Law in the Territory of Hawaii,* submitted to the United States District Court by the ILWU law firm in ILWU vs. Ackerman, Civil Nos. 828 and 836. A recent example of the importance of the defense of legal and constitutional rights for the survival of the Union is the fact that in 1949 by means of a court injunction the Union was able to delay the application of Acts 2 and 3 which had just been passed by the Territorial legislature, and thus prevented the longshore strike then in progress from being broken by Territorial operation of stevedoring facilities.

8. The immediate result of the first successful union political action campaign (in the 1944 elections) was the passage in 1945 of the Territorial "Little Wagner Act" (Hawaii Employment Relations Act) which extended to agricultural workers the same protection of the right to organization for the purpose of collective bargaining that industrial workers enjoyed under the federal statute. This made possible the rapid and complete organization of the sugar and pineapple plantations.

9. Romanzo Adams, "The Unorthodox Race Doctrine of Hawaii," quoted in Lind, *An Island Community,* p. 273.

Our Future in Hawaii

CHINN HO

THERE should be absolutely no doubt in the mind of anyone that the future of tourism in these Islands is assured. The prosperity of our nation has decreed it. Our balance of payments problem and any further restrictions on foreign travel decree it. The demands of labor for shorter hours and higher wages decree it. The introduction into service of faster and larger jet aircraft and the prospect of lower air fares decree it. And the increasing affluence of our foreign neighbors decrees it.

In 1966 over 117,505,000 Americans took a domestic holiday or a business trip and spent an estimated $23 billion in so doing. This represents an 11% increase over 1965. Of this total, 3,000,000 Americans journeyed overseas and spent over $4 billion. Hawaii was delighted to receive over $300,000,000 out of this sum and can expect to increase its share. It is probable that 950,000 visitors will have come to Hawaii by the end of this year, as compared with 700,000 in 1966 or an increase of 36%. This, of course, includes over 100,000 R&R visitors. At this rate, it is also reasonable to expect 1,100,000 visitors by 1968, inclusive of R&R; 1,500,000 visitors by 1972, exclusive of R&R; and 2,000,000 visitors by 1975, exclusive of R&R. These projections are realistic and I feel that revision to reflect higher figures may be necessary before long.

Speech to the Hawaii Newspaper Publishers Association Convention, October 6, 1967. Reprinted by permission of Chinn Ho.

The Civil Aeronautics Board is now considering the applications of 18 airlines for flight routes to Hawaii and, no doubt, additional franchises will be granted thereby opening new markets for Hawaii. This will mean, based on available information, a seating capacity capable of servicing about 2,000,000 visitors annually before 1972. When an industry like the airline industry can generate earned revenues exceeding $1 billion in 1966 for international traffic (a 17% increase from 1965) and reflect net income of $121 million (a 61% increase and a return on investment of 17%), competition for routes will always be intense. The domestic picture for the industry was equally bright. Here, total revenues exceeded $3½ billion for the first time, up 19% from 1965 and net income hit $259 million, up 69%, despite the effects of the crippling mid-summer strike. The return on investment was a sound 10.5%.

In terms of dollars and cents to Hawaii, the tourist industry in 1967 will bring in $400 million, generate more than $55 million in taxes, and create 45,000 job opportunities.

But more than tourists and dollars will come to Hawaii. Close on the heels of the tourist arrivals will follow a smaller but equally significant tide of strangers to these Islands, drawn here by the huge drain of human resources created by the need to service the expanding tourist economy or to seek retirement. We could reasonably expect over 300,000 of these strangers to arrive by 1975, to bring our total population to over 1,000,000. For the most part they will not be poor or uneducated and it will not take them one or two generations to assimilate into the mainstream of life, as in the case of my forebears. Rather, we can expect them to be adult, educated, vigorous and rather uninterested in the old lines that still define our society. Many will decide to settle in Hawaii permanently, and there is not the slightest doubt in my mind that . . . these new immigrants may contribute substantially in any change in the political structure of the Islands.

Clearly, the problem with tourism will be how to live with it. One is treated almost daily to stories and editorials in our newspapers decrying the lack of beauty and the lack of planning that distinguishes the new order of life in Hawaii. I believe that this concern is real, and that there exists ample evidence to warrant concern in specific areas.

The answer lies, of course, in bold, practical and creative planning. Many of you know that my own expectations have sometimes been disappointed because of the restrictions imposed by central planning, but while I may disagree at times with the specific results I have never wavered in my deep belief in the wisdom and the beckoning promise of this system for order.

There are many who have written Waikiki off as a total and irreparable loss. *These are foolish people.* I believe that the people of Oahu need not endure the gap between what they would like for Waikiki and what is possible. The vast lands of East Waikiki can easily be transformed by strong planning decision and wise development into a magnificent sub-metropolis. I hope and I urge that the City administration and planners will, in their infinite wisdom, decide to convert Kalakaua Avenue in East Waikiki into a mall; to extend Kuhio Avenue to Kapahulu Avenue; and to reroute through traffic over a widened Ala Wai Boulevard.

In this connection I am pleased to note that the major land estates of the State are awakening to their responsibilities, not only to their beneficiaries but to the community, by providing larger areas of their lands for resort development under more reasonable terms than have been available in the past. The increasing release of such vast tracts of land for orderly resort development is healthy and marks the beginning, I predict, of greater changes to come.

. . .

Of more immediate and serious concern to tourism is the state of our manpower and transportation facilities. The annual average unemployment for Hawaii dropped from 3.5% in 1965 to 3.2% in 1966—a figure considerably below the national average. The shortage of skilled manpower to service the industry, *particularly outside Oahu,* will be acute. Government has been alerted for several years as to this critical need and yet, to my knowledge, has not done much of anything in the way of providing adequate training facilities and programs, or even low-income housing to induce people to settle near the new outer island resort areas. All the steel, concrete, glass and money we can throw into the making of a huge luxury resort hotel is meaningless without a single housemaid. The manpower problem demands immediate solution on a crash-program basis.

And then there is the problem of our airports. There has been a great amount of criticism lately about the state of our airports, particularly Hilo. Not all of it has been deserved by those to whom this criticism has been directed. If the airlines had accepted even in principle the common fare proposals made many years ago, a more gradual and natural pattern of expansion and improvement of our neighbor island airports and a more orderly development of hotel facilities could have occurred. Instead they chose to dump the common fare decision upon the State, the counties and the CAB, and the result has been political pressure to establish Hilo as a gateway terminal. This will create urgent demands on Hilo's limited visitor facilities and cause unnecessary inconveniences to visitors. Nor is the situation at Honolulu International satisfactory, but I am confident that government will (it must) rise to the occasion and rapidly resolve the problem of receiving the new generation of aircraft.

I think that I have said enough for one day. Enough about problems, enough about plans and enough about the future. *My convictions are that Hawaii for the years ahead will have unprecedented prosperity.*

Inaugural Address

GOVERNOR JOHN A. BURNS

MY fellow citizens, four years ago, we gathered here, in this historic place, to commemorate the acceptance of high office and the beginning of a new administration. I pledged then to seek the full attainment of those goals for which you had expressed your deep desire. Indeed, in keeping with these goals, I also promised change.

Today, unlike that last inaugural day, we mark not an ending and a beginning but a continuation and an enrichment. We pause ceremoniously only to take stock and to measure our progress and then to set out afresh on our charted course.

Yet change is no less upon us and will be further required if our continuing quest for a "New Hawaii" is to be fully realized.

Today, we also dedicate ourselves to the unending search for ever new goals. While we have come far in the attainment of those ends we set forth four years ago, our progress to date is less relevant than the march before us. We now address ourselves to the task of building confidently upon past achievements and to convert new hopes and new ideas to firm reality.

Lest we forget, as a united people, we must first seek a goal that is forever new—to nurture our most precious resource, our children. Their future and the future of our State are, in essence, one and inseparable. We shall, therefore, continue to urge the expenditure of

Reprinted by permission of Gov. John A. Burns. Delivered December 5, 1966.

every available dollar to provide our children with the best education —the **very** best education—wherever they may live—in the city or in the country, on Oahu or on the Neighbor Islands, in Kahala or in Kalihi.

Indeed, in every phase of the full development of our school system and our University, we shall decline to settle for the ordinary. Rather, our commitment to educational excellence shall know no limits. We shall seek to insure that no qualified young citizen shall be denied opportunity for higher education because of lack of funds. If, as Horace Mann observed more than a century ago, education is, in fact, the "great equalizer of the conditions of men," it is only fitting that it be equally accessible to rich and poor alike.

Consonant with this, Hawaii—you and I—must also seek to assure gainful employment for every citizen who is willing and able to work. In this respect, the record of the present serves as a growing challenge for the future and its enlarged population.

We will, therefore, continue to press an aggressive program of attracting and encouraging the expansion of those industries that promise our people the widest and best employment opportunities. Under a program of selective industrial development, we shall pursue, in particular, those industries, such as those oriented to ocean sciences, which will add new dimensions to our economy and enhance our prosperity and world prestige. We shall lend such industries every assistance it is appropriate for government to offer. In fact, we shall spare no effort to generate employment opportunities which will provide increasing numbers of our citizens with a better life.

Our goal of full employment actually goes even further and strongly suggests an obligation on the part of government to assist in the maximum development of each and every individual's innate talents and abilities. A man's labor should earn him self-esteem as well as just wages. With this in mind, we are pledged to provide every worker, regardless of previous education, the opportunity to acquire new skills and new satisfaction through participation in State-supported training programs of the highest quality.

In all our efforts to build and maintain a flourishing economy, we must not lose sight of our other basic human needs. The treasures of our natural beauty must be preserved and cultivated for all to enjoy. New recreational areas and parks must be fashioned to retain our island way of life and to provide facilities for the pleasant and meaningful use of our increased leisure time.

The beauty of nature not only refreshes but invariably leads to new achievements in the fields of culture and the arts. It would be tragic, indeed, for Hawaii—with its richness in cultural understanding and appreciation—to fail in this respect. With common resolve, we will not fail.

Our concern for the orderly development of our material resources will be coupled with equal, if not greater, concern for the full flowering of our human resources. This administration has not been timorous in this pursuit. We will continue to eschew timidity in the name of political prudence, which is not to say that we will plunge brashly into new fields for the sheer glory of the game.

Let it be remembered that, in all of our pledges, we do not promise change merely for the sake of change, but only to meet the legitimate needs of our people and our changing institutions.

We must be ever mindful that our government must serve **all** our people—the young and the old, the banker and the baker, the professions and the laborers, the backward as well as the brilliant. Here, let those who question our fundamental policy be reminded that "civility," as President Kennedy said, "is not a sign of weakness." The highest office of our State should be graced with equal concern for **all** who are represented by that office.

What we seek is to elevate each to his highest standard and to insure just reward for his initiative and his imagination and his industry. For we know that:

—The forces we set in motion are as important as the gains we achieve.

—The energies we release are as important as the goals we attain.

—The minds we enlighten are as important as the money we expend.

Thus, faithful to our assigned responsibilities, we shall, through efficiency and economy, seek to utilize prudently the revenue generated by our expanding economy, and thereby avoid undue imposition of any additional burdens on our taxpayers. In brief, we shall continue, as in the past, to provide the best possible government at the lowest possible cost.

Now, out of concern with our own needs and aspirations, let us not be distracted from our vital role in the Pacific community of nations. Our heritage and Aloha spirit uniquely qualify us for Pan-Pacific leadership and new destiny. Our people have already stepped into the vanguard of Pacific affairs. But there is much more we can do and which we must do to assume our rightful place in the Pacific sun.

President Johnson, in his recent visit to Hawaii, announced his hope for an early international conference on education and cited our University, with its East-West Center, as an ideal site. Next May, the Pacific Conference on Problems of Urban Growth will be held here, under joint State-Federal sponsorship. Our community and business leaders are stirring interest in a Pan-Pacific exposition tentatively scheduled for 1973 to coincide with our 75th year under the American flag.

Can anyone doubt that exciting days of challenge and construction await us in this rapidly emerging area of the world? The fire has been kindled, the torch has been passed into our hands. Let us hold it ever higher as a beacon for all to see.

Finally, my fellow citizens, let us be ever mindful of our role in the world at large. Infant state though we are, age-old are the cultures in which we have our roots. Though we are but one part of a great nation, to millions we symbolize a separate spirit—a modern version of the New World once sought by Europe . . . a new vision of the cooperation and enlightened unity that all mankind must surely find one day. In an age of newly created nations, in a time of domestic as well as international strife and conflict, let us demonstrate increasing pride in Hawaii's past and in the lofty ideals she now provides the world. By the same token, we must not let our pride become overweening or distract us from the work at hand and the work that stretches ahead. Rather, let us be the first to be ever true to our own ideals, and the last to abandon the way to fulfill these ideals.

And so, on this inspiring occasion, save for the ever-present few who continue to cling to outdated matters, it is increasingly clear that a new day—brighter than ever in an always bright State—awaits our beloved Hawaii. Indeed, this day is so imbued with unique opportunities for the enrichment of all our lives that our mission is clear and demanding.

During the past four years, I have benefitted from your wise counsel, profited from your constructive criticisms, and been inspired by your confidence and support. Whatever progress has been made, whatever gains have been realized, and whatever opportunities remain to be seized are due to you—and you alone. Progress is not a self-sustaining matter. Political leadership can be instrumental and even crucial. But fundamentally, you, the people, must have the will to move ahead, to work for a better life, and to break the bonds of tradition when they become restrictive and inhibit creative growth.

Greatness is your heritage; the pursuit of excellence your means of attaining it.

In again taking the oath of office as your Governor, I am humbled by your continuing faith in me and in my colleagues. I am also inspired by your decision to continue the pursuit of a noble enterprise. I accept your mandate to move Hawaii forward along the course you have chosen.

Let us then move forward together with renewed vigor and vision —with new faith and new hope, both at home and abroad.

Let us join together to continue the work we have begun, to meet new duty with fresh determination, to accept future challenge with bold imagination, and, with renewed faith, to convert today's dreams into tomorrow's living reality.

Let us go forth to build the New Hawaii.

In All Hawaii, Not One Hawaiian Worthy of Trust?

SAMUEL CROWNINGBURG-AMALU

IN my column of last Thursday, I expressed for the first time my own personal observations regarding the recent appointment by the Hawaiian Supreme Court of Matsuo Takabuki as trustee for the estate of Bernice Pauahi Bishop.

At that time, I explicitly deplored some of the actions and objections taken by members of my own native race against this particular appointment. I made the statement then that I believed the rash of objections to Mr. Takabuki's appointment stemmed from the single fact that he was of Japanese extraction. I found this deplorable then. I find this still deplorable.

I had no intent to comment further on this matter because I am not unaware that the greater majority of these objections arise purely out of emotion and are without rational objectivity. . . .

This is the hour of the demagogue. The placard and the demonstration now usurp the seat of sober and reasoned judgment.

Last Wednesday, I was driving through the Civic Center in downtown Honolulu, and I noticed a number of grown men engaged in what at first I thought was a rather frolicsome Maypole dance—with the statue of King Kamehameha as the Maypole.

Reasoning to myself that May Day was already long past, I drew nearer and by such appropinquity was able to notice that they were all my fellow Hawaiians. Madly waving placards and signs. And calling out to all and sundry that ancient battle cry that first rang out on the battlefields of Mokuohai: "Hele On, Bruddah."

In *Honolulu Star-Bulletin and Advertiser,* June 27, 1971, p. D6–1. Reprinted by permission of Samuel Crowningburg-Amalu, columnist for the *Honolulu Advertiser*.

I inquired of a chance acquaintance who these were who were so obviously my own brothers of the flesh. And I was told that they comprised an ad hoc committee made up of the members of 23 Hawaiian Civic Clubs.

Impressive indeed.

I have always been fascinated by ad hoc committees because I was never quite certain what they did.

Now I know. They prance in a Maypole dance around Kamehameha's statue in the latter weeks of June and yell "Hele On Bruddah" at any and all who will pause to listen.

Well, I suppose if this be the sort of thing you enjoy, well and good. Just count me out. . . .

Instead, I quietly walked into the Throne Room of Iolani Palace and stood with bowed head before the shadows of the lords and ladies of Hawaii who once walked there.

For a long time, I stood there among those silent shadows. And I remembered them who had lived before. Liliuokalani who was imprisoned there, robbed of her throne, her crown, her sovereignty. I thought of Robert Wilcox who rose in rebellion against those who had usurped the sovereignty of his nation. I thought of my own grand uncle, Samuel Nowlein, who led so pitiable an army in defense of his Queen. I thought of Kuhio fighting to give back to his people a portion of what they had lost.

And I thought of my own grandmother weeping silently here in this very room and asking in whispers: "Aia ihea ka lahui. Aia ihea na pulapula." (Where is our race? Where are our people?). . . .

Then quietly I walked out and gazed across the Palace grounds toward the statue of the great Kamehameha. And maybe they were right who danced there, who demonstrated there. Maybe they were right.

My dearest friend in all this world, bar none, is the Rev. Abraham Kahikina Akaka, the pastor of Kawaiahao Church. I love him devotedly. I love him for the goodness of him and for the great and brave heart that is his. I love him for the comfort that he has given me, for the confidence that he has restored to me, for the gentle hand that he never fails to offer me.

And I love him best because I know that all of his love is poured out for his people. Yet I would not be fair or faithful to that love were I to refrain from speaking forth of what lies at the bottom of my heart.

My brother Abraham has been given a mission that is most rare.

From his lips must pour forth the word of the Father. And the teachings of the Son. And the grace of the Holy Spirit.

He speaks from the pulpit of Kawaiahao. And thus must he speak not only to but also for the whole people of Hawaii.

For the love of God is not given to but one race—but to all races. To all mankind. From the pulpit of Kawaiahao, the voice of Abraham Akaka thunders over the world. . . .

And this is where expressly his mission lies. In the pulpit of Hawaii's mother church. Nowhere else.

I know that Abraham Akaka has long been a leading candidate to be a trustee of the Bishop Estate. I should be very sad indeed to find him so chosen. The thunder of his voice would then be reduced to almost a whisper. . . .

Of Abraham Akaka, I ask only the thunder. The reverberating thunder of the message of aloha.

Of course, I may be mistaken. Utterly mistaken. But I do not really believe so. I am as fully capable as any of reading between the lines. And it would be extremely difficult to dissuade me from the persuasion that the objections against the appointment of Matsuo Takabuki are based on anything else but purely racial grounds.

And if this be true, I am chagrined that such bigotry should arise from among my own people. We Hawaiians have been the leaders in these Islands and perhaps in this entire world to bring about a harmony among all races. . . .

Nor has this been an easy thing for us to do. We have had to overcome our own selfish natures in order to do so. Deep within our bowels, we still may hate the differences that we find in others. . . . But we have been able to sublimate them, these petty hatreds of ours. We have not voiced them aloud.

And as a consequence, we of Hawaii have come to live together in peace and in harmony. One people before God. I would combat with my life any attempt, even the least, to cast away or overthrow the peaceful tenor of such rare harmony.

I have not the least doubt in my mind that Mr. Takabuki's appointment is anything else but one of political patronage.

But is this so rare?

Can anyone show me any other appointment that is not one of political patronage? This is exactly how the noisome game of politics is played.

But the mere fact of patronage does not persuade me that the appointment itself is invalid or wrong. I have even heard some infer wrongdoing on the part of Mr. Takabuki and impugn some of his past activities.

If this be true, then stand up and speak out. It is easy to call someone a name. They have been doing this to me for at least 40 years.

In my case, it is easily to be proven. I doubt exceedingly that the same can be done in the case of Matsuo Takabuki. . . .

As an American, I can do naught else but approve of him as a trustee of the Bishop Estate since he fulfills all of the real qualifications set forth in the will of Bernice Pauahi Bishop and under the laws of this land.

Now I have had my say as an American. I cannot but also help to plumb the depths of my heart and of my soul. I cannot forget that I am also a princeling of the Kamehameha and the Lunalilo dynasties, that I am also a child of the Hawaiian race and people. Nor can I forget that the lands of the Bishop Estate once belonged to the Kamehameha family. . . .

I cannot forget that of all the trustees of the Bishop Estate, only two have ever done anything worthy of their great trust. And neither was Hawaiian.

I speak first of Atherton Richards who had the courage to speak out against the actions of his fellow trustees and to condemn them openly, forthrightly, and publicly. I speak also of Hung Wo Ching who set aside from his own personal fortune annual funds to further the education of Hawaiian children.

As an American, I can do naught else but acquiesce to the appointment made by the Hawaii Supreme Court. But as an Hawaiian, I am insulted. I am offended, I am even enraged.

More, I am appalled that the Supreme Court of Hawaii at this late date would have the gall and effrontery to appoint a man to this trust who was not of the aboriginal blood of Hawaii. I am sickened and nauseated by the court's action.

These are the lands of Hawaiian princes. Set aside for the sole benefit of Hawaiian children. Who else should be entrusted with the administration of these lands but persons of Hawaiian blood? Can I be led to believe that in all of Hawaii, there is not one single person of Hawaiian extraction worthy of such trust? . . .

I stand in sullen dudgeon and condemn the Supreme Court of Hawaii and every single one of its judges who gave assent to this appointment.

I am twain. I cannot help this, for such are the natures of my citizenship and my birth. I am both an American and an Hawaiian.

As the first, I am forced to approve the appointment of Matsuo Takabuki.

As the second, I must deplore it.

And such is the irony of fate that all of us must face who are of Hawaiian blood and extraction. We have lost our ancient faith and religion, our culture, our sovereignty, our kingdom, our throne, our crown. We are even losing our identity as a people, as a race apart among the races of mankind.

Of the little that we have left to us, the Kamehameha lands of the Bishop Estate are among the most important. Would any of the alien races whom we have welcomed upon these shores, would any of them take even these away from us?

Dear God, even I am sometimes tempted to take to the placards and to a Maypole dance about the statue of our dead Kamehameha.

Speech to the Hawaiian Civic Club's Annual Convention

MATSUO TAKABUKI

WHEN I was first approached to address you, I had mixed feelings, but I consulted a friend whose judgment I valued, and he encouraged me to accept it.

So I am here this morning.

For many years I have avoided making a speech, and I was contented because it was the way I wanted it.

For many years I was out of the "glassbowl of public glare"—permanently retired from the public sector—to live within a fence of privacy for myself and my family, and it was a lifestyle more to our liking. I enjoyed what I was doing in my particular fields of interests, being adequately compensated for my work with people I knew who entrusted me with such work.

But eight months ago I was thrust into the center of a stage of raging controversy within our community, and but for one public statement, I refrained from making any other statement until today.

It has been six and a half months since I took office as a Trustee of the Bishop Estate. And I should like to share some of my thoughts with you.

At the outset, let me make an obvious personal commitment. You can be assured of my best efforts to perform the job I have been entrusted to do—to use whatever talents I may have to work with the other trustees of the Estate to meet the broad objectives established

Delivered February, 1972. Reprinted by permission of Matsuo Takabuki.

under the Will of Princess Bernice Pauahi Paki Bishop. You can be assured that there will be no miracles—no earth-shaking changes—only my continuous effort with the other trustees to enhance the assets of the Estate, and to generate more income to fund the educational activities of its principal beneficiary, Kamehameha School, and to assist in establishing meaningful programs in reaching out to as many of the children who are not presently receiving the benefits of her concern.

If you will allow me another brief personal note, I want to tell you of my profound admiration for the two principal benefactors of the Estate, the Princess and her husband, Charles Reed Bishop, for their foresight by creating this legacy of charity and compassion which shall continue in perpetuity. Trustees will come and go, but the Estate and Kamehameha Schools shall remain beyond any Trustee's lifetime as the lasting memorial of her concern for her people.

Now, let me get back to look at this "Takabuki problem" as it may relate to you, to me, and to our broader community. You have asked, and others have asked, and rightly so, who is this guy, "Takabuki," who is vested with this awesome responsibility by the Supreme Court of Hawaii as one of her five Trustees to do the good that the Princess wanted for her people. What is he? An unscrupulous political hack; a shrewd conspirator out to destroy the Estate; or the best thing which happened to the Estate; or anywhere in between these extremes? Only time will tell how this story will end.

Perhaps, however, an observation made by a friend in half-jest may be illuminating. In our abstract philosophical evaluation of this controversy, he sort of brightened up, grinning somewhat impishly, and said pleasantly, "You know, Matsy, I think you got a lot of charisma," and he paused, and I quickly reacted, somewhat puzzled, "Charisma?" at this very inappropriate description of me, especially in the midst of the raging controversy, and he smiled, and continued, "Yes, a lot of *negative* charisma." How right he was! I could never win a popularity contest.

Now that you know of this speaker with negative charisma, it should warn you that you could not be expecting too much from him.

Let me, however, attempt to place in some perspective the deeper issues of this controversy by quoting from an article appearing in the *Star-Bulletin* by Tomi Knaefler, in an interview with Dr. Alan Howard, a former Bishop Museum anthropologist who is now professor of anthropology at the University of Hawaii, with a three year live-in research and study in Nanakuli. The excerpts of his interview read as follows:

> The Takabuki protest symbolizes the Hawaiians' first battle cry to legitimize their ethnic identity. If they fail to gain it through this route, they have no choice but to express themselves through conflict —politically and militantly.
>
> At heart, the Hawaiian movement is no different than the blacks' fight for ethnic identity.
>
> The protest points up the myth of Hawaii's melting pot concept, which, in fact, is a boiling pot of suppressed racial differences long denied legitimate airing.
>
> The melting pot illusion simply must go. The damage it has done is to blur ethnic diversity and to allow the Anglo culture to dominate.

. . .

These are very interesting observations! Certainly they touch the sensitive vein of ethnic identity—so different from the accepted rhetoric of the "melting pot" of the Pacific—and so true in some respect—but is this battle cry for ethnic identity comparable in intensity as the "black power" movement of the militant blacks? Is this melting pot illusion called Hawaii similar to the black ghettos of Watts, Newark or Harlem? Are the Japanese, or Takabuki, the symbol of suppression as the "whiteys" are to the militant blacks? Dr. Howard, however, softens this thrust by saying that: "[But] I don't feel the protest is an expression of hostility toward the Japanese or toward Takabuki as an individual."

But is he right when he said in seeking your ethnic identity, you have "no choice but to express yourselves through conflict—politically and militantly." Can there be other options and alternates that you can choose? Or can you do it alone as one ethnic group isolated from all other groups in this society? Or is this irrelevant because we are on the threshold of a new era—a changing lifestyle from the melting pot concept to ethnicity, and an emotional need of ethnic minorities to pursue militant courses of action on ethnic lines to get a "piece of the action?"

Let me try to examine this point of view.

Anyone who has lived in Hawaii for awhile can readily give you illustrations of ethnic tensions, and yes, discrimination existing in our imperfect society, but is it boiling so much that the melting pot becomes the boiling pot of suppressed racial differences? Are you, or am I, or are we prepared to move away from the goal of making Hawaii the "melting pot" of the Pacific? Are we ready to cast aside the acceptable norm in reaching for a "homogenized blend of races," or in looking even further in the future, will there be a time when the bloodlines of our people may become so mixed as to have the "golden man" of the Pacific?

Is the "part-Hawaiian" who has grown so substantially to be this "golden man" of the future? A Hawaiian-Chinese, Hawaiian-Caucasian, Hawaiian-Japanese, or any mixture with Hawaiian is racially classified as "part-Hawaiian," and not part-Chinese, part-Haole, or part-Japanese. But will time and circumstances change this ethnic reference as it did in our recent Hawaiian history? I think back to the days of the 442nd Regimental Combat Team in the Second World War, and I can remember when many Hawaiian-Japanese were not part-Hawaiian then, but part-Japanese who can only belong to this racially segregated combat unit. Any smattering of Japanese blood made him different from other ethnic Americans at war, but I can remember also the counter-declaration by Franklin D. Roosevelt that "Americanism is not a matter of race, color or creed," and for this reason this ethnic group should be given the chance to prove themselves.

What happened since is past history, and I guess we proved that President Roosevelt was not wrong that Americanism overcame ethnic bloodlines, and perhaps, the melting pot concept is viable and the "golden man" is achievable.

Are we now, two and a half decades later, involved in a new cycle of reordering our priorities when ethnic identity becomes the rallying cry for a sense of pride and confidence? Is it not true that to deny pride in one's ethnic identity is really to deny who you really are? Or, perhaps, could it be an angry ethnic outcry born of frustration? Should we now say that "Brown, Yellow, White or Black is beautiful," as the case may be, and put the homogenized blend of races on the back burner as a myth—the bad guy of Anglo-Saxon culture who suppresses ethnic pride?

In searching for this ethnic identity, or in seeking a sense of pride and confidence in ethnic terms, is there any danger that it may lead some to reject all that is not of its color? Or, will the opportunity to openly and proudly air their cultural and ethnic differences create an understanding, appreciation and mutual respect among all the diverse ethnic groups to accept them as they are?

Is Dr. Howard right when he seeks replacement of the melting pot concept with ethnic diversity by saying:

There are those who oppose legitimizing ethnicity on grounds this would lead to racist conflicts.

Such danger exists more by denying ethnicity because to deny pride in one's ethnicity is to deny who you really are.

The need then, is a society that encourages divergence, not convergence. A recognition and respect for individual differences. And a willingness to admit that there's more than one way, more than one right, more than one truth.

But what happens when such ethnicity, such way, such right, or such truth sharply conflicts with other groups aspiring for the same thing within the same society—or it runs counter to the dominant White-Anglo-Saxon-Protestant cultural pattern—or it denies the concept of love and the brotherhood of men of the Protestant ethic —or it violates the precept of a democratically constituted political structure that "all men are created equal."

I guess this was our dilemma in this incident. But can there be an accommodation of both concepts?

When does ethnic identity become a divisive force, and not a positive one within a community? Can you be primarily ethnic in some areas like the Hawaiian Homes Commission, and yes, your major legacy as the Bishop Estate, Liliuokalani Trust and others, and yet, perhaps, reconcile these as exceptions to the rule to escape the possible backlash of the accepted mores of the "melting pot" concept?

Where is the balance one can strike on ethnic diversity, and yet maintain an equal, if not stronger, desire to seek a common denominator so we could live together in relative harmony? Can we believe ethnicity and the "golden man" concept at the same time? Are we, again, going through a useless exercise of soothing rhetoric of trying to blend the races when we should recognize openly that we will continue to have this kind of ethnic crisis so long as people have different shades of color?

Can there be a common definition of a "child of Hawaii," a *"keiki o ka aina?"* Or is this, again, the same kind of rhetoric to lead to conformity to suppress ethnicity under a WASP cultural pattern?

Can anyone of us be a "child of Hawaii" in one respect, but never in another one? Don't you, or I, or any other person, have the right to foreclose all others in doing our own ethnic thing? Isn't it your right to control your own ethnic destiny? Is it not true that only you could fully understand your own ethnic hopes and aspirations? But, then, what about a Charles Reed Bishop? Or is Abraham Lincoln irrelevant to the Blacks because he was not one of them? I wonder if there are some lessons we can learn from these questions.

Or, in evaluating another incident within a different context where the converse can be said to have occurred, should we really applaud Jesse Kuhaulua for his award by the East-West Center for his contribution to intercultural activity in gaining unprecedented stature as a non-Japanese in a purely indigenous Japanese sport called sumo? Can't he be, in one way of thinking, the shining example of "brown power" over "yellow power" in Hawaii? Or is he another example of the blending of the races, the racial tolerance, or the Aloha spirit of Hawaii? Or is Jesse Takamiyama an "Uncle Tom" for the Japanese?

I raise these hard questions to show that there are many sides to an issue, and many shades of interpretation depending on how you see it, or want to see it, and the rationale you use to justify your belief.

I raise these questions to show that any action may bring diverse reactions—good or bad, sharp or indifferent, in varying shades of intensity depending on how such action may affect the person or persons involved.

I raise these questions as possible bases for your own critical reevaluation, and perhaps, the need for careful rethinking, reexamination and reordering of your priorities and values—and I suggest it may be a time for soul-searching for all of us, seeking, perhaps, for a new accommodation, or reaffirming the old concepts, or blending the new and the old, in trying to reconcile all the variables covering the whole spectrum of our society, including our ethnicity, our socioeconomic priorities, our political cross-currents, and our individual and collective hopes for the future, and seeking somehow by our actions to create a better Hawaii for all of us.

I do not pretend to know the answers. And it is certainly not for me to try to tell you what should be done. You will have to decide what is your own way, what is your own right, and what is your own truth.

And in this difficult task that only you can decide, I wish you well.

CHAPTER FOURTEEN

Toward a New Hawaiian Consensus

AGAINST the darkness of the outgoing evening tide, the *Saihō Maru,* the "mother boat," is illuminated by a small glowing lantern. Laden with flowers, food, incense, and scrolls upon which are written the names of the departed, the miniature four-foot vessel bobs in the ocean current, its fixed sail catching the light gusts of a summer breeze as it is swept seaward. Close behind, hundreds of floating lanterns form a mass procession of holy lights following the barely visible *Saihō Maru,* lighting the way to Paradise for the spirits of the dead.

It is written in an ancient *sutra* that Maudgalyayana, a disciple of Gautama the Buddha, had a vision of great spiritual insight. His mother, suffering from the karma of past selfish lives, was seen hanging upside down in anguish; deprived of food and water, her body was wasting away. Out of pity and love, Maudgalyayana, vowing to liberate her soul from torment, practiced unselfish compassion and *dana,* charity. As Maudgalyayana offered the accumulated good karma of his selfless love, his mother was finally emancipated and was able to journey to Nirvana. Upon her entering the bliss of Enlightenment, both mother and son danced for joy.

Urabon is the annual Buddhist festival, corresponding with the July full moon, which celebrates the love of Maudgalyayana, his total concern for the spiritual welfare of others, and the attainment of Enlightenment by the departed through the good karma of the living. At this time, therefore, the ancestral dead return to share the joys and sorrows of the living, to celebrate the wisdom and compassion which are the cornerstones of the Buddha's *dharma,* or teachings. And as mother and son danced for joy, so too do the celebrants of *urabon*. On the grounds of the Buddhist temple, amidst the gaiety of colored, hanging *chōchin* (lanterns), the pulsating beat of drums, and the rich treble of song, young and old, dressed in bright *kimonos* or *happi* coats, dance the traditional and popular *bon odori*—the bon dance.

At the end of the *urabon* season, after dancing for the joy of life and salvation, the dead return to Paradise. To hasten and safeguard their journey, the spirits follow the *Saihō Maru* and the hundreds of floating lanterns, each of which bears an inscription of the name of a departed soul. Exemplifying solemnity and remembrance, simple beauty and affirmation of faith, the Festival of the Floating Lanterns ends as the final flicker of candlelight is quenched by the ocean's blackness.

The Jōdo Mission of Haleiwa, Oahu, is where the annual Floating Lantern rite is celebrated. A large grassy area is converted into a parking lot to accommodate a portion of the nearly 3,000 devotees, celebrants, and interested onlookers who travel from all parts of the island for an evening of food, music, *bon* dances, and "fireworks." But the quiet rural community of Haleiwa, with its two-lane roads and lack of traffic signals, still cannot accommodate the hundreds of cars competing for traffic space. By the time the dearly departed have returned to Paradise, the living are ensnarled in an automotive madness which is the trademark of modern entertainment.

But despite the time-consuming traffic, the shoulder-to-shoulder crowds, pleasant memories will be taken from this July evening in Haleiwa, memories which help form the collective lifestyle of an individual—fragments of customs, habits, values, and pleasures which *in toto* constitute the cultural being. The *bon* festival, the joyous ceremony of the Buddhist religion, has become a living institution in Hawaii, a phenomenon of culture which epitomizes the axiom of being "all things to all people." Religious and yet nonreligious. Solemn and yet brash. A pageant of color, tradition, and faith, and yet a bizarre carnival of lifestyles and attitudes reflective of a unique island diversity. Of the 3,000 participants, few will have the same impressions of the *bon* festival, few will attach identical meanings.

For an elderly Issei woman, the *bon* festival has a special meaning.

She dances slowly, gracefully; her agility is enviable. The kimono, colorful and neat, is proudly worn; its history, its age, are hidden behind the gentleness of tradition and respect. The old woman's lips move slightly—she is singing the words of a song to which she has danced countless times. From the *yagura* (the wooden, raised platform in the center of the dancers) boom the drums, the music of a people—remembrances of Japan, plantations, Hawaii, a family, a religion, a way of life. She has looked forward to this night—an evening of continuity with the past.

The *bon* festival also provides continuity for a middle-aged Nisei school teacher—continuity with his peers and community. Twisting his way through the mass of onlookers, he finally reaches the long concession lines. He is buying a shave ice for an old friend whom he hasn't seen for nearly a year. "Oahu is becoming too big," they lament together. "It's so overcrowded you just never run into friends anymore." Both Nisei and their wives have been dancing. They wear *happi* coats, one advertising the Fukushima Bon Dance Club, the other a popular Korean bar in Honolulu. For them the *bon* festival is a time to renew old acquaintances and make new ones—a time to reaffirm their social ties with their ethnic community.

The younger Japanese Americans seem to reflect a variety of attitudes toward the *urabon* season. One Sansei is seen in the circle of dancers, following the pattern of the Issei and Nisei. She is immaculately groomed, a member of a *bon* club, probably an active young Buddhist. Another Sansei is dancing with her—she wears a Christian crucifix. A short distance away, behind a sea wall, a small group of Sansei teenagers are huddled in a tight circle passing a "joint" of *pakalolo* (marijuana). They will remember the *bon* festival as the night they "really got stoned." While one Sansei couple sit with their parents and watch the dancing, another couple, under a blanket on the beach, "make out." Some young people seem bored, but others are laughing, "talking story," and having "good fun."

Of the numerous participants, few Japanese and non-Japanese will remember the religious significance of the evening—the old wooden mission temple filled with offerings and prayers, the beliefs in karma, wisdom, and compassion, the night of joining the dead. Most will have an entirely different perspective. Tourists photograph dancers and floating lanterns so as to remember this oddity of Orientalism in the Pacific. A University professor tape-records the songs so that he can complete his study of *bon odori* in Hawaii. A politician in *happi* coat moves among the dancers, smiles for the photographers, so that the participants will remember him on election day. Parents hover around the notables, trying to get autographs—"for the kids, of course." Young *haole* "hippies" wander in the crowd, their dogs and children in tow. Children eagerly consume hot dogs, shave ice, Coca-Cola and barbecue meat on sticks. Groups of young girls cruise the area looking for young men. Groups of young men cruise the area looking for young girls. Maudgalyayana might not recognize the *urabon* festival in Haleiwa—he might not want to claim it as "Buddhist." But even he could not deny the spirit of "joy," the vibrance of human life, generated in the Island ceremony. Even the littlest children are caught in the mood of *bon*. A small Japanese boy dressed in kimono, perhaps a year old, stumbles on the ground where the exhausted dancers are about to quit. As if at a circus, his eyes are wide, soaking in every scene of excitement and glitter. Since he hardly walks, he doesn't try to dance. But he follows the others in their last circular movements, giggling as he occasionally falls.

Many customs and cultural practices of the Japanese people have become a part of the Island lifestyle. Many Japanese values, beliefs, words, and concepts have become incorporated into Hawaii's lexicon of cultural realities. An Islander of any race doesn't enter a home without removing his shoes—an ancient Japanese practice. Rarely will an Islander forget to bring a cake or dessert when invited to someone's home—a practice of *giri,* reciprocal gift-giving. Eating *musubi, sushi, namasu, teriyaki,* or *tempura* are as natural for a Hawaiian as they are for a Nisei. *Obake, shibai, bakatare,* or *okazuya* are spoken of as freely by a Portuguese as by a Sansei. Filipino, Hawaiian, and *haole* children clamor in line with Yonsei to see their Japanese science fiction hero, Kikaider, and few Islanders have never seen a *samurai* film either in Honolulu's Japanese movie houses or on the local Japanese television channel. The tea house, the *furo* bath, karate, judo, Buddha day, or Boy's and Girl's days are as much a part of Hawaii as are the *hula, poi, mahalo, mabuhay, won ton, kim chee,* or Fourth of July. And so too has the *bon* festival, whether held in Haleiwa, Hilo, or a small temple in residential Honolulu, become an Island activity reflective of the multidimensional experiences of diverse peoples.

Hawaii in the last quarter of the twentieth century, then, remains as much a cultural laboratory of human interaction as it was in the first quarter. Despite war, growth, immigration, Americanization, and statehood, the Islands have retained much of the cultural hodgepodge of customs, habits, languages, and values which had prompted many early observers to speak of Hawaii as the "melting pot of the Pacific." But the cultural diversity of the Islands, as seen at the Haleiwa festivities, has undergone changes; the laboratory has encountered new trends and pressures. Unlike the "melting pot" of the pre-World War II era, modern Hawaii can no longer be explained as being simple, isolated, or "innocent." The dancers go through their movements, the young and old embrace the events of the night in remote, rural Hawaii, but the forces of a modern, technological world impinge on their privacy, their lifestyles.

The Pacific Ocean no longer separates Island people from the economic and political influences of the Asian or American continents. The alluring tropical climate, the idyllic paradisical setting no longer help to placate human problems, suffering, or poverty on an urbanized island. The platitudes with which Islanders have lived so long, the image of "Beautiful Hawaii," "Lucky Come Hawaii," "Hawaii no ka oi," no longer by themselves rationalize the complex social and technological changes taking place in modern Hawaii. For whatever purposes, the Issei, Nisei, Sansei, the Hawaiian, *haole,* or Filipino appreciate their Island lifestyle. But appreciation alone cannot maintain and encourage a way of life—not in a society characterized by mass media, urbanization, commercialization, and depersonalization. Instead, Hawaii's social environment requires a serious reevaluation of the dynamics of cultural living so that the ethnic laboratory of human relationships cannot only continue but become progressively more successful.

By necessity, this reevaluation of Hawaii's society in terms of its ability to meet the challenges of the future will require a series of value judgments as to what is the "good life" for Islanders. In what type of environment do they want to live? What styles of social institutions will meet their diverse needs? What kind of Island society will they want their children to inherit? The result of this questioning process will be a notion of the "good life" forming the nucleus of a new Hawaiian Consensus—a consensus of shared value judgments which functions to define for individuals, institutions, and leaders the social attitudes necessary to a harmonious Island society. And for the future, the new Hawaiian Consensus cannot rely totally on past conceptions of the "good life"—a process of making new value judgments is required. If the ultimate goal of Hawaii's people is a harmonious, culturally pluralistic society, if the notion of the "good life" includes the perpetuation of diverse and nondivisive lifestyles, what steps are necessary to achieve it? Is growth, profit and urban expansion desirable? What qualities of life are to take priority over others—natural environment or economic development? Social stability or individual freedom? A strong, extended family or the nuclear family? Suburbanization or ruralization? Resolving these issues and developing a sense of priorities which balances progress with the quality of life will involve definite subjective decisions as to what is "good" and "bad," "valuable" and "valueless," "meaningful" and "meaningless" for both the individual and the community.

The final decades of twentieth-century Hawaiian history and social thinking will undoubtedly be characterized by this endeavor to define value priorities. Doing so, the shaping of a new Consensus would need to be influenced by an extensive number of multicultural inputs. Since culture is not a static, time-locked concept, the challenge will be to identify the ethnic values and practices of Hawaii's people which are relevant for the future and those which are archaic, irrelevant, or dysfunctional. Sifting through the vast resources of the Island "cultural bank," selecting and emphasizing significant values, traditions, or aspirations, Island ethnic groups could participate in the formation of a Hawaiian Consensus which would transform the inanity of a "land of all people" into a meaningful description of Hawaii's political, economic, philosophical, and cultural milieu.

And one of the most fundamental components of this new Hawaiian Consensus will have to be the stimulation of a pervasive attitude of self-worth among Island people. In an explosive technological society of increasing personal independence and alienation, the individual, whether he be Japanese, Filipino, *haole,* or Hawaiian, seeks a secure self-identity. From social chaos and "future shock" he tries to create a self-satisfying system of personal values and ethics which help define his home and community, his goals and outlook. As technology and materialism liberalize moral institutions, the individual assumes a bewildering freedom to make ethical decisions defining "right and wrong." But freedom without a firm foundation in basic human relationships is not freedom but chaos. Without the psychological security of a sound home and community environment, the right to make moral decisions becomes a portent of alienation, disruption, and loneliness.

The most critical problem facing Hawaii's future will necessarily be human alienation as the dissolution of stabilizing institutions continues. Increasing population and the gradual urbanization of the

Neighbor Islands will upset the patterns of a more rural community lifestyle. Racial alterations due to increased Island immigration will threaten the "local" identity with an overwhelming mainland influence. With each new generation, the forces of education, media, and commercialization will eventually undermine the influence of ethnic institutions. And as these developments redefine the family, the peer group, the culture of the individual, the Hawaiian Consensus must be prepared to counteract disorientation with a new emphasis on humanism.

In this regard the Consensus should reexamine the concept of spirituality and its relevance for the individual and community. If religion embodies a complexity of psychological releases satiating the emotional strains of human existence, certainly the Islander will need a spiritual component of belief to complement materialism and technology. If religion promulgates a philosophy of love and tolerance, a respect for the dignity of the human being and a socially just and humane community, certainly modern man will need a tenet of social and personal interaction which will soothe hostilities and perpetuate a tolerant and compassionate society. If religion gives personal meaning and identity to the individual, a sense of belonging in the mazeway, certainly modern man will have a need for equilibrium and self-worth to mitigate the detriments of alienation.

Religion as it was defined for the Issei or Nisei has simply become inapplicable and irrelevant to future generations. Traditional Buddhism and Christianity and folk beliefs and practices no longer wield the power, respect, and reverence they once possessed. Nor should they, necessarily. The challenge of tomorrow will be to explore a diversity of spiritual dimensions which will satisfy new social demands and provide a humanistic framework of individual identity. While the traditional religions can provide much of the direction, the spiritual outcome must be appealing, innovative, and forward-looking.

In the shaping of this "new religion," the people of Hawaii must look beyond their apathy, their uninvolvement; they must become aware of modern humanistic concerns. And the traditional religions must be prepared to look beyond the prejudices and intolerances of the past to enhance their similarities, develop their unique spiritual alternatives, and thereby begin to offer relevant insights into modern life. Both the Buddhists and Christians must reexamine their dogmas and their limitations, and cooperate in the rejuvenation of spirituality in Hawaii's future.

To this end, many Buddhists have come to recognize that if their religion is to contribute to Island living, then its teachings, its values, and its outlooks must be updated aggressively. "The Buddhist church must come to recognize," writes a concerned Sansei, "the fundamental changes in needs and ideas of people today and meet them in vital, informed, and compassionate ways."[1]

If actively incorporated as a religious outlook, Buddhism could have pertinency to the evolution of the Hawaiian Consensus. Hawaii's people, living in an atmosphere of intense human contact and rapid urban changes, could benefit from aspects of Buddhism which teach the interdependency of all life, a respect for nature, and a pervasive humanism. Indeed, the recognition that the actions of each individual have repercussions on others instills a sensitivity in human beings and institutions allowing for an increased cooperative spirit in solving social problems.

And in an environment characterized by sedate beauty and healthy charm, the Islander must continue to appreciate nature and respect both her enduring and fragile features. The Buddhist outlook places man in nature and views him as dependent on the natural elements, a dependency which predicates ecological reverence and technological sanity. Without this sane attitude toward the Islands' natural beauty and the controlled development of economic and urban systems, the Hawaii of the future will no longer be able to provide an environmental haven for its residents. Priorities of growth and the myopic perspective that "nature can take care of itself" will gradually destroy the ecological balance.

Finally, Buddhism advances an outlook on the social condition which is basically humanistic. Certainly life is not ideal—suffering, starvation, death, and evil are integral to worldly existence. But in Buddhist teaching, man is not doomed to such a dismal earthly state. Salvation lies not in a benevolent Absolute Being but in the self-enlightenment of the individual—man need not seek the forgiveness of the Divine but can act independently to correct his life and community. As one Christian theologian has postulated, "Buddhism trusts in man's ability not only to come to an understanding of things as they really are but also to act in terms of that understanding."[2]

The application of these Buddhist values and attitudes to the dilemmas of modern society has been the concern of thirty-year-old Reverend Ryo Imamura. Grandson of Reverend Yemyo Imamura, and son of Reverend Kanmo Imamura, former Bishop of Hawaii's Honpa Hongwanji from 1967 to 1974, Reverend Ryo Imamura was involved in several community issues ranging from the dissemination of Buddhist literature and concepts to social change through community action projects. In August, 1972, Reverend Imamura, with other Sansei Buddhists, established the Buddhist Study Center (BSC) which aims at informing the public and youth of Buddhist history, culture, and thinking. The BSC, through newsletters, books, group discussions, films, and public lectures attempts to revitalize religion as a spiritual support to social change.

For Reverend Ryo Imamura, Buddhism can serve as a potent spiritual force in the Island community. The humanism, the respect for nature, and the interdependency of life are three themes which reemerge in his thinking. His sermons, which are direct and uncomplicated in style, often bespeak of an attitude toward the self and the community which could provide the people of Hawaii with one plausible alternative to a growing, inuring apathy.[3]

He states:

> We all want and need a greater sense of community, yet we spend our lives resisting it because we've fallen blindly in love with convenience, mobility, and privacy. . . . We are moving to the opposite extreme of isolationism, and insensitivity toward others.

What can be done? Stressing the interdependence of life, Reverend Imamura believes the answer lies in human involvement. "How does one create a community? Well, community is people. I find community only when I find other people."

The recognition that man is responsible for all of his actions and the tolerance of Buddhist thought which allows the individual to accept those who by race or creed are not the same are attitudes which can have meaning for modern America. And always, man is capable of changing the human and social conditions. "The solution to all of our problems, both inner and outer," Reverend Imamura concludes, "lies in each one of us. We have the strength and energy necessary; we have only to redirect them."

Christianity can also play a predominant role in the formation of the "new religion" and the humanization of the Hawaiian Consensus. While many observers have recognized the waning of Christian institutions in a community once sculptured by missionaries, Judeo-Christian principles remain a reservoir of spiritual understanding and comfort. Even as traditional beliefs become muddled by modernization and religious establishments lose congregations and monetary support, the metaphysical concepts with which Western man has wrestled for over two millennia have not staled or become irrelevant. Blended with the truths and insights of Eastern religions, Christianity can emerge from the confines of the church to instill humanistic love and tolerance.

With this in mind, sociologist Andrew Lind attempted to apply Christian concepts of humanistic love to Hawaiian race relations in an article entitled "When Racism Is Laudable."[4] Combining sociology, theology, and anthropology in an investigation of the dimensions of ethnicity in Hawaii, Dr. Lind discussed the recent revivals of "ethnic identity" among Hawaii's people and the resurgence of racial pride and heritage. Realizing that if left unchecked such attitudes could be destructive, he also believed that such pride in ethnicity reinforced individual and community stability and actually enhanced equitable race relations. And Judeo-Christian principles sanctioned this pride in one's cultural background. The Jews after all were the Chosen People and Jesus was an "ethnocentric." Christian humanism understands that man, as he strives for love and tolerance, will also find roots of self-identity in "racism" or ethnic pride.

Moreover, humanism seeks to undercut the differences arising from culture and race. But "any religious fellowship," Dr. Lind warned, "which aims to cut across racial and ethnic lines must at the same time retain a high degree of sensitivity to and appreciation for the various cultural traditions represented in this community." The outcome, consequently, will be a worthwhile pluralism of cultural beliefs and attitudes.

Hawaii, Dr. Lind concluded, is entering a decade of endangered race relations. The peaceful plurality of Hawaii's people is once again being challenged by unpredictable forces. During this period of rapid growth, alienation, and social change, Christianity needs to play a greater role in balancing the tendency toward ethnic identity and the demands for social harmony. Tolerance and love, the cornerstones of Christ's humanism, in collaboration with the humanism found in Hawaii's other religious systems, must be utilized to perpetuate Island cultural pluralism:

> In a time of such rapid and unprecedented social change as our Islands have recently experienced and will undoubtedly continue to experience, the principles of conduct most needed will be those of

moderation and tolerance inherent, although not always recognized, in each of the major religious systems known here—an ability to penetrate behind the external labels of race and class to discover and treasure the broadly human elements which exist there.

Beyond Imamura's and Lind's religious ideas, the spiritual humanism needed to pervade a new Hawaiian Consensus must also be accompanied by a reinforcement of social institutions. Values in the Island culture enhancing patterns of family structures, intergroup relationships, and individual freedom need to be identified and strengthened. Accordingly, in the summer of 1970, artists, novelists, sociologists, historians, ecologists, political scientists, humanists, politicians, businessmen, and concerned community leaders assembled for a symposium to study the institutions, values, and future of Hawaii. At the Governor's Conference for the Year 2000, the impressive array of scholars explored a breadth of topics. With excitement, sober judgment, and not a little idealism, the futurists foresaw advantageous developments in Hawaii's economy, ecology, cultural pluralism, racial relations, artistic spirit, and political process which would enhance the Island "good life."

As his contribution to the Conference, Dr. John F. McDermott, Jr., then a psychologist at the University of Hawaii, addressed himself to the human dimensions of Island future life. His article, "The Quality of Personal Life 2000,"[5] was an attempt to unravel the nature of Island social relations as they would exist by the year 2000. What would be the status of the family and ethnic community in the process of evolving social systems? What relational values would be essential not only to economic well-being but to personal security and racial harmony? How can we rechannel our energies into preserving the quality of human life in a maturing Island environment?

The sources of the danger which threatens the personal quality of life in Hawaii, Dr. McDermott stated, are the impersonality, the psychologically disintegrating effects of urban society. Technology has especially had an alienating force, upsetting familial relationships, producing ecological disasters such as Waikiki, and eroding a personal sense of belonging and affiliation instilled in the "simple world." Dr. McDermott observed in Hawaii a growing generation gap, and the disappearance of goodwill and *aloha,* trends he accredited to overgrowth, technology, and urbanization without consideration of human relationships. "We must redirect our attention," the concerned psychologist warned, "from the measure of quantity to the quality of life."

Technological influence, plus an attitude of independence and equality, has also had an effect on the dissolution of the primary socializing institutions. "Marriage and the family," Dr. McDermott saw in Hawaii, "will no longer enjoy the stability they have in the past, but rather may be fragmented, revolving, serial, partial, and semi-permanent as well as permanent." The new generations will find secondary institutions—the school, the community—greater influences in shaping their personalities and world views as the family undergoes deemphasis and reorientation.

Because McDermott believes the family is a passé institution, he feels the responsibility for the enculturation of relational and independent values will have to be assumed by the school and government. Education for social and moral values needs to be improved and made more relevant. The welfare system needs reformation to return respect to familial authority. Childrearing techniques can be patterned after planned group infant-care centers such as those functioning in Israel. New family substitutes, such as communes, should be encouraged as social experiments having worth, and the society should be inundated with efforts to promote the reevaluation of value priorities.

The primary objective of these suggestions is the counterbalancing of any unyielding alienation and rampant social change with a reemphasis on the humanistic values of interpersonal relationships. And as Dr. McDermott stated, "Society has a responsibility to maintain a balance in its value systems just as it does in its economic system." Values must be accentuated which do not deny technological reality but give policy-makers the insights to utilize knowledge humanely with a spirit of affiliative purpose.

Certainly, Dr. McDermott's analysis offers valuable alternative insights into the future. However, notwithstanding his judgment that the family will be fundamentally weakened by 2000 A.D., the study of the Island Japanese American family suggests a possibly different picture. The family need not weaken but can expand in scope and influence. The modified extended family, a sense of community in an assimilated urban setting, has found roots in the Island lifestyle—roots unifying the ethnic group and pervading the commonness of the intercultural community.

The modified extended family, the affiliative spirit, will not always be the panacea of social ills. Personality disorders, crime, alienation, loneliness, and technological malaise will not be totally eradicated. The youth, the elderly, the "misfits," the mother, and the father will continue to encounter complex problems in an expanding Hawaii.

But with her "small town" qualities, her island intensity of relationships, the rurality of her roots and lifestyles, the lack of mobility, and the proximity of families, Hawaii can truly continue the modification of her social systems with the humanism of the intuitive family organism.

This familial unity, the affiliative spirit, can for future generations be protected and nurtured by the Hawaiian Consensus. Tax incentives to encourage extended family households; or the care of the aged, educational programs, and community workshops to facilitate family democratization; immigrant assistance programs designed to ameliorate disruptive family problems; a revamping of the welfare system to encourage the family integrity and self-autonomy are but a few measures which an enlightened Island leadership could explore as means to insulate and uphold the family structures.

Other suggestions to strengthen the cultural lifestyles and institutions of Hawaii's diverse people were offered by Douglas S. Yamamura and Harry V. Ball in their article "Hawaii's People and Lifestyles 2000"[6] presented at the Governor's Conference. The major thrust of their article was to discern ways in which Island people can perpetuate their "individual freedom and local community autonomy in a world which will be increasingly centralized, bureaucratized and standardized." By allowing each ethnic group and each local community the power to determine their own lives and futures, Yamamura and Ball felt the threats of mediocrity and standardization to Hawaii's lifestyles could be mitigated.

Part of the expansion of personal freedom, the authors believed, could be promoted through a reduction in the notion of "privacy."

> We seriously propose that Hawaii 2000 be characterized by a great reduction in privacy generally. . . . We recognize that invasion of privacy has been equated with abuse of centralized or privileged power, but we do not believe that such need be the case. We further suggest that openness in interpersonal dealings is a major contribution of the original Hawaiian culture to our future potential. We believe that personal and interpersonal security is premised upon such openness, and that is the essence of constitutionality in any community.

In other words, the crass individualism and alienation of "privacy" must be counteracted in the future with a permeation of humanism, the bonds of family and community which link the individual to a meaningful world. But in the process of "opening" society, a sophisticated style of freedom to allow for diversity is also vital.

Diversity in Island society will allow for experimentation so as to continually discover more fruitful ways in which cultural lifestyles can meet future demands.

Education plays an especially dominant role in this process of diversity. Many ethnic groups in Hawaii, most notably the Hawaiian and Filipino, have recognized that the school can obscure diversity by a means of cultural and socioeconomic suppression. While the Japanese, *haole,* or Chinese might have adapted extremely well to the culture of the school, other groups have found home lifestyles to be in serious conflict with the style of aggressive independence required in an American classroom. Consequently, successful ethnic groups consistently maintain their status through education, while other less-adaptable groups continue to meet socioeconomic barriers. To counteract this detrimental situation, diversity and local autonomy must reshape the school and educational process—the local community must increasingly have the power to determine curriculum and school lifestyles which have relevancy to their particular needs.

Among Yamamura's and Ball's recommendations for steps to implement an open, diverse Island community, the decentralization of educational authority and expansion of education resources stand out. Yamamura and Ball also recommended the ownership of all land in Hawaii in the name of the politically organized community. Only by direct control of land in an island environment can the community protect lifestyles eroded by rampant development and uncontrolled investment. Islanders must also begin to plan future diverse communities so as to perpetuate the type of lifestyles which they feel will maximize the humanism and the extended familial spirit existent within their ethnic cultures. In this way, the future will be characterized by the same democratic trends of the past:

> In the process of living and working together, the people of Hawaii have forged a life system and orientation that reaffirms the essential dignity and integrity of every human being, irrespective of race, color or creed.

The process of forging this special Island way of life, symbolized in the concept "local," becomes then for Hawaii's people the key concern for the future. Can the cultural pluralism engrained in an Island lifestyle be perpetuated? Can outsiders, yearly swelling the population, be adapted to a system of Hawaiian race relations? And, more importantly, can local ethnic groups continue to ameliorate the undercurrents of racial injustices still a part of Island living? This maintenance and expansion of cultural pluralism will not be as simple as perpetuating ethnic foods or festivals. One cannot simply build a shopping center with Hawaiian, American, Chinese, Japanese, or Filipino goods and foods and say complacently that Hawaii is perpetuating cultural pluralism. Cultural pluralism involves not just the cohabitation of artifacts and customs but the free interaction of behaviorally diverse people. Not merely the creation of a smorgasbord of cultural embellishments but human beings with different backgrounds intermingling peacefully, rewardingly, and equitably in the same community is the gist of cultural pluralism.

One of the more interesting notions of cultural pluralism as it operates among the people of Hawaii was included in a 1974 study of Island children by a University of Hawaii researcher, Glen Grant. Specifically studying the adjustments of the *haole* newcomer to the culture of the Island school, Grant's study has important implications for understanding the mechanisms of cultural pluralism in Hawaii and its relevancy for the Japanese, Hawaiian, and Filipino as well as the *haole* newcomer.

In his synopsis of the study, "Race Relations in the Hawaiian School: The Haole Newcomer,"[7] Grant suggested that common assumptions about race relations are perhaps faulty. Too much concern has been placed on negative attitudes instead of actual behaviors. Rather than determining "racial stereotypes," the study concentrated on the interracial behaviors between children and found generally that no two *haole*s had developed identical race relations. Racial attitudes and assumptions, though existent, did not distort friendly race relations. Although some *haole*s were treated by local children as stereotypically "dumb," most had adapted very well to the culture of the school. As Grant stated, "race in itself is a secondary factor in race relations."

What is crucial to the development of friendly race relations are "points of commonality" established between children of varying races. Essentially, "points of commonality" are common behaviors where individuals "see the world" in mutually rewarding ways. Thus, for example, the *haole* child who gives tutorial assistance to the local child, who in turn responds with friendship behaviors, is seeing the world congruently with local children at this point in their behaviors. Both are reaching desired ends through interdependency of their behaviors. Neither are culturally nor racially alike. They do not have common motives or interests. And it is not necessary for them to learn each other's cultures for healthy race relations to occur over a period of time. What is necessary is the development of "points of commonality."

As Grant suggested, the negotiation of "points of commonality" between Hawaii's ethnic groups had been the continuing basis for the historical development of "local" culture. How else could ethnic groups at once remain culturally diverse and yet interact in a commonality of spirits? Each individual, Grant stated,

> . . . can remain culturally distinct in the process of developing points of commonality. It is not necessary for them to abandon cultural ties with others of their own ethnic origin for friendly interethnic relationships to be possible. Sharing a local Hawaiian lifestyle for these children is in actuality sharing points of commonality in their diverse behaviors. Becoming local was the end result of a process of negotiation which each immigrant has undergone and which continues operative to this day.

The implication for the future of cultural pluralism and the Hawaiian Consensus is clear. The *malihini* as well as the *kamaaina* can be incorporated into a naturally evolving system of race relations, seeking the "points of commonality" between people. No one need abandon his culture in Hawaii for harmony and mutually rewarding interdependency to be achieved. The darker undercurrents, the racial stereotyping and inequalities of Island systems, will most likely remain in the future. But they can be ameliorated without sacrificing fundamental ethnic values, systems, and institutions. The new immigrant—whether *haole,* Korean, Vietnamese, or Filipino—must learn to negotiate with the local resident the skills, knowledge, and resources needed for the betterment of an Island life. The Islander who is dispossessed from power, who seeks greater involvement in local society, must learn to negotiate the valuable resources of his ethnic heritage for a better position in Hawaiian systems. And as the new immigrant and dispossessed Islander increase their interdependency in a local culture and way of life, they can maintain their unique world views.

In the process of developing the new Hawaiian Consensus, in the evolution of ethnic groups negotiating increased equality and interdependency, the most highly valued "points of commonality" will be the commonness of the democratic, extended family unit, the spiritual humanism, the affiliative emotions, the obligations to friend and neighbor, the human creativity and open personal responsiveness at the core of each ethnic group's lifestyle. The Hawaiian Consensus of tomorrow will need these human commonalities as the focus of a "good life" for all Islanders—as a means to elevate not only the standard but the quality of living, for without these feelings, obligations, responsibilities, and interdependencies, without our "points of commonality," we are not truly human. Without the spirit of love and dependency between individual, family, friends, and neighbors, we become only empty caricatures of lonely men and women.

NOTES

1. Gail Miyasaki, "The Role of the Buddhist Church in the History of the Japanese in Hawaii," *Hongwanji Newsletter,* June 1974, p. 6.

2. Donald K. Swearer, "The Appeal of Buddhism: A Christian Perspective," *Christian Century,* (November 3, 1971) p. 1290.

3. Reverend Ryo Imamura, "Selections of Sermons."

4. Andrew W. Lind, "When Racism is Laudable," speech given at the Church of the Crossroads, January 26, 1975.

5. John F. McDermott, Jr., "The Quality of Personal Life 2000," *Hawaii 2000: Continuing Experiment in Anticipatory Democracy,* edited by George Chaplin and Glenn D. Paige, Governor's Conference on the Year 2000, Honolulu, 1970, University Press of Hawaii, Honolulu, 1973, pp. 162–75.

6. Douglas S. Yamamura, Harry V. Ball, "Hawaii's People and Life-styles 2000," *Hawaii 2000: Continuing Experiment in Anticipatory Democracy,* edited by George Chaplin and Glenn D. Paige, Governor's Conference on the Year 2000, Honolulu, 1970, University Press of Hawaii, Honolulu, 1973, pp. 141–61.

7. Glen Grant, "Race Relations in the Hawaiian School: The Haole Newcomer." From *The Interaction of the Haole and Local Child: A Study of Race Relations in Hawaii's Schools,* University of Hawaii master's thesis (Educational Foundations, 1974), under the chairmanship of Dr. Royal T. Fruehling.

Selection of Sermons

REVEREND RYO IMAMURA

EACH new year is a time of rejuvenation, of rebirth. We've made it a custom to look back and evaluate the just-completed year and, at the same time, to look ahead and examine the prospects of the coming year. Nineteen seventy-three was a strange and disruptive year. With Watergate, the fuel shortage, the resignation of the Vice President, spiraling costs, the Israeli–Arab War, the continued fighting in Southeast Asia, and so on, it's no wonder that many of us prefer to look ahead in hopes of improvement rather than looking back at the confusing and frustrating mess that was 1973.

Most of us are wondering in what direction we're headed. More people are questioning and examining all that has been taken for granted until now. I'm sure mankind will benefit from this much-needed period of reevaluation. From what I've read, these turbulent and searching times closely resemble sixth-century B.C. India which produced Gautama Buddha, and the Kamakura Period of Japan which produced Shinran, Honen, Dogen, Nichiren, and other important religious figures. So reevaluating 1973 from this perspective, it could be considered a very good and promising year—a starting point for resuming our search for our identity.

But of course search is always arduous, time-consuming, and usually painful. Man, as lazy and timid as he is, would rather wish for the "good old days" rather than strive for new solutions which require insight, creativity and dedication. He would rather talk about how nice, simple, clean, friendly, safe, and so forth, it used to be, rather than earnestly searching in the present for answers. Maybe it was really great way back then . . . I don't know. But you have to admit that life today is more convenient and none of us would be willing to give up all of our modern conveniences in exchange for the "good old days." In other words, we've sold ourselves out. For the three things we cherish most—mobility, privacy and convenience—we've given up our sense of community, that is, the closeness and intimacy we used to share with our relatives, our neighbors, the barber, the grocer, the minister, the other people in the community.

It's a confusing and frustrating situation. We want the friendliness of a close community, yet we're not willing to get involved. We hate being unknown to each other, yet we crave anonymity. We yearn for a simpler, more communal life, yet we're not willing to sacrifice any of the advantages that mass society has brought us.

For example, we all like the idea of the small independent family-owned grocery store. Yet we shop at the supermarkets because there's a better selection, prices are usually lower, it's faster, and no one knows you enough to ask you personal questions. Convenience, mobility, and privacy are more important to us than the communal feeling offered by the small neighborhood store.

Even in the home, the sense of community is disappearing, not by accident but by choice. How often does your family sit down and eat and talk together? How many families eat in front of the television rather than have to face each other's company? How many families wash the dishes in the dishwasher rather than wash dishes together by hand? Would you hassle with your family over what kind of cereal or pudding to eat, or would you rather just buy the variety pack of individual servings and avoid what we consider to be needless interaction? Do you discuss which television programs to watch or do you just get a television set for Mom and Dad and one or more for the kids? I ask these questions to underline the fact that, even within our homes, we are losing the closeness, the intimacy, the feeling of sharing which used to exist. And again this is by choice, not to be simply written off as a modern phenomenon.

We all want and need a greater sense of community. Yet we spend our lives resisting it because we've fallen blindly in love with convenience, mobility, and privacy. In rejecting the suffocation of total community that intermingled place, kin, work, and friends, we are moving to the opposite extreme of isolationism, and insensitivity toward others.

One of the basic and practical teachings of Buddhism is the Middle Path—that reality always lies between extremes or opposites. Nothing is black or white, but a mixture of black and white. Nothing is good or evil, but a mixture of both good and evil.

To satisfy our need for communal life, we cannot recreate the communities of the good old days, nor can we continue on this trend toward isolationism and impersonalness. We must open our eyes to what is today and consider the possibilities and limitations.

The greatest problem or fear seems to be "How can I maintain my individuality in a community?" or "How can I enjoy the friendliness of a close community and not be swallowed up in the process?" This is an unreal fear. There is nothing stronger or harder to lose than one's individuality or one's ego. In fact, individualism is a terrible burden and when it is exchanged for submersion in a group, we're ecstatic, reborn, free at last from the tyranny of our illusory selves.

So the villains who are destroying community are ourselves—our strange desire not to get too close when we have the undeniable need to join together. Yes, this is our ignorance—our foolish prides which won't allow us to make that humiliating admission that I can't live alone, that I need people, that we are all interdependent.

How does one create a community? Well, community is people. I find community only when I find other people. And I can find other people in my normal everyday life. Perhaps, I can begin in my home by trying to interact more with my family. Maybe I can try to cut down on the use of my car. I can go a little out of my way to patronize the smaller family businesses who need my patronage more. As a minister, I can try to interact more openly with all the temple members. There's no end to the possibilities of creating a greater communal feeling. Once I take the risk and break the ice, it's amazing how many others turn out just to have been waiting their turn. That's how the community begins.

. . .

Comparatively speaking, Honolulu isn't nearly as polluted as some of the other places I've lived in the past few years. But it's no lie when I say that we are catching up to the problems of more polluted cities and catching up fast. How often have you heard the remark "Wow, has Honolulu changed!" from someone who had been away for a few years. That remark is very rarely a compliment. He's probably referring to our skyline of instant high-rise buildings, our roads which are just as congested as those of any major city, our sprawling growing suburbs, the neon signs, the roar of jet airliners, and the odor of carbon monoxide fumes.

Here are a few statistics compiled by the City and County of Honolulu for the year 1970:

1. 1,700 tons of impurities discharged into air of Oahu each day; 69 percent caused by automobiles.
2. Over 340,000 vehicles registered on Oahu for 630,000 people. Less than 2 people (children included) per car.
3. Each resident of Oahu produces an average of 7.8 pounds of refuse a day.
4. Sewage is 103 million gallons per day and more than half is discharged into the ocean untreated.
5. We are gradually but surely losing our hearing. Many Honolulu residents cannot even hear the buzz of a mosquito. And to think that there's an African tribe whose members speak in whispers and can hear a mosquito at twenty feet.

I assume that we can go on from this point with the consensus that we do indeed have ecological problems here in Honolulu. Now how can we relate Buddhism to the current environmental dilemma?

The Buddhist teaching which points out to us the interrelatedness of man and nature, of all forms of life, provides us a solution to the ecological crisis. For, if man understands the interrelatedness and interdependence of man and nature, he would feel deeply responsible for the welfare of the world and be more wise and compassionate in his attitudes and actions toward all of mankind and nature. All forms of life have a common essence—Buddha-nature. To do harm to one form of life is essentially to do harm to oneself as well. Plants and animals (man included) live in a balanced relationship with their environment. Nature is a force that demands retribution from all who disturb the balance and harmony of the environment. Man has disturbed and continues to disturb the balance of nature either intentionally or through sheer ignorance. Man is reaping his reward in respiratory troubles, chemical poisoning, deafness, extinction of various forms of animal and sea life, the disappearance of trees, and overpopulation.

Pollution is a man-made problem and it is becoming increasingly clear that we cannot live with it much longer. We must either solve it or suffer because of it. To solve it, man must realize his oneness with

Nature, his interdependence with Nature, and be more responsible for his attitudes and actions toward the world.

. . .

I especially appreciate the spirit of tolerance and understanding in Buddhism. In its long history of over 2,500 years, there is not a single instance of religious persecution or the shedding of a drop of blood in its propagation. Within Buddhism, there is a multitude of schools and sects coexisting, often with seemingly directly opposite points of view, from our Western way of looking at it. But there is an agreement to disagree and this is the unity, the oneness within Buddhism. The acceptance of Manyness is the oneness within the Buddhism tradition.

Tolerance has been an important guideline to living from the inception of Buddhism. The Buddha said, "To be attached to a certain view and to look down upon other views as inferior—this the wise men call a fetter." In the third century B.C. the great Buddhist Emperor Asoka said

> One should not honour only one's own religion and condemn the religions of others, but one should honour others' religions for this or that reason. So doing, one helps one's own religion to grow and renders service to the religions of others too. In acting otherwise one digs the grave of one's own religion and also does harm to other religions. Whosoever honours his own religion and condemns other religions does so indeed through devotion to his own religion, thinking "I will glorify my own religion." But on the contrary, in so doing he injures his own religion more gravely. So concord is good: Let all listen, and be willing to listen to the doctrines professed by others.

Are we as Buddhists practicing tolerance in our daily lives? By tolerance, I don't mean "Well, okay, anything's okay with me." We all have responsibilities to care for ourselves. And in caring, we must form opinions and make decisions. There's nothing evil or wrong in forming opinions or making decisions. But opinions and decisions arising from intolerance and misunderstanding inevitably cause conflict, strife, suffering.

Do you practice tolerance in your daily lives? You'll have to answer that for yourself.

. . .

Where do the problems of the world, of our society, come from? And where can we find the solutions to these problems? In ourselves, obviously. For is not the individual the society? You and I have created this society with our greed, with our ambitions, with our nationalism, with our competitiveness, with our brutality and our violence. That is, what we have outwardly is only a reflection of what we are inwardly. The outrageous war which is still going on in Vietnam is *our* responsibility because *we* have accepted war as the way of life. The racial and class conflicts in our society are only the collective *individual* racial and class prejudices we all have. The growing rate of crime in our streets is only the manifestation of the violence each one of us carries with us at *all* times. And the spiraling problems of pollution are caused by *our* neglect, *our* laziness, *our* insensitivity to our surroundings.

Realizing that the outside world is only a reflection of our inside worlds, and that the solution of a problem is invariably found in the cause, we must look into ourselves without fear. By observing ourselves in relationship with things, with property, with people, with ideas, with nature, we can become free of the fear and violence that possesses us. By watching, by learning, by understanding the whole thing in ourselves, we can free the love and wisdom that we lack so much in our world today.

Do you have the strength and energy necessary to change radically, basically, so that you can look at the world through different eyes, with a different heart, no longer filled with hatred, antagonism, racial prejudices, but with a mind that is clear and loving? You would probably think that you don't, that only Siddhartha, Gautama, and Shinran have that much strength and energy. But think about it. Maybe if you just redirected your strength and energy. . . . After all, man has enough energy to hate; when there is a war he fights; when he wants to escape from what really is, he has the energy to run away from it through amusements, ideas, through gods, through drink. When he wants pleasure, sexual or otherwise, he pursues these things with great energy. He has the energy to overcome his environment, to live at the bottom of the ocean or in the sky, even to go to the moon. With all this obvious energy, man still says that he has not the energy to change even the smallest habit.

So what keeps us from looking into ourselves? What keeps us from transferring just a fraction of the energy we expend in our usual interests to studying and thereby understanding ourselves. It is fear. It is fear that destroys love. It is fear that causes anxiety, attachment, possessiveness, domination, jealousy, and violence. As one can observe in large cities with growing populations, there is insecurity, uncertainty, fear. And therefore we have a great deal of violence in the large cities. There is the fear, the insecurity, that our husbands and wives, our boyfriends and girlfriends, our sons and our daughters will one day leave us, so we become possessive, domineering, and jealous. We are insecure and uncertain in our relationships with other people, so we become defensive, withdrawn, and insensitive; that's why we are forever playing games with people and not being honest and open. But, most of all, it is fear, insecurity, uncertainty, which keeps us from dealing with ourselves freely and honestly; that is, from studying and thereby understanding ourselves.

This fear and insecurity in living in this world and in oneself can be overcome only through earnest and time-consuming self-examination. After all, when we really look at and know what was formerly causing our fear, there is no more fear, isn't that right? And the solutions to all of our problems, both inner and outer, lies in each one of us. . . . We have the strength and energy necessary; we only have to redirect them.

When Racism Is Laudable

ANDREW LIND

MOST of the members of this congregation have doubtless concluded that there must have been some error in the phrasing or spelling of the topic for this discourse. "When *Race* Is Laudable," perhaps, or "When Racism Is Laughable," or "When Racism Is Horrible," but surely no one in his right mind would presume to speak to a Christian congregation on the topic, "When Racism Is Laudable."

For most people racism is a bad, really a dirty, word. It has assumed the character of an obscene epithet to be flung at persons or groups of whose acts or existence the speaker strongly disapproves, and it commonly implies an evil or wicked disposition among those to whom it is applied. Like so many other designations for groups of people with distinctive life styles, such as communists, Maoists, fascists, or capitalists, the term racist has become in the modern world a device for both condemning and excluding from normal association those outside the pale.

Some social scientists and journalists have sought to give the word some respectability and objectivity by defining it in the language of the U.S. Commission on Civil Rights in their January 1970 Report as "any attitude, action, or institutional structure which subordinates a person or group because of his or their color." This was the definition accepted by the YWCA, both locally and nationally, in its

An address to the Church of the Crossroads, Honolulu, January 26, 1975. Reprinted by permission of Andrew Lind.

widely publicized campaign several years ago "to eliminate racism wherever it exists and by any means necessary."

Such an attempt to identify what is commonly known as racism with the discriminatory dispositions associated exclusively with differences in color fails, of course, to correspond with common usage by excluding such forms as anti-Semitism in White America and Europe, the tensions between Chinese and Malays in Southeast Asia, or between Hawaiians and Samoans in these Islands. Other definitions, no matter how precisely or objectively they are stated, invariably imply criticism and derogation of the persons or actions to which they are applied—terms deemed appropriate in describing objectionable "outsiders," but not respectable insiders.

Insofar as this term has crept into the vocabulary of Islanders in recent years—and an examination of newspaper articles, editorials, letters to the editor, and ordinary conversations clearly confirms the impression of such a trend—it reflects an increasing tendency in certain segments of our population toward divisiveness, to increase the barriers between themselves and others, not necessarily on the basis of their skin color, but rather because of real or imagined differences in speech or conduct.

The fact that the term is so loosely and variously employed, but always with a critical or invidious connotation, means also that it is subject to serious abuse and misunderstanding. When a competent school principal of Japanese ancestry, rather than one of several competitors of other ancestries, is advanced to a preferred post, the charge of racist discrimination is all too frequently sounded. The newly arrived mainlander who is given a ticket for speeding by a local traffic officer may insist that he is the victim of Island racism, just as a similar charge may arise in connection with difficulty in securing satisfactory housing or employment, or in getting prompt service in local stores. This is not to suggest that discriminatory racial or ethnic attitudes are necessarily completely absent from such experiences, but to attribute the difficulties wholly to the ill-will of strangers, labelled "racists," is simply to delude oneself.

Because the terms racist and racism commonly imply such opprobrium toward those so described—and this is true even when they are applied to institutions, like the nation, the church, or the school of which the critic is a member—this approach avoids a realistic confrontation with the problems of divisiveness or lack of communication with outsiders. And it is this which lies at the root of so-called racism. It would seem wiser to avoid the use of such terms entirely as reflecting an evasion of the real issues, and instead to make an effort to examine honestly and dispassionately the problems involved in the meeting of diverse ethnic groups.

Why talk about racism at all, then, especially as if it were sometimes laudable? I must confess that I selected the topic as it is phrased partly for the purpose of emphasizing a closely related and commonly neglected principle, namely that many of the so-called evils of the world contain elements of positive significance and validity. We should remember that no people, large or small, have ever made a significant impact upon the history of the world without their achieving somehow a sense of their own dignity and worth—attitudes which could be interpreted by other people, particularly their rivals, as evidence of the rankest "racism" in its derogatory meaning.

There have probably been few people anywhere who during the past several thousand years have maintained a higher conception of themselves as the elect and chosen of God than the Jews. But because of their adherence to modes of life consistent with that belief, they have also been continuously vilified by outsiders as "racists" or by whatever comparable epithets were current at that time. Gentiles and Jews too have wondered in the language of what is probably the world's shortest poem in English, "How odd of God to choose the Jews." But no one familiar with that history can fail to recognize that what has sustained this small, war-ravaged, and beleagured people over the more than three thousand years of their separate existence has been the assurance, so frequently and variously expressed in the Book of Psalms, "The Lord of hosts is with us; the God of Jacob is our refuge." Most Christians simply forget that so much of what they assume to be their own heritage of religious trust and exaltation has been borrowed from the Jews. The comfort Christians derive from such familiar promises, as contained in the 95th Psalm, "He is our God, and we are the people of his pasture and the sheep of his hand" was supposedly because "He had made known his ways to Moses, his acts to the people of Israel."

We are reminded of another people, the Japanese, whose primordial estimate of themselves was scarcely less exalted than that of the Jews, and they also have been widely accused of racism. According to their tradition, "the Japanese are one people, united through descent from the *kami* (gods) and ruled by a single ruling family for ages eternal."

As illustrative of the universality of the principle that outstanding achievement by any people demands a high degree of group confidence, seeming even to border on arrogance, I should like to quote a statement from a book by Harry Kemmelman, attributed to a fictional Jewish rabbi. The rabbi was attempting to defend the conception of the Jews as a Chosen People before a group of emancipated and hypercritical Jewish college students.

> "I suppose that to your modern, rationalist, science-oriented minds, the thought of the Almighty making a compact with a portion of his creation is hilariously funny. Well, I can understand that. . . . You can doubt that He offered such a compact; you can even doubt His existence, but you cannot doubt that Jews believed it and acted accordingly. That's fact. And how can one quarrel with the purpose and goal of Chosenness; to be holy, to be a nation of priests, to be a light unto a nation?"
>
> Here a student breaks in, "But you've got to admit it's pretty arrogant."
>
> "The idea of being Chosen? Why? It's not confined to the Jews. The Greeks had it; the Romans too. Nearer our own time, the English felt it their duty to assume the White Man's burden; the Russians and the Chinese both felt obliged to convert the world to Marxism; while our country feels it must prevent the spread of Marxism and indoctrinate all people to democracy. The difference is that in all these other cases, the doctrine calls for doing something to someone else, usually by force. The Jewish doctrine alone calls for Jews to live up to a high standard so that they might become an example to others. . . . It manifests itself in restraints which we impose on ourselves. . . ."

Rather than label such sentiments expressive of confidence in the rightness and even the superiority of one's own cultural heritage by the odious term of racism, the more descriptive and nonjudgmental term of ethnocentrism seems more appropriate and accurate. Such confidence and pride of heritage come then to be conceived as a perfectly natural phenomenon, essential indeed to the survival of any society. It is only when such group loyalty becomes excessive—overbearing and truculent, demanding more of privilege from outsiders than is given in return—that it becomes a positive threat to the common welfare, deserving of extermination, either by insiders or outsiders.

In the wake of similar developments on the Mainland, we in Hawaii have witnessed within the past decade an unusual outburst of interest and concern among several ethnic groups in their own peculiar traditions and values. The most spectacular expressions of cultural revival have occurred among the Hawaiians, who previously had shown the least evidence of wanting to preserve their own heritage and who had diluted their biological purity to the greatest degree by outmarriage. Over earlier years the various immigrant groups, notably the Japanese and Chinese, had engaged in a constant struggle to educate their children in the language and moral values of their homelands. This has frequently been accomplished in the face of strong opposition from the larger community on charges of being "un-American"—the parallel stereotype to today's charge of "racism."

Much of the present-day emphasis upon ethnic revival springs paradoxically from the concern, so rampant these days in the Western world, with the discovery of "personal identity"—with answering the question, "Who am I?" Unfortunately the answer is frequently sought on the questionable assumption that personality or "self-fulfillment" is to be achieved exclusively from one's ancestral heritage. There is, of course, no more reason for damning such an exercise as "racist" than the earlier ones as "un-American," although every such movement probably faces the danger of indulging in exaggerated claims for recognition or for the restitution of alleged past injustices.

Christians need especially to be reminded that their exemplar taught his disciples the crucial importance, on the one hand, of preserving the basic values of the Jewish tradition. "Think not that I came to destroy the law or the prophets; I came not to destroy but to fulfill. Till heaven and earth pass away, one jot or one tittle shall in no wise pass away from the law." From that point of view, it might be said that Jesus was ethnocentric. He was throughout his life a Jew and insisted always upon the sanctity of Jewish values. On the other hand, he was more than a Jew and his compassion for the non-Jews and for the Jews who failed to measure up to the strict expectations of Jewish law is perhaps what is valued as most centrally Christian and broadly human. His parables, for example, of the Prodigal Son and the Good Samaritan, and his encounters with the tax collector, the woman taken in adultery, and the Samaritan woman at the well, to mention only a few, testify to his all-embracing fellow-feeling and understanding of those outside the law, as well as those within.

In a more direct reference to the contemporary situation in Hawaii, particularly as it affects this and other similar congregations, I would suggest that our peculiar tradition of an open, nonracially oriented fellowship should be continued as coinciding most closely with the long-term trends toward the obliteration of racial lines, both locally and in the world as a whole. Certainly in our Island community where even the most crudely defined racial analyses indicate a population of whom at least one quarter are of mixed ancestry, color-blindness must simply be taken for granted in any institution with its outlook on the future. At the same time, however, there must be recognition that the great majority of Hawaii's people are still at least *partially* identified with one or another of the six or eight major ethnic groups, from which many of the basic moral values are derived, some of them quite unconsciously. For this reason, if for no other, any religious fellowship which aims to cut across racial and ethnic lines must at the same time retain a high degree of sensitivity to and appreciation for the various cultural traditions represented in this community. The striking surge of interest in ethnicity, locally as well as on the Mainland, provides an opportunity for becoming acquainted with and giving recognition to the common values which inhere in many of these cultural strains.

It goes without saying, however, that life in the modern world is made up of so many different and frequently more compelling interests than those associated with racial or ethnic heritage. Man himself has become, as one observer expressed it, "a coalition of interests and aspirations, as varied as the groups to which he belongs" —occupational, religious, artistic, educational, recreational, and many others. The ethnic affiliation may indeed appear the least important to him. Religious institutions, as representing the broadest and most inclusive morale-building concerns of man, should most certainly avoid becoming captives of any single interest group, ethnic or any other.

In conclusion, perhaps the chief justification for the quasi-sociological-religious discourse lies in its bearing on the changing social scene in the Islands during this decade. Largely as a consequence of the shifting character of our economy, with a mounting impact of tourism, displacing agriculture as the principal source of livelihood, and the attendant pressure of Mainland standards, the Hawaiian traditions of race relations have been subjected to more serious strain than at any time since World War II. The introduction and local use of terms such as racism and racist with their invidious connotations reflect tendencies toward fragmentation and alienation which all institutions concerned with the "wholeness of life," ought to recognize as a serious challenge, and which Crossroads with its peculiar history and emphases simply cannot disregard.

On the other hand, the awakening recognition throughout the Islands of the richness and worth of the cultural traditions in all the major ethnic groups has set in motion tendencies toward racial and ethnic glorification which are indeed laudable when they are cultivated in moderation and with due regard for the just claims of other values. Unchecked, however, they assume exaggerated and even dangerous proportions. In a time of such rapid and unprecedented social change as our Islands have recently experienced and will undoubtedly continue to experience, the principles of conduct most needed will be those of moderation and tolerance inherent, although not always recognized, in each of the major religious systems known here—an ability to penetrate behind the external labels of race and class and to discover and treasure the broadly human elements which exist there.

The Quality of Personal Life 2000

JOHN F. MCDERMOTT, JR.

Introduction

As important as our conclusions is the process through which they have evolved. It expressed the capacity of the people of Hawaii to be concerned about the future and to attempt to understand and control the forces shaping it. Our single underlying premise is that the concept of quality control is even more important to apply to our biological, personal, and social experience than it is to our automobiles and refrigerators. Quality control can be engineered into our life experience in Hawaii if we are aware of just where we wish to be thirty years hence, and if we assess the means of getting there. One principle appears clear: we must change some of our current ways of life. A linear extension of more and more of what we already have and do will bring us more and more of the problems we are finding so intolerable today. We must redirect our attention from the measure of quantity to the quality of living.

Some of Today's Problems

The scientific revolution of the midtwentieth century has produced a significant disruption of the balance among the individual, the family, and society. The stunning advances of technology promise to

In *Hawaii 2000: Continuing Experiment in Anticipatory Democracy,* ed. by George Chaplin and Glenn D. Paige, Governor's Conference on the Year 2000, Honolulu, 1970 (Honolulu: The University Press of Hawaii, 1973), pp. 162–175. Reprinted by permission of The University Press of Hawaii.

accelerate at a breathtaking pace during the next thirty years, producing an even greater gap between our scientific and our human capabilities. Technology, which once was the slave of man, now threatens to become his master, and it is crucial to consider the consequences. For example, technology has permitted man to subdue nature, but it has also made him insensitive to it, with the result that massive pollution threatens our existence. For this reason, some critical values must be applied to technology so that it is not viewed as a creature of the new environment independent of the old. Rather, technology must be viewed as an extension of man and must be in harmony with overall objectives which consider the quality of his personal life.

Examples of Technological Fallout

The computer allows for instant sharing and dissemination of information stored in central computer files located throughout the country. Technological eavesdropping, recording of our vital statistics, and even more personal data giving a complete description of the outer self of every individual is argued by some as necessary for national planning. Person-to-person relationships are being replaced by more remote impersonal connections of ever-proliferating state agencies and institutions which operate less and less through identifiable persons and more and more through computers. We have been losing the race to preserve the dimension of physical and geographical privacy in our lives. Waikiki is a good example of this loss, and a constant reminder of what must be planned against. As an island state we are exquisitely sensitive to population growth, and to the limit to physical expansion which is constantly visible. The loss of physical space and beauty is particularly hard for a people who are still in union with their surroundings, and where nature, the mountains, and the sea have daily meaning to everyone. Hawaiians do not live in an anonymous concrete city. That is why development and expansion such as Waikiki arouses such intense feeling in Hawaiians. It intrudes into their relationship with a nature which is a part of their lives. We are well aware of the implications of such growth for our well-being.

The Hidden Crisis

But the problems of pollution, privacy, and even population are only the most visible parts of the iceberg. Erosion of relationships and alienation of groups have become an expected part of fallout from technological advances. It has been generally agreed that, over the past century, technological development of a modern nation has required that the values of competition, achievement, self-advancement, individualism, and independence be allowed to flourish and be promoted. These "modern" values of an urban society needed for the technological age have replaced the predominant values of the older society in which large extended families or groups predominated and required the allegiance and commitment of the individual. The shift in priority away from such values as respect, a sense of responsibility and obligation toward others, and affection (aloha) can be traced in part to the shift from the old extended to the modern nuclear family with its mobility. However, it would appear that an exaggerated emphasis on the value orientation of the technological age has exceeded the natural evolvement in which a blend of the two sets of values, old and new, would occur, and the new one is becoming pathologically destructive in its overgrowth. In one sense it is seen in the so-called generation gap, a symptom of the conflict between, and a polarization of the points of view of, young and old. The erosion and dilution of relationships between groups of people, the very qualities which humans in all parts of the world developed and redeveloped over thousands of generations, discovered and transmitted to new generations, rediscovered and modified through the long history of mankind—these qualities threaten to vanish. It is questionable how man will survive if they do. Certainly the pleasant, relatively easygoing way of life in Hawaii has given way to more and more pressure, confrontation, and competitive activities, more and more distress and hostility, so that much of the warmth and genuine charm of people, the goodwill and selflessness that was once typical of many residents of Hawaii seems to be disappearing.

A Second Major Force in This Direction

Superimposed upon the values associated with and promoted by the technological explosion of the scientific age, major powerful social movements have arisen which will unquestionably shape the relationship of the individual, the family, and society in the next thirty years. They will significantly add to the stresses on the institution of the family, which, for the purposes of this inquiry, we are utilizing as a model to be studied. Women's liberation and the youth movement throughout the nation emphasize individuality, independence, and freedom of choice, attacking the structure of the established institutions as authoritarian, and further shifting the values from the group to the individual. At present society has accepted the *principle* of these movements as pointing in a healthy direction if controlled in their implementation (that is, increased freedom of choice for the individual regarding his own personal functioning). Legislative trends toward the promotion and underwriting of modern contraceptive practices, the availability of unrestricted abortion, and the liberalization of divorce laws are examples of a trend which is likely to continue throughout the next decades. Here in Hawaii recent pioneering legislation has not only recognized but further developed this important trend toward individual autonomy versus legislative control over intimate areas of personal decision-making; that is, abortion is now a matter of individual (and family) choice.

By 2000 contraception and abortion will be universally practiced, and society will likely have imposed restrictive laws or positive incentives for the control of the size of families. A series of marital models will be available, ranging from 1) trial or temporary relationships, 2) those marked by one-, three- or five-year periods, and 3) those which are permanent and with which the option of bearing and raising children will be associated, perhaps even licensed. Those individuals not oriented toward a permanent, stable relationship in which mutual sharing has replaced romantic excitement will not be denied any form of sanctioned relationship or forced into a single model of marriage. Thus, while divorce will be readily available without the punitive induction of an adversary system of hostility and guilt, it will not be utilized in the sense it is today. Rather, it will be less important as the only exit because of the varying permanence and intensity of marital relationships receiving official sanction.

The Price We Must Pay

While these trends have already begun to be implemented because of their inherent merit—for example, individual choice versus coercion—they will add further serious, perhaps even critical, stress to the institutions of the past and present, on which we depend. Marriage and the family will no longer enjoy the stability they have in the past, but rather may be fragmented, revolving, serial, partial, and semi-permanent as well as permanent. The shift in the primary function of the family from the rearing of children to the self-fulfillment of the individual partners will seriously affect the new generation of children. The family has been the primary group through which values have been communicated to new generations and in which capacity for relationships with others is laid down. In the past the primary group (the family) has been responsible for the building of character and associated values in the individual child who will become a member of that society. The child's primary group identification is the oldest and most powerful in its imprint on him. The secondary identifications he makes in the outside world also shape his values, but are more recently acquired and more modifiable by changes in the social structure. As discussed above, the secondary group (society) has been shifting more and more in its value orientation and the primary group is undergoing serious stress (and even disorganization) with regard to its major role in character formation of the individual.

Toward Solutions

It is thus apparent that considerable attention must be given to primary and secondary group functions, their futures and their complementarity. To some extent the functions of primary and secondary groups must be blended and mixed in the future, the one complementing the other, rather than remaining separate from each other. For example, by 2000 society will take more responsibility for the value system which the individual acquires both early and later in life. In this fashion our society will attempt to restore the balance and to blend the competing demands of individual expression, self-interest and privacy, with those of cooperation and close relationships with others. Because of the speed with which technological change is occurring, certain of the values of society are shifting dangerously from those maintaining harmonious group interrelationships toward those of individual autonomy (an overbalance which threatens to topple the family as an institution). Society has a responsibility to maintain a balance in its value system just as it does in its economic system.

A Unifying Force

Perhaps more than in any other state in the union, the citizens of Hawaii identify themselves together, bound by unique customs, music, geography, and dress. Thus, a common bond, although loose and at first glance superficial, allows the citizens of this state to consider themselves "Hawaiian," an identification with a larger and earlier culture, unique to us as a group within the United States. This, as an example of a secondary social identification beyond that acquired in the family, may provide a base upon which to build certain values and attitudes which will enhance the quality of personal life for the people of this state. It is to be emphasized that the identity "Hawaiian" is to be one that is borrowed and shared rather than taken. It may already have provided the bridge through which multiple ethnic groups have related effectively.

It is highly unlikely that by 2000 we will be a "golden people," a true melting pot free of conflicts. The dream of complete acculturation and homogenization of the various racial groups of Hawaii will not be achieved by 2000. Rather, our ethnic groups will still retain some measure, although diminished, of their own identity, providing a series of balanced contrasts, and it is to be considered that the survival of these differences may be a source of cultural enrichment to be maintained. The coexistence of several races has been a significant factor in the success of Hawaii, perhaps because of the delicate balance of all as minorities, thus denying to any race the permanent fixed position of dominance. Yet further rubbing off of the sharp edges of conflict and antagonisms will continue for the next thirty years and will provide a laboratory for study of adaptive mechanisms which enable one race to deal effectively with another, a model for ourselves and for the rest of the world to study. One essential feature, however, will be the continued giving up by each group of a certain amount of its own cultural uniqueness in order to come together in a common commitment toward a shared "Hawaiian" identity. It is obvious that we identify ourselves more as "Hawaiians" than residents of other states do with their own statehood. It is the values of this Hawaiian identity which, without idealizing any one culture, take the best from each and provide a composite from which the others may draw, and thus find further common identifications. Here then is a form of ethnic difference which the individual and his group must voluntarily be willing to dilute to provide improved and extended relationships between Hawaiian peoples, a community group spirit of sociability which becomes embedded in everybody's lives.

Ancient Values for the Future

The historical traditions and racial configuration in Hawaii have produced values that are peculiar to Hawaii. Many of the old values have been forgotten. They may need to be reexamined and when appropriate reintegrated into the society of 2000. This is not to say that we are to revive the old Hawaiian society and attempt to integrate its social rules and regulations into the very complex society of 2000.

Rather, we should consider an attempt to reconstruct old values which can be rebuilt into newer social structures and provide newer mechanisms for relationships among people, very much as the old Hawaii has been blended into our architecture, music, and dress. For example, it may well be that we could profitably study the Hawaiian concept of *'ohana,* which has been described as a highly structured system of relationships among members of an extended family living in a given geographical area. Within the *'ohana* there was room for a display of considerable independence by men and women of strong character. However, in all matters of major concern, the *'ohana* always functioned as a unit. For example, land or fishing grounds were not owned privately but by the *'ohana*. This was a recognition that in a closed ecosystem the ownership of a resource must be secondary to the use of that resource for the greatest good of the whole. A second Hawaiian value, *ho'oponopono,* was a problem-solving technique evolved within the *'ohana*. *Ho'oponopono* means "setting to right of wrongs" and provided an opportunity for problems to be brought into the open in the presence of all the people involved in the problem. Each person had a chance to speak out in the most personal terms and when everyone was aware of how each felt, the group reached a solution of the problem and that solution was binding on all parties. In old Hawaii it provided for integration of nature, the old, the young, and ancestors. A statewide computerized *ho'oponopono* via television might be created for the future. It would have assisted the statewide discussion which occurred prior to abortion legislation in 1970.

A third Hawaiian value, the concept of *kokua,* provided the foundation for an economic system based primarily on cooperation, but with considerable elbow-room for competition. Under this system it was important that one expression of *kokua* be repaid with another expression of *kokua* because such payments or gifts determined status within the *'ohana*.

Recommendations For the Future

The following recommendations are made as serious attempts to begin to plan for a society in 2000. They take into account the effects of social and scientific trends that are shaping our institutions, such as the family, to a significant degree and which may topple them unless they are modernized by 2000.

Two major factors are to be considered: 1) the value system built into the developing individual (both because of the present structure of the family and society) is overbalanced toward self-interest and away from group-interest; and 2) the family as we have known it as the primary group shaping the individual's character and his attitudes is under serious assault and will no longer exist in the same form in 2000. It is thus important that society restructure its role and anticipate sharing with the family certain of its responsibilities—that is, childrearing. Childrearing, previously the most important function and the cement that held the family together, may not be the primary function in many families now, and may not be for most families in 2000. The control of population by the promotion of childless and one-child families, the new forms of officially sanctioned relationships between adults which are less permanent than the single marital model offered today, the mobility of families, the individuality and independence promoted among its members by social trends today, are all to be considered serious stresses. We must anticipate the problems created by these trends and compensate for them by modernizing our system. It is thus recommended that:

1. The school experience be considered an extension of the family experience, and thus share with the family the dimensions of education in attitudes and values. It is crucial that by 2000 citizens will have worked together with the Department of Education to shape the precise values to be transmitted so that this vital area of character formation will not be ignored, or left to the idiosyncratic approach of the individual teacher. Now is the time to study the role of the school in the socialization of the child.

2. The welfare system, which has helped shape the individual personality and the family structure of so many, is universally agreed to be in need of great reform. It should be restructured to blend primary (family) and secondary (community) group functions for the future, to promote in the people it serves values, characteristics, and attitudes which are important for their development and successful adaptation. Thus economics should be the independent variable, the means and not the end.

It is agreed by most that certain personality characteristics are influenced and even shaped by a welfare system—for example, dependence versus independence. Thus a planned approach toward this issue and experimental programs seem crucial. For instance the concept of "work" may need considerable reassessment and modification by 2000. A major work within the family, especially for the mother, has been childrearing. Today it is often compared unfavorably with work outside the family, and equated with drudgery because of its tedious, unrelenting, and sometimes discouraging character. However, to insure that the highest priority of society is toward children, its greatest natural resource, it may become necessary for childrearing to be socially, legally, and economically defined as work. In this way it would achieve a status as important as other forms of careers, with extrinsic as well as intrinsic rewards.

Training for childrearing (just as for any other occupation) would be available, and appropriate pay and vacation periods would be marked off to further define and recognize its crucial importance. Not only would its importance be guaranteed as a role equal to any other career, but also society would share responsibility with parents who currently experience lonely frustration because total childrearing becomes a burden which they cannot adequately discharge twenty-four hours a day over a period of years by themselves. In sharing this responsibility, society will need actually to assume the role of parent in some cases. Inevitably, many children will be born for whom full-time mothering in the usual family structure will not be available. This may occur for a variety of reasons—for example, the wishes of the mother to work at another role, psychological interferences with full-time mothering capacity, separation and divorce, and so forth.

To provide adequate care for the emotional development of these children, a combined home-school experience, a family substitute organized as group childrearing experiences, should be available. Sufficient experience with childrearing centers in Israel has now clearly demonstrated that through planned group childrearing (provided when the mother-child bond is not available or practicable except on a part-time basis) personalities can be shaped in positive rather than negative directions. (It has been discovered that there is a particularly desirable extra dividend of enhanced outward or extended attachments, strong loyalties and sense of responsibility, developed by the youngsters toward the larger group.) Various levels and degrees of parental participation in these childrearing centers would be available, so that some mothers who were not ready for mothering could be released for different work, others involved in a partial way most satisfying to them and the children, and others devoting all of their time to childrearing, not only with their own but with other children as well.

A new profession, that of childrearing specialist, would be developed, consisting of individuals who would live with the children and serve as ongoing parental substitutes for youngsters without adequate family lives. The centers would also serve as training sites. The specialists there would serve as trainers for parents who were planning to have children, and for those who were already raising children of their own. Prevention of problems would begin to replace the rehabilitative measures of today which are so expensive, time-consuming, and only partially effective. The most important considerations would be that a) those who are not equipped for child-rearing or do not wish to rear children, would not be employed in this role, a rule of thumb that applies to other occupations; and that b) other options for assistance in the rearing of children would be available to those families either on a full-time or a part-time basis.

3. New groups, often serving as family substitutes, are spontaneously springing up all around us, as, for example, in communes. Often they develop for specific purposes, are sometimes semipermanent and sometimes temporary. The effect of such activities is the creation of new cultures. One would expect that a place like Hawaii, with its multiethnic population and its commitment to racial harmony, would be the most tolerant to diversity as it arises from the appearance of such groups. But we all know that Hawaii's tolerance is limited to some specific types of diversity, so that the reaction to new experimental groups, especially when they profess to values and develop living styles which are in conflict with those of established groups, are received without enthusiasm, or at best with very mixed reactions. It is recommended that experimental, naturally occurring groups be encouraged, especially those which do not harm individuals in the group or threaten directly other established groups through unwanted encroachment or profession of violence. Once experimental living groups are encouraged, we may expect all kinds of interesting communities to develop. It is most important that we study and allow these groups to communicate their experiences to us in order to evaluate possible new models for the future. The university might sponsor as a major intercollege effort the study of such groups that already exist in the military, university, yacht basin, and various other housing clusters.

4. Individual efforts by those who feel the need to establish their own new patterns of relating to others can be contagious. Large-scale community and media efforts toward improving individual relationships and improving values may be encouraged. A very basic example which achieved substantial support at the governor's conference consisted of an attempt to lessen the strained relationships between drivers and pedestrians by encouraging that hitchhikers be picked up. Some suggested that a shift in role from driver to hitchhiker would be helpful in promoting flexibility.

Hawaii's People and Life-styles 2000

DOUGLAS S. YAMAMURA AND HARRY V. BALL

WHETHER we like it or not, to a considerable extent the Hawaii of 2000 is already here.[1] The decisions that we and others have made and are making now about our physical and social environments have and will continue to set important constraints upon our future options. More importantly, however, Hawaii 2000 is now here in the sense that the realities of Hawaii 2000 will be only as rich (or as sparse), only as beautiful (or as ugly), as the visions which men are willing to dream now—and, in the dreaming, create.

Given this, we as members of the task force on "People and Life-styles" feel a special burden. We honestly believe that Hawaii has a significance—even a preeminence—in the world today that is all out of proportion to its size or material wealth (or even its climate); and that this importance is due to its people and their ways of life. We of Hawaii, both those who have been born here from an act of love and those who have moved here as an act of love, are all aware of the tarnishes on our halo, the blemishes on our surface, the serious rents in our social fabric. Yet we believe that these facts, which we know and acknowledge (without passive acceptance), and our worldwide image, when taken together, only serve to document the tragic state of

In *Hawaii 2000: Continuing Experiment in Anticipatory Democracy,* ed. by George Chaplin and Glenn D. Paige, Governor's Conference on the Year 2000, Honolulu, 1970 (Honolulu: The University Press of Hawaii, 1973), pp. 141–161. Reprinted by permission of The University Press of Hawaii.

most of the world and the importance of what does happen to the few important beacons, of which we are one.

Where We Have Been and What We Are

Hawaii's peculiar social organization is all the more dramatic given the fact that in less than two hundred years it has moved from being an isolated, homogeneous, preliterate stone-age society, to being one of the most modern communities in the world. During this transformation it has brought into potentially promising union some, if not most, of the major cultural traditions of the Pacific: American, Polynesian, Sino-Japanese.

The culture of the first Hawaiians stressed kinship, community, and harmony with nature and the gods. Property, in the sense of use-rights and access-rights to those things necessary to sustain life, was basically communal. A very high level of interpersonal security was achieved through one's kinship group and through one's membership in larger community groupings and political unions. This was so even though some warfare appears to have been chronic—some of which could be devastating to the losers. Taxes were paid in kind, that is, in work and service, and no market relationships disturbed the basically egalitarian and open relationships among men. While some privacy obtained between the sexes, there was very little concern for privacy in the modern sense. This lack of privacy, while it constituted a constraint upon individuals, was also a source of interpersonal security. Work was viewed as a necessity and not as an end in itself; it was usually executed in social settings in which the personal interaction provided the sustaining gratifications. A very high degree of ecological balance had been obtained, and it is presumed that the population was stable at roughly the size of the population of Honolulu in 1950.[2]

The first half of the nineteenth century was marked primarily by two developments: first, the decimation of the original Hawaiian population through diseases; and second, the reorganization of the society upon the basis of egalitarian-individualistic small-community premises that were produced by virtually the same social forces that produced the anticity, anti–mass-manufacturing, anti-plantation, and antislavery movement in the United States. This culminated in the Great Mahele, which was to free the Hawaiian common man from feudal abuses.

The next fifty years, the second half of the nineteenth century, were (most ironically) dominated by the development of sugar plantations and the importation of contract laborers, producing a vast rural proletariat of foreigners, many of whom did not come to Hawaii with the intention of remaining permanently. This phenomenon proceeded at a pace beyond anyone's expectations. At least five homestead programs that were restricted to natural-born Hawaiians failed to counter the dominance of these land-factories, which were worked by imported labor and controlled by a small elite of Americans and Europeans through their privately owned corporations. The overthrow of the monarchy and annexation in 1898 by the United States secured these forms, and left the native Hawaiians with not much more than a terrible sense of deprivation and some estates dedicated to their welfare.

The next major development was the migration of plantation laborers to the cities and towns where, because of their numbers, they could establish small businesses and farms and become a newly emergent middle class with considerable autonomy from the power elite. As a divided elite increased public educational opportunities and the depression slowed immigration, concern was voiced in some quarters that the haoles were disappearing.

The continuing efforts of the elite to develop a rational-industrial type society, while still perpetuating the archaic prejudices of the nineteenth century, broke with the events of World War II. Modern industrial organization of the plantations, with the inevitable internal pressures toward rationalization that its organizational form creates, produced commensurate pressures for an individualized meritocracy and the development of organizations of wage earners as a countervailing force to organized management. World War II released these tendencies as if there had been an eruption. It brought new outside influences into the islands. Wartime experiences and the educational programs of the G.I. Bill produced a new group of trained and cosmopolitan persons who were no longer disposed to accept the previous status system and who provided the organization and much of the leadership to demand equal opportunity and full participation.

The model now became the organizationally dominated, merit-selecting, rationally oriented bureaucracy, in both the public and private sectors—which continued to be intertwined. Unionization in the private sector and civil service in the public sector carried forward these principles of bureaucratic rationality and at the same time introduced new principles of due process, justice, and job security (the vested interest in bureaucratic positions).

Formal education was seen as the new basis for preparing persons to enter into and to make claims upon these large organizations, and the same organizational models were applied to the educational ventures. Larger and larger units were established under centralized control to provide uniform treatment and equality of opportunity.

In this competition, the educationally and bureaucratically oriented descendants of plantation laborers fared rather well in the public sector, and in those previously public sectors which had become increasingly quasi-public, in contrast to the native Hawaiians, who were oriented more toward apprenticeship and interpersonal harmony.

In recent years another factor has intruded itself into the sector of the private economic bureaucracies. These have tended to become components of the largest mainland corporations and international in their operations. Thus, to be vertically mobile a person must be loyal primarily to the corporation and not to a kinship group, a community, or a locale. The personnel rotation of the military has become a powerful model in the name of the rational utilization of human resources. Yet many persons born in Hawaii are oriented primarily toward Hawaii as a place to live and as a way of life; these have been joined by many others who came here first under corporate or federal bureaucratic sponsorship and subsequently "jumped ship." As private exclusionary arrangements and public residency requirements are being declared illegal on various grounds with increasing regularity, many modern Hawaiians of every ethnic background are beginning again to share a feeling of invasion, outside threat, and deprivation.

While these trends have proceeded, the local responses seem to have concentrated overwhelmingly upon the contradictory policies of assuring the security of every man through the private ownership of his land, while imposing controls upon land utilization (for a combination of economic and conservationist ends) which have turned the land market into a highly inflated and speculative operation. Again the cry is raised to solve this problem by opening up more state and estate land for fee-simple ownership, the late twentieth-century version of the now outdated homestead programs. The proposed answers to a speculative nightmare and to increasing outside control seem to be that everyone can get into the game, with Hawaii becoming a means to an end for an increasing number of organized interests. On the contrary, other tools are being increasingly indicated by the "law explosion" and the "justice explosion"—the awareness that in the future human security must be based upon the introduction of the rule of law into all large-scale organizations (local, national, or international) and the implementation of the worldwide demands of all for at least minimal justice. Thus, many of the challenges in the area of social organization, now faced by Hawaii, are the same as the challenges that face most of the rest of the world.

Hawaii's Special Challenge and Value Choice

If, as indicated above, we share many of the organizational constraints and opportunities of the rest of the world, we believe that Hawaii also has its own particular value orientation that operates as its special challenge, opportunity, and constraint. In the process of living and working together, the people of Hawaii have forged a life system and orientation that reaffirms the essential dignity and integrity of every human being, irrespective of race, color, or creed. While many people are inclined to disparage Hawaii's achievement in the field of interpersonal and intergroup relations, there is ample evidence of a fusion of racial types and a blending of cultures that is unique. Of course, the Hawaiian social structure has undergone severe stresses and at times seemed to move away from the ideal of the social equality of all men. Yet it has been possible for men of superior ability, character, and energy to achieve positions of authority and dignity without limitations as to race. Personal position and status in Hawaii has come to depend more on personal merit and less on racial or cultural antecedent. While we are far from perfect, the existence of this public code of racial equality has been crucial in promoting the ideal.

The "aloha spirit"—however it is defined—is a basic ingredient of a style of life based on the essential equality and dignity of all human beings. The basic qualities of this way of life are perhaps best characterized by such terms as openness, hospitality, neighborly concern, tolerance, general acceptance of others, emotional warmth, genuine love for other people, and friendliness. This state of mind, introduced to visitors and incoming residents from all parts of the world by the Hawaiians, nurtured however imperfectly through the stresses of successive waves of immigrants has enabled Hawaii in its doctrine and practices about human relationships to develop as a unique area of the modern world. Hawaii as an image and as a state of mind is heavily indebted to the original Hawaiians.

There is danger, of course, in clinging to outworn clichés rather than reality. Will the aloha spirit become passé? What will happen to the traditional hula? Will the giving of a flower lei disappear, or will this practice become hollow ritual? For, to remain relevant, the state of mind which we call the aloha spirit must demonstrate its viability in the terms of the twenty-first century. This guiding principle in our style of life, however imperfectly practiced, is one of the more basic elements of the identity of Hawaii.

. . .

We also tend to think that the next greatest problem we face in the area of social organization generally is that of imposing personal controls over the ever larger and ever more impersonal bureaucracies. We are indebted to the great German sociologist, Max Weber, for his analysis of the power of this social form to sweep over all competitors because of its deification of the goal of efficiency and of the fact that the modern world requires such a level of efficiency. At the same time, Weber spelled out in great detail the dangers inherent in secrecy within these bureaucracies and the great contribution that this form of social organization can make to tyranny, as well as to the development of mass society, in which we find a world crowded with strangers. If we cannot survive today without the bureaucratic form, then we must also ask how we can survive with it? We suggest that the answer must lie in the seemingly paradoxical statement that we must harness the bureaucratic form to enlarge and enhance the human values implicit in our concept of aloha.

. . .

What We Should Aim For

. . . The basic issues for consideration at State and county levels are those relating to the perpetuation of individual freedom and local community autonomy in a world which will be increasingly centralized, bureaucratized, and standardized. Will the world become like an army, or will there be full freedom for the differing communities in which people will wish to live? How do we implement individual and group freedoms for citizens of the world?

Our basic answer to this question is that a person must become a citizen of each of his important social groups. Citizenship entails full participation in and commitment to each group, and also a full quota of commensurate rights and the protection of these rights.

The significant identity for everyone must be his world citizenship.

To avoid the development of a colorless uniformity and to guard against totalitarianism, world organization should be limited to basic production, enlarged only as is necessary to provide for each man's basic sustenance and for the worldwide communications system. It is precisely this industry that is today organized into the greatest bureaucracy, and the one in which the bureaucratic form makes its greatest contribution to efficiency. Work in such organizations will have to be not the basis for securing special power and control over others, but a major contribution that members of the world community make, for each other and for themselves. One's commitment would have to be to the world community, not to any particular bureaucratic structure.

Participation in such organizations should have the character of a form of national service. Each person would be expected to prepare for such service, and would be provided opportunities in line with his wishes and demonstrated abilities. No one can properly identify with a community that does not permit and demand that he contribute on a membership basis, and the world community can be no different.

It is possible—even desirable—that some manual labor will be required of all, especially such labor as maintains the humility of man in his relationships with the rest of the world. For example, it is possible that all adults will periodically engage in such activities as weeding—even if much of our future food can be raised by hydroponics. In Hawaii such basic duty might well include staffing our hotels, for it is difficult to think of any service that is more symbolic of our pride in Hawaii and of our human kinship than sharing the beauty of the islands with guests, provided the duty is voluntary (for the role of servant, especially in domestic service, is the lowest-status work we have yet devised).

Movement into and out of worldwide bureaucracies, even at the highest levels, would be mandatory, and would be the major restraint against any person's seeking to dominate the world through perpetuated control of organization. Those who control the bureaucracies would thus not be able to divert an organization to their own personal ends—not in any narrow sense of pecuniary gain, but in the broader sense of ego gratification. It is, of course, possible that such rotation might result in some loss of efficiency; however, we not only doubt this but suggest that if it did occur, the loss would be more than compensated for by the much higher level of personal security that the world would enjoy.

We readily admit that it takes considerable boldness to seriously propose a rotating structure of this kind to deal with mankind's basic resources. We can only ask that, before rejecting these suggestions, each skeptical reader examine Weber's work on bureaucracy and Galbraith's analysis of our bureaucracies in *The New Industrial State.*[3] We do not believe that man can afford to abandon the bureaucratic form as a device for coordinating large-scale activities; we merely believe that it must be modified so that it is not an instrument of unaccountable power organized for the personal ends of permanent agents. Many who have been concerned with this problem propose socialism as the solution, but we suggest that most evidence indicates that these persons simply misunderstand the basic nature of the problem. We feel that our proposal of a randomized entrance and exit at all levels goes more to the heart of the problems.

Next we may ask if this principle of organizational openness should stop with bureaucracies? On the contrary, we seriously propose that Hawaii 2000 be characterized by a great reduction in privacy generally. It is understandable that privacy is in great demand in a world in which more people are demanding a greater range of free choice from a society that is basically constraining. If, however, constraint is less, then the demand for privacy should be less. We recognize that invasion of privacy has been equated with abuse of centralized or privileged power, but we do not believe that such need be the case. We further suggest that openness in interpersonal dealings is a major contribution of the original Hawaiian culture to our future potential. We believe that personal and interpersonal security is premised upon such openness, and that this openness is the basis of the kind of accountability that is the essence of constitutionality in any community. In a rational world the answer to private abuse is not more privacy, nor even more publicity at some levels and more privacy at others, but less privacy at all levels.

There is, of course, an additional requirement for this proposition to be behaviorally effective; that is, for reduced privacy and full disclosure to increase both personal and group security. It is that both individuals and communities be highly tolerant and supportive of individuals who are self-consciously "different," so long as they contribute to the richness of living in the society. This qualification is very important, and is an explicit rejection of nihilism. At the same time it carries the implication that, as we become increasingly open, our rule of law will move toward more inclusive definitions of tolerable conduct, just as it has in our own lifetimes.

We recognize that this suggestion to reduce privacy runs counter to the concern voiced in many quarters (a concern which we share) about the files on individuals being developed by public and private agencies. Nevertheless, we think that detailed, computerized social histories will be available on just about everyone in Hawaii 2000, and that they will also be public in the fullest sense. A step in this direction was taken by recent federal legislation requiring agencies that conduct credit investigations to permit any person about whom they have information to see his own file. Already debate is being joined about whether or not a citizen should be allowed to inspect his own FBI file. Files will be kept in a bureaucratically organized world because individuals have histories on which decisions must be made and new knowledge produced. Files are threats—or perhaps we should say, unreasonable threats—to a person in a world of secret decisions and unaccountable power, but immediately available information about persons can be a source of great security in a society with other primary principles of organization.

Such files in Hawaii 2000 will be necessary supports for the high level of interpersonal and intra- and intercommunity tolerance that are central elements of aloha. Tolerance of differences between individuals and communities cannot be achieved to any substantial degree under conditions of secrecy, unknowns, and strangeness. To the contrary, these are the conditions of distrust, suspicion, anxiety, and fear.

If, and admittedly it is a big if, such arrangements as the above can be obtained for Hawaii 2000, then each individual will face a rich variety of choices in structuring his life and can in fact exert a very large control over his own fate. In a sense that is almost inconceivable today, a person can create himself.

First of all, he will be able to be a part of several small but worldwide groupings which share one or more of his interests—the activities or ideas that excite him. This will be possible because of the system of satellite-linked communications that will be available. Already the picturephone connects Pittsburgh and Washington, D.C.; already a planning expert employed "in" Washington, D.C., works and lives in Colorado with his wife, a psychiatrist, who maintains her practice in San Francisco. With additional satellite development, persons who want to will be able to regularize face-to-face communication on a worldwide basis.

This means that place-of-residence and place-of-work, or at least some of them, will become increasingly independent decisions. However, in line with our earlier value choices, we do not believe that Hawaii 2000 should become only a collection of apartments in which almost all social interaction takes place by means of electronic transmission. Provision should be made, however, for this kind of lifestyle, and in time it might encompass an increasingly large segment of the population. We anticipate, however, that Hawaii 2000 will have achieved a wide range of diverse communities to constitute the social settings in which individuals carry out most of their activities. Membership in any of these communities will be by choice.

The amounts and kinds of diversity that will be possible among these communities will depend considerably upon the fullest implementation of tolerance and the necessary conditions for such a norm to be a substantial influence over behavior. We anticipate that communities may be as diverse as the most radical Israeli kibbutz on one hand, and some of our modern high-rise apartments on the other, as diverse as the Banana Patch and Waipahu.[4] Some of them will undoubtedly embody counterculture and be highly self-conscious efforts to reject the most central elements of modern American, urban, middle-class culture. Others will have even a higher level of sophistication and will seek a certain quality of life from various theoretical perspectives. Some may be self-consciously ethnic communities, but operating on a more creative future-oriented base than at present, because all will be aware (through the worldwide communication system) that none of the ethnic cultures have the degree of homogeneity that characterized even the year 1900. We will thus find a range from unisex roles to diverse bisexual roles at the adult level; we will have considerable diversity in childbearing and childrearing practices and responsibilities. The creation of such communities will require a continuation of the present trend to systematically make our formal regulations of marriage and parenthood more diverse.

It should be stressed that these communities will be of a genuinely experimental character. Most evidence today suggests that we do not know enough about child development to design any single best set of childrearing practices. In return for the support for self-choice that each community will offer the other, all must be committed to providing systematic information to the public data banks on the results of their practices. Thus, once again we may return to the social experimentation, once dreamed about in the United States, in the form of permitted diversity among the states. The possibility that each community could be a self-correcting institution within the range of its ideals might be given a very substantial boost by our required systematic, public evaluation. This would be possible because our reorganized bureaucratic structure and assurance of minimum necessities would enable each community to have primary values different from those of any other without fear of handicapping their children in a lifelong competition with others.

The problem then is to provide each individual and community with as much free choice in lifestyle and social organization as is conceivable (under conditions of high interpersonal and intercommunity security) and to provide each with a fair share of the needed resources to implement such free choice. Central here is control of educational resources and organization, so that each individual and community would have access to vast stores of computerized information and instructional materials. Such technology in itself, however, does not dictate the nature of the educational organization nor the specific content for each person. With each passing year, of course, content would become increasingly self-selected by the learner. It is probable that what we think of today as basic education (whatever its equivalent in Hawaii 2000), and some specialized education, will end at about age sixteen.

Since the stability of each community, and thus of the world, would be based substantially upon each individual's creating himself by consciously choosing his community and interest group, it would probably be necessary to have the next period of socialization by the young include a maximum of travel and participation in relatively small, and probably highly specialized, educational communities. This projection for the young is made because we believe that there is for them a very intense peer-group orientation and a need for social supports while working through their initial identity crises.

The principle of continuous learning based on self-choice would also be implemented throughout adulthood—as, for example, in that dramatic, even revolutionary experiment in twentieth-century America, the Veterans' Education Bill, immediately after World War II. One of the amazing features of the 1950s and 1960s is the manner in which hundreds of young legislators throughout the United States, including Hawaii, experienced the choices available through this Bill and then turned their backs on it in favor of bureaucratic models in which a man is supposed to gain his freedom by having most important decisions made for him by others. The bureaucratic principle should be employed to guarantee and to provide maximum equality of opportunity, but it should not be used to dictate what should be learned and where or how it should be learned. This is the lesson we learned and then forgot or rejected in favor of secondary values. This lost principle must be reaffirmed and reimplemented; hopefully, new technologies and less intercommunity suspicion will greatly facilitate this task.

We recognize that education is today embroiled in a vast public debate. Some persons identify social, especially racial, integration with the immediate problem of placing children of diverse ethnicities into larger and larger administrative and educational organizations. The current effort to solve this problem by larger bureaucracies is not very successful because the effort itself generates a vast number of additional problems associated with coercion. So far as public resources are concerned, we could maintain at least as high, if not a higher, degree of reduction of ethnic and socioeconomic discrimination by a system using small, personal, and specialized units that provide each person with great freedom of choice.

Such choice is also necessary to provide effective education in a world with a highly mobile population. Today we worry about the manner in which we program the sequence of educational activities for our children. Because sequencing is accepted as crucial, we even talk about integrated planning for elementary, middle, and high schools in a "feeder system." But our children move all over Hawaii and all over the world. Sequentially planned education for them cannot be organized on a territorial basis, but must be organized by private organizations that offer their services in those communities among which people are moving. The nonpublic organization offers the best format for educational integration in the emerging world.

Immediate Steps For Hawaii

To attain the most desirable Hawaii 2000 we propose that the following steps be taken now.

1. Support all steps to internationalize basic production on the principle of bureaucratic organization, with rotating assignment of workers at all levels. Clearly, an important step in this direction will be to support this principle in the development of ocean resources.

2. Resist all efforts to release more State land to fee-simple ownership or to break up the large estates, while initiating a program to reacquire ownership of all land in Hawaii in the name of the politically organized community. Since our land-use controls are an inflationary factor as things stand now, we should control the price of land under the principle of unjust enrichment. Reacquisition would then no longer be a hopeless dream within our constitutional constraints.

3. Begin the planning immediately of diverse communities. If a large estate really wants to donate land for a second Oahu campus for the University of Hawaii, insist, for example, that it contribute to diversity by designing a community intended to realize the goals of women's liberation. Although we are already ahead of many communities in some dimensions of liberation, let us proceed systematically to find out now what are the full implications of this movement for physical and social community planning.

4. Move dramatically to match our centralized control of educational resources with the decentralization of education. Serious experiments in this area are underway, and we should get actively involved. We should, for example, facilitate progress in our own university's work in sequential integration, at the same time as we enlarge our horizons to prepare for the day of greater variation, and nonterritorial sequential integration, within a quasi-public sphere.

Postscript

We hope that each reader will recognize the extent to which many of us feel rooted in the past in that we believe that the basic problems of human organization will not be greatly different in 2000 than they are today.

Nothing contained in this paper should be assumed to represent the firm conviction of any member of our task force; we share only our conviction that the problems we have discussed will be areas for decision that will, more than any others, serve to determine what kinds of people we citizens of Hawaii will be in 2000, and what kinds of lives we may live. But we do share our feelings about aloha.

A last word of caution: values change. In 1985 we may prefer some other alternative for 2000 than we do in 1970. In 1985 we may see new consequences for 2030 of the alternative futures in 2000. We may look further ahead and discover that we would rather travel on a different road than the one which appeared to us preferable in 1970. Decision theory may help us with this problem; it shows us how to estimate whether we should defer our decisions in some areas until 1985, and what the social costs or consequences might be for postponing the option to change directions now. Other changes in our preferences may not be attributable to new foresights, but rather to new insights. Under these conditions, it seems essential that Hawaii, as it looks toward its future, continuously reassess its values and goals and make appropriate changes in possible courses of action.

NOTES

1. Because of space requirements we removed the thirty-five pages of our initial working paper [see *Preliminary Task Force Reports (July 1970)*] that carefully reviewed the slow progress man has made in producing new social forms that increase his capacity for a full, secure, and varied life. Many persons missed our point entirely in the first draft—that the number of pages consumed represented the length of time that each step of progress in this area consumed in the past. In this version we have concentrated upon elaboration of the areas that struck us as representing the major decisions that must be made today if we are to avoid worldwide disaster, and gain substantial control over our fate by 2000. Many of us prefer our first version, for it is our firm conviction that under even the best of circumstances man will always be backing into his future.

2. City: 248,034; county: 353,020

3. Baltimore: Penguin Books, 1969.

4. Maui's Banana Patch attracted disillusioned young people searching for a slow-paced life of natural simplicity in gardening, sunbathing, and meditation. For five years owner David Joseph welcomed into his lush valley these "children of God," who built some twenty small dwellings and went on their own "trips" of sharing or solitude.

Waipahu is a rural town, built around a sugar mill, celebrating its seventy-fifth anniversary in 1972—Editors.

Race Relations in the Hawaiian School: The *Haole* Newcomer

GLEN GRANT

AT Rural Elementary School,[1] in the fifth grade class of Mrs. McDonald, three *haole* children could be observed: Joseph, who sat quietly with his Filipino peer group; Gary, who fidgeted in his chair making grotesque faces at snickering local children; William, who quietly sat alone, shunned by children around him. Physically, their appearances were nearly identical—blond hair, blue eyes, fair skin. They had each been in Hawaii for less than a year. But their adjustments and relationships with local children were each uniquely different—Joseph, part of a Filipino peer group; Gary, in the process of developing friendly relations with some local children; and William, the outcast.

In the classroom a local boy was wearing a dark blue T-shirt with white stenciling. There was a funny cartoon character of a long-haired surfer and the huge wording "Dumb Haole!" In conversations with each other, in verbal fights, the worst insult a local child could think of was, "You one *haole*!" Yet the same local children who could express such attitudes had friends who were *haole*. Some Filipino children had accepted Joseph as a part of their network of friends; Gary sometimes could be seen playing with Hawaiian boys in friendly sports. Then, of course, there was the "dumb *haole*" who

From *The Interaction of the Haole and Local Child: A Study of Race Relations in Hawaii's Schools,* University of Hawaii master's thesis (Educational Foundations, 1974), under the chairmanship of Dr. Royal T. Fruehling. Reprinted by permission of Glen Grant.

received the brunt of physical attacks and verbal abuse—William could not sit through an hour of class that someone didn't pinch, tease, hit or insult him.

David, a Filipino youngster, threw spit balls at William, called him an "ass" and tried to poke him with a pencil. David then sought the help of Joseph on an assignment which the teacher insisted he finish. Later he was seen with Gary, arm in arm, talking, disrupting class, laughing and, when possible, insulting the teacher to the delight of many.

Even the most casual observer would have to be puzzled if he had any precognitions of "typical" race relations. In this classroom the ethnic and racial boundaries seem obscured on the personal level. How could three children of the same race have developed so markedly different racial interactions? How could a child of one race be so diverse in his treatment of children of another race? Aren't our standard assumptions operative that the existence of racial prejudices lumps individuals into a single category of behavioral treatment? And what about the popular notion that *haole*s are hated by locals, that they receive the frustrations and vengeance of local people undergoing social upheaval? Or the complaint by parents that *haole* children are racially picked on, teased, or insulted indiscriminately by prejudiced local children?

For three months the race relations between local children and the *haole* in the Rural Elementary School were observed, attempting to discern the cross-cultural interactions in the classroom. How had friendly interactions between children of different racial backgrounds been established? How had hostile relationships developed between certain children? How had the various local and *haole* children learned to adapt to each other's cultures and behaviors? How could children with such similar racial backgrounds as Joseph, Gary, William, or David have been involved in such diverse interethnic relations?

The classroom in the Island school can often be a microcosm of the processes and dynamics of social, economic, and political forces on the state-wide level. In terms of ethnic interactions, analogies or comparisons can be drawn with the processes of Hawaiian race relations which have characterized the multiethnic environment of the Islands. Philosophical or sociological outlooks could be suggested which give depth to a comprehensive understanding of cultural pluralism in Hawaii.

The Rural Elementary School, accordingly, approximates many

of the social changes and economic–racial stratifications found in the broader Hawaiian system. The area which the Rural Elementary School serves is a constantly changing one, with an influx of mainland transients, military families, and new *haole* middle-class residents as a result of recent nearby housing developments. The socioeconomic status of varying ethnic peoples in the areas also shows diversity. While the incoming *haole* families are generally middle class, the school has a significant portion of children from homes of lower-middle or lower-class economic status. Two hundred forty students or over one third of the student body qualifies for a free lunch under unemployment or welfare benefits. The racial composition of the Rural Elementary School also typifies Hawaii's ethnic pluralism. Out of a total of 680 students, 35 percent are Hawaiian or part-Hawaiian, 30 percent Japanese, 20 percent Filipino, 10 percent *haole* and 5 percent Chinese, Korean, and Samoan.

In this multiethnic school environment, as in the pluralistic society, friendly race relations are essential for the continued performance of necessary roles and functional behaviors. People of various ethnic backgrounds or racial origins must be able to cooperate and interact with one another for the perpetuation of the social group—otherwise hostility would lead to conflict and social disruption.

While a simple enough proposition, multiethnic harmony has not always been so simply achieved, or understood. Hawaii, as a plurality of cultures and races, has generally been viewed by historians, sociologists, and novelists as the "Melting Pot of the Pacific," a system of "racial unorthodoxy" and an environment where the various ethnic groups live with one another in relative peace. But racial upheavals instigated from without, the influx of newcomers from the mainland, Philippines, and Samoa, have caused some observers to be wary of the durability of the Islands' multiethnic harmony. Will these newcomers, specifically the *haole,* be able to interact and cooperate with local people? Will they increase racial hostilities and distrusts? Can they assimilate local ways, be incorporated in a local lifestyle?

But to understand the nature of race relations between the *haole* and the local child is to first recognize the cultural and behavioral differences between the two groups, for the *haole* and the local child are indeed culturally different. Home environment, cultural training, past school experiences, and values vary between the child reared in a *haole* family on the mainland and the child reared in a Japanese,

Filipino, or Hawaiian home in Hawaii. When they find themselves in the same Island classroom, on the same playground, or sitting next to each other in the cafeteria, when they find that they must engage in interactions cross-culturally, they do so with a set of cognitive maps, or cultural mazeways, which are unknown to each other and at times mutually incompatible.

The *haole* student entering the Rural Elementary School classroom would encounter a network of local children's behaviors which have been developed as a consequence of adapting to the Island culture. At home or in the community, folk patterns of "local Hawaiian culture," including an emphasis on affiliation, reciprocal obligation, and strong peer group influences, shape the child's "world view." In addition the local child has also learned a series of coping strategies used to adapt to the expectations of the school culture. Island children tend to relate better in terms of peer group work rather than the teacher–child relationship; verbal expression is inhibited so as not to "make ass" or outdo the peer group. "Playing" or "clowning around" are behaviors learned to ease the frustrations of an environment highly competitive and goal driven. The demands of the academic subject matter, the authority of the teacher, and the schedule of daily activities become cultural pressures on many local children alien to their home environment and demanding of adaptation or sublimation. Behaviors which become valuable for local children, then, are getting peer group help when needed to meet the demands of the subject matter, accommodation to the classroom environment of quietness so as not to jeopardize peer group equalitarianism, venting frustrations of teacher discipline and expressing themselves physically on the playground after time spent sitting in class. For both males and females, these behaviors have an important priority as was determined through observation.

The *haole* child, on the other hand, possesses quite a different view of the school culture. The relationship of prime importance is the teacher–student dialogue, not necessarily the peer group. Giving help to classmates can sometimes be interpreted as "cheating," violating the ground rules of healthy competition. One must outdo his peer group, excel in study and self-expression while maintaining obedience to the teacher's authority. While certainly physical exertion helps to release the tensions in the classroom, such activity must never jeopardize the teacher–student rapport.

When the *haole* newcomer enters the classroom of local children, he quickly learns that his behavioral normality is frequently aggravating to the local. But being a newcomer, the *haole* wants to become part of the majority or "in-group." Consequently, the *haole* can be seen frequently initiating interactions with local children so as to gain peer group acceptance. In turn, the local child is willing to enter into interaction with a *haole* if the outcome of that continued interaction is a relationship which allows the local child to in some way enhance the coping strategies he employs in the culture of the school. If the *haole* can provide academic help, if he enhances "fooling around" or if he is a good athlete or active physically, then a local child would be willing to initiate and continue an interethnic relationship.

In the context of these valued rewards, the basis of the diverse *haole*-local interactions can be examined. If a friendly interaction between a local and *haole* child occurred, then the performance of behaviors by the participants was rewarding to each other's needs. Thus the *haole* who was a tutor, performed a helpful behavior for local children which enabled them to do better in school. Because local children in turn showed the *haole* friendship or at least neutral acceptance, he was able to be passively accepted by some local children or avòid hostilities from others. Other *haole*s based their interactive behaviors on their ability to participate in "fooling around" behaviors which enabled local children to "fool around" themselves or laugh. Again, these *haole*s were able to join local peer groups due to their predictable, friendly behaviors. Finally, some *haole*s based their interactions on their athletic abilities, enabling local children to win at games or have more competition on the playground.

For friendly interactions between the *haole* and local child to continue over a period of time, the predictability of behaviors as being mutually rewarding is basic. Local children must learn that by giving certain *haole* children friendship, those *haole* children would always be willing and capable of enhancing the coping strategies of local children. In turn, the *haole* children must know that local children will predictably provide accepting or friendly behaviors when they perform their respective interactive behaviors. It is not necessary that either child in a *haole*-local interaction know what the other child is thinking or why. It is not necessary to share the same cognitive maps, cultures, or motivations. But it is necessary that the behaviors of the *haole* and local child be viewed by them as being predictable, friendly, and rewarding. In this sense the *haole* and local will share a "point of commonality" in their cultures, a common reciprocal understanding enabling them to engage in mutually rewarding behaviors.

At least a minimum of these "points of commonality" is necessary if friendly ethnic interaction over a period of time is to develop. In the interactions of *haole* and local students, for friendly behaviors to be engaged in, only one well-established "point of commonality" is really necessary. Some *haole* children predominantly engaged in only one kind of behavior with locals—the giving of academic assistance. This one "point of commonality" was capable of establishing friendly interactions with locals for these *haole*s. It was also clear from the results of this study that a multiple of "points of commonality" might be desirable, but is not necessary for the continuation of friendly interethnic relations. Speaking pidgin, dressing locally, "fooling around," trading marbles, playing dodgeball, the whole gamut of the local child's daily activities, need not be emulated or negotiated as a basis of interaction. The *haole* child need not become "local" for friendly long-term interactions between races to take place.

However, many times "points of commonality" do not implicitly develop. Many times the *haole* child finds that his behaviors are not necessarily rewarding or predictable to local children—he must negotiate behaviors for the condition of friendly interaction to occur. So the *haole* children who were observed in this study were continually involved in developing mutually rewarding behaviors for the creation of more durable or numerous "points of commonality." Some *haole*s tried to strengthen friendships with "joking" or "talking story"; others learned to use heavy pidgin to establish behavioral commonalities; some used marbles to try to establish behavioral "points of commonality."

Sometimes a *haole* child, though, incapable of negotiating "points of commonality" encountered a situation of hostile, unfriendly, and exploitive interactions. Possibly the punishment he received in itself became a reward worth perpetuating—at least he was receiving some attention and not being totally ignored. But the costs of punishment, of being an outcast, were frequently too high and unpredictable. Other *haole*s avoided the child because he became a liability affecting their own negotiations or friendly interactions. Generally unfriendly interactions stemmed from behaviors which exacerbated the misunderstandings of local children for the *haole*. The outcast, William, for example, consistently refused to give help to children who asked for it; on the playground, William didn't play team games; he made errors when he did. In classroom interactions when local children "fooled around" William didn't laugh; he remained aloof; he responded to good-natured teasing with anger which reinforced the teaser. As a consequence, day in and day out William exploitively received hostile behaviors from local children. Teasing William became a source of fun, and a means to react to William's nonrewarding behaviors, while William received nothing.

Once the pattern of nonrewarding and nonpredictable behaviors was established, the evidence suggested that breaking that cycle was exceedingly difficult. Negotiating explicit contracts for those children involved establishing new behaviors which were not only rewarding but predictable over a long period of time—the old predictabilities of behavior had to be supplanted by positive, rewarding predictabilities. Other children, local or *haole,* were going to have to find the rewards for interacting with *haole*s deemed outcasts greater than the costs of associating with them. Evidence suggested that such costs were usually greater than anything which the *haole* under observation could offer local or *haole* children. In addition, in the "closed system" of the school, the child could not break off, avoid, or terminate such hostile or exploitive relationships.

As a consequence of these various processes and inputs, the individual *haole* has developed a variety of adjustments and behavioral contracts with local children. Since there are innumerable "points of commonality" which can or cannot be negotiated, innumerable contracts to be established or broken, the nature of *haole*-local relationships is also widely variable. If a minimum of "points of commonality" can be established, friendly interactions, from passive acceptance, individual relationships, peer group acceptance to wide popularity, can be possible. If not, then hostility, unfriendliness, or exploitation is possible. At any rate, the process of explicit negotiations of "points of commonality" is a constant interpersonal dynamic which constantly shifts the nature and meaning of *haole*-local interactions and the various styles of *haole* adaptation to the school culture of the local child.

The implications these conclusions have for understanding race relations in the Hawaiian classroom are significant. Most importantly, an understanding of the interactions of local and *haole* children as described in this study necessitates the conclusion that race in itself is a secondary factor in race relations. Granted that general ethnic groupings, respecting boundaries and common interest, were maintained at Rural Elementary School. Granted that children used the terms "Jap," *"haole,"* and "Portogee" in derogatory tones. But as evident in the diversity of adaptation between Joseph, Gary, and William, being *haole,* in and of itself, had little to do with the resulting behavioral patterns. Behaviors, what one individual could offer another, skills of negotiation, were the dominant basis upon which friendly or unfriendly behaviors were determined. The quality, then, of interethnic relations on the personal level is clearly the result of the establishment of "points of commonality" that make mutually rewarding contracts possible in behavioral relations and not the texture of the hair, the color of the skin or the genetic composition of the chromosomes. The *haole*s in this study did not receive hostile behaviors from locals simply because they were *haole,* but because they performed specific behaviors and failed to negotiate specific contracts which would create the conditions for friendly interracial contacts.

Furthermore this study revealed that what is necessary for friendly interaction to occur is only a minimum of "points of commonality." The *haole* need not assimilate the entire ways of the local child; the local need not become "haolefied" for friendly interaction to take place interethnically. The *haole* can remain culturally a *haole,* the Japanese a Japanese, the Filipino a Filipino, the Hawaiian a Hawaiian and still mutually rewarding and predictable relationships can be developed and perpetuated.

The meaning this gives to race relations in Hawaii is significant. General observations revealed that in the school, ethnic groups maintained their boundaries and divisions. Hawaiians, Japanese, Filipinos, Chinese interacted to a great extent with their own kind. While this might negate the "integrative" notion of race relations or the notion of "cultural pluralism," in reality it points to the fact that each of those individuals can remain culturally distinct in the process of developing "points of commonality." It is not necessary for them to abandon cultural ties with others of their same ethnic origin for friendly interethnic relationships to be possible. Sharing a "local Hawaiian lifestyle" for these children is in actuality sharing "points of commonality" in their diverse behaviors. Becoming local was the end result of a process of negotiation which each immigrant to Hawaii has undergone, and which continues operative to this day. Except for the native Hawaiian, each immigrant group has been viewed as a "newcomer" by local residents and has had to undergo the same process of negotiating "points of commonality" which was studied in the Rural Elementary School. As seen in the sharing of the "local

Hawaiian lifestyle," the generational development of local ethnic groups has resulted in shared "points of commonality" which allow for friendly interethnic behaviors while at the same time maintaining cultural and racial diversity.

The newcomer entering Hawaii will as a member of a group encounter various social difficulties and will encounter various racial attitudes and prejudices. But on the individual level, he will frequently need to interact with the "locals" which for both participants must be based on mutually rewarding and predictable behaviors. Since he enters a local system which is generally satisfying, the newcomer must show the local how he can make the system more rewarding. "Points of commonality" in their behaviors on a daily basis will possibly be established, though they need never share common cognitive maps or cultural realities. The newcomer will remain a *haole,* a Filipino, a Samoan, a Hawaiian, a Puerto Rican, a Chinese, a Korean or a Japanese. But he will be capable of eventually engaging in interactive behaviors which all parties will find rewarding and predictable. There is no need to "become" anything they are not, to acculturate totally to any lifestyle or cultural mold for a society of diverse people to live peacefully and rewardingly together. Essentially this process is the foundation of interpersonal race relations in Hawaii and it is a process which this study suggests is durable, capable of incorporating diverse peoples, and, if left untampered, will be the continued basis of the dynamic style of cultural pluralism found in Hawaii.

NOTE

[1.] Located in the rural district of the island of Oahu.

Kodomo no tame ni

MOST of the inhabitants of the city were bronzed, with shining black hair and pleasing features. Their dress appeared to be borrowed from the Chinese, the men in loose flowing pants and shirt similar to the higher class of China. Correspondingly, the women were wearing Chinese garb of loose pants and an over-dress decoratively colored. The more elegant ladies wore white wreaths instead of bonnets on their black hair. Each lady was followed by a servant who carried a monstrous umbrella to shield her mistress from the tropical sun. Even the language they spoke was a strange blend of tongues. Evidently the entire population was a racial mixture of European and Chinese peoples existing in a community of 80,000.

About twenty miles away from this city called Honolulu, toward Ewa, was a larger metropolis of 100,000. Reached only by the Oahu Insular Railway, Helopolis was the capital of Hawaii. The houses of the city were constructed out of coral stone and extended back into the reaches of several valleys, terraced with olive groves and vineyards. The city was composed of enormous five-story buildings of stone and glass. The city of Helopolis was dependent economically on the great harbor which had been cut through a reef in 1910. The harbor became an international port for trade between China and America, carrying principally oil. The great steam sailing ships ran a regular monthly line between Helopolis and the rest of the world. Indeed, the trade in oil had built the metropolis and turned it into the bustling seaport of men, ships, and visitors.

Within the Islands, life had appreciably changed due to the development of Helopolis. Every interisland ship was outfitted as a steamer with a regular daily run to each outer island. Telegraphic lines had been established between each island and also with the mainland. News in Europe took only one hour to reach the remote islands of Hawaii.

Such was Hawaii, the "greatest emporium in the world," in the year 1956. Or that is, such was the Hawaii of the future predicted in the year 1856, for in that year the *Pacific Commercial Advertiser* published a futuristic projection of what the Hawaii of tomorrow would be like.[1]

If anything, the futurism of 1856 teaches a lesson in humility. Man's soothsaying powers might be entertaining, but they are also restrictive. The future is invariably seen with the eyes of the present, ignorant of unpredicted yet certain-to-occur events. To the individuals of 1856, the Hawaiian peoples of the future were to be an amalgamation of European, Polynesian, and Chinese stock—the maintenance of ethnic boundaries, the immigration of Japanese, Filipino, or Koreans were unforeseeable. Honolulu and Helopolis were to be linked solely by railway—the invention of the car was unimaginable, as were freeways. The major industry of Hawaii was to be the trade in oil—the shipping of sperm oil in the whaling industry was seemingly the only economic resource open to the Islands. Sugar production, labor importation, tourism, air travel, world wars, and the media were developments wholly alien to a past generation naive to the dynamic skills of the technocrats, politicians, and "city-builders."

Futurists of 1975 are more sophisticated, using computers, technological genius, and charted "trends." Still, human beings continue to view the future, as Marshall McLuhan so vividly explained, as if they were driving a high-speed car eighty miles per hour while looking only in the rear-view mirror. The human condition is still limited by the ignorance of foresight, the incapacity to divert our eyes from the rear-view mirror to the road ahead.

Any prediction of the future of Japanese in Hawaii seems similarly overly reliant on the past. The fourth generation, the Yonsei, and the fifth generation, the Gosei, cannot be described based on the experiences of the Issei, Nisei, or Sansei. Will there even be a culture known as the Japanese American by 2000 A.D.? Will the Americanization of the media or intermarriage obliterate ethnic lifestyles and boundaries? Will Hawaii's people evolve into a new form of social community exemplary of international patterns? As tempting as the possibilities of fortune-telling might be, to predicate a Helopolis for posterity ultimately creates for the soothsayer an embarrassing reputation.

The concept of the Hawaiian Consensus, on the other hand, should not be viewed in terms of fortune-telling but future building. For the problems, the technology, the social revolutions which Hawaii and the Japanese will encounter by the year 2000 A.D. will not require prophecies but sound attitudes. The values Islanders employ to seek the "good life" will become the major philosophic resource upon which a beneficial future will rely. Most importantly, then, it is essential that the inherent relational and humanistic values in the diversity of Island "points of commonality" prevail. In particular, Islanders must place high priority on a "point of commonality" shared by all of the ethnic groups—a drive for an improvement in life. The Japanese have called it a spirit of *"kodomo no tame ni"* (for the sake of the children). And for Islanders, such commitment to *kodomo no tame ni,* a recognition of its role in the Hawaiian Consensus, will necessitate an acceptance of the evolving pluralism of Island economic, political, and cultural systems. Those in power—businessmen, administrators, and legislators who have gained economic stability—must realize that the same motives which drove their parents and grandparents to succeed are driving the newer immigrants and even the new ethnically conscious native Hawaiian community. The strategies of community cohesiveness which helped the earlier groups achieve their social status and influence in Island affairs are now being employed by other ethnic groups desirous of a better future for their children.

Such an acceptance of social change, a redistribution and equalization of power for the improvement of all Island life, eventually involves a new meaning of ethnicity and humanism. It means a Hawaiian Consensus which can stimulate a transformation of ethnic jealousies and apathy into a serious reappraisal of belief systems. The educational system, the political system, the corporation, the family, and the layman—indeed all facets of Island life—would be affected by a reevaluation of attitudes and the encouragement of new outlooks. Ultimately, the humanization of Island life will mean that all become more open to new and diverse insights; that all will make choices based on the broadest cultural alternatives as to what they feel is best for themselves, their families, and their communities; that all will become cognizant of the values consciously and unconsciously enculturated in their children, providing them with the necessary tools to deal with their futures; that all will simply become involved in living.

Incumbent upon Island people will also be the cost of this social involvement. Once the future becomes malleable through the concerned efforts of an involved populace, random chance can no longer be totally blamed for social futures. The creator who has chosen the design must be held accountable. At no other time in their history have the people of Hawaii been more in control of social and cultural evolutions. At no other time have the responsibilities of future directions been so awesome. No longer can they thoughtlessly drift as simple bobbing candles following the *Saihō Maru* through paternal currents. No longer can they trust the gods to descend from the heavens to implement divine schemes. The choices for the future, for the children, are theirs alone—choices of moral and spiritual values underlying the concerns of family, ethnic community, and cultural pluralism. Ultimately it will involve a full commitment to either apathy or action. Emptiness or meaningfulness. Indifference or purpose. Boredom or human creativity.

NOTE

1. *The Pacific Commercial Advertiser,* July 2, 1906, pp. 17–18.

Bibliography

I. Secondary Works

Adams, Romanzo. *Interracial Marriage in Hawaii: A Study of the Mutually Conditioned Processes of Acculturation and Amalgamation.* New York: The Macmillan Company, 1937.

Allen, Gwenfread E. *Hawaii's War Years, 1941–45.* Honolulu: University of Hawaii Press, 1950.

Anesaki, Masaharu. *History of Japanese Religion.* London: Kegan, Paul, Trench, Trubner, 1930.

Burrows, Edwin Grant. *Chinese and Japanese in Hawaii During Sino-Japanese Conflict.* Honolulu: Hawaii Group American Council, Institute of Pacific Relations, 1939.

Chaplin, George, and Glenn D. Paige, eds. *Hawaii 2000: Continuing Experiment in Anticipatory Democracy.* Governor's Conference on the Year 2000, Honolulu, 1970. Honolulu: University Press of Hawaii, 1973.

Coffman, Tom. *Catch A Wave: A Case Study of Hawaii's New Politics.* Honolulu: University Press of Hawaii, 1972.

Compilation Committee for the Publication of Kinzaburo Makino's Biography, eds. *Life of Kinzaburo Makino.* Honolulu: Hawaii Hochi, 1965.

Fuchs, Lawrence H. *Hawaii Pono: A Social History.* New York: Harcourt, Brace and World, 1961.

Gray, Francine Du Plessix. *Hawaii: The Sugar-Coated Fortress.* New York: Random House, 1971.

Hunter, Louise. *Buddhism in Hawaii: Its Impact on a Yankee Community.* Honolulu: University of Hawaii Press, 1971.

Kitano, Harry H. L. *Japanese Americans, The Evolution of a Subculture.* Englewood Cliffs, New Jersey: Prentice-Hall, Inc., 1969.

LaViolette, Forrest E. *Americans of Japanese Ancestry, A Study of Assimilation in the American Community.* Toronto: The Canadian Institute of International Affairs, 1945.

Lind, Andrew W. *Hawaii, The Last of the Magic Isles.* London: Oxford University Press, 1969.

______. *Hawaii's Japanese: An Experiment in Democracy.* Princeton: Princeton University Press, 1946.

______. *Hawaii's People.* Honolulu: University of Hawaii Press, 1967.

MacDonald, Alexander. *Revolt in Paradise: The Social Revolution in Hawaii After Pearl Harbor.* New York: Stephen Page, Inc., 1944.

Samuels, Frederick. *The Japanese and the Haoles in Honolulu.* New Haven: College and University Press, 1970.

Simpich, Frederick, Jr. *Anatomy of Hawaii.* Toronto: Coward, McConn and Geoghegan Inc., 1971.

United Japanese Society of Hawaii. *A History of Japanese in Hawaii.* Ed. by Publication Committee, Dr. James H. Okahata, Chm. Honolulu: United Japanese Society of Hawaii, 1971.

Wakukawa, Ernest. *A History of the Japanese People in Hawaii.* Honolulu: The Toyo Shoin, 1938.

Wright, Theon. *The Disenchanted Isles: The Story of the Second Revolution in Hawaii.* New York: Dial Press, 1972.

II. Articles, Unpublished Dissertations and Theses

Agena, Masako, and Eiko Yoshinaga. " 'Daishi-Do'—A Form of Religious Movement," *Social Process in Hawaii.* V. 7 (November 1941), pp. 15–20.

Akinaka, Amy. "Types of Japanese Marriages in Hawaii," *Social Process in Hawaii.* V. 1 (May 1935), pp. 32–3.

Araki, Makoto, Marjorie H. Carlson, Kazuichi Hamasaki, Blossom M. Higa, Betty Ann W. Rocha and Hiromi Shiramizu. "A Study of the Socio-Cultural Factors in Casework Services for Individuals and Families Known to the Child and Family Service, Honolulu, 1954." M.A. thesis (Social Work), University of Hawaii, 1956.

Arkoff, Abe. "Male Dominant and Equalitarian Attitudes in Japanese, Japanese-American and Caucasian-American Students," *The Journal of Social Psychology.* V. 59 (1964), pp. 225–9.

Bell, Roger J. "Admission Delayed: The Influence of Sectional and Political Opposition in Congress on Statehood for Hawaii," *Hawaiian Journal of History.* V. 6 (1972), pp. 45–68.

Glick, Clarence E., Alice T. Higa, Irene S. Nose, Judith M. Shibuya, "Changing Attitudes Toward the Care of Aged Japanese Parents in Hawaii," *Social Process in Hawaii.* V. 22 (1958), pp. 9–20.

Glick, Clarence E., and students. "Changing Ideas of Success and of Roads to Success as Seen by Immigrant and Local Chinese and Japanese Businessmen in Honolulu," *Social Process in Hawaii.* V. 15 (1951), pp. 56–60.

Gushiken, Chiyo. "Wedding Ceremonies: 1938–1945," *Social Process in Hawaii.* V. 12 (August 1948), pp. 8–11.

Henderson, C. J. "Labor—An Undercurrent of Hawaiian Social History," *Social Process in Hawaii.* V. 15 (1951), pp. 44–55.

Hilo, M., and Emma K. Himeno. "Some Characteristics of American and Japanese Culture," *Social Process in Hawaii.* V. 21 (1957), pp. 34–41.

Hormann, Bernhard L. "The Contemporary Family in Hawaii." Partly revised paper given to Hawaii Social Work Conference, Honolulu, 1964.

______. "The Problems of the Religion of Hawaii's Japanese," *Social Process in Hawaii.* V. 22 (1958), pp. 5–8.

______. *The Revival of Buddhism in Hawaii.* War Research Laboratory Report No. 12, Honolulu: University of Hawaii Press, 1947.

Inamine, Otomi, Phyllis Kon, Yan Quai Lau, and Marjorie Okamoto. "The Effect of War on Interracial Marriage in Hawaii," *Social Process in Hawaii.* V. 9–10 (1945), pp. 103–9.

Johnson, Colleen L. "The Japanese-American Family and Community in Honolulu: Generational Continuities in Ethnic Affiliation." Ph.D. dissertation (Anthropology), Syracuse University, 1972.

Kikumura, Akemi, and Harry H. L. Kitano. "Interracial Marriage: A Picture of the Japanese Americans," *Journal of Social Issues.* V. 29, no. 2 (1973), pp. 67–81.

Kimura, Sueko H. "Japanese Funeral Practices in Pahoa," *Social Process in Hawaii.* V. 22 (1958), pp. 21–5.

Kimura, Yukiko. "Rumor Among the Japanese." *Social Process in Hawaii.* V. 11 (May 1947), pp. 84–92.

______. *Socio-Historical Background of the Okinawans in Hawaii.* Romanzo Adams Research Laboratory Report no. 36, Honolulu: University of Hawaii Press, 1962.

______. "Some Effects of the War Situation Upon the Alien Japanese in Hawaii," *Social Process in Hawaii.* V. 8 (1943), pp. 18–28.

Kitano, Harry H. L. "Mental Illness in Four Cultures," *The Journal of Social Psychology.* V. 80 (April 1970), pp. 121–34.

Lind, Andrew W. *Japanese Language Schools, 1948.* Hawaii Social Research Laboratory Report no. 15, Honolulu: University of Hawaii Press, 1948.

______. "Some Problems of Veteran Adjustment in Hawaii," *Social Process in Hawaii.* V. 12 (August 1948), pp. 58–73.

______. *Trends in Post-War Race Relations in Hawaii.* Romanzo Adams

Social Research Laboratory Report no. 25, Honolulu: University of Hawaii Press, 1959.

Lum, Doman. "Japanese Suicides in Honolulu: 1958–1969," *Hawaii Medical Journal.* V. 31, no. 1 (January-February 1972), pp. 19–23.

Masuoka, Jitsuichi. "Changing Moral Bases of the Japanese Family in Hawaii," *Sociology and Social Research.* V. 21, no. 2 (November/December 1936), pp. 158–69.

______. "Race Preference in Hawaii," *American Journal of Sociology.* V. 41 (1936), pp. 635–41.

Mitamura, Machiyo. "Life on a Hawaiian Plantation: An Interview," *Social Process in Hawaii.* V. 6 (July 1940), pp. 50–8.

Miyasaki, Gail. " 'Hole Hole Bushi': The Only Song of the Japanese in Hawaii," *The Hawaii Herald.* February 2, 1973, pp. 4–5.

______. "The Role of the Buddhist Church in the History of the Japanese in Hawaii," *Hongwanji Newsletter.* May, 1974, p. 5; June, 1974, p. 6.

Nakahata, Yutaka, and Ralph Toyota. "Varsity Victory Volunteers," *Social Process in Hawaii.* V. 8 (1943), pp. 29–35.

Ogitani, Ronald Kazuo. "Attitudes Toward Aged Parents: Symptom of Social Dysfunction." Senior Honors thesis (Sociology), University of Hawaii, 1969.

Ogura, Shiku. "Familial Survivals in Rural Hawaii," *Social Process in Hawaii.* V. 2 (May 1936), pp. 43–5.

Onishi, Katsumi. " 'Bon' and 'Bon-Odori' in Hawaii," *Social Process in Hawaii.* V. 4 (May 1938), pp. 49–57.

______. "The Second Generation Japanese and the Hongwanji," *Social Process in Hawaii.* V. 3 (May 1937), pp. 43–8.

Robinson, F. Everett. "Participation of Citizens of Chinese and Japanese Ancestry in the Political Life of Hawaii," *Social Process in Hawaii.* V. 4 (1938), pp. 58–60.

Stokes, John F. G. "Japanese Cultural Influences in Hawaii," *Proceedings of the Fifth Pacific Science Congress, Victoria and Vancouver, B.C. Canada, 1933.* Toronto: University of Toronto Press (1934), pp. 2791–803.

Tanaka, Masako. "Religion in Our Family," *Social Process in Hawaii.* V. 12 (August 1948), pp. 14–18.

Yamamoto, Tamiko. "Trends in Marriage Practices Among the Nisei in Hawaii," *What People in Hawaii are Saying and Doing: Report No. 21.* Hawaii Social Research Laboratory, University of Hawaii, 1952.

Yoshizawa, Emi. "A Japanese Family in Rural Hawaii," *Social Process in Hawaii.* V. 3 (May 1937), pp. 56–63.

III. Government Publications

Bennet, Charles G., George H. Tokuyama and Paul T. Bruyere. "Health of Japanese Americans in Hawaii," *Public Health Reports.* Public Health

Service, U.S. Department of Health, Education and Welfare, v. 78, no. 9 (September 1963), pp. 753–62.

Honolulu, City and County, Office of Human Resources. *Profile of Oahu's Aging Population.* Honolulu: 1973.

Honolulu, City and County, Office of Human Resources. *Profile: Oahu's Women.* Honolulu: July, 1973.

Rice, William M. *Immigration of Japanese.* United States House of Representatives, House Document 686, 56th Congress, 1st session, Washington: 1900.

U.S. Congress. *Hearings Before the Joint Committee on Hawaii Statehood.* 75th Congress, 2nd session (October 6 to 22, 1937).

______. *Pearl Harbor Attack.* Hearings before the Joint Committee on the Investigation of the Pearl Harbor Attack, 79th Congress, 1st session.

______. *Statehood for Hawaii.* Hearings Before the Subcommittee on Public Lands. United States Senate, 80th Congress, 2nd session, January-April 1948.

______. *Statehood for Hawaii.* Hearings Before the Subcommittee on Territories and Insular Affairs of the Committee on Interior and Insular Affairs, 85th Congress, 1st session, April 8, 9, 16, 1957.

U.S. Department of Health, Education and Welfare. *A Study of Selected Socio-Economic Characteristics of Ethnic Minorities Based on the 1970 Census, Vol. II: Asian Americans.* Washington, July, 1974.

IV. Primary Sources

Balch, John A. *Shall the Japanese Be Allowed to Dominate Hawaii?* Honolulu: 1942.

Kauai Morale Committee. *The Final Report of the Kauai Morale Committee.* Lihue, Kauai: 1945.

New Americans Conference. *Proceedings.* 15 vols. Honolulu: 1927–1941.

Okumura, Takie. *Seventy Years of Divine Blessings.* Kyoto: Naigai Publishing Co., 1940.

______. *Thirty Years of Christian Mission Work Among Japanese in Hawaii.* Honolulu: Takie Okumura, 1917.

Okumura, Takie, and Umetaro Okumura. *Hawaii's American-Japanese Problems. A Campaign to Remove Causes of Friction Between the American People and Japanese, Report of the Campaign, January 1921 to January 1927.* Honolulu, 1927.

Porteus, Stanley D., and Marjorie E. Babcock. *Temperament and Race.* Boston: Gorham Press, 1926.

Westervelt, Reverend W. D. *The Japanese Consul.* Honolulu: Paradise of the Pacific Print, 1904.

Young Women's Christian Association. *Silver Anniversary Review of the Young Women's Christian Association of Honolulu, 1900–1925.* Honolulu Star-Bulletin, 1926.

V. Newspapers and Magazines

The Friend
Hawaii Shimpo
Hawaii Tribune-Herald
Honolulu Advertiser
Honolulu Record
Honolulu Star-Bulletin
Nippu Jiji
Nisei in Hawaii and the Pacific
Pacific Commercial Advertiser
Paradise of the Pacific

Index

People

Subject

Production Notes

This book was designed by Roger J. Eggers. Composition was done on the Unified Composing System by the design and production staff of The University Press of Hawaii.

The text typeface is English Times. The display face is Oracle.

Offset presswork and binding were done by Vail-Ballou Press. Text paper is Glatfelter P & S Offset, basis 55.